SOME SOUTH CAROLINA
GENEALOGICAL RECORDS

COMPILED
by
JANIE REVILL

SOUTHERN HISTORICAL PRESS, INC.
c/o The Rev. Silas Emmett Lucas, Jr.
P.O. Box 738
Easley, South Carolina 29641-0738

ISBN 0-89308-539-1

INDEX OF COUNTIES

INTRODUCTION

These abstracts are a panorama of available records,
such as jury lists, wills, estate records, deeds,
plats, tombstone inscriptions, etc., of some twelve
South Carolina counties. These records cover a
period prior to and after the Revolutionary War, often
reaching into other counties and states citing the
author's source. Janie Revill's records are known
for their fairness and accuracy.

For the first time, her renowned card abstracts
of Edgefield County, South Carolina, heretofore
housed in the Washington Memorial Library, Macon,
Georgia, were published in 1985.

This is the second volume of records taken from
the index cards of Miss Revill which are housed in
the Washington Memorial Library in Macon. The counties
covered in this volume are as follows: Abbeville,
Anderson, Barnwell, Chester, Fairfield, Greenville,
Laurens, Newberry, Richland, Spartanburg, Union and
York.

ABBEVILLE COUNTY, SOUTH CAROLINA

AGNEW, SAMUEL▾- 96 Dist. Rec. Index (309-347-351-388)

ALEXANDER, WILLIAM--96 Dist. Rec. Index (503-538
    AARON--(532-576-56-*

ALLEN GRANT--See Will John Marshall 1784. Abbeville

ALLEN, JOHN--Of Granville Co. (Had sd infant's money) and Elizabeth
    Cockran, alias McIntosh--Infant. He owed her 111 lbs. which he
    had borrowed from her mother which the infant was to have at age
    18 or married. Mtg. Cattle. Wit: Wm. Coursey, Jacob Summer-
    all, J. P. Satisfied by Ann Allen also "Nanney". 19 Oct. 1768
    24 June 1766. Abbeville File Mtg. 22-631/2

ALLEN, JOSIAH--Will Oct. 31, 1857 Talbot Co. G. Wills Bk. A-295/7
    Wife: Elizabeth--All for life or until ch. of age.
    "My Children"--To be educated

ALLEN, ROBERT, SEN'R--Dec'd. Will 7 Sept. 1815
    Son: James Allen
        Lewis "
        Robert " --Wearing apparel
    Dau: Hannah -w- John Gray-- 2 tracts land
    Son: George B. Allen
    Gr. Son: Robert H. Allen
    "   "   Arthur A. Gray Abbeville Wills Bk. 3 Pg. 44

ALLISON, THOMAS--96 Dist. Rec. Index (45)

ANDERSON, CHARITY-20, WILLIAM-42, JAMES-177 96 Dist. Rec. Index

ANDERSON, MRS.--Will of Dr. James Moore mentions: Property "to come
    to me at death of Mrs. Anderson". His wife was probably Mrs.
    Anderson's daughter. Abbeville Wills Bk. 1-387. 1809

ANDERSON, JAMES--of 96 Dist. Abbeville File. C. T. Wills
    Wife: Agnes--Preg.
    Son: Stephen Anderson
    Bro: Stephen Anderson
        Colbert "
    Dau: Sarah "
        Rebecca "
    Bro-in-law: John Murphy

ANDERSON, WILLIAM--Son-in-law of James Clahoun, Sen'r. Will 1786.
                                                    Abbeville
APPLETON, THOMAS--96 Dist. Rec. Index 25 and 186

ARDIA, CHRISTIAN--96 Dist. Rec. Index 10

ASKINS, SARAH--Wife of George Askins. Dau. of Charles Mulhern. Will
    1786. Their Dau.: Elizabeth Askins. Abbeville

ASTON, JAMES--of Abbeville Co. Abbeville Wills Bk 1-19
    Wife: ?
    3 youngest sons: John, Samuel, William
    Dau: Mary, Sarah, Elizabeth. 24 Aug. 1788. Prov. Oct. 5, 1789

ATKINS, JEAN--Dau. of Robert Yeldell of Abbeville. Will 1789

BAIRD, JOHN--Dec'd. Abbeville Inv. and Sales 4 June 1798
    Purchasers: Martha Baird, Simon, Mary, Hugh, Adam, Mara Baird.

BALL, ELIZABETH--96 Dist Rec. Index 145
    MARK 505

BANKS, JAMES--96 Dist. Rec. Index 470-444

BARKSDALE, MARY--96 Dist Re. Ind. 143
       Henry 163

BARNEY, ANDREW--96 Dist. Rec. Ind. 38

BARTON, JAMES B. 96 Dist. Rec. Ind. 145

BASKIN, JAMES--96 Dist. Rec. Ind. 273-295
      HUGH 609

BASKINS, ANN--Wife Capt. Wm. Baskins. Dau. of George Reid. Will 1786

BATES, STEPHEN--Abbeville Bk. 1-9
    Wife: Anne
    Son: James Alexander Bates--minor
    25 Aug. 1788. Prov. Oct. 8, 1788
    STEVENS--96 Dist. Rec. Ind. 308

BATES, MARGARET--Dau. of Moses McCarter. Will 1787. Fleming Bates
one of Exor's.

BEAZLEY, EDMOND--Dec'd. Columbia Telescope. Oct. 20, 1838
    Abbeville Dist Equity Case: Robert Anderson -vs- Nancy Beazley,
    Benj. C. Beazley, William Beazley, and Washington Beazley. Last
    4 out of state

BEATTY, ANN--intestate. Abbeville Prob. Pg. 3
    Summons: James Beaty   Thomas Beaty
             Samuel Wideman   Peter Leroy
             Edward Carter

BENNIT, JOHN--96 Dist. Rec. Ind. 41-5-

BENTLEY, HENRY--Minor. John Moore Appt. Gdn. Abbeville Prob. Bx-66
                                         Pk-1622
BERRY, WILLIAM--96 Dist. Rec. Ind. 48

BIBLE, RICHARD--96 Dist. Rec. Ind. 144--Mar. Lic.

BLACK, ARCHIBALD--96 Dist Rec. Ind. 178

BLAND, ROBERT--Of Edgefield Co. 21 Dec. 1786. Abbeville Wills Bx-11
    Wife: Ann   Pk-208
    Son: John Bland -w- Mary. To: "My Gr. son"Micaja--The home place
         James, Pressly, Wormley, Elisha, Payton
    Dau: Lividey--50 A. Abbeville Wills Bx. 11 Pk. 208

BOLE, JOHN--Land Gr. Vol. K 11-600 27 Aug. 1764
        200 A. surv. for him 7 Apr. 1764 Br. N. W. fork Long Cane Cr.
        sd Br. abt. 6" deep and 20 links Broad. Bd. N. E. Mr. Carmichael
        and vac. S. E. Hugh Heron and Vac. Surv. Cert. July 3, 1764

BONCHILLON, JEAN--96 Dist. Rec. Ind. 143

BONCHILLON, JOHN--of Hillsborough Township. Abbeville Bk 1-17
        Eldest Son: John
                Son: Joseph   ) Minors
                Dau: Elizabeth)
                Wife: ?
                Bro: Joseph--Gdn. and Exor. 14 Apr, 1778. Prov. July 7,
                                                                        1787

BOND, ROBERT--96 Dist Rec. Ind. 367-319

BONDLATE, BOZALL--96 Dist. Rec. Ind. 27

BOWIE, ROSE -w- John Bowie, Dau. of George Reid. Will 1786. Abbeville

BOWMAN, JACOB--96 Dist. Re. Ind. 22-57
        John--326
        James--369

BOWMAN, JOHN--Abbeville Bk-1-26
        Wife: Jean. Dau: Margaret, Son: William. 2 Nov. 1789
        Prov: May 10, 1790

BOWMAN, WILLIAM--Of Abbeville Bk 1-30
        Gr-son: William Bowman--Minor
        "   "   Samuel Moon Wardlaw--Minor
        Dau.-in-law: Jean Bowman
        "My ch and gr-ch"
        Exor's: Samuel Reid Wardlaw, Jr., Hugh Wardlaw
        4 Nov. 1789. Prov. Apr. 6, 1790

BOYD, JANE--Abbeville Dist. Misc. L-326   21 Feb. 1841
        "Whereas Leonard T. White hath this day become jointly bound
        with Wm. Campbell of the Dist. and State aforesaid by reason of
        a note of hand given to Hugh Boyd for $200.00 for the better
        securing the sd Hugh Boyd against his liability to pay a joint
        bond with the sd Wm. Campbell for the gdnship of Robert Boyd--
        Minor and for the liability of the sd Hugh Boyd to pay unto Jane
        Boyd fifty dollars, the sole debts of the sd Wm. Campbell.
        Mtg: stock, cattle, etc--21 Feb. 1841
        Wit: Gifford Waller, Samuel Felt, Prov. Abbeville Dist.

BOYD, ROBERT--96 Dist. Rec. Ind.--3-11-189
        JOHN--40

BOYER, ARTHUR--96 Dist. Rec. Ind.--15-189

BAXTON, SAMUEL--96 Dist. Rec. Ind. 18

BOOZMAN, EDWARD--96 Dist. Rec. Ind.--134

BRACKENRIDGE, JOHN--96 Dist. Rec. Ind. 590-618

BRANYON, H. J.--96 Dist. Rec. Ind.--163
        Henry--164
        H. Y.--166

BRASWELL, DAVID--96 Dist. Rec. Ind.--35-59

BREADIN, JAMES--96 Dist. Rec. Ind.--238

BREAZEALE, HENRY--Of Hillsborough Twp. Will 16 Jan. 1767. C. T. Will
    Ch'n: Sarah Baker
          John Breazeale
          Elizabeth Baker
          Elijah Breazeale, his son Henry, wife, Patty
          William Breazeale
          Willis, Enoch, Drury, Joel Breazeale.
    Wit: John Giles, David Alexander, Robert Giles
    Prov. before Patrick Calhoun. 23 May, 1770 Abbeville File.

BREAZEALE, WILLIS--96 Dist Rec. Ind.--525-472

BRISKY, ELIZABETH -w- Nicolaus B. Dau. of John Balthaser Marck.
    Abbeville Will 1789

BROOKS, ELISHA--96 Dist. Rec. Ind. 13-188-
    CHRISTOPHER--166

BROWN, WILLIAM--96 Dist. Rec. Ind.--369
    CORNELIUS--412 etc to 594

BROWNLEE, JOHN--of C. T. Will 1827 Misc. 5-E 289
    Half sister--Elizabeth Lindsay -w- John L.
    9 Ch: Sarah -w- James Pratt
          Mary -w- James Martin
          James Lindsay and "six others"

BRYANT, ROBERT--96 Dist. Re. Ind. 13

BRYAN, ROBERT--96 Dist. Rec. Ind. 191

BUFORD, WILLIAM--A gr son of William Brown. Will 8 Jan. 1791
    Abbeville Wills Bk 1-82

BULLOCH, ELIHU--96 Dist. Rec. Ind. 142-156-459-164-165-173

BULLOCK, WILLIAM--Dec'd. Summons to: Vincent Griffin -w- Agnes
    10 Oct. 1832. Wm. Bullock-minor, Luther M. Bullock-minor.
    John White--Gdn. Abbeville Prob. Pg. 85

BURDEN, JOHN--Dec'd intestate. Abbeville Prob. Pg 38. Summons:
    7 Feb. 1827. Henry Gray, Gdn for minor ch. and Wm. Burden,
    Abraham Burden, Kenedy Gibson -w- Mary

BURDINE, REGIONAL,--96 Dist. Rec. Ind. 218

BURDIT, GILES--Dec'd. Widow: Averilla -m- Henry King of Little
    Saluda. A't (?) to gnd Henry King. Feb. 1, 1783 96 Dist Bk.

BURDITT, JAMES--96 Dist. Rec. Ind. 43
    Giles--60

BURDSHAW, JOHN--96 Dist. Rec. Ind. 147-156

BURNEY, ANDREW--96 Dist. Rec. Ind. 120

BURNS, GEORGE--Of St. Paul's Par. Greenville Co. Will 26 July, 1770
    Wife: Elizabeth--Ex.
    Sons: John, Robert, George, William
    Wit: John Heard, Sr. also Exor.
        Wm. Martin   "   "
        Elizabeth Heard. Abbeville Wills C. T. Will

BURNS, LULA--96 Dist. Rec. Ind. 155
    LUKE--158

BURTON, JOHN--Will July 9, 1836 Abbeville Equity Bx-60-3391 18 Nov. 1846
    Wife: Caroline C. -m- (2) John F. Gray
    Dec'd son: James--widow--Margaret. 1 ch.--Mary Ann
    Son: Joseph--res. Abbeville
         John A.--res. Alabama
         William--Res. Texas
    Dau: Margaret--d. 16 Jan. 1840. -w- George Foreman. Res. Ala.
         Mariah -w- Jesse Chandler. Res. Abbeville
         Mary -w- Isaac Thacker. Res. unknown

BUTLER, JAMES--Dec'd. Widow -m- Rissell Wilson of Richland Dist. Cit.
    30 Oct. 1782. 96 Dist. Book
    96 Dist. Rec. Ind. James Butler--33-190-312

CAINE, RICHARD--96 Dist. Rec. Ind.

CALDWELL, JOHN--96 Dist. Rec. Ind
        WILLIAM--Mar. License
        JOSEPH--Col.
        EZEKIEL
        WM. T.--Mar. Elizabeth Williams, Spinster. Msr. 18, 1783

CALHOUN, JAMES--Of 96 Abbeville Co. Abbeville Bk-1 Pg-3
    Wife: Jennet
    Legacy: James Calhoun, son John Calhoun
    Son: William
    Legacy: Andrew Chalmers
    Dau: Martha
    Son-in-law: William Anderson
    Legacy: James Calhoun, son of Wm. Calhoun
    9 May, 1786. Prov. Oct. 21, 1787

CALVERT, LUCINDA--Was a daughter of Wm. A. Moore. Abbeville Wills 1843
                                            Bk-3-82
CAMERON, ARCHIBALD W.--Dec'd. Abbeville Prob. Ord. Bk. Pg-1 1825
    Summons to: John Cameron, Sam'l Cameron, Angus Cameron--all out
    of state. John McLennon, Applicant. Undiv. ½ lot in Cambridge.

CAMERON, JOHN--Native of Argyle--Pet. Citizenship and Oath of Alleg.
    Abbeville Dist. Misc. D-108 1819

CAMPBELL, DUNCAN--Dec'd. Intestate. Abbeville Equity Bx. 65-4231
    Widow: Mary   66-4277
    Ch: William

    Isabella -m- Obadiah Cones
    John--Widow-Elizabeth. No children
    Jesse
    Polly -m- Howell L. Smith
    Selly (Sally or Seely) -m- Thomas Graves
    Enos
    Elinor   Filed 15 Nov. 1797

CAMPBELL, ELIZABETH, Will 23 Jan, 1807. Prov. 7 Feb. 1807 Abbeville
    To: John Edmiston--a cow   Wills
    Dau: Lydda
    Son: John and James
    To: Lucy Edmiston
    Exor's: James Campbell and Wm. Phillips

CAMPBELL, JOHN--Will 13 July 1786 Abbeville Wills
    Wife: Dec'd. 3 sons. 2 daus: Easter, Mary

CAMPBELL, JOHN--Will 21 Apr. 1821. Had land in Pendleton Dist.
    GR-dau: Arabella Chambers of N. C.
    Gr-son: John G. Simmons
    To: Elizabeth -w- George Miller
    Dau: Charlotte Cobb -w- James Cobb
    To: Jane--widow of Wm. McKee lived in Pendleton
    Dau: Mary A. -w- Thomas Simmons
        Peggy -w- Isam Edwards of N. C.
        Arabella -w-   Martin. Son: John C. Martin

CAMPBELL, MARGARET -w- Jesse. Dau. of James Crawford. Abbeville 1780
    96 Dist. Bk.

CARGO, SAMUEL--96 Dist. Ind.

CARMICHAEL, WILLIAM--96 Dist. Ind.

CARTER, JAMES AND ROBERT. 96 Dist. Ind.

CASSIDY, MICHAEL--96 Dist. Ind.

CHALMERS, ANDREW--See Will James Calhoun. Abbeville 1786

CHAMBLIN, JOHN, and Chambers, James. 96 Dist. Ind.

CHEVAS, THOMAS--96 Dist. Ind.

CHILES, BLUFORD, Dec'd. Summons to: Robert Y. Jones for himself.
    19 Feb. 1830 as gdn. of Miss Emily Chiles, minor. Abbeville
    Prob. Bk. Pg-56

CHILES, GARLAND--Dec'd. Summons : Miss Elizabeth Chiles--app. 1827
    Abbeville Prob. Pg-31

CLARK, REV. DR.--96 Dist. Rec. Bk.

CLEM, JOHN--96 Dist. Rec. Ind.

COCHRAN, JAMES,--Bro-in-law of John McElwee. Will 1787. Abbeville

COLLIER, CORNELIUS--Abbeville Box 20 Pg-442. Elizabeth Collier, Adm'x
    Adm. Bond 7 July 1790. Wm. Pettigrew and Edward Collier warrant
    of Apprs.--20 July 1790. Cit: 19 June, 1790
    Inv. and appraisement of Estate returned 5 Oct. 1790. Total
    value 618 lbs-11-5. Apprs: Wm. Stanfield, Vel. Hill, Adam Wideman
    Will Bk-1 Pg-35 "Adm. of Cornelius Collier's estate was gr. to
    Elizabeth Collier 7 July A. D. 1790"

COLLIER, DEATRIX--Joseph Collier, Gdn. Shows James. Abbeville Bx22-509
    Board Jr. 2 Oct. 1815 to 25 Dec. 1816

COLLIER, EDWARD--Abbeville Will Bk-3 Pg-185
    Wife: Mary
    Dec'd Bro: James and his children and Gr. ch. in Ala.
    Dec'd Bro: William and his ch--Beatrix Herring
    Dec'd Bro: John and his son Dr. Wm., also dec'd. Widow: Sarah
            Ch: Wm. E. Collier
                Maria V. "
                Patrick Henry Collier
                James G. Collier
    Nephew: Edward W. Collier
            Ch: Thos. R.
                Mary E.
    Nephew: John Hill and son Joshua   23 Aug. 1837

COLLIER, WILLIAM--Abbeville Will Bk 1-418
    Dau: Beatrix--All if she lives--if she die-no issue-to:
    "My three nephews": William Collier
                       William Edwarde Collier
                       William Wiatt Hill
    28 Oct. 1803. Prov. 4 Jan. 1813
    Wit: Joshua Hill, Joseph Williamson, William Blair.
    Box 22 Pk-509--shows James Collier apt'd. Gdn. Gdn. Bond by
    James Collier dated 3 May, 1813 and states minor is under 14 yrs
    of age. Return made by James Collier, Gdn. dated 15 May 1818 shows
    minor "now Mrs. Herring".
    William--Box 21-458--James Collier and Joshua Hill applied for
    letters of Adm. Cit. gr. 4 Jan. 1813. 16 Dec. 1819--William
    Herring in right of his wife, brought suit -vs- James Collier,
    Adm'r and Gdn.

CORN, GEORGE--96 Dist. Rec. Ind.

COWAN, ANDREW Abbeville Un1l-19   Nov. 7, 1786. Prov. Apr. 7, 1789
    Wife: Ann
    Sons: John, William, Isaac
    Daus: Elizabeth, Ann, Leany, Mary

CROZIER, JAMES Abbeville Bk 1-15
    Wife: Not named
    Son: Samuel
    Dau: Agness
    Ex: Thos Crozier and Wm. Prestly.   27 May, 1778

DAVENPORT, JANE -w- of _____. She was the dau. of Rose Moore.
    Abbeville Wills Bx 3-67   1839

8

DAVENPORT, JOHN--Will 7 May, 1798. Had legacy from his father's
    estate in Va.
    Son: Richard
    Daus: Peggy, Patty,
    Son: Charles. All minors Prov. 13 Sept. 1798
    Exor's: John Arnold, George and John Connor.
    Wit: James Pettis, John P. and Wm. P. Arnold. Abbeville Wills

DAVIS, WILLIAM--Of Monroe Co. Ga. M. set 17 Jan 1842 Miss Elizabeth
    Yarborough of Abbeville. Abbeville Misc. M-92
    Trs: James Murray and Littleton Yarborough. If she die without
    ch. the property to go to:
        Frances -w- James Murray
        Cornelia -w- Joseph Wetherall
        Amanda Murray -dau- James Murray
        Fanny Nelson -dau- of Sarah Nelson
        Wm. Yarborough
        Drucilla Taggart -w- Oliver Taggart
        Mary -w- Nicholas Miller
        Thomas Yarborough -son- of John Yarborough
        Francis   "   "   "   "   "

DAY, LUKE--Dec'd. Abbeville Wills Vol 2-309
    Settlement Est. Receipt 1837
    Heirs: Edmond, Philip, John, William Day

DELECHAUX, JACOB--Of Hillsborough Twship. Abbeville Co. Will Bk 1-34
    Wife: Elizabeth
    Sons: James and Peter
    Daus: Suzanna, Sarah, and Elizabeth
    Y-son: Jacob. 17 March 1790. Prov. July 6, 1790

DENNIS, JOSEPH--Son-in-law of Robert Yeldell. Will 1789 Abbeville

DICKSON, STARLING--Dec'd. Abbeville Prob. Bk Pg 33.
    Summons: James N. Dickson, Appl. -vs- Wm. Pettigrew in right
    of wife. Ellis Dickson and Freeman Dickson--minors--John McFar-
    land, Gdn.

DONALD, JAMES D.--Dec'd. Abbeville Prob Bk. Pg-68
    Summons: Mary Donald, Widow. Minor Ch.??. 18 Nov. 1831

DONALDSON, MATTHEW--Will 13 Nov. 1802. Prov. 11 Dec. 1802 Abbeville
    Wife: Jennet   Bk 1-271
    Niece: Jean -w- Robert Campbell
    Nephew: Andrew Cowan and Mathew Cowan in Ireland

DRENNAN, NATHAN--Dec'd intestate. Abbeville Prob. Bk Pg 66-67
    Summons: Wm. Drennon--Appl. -vs- Representatives of Nathan
    Drennan. Dec'd.

DULPH, STEPHEN-"Late of C. T. but now residing in the Dist. of 96"
    24 May, 1774 Archives Dept. Misc 22-72

EDMINSTON, JOHN (EDMISTON?) Abbeville Bk 1-23
    Wife: Elizabeth
    Sons: Andrew, John James, "my hole cln"
    17 March, 1789. Prov. Oct. 8, 1789

EMERSON, JOSEPH --Of C. T.. Archives Dept. B/S 22-384
    Widow: Martha -m- John Mitchell res. 96 Dist. Deed gift for
    Eleanor Porter--1 slave, Sarah--2 Oct. 1770
    B/S By John Mitchell of 96 -w- Martha. 16 March 1784

EVANS, CATREN(or Catherine) Dau. of Moses McCarter. Will 1787.

EDWARDS, THOMAS--Dec'd. Abbeville Prob. Bk. Pg-95
    Summons to: Jane Edwards
             Thomas Edwards
             George Coleman -w- Margaret
             Andrew Hamilton -w- Jane
             John A. Edwards
             James Edwards
             John Neely -w- Rebecca
             John Buchanan -w- Jenny
             Nicholas Thomas -w- Sarah

FISHER, SAMUEL--Dec'd. Abbeville Prob. Bk. Pg-32 Nov. 3, 1877
    Summons: James Fisher, Stephen Fisher, Thomas Fisher
           George Higgs -w- Sarah
           Isaac Stuckey -w- Elizabeth
           David Cummings -w- Susan
           Reuben Fisher -w- Mary
           Matthew (or Martha Fisher, Jemima F. Francis F. Matilda F.

FOSTER, ROBERT--Dec'd. Abbeville Prob. Bk. pg-63 Summons: (not complete)
                                               1830

FRASER, DONALD--Will 12 Aug. 1807 Abbeville Wills
    Wife: Mary Allen Fraser
    2 ch: John and Margaret
    Bro: John Fraser of C. T.--Exor.
           William "
    Sister: Isabella

FREEMAN, JOSEPH--Of 96 Dist. Will Oct. 20, 1775. Abbeville File
    Wife: Sarah   C. T. Wills
    Daus: Alice, Ann, Sarah
    Exor: Wm. Wilson, Wm. Martin
    Wit: Wm. Freeman, Mary Owens.

GHANT, JOHN--Dec'd intestate. Abbeville Prob. Bk. Pg-23
    Summons: Widow. Minor ch. 7 Dec. 1827. E. Hunt, Gdn.

GLASGOW, MRS. MARY--Dec'd. Abbeville Prob. Bk. Pg-60

GLASGOW, WILSON--Dec'd. Pet. for Part. Newberry Bdl. 2 Pk 22 1830
    7 ch: Robert Glasgow
          Ruth   " Now widow of Absolom Glasgow
          Naomi -m- Samuel Abrams
          Matilda -m- Richmond Glasgow
          Hiram Glasgow
          Alminer Glasgow
          Marian -m-William McCracken

10

GLOVER, ALLEN--Dec'd. Abbeville Prob. Bk. Pg-73
    Summons to: Lydia Glover--widow
                 Jared   "
                 Timothy Russel -w- Edney
                 Samuel Edney -w- Olive
                 Giles Glover
                 Newton   "
                 Ichabod and Lemuel--minors. George Pressley, Gdn.

GOORLEY, JAMES (or Gorley) Abbeville Wills Bk. 1-33
    Bro: Robert Gorley
          Thomas   "
    Bro-in-law: Samuel Keowe and James Fell
    Bro: Hugh Gorley
    Legacy: Andrew Cochran--six shillings
             David Hawthorne McCreery--Coat
             Margaret McCreery. 17 Sept. 1789--Prov. July 6, 1790

GOWEDY, ROBERT--Of 96 Dist. Abbeville Wills Bk 1-36
    Wife: Mary
    "My 2 Ch." James and Sarah
    "My 3 Indian Daughters: Peggy, Krianague, Nancy
    Ex: Robert Waring and Robert Dickie
    2 July, 1775. Prov. Oct. 4, 1790

GRAHAM, JAMES, JR.--Dec'd. Abbeville Prob. Bk. pg-39
    Summons: Wm. Graham -vs- J. W. Graham 23 Aug. 1827
              Benjamin Jones -w- Mary
    Josiah Campbell, Gdn. of minors

GRAHAM, TUSDAY--Dau. of Robert Moors. Abbeville Wills 1846. Bk 3-151

GRAVES, GEORGE--Of Jefferson Co. Fla. Abbeville Dist. Misc. N-297
    M. set 30 Jan. 1844. Caroline S. Tatom of Abbeville Dist.
    Heir to 1/3 est. Orville Tatom.
    M. set William Tennant and Patsy Middleton. Set 3 Dec. 1795
    Wm. Tennent, and Wm. J. Lomax, Trs.

GRAYHAM, CAROLINE MRS.--Wife of _____? She was the dau. of Rose Moore
    Abbeville Wills Bx 3-67 1839

GUNNIEN, BENJ.--Oct. 6, 1811--Abbeville Bk 1-400 Prov. 4 Nov. 1811
    Wife: Jean
    Dau: Hannah W., Isabella, Mary
    Son: James
    Ex: James Wardlaw, Gilbert Mann
    Wit: Wm. McGraw, John Mann, Allen M. Gillespie

HADDON, ANDREW--Dec'd. Abbeville Prob. Bk. Pg-53 23 Nov. 1830
    Summons: John Norwood -vs-
              Isaac Haddon
              _____? Gaston -w- Elizabeth--out of state
              Washington R. Gray -w- Lucinda
              Ebenezer Smith -w- Polly Ann
              William and David Hadden--minors. Andrew Miller, Gdn.
              Lewis and Jane Hadden--minors--Glynn Smith, Gdn.

HAGAN, THOMAS -vs- Wm. Hagan, et al. Land sold to Agnes Hagen.
    Oct. 1835. Abbeville Prob. Bk. Pg-97

HAIRSTON, MARY--Dau. of Robert Yeldell, Sen'r. Will 1789. Abbeville

HANKS, LUKE--Of Pendleton Co. Abbeville Wills Bk 1-22
    Wife: Ann Hanks
    "All my children"--not named
    21 May, 1789. Prov. Oct. 7, 1789

HARRIS, JOHN, HANDY, THOMAS wit. will of William Little of Abbeville
    1788.

HASLET, JOHN--Dec'd. Abbeville Prob. Bk. Pg-28
    Summons: Newton Haslet--App. 17 Feb. 1827 -vs-
            Hannah Haslet--Gdn. of James, Moses and Caroline Haslet
            David   "
            Anne   "

HEARD, STEPHEN--"In Georgia"--owed note to est. of James Calhoun. 1794
    Abbeville Inv. and Sales Pg 1 1787-1811

HEARD, WILLIAM--Nephew of Andrew Logan. Will 1788 Abbeville

HERNDON, RUTH--Dau. of Lawrence Rambo. Abbeville Will 96 Dist Bk. 1775

HILL, JOHN SEN'R.--Dec'd. Abbeville Prob. Bk. Pg 54
    Summons: Charles Cullens--App. Nov. 24, 1830 -vs-
            Benj. Rosemond, et al.
            Benj. Hodges -w- Rebecca --out of state
            Wm. C. Hill, John Calvert--Gdn.

HILL, SAMUEL--Dec'd. Abbeville Prob. Bk. Pg-4 Summons: 18 July, 1825
    Widow: Elizabeth--1/3
    Ch: Nancy Elizabeth Hill and Susana Elvira--Minors
    Wm. Barmore--Gdn.

HOLLOWAY, ROSA ANN--Dec'd. Wife of____? Dec'd dau. of Rose Moore
    Left ch: Jane Holloway, Joseph Holloway, John T. Holloway
    Abbeville Will 1839

HOWELL, LUCY--Will Abbeville Wills Bk 3-224
    Son: John Poston
    Daus: Nancy Walton, Mary Elliott, Rebecca Brown, Katherina
           Howell
    Son: James Poston $100 Each
    Gr. Dau: Sarah Ann Elizabeth Mitchell-Spinning Wheel, Kit. furn.
    Dau: Lucy B. Mitchell--All money left me by my Father. Wm. Jenniings
    Ex: Samuel Mitchell 18 May, 1844
    Wit: Thos. Gantt, J. H. Chaspings, J. F. Underwood. Prov. 12 Oct.
                                       1848

HUBBARD, WILLIAM--Advertised for indentured apprentice--James Clain--
    a boy--ran away 18 Nov. last. Deliver to "Me residing on eighteen
    Mile Creek" Reward--6¼ cents. Pendleton Mess. Dec. 5, 1827
    WILLIAM--Advertised that he has opened the house formerly kept by
    him in Pendleton for Boarders and Travellers--house has been en-
    larged and remodeled. Drovers will be provided with lots and pro-
    vender on reasonable terms. Pendleton Messenger Jan. 10, 1845

12

JACKSON, WILLIAM--Dec'd. Abbeville Prob. Bk. Pg-27
   Summons: Nancy Jackson--App. -vs- George Allemburger -w- Esther
      Minor ch. Robert Conn, Gdn.

JAY, WILLIAM --Of 96 Dist. Will 23 Nov. 1772. Abbeville File. C. T.
   Wife: Mary--Ex.   Will
   Son: John Jay--land adj. home place
      David Jay--Home pl. pur. from Rob't Ball and David Mott
   "My 3 Daus": Mary, Rachel, Lydia

JOHNSON, BENJAMIN, SEN'R.--Dec'd. Abbeville Prob. Bk. Pg 56 1830
   Summons: Benj. Johnson--App. -vs- Mark Johnson, Wm. Gains, et al

KEOWE, SAMUEL--Bro-in-law of James Gorley. Will 1789. Abbeville

KING, BENJAMIN--"Merchant" of Cambridge 96 Dist. Abbeville Wills 1-5
   Son: Benj. King--Land in Cambridge and on Mtn. Cr. a Br. Turkey
      Cr.
   Son: John Cogdell King--In Cambridge and on Cuffy Town Cr. and
      Halfway Swamp.
      In business with Thos. Everleigh of Charleston.
   Ex: Wm. Moore, Wm. Swift. Also Gdn. of sons. Sons not 21
   Date: 1 July 1788
   Wit: Robert G, Harper, Davis Moore, Wm. Moore, Sr.
   Prov. 8 July 1788

LEARD, ANDREW--Abbeville Prob. Bk. Pg-16   -vs-
   Summons: Widow--Jane -m- Isaac Dansley. Ch: Samuel and Nancy
   Leard. 7 Aug. 1876

LESLY, JOHN--Adm. Wm. Lesly, Sr. Lett. Gr. 8 Apr. 1788. Abbeville
                                           Wills 1-4
LIDDELL, GEORGE--Will 28 Dec. 1789. Abbeville Wills Bk-1-32
   Wife: Rachel--Preg.
   Sons: James Liddell, George Washington Liddell. Prov. Apr 6, 1790

LINDSAY, JOHN L.--M. Elizabeth--half sister of John Brownlee of C. T.
   Ch: Sarah Lindsay -m- James Pratt
      Mary   "   -m- James Martin
      James Lindsay. Abbeville File. Misc. 5E-289

LIPPORD, ASA--Dec'd. Abbeville Prob. Bk. Pg-10 Summons: 2 Apr. 1826
   Daniel Weed -w- Martha
   Ch: Polly, Henly, Fanny, William Lippord--minors
      Joel, Jr.--Gdn.

LITTLE, WILLIAM--Of Abbeville. Abbeville Bk-1 Pg-24 4 Sept. 1788
   To: Mary Little, alias Smith--1 shilling
   Dau: Anne
   Son: John Prov. Oct. 8, 1789

LIVINGSTON, BRUCE--Dec'd. Abbeville Prob. Bk. Pg-51 Summons: 10 Dec.
   Mrs. Agnes Livingston   1829
   John C.   "
   John Yarborough -w- Mary
   Jane Livingston
   John J. "   As Gdn of:
   Mary Adeline and Wm. L.--Minors

LOCKHART, JOEL AND MARY--Heirs of Wm. Moore. They lived, it seems in
    Ga. He left them lot in Town of Petersburg, Ga. Abbeville
    Wills Bk 1-321 1803

LOGAN, ANDREW--Abbeville Bk. 1-10 25 Aug. 1788. Prov. Oct. 10, 1788
    Wife: Lidy
    Son: John and Isaac
    Nephew: Wm. Heard

LOGAN, JOHN and his children. See will of Charles Mulhern or Mulhewin
                                                                1789
LOGAN, ALEXANDER--Adv. for Indents stolen from his home "White Hall"
    in Abbeville County. All for Militia duty and supplies issued
    to Alex'r Loggan, John Loggan, Thomas Loggan, dec'd, David Loggan
    and Newby Mans. College of C. T. City Gazette Nov. 11, 1790

LOMAX, ABSOLEM--Dec'd intestate. Summons 27 Nov. 1826. Abbeville Prob.
    Widow: Cloe Lomax. Minor Ch. Geo. Lomax, Gdn   Bk. pg-22

LOMAX, JAMES -w- Lucy -vs- Rose Moore, Nancy Norris, Joseph Adams.
    Bill for Part. Abbeville Dist. Columbia Telescope. Mar. 13, 1829

LONG, MARTHA--96 Dist Bk.--Abbeville 1780. Dau. of James Crawford.

LONG, MATHIAS, D. S.--For land Gr. to James Pettigrew of Abbeville--
    Cert. May.1, 1772. Archives Dept. Mem 11-379

LOWERY, WILLIAM--96 Dist. Bk-1779. Nephew of James Magill

MAGILL, JAMES--Will 8 Feb. 1779. 96 Dist. Bk-Abbeville
    Gr. Ch: James Golding, William Golding, Anthony Golding
    Son-in-law: Anthony Golding
    Land owned in Va.--Frederick Co. Nephew--Wm. Lowery. Had Nephews
    in Ireland

MARCK, JOHN BALTHASAR. Abbeville Bk1-25   21 March, 1789
    Son: Henry
    Dau: Elizabeth -w- Nicolaus Brisky
          Philipina
          Elizabeth Margaretha   Prov. Oct. 3, 1789

MARSH, JOHN--To wife, Frances, sole trader--23 Feb. 1816. Misc.C-266

MARSHAL, JOHN--Abbeville Bk-1 Pg-9
    Legatees: Wm. White   Wm. Marshall
               Mathew Marshall   Peggy Marshall
               Grant Allen   Richard Moore
    Bro: Dixon Marshall
    Legacy: John Wortham--10 shillings 10 Mar. 1784. Prov. Oct. 8,
                                                                1788
MARTIN, ABRAHAM--Of Cornwall Parish--Charlotte Co. Will Nov. 27, 1769
    Wife: Betty   Dau: Letty
    "My sons and Daus"
    Exor: Edward Wade, Wm. Martin, James Martin
    Wit: Margaret Mullins, James Mullins, Wm. Matthews

MARTIN, ALEXANDER--Of Newberry Dist. Will 30 Jan. 1814.
    "Being called in service United States of America"
    Wife: Agnes. "My children".
    Ex: John Martin and James Caldwell
    Wit: Jno. M. Moseley, M. Weatherford, Thomas Gordon
    S. C. Newberry Dist: "I do hereby relinquish my right as Ex-
    ecutor xxx James Caldwell. Nancy Martin and Robert Gilmore asked
    for Letters 19 Dec. 1831
    ALEXANDER--Dec'd Abbeville Part. Bk 1-79

MARTIN, CHARLES--Will 28 June, 1808. Abbeville. Prov. 25 Oct. 1808.
    Son: Jacob--Ex.   Bk. 1-369
          Geo. Washington Martin--Ex.
    Wife: Pattey--Ex. Home place for life--289 A.
    Dau: Suckey Moore
    Son: William
    Gr. Sons: James and Thomas Cobb
    Gr. Dau: Patsy Bibb
    Dau: Salley Nichols--no property
    Wit: Nath'l Bowes, Sam'l Linton, Wm. Dunkird

MARTIN, GEO--Abbeville Box 58-1376
    Sarah Martin--Adm'x. apt. 5 Dec. 1820
    Bond: 5 Dec. 1820
    S: Wm. Thompson, Jacob Thompson
    Sale--22 Dec. 1820. Pur: Nancy Martin, Geo. Martin, Jr.

MARTIN, JANET--Will 4 Dec. 1811. Abbeville Bk 1-402
    David Pressly sole executor and "That he take care of my children
    and do the best he can for them". Prov. 14 Dec. 1811

MARTIN, PETER--Est. Abbeville 27 March 1797. Bk 1-168
    Adm: Robert Martin of Savannah River. "Father sd dec'd".

MARTIN, ROBERT "Of Abbeville" Abbeville Bk 1-389. 9 May, 1810
    Wife: Jannet--Ex.   Prov. 3 Sept. 1810
    Son: James
    Daus: Jean and Mary
    Wit: David Pressly, Thos. Gillespie, Anny Gillespie--Minors

MARTIN, WILLIAM --Abbeville Bk 1-204. 25 Jan. 1793 Prov. 27 Mar. 1798
    Gr. sons: Wm. Joseph, John, James McMurtrey
    Son-in-law: Samuel McMurtrey
    Gr. Dau: Sarah Watts and Jenny McMurtrey
    Dau: Jean
    Money in hands of Thos. Lessly and Thos. Martin. to be collected.
    Ex: Samuel Watts and Wm. Lessly
    Wit: Robert McCrone, Matthew Wilson, Robert Simmons

MAXWELL, CHARLES--Dec'd. Abbeville Prob. Bk Pg-90 Summons:
    Austin Pollard -w- Sarah F.
    John M. Maxwell   )
    Charles D. Maxwell) Minors. Austin Pollard, Gdn.

MAYFIELD, SUSANNA--Abbeville Wills Bk 1-109
    Ch: Jean, Agnes, Elizabeth, Nancy, William. 10 Sept. 1790

McADAMS, JAMES--Dec'd. Abbeville Prob. Bk. Pg-59 Summons 28 Feb.
    Mrs. Charlotte McAdams, Gdn. of: 1831
        Robinson McAdams
        John McLean -w- Polly
        Wm. McAdams
        James   "
        Bennet "
        Dempsey Calahan -w- Hannah
        Thomas McAdams
        Wm. R. Rany -w- Nancy

McALPIN, MARY--Abbeville Wills Bk 1-321 1803
    Was Mary Moore, sister of Wm. Moore

McBRIDE, MARTHA--Wife of Hugh McBride, dau. of Robert Ross. Will 1790

McCANTS, TELITHA ANN, wife of D. W. McCants. She was dau. of Wm. A.
    Moore. Abbeville Wills Bx. 3-82. Will 1843

McCARTER, MOSES--"Farmer" Abbeville Wills 1787. Bk 1-6
    Wife: Catren   Sons: Robert and Moses
    Daus: Anne York, Catren Evans "   John and Wm.
     "   Mary McCarter   "   James
        Agnes Crawford
        Margaret Bates
        Jennet McCarter
    Ex: John McCarter, Fleming Bates 5 Feb. 1787
    Wit: Mary McCarter, Margaret Bates, Joseph Crawford
    Prov. 9 Jan. 1788

McCLELLAN, WM.--Of Long_Cane_? C. T. Wills
    Wife: Ann McClellan--Place on Catawba R. Where I Formerly lived.
    Exor: Thomas Lindsay. 14 Jan, 1782. Codicil--Sis. son-John Swansy

McCOMB, ANDREW, SEN'R.--Abbeville Bx. 67-1628
    John McComb--Adm'r. Cit: 20 May, 1819. Pub. by Jesse Calvert
    Adm. Bond: 11 Dec. 1819   7 June, 1819
    S: Rebecca McComb and Andrew McComb

McCRAVEN, JOHN--Dec'd. Abbeville Prob. Bk. Pg 43-100-101
    Summons: 12 Nov. 1823. James McCraven, App.
    To: Robert McCraven, Sr. -w- Jane
        Joseph Boyd -w- Mary
        John Gilespie -w- Elizabeth
        Wm. M. Rogers--minor--Paul Rogers, Gdn.
        Wm. McCraven
        Robert McCraven, Jr.
        Jean   "
        Ann   "
        Andrew M. " Minor

McCRADY, JAMES--Dec'd. Abbeville Prob. Bk. Pg-47 Summons 5 Dec. 1829
    Milly McCrady, Gdn. of James McCrady
    Jabez W. Johnson, Gdn. of Mary Frances McCrady.

McELWEE, JOHN--Abbeville Wills 1-2. Will 1787   9 Feb. 1787
    Wife: Sarah   Prov. 2 Oct. 1787
    Dau: Agnes
         An unborn child. Wife pregnant.
    Sister: Elinor--a widow
           Martha
    Son-in-law: James Cochran--clothing
    Father-in-law: John Cochran and Sam'l Foster of Long Cane. Exors.

McGHEE, ANN--Of Virginia--Dau. of Francis Meriweather. Will 7 June, 1783
    Also dau. Mary Meriweather--Will 1809 Abbeville Wills.

McGHEE(McGHIE), PATRICK--Will 1750. C. T. Wills
    Wife: Charlotte
    Dau: Henrietta--Should she die, to go to people in Scotland

McGILL, ANDREW--Minor. E. and Wm. and Sarah Moore aptd. Gdn.
    Abbeville Prob. 1818 Bx-66 Pk-1612

McQUEANS, ALEXANDER--Dec'd. Summons 6 Jan. 1834 to Mrs. Agnes McQueans
    Minor Ch. Abbeville Prob. Bk. Pg-94-96

MILLER, ANDREW--Dec'd. Abbeville. See Will of Andrew Moat 1787
    Ch: John, Jr. Margaret, Esther

MILLER, JAMES S.--Dec'd-intestate. Abbeville Prob. Bk. Pg-14
    Summons: 27 July, 1826 Wm. Hall, App. -vs-
        Joshua Brown -w- Elizabeth
        John Endsley -w- Elinor)
        George Miller   )
        Jacob   "   ) Out of State
        Archibald "   )
        Robert   "   )

MILLER, GILBERT--Abbeville Wills Bk 1-33 3 Nov. 1789. Prov. Apr. 7
    Wife: Martha   1790
    Son: Alexander Mills
          William   "
    "My wife and children"
    Ex: Matthew Mills, Wm. McGraw

MISCAMPBLE, JAMES--Of Long Cane. Will 27 Sept. 1775. C. T. Wills
    Wife: Ann   Abbeville File 1774-1779-516
    "My 3 sons": John, James, Robert
    Exor: John Foster
    Wit: George McCombe, James Foster, John Foster.

MITCHELL, JOHN and wife, Martha. 96 Dist. Misc. 22-384
    Martha late widow of Joseph Emerson. Late of C. T. 16 Mar. 1784

MITCHELL, ISAAC of Abbeville Co. Abbeville Wills Bk 1-21
    Wife: ?
    Son: Isaac--a minor
    Daus: Ursula, Catherine, Mary, Sarah.
    All my other sons--not named. 27 June 1789. Prov. Oct. 6, 1789

MOAT, ANDREW (Mote or Motte). Will. Abbeville Wills 1-3
    John Miller, Jr. Son.
    Andrew Miller, Dec'd
    Wife: Elizabeth
        Margaret Miller and Esther Miller--Daus. of Andrew Miller
    Ex: Ezekiel Evans, Jno. Lesly, Sam'l Wall
    19 Aug. 1787. Prov. 8 Jan. 1788
    Wit: James Evans, Samuel Evans

MOORE, HARRIET--Minor--Gr. dau. of Pheba Shanklin. Formerly widow
    Phebe Covington. Will 12 March 1801.
    Sons: Wm. and Richard Covington
    Dau: Nancy Fuqua

MOORE, JAMES--1780 Abbeville--96 Dist. Pg-39
    Wife: Anne Moore
    Son: Davis   "   Not 20 yrs.
        James   "
        Jonathan"
        Wm. Drayton Moore
        Unborn child, if any, and he believes so.
        Mentions slave "in care of Mother Pratt, My Mother,
        Susanna Moore--
    Ex: Wife, with Wm., John, and Richard Moore.
    Date: 12 Jan. 1780. Wit: Wm. Neal, Wm. Wilson
    Prov. by Wm. Neal. 23 Sept. 1782

MOORE, DR. JAMES--Of Abbeville Dist. Abbeville Wills Bk 1-387 1809
    Wife: Frances
    Sons: Edward, James
    Dau: Frances Louisa Moore
    Bro: Jonathan Moore (Ex. only)
    Mentions property to come to me at death of Mrs. Anderson.
    Ex: Bro. and Archy Mayson, John C. Mayson, and Washington Bostick
    Date: 26 July, 1809
    Proven: 4 June 1810
    Wit: Taleafero Livingston, Thos. Chiles, Jos. Coleman

MOORE, _____? --Dec'd C. T. Deed K-10-137
    Widow: Mary -m- Charles Newman
    Dau: Ann Moore, spinster, of C. T. d. 24 Nov. 1822, intestate
    Bro: James Moore of Abbeville
        George Moore of Charleston
    Joint conv. by Mother and Bros. of Ann to John Taylor Bowles of
    C. T. Lot in _____? St. Conv. 22 Nov. 1823

MOORE, ROSEY, --Dau. of Wm. Adams--Will 1794. Abbeville Wills

MOORE, MARTHA--Dau. of Peter Green. Will 1794. Abbeville Wills
    Julius Nichols, Jr. a Wit.
    Polly Moore -w- George B. Moore
        Dau: Harriot Moore
    Polly--dau. of Wm. Covington--Will 1790. Harriot Moore--Gr dau.
    of Phebe Shanklin--formerly wife of Wm. Covington

MOORE, SAMUEL--A Gr. son of William Bowman. Will 4 Nov. 1789
    Abbeville Wills Bk. 1 *g 31. Samuel Moore Wardlaw

MOORE, SUKEY--Dau. of Julius Nichols. Will 23 Jan. 1803 Abbeville Wills
    Wife (of Julius): Patty
    Son: Julius and William
    Dau: Lucy Marshall and Sally Nichols
    Gr. Ch: Ch of dau. Sukey Moore
        Sukey Moore
        Betsy Cooper
        Molly Jones
        Bobby Hunt
    Son: Thomas

MOORE, SUCHEY--Dau. of Charles Martin--Will 28 June, 1808
    Wife: (of Charles) Patsy
    Sons: Geo. Wash. Martin, Wm. Martin, Jacob Martin.
    Gr. sons: James and Thomas Cobb
    Gr. dau: Patsy Bibb
    To: Salley Nichols--$100.00

MOORE, AMANDA--"Miss, of Abbeville Mar. John Brown. On 3 Jan. 1861
    At residence of Wm. Magill by John G. Baskin, Esq. All of Abbeville
    The Charleston Mercury Jan. 15, 1861

MORGAN, THOMAS--Dec'd intestate. Abbeville Prob. Bk Pg-40
    Summons: 19 Feb. 1828--Widow: Nancy--1/3 Land
    Ch: Wm. Morgan, John, Thomas, Mary Morgan.

MORRIS, JOHN--Dec'd--int. Abbeville Prob. Bk. Pg-49 Summons: 24 Dec.
    Mrs. Sarah Morris, Jonathan Lyon and wife.   1829

MORRIS, WILLIAM--Abbeville Wills 1-7
    Adm: Gr. Eleanor Morris and Wm. Black. 9 July 1788

MORROW, GEORGE--Of Abbeville Co. Abbeville Bk 1-29 10 March 1790
    Wife: Mary   Prov. Apr. 6, 1790
    Son: John Morrow
    Dau: Jane   "
    Son: Hugh   "
    Dau: Margaret Morrow
        Mary Ann   "
    Son: Geo. Mecklin Morrow
        James Morrow

MORROW, JAMES--Abbeville Wills 1788 1-7 Adm. Gr. Thos. Morrow 9 July
                                              1788

MULHERN, CHARLES--Will 17 March 1789. Abbeville Bk 1 Pg 13 (Mulherin?)
    Gr. dau: Elizabeth Askins, dau. of Sarah and George Askins
    Dau: Jean
    Son: James and John
    Legacy: John Logan's Daus: Margaret and Sarah
       "   "   "   Sons: John Jun'r. and Andrew
    Wit: John Meriweather, Larky Meriweather Wm. Heard. Prov. Apr 7
                                                  1789

NICHOLS, JULIUS--Abbeville Bx 64 Pk 1531 1791. A relative of
    Wm. Moore, Dec'd and an Adm.

NORWOOD, PHEBE--Abbeville Wills Bk 1-470 1791. Adm. of Quinton Moore

NORWAY, SAMUEL--Abbeville Bk 1-57 Will 16 Nov. 1789. Prov. Oct. 29
    Wife: Elizabeth   1790
    Sons: John, Thomas, Blakely, William, Robert, Joseph, Theophelus
    Norwood's 3 Children: Samuel, John and Richard
    My 3 Daus: Elizabeth Porter, Agnes Watts, Mary Watts

NORWOOD, THEOPHILOS--Abbeville Will Bk 1-18 13 Apr. 1787 Prov. July 9
    Wife: ?   1789
    Sons: Samuel, John Middleton, Richard Norwood
    Ex: John Middleton and Sam'l Porter

PARKS, ELIZABETH--Widow. -m- John B. Byrd, Sr. (it seems, see Will
    John B. Byrd) Her Parks ch: Lewis, James, John T., Wm. and
    Elizabeth -w- John Banett. 1856

PORTER, ELIZABETH--Dau. of Samuel Norwood of Abbeville. Will 1789

PRATT, WILLIAM -m- Mary Drennan. Lic. Jan 28, 1783 96 Dist. Records

PRATT, JOSEPH, JUN'R. intestate. Abbeville Prob. Bk Pg 41
    Summons: 25 Feb. 1828 William Pratt, App -vs- Wm. Gormy and
    wife____?. Samuel Young -w- Emma

PRESSLY, DAVID--Of Long Cane now in C. T. Will 5 Jan. 1785
    Eldest Son: Samuel
                  David--L. Gr. to "me and Wm Pressly"
    Eldest Dau: Agnes Pressly-alias
                  Her eldest dau: Elizabeth Wyly
    Dau: Mary Ann Pressly
    Sons: William and John
    Dau: Esther
    Son-in-law: Henry Wyly Abbeville File C. T. Wills A.

RAIFORD, WILLIAM--Gr. son of Wm. Brown, Sr. Will 1791. -w- Isabel
    Son: Wm. Brown
           Son: John
    Gr. son: David Black, son of James Black
    Dau: Isabel Brown, Mary Brown, Sarah Brown, Martha Brown
    Dec'd Son: John Brown
          Ch: Margaret, Elizabeth, Frances

RAMPEY, JOHN--Dec'd. Abbeville Prob. Bk. pg-52. Summons 1 Feb. 1830
    Mordecai McKinney and Wife -vs- James Steefle-Gdn of minors

REAGAN, JOHN--Dec'd. Abbeville Prob. Bk. pg-76. Summons: 10 Jan, 1832
    To: Rachel Reagan, the widow, Young Reagan, Bailey, Allen, Esward
    Tabitha--minor. Appl: John Robison, Jr.--gdn for Minor.

REID, GEORGE--Of 96 Dist. Abbeville Will Bk 1-27. 23 Nov. 1786
    Dau: Rose -w- John Bowie of 96 Dist
          Ann -w- Capt. Wm. Baskins
          Margaret -w- Hugh Reid
    Son: Samuel, Alexander, Joseph Reid
    Legacy: Polly McGee. Prov. Apr. 6, 1790

REYNOLDSON, WILLIAM--Dec'd. Abbeville Prob Bk. pg-8. Summons
    21 Dec. 1825 To: Mrs. E. Pennington, Appl. -vs- Andrew Reynold-
    son, Wm., James, Thomas Kennedy, Wm. Anderson -w- Martha
    Peggy B. Kennedy, John Boyd -w- Polly, Jane ann Kennedy
    James Clements -w- Sarah, Senia Kennedy

RICHEY, WILLIAM--Dec'd. Abbeville Prob. Bk. pg-74. Summons 4 Dec.
    To: Joseph Lyon --w--   1831
         Thos. Hawthorn --w--
         John Weir, Gdn for minor children

ROBERTSON, JOHN, SEN'R.--Abbeville Bk 1 Pg 1 30 May 1782
    Wife: Jean (or Jeen)
    Sons: William, Robert, John
    Oldest son: Andrew   Prov. 3 July 1787

ROBISON, HENRY--Dec'd. Abbeville Prob. Bk. pg-99/100 Summons to
    Nancy Robison-widow adv. Wm. Robison-Gdn. Appl. 3 Feb. 1834

ROBISON, JANE--Dec. Abbeville Prob. Bk. Pg 78/9 25 Jan. 1832
    Summons to: Andrew Robison--Appl.
    Joseph Richey -w- Jane
    John McCord -w- Elizabeth
    Dec'd Polly Stone's Children. Benj. Mosely, Gdn.
    Wm. Richey, Sen'r.
    Richard Maddox -w- Peggy
    Augustine Maddox -w- Letty
    John Robison

ROLAND, MARY MRS. Wife of_____?. Was a dau. of Rosa Moore.
    Abbeville Wills Bk 3-67

ROSS, ROBERT--Abbeville Wills Univ 1-60. 12 July 1790. Prov. Oct. 5
    Gr. Ch: Robert McBride and James McBride--minors   1790
          Children of dau: Martha
    Son-in-law: Hugh McBride
    Dau: Martha McBride
    Exor's: James McBride, and Andrew McComb

ROWELL, GRACE--Son. Times and Gazette. Aug. 9, 1830. Columbia, S. C.
    -vs- George Z. Twiggs and Valentine Walker as Exor's of Edward
    Rowell, Dec'd. Richmond Superior Ct. Georgia
    Mary A. Rowell   Nancy W. Rowell
    Elizabeth Foreman   Milly E. Rowell
    Sarah C. Rowell   Benjamin D. Rowell
    Hannah T.   "   Margaret C.   "
    William   "   Edward   "
    Eliza Williamson   Catherine   "

Sarah Rowell	Randolph Rowell
Mary "	Dorcas "
Jane "	Mary Davies
Benj. Strange	Patsy Foreman
Randolph Strouge	Edward Strouge See Card #2
#2 Hubbard Strouge	E. S. Sibley -w- Elizabeth
Arthur Westbrook -w- Mary	Benjamin Jackson -w- Rebecca
Lucy Ball	John Stanley
John Horton -w- Elizabeth	Jesse Westbrook -w- Susannah
William Coombs -w- Winifred	Nathaniel Stanley-out of state
James Stanley, Jr.--resides in Lawrence Co., Georgia	

RUSHTON, JOHN AND PRISCILLA--Dec'd. Summons 1827 --Gaines F. Rushton,
     Eliphar Rushton--both minors. James Carson and Geo. F. Caldwell,
                                                                 Gdns.

RUSSELL, ROBERT--Dec'd. Abbeville Prob. Bk. Pg-20Summons 4 Sept, 1826
     John Brown -w- Jane--Appl. -vs-

*James Smyly -w- Margaret	*William Russell
Jane C. Russell	John Richey -w- Elizabeth
*Robert Russell	*Alexander Russell
*John Russell	*James Russell (*out of state)

SANDERS, ANN--Abbeville Misc. Bk. 1826 pg 101. John Little, gdn of
     the minor children of Ann S. -vs- Joseph Davis, Adm. of est. sd
     dec'd. 8 july 1823. Page 102: Sanders, Donald--Dec'd. Thos.
     P. Martin adm. Sale Bill recorded

SANDERS, JOSEPH--Abbeville Wills Bk 1-308   20 March, 1805
     "My 3 sons": Joseph.Frazer, Donald Frazer, Thomas Adams-all minors
     Wife: Sarah R. Sanders
     Dau: Polly
     Child wife is preg. with--if any.
     Wit: Jno Lowy, Wm. Baird. Prov. 6 May, 1805

SEAWRIGHT, JAMES--Of Abbeville Co. Abbeville Wills Bk 1-29
     "My children"--not named. Ex: Samuel Agnew and Hugh Wardlaw
     29 Oct. 1789. Prov. Apr. 6, 1790

SHACKLEFORD, FRANCIS--Dec'd. Intestate. Abbeville Prob. Bk. pg-71
     Summons to: Mary Shackleford-widow 10 Dec. 1829
                  Ethel Shackleford -w-John F. Green

SHELLY, AGNES.--Abbeville Wills Bk 1-31. Prov. Apr. 6, 1790
     "My child"--a minor to be cared for.
     Sister: Margaret Shelly
     Exor's: Joseph Crawford, Wm. White

SHIRLEY, JOHN--Dec'd. Abbeville Prob. Bk. pg 88. Summons 5 Nov. 1832
     Obadiah Shirley--Appl. -vs- Benj. Shirley, et al

SIMPSON, JOSEPH AND POLLY--Dec'd. R. E. Sale on Sawney's Cr. of Little
     River. Heirs: Henry, Thomas, Joseph, John James, Jemima, David
     Simpson. Adv. Andrew Milligan, Appl. Land sold to Meredith McGee
     Abbeville Prob. Bk. pg-5.

SMITHERS, CHRISTOPHER--Abbeville Wills-1781. Wife: Caroline. Son-James

SMITH, JOHN--Dec'd. Summons to Heirs--? Names not shown. 1827

SMITH, PETER--Dec'd--Left Will. Abbeville Prob. Bk. Pg-82/3
    Summons Peter Smith, Charles Smith--Appl's. -vs- ??

SPRAGINS, WILLIAM--Dec'd. Summons: 5 Nov. 1827 Thomas J. Spragins--App.
    -vs- Thomas Atkinson -w- Tabitha, Wm. Spragins and John Meeks,
    Gdn. of minor children of Sarah Meeks, Dec'd. John out of State.
    Abbeville Prob. Bk. Pg-42

STARKE, SAMUEL C.--Dec'd. Abbeville Prob. Bk. Pg-81/82
    Summons Sept. 10, 1832 Ezekiel Frible -w- Rosanna
    Charles Starke--Gdn of Samuel J. W. Starke-minor

STEEL, AARON--Mar. Lic. Nov. 15, 1782. Elizabeth Corly. 96 Dist.

STEWART, JOHN--Dec'd. Abbeville Prob. Bk. Pg-77
    Summons 1825: David M. Stewart,
                  Margaret, Alesander, Mary and John--Minors
    John Weir--Appl. and Gdn.

STONE, POLLY--Dec'd. Abbeville Prob. Bk. Pg. 80/81
    Summons June 7, 1832 to: Wm. Richey--Appl. -vs-
    John Stone, Benj. T. Owens -w- Jane
    Melinda Stone--Minor Benj. Mosley, Gdn.

SULLIVAN, MARGARET P. And John Cameron -vs- John Miller and John
    McMahan. In equity--Abbeville Dist. Col. Telescope. May 29, 1824

SOUTHERLAND, FRANCIS--Dec'd. Abbeville Prob. Bk. Pg.-12
    Summons 20 Jan. 1826-- Jennett Southerland--Appl. -vs-
    Wm. C. Mills -w- Elizabeth
    Wm. Robison -w- Anna
    Wm. Southerland
    Andrew W. Southerland
    James Welch -w- Mary
    John Hemmenger -w- Jane

TAYLOR, ANN -vs- Her husband, Wm. Taylor. Suit for Alimony
    A wit. John Taylor, father of Wm. Taylor, and testified in behalf
    of the wife. Mrs. Sturgennegger, sister of Ann Taylor, lived
    with the Taylors from 1795 to 1804, and Mrs. Myers, a cousin.
    Allen Nesbitt, a son-in-law of Ann Taylor. Hugh Nesbitt, a wit.
    Mrs. Clarke, a sister of Ann Taylor. Mrs. Susannah Taylor and
    Ann Flint, Wit. In Georgia by depositions. Mr. Galphin, a re-
    lation. Rev. James Holcomb and Mr. Owens waited on defendant to
    persuade him to agreement. A nasty case.
    June Ct. 1811. Abbeville Case. Desaussure's Rep. Vol. 4-165

TAYLOR, THOMAS--Of Co. of Culperrer. Abbeville Bk 1-23 Dec. 2, 1787
    Wife: Johannah
    "All my Children"--not named
    Exor: William Miles and John Taylor. Prov. Oct. 7, 1789

TERRY, CHAMPNESS--Of 96 Dist. Abbeville Firl. C. T. Wills Sept. 14
     Wife: Sarah--ensient   1775
     Dau: Sarah Champness Terry
     Son: Champness Terry
           David Terry
     Exor: John Lewis of Va. Robert Stark

TILLY, JEAN--Dau. of James Pettigraw. Abbeville Will 1784

THOMAS, ELIZABETH--Of 96. Will 22 Aug. 1769. Prov. 18 july, 1770
     Gr. son: John Hawkins--The plt'n on 96 Creek and land on Half-
     way Swamp.
     "My own son": James Jones--2 shillings
     Exor: John savage--Gr. 18 July 1770
            Andrew Logan, Sen'r.
     Wit: Robert Dickie, Batt O'Brien, Susanna Dickee

THOMPSON, JAMES -w- Jean. 1768-Conv. Gr. 28 Aug. 1767. To Thos.
     Wilson. Long Cane Mem. 10-74   1

VAUGHAN, E. P. -m- Frances Byrd. Dau: Thos. B. Byrd and sister of
     Dudley Byrd. 1836

VERNER, MARY--Dau. of James Pettigrew. Will 1784. Abbeville

VERNON, JAMES, JUN'R. of Abbeville Co. Abbeville Univ. 1-13
     Legacy: Jane Kerr (Another card lists James Kerr-Bay Mare)
     Bro: Nehemiah   Isaac
           Robert   Joseph --Ex.
           Richard --Ex.
     Sister: Sarah   Hannah
     Nephew: John Vernon
     Father: Legacy--Linen Coat
     Wit: Felix Hughes, Robert Houston, Mary Kerr
     1 Sept. 1787. Prov. July 9, 1788

WAKEFIELD, JOHN--Greenville Deed Bk A-165 1789 to Thomas Wakefield

WALKER, JOHN--Mar. set Mary Ann Williamson. Old Index YY-112 Abbeville
     Thomas Hooper, Andrew Williams, David Oliphant

WARDLAW, HUGH--Dec'd. Will. Abbeville Prob. Bk. Pg. 98
     Summons 13 Dec. 1833 to: Joseph Wardlaw--Appl.
     William Wardlaw   James Wardlaw
     John   "   David   "
     James   " -w- Margaret
     Hugh H. Calvert
     James Dunn -w- Caroline
     Wm. Smith -w- Frances
     Wm. Leek -w- Eliza
     Mary Calvert
     John Calvert and Lucy Calvert--minors--Jesse Calvert, Gdn.
     Hugh Wardlaw
     David R. Caldwell -w- Elizabeth
     Benjamin Hodges -w- Mary Ann

WARDLAW, JOHN--Dec'd. Abbeville Prob. Bk. pg-37
    Summons 17 Sept. 1822 To: James Devlin--Heir--Appl. -vs-
    Col. John Hearst and Margaret Wardlaw
    Pg-44-50
    John Devlin--App. -vs-
    Wm. McClinton
    John Devlin and his children
    Esther McCullock --out of state
    Charlotte McCullock--Out of state.
    R. E. of Martha Smyth, dec'd to be sold

WARDLAW--Abbeville--See will of Wm. Bowman. 1789

WATKINS, JOHN AND Wife Greenville Deed Bk A 139/40 1787
      JANE To: Drury Morris

WATTS, AGNES--Dau. of Samuel Norwood of Abbeville. Will 1789
    Mary Watts--another daughter

WEEMS, JAMES--Dec'd. Abbeville Prob. Bk. Pg-45
    Summons 25 July 1829 to: Thomas J. Weems, Appl. -vs-
    Mrs. Agnes Weems--Adv. and Gdn. Pur. land.

WELLS, MOSES--Dec'd. Abbeville Prob. Bk. Pg-64/5
    Summons 28 Oct. 1831 To: Mary Wells
    John W. Anglin -w- Polly
    Walter Anderson -w- Susan
    Washington Wells
    Martha Ball -m- Bell?
    Brexton Smith -w- Rebecca
    Pamela Wells--Minor   John W. Anglin, Gdn.

WHITE, SARAH--Dau. of Robert Yeldell. Will 1789 Abbeville

WILEY, THOMAS--Dec'd. Abbeville Prob. Bk. pg-35
    Summons 6 Feb. 1828 to: Margaret Wiley, Appl.
    Samuel Young, Gdn of minor heirs. Ch.

WILLIAMS, JAMES.--Est. Partition Bk 1-136. Abbeville
    To: Mary Williams-widow, William Williams
    David Robinson and Eliza his wife.
    Archibald F. Hamilton and Owealine his wife.
    Mary Williams, Gdn of Sarah M., John, Margaret S., James N., and
    Samuel L., to appear. 14 Nov. 1837. Real Estate on McCord's Cr.
    Waters Long Cane. 120 A. Bd. L. James McCord, Henry Riff,
    Archibald McCord, et al

WILLIAMS, JAMES. Abbeville Bk-2-388. 11 Aug. 1836
    Son: James--All. Prov. 6 Aug. 1837

WILLIAMS, MAHOLY--Dau. of Robert Moore. See Will R. M. Abbeville Wills
                                              Bk 3-151 1846
WILLIAMS, SIMEON--Of Abbeville 8 Apr. 1801
      Wife: Edny. Bro: Arthur.--Exor's.--To sell 100 A. in Greenville
    to pay debts. Wife's son, Sheridan, equal share. "my children"
    not named. Wit: Chas. Dodson, John Williams. Prov. 23 Sept.
                                         1801

WILSON, CHARLES--Dec'd. Will 20 Nov. 1809. Prov. 27 March 1811
    Ch: Minors. Sons: Michael, James, John, Andrew, Elizabeth,
    Margaret--Minors. Abbeville Bx 95-2355. 1811

WILSON, JOHN--Dec'd. Will 9 June, 1783. Abbeville Bx 95-2346 1783
    Elsest Dau: Ann--The home place
                Jean--100 A. Gr. To Robert Castle in 1768
    1794 Bx 95-2345--John Wilson--Dec'd. Will 30 Aug. 1796
    Widow: Ruth
    Son: John
         James--minor
         Jacob
    Dau: Betsy

WILSON, THOMAS--Dec'd. Abbeville Prob. Bk. pg-69
    Summons to: Wm. H. Jones, Appl. 14 Nov. 1831
    Hannah Wilson--1/3
    Lorenzo Wright -w- Jane
    Minor Ch. Wm. H. Jones, Gdn.

WILSON, JAMES--Dec'd Page 75. Summons: John R. Wilson--Appl.
    Matthew Wilson, Thomas, Margaret, Sarah, Jane Wilson
    James Bigham -w- Mary
    Theophilus Norwood -w- Elizabeth

WINN, LETTICE--Dec'd. Intestate. Abbeville Prob. Bk Pg 18.
    Summons 1 Jan. 1827: Henry G. Walker -w- _____? Appl.
    James Baird -w-   Jeremiah G. Walker
    Burrel Boykin   Faris Carter
    John W. Walker   Faris C. Walker

WINN, LEWELLEN--Dec'd. Abbeville Prob. Bk. Pg 47/48
    Summons 28 Sept. 1829 to: Burwell E, Hobbs. Appl.
        14 Dec. 1829   -vs-
    Stephen J. Blackwell -w- Maria
    Elizabeth H. Winn   - Warren F. Winn
    Susan Winn   Sarah Winn

WITHERSPOON, MARTHA--Dau. of James Pettigrew. Will 1784-Abbeville

WOOD, WILLIAM AND WIFE ELIZABETH--To James Southern. Greenville Deed
    Bk. A-103. 1787

WOOD, WILLIAM and Wife Elizabeth to John Pyle. Greenville Deed Bk A-70

WOODIN, REBEKAH--Of St. Phillips Parish. City of C. T.
    Legacy: Dr. John De La Howe of C. T.
            Daniel Bourdeaus and wife
            Miss Elizabeth Bourdeaux
            Mrs. Matthews.
    20 Nov. 1784. Prov. Oct. 8, 1788. Abbeville Wills

WOODS, RACHEL W. -vs- Martha B. Drinkwater, John Gray and James Woods.
    Adm'rs. Out of state. In Equity--Abbeville Dist. May 29, 1824
    The Columbia Telescope

26

WOODS, MRS. SUSANNAH--Dec'd. Abbeville Prob. Bk. Pg-46
    Summons 5 Nov. 1829: Wm. M. Smith and wife. -vs-
    *James Woods   *Robert W. Woods
    *Wm. L. "   *Andrew C.   "
    *Michael "   *--Out of State
    Martha B. Drinkwater

WORTHAM, JOHN--Legatee John Marshall. Will 1784. Abbeville

WRIGHT, GEORGE--Of 96 Dist. Abbeville File. C. T. Wills
    Wife: Sarah   Will 14 May, 1774
    Dau: Mary Ann Wright--Grist and Saw Mill
          Sarah Wright--Land in Frederick Co. Va.
          Susannah Wright--Still and 150 acres.
    Son: George Wright--Home Place

WRIGHT, ROBERT--Dec'd. Abbeville Prob. Bk. Pg-77
    Summons 10 Feb. 1832 to: Anna Wright--Gdn. of
                    Vincent T. Wright, and Turner T. Wright

YARBROUGH, BUFORD--Dec'd intestate. Abbeville Prob. Bk. pg-93
    Summons 19 Nov. 1833 to: Wm. D Yarbrough-minor
    Elizabeth Yarbrough
    Mary   "
    Sarah   "
    Drusilla Taggart

YELDELL, ROBERT, SEN'R.--Will 29 June, 1789. Abbeville Bk-1-20
    Son: James, dec'd--To his heirs
    Dau: Jean Atkins and Sarah White
    Gr. Dau: _____? dau. of Joseph Dennis
    Dau: Mary Heirston and Gr. son Robert Heirston
    Sons: Robert Yeldell and Anthony Yeldell
    Dau: Phebe Yeldell
    Gr. Son: Robert Yeldell. Prov. Oct. 6, 1788

YORK, ANN--Dau. of Moses McCarter. Will 1787. Abbeville

ZUBLY, JOHN JOACHIM--Of Savannah Georgia. Dau: Ann "Wife of Mr.
    Peter Bard of New York. See Codicil 25 May 1781.
    C. T. Wills Univ. Vol. 19-311

ANDERSON COUNTY, SOUTH CAROLINA

ADAIR, JOHN -- "S. C. Pendleton District" Anderson Wills Bk A-176 Roll 3
    Wife: Jean -- 200 A. The line to cross at the flat shoal Little
                  River below Fish Trap called Walter's Trap to Kyes
                  line.
    Son: Samuel --
          Walter -- Debts due by Cherokees
          Thomas B.
          John -- Land on Connerose-200 A.
          Edward
    Dau: ? See will in file if necessary
          Jean
    Son: James -- Land on Cane Creek. Part Home Place
          William Henry
          Charles D.
          Elbert Earle
    Dau: Mary Ann
    Son: Benjamin Franklin
          John Alexander 4 Nov. 1815
    Ex: Entire family
    Wit: Joseph Reid, Sam'l Boyd Sloan, Thos. Lamar, Capt. David
    Proven: 4 Dec. 1815

ADDIS, WILLIAM --Dec'd. Pendleton Messenger Mar. 30. 1849
    Sale of R. E.
    Samuel Addis
    Elizabeth -w- Pinckney Mason
    John Addis
    Sarah -w- John Thomas
    Nancy C. -w- Thomas Smith
    William Addis -vs- Heirs of James Addis Dec'd.
        Mary Addis
        Jane -w- George W. Fuller Both out of state

ANDERSON, DAVID and MARGARET -- Children of Elizabeth Crook. Heirs
    of David Moore Will 1836

ANDERSON, DAVID Anderson Wills 20-21 Will 23 June 1860 -- 5 July 1861
    Wife: Lucinda Matilda
    "My 2 f'st ch'n: Edward M. Anderson
                  James G. Anderson
    Son: Robert Anderson
    Dau: Mary   "
    Son: David   "

ARMSTRONG, ARCHIBALD Will 4 Apr. 1862 Anderson Wills Bk 3-94
    Wife: Mary Ann
    Dau: Arty E. (a Cripple)
    "9 Ch: Elizabeth Shirley
           Daniel B.
           Isabella I. Ellis
           Mary J. Shamble __(Arty was fifth child. Comes in here)
           Margaret L. Hays‐
           Andrew G.
           Rachel R.
           John A.

ARMSTRONG, JAMES Anderson Gard. Bk. 2-482 19 Dec. 1856 Guardian for:
    Archibald P Armstrong, Narcissa, Elizabeth, Margaret, Minerva
    William C., Palestine and Mary a minor.

28

ARMSTRONG, JAMES, SR. Anderson Will Bk 3-79
    Wife: Polly
    "My 4 Sons": William B., John R., N. H., C.C.,
    "My 4 Daus": Margaret S. -w- Benjamin W. Chambliss
               Lucinda -w- James C. Williams
               Polly A. E. -w- H. A. Cobb
               Elizabeth Armstrong
    4 Dec. 1857 Prov. 24 Oct. 1860

ARMSTRONG, JOHN of Pendleton Dist. Anderson Wills Bk A-98 Roll 6
    Son: John
    Dau: Mary: Called Polly it seems
    Son: Charles
    Dau: Isabella -m- Isaac Bradley of Pendleton
          Sarah -m- Isaac Bradley (This is not an error. F. C.)
    Remainder to "All my Children" not named.
    Ex: Joab Mauldin, John Bowen
    Date: 6 Mar. 1808 Proven: 1 Aug. 1808
    Wit: James Fleming, Jos. Pressly, Andrew Hughs
    Receipt 18 Feb. 1811 Jonathan Bruce -w- Mary
        "   12 Aug. 1814 John Armstrong
        "   Oct. 1808 George Armstrong, son of Dec'd
        "   9 Aug. 1809 Charles Armstrong, a son
        "   22 Oct. 1808 Joseph Gibson -w- Elizabeth of Tenn. (a Dau.)
        "   23 Nov. 1808 Isaac Bradley -w- Isabella of Pendleton
        "   23 Nov. 1808 Isaac Bradley -w- Sarah

ATKINSON, M. D. Anderson Probate 1843 --Children of -- Heirs of John
    Morgan Moore d. 1843

BALLENTINE, ELIZABETH --Heir of John Morgan Moore D. 1843 Anderson Pro.

BOWMAN, ARCHIBALD -- Indicted by the Grand Jury of Pendleton for
    Bastard on body of Margaret Pickens. Has fled to N. C. and this
    is request for his return for trial. 16 Dec. 1807 Gov. of N. C.
    Anderson File Misc. B-497

BRUCE, JAMES A. Will 13 June 1861 Prov. 2 March 1863. Anderson Wills
    Mother: Vancy Bruce   24/25
    Bros: P. S. F. Bruce, C. C. M. Bruce, S. P. Bruce
    Sister: Elizabeth L. Bruce

CLINKSCALES, WILLIAM F. Will 17 Nov. 1852. Prov. Nov. 25, 1859
    "My 5 Children" Asa, Stephen, Polly Clement
    Betsy -w- W. P. Hunnicutt--reside in Gwinett Co. Georgia
    Chloe Townes -w- Wm. W. Towne --Land on Hen Coop Cr.
    Exor: Franklin D. Towne at age 21
            Son: Berry Clinkscales Anderson Wills 10/11

CROOK, ELIZABETH -w- Jesse Crook. Heir of David Moore W. 1836
    Anderson Probate

CUMMING, THOMAS J. Will 1 Sept. 1861 Prov. 20 Sept. 1861 Anderson 19/20
    Wife: Name not clear--½
    To: Miss Rosa Hanah Duglas--a friend
    To: The Children of Adaline Allen--House and lot in Charles
        Town to be sold.
    Bro: George A. Cumming
    Sister: Agnes Cumming

DAY, BALLARD Sen'r Anderson Willa Bk A-168 Roll 171
    Wife: Silvey
    Son: Johnson--married
    Dau: Mary Breazeale
    Son: Middleton (Had other children it seems)
    Ex: Wife and Abraham Mayfield 13 Jan. 1815
    Wit: Reuben Clements, J'n Burford, Rich'd Harrison

DICKSON, JANE (x) Will 5 June 1859 Prov 27 Apr. 1861 Anderson Wills 22
    Sister: Margaret C. Smith--Land left to me by my father Mathew
          Dickson where we now live. At her death to: Alexander
          Dickson and Permelia Dickson

DICKSON, MATHEW, SEN'R -- Pendleton Messenger July 21, 1830
    Died 10th inst. 99 yrs age. Native of Ireland--came to America
    in 1762. 60 yrs citizen of S. C. A Rev. patriot. 4th generation
    of descendants. Aug 18 est. notice--Hugh Gaston, Exor.

 DRENNON, WILSON and Wife Keowee Courier April 3, 1858
    Prudence Drennon and Edwin Rogers
    Temperance McWhorter
    John and wife Sarah
    Amos Robinson and wife Nelly
    Hugh Rogers
    Heirs of John Rogers and his widow
        Emmerson Black and wife Elizabeth
        ____ Moore and Wife Sarah
    James, Zachariah, William, John. David and the state and James
    Rogers. Heirs of: Bill for partition

DRENNAN, WILLIAM, JR.--Wit. deed from Elijah Brown to Wiley Brown of
    Lincoln Co. N. C. Anderson Deed A-69

EDWARDS, JAMES WESLEY Will 13 May 1861 Prov. 24 May 186. Anderson Wills
    Wife: Martha Ann   21/22
    Bro: John M. Edwards--To his Children
    Exor: John Wilson

ELLISON, FRANCIS--Heir of John Morgan Moore d. 1843 Anderson Pro.

FEATHERSTONE, JOHN WESLEY Will 11 Feb. 1858 Prov. 31 May 1858
    Son: L. P.   Anderson Wills Bk 3-1
    Dau: Helen H. Williams
          Emma E. Young
    Son: John C. C.
    Also younger children-minors-not named. To be educated
    Wife not mentioned.

GRINDWELL, JOHN--Farmer of "sd Co". for Solomon King of Abbeville Co.
    200 A. Seneca River. Anderson Deed C-104 2 Jan. 1796

GROGAN, THOMAS Anderson Deed M-527 8 Apr. 1810
    For Abram Anderson of Pendleton 105 A. Samuel Jackson Mill.
    Wit: John Field Jr. and Jas. T. Baker

GROGAN, THOMAS Of Pendleton Dist. Anderson Deeds L-56 10 Dec. 1810
    To William McFarland 106 A. Crow Creek--Waters Keowee R.
    Wit: Richard Grogan and Lucy Grogan. Prov. by Richard Grogan
    1 Feb. 1811

GROGAN, THOMAS Of Pendleton.   Anderson Deeds P-256 28 March 1821
    To Elisha Alexander of Pendleton 234½ A. Crow Creek--Purchased of
    William Anderson--Keowee River--Whereon I now reside. Also 175 A.
    adj. above gr. sd. Grogan 3 July 1809 by John Drayton. Wit:
    William Grisham, Prier Alexander

HAYNE, HARRISON--Pendleton Messenger Mar. 31, 1843
    Charged with stealing cotton. Found guilty. For Edgefield Adv.

HEAD, JOHN--Anderson Deed E-126
    To Fanny Waters--Dau. of Charles Waters and wife Mary--Consid-
    eration Pd. by Charles Waters $100.00 - 76 A. Pt Gr to Alex'r
    Maham who conveyed to Charles Waters and from sd Waters toJohn
    Head. Also pt gr to Robert Brasher who conv. to Ed Maxwell
    who conv. to John Head. Including the plantation where the
    said Waters now lives--reserves life estate for sd Waters and
    Wife, Mary. 5 May 1799 Wit: James Head, Peter Head sd John
    Head

HILL, ABRAHAM Anderson Probate 1841
    Wife: Polly-widow
           Newport Hill -w- Elizabeth
           T. I. Hill
           David Argo -w- Polly
           Ann David Hill
           Emmaline Hill
           Abraham Hill
           John Hill

HOLLAND, WILLIAM Anderson Wills 16/17 Will 10 Feb. 1859 Prov. 15 Mar
    Son: William Davis Holland--Not 21   1859
    "All my Children"
    Exor: Benj. F. Mauldin

INGRAM, BENJAMIN of 96 District Anderson Deed B-83 18 Dec. 1792
    To: Patrick McDowell and Alexander McDowell 640 A. 12 Mile Creek
    Waters of Savannah River--Gr 6 Nov. 1786 to James Millwee. Wit:
    Wesley Glover, Thos. Robertson. Prov. in Abbeville Co 26 Mar. 1792
    by Thomas Robertson
    Anderson Deed F-396 10 Feb. 1802 Benjamin Ingram to Lewis D. Martin
    235 A. on Conneross--Keowee River. Dist Pendleton formerly 96 Dist.
    Bd. Austin's Land, Chas. Hunt, Lewis D. Martin. East by James Ingra m

HUNT, SARAH -m- Nicholas Hunt 20 Dec. 1811. Anderson Equity 4 1820
    Suit for separation alleging cruelty of _____? and adultry with
    Betsy Turner. They had sev. children. He alleged Betty was his
    niece.

JOHNSTON, FREDERICK Anderson Deed Bk A-75--Stock Mark: "Frederick
    Johnston's Mark--a swallow fork and an underbit in each ear.
    Recorded 7 April 1806".

JOHNSTON, FREDERICK Anderson Wills 1-48 Roll 74 A-55
    Mentioned as being or having a step-son (seems that Elijah Smith
    is his step-son in will of Willoughby Broughton. James Garvin
    is executor.

JOHNSON, JOHN of Pendleton Co. Anderson Wills Bk 346
    Wife: "And her children"
    Son: Joseph--Land on Great Saltcatchers, Winton Co. Orangeburg Co.
    Dau: Elizabeth--Land on 3 mi. Creek--waters of Saltcatchers
    16 Aug. 1790 Prov. 8 Nov. 1790
    Wit: Stephen Sullivant and Elizabeth Jones, Joseph Dunklin

LAHOON, PETER Anderson Wills Bk A-1 7 June 1800
    Wife: Hannah
    Daus: Catherine, Elizabeth
    Son: Peter
    Dau: Mary Waters

LEWIS, DAVID--Anderson Wills A-270 Pendleton Dist. Will 19 Jan. 1820
    Wife: Penelopy
    Son: Isaiah
    Dau: Priscilla -w- Thos. Field
    Sons: Jacob, Joab, Noriah, Benjamin
    Dau: Elizabeth -w- Micajah Alexander
        Cozby (?) -w- John Wodall
    Son: Tarkton Lewis
    Dau: Hannah -w- Ezekiel Norton

LIDDELL, MARY--Widow of A. J. Liddell Will 17 Nov. 1849 Anderson Wills 3
    Dau: Mary Caroline
        Amanda--widow of Alex'r Dickson of Miss
        Rachel Emily Stephenson -w- James S. of Miss.
        Eliza Reeves -w- R. W. Reeves

MAYFIELD, PEGGY--Equity Notice Pendleton Messenger 14 Mar. 1845
    -vs- William Magee et al--Pet. for sale of lands
    Out of State: Austin Mayfield, Silvy Day, Jonathan Reeves -w-
    Thassey, Ephraim Mayfield

McPEYON, WILLIAM Anderson Probate 1833--Citation in file of Samuel
    E. Moore

MERITT, OBADIAH--Anderson Wills 13/14 Will June 13, 1860 Prov. Aug. 21
    Dau: Lucy Meritt and her 2 daus. Mary and Florence   1860
        Sarah
        Nancy and her children
    Exors: Richard T. Elrod

MILLER, SARAH--Anderson Wills 4/5 Will 6 Jan. 1858 Prov. Mar. 10 1858
    Dau: Maria Jane Coffee of Cherokee Co. Ga.
        Mary Ann Bright -w- William B.
    Son: Andrew Jackson Lowery
    Dau: Theresa -w- Leroy Rillen
    Son: John Franklin Miller

MOORE, AGNESS--Dau. of Samuel Findley Anderson Wills C-46 1 Sept 1794
    Jane Moore--Dau of David Alexander Univ. 1-23

MOORE, AGNESS--Pendleton Messenger 9 Dec. 1836 -vs- Thomas Moore
    Pickens Dist. Out of State: Thomas Moore in re estate of
    Lazarus Moore, Dec'd

MOORE, JAMES -w- wife, Lucinda, formerly Lucinda Brown dau. Randolph
    Brown in re Est. Elias G. Brown -vs- Rebecca Brown et al
    Anderson Equity Box 7 #116 1851

MOORE, LEAH -vs- Th. Williams -w- Jane Bill for Partition 142 A. on
    Rocky River adj. L-Jonas Thomason; C. Wakefield et al.
    Pendleton Messenger Equity Oct. 30, 1846

O'NEILL, MICHAEL --Will 28 Oct. 1857 Prov. 27 Sept. 1858 Anderson Wills 4
    Wife: Catherine -- Home Place in Anderson and all other

ORR, CYNTHIA--Heir of John Morgan Moore d. 1843. Got land on Hurricane
    Creek. 230 A. adj. S. T. Richardson, Sam'o Elrod et al

PARROTT, NATHANIEL--Will 4 June 1860 Prov. July 11, 1860 Anderson Wills 17
    To: Martha C. Watt -w- Samuel S. Watt
        Wm. D. Hewin
        Louisa Watt -w- John W. Watt
        John Mc Hewin
        Elvis A. Keown -w- Robert Keown, Jr.
        Postell Hewin
        Olin T. Hewin
        Pinckney W. Hewin

PERKINS, ISAAC of Pendleton Dist. Anderson Wills Bk C-53 10 Feb. 1794
    Wife
    Son: Richard
    Wit: John C. Kilpatrick, Alex Kilpatrick, Bartholomew Wollom(?)

PETTICE, JANE --Will 22 Feb. 1858 Prov. Aug. 5, 1858 Anderson Wills 5
    To: Mr. Daniel Osborne--All for life then to "My Brother" Murry
    Woodson -w- Katy and their children.

PERKINS, WILLIAM Anderson Wills Bk Pg. 353 (Of Pendleton Dist.)
    Dau: Rutha Philips--1 Shilling for her disobedience
    Son: Moses Perkins--1 Shilling for his disobedience
        Josiah and Joshua--Land where on my mother now lives after
        her death.
    Mentions other children but doesn't name them.
    Ex: John C. and Peter Kilpatrick   29 Mar. 1816
    Wit: R. H. Grant, Aaron Terrell, Aaron Shannon

POOL, ADAD -w- Easter of Pendleton Co. Anderson Deed N-21 16 Dec. 1797
    To: Thomas Shelton--135 A. Gr. to John Roland 31 Aug 1774--on
    Lick Br. of Broad River

PRICHARD, LEWIS--Will 3 Feb. 1858 Prov. Aug. 13, 1858 Anderson Wills 10
    Wife: Hariet
    Son: James and Berry
    Dau: Nancy Bolt
    Sons: William L., Cornelias T., Lemuel M.,
    Dau: Martha Ann, Sarah E., Ada B., Mary C.
    Exor: Bryan Borough

PRINCE, EDWARD C. of Anderson Anderson Wills Vol 3-194 10 Jan. 1862
    Wife: Mary E. Prince--All   Prov. 7 Oct. 1864
    No children. 110 A. stock, etc.
    Exor: Wm. Sherard

RICE, HEZEKIAH--Will Apr. 5, 1846 Prov. Jan. 18, 1860 Anderson Wills
    Wife: Polly Rice   18/19
    "My Children": Polly Clinkscales
                       Ibsan Rice
                       Thomas Rice
                       Amaziah Rice
                       Asinoth -w- Wm. Magee
                       Ch. of dec'd son, Hezekiah Rice
                       Louisa -w- Abner H. Magee
                       Fleetwood Rice
                       Wiley Latimer -w- Irina Smith

RILEY, RUTH--Will 27 Apr. 1858 Prov. 18 May 1861 Anderson Wills 14
    Nephew: Sanford V. Gentry
    Niece: Malissa Wilcox -w- James B. Wilcox

ROBINSON or CLAYTON Graveyard near Liberty, S. C.
    Robinson, Charles S. b. Jan 23, 1846 d. 1896
    His wife: Louisa E. Clayton b. Apr. 22, 1846 d. 1928
    She seems dau. of Carter Clayton

ROGERS, LARKIN--Will Mar. 19, 1862 Anderson Wills 25/26
    Children--Wife--Living
    To: W. P. Rogers, Sarah E., D. J. S., Eben Z., Thos., Benj. H.
    John S., Joseph W.-not of age, Ruby A., Matilda M., W. N.,
    David C., George F.

SHERIFF, LETTY AND CHARITY--Daughters of John Morgan Moore d. 1843
    Anderson Probate 1843

SILMON, BENJ. --(1800-1834) 15 Dec. 1802 Anderson Wills 1-26
    Wife: Isabel
    Sons: Benjamin and David
    Daus: Rosy and Judy
    Bro: Thomas, Exor. Landon Torrans Br.

SLATER, ANNA Anderson Probate 1839--Ward of John M. Moore d. 1843
    She was heir of Wm. Slater, dec'd.

STANTON, C. B. Will Sept 9, 1875 Anderson Prob. Will Bk 5-379
    Legacy: Francis E. Slines
    Dau: Synther K. Stone $1.00
          Rachel C. Ford $1.00

STANTON, CATHERINE AND MATHIAS--Anderson Deed W-420 1843
    To: Wm. Welborn--260 A. Saluda River. 1840

STANTON, GEORGE --Of Anderson Anderson Bk 1-199 1845
    Wife: Lurance
    Dau: Elizabeth Payne (dec'd) children
    Ex: Caleb Payne "The whole of my Children".
    Wit: James Donthit, Berry Durham, Andrew Durham
    Dated 4 Aug. 1837 Prov. 21 Apr. 1845

STANTON, JAMES to Caleb Payne--100 A. Craven's Creek Pt. l. conv.
    Christopher Stanton by John Tripp who conv. to John Stanton.
    Wit: Geo. Stanton, Elijah Satterfield R-105 1825

STANTON, MATHIAS "Of Anderson" Anderson Wills Bk 3-299 Roll 2310
    Wife: Mary Ann
    "My four children"
    Bro: R. B. Stanton--Ex. with Wife
    Dated 5 July 1862 Prov. 27 Apr. 1868

STANTON, THOMAS Anderson Probate Roll 677
    Cit: 6 July 1815 Maj. Adam Carruth and Thos Payne applied for
    Letters of Administration. Bond: Sept. 13, 1813
    Surety: Wm. Hamilton

STANTON, WILLIAM--Anderson Deed F-430 12 Oct. 1801 from Hezekiah Rice
    175 A. on Hiram Cr. 12 July 1800

STANTON, WILLIAM--Anderson Deed G-70 12 Oct. 1801 from Wm. Lowe and
    wife, Margaret Lowe 88 A. on Saluda River

STANTON, WILLIAM--Anderson Deed Bk A-73 Stock Mark
    "William Stanton's Mark is two crops and two over keels. Re-
    corded 14 Oct. 1801

STANTON, WILLIAM Anderson Deed Mar. 3, 1804 G-509 From Watson
    Allison of Jackson Co. Georgia. 400 A. on Bushy Cr. Pt Gr sd
    Allison 4 Dec. 1786. Wit: Robert Allison, Frank Thompson

STANTON. William Anderson Deed I-277 21 Oct 1808 from Benj Clardy
    140 A. Gr David Clark June 13, 1809 262 A. on Hurricane Cr.
    K-130 Apr. 12, 1810 100 A. Hurricane Cr.
    M-96 22 Mar. 1813 To James Merritt of Pendleton 400 A. on
    Brushy Creek. Pt 400 A. Gr to Watson Allison 4 Dec. 1786
    P-328 1 Oct. 1821 from Cain Broyles 938 A. on waters Saluda R.
    Apr 24, 1821. Dower, Lucinda Broyles
    R-468 4 Sept 1826 to Mark Littleton 161 A. on Hurricane Creek
    waters of Saluda R. 10 June 1825. Dower: Caty Stanton Apr 21,
    R-496 3 Oct. 1826 from John Vandiver 246 A. Big Mouth Cr 1826

STANTON, WILLIAM d. intestate Anderson Equity Roll 63
    Widow: Catherine
            Charity -w- Jeremiah W.
            Fanny -w- John Murphy
            Lettice -w- Grant A. Moore
            Betsy -w- John A. Moore
            Catherine -w- Abner Cox
            Melissa -w- Wm. Telfornes
            Thomas, William, and Christian B. Stanton
            Richardson, Cynthia, Matthias Stanton--minors
            Cynthia -m- Reuben B. Cox

STEGALL, HENSLEY--Of Pendleton District Will Anderson Bk A-329
    "I Will and Bequeath all my estate, both real and personal to the
    children that I have had by Fanny Holeman, the woman with whom I
    now live, viz; Spencer, Caroline, Mary, Elizabeth, and William
    Warren". If my father, Richard Stegall, who is now living,
    should at his death, bequeath any part of his estate to me,
    (same disposition as above) 10 July 1826

STEGALL, RICHARD Pickens Deed B-2 84--To his children; Bird, Spencer,
    Blackwell, Linny, Yancey Artemus, Susan, Benj. Thelly, Nancy
    Patsy (dec'd) Hensley

STEGALL, RICHARD Anderson Deed H-468 1807 from Robert Bowman 600 A.
    Bd. N. Robert Henderson E. Wm. Bowman. 8 Oct. 1805

SUBER, ANDREW H. Will 28 Dec. 1861 Prov. 23 June 1862 Anderson Wills 24
    Wife: Ellen C. Suber--All
    Exor: H. H. Vandiver

TAYLOR, NANCY--Widow of Joseph Taylor Anderson Wills 23/24 1853-1862
    Son-in Law: William Poe
            "My dau. Ellen C. Poe
    Son: Dr. Joseph Taylor
    Dau: Susanne M. Lewis
    Son: Samuel J. Taylor
          John A. E. Taylor
          William S. Taylor
          David S. Taylor

TAYLOR, JAMES Will 19 Dec 1857 Prov. 26 Feb 1858 Anderson Wills 9
    Wife:_____ and her 3 sons, and 3 sons not with her--190
          A. the Homestead, etc
    Son: Robert C   )
    Dau: Caroline   ) Children of 1st wife.
    Sons: George B. and James H.)
    8 children by 1st wife being 4 sons and 4 daus.

WATKINS, THOS. C. Will 15 Jan 1862 Prov. 14 Oct. 1862 Anderson Wills
    Wife: and her children or their heirs   22/23
    Exors: B. J. Watkins, Warren J. Martin, Aaron John Smith

WEBB, WARREN H. Will 26 Sept 1859 Prov. 23 Mar. 1860 Anderson Wills 18
    5 Shares: Samuel J. H. Webb
               Charles L. Webb
               Charlotte A. C. T. Webb
               Benjamin F. Webb
               Ann W. Pepper -w- John H. Pepper

WILSON, HUGH Will 4 Sept 1862 Prov. 6 Dec. 1863 Anderson Wills 6
    Wife: Elizabeth
    Son: James R. Wilson--Exor.
    Dec'd son: John H. Wilson's Dau: Mary Wilson (Dau?)

Wilson, James--Will 13 Aug 1853 Prov. 13 Oct. 1858 Anderson Wills 8/9
    Wife: Not named
    Eldest Dau: Sarah Avery and her only dau.
    Dau: Elizabeth Avery widow of Jesse Avery
          Margaret D. Coker -w- Edwin A. Coker
    Son: John Wilson, M. D. Exor.
    Exor: George B. Telford

WILSON, ROBERT--Anderson Equity Roll 10 -vs- John Lewis et al
    Alleges: Gen Assemb. authorized relief of persons who sus-
    tained loss by fire at pickensville

WYATT, JAMES--Anderson Probate 1843--Heir of John Morgan Moore d. 1843

BARNWELL COUNTY, SOUTH CAROLINA

AARONS, MARY ELIZABETH--Dau. of Robert Kennedy. Will 1834 Barnwell

ADAMS, WILLIAM (X)--Will   Barnwell A-61
    Wife: Joanna Adams
    Son: John Adams--Exor.
           William Adams
    Dau: Susanna Alfred and son-in-law, Jacob Alfred, Exor.
    Son: James Adams--a minor
    Dau: Elizabeth Adams
           Polly   "
           Sally   "
           Nancy   "
           Hannah   "
           Rebecca Poste Adams

ADKINS, HARRIET (also called Harriet Smithhart)--dau of Eleanor Newson
    Will 1837

ALEXANDER, RAIN--Native of Rochelle, France, now of Barnwell Dist. Will
    20 July, 1803. "my 2 sons": Mathew and Reuben. Land on Savannah R.
    Barnwell Wills A-4/5

ALFRED, SUSANNAH--Dau of Wm. Adams of Barnwell. Will abt. 1803

ALLEN, ANN--Dau of Sarah Dewees of Barnwell. Will 1816

ALLEN, JOSEPH--Gr-son of Joseph Duncan of Barnwell. Will 1820

ALLEN, JOSEPH--Gr-son of Mary Woodroof of Barnwell. Will 1822. "Son"
    Orasmus D. Allen. Caroline W. Allen--Now Mrs. Hamilton

ANDERSON, ELIZABETH--Dau of Moore Johnson. Will 1825 Barnwell

ANDERSON, SARAH MARY--Gr-dau. of Sarah M. Johnson. Will 1844. Barnwell
    Catherine Anderson--dec'd dau. of Testator. Her dau: Margaret--
    Legatee also, and sev. sons.

ANTHONY, JOHN -vs- Richard Dillon and Richard Jones, Partition. Barnwell
    Ct. Com. Pl. Bk.-1-30 1800 March 10, 1802

ARMSTRONG, JAMES--Nephew of Elizabeth Lord. Barnwell Will 1843

ARMSTRONG, TABITHA--Dau of Adam Lard, Sr. Barnwell Will 1828

ARINGTON, BUREL--Bro. of Nancy Skiper of Barnwell. Will 1816
    Arthur Arrington--another Bro.

ARNOLD, MARTHA--Dau. of Eleanor Newsom. Barnwell Will 1837

ASH, CATO--Gr. son of Andrew Deveaus of Barnwell. Will 1812. Son-in-
    law: Richard Ash.

ASHLEY, AUSABEL--Dau. of Taliafferro(sp) Martin. Barnwell Will 1832

ASHLEY, NATHANIEL--Will Barnwell Bk-A 246 Oct. 11, 1813
    Wife: Elizabeth--Ex.
    Ch: Wilson, Ex.
    Joshua--a minor
    William, Polly, Ann, John, Charles, James, Sally

AYER, HENRY--Will--his 3 Ch. of 1st. wife Rebecca--Legatees of Susannah
    Sutton. Barnwell Will 1833

BACON, EDWARD, ESQ.-"Late a citizen of Georgia, who has settled in this
    State". Admitted to Practice of Law in S. C. Barnwell Bk-1 P 154
    21 Oct. 1806

BAKER, WILLIAM--Will 13 Feb. 1786 Barnwell Wills, C. T. File
    Gr. dau-in-law: Elizabeth Ladson
    Bro-in-law: Mark Harden
    Bro: James Baker
    Sis: Temperance McDonald
          Rachel Mallett(see Edgefield Deeds)
          Judith Harden
          Sarah Johnston, Niece

BALDWIN, BETSY--Dau of Wm. Stringfellow of Barnwell. Will 1812

BARFIELD, WINNEY--Dau of James Roberts of Barnwell. Will 1802

BARNEY, JAMES H.--"son" of Willis Weathersbee. Barnwell Will 1827

BATES, ANDREW, SR. Will 19 Sept. 1799 Barnwell Wills A-21/2
    Wife: Elizabeth
    Sons: Richard, Andrew, John, Jacob
    Daus: Martha, Mary

BATES, SARAH--Dau. of Henry Snelling of Barnwell. Will 1819

BAXLEY, WILLIAM--Father-in-law of Darling Bloom. Barnwell Will 1830

BEACH, LAVINIA--Dau. of John Cochran Barnwell Will 1837

BEAL, ANN--Dau. of Richard Kirkland of Barnwell. Her son--Richard
    Beal. Will 1812

BEAL, NATHAN--Provision in will of Edward Kirkland of Barnwell, states
    his Mother, Mary Kirkland, must disown Nathan Beal as her husband.
    Names Ann Beal as his sister. 1807

BEAL, RICHARD K.--Richard C. Kirkland of Barnwell. Will 1817

BECK, ELIZABETH--Step Dau. of Burrel Parker. Barnwell. Will 1833 or 35

BECK, MARY--Dau. of Reuben Morgan of Barnwell. Will 1818

BELL, MARY AND HANNAH--Daus. of Joseph Hayse of Barnwell. Will 1799

BELL, RHODY--Dau. of Thomas Lee of Barnwell. Will 1815

BENTLEY, ELIZABETH--Dau. of Solomon McClair of Barnwell. Will 1814

BESSELIEN, ELIZABETH--Gr. Dau. of Sarah Deween of Barnwell. Will 1816

BEST, JOHN B.--Land he lived on at time of his death. 25/96 parts be-
    longed to John A. Best, in year 1860. Barnwell Misc. 2B-232
    796 A. Barnwell-- on King Creek

BLACKMAN, WINIFRED--Dau. Robert Lee of Barnwell. Will 1789. Gr. Dau:
    Zelpha Blackman

BLALOCK, SARAH--Dau.(?) of John Blitchendon of Barnwell. Will 1803
    See Will of Levi Long of Barnwell--1803

BLAND, MARY--Dau. of Moore Johnson. Will 1825. Also Dau. Sophia Bland

BLITCHENDON, JOHN--Will 18 Sept, 1803 Barnwell Wills A 59/60
    Gr. Son: John Hickman--land on Half Moon Br.
    Dau: Rebecca Hickman
        Mary Day   )
        Ann Taylor   ) Have already received their share
        Sarah Black   )
        William Blitchendon)
    Son-in-law: Thomas Hickman--Exor.
    Wit: John Hickman, Elizabeth Hickman, Anna Hickman (All sd X)

BLUME, JOHN, SR.--Will 7 March 1814. Deed Bk 9 Pg. 109/10 Barnwell
    Wife: Sarah
    Son: Darling (Blume)
    Pg. 107: J. B. Sr. to Dau. Sarah B. Jr.

BOYD, MARY--Dau. of Elisha Chavous of Barnwell. Will 1826

BOYLES, PRISSA -w- Henry Boyles. Legatee of John Steel. Barnwell Will 1835

BOYLSON, SARAH--Dau. of Robert Willis. Barnwell. Will 1843 (44)

BURKALTERS, WILLIAM AND JAMES--Sons-in-law of John Canady, Sr. of Barn-
    well. Will 1819

BUTLER, FRANCIS -w- Louisa A. Son in law of Elizabeth Ford of Barnwell
    Will 1824

BRABHAM, SARAH--Dau. of Reuben Kirkland of Barnwell. Will 1822

BRELAND, ABRAHAM-w- Elizabeth--Dau. of John Varn. Will 1827

BRELAND, MARY-w- Wm Breland. Dau. of Wm. Kearse. Will 1838 Barnwell
    Also: Nancy -w- James Breland. Another dau. of testator.

BREWTPM. REBECCA--Dec'd dau. of Daniel Odom. Will 1836

BRIGHTWELL, SARAH--Dau. of Anderson Winger of Barnwell. Will 1811

BRISBANE, WILLIAM --SOn-in-law of Andrew Deveaux of Barnwell. Will 1812

BROWDWAY, LYDIA--Dau. of Peter Banner of Barnwell. Will 1799

BROOKER, MARY--Dau. of John Jackson. Will 1829

BROWN, BARTLETT--Will 10 Oct. 1815 Barnwell Wills
    Ch: MichaelBrown, Barnett H. Brown. Jacob G. Brown
    Benj. B. Brown--Will 1827 -w- Experience. No ch.
    Dau: Cynthis W. Brown -m- Calhoun
    Exors: James Overstreet and John B. Best

BROWN, BARTLETT, SR. OF sd Province. Barnwell--Winton Co. Deeds Al-Pg 246
    Son: Bartlett)
            James   ) Conv. to Christion Bear (sd Barr) dated 10 Jan. 1775
            200 A. at mouth of Fishing Creek, Sav. River--Gr. to sd.
            Christian Bear. Wit: James Garvey, Bartlett Brown, Sr.
    Page 251: Benjamin Brown--of Burke Co. Ga. to his Brow: James and
    Bartlett Brown, 11 Dec. 1786. 540 A. Co. of Winton, near Matthews
    Bluff. Orig. Gr. to Bartlett, Dec'd. Gr. 21 Jan. 1785, Wm. Brown
    a witness

BROWN, ELIZA--Dau of Joseph Duncan of Barnwell. Will 1820

BROWN, JANE--Dau. of Peter E. Brown. Niece of Jane Maxwell of Barnwell.
    Will 1822

BROWN, JOSIAH E. and CHARLES I.--Gr. sons of Sarah Overstreet of Barnwell
    Will 1818.

BROWN, MARY--Legatee of Charles Beck, Sr. of Barnwell. Will 1823

BROWN, SUSAN E.--Dau. of Mary Mixon Barnwell. Will 1837

BROWN, TARLTON -w- Amelia of"Co. of Winton". 2 Feb. 1790 to Aaron Smith
    100 A. near Murdock's Br.--btn sd br. Gr. to Thomas Standland.
    Bd. Joseph Jackson and vac. Winton Co. Book Pg. 84.

BROWN, COL. TARLTON and Elizabeth Johnson--adv--Robert Grimble and
    Elizabeth, his wife. Partition suit. 1811-March.
    Ct. Com. Pleas Misc. Bk. 1 Pg. 317 1800

BROWN, TARLTON--Will 9 June, 1842 Barnwell Wills
    Gr son: Raymond R. Dopson
    Gr. Dau: Sarah F. Peyton (dau of Frances C. Peyton, wife of Wm. H.
    Peyton.
    Son: Austin B. Brown, Wm. D. Brown
    Dau: Almedia widow of Preston Harley
    Son: Lewis M. Brown

BROWN, WINNY--Dau of Taliafferro Martin. Will 1832. Barnwell

BRYAN, FORTUNATUC--Will 12 Feb. 1821. Barnwell Will Bk B-149
    Wife: Ann
    Son: Anderson-Had slaves from his uncle Abraham DeProng
          Josiah D. (Both minors.
    Land in Darlington in hands of Major George Bruce to be sold.

BRYAN, Rebecca--Dau of Sarah Dewees of Barnwell. Will 1816

BRYANT, JOHN--Will April 6, 1805. Barnwell Wills A-47
    Wife: Home place for life or widowhood
    Son: Evan--not of age--"which I had by my wife before we were
          married".
          William
    Dau: Elizabeth--not 21--"which I had by my wife before we were
          married".
          Mary
    Exor's: Esaac Bush, Edward Buchley, and Benjamin Williamson.

BRYANT, WILLIAM--Legatee of John Cannady, Sr. of Barnwell. Will 1819

BUSH, JOHN (X)--Will April 4, 1807. Wife: Mary. "My sons and Daughters"
    Exor's: Isaac Bush, Thomas Newman. Barnwell Wills A-26

CAIN, SARAH ANN -w- Edward Cain and dau. of Benjamin Ray. Will 1845

CALHOUN, JOHN EWING "late of St. John's Paeish" Atty. at Law. Will 20
    May, 1802. Barnwell Deed Bk E-247

CALHOUN, MICAJAH and dau. Elizabeth. See will of Samuel Moore of Barnwell
                                                                         1812

CANFIELD, FELIX PASCALIS, Theodocia, Felicia Hemans, Lucy Williams.
    nephews and nieces of Cyril O. Pascalis. Will 1835

CANNON, POLLY--Dau. of Taliaferro Martin. Will 1832   Barnwell

CARREL, THOMAS--Will 30 Nov. 1779 Barnwell Wills A-2
    Son: Jacob--½ land
         Thomas--½ land
    Dau: Elizabeth--1 guinea
         Mary

CARROL, WILLIAM--Nephew of Elizabeth Lard. Will 1843 Barnwell

CARTER, ANN -Widow- Dau. of John Tucker. Will Rec'd 1835
    Her son: William Carter--minor
        Dau: Margaret   "   "
        Son: John D   "   "   Barnwell Bk C-134

CARTER, ISHAM--Age 66 yrs. At abt age 19 he entered under Capt. John
    Wickly--Regt. Cpt. under Col. Roberts--served 5 years--was in
    battle of Storo: Seige of Savannah; Charleston;
    Barnwell Ct. Min. Pg.-391 Apr. 5, 1821

CARTER, JACOB of St. Bartholomew's Parish to son, George Carter.
    Deed Gift 50 Acres E-s Little Saltcatcher's. C.T. Deed Y-5-35
    Y-5-A71--George Carter to Joel Paget. 50 A. April 7, 1787

CARTER, CATHERINE--Dau. of Richard Johnson, Sr. Will 1824. Bk B-236

CARTER, JAMES Dec'd intestate. Part. was in 1808. Adm'r. William Carter
    Adv. R. B. (or R. Q.) Andrews and wife per prop. $1368.46
    Pg. 137 Rev. R. B. Carter Gdn. for R. B. Andrews and Sarah Carter.
    Barnwell Equity Report Bk Pg 127

CARTER, JOHN J.--Wit. Will of Mary Mixon. 21 Aug. 1837.
    Barnwell Bk C-203   Bdl. 71 Pkg-5

CAVE, NANCY and Elizabeth--Ch. of Burrell Parker. Barnwell Will 1835

CHERRY, JESSE Will 13 March 1843. Barnwell Will Bk D Pg.-97
    Wife: Elizabeth
    Bro: James--Res. Alabama
    To: Charity Roberts -w- Ervin Roberts of Stewart Co. Ga.
        Her Gr. son: John C. Roberts
    Bro: Joel Cherry of Tennessee
    Sis: Penelope Butler of Ala.

CHEVELLETTE, LOUISA--Legatee of Geo. Robson of Barnwell. Will 1803

CHITTY, CYNTHIA--Dau. of William Hughes. Barnwell Will 1843

CHITTY, ELIZABETH M.--Adopted dau. of David Rice, Sr. Barnwell Will
19 Apr. 1838

CHITTE, JOHN--Will 23 Oct. 1805 Barnwell Wills A-11
Wife: Frances
Son: John, William
Dau: Polly Sanderford, Winnefred Mathis
Son: James, Edward, Robert, Jephey, Willis
Dau: Seley McMillon, Priscillah Thurston

CHITTY, MARY AND REGINA--Legatees of Leonard Seare. Barnwell Will 1840

CLARK, EDMOND--His widow Elizabeth -m- Daniel Darby (see Darby)

CLAYTON, ISHAM--Orig Will 16 Jan. 1798 Barnwell
Wife: Anna (same file. Ex. 1806)
Sons: James, Isham, George, Joseph
Daus: Sarah, Anna, Mary, Rebecca

CLAYTON, ISHAM and Jene Clayton with Micajah Rice Wit. deed--Abigail
Williams "spinster" of Winton Co. Barnwell--Winton Deeds I-257
5 May, 1787

CLENDOL, WINNIFRED M. C. (or McClendon of McClendol). Dau. of Levi Lee
Will 1845

CLIFTON, JONATHAN -w- Levina of Pr. Wm's. Parish. Barnwell File C.T. T-5
To Wm. Davis: 200 A. on Savannah River called Perkin's   469
Bluff--Sur. for and Gr. to Hannah Clifton. Wit: Wm. Kiry
Wm. B. Davis (Wm. Brewster Davis)

COATS, POLLARD--Gr. son of John Hickman of Barnwell. Will. Emelia Coats
a Gr. Dau. Helena Coats, a dau.

COCHRAN, MARY--Dau. of Adam Lard, Sr. Will 1828 Barnwell

COLDING, SAMUEL, Dec'd. Barnwell Ct. Com. Pleas. Misc. 1800
Mrs. Mary Booth--one of heirs
Rachel Cone--Dec'd." "   "
4 Ch: Zilphs Cone. Cone of Beaufort Dist. Adm't. of B.
Conchord Colding, Jacob Kettles and others. Pg. 269
-vs- Elizabeth Colding, Adm't. of James Colding. Job Rowley, one
of heirs was of full age and was not served. Pg-288: Thos. Colding
et al -vs- Same Part. suit.

COHEN, BARNETT A. Will 28 Jan. 1837 Barnwell C-221-223
"my 6 sons": Moses A. Cohen--Mason's Branch
Samuel   "   Gold Watch
Eleaser H. "
Isaac   "
Jacob G.   "
Michael   "
Dau: Catherine Elizabeth Cohen
Elsa Cohen and dau. Cochia
Mother-in-law: Cecelia Solomon--if living.
Requests he be buried in Hebrew burying ground near Charleston.
Also to have body of his wife, Isabella Cohen, removed there.

COLLINS, ANN--Dau. of Patt Mackelmurray of Barnwell. Will 1815

COLLINS, JAMES--Barnwell Wills Bk 1-77 1-26 Rec'd 9 Jan. 1790
    Son: James--the eldest. Home Plantation
    Dau: Lydia Collins
    Son: John
          Major Croom Collins
    Dau: Mary Collins
    Son: Daniel Collins
          William Winwright Collins
    Ex: Leven, James, Joseph Collins
    Wit: Daniel Odom, Ben Odom, Leven Collins

COLLINS, NANCY -w- David Collins, dau. of Jacob Free. Will 1822 Barnwell

COLOMOM, ELIZABETH--Dau. of Peter Banner of Barnwell. Will 1799

CONGHRAN, ANN--Dau. of Samuel Still, Sr. Will 1830 Barnwell

CONNOWAY, HEMP-Alias Simmons by next friend Wm. Gordon -vs- Ann Connoway
    Adm'r A. Connoway. Barnwell Ct. Com. Pleas. Bk-1 29 Apr. 1, 1802

COOK, MARY -w- Abraham Cook, dau. of George Walker of Barnwell. Will 1799
    Cook, Pershney, -w- James Cook. Dau of same.

COOPER, NICHOLAS--Will A-27
    Wife: May be encient
        Her son and dau: Jane and William Lester ch. of George Lester.
    Son: James
    Archibald Campbell of Glasgow is Partner in Store at Campbelltown.
    Bro: Agrippa Cooper
    My ½ Bros. and Sisters.
    Father and Mother--"suit of mourning"

COPELAND, JACOB--Son-in-law of Catherine Shubert. Will 1834 Barnwell

COULTER, DAVID -w- Anna--dower. Conv. land on Edisto. Jan 20, 1815
    Pg. 239/40 Josiah G. Allen -w- Elizabeth Conv. 1815
    Pg. 241 Re. Est. And Grs. to Joseph Allen,Thomas Allen--Conv. by
    Giles Miller
    Pg. 384 David Coulter of Richland Dist. Conv. 1815. -w- Ann
    Pg. 100 Coulter, David--Dec'd vs Lark Robinson. Barnwell Equity 1821

COULTER, JAMES -w- Susannah: March 22, 1832 Notice to the Public: That
    he will not pay wife's debts as she has left him and refused to
    "accompany me to the Western Country".

COUNTS, ELIZABETH--Dau. of John Absten. Will 1825. Barnwell

COWARD, SARAH--Dau. of Adam Lard, Sr. Will 1828. Barnwell

CREIGHTON, LASHLEY -m- Thos. Gough. See Will of Elijah Gillett of
    Barnwell. 1817--Codicil.

CUMBAA, REBECCA--Dec'd dau. of Josias Keadle. Will 1839. Barnwell

CURLEE, DORCAS--Dau. of James Roberts of Barnwell. Will 1802

DANIEL, MARGARET--"Who has lately inter-m- with Samuel Carlton. Barnwell
    Ct. Com. Pleas 1800. 2 Mon. April 1812 Bk-1-335
    Adv. Sam'l Solomon & Co. Pg. 339

DARLINGTON, MARY H. -w- James Darlington-Dau. Mary Mixon of Barnwell. Will
                                                                          1837
DAVIS, ANN R.--Dau of Levi Lee. Will 1845 Barnwell

DAVIS, CHARITY--Dau. of James Moody of Barnwell. 1809

DAVIS, ELIZABETH--Spinster--m--Apl. 23, 1753 Henry Jackson. Son of
    Henry and Elizabeth Jackson. St. Helena's Par. Reg.

DAVIS, JAMES--His wife Mary--Dau. of John Clayton. Will 1842. Barnwell

DAVIS, WILLIAM Of Pr. William's Par. to John Hunt. Mtg. to sec. Bond of
    18 June 1770 278 A. Pr. Wms. Pur--Bd. Capt. John Jackson, Joseph
    Wragg and vac. Wit: Benj. Whippy and John Jackson, Jr.
    Barnwell File. C.T. R-3 140

DAVIS, COL. WILLIAM--owed 28 lbs-15 sh. rent due 15 Dec. 1786 to John
    Wyld--for house and plantation on Perkin's Bluff. Orig. Gr. to
    Hannah Clifton. John Wylds _____? Henry Mills to distrain
    for the rent-5 May, 1787. Barnwell Plat Bk 1 Pg-80

DAVISON, PATIENCE,--Sister of Nancy Skiper of Barnwell. Will 1806

DAY, MARY--Dau. of John Blichendon of Barnwell. Will 1803

DELOACH, SARAH SMITH--Dau. of James Garvin of Barnwell. Will 1822

DEPONT (g), ABRAHAM--Uncle of Anderson Bryan--son of Fortunatus Bryan of
    Barnwell. Will 1821

DILLARD, BARNABA--Will 22 Nov. 1800 Barnwell Wills A-9
    Wife: Polly
    2 Sons: Oen (Owen?) Dillard
             Coelan   "
    Dau: Milbery
          Elizabeth

DOLITTLE, JOSEPH--100 A. Orangeburg Dist. on Middle fork of Dean Swamp
    of S. Edisto. Cert. 22 Jan, 1785. George Renorson, Dep. S. .
    Plat Bk 1-184. Pg. 194--100 A. on Holmes Camp of Edisto. Cert.
    22 Jan. 1785. All vac.

DOMINIS, SUSAN C.--Legatee of Leonard Seare. Barnwell. Will 1840

DOPSON, RAYMOND R.--Gr. Son of Tarlton Brown. Barnwell Will 1842

DOPSON, REBECCA, et al -advs- James Higginbottom and Preston Harley and Co.
    Out of State: Alex'r T. Dopson. Barnwell Dist. Sept 20, 1830

DOUGLAS, JOHN Will 29 June, 1816. Barnwell Wills A-251
    Wife: Molly
    Sister: Moleys Gram's Children
    Bro: James Douglas's Children

DOWLING, E (ELIJAH?) Barnwell Equity Pg. 21 1821-Rec'd 1823
    Heirs: Decana, William, Elizabeth, Aaron, Ann, Charles Dowling

DOWLING, ELLENDER--Dau. of Elijah Dooling of Barnwell.   Will 1816
(Dowling)
DOWLING, MARIA--Dec'd. dau of Magdalen Holman. Will 1842. Her ch:
    Elizabeth Dowling
    Emily M.   "
    Ellen M.   "   Barnwell

DUDLEY, MARY MAGDALLEAN HARVEY--Gr. dau of Jonathan Thomson. Will 1842
    Also dau of Mary S. Fibbeon.

DUKE, ELIZABETH--Sister of John Burnley of Va. Will at Barnwell, S. C.
    Will made in London 1778. Keziah Duke, another sister. Ann
    Littlepage -w- Thos. L. another sister

DUNBAR, CATHERINE--Dau. of Wm. S. Johnson and Gr. dau of Sarah M. Johnson
    Will 1844 Barnwell

DUNBAR, FRANCES--Dau of Joseph Duncan of Barnwell. Will 1820

DUNBAR, GEO. ROBISON. and Lucy D.--Gr. Ch. of Elizabeth Ann Stewart.
    Legatees of Geo. Robson of Barnwell. Will 1803

DUNBAR, LUCY--w-- F. F. Dunbar. Dau. of Stephen Smith. Will 1840

DUNCAN, ELLEN BARLOWE--Widow of Willis J. Duncan and Daughter of John
    S. Bellinger. Will 1842. Sister of one Edmund Bellinger, Lucius B.
    and John B. Barnwell

DUNN, WINNEFORD--Dau. of Eli Myrick. Will 1840 Barnwell

DWYER, MARY--Of Ireland--Aunt of Cornelius Tobin. Will 1829 Barnwell

DYKES, BARBARY, Sister of John E. Steivender of Barnwell "Ashepoo"

DYCHES, ESTHER -w- Seth Dyches--Dau. of Moses Duke of Barnwell. Will 1820

DYCHES, MARTHA--Dau. of Levi Lee. Will 1845. Barnwell
    GEORGE--Mentioned

DYESS, WILLIAM--Wife--Elizabeth(Or Wm. Dyches) son in law of Wm. Everitt
    of Barnwell. Will 1788

DYES, WINNIFORD--Dau. of William Bozit of Barnwell. Will 1808

EAVES, ELIZABETH--Dau. of Henry Kennedy. Will 1840 Barnwell

EAVES, ELLEN E. -w- Jackson Eaves and Sau. of Henry Hartzog. Will 1846

EAVES, MARY--Legatee of Leanord Seare. Will 1840. Barnwell

EVES, SARAH--Mother of Josiah Walker. See Will of Nathaniel Walker of
    Barnwell. 1819

EASTERLAND, JOHN--Nephew of Elizabeth Lard. Will 1840

EASTERLING, MARGARET--Dau. of Adam Lard, Sr. Will 1828. Barnwell

EDGERTON, ELIZABETH-and George W. Muse of 1st part-and-James W. Maxwell,
all of Barnwell Dist-of 2nd part. Marriage between Elizabeth and
George W. Muse. Elizabeth is entitled to an undivided share of
estate of Otis Edgerton, dec'd, her late husband, and also to a
certain negro slave now in possession of the adm'rs of estate of
John Wolfe, dec'd, and also sums due by sd adm'rs and by Jacob
Wolf. Remainder to children of said union, if any, if not to all
children of said Elizabeth. Wit: John W. Rush, Wm. Hughes.
Probate Barnwell Dist. 2 May, 1831 Misc. Rec. G-370
Edgerton, Henrietta C., et al. -vs- Geo. W. Muse and Elizabeth
his wife. Partition of Estate of Otis Edgerton between plaintiffs
and defts. his heirs. Shows: Elizabeth Edgerton-widow-married
George W. Muse. Heard at Barnwell Feb. 1834.

ELKINS, LOUISA (or Lusina) Dau. of Wm. Stringfellow of Barnwell. Will 1812

EMEKS, SARAH D.--Dau. of Robert Bradley of Barnwell. Will 1816

ENECKS, JEMIMA--Dau. of Micajah Calhoun of Barnwell. Will 1823

ENNEKS, THOMAS--Will 13 Oct. 1802. Barnwell Wills A-53/54-5
    Wife: Sons: Isaac, Thomas, William

EUBANKS, ELIZAR--Dau. of Eleanor Newsom. Will 1837 Barnwell

EVANS, ELIZABETH--Eldest dau. of Francis Shaw who was wife of Thomas
    Shaw of Barnwell. Will 1801. John Evans, a son.

FAIL, NANCY--Wife of Wm. Fail and dau. of Osborn Lain. Will 1841.
TANT
FANT, CATHERINE--Dau. of Henry Zorn of Barnwell. Will 1821 (Tant?)

FAUST, ANN--Dau. of Eli Myrick. Barnwell Will 1840

FAUSTER, DANIEL--Legatee of John Absten. Barnwell Will 1825

FELDER, DAVID--Son-in-law of John Guess of Barnwell. Will 1817

FIBBON, MARY--Dau. of Testator. Legatee of Jonathan Thompson. Will 1842

FISHBURNE, MARY--Dau. of Mary Bellinger of Barnwell. Will 1811. Gr. dau.
    Sarah Fishburne.

FITTS, JOHN--Will 14 Feb. 1799 Barnwell Wills A-18
    Wife: Sarah (encient)
    Son: William-1 shilling. To his ch'n.] share
         Mitchell Fitts
         "All my Ch'n"

FOGLE, EXPERIENCE G. -w- Jno. J. Fogle. Dau. of Mary Mixon. Will 1837

FOGLE, MARY W.--Formerly widow of John A. Owen-son of William Owens.
    Will 1835. Her Ch: William, Edward, Sarah Owens. Barnwell

FORTUNE, BARABY--Sister of Nancy Skipin of Barnwell. Will 1816

FORTUNE, JOHN--Gr. on Rd. from Winnsboro to C. T. and Gr. 150 A. to Wm.
    Fortune, conv. by Richard Winn to John Winn. 1 Feb. 1786
    Winnsboro Deed A-250

FORTUNE, RICHARD--Wit Deed 22 Apr. 1797 by Benj. Odom, Jr. to Walter
     Robinson. Barnwell Deed 3-126

FORTUNE, WILLIAM--Will Barnwell Probate. Case 115-pg 1
     All to Sarah Onelia Mosely--Love and affection. 9 Jan. 1853. Est.
     was adm'd by John G. Smith. Shares pd. James Fortune, Jesse Fortune
     et al. Pd. J. and R. McCrary on Judgment.

FOSTER, BENJAMIN--Will 8 June 1804. Barnwell Wills A-10
     Wife: Mary Catherine
     "my 2 Ch." Benjamin and Mary Catherine

FOWKE, SARAH--Dau. of Richard C. Fowke a Legatee of Sarah M. Johnson.
     Barnwell Will 1844

FRANCES, FREDERICK to Joseph Vince. Winton Bk 1-pg 1. Jan. 10, 1787

FRASURE, HEZEKIAH--Deed Adm'r--John H. Hasley. Barnwell Probate Box-40-2

FRASER, SOPHIA M.--Gr. Dau. of Ann O. Hagood. Will 1842. Barnwell

FRAUST,JOHN, Mary, Sarah, Elizabeth, William. Ch. of Jesse Fraust, dec'd
     son of Mary Peacock of Barnwell. Will 1814

FREEMAN, THOS Susannah, and their son George, of Culpepper Co. Va.
     Legatees Geo. Latham of Barnwell. Will 1806. Calls Geo. his nephew.

FURSE, EDWARD -w- Louisa--Dau. of Stephen Smith. Will 1840 Barnwell

FURSE, JAMES -w- Julia A.--Dau. of Stephen Smith. Will 1840

GALPHIN, DR. MILLEDGE--Adopted son of John Milledge of Barnwell. Will 1818
     Cousin: Mary Milledge

GALPHIN, SARAH--Dau. of Stephen Smith of Barnwell. Will 1788

GANTT, SARAH--Dau. of Mary Woodroof of Barnwell. Will 1822. Sarah
     Gantt now Mrs. Stone

GARDNER, RHODA--Dau. of Welcome Ussery. Barnwell Will 1834

GARVIN, ELIZA--Dau. of Rich'd Kirkland of Barnwell. Will 1812

GARVIN, JAMES M. dec'd. Barnwell Eqty. Repts. Pg-12. 1839
     Widow: _____ -m- James Copeland, moved to Fla.
     Ch: Lydia Louisa--age 6 or 7 yrs.
     Bro: W. Garvin. (Widow dau. of S. R. Cannon)

GASKIN, ELIZABETH--Dau. of Taliaferro Martin. Will 1832. Barnwell

GIDDINS, JAMES to Niece, Mrs. Hepsibeth Davis--formerly Miss H. Anstead.
     Land on 3-Runs. Bd. Joseph Harly and vac. Barnwell I-Pg 9
     21 Nov. 1814

GILBERT, MARY ANN, Ro_____?, Catherine--all minors. Pet. apt. friend
     Joel Anthony as gdn. in re their home and lot on corners of George
     and Meeting Streets in C. T. which Thos Lee claims he pur. as
     _____? property. Barnwell Ct. Min. Pg-486. April 1, 1822

GILL, ELIZABETH--Dau. of James Mirick of Barnwell. Will 1814 (Myrick?)

GILL, ELIZABETH--Dau. of Benjamin Banner. Barnwell Will 1827

GILLETT, WM. SCARBOROUGH--Gr. son of Lucy Scarborough of Barnwell.
    Will 1815. Others: Alexander Gillett, Aaron G., Julia G.,
    and Elizabeth Gillett, their mother.

GILLETT, ELIZABETH--Dau. of Wm. D. Scarborough of Barnwell. Will 1810

GLOVER, NANCY--Dau. of John Hickman of Barnwell. Will 1798

GOMILLEON, CINTHA--Dau. Josias Keadle. Will 1839

GOMILLEON, VICEY--Dau. of Taliaferro Martin. Will 1832. Barnwell

GOVAN, ELIZABETH ANN and Andrew--Legatees of Geo. Robson of Barnwell
    Will 1803

GRAHAM, ZACHARIAH--Son-in-law of Elijah Dooling of Barnwell. Will 1816
                                 (Dowling?)
GREEN, ABSOLEM--Bro.-in-law of James Stallings of Barnwell. Will 1803

GREEN, FRANCIS M.--Dau. of John Hogg. Will 1846

GRIFFIN, SUSANNAH -w- Moses Griffin. Dau. of George Walker of Barnwell.
                                                         Will 1799
GRIMES, JINSY--Dau of Wm. Breland of Barnwell. Will 1819

GRIMES, JOHN D.--Gr. son of Daniel Odom. Will 1836. Dau: Polly Grimes

GRUBBER, HENRIETTA -m- Isaac Pearce. Lic. 6 Aug. 1791. Augusta Ord. Ct.

GRUBS, MARY--Dau. of Mary Peacock of Barnwell. Will 1814. Her Ch: Ralph

GUNNELS, WINNEFRED--Dau. of Kinched Delk of Barnwell. Will 1818. Wife
    of Allen Gunnels.

HAGOOD, HARRIETT--Dau. of Susannah Yonge of Barnwell. Will 1817. Wife
    of Gideon Hagood. Gr. Ch: Harriett Amanda, Elvira, Susan Julia,
    Johnson, Thomas Gideon, Yonge I. all Hagood

HAINS, EDEY--Dau. of Wm. Green of Barnwell. Will 1809

HALL, WILLIAM AND UNICEY--Gr. dr. of Mary Weathersbee. Will 1822

HAMILTON, CAROLINE W.--Formerly Allen. See Will of Mary Woodroof of
    Barnwell. 1822

HANKINSON, ANN--Wife of Richard. Sister of John Williams of Barnwell.
                                                           Will 1817
HANKINSON, RICHARD--Will Barnwell Eqty. Rep. Pg. 212
    Wife:
    Son: Milledge
    Dau: Mehala-d-1 dau. Cornelia. Wife Thos. Alexander.
    Son: Robert--Nothing--already has his part.
    Ch: Richard, Jane, (died unmar.)Elizabeth, Ann,
          Mary -w- Wm. Green
          Sarah -w- G. H. Green
          Caroline -w- L. Eubanks

HARDEN, DELIA ANN--Dau. of Nathaniel Badger. Will 1842 Barnwell

HARDEN, SARAH -w- Abi___? Harden. Legatee of John Jackson. Will 1829

HARDIE, THOMAS--Age 67. Enlisted in Va. Albermarle Co. under Capt.
     Matthew Dewitt--Regt Col. Nelson Va. line--marched to Gwyne Island
     where Lord Dunmore had hdgts. Discharged at Valley Forge.
     Barnwell Nov. 3, 1825. Misc. #2 Pg. 299

HARGROVE, SUSANNAH--Dau. of Solomon Owens of Barnwell. Will 1818

HARKNESS, HENRY--Bro.-in-law of Andrew Dunbar of Barnwell. Will 1819
     of Mississippi, Co. of Amite

HARNY, MARGARET--Dau. of John Thompson of Barnwell. Will 1809

HARP, IELILA--Sister of Nancy Skiper of Barnwell. Will 1816

HARRISON, WM. H. M. set Elitha Harvy 26 March 1861. Barnwell Misc Bk-314

HARTZOGG, WILLIAM--Legatee of Jacob Free. Will 1822

HATCHER, MARY -w- Archibald Hatcher of Ga. Legatee George Robson of
     Barnwell. Will 1803

HAWKS, MARTHA ANN--Dau. of Lewis S. Hay. Will 1838 Barnwell

HAY, HARRIET Y.--Niece of Sarah M. Johnson. Will 1844

HAYNE--See Harriet Y. Hay in will of Sarah M. Johnson 1844 for possible
     error. Chas. Hay an Exor.--seems Hay is correct

HAYS, EDWARD "late of city of Waterford, Kingdom of Ireland. Barnwell
     Min. Bk. 892 Nov. 6, 1815
     Pg. 93--John M. Tarver--late of Kingdom of Great Britain.

HAYSE, JOSEPH--Will 20 Aug. 1799 Barnwell Wills A-58/9 of Winton Co.
     Wife: Anney (also Anna)
     Son: John Hayes
     Eldest Dau: Mary Bell
                  Hannah Bell and her eldest dau. Delany
                  Patsy Bustion
                  Nancy Hayse

HEARD, JOHN of Barnwell. M set 15 July, 1809--Jane Barnard of Edgefield
     Land called Pine Grove. Next page shows they have married. Misc B-
                                                                      589
HEARD, NANCY--Dau. of Jacob Foreman of Barnwell. Will 1823

HEATH, BENJAMIN--Will 19 July 1804 Barnwell Wills A-42/3
     Wife: Sarah--Ext.
     Dau: Zilpha Heath)
     Son: James Heath) To be reared or maintained
           Joseph   "
           Benj.   "   ) Not 21
     Dau: Lucretia -w- Isaac Williams
     "My Gr. Ch." James Williams
                   Benjamin   "
                   Nancy   "
                   John   "

HULETT, MARY E. (or Hewlett)--Dau. of Richard Johnson Sen'r. of Barnwell
Will 1824

HEWLETT, MARY E.--and her daughters, Mary, Catherine, and Sarah. The
dau's Legatees of Sarah M. Johnson. Will 1844

HEXT, BETSY -w- Wm. Osborne Hext. Dau. of Joseph Vince of Barnwell.
Will 1810

HICKMAN, JOHN--Gr. son of John Blichendon of Barnwell. Will 1813.
Dau. Rebecca Hickman -w- Thomas Hickman

HIGHTOWER, MARY--Dau. of John Guess of Barnwell. Will 1817. Her son
Jesse Hightower

HINDS, JOHN--Age 65. Act Congress U. S. 18 March 1818. Ct. Min. Pg 253/4
Served under Capt. Mayson - Regt. of Col. Isaac Motte --S. C. Cont.
Line. Has wife and 2 ch. 1 a son, married and has a family of his
own. 2 a boy age 7. In battles of Sullivan's Island and Parkers
Ferry. Has discharge by Col. Isaac Motte. 1820, Nov. 4

HITT, HENRIETTA NEAL--Dau. of Samuel Still, Sr. Will 1830 Barnwell

HOLMAN, MARY--Dau. of Levi Lee. Barnwell Will 1845

HOLLY, JERUSHA--Legatee of John Steel. Will 1835. Barnwell

HOLLEY, PRUDENCE MOODY--Dau. of Solomon McClain of Barnwell. Will 1814

HOLLY, RACHEL--Dec'd wife of John Holly. Dau. of Nathaniel Sanders.
Will 1834. Her Ch. John, Calvin, Alfred, and Julian Feraby Holly.

HOOVER, JOHN MILLS--Adopted son of John Harrison, Sr. Will 1814 Barnwell

HUFFMAN, SOLOMON--Will 20 Nov. 1804 Barnwell Wills A-45/6
Son: Syllas Huffman -w- Sally (also sp. Sillas)
Gr. son: Solomon Huffman, Jr.
Son: John Huffman
Gr. Ch: ?
Gr. Dau: Marianne Huffman

HUGHS, MARGARET--Dau. of Simon Rentz of Barnwell. Will 1815

HUGHES, MOSES D.--Son of Micajah H., nephew of Moses Duke of Barnwell.
Will 1820

HUNTER, ELIZABETH--Dau. of Wm. Hughes. Barnwell Will 1843

HUNT, JOSEPH of St. Bartholomew. Barnwell File--C. T. Will 7 Oct. 1763
Dau: Elizabeth Hunt)
Sarah   ")
Rebecca   ") To be maintained
Martha Brown
Mary Jackson
Son: Joseph Hunt--not 18
Exor: Dr. Wm. Day, Charles Jones, John Hunt

***** HARLEY *****

ALMEDIA -widow- of Preston Harley and dau of Tarlton Brown. Will 1842
                                                         Barnwell
ANN -widow- marriage set Wm. G. Finley. Andrew Harley, Tr. All of St.
    George's. Archives Dept. Mar. Bk. 8-231

CHRISTIAN (A?) -vs- Joshua McCreary. Judgment for Prop. $2034.90 1875
    Barnwell Judgment A-307

ELIZABETH--Dec'd. Cit. 2 Dec. 1822. Barnwell Case 40-pk 9
    Adm'r: Preston Harley and Pet. "my dear Mother", Columbia Mott.
    Bond: John A. Hayes and Joshua Mosely. Inv. val. $1494.31
    Sale Bk. Pg. 59. Sale 20 Jan. 1823. Pur's: Preston H., James H.,
    Joseph J. H., Tristram Covington, Jane H., Ann H.

HENRY--To Preston Harley--Pd $100.00--100 A. undiv. mortg. of 400 A. belg.
    to sd H. H. by his dec'd father, Joseph Harley--on Lower Three Runs.
    Barnwell Deed 1-33. Dec. 20, 1814

HENRY--Will 20 Jan. 1815 Barnwell Wills Bdle 24-Pk 2. Book B-pg-44
    Wife: Zilpha--all for life   Prov. 1 Feb. 1815
    Son: William
    Dau: Ann Elizabeth Harley
          Rebecca Harley
    Exor: Friend Adam McCreary, and Bro. Preston Harley.

J.--Adm: J. J. Harley. Barnwell 2 Nov. 1838 Case 72 Pg 7

JACKSON--Barnwell Plat Bk 8 Pg's: 466,593,609A, 291A Feb. 12, 1808
    2-15--609 A. on Sou. Br. of Lower Three Runs. Bd. Rankin and Alex'r
    Newman and unknown, also Henry Harley-Jas. H. 9 Jan. 1811
    2153-- 291 A. Bd Lower Three Runs and Big Salt. Near a Great Sw.
    Bd. Survey for Joseph H. and Miles Riley and Isham Cowarde.
    Ch-b_.- Wm. Parker, Preston Harley

JACKSON, H. Barnwell Case 93, Pk 10. Sept 20, 1847. Adm. James E. Harley

JACOB, R. et al -vs- Jos. E. Robinson et al. Bill for debt. Pendleton
    Messenger Equity--Mar. 14, 1845

JACOB R. --in regard estate of George Braton "on Edisto" Land. Heirs:
    Jacob Harley and Wife 1/18
    Charles DeWitt 1/9 or 2/18
    My Daus. 3 Ch. 1/18 each   Barnwell Equity Bk Pg 313. 1821
    Also: Bk 1831-etc Pg-18. George Buwton-intestate. Widow and 1
    Child 2 or 3 yrs. old when his father died. (Jacob R. Harley)
    Legatee of Mrs. Odorn or Adorn.
    Pg. 30: Preston Harley, Dec'd.
        Heirs: Widow: Almedia Harley
                Mrs. I. Sarah Langley
                Joseph T. Harly
                Eliza B. Harly
                James P. Harley-minor
                Susan Frances Harly-minor
    Pg. 170: Josiah Stalling d. Aug. 1836. Adm'r: Preston Harley.
        Died Fall of 1827

JAMES -w- Ann of St. George's Parish, Berkley Co. Charleston Deed W-4-296
   To: Allen Miles of St. Paul's Parish. 665 A. Pt. pltn Gr. Tobias
   Fitch on 22 Apr. 1735 S. side Four Hole Swp. in St. James Parish.
   Bd. by lands of Edward Perry, John Fullerton, and James Lindsey,
   and Fred Hooks.

JAMES "of St. George Par. Dorchester. Wife-Ann. 1776 conv. lands at
   Four Holes. Wit: James Harley, Jr. C. T. Deed A-5 Pg. 176

JAMES--Will 10 Feb. 1776. C. T. Wills
   Wife: Ann--Plt'n "Springfield"
   "my 5 sons": James, Francis Lemon, John Osgood, William, Allen.
   Dau: Sarah Ann Harley, Rachel Harley

JAMES--Barnwell Plat Bk 8-739. Feb. 10, 1814. 67½ A. Bd. sd J. H.,
   Stephen Collins, and Michael Suscord. C. B.--Gideon Nobles and
   Howard Anderson. J. E. Carstaphen-D. S.

JAMES--Dec'd. Barnwell Equity Rep. Pg 350 to -1821. Adm'r: Jane A.
   Harley, and John A. Harley. Accting--Firm Geo. W. Collins and James
   Feb. 6, 1826--Cit. Case 46 Pk 3   Harley
   1830--Jane A., Adm'x. and John a Hayes, Adm'r. Adv. Ann Hankinson
          Barnwell #2 Misc. 542

JAMES--Dec'd 1836 Barnwell Equity Pg-306
   Widow: Jane A. Harley (has died)
   Dau: Jane -m- Dr. J. J. Harley
   Dau: _____ Dec'd -m- John A. Hayes
   Dau: Elizabeth -m- J. G. Barker
   Son: Richard W.
   Dau: Martha died before June 1841
          Susan and Rebecca--died before 1845
   Son: James M.

JAMES--Dec'd Barnwell Case 79-pkg 9. Aug. 7, 1841. Adm. J. J. Harley

JANE--Barnwell Case 87 Pk 12. Sept. 18, 1844. Adm: Wm. P. Harley

JANE--Will 17 Oct. 1835. Barnwell Will Bk C-154 Prov. 24 Nov. 1835
   "my 3 sons" Jackson H. Harley, James M. Harley, Richard W. Harley

JEAN--Formerly relict of Capt. John Jackson--late of Pon Pon. and Geo.
   Jackson exor. of Will Capt. John Jackson. To: John Laird. Lot in
   Jacksonborough. C. T. Deed TT-16 20-slot. Apr. 22, 1752

JOSEPH--Gr. 2 March 1711. Son Joseph. Colleton. Barnwell File Mem. 10
                                                                      514
JOSEPH--Mar. set 7 Dec. 1749. Jane Jackson Misc. File. KK-272

JOSEPH--Mar. set 9 Feb. 1768. Elizabeth Jackson. NN 145/7
   James Skirving, Wm. Skirving, Trs.

JOSEPH--Estate-Paid inv't rent 410 A. in 1768. Rent Bk 1760-pg 253

JOSEPH--200 A. E-s Lower 3 Runs. Bd. sd Harley. Sur. for D. Corbett and
   Sur. for Tarlton Brown. Barnwell Plat Bk 8-57. Apr. 11, 1785

JOSEPH--w- Elizabeth To: (?I think to Wm. Davis) for 50 lbs. 7 sh. 6
    pence sterling, ½ undiv. 250 A. on Saltcatchers. Orig. Gr. to
    Andrew Worster. 18 Oct. 1757. Later owned by Henry Jackson. Wit:
    Wm. Buford, Thos. Crawford, Alex'r Wood. C. T. Deed T-5-470
    1785 May 23/24

JOSEPH--Uncle of Charles J. Brown of Barnwell. Will 1798. Joseph
    Harley, Jr. a cousin

JOSEPH, SEN'R--To: 28 May, 1801, Love and Affc. Son: Jackson Harley.
    200 Acre Gr. sd Joseph Harley in year 1774. Wit: James Harley.
    Barnwell Deed Bk #2 1801-1802 Pg. 113 and 114

JOSEPH, SEN'R--To son Joseph Harley, Love and Affc. 200 A. near and S.
    sideLower 3 runs. Adj. James Giddings. Wit: Jackson Harley and
    William Harley. Barnwell Deed C-197 May 7, 1803

JOSEPH--48 A. on Lower 3 Runs of Sav. R. Bd. Tarlton Brown. Est. of
    Joseph Harley, Sen'r. Bd. Jackson Harley. Ch-B Mr. McMahon,
    Preston Harley, Jane Harley. Barnwell Plat Bk 2-22. Mar. 2, 1808

JOSEPH, SEN'R.--Will Orig. 14 Nov. 1790. Son Exor. Joseph Harley, Jr.
    Pet. as surviving exor. for sale June 8, 1815. Henry Jr. Exor.
    Barnwell Case 12-Pk 4. Prov. Aug. 20, 1807. Filed original
    Barnwell Apr. 20, 1809
    Purchasers: Elizabeth Harley, JosephL. Harley, Preston H., Robert
    McCreary, Silpha Harley, James Harley, Rebecca Harley, Tristram
    Covington, Fred J. Hay, Adam McCreary,

JOSEPH--and Miles Riley 738 Acres on the Great Savannah near Savannah
    Br. of Lower Three Runs--Bd. Wm. Parker, Jackson Harley, Chain
    Carriers: Wm. Parker, James Harley D. S. Preston Harley.
    Barnwell Plat Be. 2-121 Dec. 22, 1810

JOSEPH--Dower--Jane Ann to George Philpot. 44 A. Pt Gr. to Richard
    Creech/ Barnwell Deed 1 (or I) Pg 85/7 Jan. 14, 1813

JOSEPH--Cit. 6 Oct. 1820. Adm. Mrs. Jane Harley. Bond 26 Oct. 1820.
    Barnwell Bdle 35-pk-2

JOSEPH J.,--James S., William J., Jacob R., John H., to Mrs. Rebecca F.
    Peyton, W. H. Peyton and J. J. Wood, Trs. 200 A. Adj. Est. Jackson
    Harley

JOSEPH J.--Died March 1857 intestate. Bro. Jacob R. Harley Appld Lets.
    Barnwell Min. Bk. Pg 452

PRESTON--460 Acres on Head Waters of Savannah Br. of Lower Three Runs.
    Bd. Joseph Harley-Gr. sd P. H. Cert. 4 May 1831. Barnwell 1831
    Plat Bk 3-

PRESTON--Dec'd. Adm'r.--Wm. J. Bk. Pg. 74 "Est. Capt. Preston Harley"
    Bond 12 Dec. 1837--Penalty $14,000.00. Alemedia Harley, J. T.,
    Jos. J. Apprs: Dr. Jos. J. H., Jackson H., Wm. H.,Peyton, John
    Canady, and Benjamin Owens

SUSANNAH--From Samuel Davis. Gift: 1 slave. 14 May 1713. Misc. LL-609

SARAH--Widow of Joseph. Son: Joseph Harley-Will 25 May 1741. Gr. dau:

Mary Rondells, Dau: Sarah Rondalls. Prov. Jan 4, 1743. Wit:
Sam'l Davis, And'w Brown, Wm. Cathcart. C. T. Wills

SARAH--Gr. Dau. of Wm. Cave. Will 11 May, 1849. Barnwell Wills
Gr. Ch: David Bradley
         Jane
         James
         Eliza
         Priscilla McMillan
         Martha Cave
         Mary Cave

THOMAS--Served as Mayor of London in Year 1768. Misc PP Pg-70 Barnwell

TIMOTHY WALTON, DR. of St. Georges Parish. -w- Sarah Amanda--Separation
James W. Martin, Tr. 23 Dec. 1856. Misc 5H-137

WILLIAM P.--Dec'd. Adm'x: Adaline Harley. Barnwell Case 99-pk 5
June 9, 1849

ZILPHA--Dau. of John Drummon of Barnwell. Will 1809

JACKSON, JAMES, SEN'R. Will Dec. 10, 1803. Barnwell WillsA 5 and 7
    Wife: Ferebia
    "My 4 ch'n": Ruthy Jackson
               Juda   "
               Joshua   "
               Joy   "   Exor: Stephen Green

JACKSON, MARY--Dau. of James Mirick (Myrick) of Barnwell. Will 1814

JACKSON, SARY ANN ELIZABETH--Gr. Dau. of Leah Brooker of Barnwell.
    Will 1819. Wm. D. Jackson, and Jesse C. Jackson, Gr. Sons.

JEFCOAT, NELLY -w- Wm. Jefcoat, Legatee of John Steel. Will 1835
    MARY -w- David Jefcoat
    SARAH -w- James Jefcoat

JENKINS, DOROTHY--Dau. of Wm. Stringfellow of Barnwell. Will 1812

JENKINS, ELIZABETH--Will 15 Dec. 1802 Barnwell Wills A-4
    Son: Joseph Parker, and Ashford Jenkins
    Dec'd husband, Arthur Jenkins. Exor's: Miles Ryley, Thos. Ryley
    Wit: Owen Ryley

JENNINGS, JOSEPH--Gr. son of Ann Daniel. Will 1827. Barnwell
    Dau. of Testator: Ursula Jennings

JETER, JOSEPH--Will 24 Dec. 1810 Barnwell Case 18 Pk-1
    Wife: Mary
    Ch: Levina Jeter $50.00
        Louisa Jeter $50.00 Ex: Sterling and Thomas Jeter

JETER, MARY -w- Sterling Jeter. Dau. of Jacob Free. Will 1822.

JETER, THOMAS, --Dec'd Barnwell Wills #I 120/21
    Widow: Susannah Jeter
    Mother: Mary Jeter--Land divided between them

JEWEL, SARAH--Barnwell Wills #I Pg 116-117 1815
    To her Ch: Mary Jackson, Martha, Thomas, Edward Jackson, and
    Henry Jewel. Deed gift.

JOHNSON, FEREBY--Dau. of Josiah Horn, Sen'r. of Barnwell. Will 1817

JOHNSON, JENNY--Dau. of John Jackson, Will 1829 Barnwell

JOHNSON, LEELY--Dau. of Isaac Dyches of Barnwell. Will 1807

JOHNSON, MARY--Dau. of Sarah Overstreet of Barnwell. Will 1818

JOHNSON, MOORE--Will 24 Nov. 1825. Barnwell Wills Bk C-146/7
    Wife: Charity--582 A. in Barnwell Dist.
    Son: Haley Johnson--Land after her death
    Dau: Charity Johnson
        Elizabeth Anderson
        Mary Bland

JOHNSON, WILLIAM of Barnwell. Bdl. 14-1 Bk A-82
    Nephew: Wm. Johnson Jr., (not 16) son of Richard
    Wife: Catherine
    Son: Elijah
          Harriet
          Yonge
          Hannah B___? Johnson
          Catherine Rhodes Johnson
          Sarah, Susannah, and Evelina Rebecca Johnson. 9 Feb. 1808

JOHNSTON, WILLIAM T.--Son-in-law of Joseph Trowell, Sen'r. Will 1836
JONES, ANN R.--Dec'd dau. of John Hogg. Will 1846

JORDAN, JAMES--Gr. 27 Dec. 1796 on Whippy Swamp of Saltcatchers. To
    Alex. M. Foster 2/3 July 1778--Bd. Wm. Davis, Benj. Gordon, Wm.
    Freeman. Now conv. by Wm. Davis and Alex. M. Foster--Both of
    Greenville. To: John Hughes and Richard King. 17 Feb. 1772
    Barnwell File C. T. Y-5-375

JOWERS, ELMS--Gr. Son of Rolin Hutson. Will 1838. Son-in-law of
    Testator: Wm. Jowers

KEARSH, REBECCA--Dau. of Solomon McClain of Barnwell. Will 1814

KEEL, RICHARD--Gr. son of Richard Treadway of Barnwell. Will 1805

KELLY, JAMES--"Of the County of Greenville" Will headed "New Winds"
    Mother: Mary Kelly   Nov. 27, 1737
    Wife: Jean 1/3
    Son: Brian Kelly--Land on Pon Pon, Colleton
    Dau: Elizabeth
    Sister: Mary Cragg
    Niece: Mary Bynom
    Niece: Ann Welsh
    Exor: John Cragg--storekeeper of New Windsor
          Thomas Barr of Pon Pon..C. T. Wills 1736-40 Pg-413
    Pg--213: Jno Cragg, James Killy, Edward Clossens Wit. Will of
          P. Nillimon Parmenter 27 Oct. 1737 in New Windsor
    Pg--319: John Charnock--Will 23 Aug. 1737. To Mary -w- John
          Cragg. and To Mary -w- of Martin Campbell. Both of New Windsor.
    Pg--391--Bk 1736-1740 Shows John Cragg as sales legatee of Darby
          McLaughlin of New Windsor. Will 2 Apr. 1739
    Pg--129--1745-1747 "Kelly Plt'n" in collection pur. from Wm. Guy
          by James St. John who willed it to son Miller St. John

KENADY, JOHN J.--Son of Alphia Parker. Barnwell Will 1840

KENADY, WILLIAM and JOHN--Step sons of Burrel Parker. Will 1835

KENEDY, ELIZABETH -w- Wm. Kenedy and dau. of John Clayton. Will 1842.
    Also Sarah -w- of John Kenedy a dau.

KENNY, ELIZABETH--Dau. of Thomas Lee of Barnwell. Will 1815. Joseph
    Kenny seems hus.

KERSH, ELIZABETH--Legatee of Leonard Searce of Barnwell. Will 1840

KILLINGSWORTH, ELIZABETH--Dau. of Wm. Anderson of Barnwell. Will 1820

KIMBERHIDE, MARTIN--Will 6 June 1787. Barnwell--Winton 1-pg-3
    To: Reuben Brunton, Margaret Brunton, and Jacob Brunton.
    Exor: Arthur Jenkins

KINARD, EVE--Legatee of Leonard Searce of Barnwell. Will 1840

KINARD, JACOB--Son-in-law of Catherine Shubert of Barnwell. Will 1834

KING, JOHN--Son-in-law of Benj. Tarrant of Barnwell. Will 1820

KINZIE, ELIZA M.--Dau. of John Hogg. Will 1846. Also written McKinzie

KIRKLAND, BENJAMIN of Winton Co. Will 13 March 1796. Barnwell A-Pg 15
    Wife: Alce--Had Grant 1774 etc.
    Dau: Susanna
    Sons: Benjamin (eldest), Caleb-land where he now lives, Richard,
        Jonathan, Moses
    Gr. Dau: Patience--1 cow and increase
    Yst Son: William

KIRKLAND, DORCAS--Dau. of David Cave. Will 1834

KIRKLAND, LAVORICE -w- Rob't Kirkland. Dau. of Mary Mixon. Will 1837

KITTLES, MARY-w- Michael B. Step Gr. dau. of Burrel Parker. Will 1835

KITTLES, MARY--Gr. Dau. of Alpha Parker. Will 1840. Gr. Gr. Son: Benj.
    Kittles. Barnwell

KNIGHT, JACOB--Wit 1789. Barnwell Will Bk I-37

KNIGHT, JAMES--61 A. in Orangeburg Dist. Little Bull Swp. of N. Edisto
    Bd. Dan'l Stroble, John Lysarth, Paul Stroman. Surv. Oct. 19,1791
    Archives Dept Plats 103-123

KNIGHT, ROBERT W. -m- set Julia Cornahan. Barnwell Deed Bk X-157

KNIGHT, THOMAS And wife, Susannah: Conv. 1 Oct. 1795 to David Adkinson
    Gr. to sd T. K. 16 Jan. 1786--on waters of Allegato.
    Barnwell Deed Bk E Pg-273/5

KNIGHT, WILLIS -w- Sarah Conv. 19 May 1807 to Wm. Bassett 100 A. on
    Alligator Br. of Saltcatchers. Orig. Gr. to Abigail Williams
    Barnwell Deed F-202

KNIGHT, ZACHARIAH 1785 (2)
       WILLIS   1785 (2)
       THOMAS   1785 (4)
       HENRY   1792 and 1801
       JOHN M.   1796   Barnwell Plats Bk 1 and 8

LAFFITTE, JOHN -w- Martha--Dau. of Stephen Smith. Will 1840 Barnwell

LAMAR, THOMAS G.--Bro-in-law of John Milledge of Barnwell. Will 1818

LAMBRIGHT, JAMES-m-set 23 June, 1814 Martha S. Collins. Trs: Stephen Smith, George W. Collins. Mixc. C-139 Barnwell file.

LANCASTER, MARY--Dau. of Samuel Still, Sen'r. Will 1830. Barnwell

LARD, PHEREBA--Dau. of Jane Thomas. Barnwell Will 1843

LARD, WILLIAM--Bro. of Mary Cochran. Will 1830. Barnwell. Her dec'd. father: Adam Lard

LASSITER, MARMADUKE--Dec'd. Adm'r. James Harley. Barnwell Prob. Bx-66-5

LATHAM, GEORGE--Will 20 March 1801. Barnwell Wills A-49/50
All to Nephew: Gabreal Freeman, son of Thomas and Susannah Freeman of Culpepper Co. Va. Land lately obtained by a writ of Partition between the late William Minor and myselfxxxxxxxx½ partxxxxxxx.

LECHMERE, RICHARD and his sister Catherine. Gr. Ch. of Andrew Deveaux of Barnwell. Will 1812

LEDLEY, MARY--Dau. of Jonas Keadle. Will 1839 Barnwell

LEE, ELLEANOR--Dau. of John Absten (sp?) Will 1825, Barnwell

LEE, ELIZABETH--Dau. of John Drummon of Barnwell. Will 1809

LEE, MARY--Sister of Nancy Skipis of Barnwell. Will 1816

LESLIE, GEORGE and Archibald Campbell of Glasgow--Partners in Store at Campbellton--and Wm. Campbell claims interest also. George Dec'd--widow -m- Nicholas Cooper. Jane Leslie, Wm. Leslie Barnwell Wills

LESLIE, GEORGE AND ARCHIBALD CAMPBELL as George Leslie and C. from Barkley Martin--3 lots in Campbelton. Edgefield Deed 12-411 & Oct. 1795

LESLIE, JANE AND WILLIAM--Ch. of George Leslie and Step ch. of Nicholas Cooper of Barnwell. Will 1803

LESLIE, WILLIAM--Dec'd. Pd. John Wilson, Coroner for holding inquest over the body of William Leslie. Pg. 43--Wm. Leslie--Mgr. Elec. in Abbeville Co. Aptd. 20 Dec. 1793. At Abb. Ct. House. Dec. 19, 1793-Pg18
Vo. 1815-88-Dec. 5, 1815--Wm. Lesley, Alex'r Hamilton com'rs to approve the _____ ? _____ ? of shffs. of Abbeville Dist.

LESLIE, WM.--Wit Deed in Barnwell Dist. 10 Oct. 1814. I Pg-61

LITTLEPAGE, ANN -w- Thos. Sister of John Burnley--Will at Barnwell 1778 Of Va. Will made in London.

LONG, LEVI--sd X Will 16 March 1803 Wife-Sarah Long Ext. Barnwell Wills
To the 5 Ch. of Israel Andres: A 30/31
   Harriot, James, Juliet, Nancy, Sidney--300 A. on Toomer's Bay
Son: Fashant--100 A., cattle, the home place
Dau: Fanny--Negro girl, 100 A.
Son: Nathaniel Long--100 A. and cattle
Dau: Sarah Long--100 A. And cattle   continued:

58

To: James, Levi, Valentine, Jonas, David, Alford Rowel--"6 sons of Elizabeth Rowel" dec'd--200 A. to be divided among them. Adj. above land. And cattle.
To: Sarah Long's 2 ch. Mahala and Mark Lazarus
To: Hardin Black's wife, Mason, "my daughter" 150 A.
To: Richard Black's wife, Martha, "my daughter" 150 A.
Son: Lewis--100 A. and cattle
Exor's: Thomas Long, and Thomas Long, Jr.

LOTT, WINNEY--Dau. of Robert Willis. Barnwell Will 1843/4

LOWERY, PRISCILLA--Dau. of Joseph Sandifer. Barnwell Will 1838

MACKAY, THOMAS--Legatee 25¢--of John Canaday, Sen'r. of Barnwell. Will 1819

MALLORY, LOUISA--Niece of Mary Bellinger of Barnwell. Will 1811

MANER, SAMUEL--of Screven Co. Ga. Barnwell Deed 1815 #I Pg 225/6/7
To: Gr. Dau: Sarah Ann Eliz. Robert (not 16) dau. of Wm. A. Robert
Julia Caroline Robert
Mary Emily Robert
Ulysses Maner Robert--all ch. of Wm. H. Robert

MARSH, WILLIAM--Dec'd Brother of Sarah Harden. Barnwell Will 1846
His ch. Legatees

MARTIN, HARRIET--Dau. of John Hogg. Will 1846

MATHENEY, SARAH -w- John Matheney. Dau. of George Odom. Will 1830

MATHEWS, MARTHA--Dau. of Robert Willis. Barnwell Will 1843/4

MATHIS, WINEFORD--Dau. of John Chette (or Chitty) of Barnwell. Will 1805

McANNALLEY, ANNEY--Dau. of Marbil Stone of Barnwell. Will 1788

McELHANNEY, ELIZABETH--Dau. of Thomas Filput of Barnwell. Will 1787

McELHENNEY, JENNETT, RICHARD, FRANCIS--Cousins of Rich'd Newman of Barnwell. Will 1806

McELMURRAY, SARAH (or Sary)--Dau. of Isaac Bush. Barnwell Will 1835

McRENZIE, CORNELIA G. --Dau. of Jane Miller of Barnwell. Will 1820

McKENZIE, ELIZA M.--Dau. of John Hogg of Barnwell. Will 1846

McKOWN, GEORGE of 96. Edgefield or Abbeville C. T. Wills
Wife: Tabitha
Bro: William 28 June, 1781

McMILLIAN, GATSEY--Dau. of Matthew Moye. Barnwell Will 1829

McMILLAN, JOEL--his wife, mary a dau. of Osborn Lain. Will 1841

McMILLEON, SALLY--Dau. of John Chette (or Chitty) of Barnwell. Will 1805

McMILLAN, SARAH--Dau. of Eli Myrick of Barnwell. Will 1840

McNEELY, PATRICK--Will 25 Dec. 1803 Barnwell Wills A-24/25
    Wife: Provadence 1/3 of all
    Son: Paul Gimble McNeely 1/3
    Dau: Sarah McNeely 1/3
    Exor: Wm. Murdach. Wit: Elinor McNeely--50 Acres
    Codicil: Mother--Margaret McNeely

McPHERSON, ANN -w- James McPherson. Dau. of Gideon Haygood. Will 1824

MEADOWS--See Will of William Teuten of Barnwell. 1814

MERIWEATHER, JUDITH -w- James M. Sister of John Bumley--Will at Barn-
    well. Will made in London 1778. Her ch. David, James, William

MILEY, DANIEL AND ELIZABETH--Gr. Ch. of Catherine Shubert. Will 1834

MILLEDGE, SUSAN G.--Dau. of Stephen Smith. Will 1840

MILLER, JANE--Will 1 Jan. 1820 Barnwell Will Bk B and G 1 and 2
    Dau: Cornelia G. McKenzie, Martha M. Miller,--"my thirds of the
    estate both real and per. of Robert McLaroth-Dec'd. Also my
    thirds of the estate of their father David Miller, Dec'd. Son in
    law--Solomon McKenzie. Wit: Peter Provost, Wm. R. Bale, Wm.
    Provost, J. P.

MILLS, SARAH--Legatee of Geo. Robson of Barnwell. Will 1803

MINOR, ROBERT--Son of Sarah Dewees of Barnwell. Will. Elizabeth a
    dau. 1816

MITCHEL, ELIZABETH--Dau. of Drucilla Turner of Barnwell. Will 1817

MIXON, MARY--Widow of John. Will 21 Aug. 1833 Barnwell Wills
    Dau: Lavorice -w- Robert Kirkland
    Ch: A. K. Mixon, James J. Mixon, Edward M. Mixon, Chas. J. Mixon,
    J. Mixon, Wm. Mixon. Susan E. Brown. Mary H. -w- James Dar-
    lington. John Mixon wit. Will of Richard Kirkland in 1812
    Vol. 1-pg 143 (or 3) and of Mary Kirkland in 1814. Vol. 1-146

MOORE, ELIZABETH--Sister of Dixon Calhoun of Barnwell. Will 1823. She
    lived on plt'n on Savannah River. See also will of Samuel Moore
    of Barnwell -w- Elizabeth. Will 1812. Wm. Moore a Nephew.

MOORE, JANE-w- Mathew Moore. Dau. of Thomas Hightower. Will 1830

MOORE, MARGARET--Dau of Sarah Dewees of Barnwell. Will 1816

MOORE, MARY--Dau of Solomon McClain of Barnwell. Will 1814

MORGAN, MORGAN et al -vs- Nathaniel Powell. Part. ____? 4 Apr. 1812
    Land to be sold. Barnwell Ct. Com. Pleas Misc. J. Bk 1-385

MORRIS, ELIZA -w- Thomas Morris--Dau. of Needham Green. Will 1839

MORRIS, MARY--Dau. of Henry Snelling of Barnwell. Will 1819

MORRISON, JAMES HAMILTON--Nephew of Sam'l N. Hamilton of Barnwell. Will
    1825

MOYR, WILLIAM AND MATHEW--See Will of Wm. Bassett. 1810 Barnwell

MOYE, MATTHEW and Susannah and their 6 ch.--Legatees of George Ward
    of Barnwell. Will 1813

MURPHEY, ANN and Susannah McMurphey--Daus. of Wm. Crosale of Barnwell.
    See Will 1787

MURPHEY, MARY--Widow of James Murphey of Ireland. Sister of Cornelius
    Tobin. Will 1829. Barnwell

MURRAY, LUCIA--Late of Savannah, Ga. Mother of Mary Bellinger of
    Barnwell. Will 1811

MYRICK, MARY -w- Elias Myrick. Dau. of Wm. Creech. Will 1833

NAIL, DANIEL--of New Windsor. Will 29 Oct. 1772. C. T. Wills 1771-1774
    Wife: Barbara
    Sons: John, Cooper, Daniel,
    Dau: Ann, Elizabeth. Ex'x: Wife. Exor: John Sturzenegger

NAIL, ELISHA--"of Jefferson Co. Ga." Conv. 18 Jan. 1800. Barnwell Deed
                                                            A-161
NEILSON, ELIZABETH -w- John Neilson. Son: Cornelius--Legatee of
    Cornelius Tobin who called him "Natural Son". Will 1829

NEWMAN, MARY--"Now Mary Wimberly"--Legatee of Patt McElmurray (Or
    Mackelmurray) of Barnwell. Will 1815. Wm. Newman, Patrick
    Newman, Letty Newman

NEWMAN, RICHARD--Will 16 Jan. 1806. Barnwell Wills A-13
    Cousin: Elizabeth Pettis, Jennett McElhenny, Richard McElhenny
    Frances McElhenny. Neice: Mary Newman. Nephew: George and
    William Newman

NEWMAN, THOMAS--Barnwell File Misc. B-488
    Ch: John, Eliza, Susannah, Alger, Isaac
    Deed gift 29 Feb. 1808--Land-Home place. Orig. Gr.--David Holmes
    Thos. Galphin, Isaac Bush--Trs.

NIX, ELIZABETH--Dau. of David Cave. Barnwell Will 1834

NOBLES, MARY A.--Dau. of John Hogg of Barnwell. Will 1846

NOBLES, NICHOLAS--Will 10 July 1816. Barnwell Wills A-249
    Wife: Elizabeth
    Son: James--to be schooled
    Daus: Mahala, Julia

OAKMAN, ANN--Dau. of Ann O. Hagood. Barnwell Will 1842

O'BANNON, JENNINGS and his ch. Legatees of Jane Maxwell. Will 1822

O'BANNON, JENNINGS--Son-in-law of Elizabeth Ford of Barnwell. Will 1824
    Wife: Harriet C. O'Bannon

ODAM, ABRAHAM, SENIOR of Granville. 30 Jan. 1771. Prov. 6 Apr. 1771
     Son: Abraham, Jacob, Demsey, David- ½Home place on Pipe Cr.
     Dau: Mary Carradine, Sarah Rooks, Nancy Deloth.
     Barnwell File. Copied Vol-orig 1767-71 Pg-594

ODOM, ABRAHAM. Barnwell--Bdl 77 Pk-3 Bk D-1
     Y-Sons: William and Richard
     Son: Wyatt Odom
     Wife: Mary Odom. 10 Sept 1840. Wit: R. W. Walker, Thomas
     Carvel, A. Hart. Abram Odom wit. will Thos Carvel in 1799

ODOM, BENJAMIN--Winton Co. Ct. Min. Pg-42. The State Vs Benj. Odom.
     Larceny--July 18, 1787. No defense appeared. Found guilty.
     39 lashes on bare back. Pg-45 Thos. Night Esq. -vs- Benj. Odom
     Judgement to be paid out of effects of Mich'l Odom, dec'd that
     comes to the hands of defendant--who pledges no effects.
     BENJAMIN, JR.--A Petit Juror 5 Aug. 1788
     BENJAMIN, SR. -vs- Wm. Ashley 6 Nov. 1788. Judgement by default.
     BENJAMIN (Prob. shows Junior) to Adam McCreary--Pd $100.00 100 A.
        on Rosemary Br. Barnwell Deed C-138/9 March 9, 1807

     BENJAMIN, SR. Wit. Will of John Blum, Sr. on 7 March 1814. Other
        Wit.-C. Tobin. Legatees--Widow-Sarah Blum, Son-Darling Blum
        Bdl 25 Pk 9 and Bk B-Pg 33
     BENJAMIN, SR. Dec'd. Let, 12 Feb. 1823. Adm'rs: Benjamin O'Dom.
        William Walker. Barnwell Let. Bk Pg 213
     BENJAMIN, MAJOR, dec'd. Late of Barnwell Dist. 19 Feb. 1823
        Appr: Wm. Matheny, Isaac Walton, Robert Brown, Ezekiel Perry,
        Abram Odom. Value: $2436.10. Sale 24 March 1823. Bk 73/4
        Pur: Benj., Julia, Owen, Levica, Sarah, M. W.,.Abraham, Sabert

ODOM, DANIEL--of Barnwell Dist. Bdl 76 Pk 12, Bk C Pg 210
     Wife: Elizabeth
     Son: John D. Odom--All lands
     Gr. son: John D. Grimes--Not 21
     Dau: Harriet Rice
           Polly Grimes
     Dec'd Dau: Rebecca Brewton and her ch. 18 Aug. 1836. Pres: Geo.
     Odom, Allen M. Odom. Daniel Odom wit Will of Benjamin Foster 1804

ODOM, DARLING--Let Gr. Bond 30 Aug. 1839. Mrs. Sarah Odom Adm'x.
     S: Reason Youngblood, Ezekial Wooley. Barnwell Let-Bonds 69

ODOM, GEORGE W. Dec'd. Inv: 7 Feb. 1827. Value: $547.87½. Inv. Bk
     Appr: Jesse Rice, David Zorn, James Kemp   Pg-152
     Sale: 22 Feb. 1827 Sale Bk Pg 8
           Cloak--Nicholas Zorn
           2 Pr. socks--John Joiner
           1 Pr. shoes-- "   "
           1 Pocket book--Nicholas Zorn
           1 Pr. Pantaloons--John Joiner
           1 Negro man, Bachus--Wm. Connell

ODOM, GEORGE--of Barnwell Dist. Barnwell bdle 74 pk 4 Bk C-230
     Sons: George R. and Allen Madison Odom. Daus: Sarah -w- John
     Matheny, Lucy D. Peebles. Sister: Elizabeth Zachery
     Ex: Son George and Willie I Duncan. Pres. John Joiner, Harriet
     Moye, A. Patterson.

ODOM, GEORGE--Wit. Will of Drusilla Turner on 24 Nov. 1817
     GEORGE, SR.. Inv. 10 Oct 1839. Value $2827.50. Appr: James W.
     Hutto, William Hutto, D. Rice, Sr. William Nimmons.
     Barnwell Inv. Bk Pg 198

ODOM, LEWIS--Dec'd. Inv. 30 Nov. 1812.. Appr: Adam McReary, Wm.
     McDaniel, John Riley, James Kirkland. Inv. Bk Pg 63. Barnwell

ODOM, LYDIA--Dec'd. Let--20 May 1814. Adm'rs-John O'Bannon, James
     Collins. Barnwell Let. Bk Pg 69

ODOM, MRS MARY--Intestate. Let--5 Aug, 1816. Adm'r--Benajah Bert.
     Barnwell Let. Bk Pg 105

ODOM, MOSES -vs- Bartlett Brown. Postponed--Ct 17 Apr. 1787. 1st
     Feb. 1787--Execution. Wm. Brown -vs- Moses Odom, Postponed
     Ct. Apr. 17, 1787. Richard Kirkland -vs- Whitmill Odom--Ct
     17 Apr. 1787--Postponed

ODOM, MICHAEL--Mentioned in Will of Benjamin Kirkland as being the
     original Grant owner of 100 A. land in Barnwell Dist. Will dated
     13 March 1796. Barnwell Bk A-15

ODOM, OWEN--Dec'd. Let--1 July 1816. Adm'r--Arthur Conaway. Barnwell
     Let Bk. Pg 106

ODOM, PRISCILLA--"This indenture made the 27 day of Oct. in the year of
     our Lord 1786 between Sarah Powell and Priscilla Odom, Jointly--
     of the Parish of St. Bartholomew--Widows-- in the State of S. C.
     Seamstresses--of the one party--Zilphy Williams and Mary Odom,
     Gr. Daus. of sd Sarah Powell and daus of sd Priscilla Odom.--
     infants--Deed gift--2 slaves Sary and Doll, Cattle, etc.

ODOM, PRISCILLA -vs- Malachy Powell. Dismissed at pltf's cost. Winton
     Co. Ct. Min. Pg 163

ODOM, SABRAD--Sued by Charles Wheeler, Prop. executed according to law.
     1 horse, bridle, and saddle, the property of Sabrad Odom. By Wm.
     Woodcock, D. Shff. Mar. 28, 1787

ODOM, SEYBERT--Inv. 15 Oct. 1824. Value 3545.05½. Inv. Bk Pg 113
     Appr's: George Odom, Thos. Kennerly, David Zorn, Jesse Rice.
     Sale 22 Nov. 1824 Sale Bk 130 and 162
     Pur: Daniel Odom   John D. Odom
          George Odom   Daniel D. Odom
     Let. Gr. 4 Oct. 1824 Adm'r John Turner Let Bk 241

ODOM, WILLIAM--Dec'd Inv. 4 Mar. 1824. Value $943.37½. Sale bk Pg 122
     12 April 1824. Pur: Jane Odom. Let-27 Feb, 1824. Josiah Dicks
                                                            Adm'r.

O'HEAR, ANN--See Will of Johnson Hagood of Barnwell. 1814

OVERSTREET, JAMES--Dec'd. Widow: Agnes Overstreet. 6 ch. by former
     mar. (1) Wm Overstreet, Dec'd. Barrett Brown, Adm'r. Barnwell Eq.
                                                            Page 167

OVERSTREET, SARAH--Will 29 Nov. 1818 Barnwell Wills
    Sons: James, John, Henry
    Dau: Mary Johnson
    Gr. Son: Josiah E. Brown
          Chas. I. Brown
    To: Jabez G. Brown
        Cynthia W. Brown
    Gr. son: Samuel Overstreet
    Wit: John McFail, Bartlett Brown, William Overstreet

OWEN, CIVIL--Dau. of Wm. Green of Barnwell. Will 1809

OWENS, ELIZABETH--Dau. of Josiah Keadle. Will 1839

OWENS, LUCY--Dau. of Alpha Parker. Will 1840
        Step Dau. of Burrel Parker. Will 1835

PAGE, JACOB--Will 7 March 1805. Barnwell Wills A-52/3
    Wife: Lurania--The home for life.
    "my 5 small ch." Beda, Jacob, Delania, Barnaby, Fereby.

PAGE, SELY--Gr. Dau. of Thomas Lee of Barnwell. Will 1815. Son Hiram

PAREMORE, MARY--Dau. of James Roberts of Barnwell. Will 1802

PARKER, JOSEPH--Son of Elizabeth Jenkins of Barnwell. Will 1802

PARSON, SARAH--Legatee Wm. Stringfellow of Barnwell. Will 1812

PARKENSON, JOHN--Will 3 Oct. 1803. Of RichmountDist. S. C.
    Wife: Sarah--Plt'n I now live on called Richmount--150 A.
    To: Francis H. Godfrey (a man) 2 acres "whereon his house is
    erected, slaves, etc" if no heirs by his present wife. If
    heirs dis. to: Edw'd Wolferden (sp) of Ireland.
    To: Thomas Galphin, Esq.--A book--Friend
    To: Samuel Dunbar--Letters--Friend

PATRICK, SAMUEL--Son-in-law of Joseph Tucker. Barnwell Will 1843

PATTERSON, ELIZABETH--Dau. of John Turner of Barnwell. Will 1806

PEEPLES, LUCY D.--Dau. of George Odom. Barnwell Will 1830

PENDARVIS, JAMES--Dec'd son of Ann Daniel. Barnwell Will 1827

PEOPLES, SARAH--Dau. of Robert Lee of Barnwell. Will 1789

PERRY, CAROLINE MARY--Aunt of Perry Hasell. Barnwell Will 1840

PETTICE, WM. JOHN--See Will of Robert Bates of Barnwell. 1815

PETTIS, ELIZABETH--Cousin of Richard Newman of Barnwell Will 1806

PETTIS, ELLY ANN BURAQUE--Gr. Dau. of Saray E. B. Futch. Will 1832

PEYTON, SARAH F.--Gr. Dau. of Tarlton Brown. Will 1842. Barnwell
    Dau: Frances C. -w- Wm. H. Peyton

PINCKNEY, LUCIA--Dau. of Mary Bellinger of Barnwell. Will 1811
    Wife of Miles B. Pinckney

PORTER, ELIZA--Dau. of Spires Broxton of Barnwell. Will 1844

PURNAL, PETER--Barnwell File Misc. B-487. 15 Feb. 1808
    Wife: Elizabeth--"late relict of John Lark-Dec'd and Dau. of
    John Darlington". He made over her inheritance from father and
    former husband. Stephen Collins, Job Darlington, Trs.

PURNAL, SARAH--Gr. Dau. of Eleanor Darlington. Will 1815. Her Bros:
    James Purnal and Solomon Purnal. Barnwell

PHILLIPS, SARAH--Dau. of Peter Hare of Barnwell. Will 1813

PLATTS, DAVID--Dec'd Barnwell Equity Bk Pg 184. 1839
    Widow: Sarah Platts
    Dau: Mary -w- George W. Bishop
        Charity -w- Stephen Creech
    Gr. Dau: Mary Creech
    Gr. Son: Josiah Creech
    Dau: Anna Platts
    Son: George Platts
    Adm'r: John Platts

PLATTS, ELIZABETH--Dau. of Catherine Shubert. Barnwell Will 1834

PLATTS, JOHN--Will 6 Nov. 1799. Barnwell Wills 1797-1816 242/3
    Wife: Sophia
    Sons
    Daughters
    Exor's dec'd--son John Platts, Jr. aptd. 15 March 1815.

    PREACHER, SARAH--Dau. of Ezekiel Stokes Barnwell Will 1836

PRICE, FRANCES--Dau. of Samuel Still. Will 1830 (or Rice)w of Charles

PRIESTER, ELIZABETH--Dau. of Matthew Moye. Barnwell Will 1829

QUARLES, JOHN AND DAVID--Gr. Ch. of Sarah Harden. Will 1846. She
    was sister of Wm. Marsh.

RAGIN, SARAH -m- John King. His 1st wife. Will 1821 at Barnwell.
    His 2nd wife--Rachel

RAST, ELIZABETH I.--Dau. of Sam. Daniel. Will 1833. Wife of John Rast

RAY, SUSANNA--Dau. of Henry Kennedy. Will 1846. Wife of Charles Ray

RED, RICHARD (or Reed)--Legatee of Richard Treadaway of Barnwell.
    Will 1805. Patience Red--a dau. and Legatee of William Boyet of
    Barnwell. Will 1808

REED, MATILDA--Dau. of Robert Willis. Barnwell Will 1843/4

REEVES, PEGGY--Dec'd dau. of Joseph Tucker. Will 1843. Also Nancy
    Reeves--another Dec'd dau. Legacies to their ch.

REYNOLDS, EPHRAIM--Age 58 yrs.--Made Off. 31 Oct. 1820 of his Rev.
    Service. First under Capt. Hill--who sent him to Maj. Dennis
    who transferred to Capt Rhodes of Maj. Lamb's Battalion of Col.
    Armstrong's Regt. of Line of Genl. Lincoln. Served in all, 7
    mos. and discharged when under Capt. Jones. Maj. McCloss, Bat.
    of Col. Little Regt. of Gen'l. Greene and discharged by him
    At Ashley Hill near C. T.. A res. cit. of W. S. 18 March 1818

RICE, ANN--Dau. of John Guess of Barnwell. Will 1817. Wife of John R.
    Dau: Theny Rice--Dec'd and her dau. Sarah Rice. Wm. seems S-in-L

RICE, FRANCES--Dau. of Samuel Still, Sr. Will 1830 (or Price)

RICE, HARRIET--Dau. of Daniel Odom. Will 1836

RICE, JOHN and Wife--Legatees of Elijah Dooling of Barnwell. Will 1816

RICE, MARY R.--Dau. of Sem Daniel. Will 1833. Wife of Charles H Rice

RICHARDS, JAMES LIGHTON--Will 13 Jan 1799. Barnwell Wills A-57
    To: Friend Wm. Fishboarn's sons--800lbs.
    To: Mr. John Logan's Children--½ remainder
    To: "my daughter, Sarah"--the other ½

RICHARDSON, MARY ANN--Dec'd dau. of William Hughes. Will 1843.
    Her Ch: Wm. F. Richardson, Thomas and Mary Richardson

RIGDON, MARY--Dau. of Solomon Owens of Barnwell. Will 1818

RILEY, MILES--Legatee of John Jackson of Barnwell. Will 1829

RILEY, WM. G. -m- set 13 April 1843. E. M. Bryan. Wm. W. Bryan, Tr.
                                              Misc. N-96

ROBERSON, GEORGA--Will 31 Oct. 1803 Barnwell Deed Bk A 33 to 41
    To: Elizabeth Ann Stewart--the home plt'n
       George Stewart, son of Elizabeth ann--Stock pur. from Thos.
       Nightingale, etc.
       Ann Squires--Her part in trust
       Louisa Chevellette
       Sarah Mills
       Mary Hatcher
    To: George Roberson Dunbar and Lucy Dunbar--Gr. Ch. of Elizabeth
       Ann Stewart
    To: Elizabeth Ann Govan and Andrew Govan--1 share
       Betsy Dunbar's children--Geo. R. Dunbar, and Lucy Dunbar
    To: Betsy Roberson Squires--dau. of Ann Squires

ROBERTS, JAMES--Will 29 Nov. 1802. Barnwell Wills A-1
    Wife: Ann
    Dau: Dorcas Curlee
    Son: Roger Roberts
    Dec'd Son: James--"to his heirs"
    Daus: Elizabeth Stansel, Mary Paremore
    Sons: Roland Roberts, Irwin Roberts
    Dau: Winny Barfield)
    Son: Stephen Roberts) Land on Land on _____? Cr.

ROBERTSON, SAMUEL D.--Late of Long Island, N. Y.   Will   Barnwell Bk A-
     Bro: John T.'s eldest child.   206
       "   Benjamin--Legacy from father. 26 Aug. 1817

ROBERTSON, WILLIAM--Gr. 2 May 1785. Part. Con. Joseph Reid and Wife 1/3
     -vs- Lark and Geo. Robinson. Barnwell Ct. Com. P. 1800 Bk-1 pg 26

ROBISON, WM. To Mary Mitchel--Slave Sylvia. Winton Bk 1 pg 2
     Wit: R8d. Vince, Lark Robison. Barnwell Deed 9 Apr. 1787

ROSE, JOHN--Will 22 March 1816. Barnwell Wills Bk A-4/5
     Wife: Mary--1700 Acres whereon I now live.

ROSHER, MALIKIAH--Son-in-law of Thos. Weathersbee of Barnwell. Will 1815
     Wife: Elizabeth

ROTTEN--see Wrotten and will of John Hickman of Barnwell. 1798

ROTTENBERRY, NANCY--Dau. (?) Legatee of James Moody of Barnwell 1809

ROUNTREE, MARGARET--Wife of Jordan Rountree. Sister of John D. Minor
     of Barnwell. Will 1816

ROWEL--See will of Levi Long of Barnwell. 1803

ROWLAND, WILLIAM--Gr. sd Gdn. of son: John Rowland--heir of his Gr-
     father Jeremiah Wood. Bond to be double value of prop. Barn-
     well Ct. Min. Pg 237. 29 March 1819.
     Pg 245--Jeremiah Wood--Dec'd. Son: Edmond Wood--under 21.
     Pet. Jeremiah Darby--Gdn. for Partition proceedings.

RUD, LOTTY--Dau. of Welcome Ussery. Barnwell Will 1834

SAMUEL, BEVERLY -w- Susan S. Samuel. Bev. son-in-law of Elijah Ford
     of Barnwell. Will 1824

SANDERFORD, POLLY--Dau. of John Chette of Barnwell. Will 1805

SANDERS, JAMES--"Son"of Charles Steed of Barnwell. Will 1807

SANDERS, JOHN AND MOSES--Step sons of William Fannon. Will 1832

SANDERS, SINABESS--Gr. dau. of Stephen Roberts of Barnwell. Will 1836

SEXTON, EDMOND--Dec'd Ct. Min. Pg 425. 7 Apl. 1821
     Heirs: Fernnel H. Thurston -w- Penelope
             Michael Heirs -w- Sylvia
             Nathan Jordan -w-
     Page 508/509--E. S. had not lived with his wife for 25 years. She
     is living and has had several children born since the separation.
     E. S. was living in adultery with Mary Bennet

SCARBOROUGH, WILLIAM--Bro-in-law of Elijah Gillett of Barnwell. Will
                                                                   1817
SCARIVEN, BARBARA--Dau. of Stephen Smith of Barnwell. Will 1840

SCOTT, DIOCIUS--Age abt. 62 yrs. Enlisted in Virginia under Capt.
    James Millikin abt. 1779 and was in the Southern Army under Gen'l.
    Lincoln with the fall of C. T. when he served under Gates, and
    afterwards under Gen'l Greene. Wounded in Ankle at battle of
    E_____? moved to James Island there discharged. Placed on
    Pension in 1798. Barnwell Rev. Claim 5 Nov. 1824

SCOTT, DRURY--Age 65. Enlisted in Northampton Co. N. C. under Capt.
    Walton. Discharged at James Island in S. C. and some years later
    to Western Country and lived there some years. Is illiterate.
    2 Apr. 1828. Barnwell Rev. Claim Min. Bk Pg 388/9

SELLERS, JOHN--Legatee John Canady, Sr. Will 1819 Barnwell

SHAW, THOMAS--Will 5 Sept. 1801. Barnwell Wills A-65
    Wife: Frances
        "My wife's eldest dau. Elizabeth Evans, a child and her
        son, John Evans".
        Ezekial Lester to be Gdn. of ch.

SHEELY, WILLIAM G.--Legatee of Rachel Taylor. Will 1829 Barnwell

SHELLY, MICHAEL--Son of Drusilla Turner of Barnwell. Will 1817

SHINGLETON, MRS. JANE--Bd. Gr. to Benj. Odom, Jr. 200 A. S-side
    S-Edisto. Also Bd Ambrose Walker. Also shows same for James
    Shingleton known as Kellis Cowpen. Barnwell Plat bk 1-165
    27 July, 1774

SHUTE, ANNA--Dau. of Peter Banner of Barnwell, Will 1779

SIMS, WILLIAM GILMORE.--B. Dec. 14 1883. D. Aug. 8, 1954. Son of
    Emma Gertrude Hartzog, and William G. Sims. Eldest child
    Chivellette--b. Jan 20, 1880 d. July 28, 1890
    Beverly Hartzog, infant son 1886-1887

SMITH, ANN--Dau. of Stephen Hankinson. Will 1828 (Smith-middle name)

SMITH, AARON Aptd Clerk of Ct. John Caraway Smith, Sec.

SMITHHART, HARRIET--Dau. of Eleanor Newsome. Will 1837. (also H. Adkins)

SMITH, JOHN CARAWAY, Daniel Green, Thomas Knight, James Farr, William
    Buford--"Being a majority of the Judges" held Ct. at "Place called
    and known by the name of the Big Horse on the Plt'n of Charles
    Brown"..Winton Co. Ct. Bk. 17 Oct. 1786

SMITH, JUDITH -w- Stephen Smith. Dau. of Joseph Vince of Barnwell. Will
                                                                    1810
SMITH, LINNA--Gr. Dau. of Wm. Stringfellow of Barnwell. Will 1812

SMITH, WILLIAM--Gr. son of Wm. Teuten of Barnwell. Will 1814

SNELLING, MARY--Dau. of John Drammon of Barnwell. Will 1809

SNELLING, SARAH ANN--Dau. of William Parker. Will 1835 Barnwell

SOBESKI, TADEUS,--Son of Henry Zorn of Barnwell. Will 1821

SOUTHWELL, CHARITY--Dau. of Solomon McClain of Barnwell. Will 1814

SOUTHWELL, MARY--Dau. of Eli Myrick of Barnwell. Will 1840

SPEARS, GINCY--Dau. of Welcome Ussery. Will 1834

SPIERS, SARAH--Dau. of John Drummon of Barnwell. Will 1809

SQUIRES, ANN--Legatee of Geo. Robson of Barnwell. Will 1803

STALLINGS, JAMES --Will 9 Oct. 1803 Barnwell Wills A-33
     Wife: Sarah may be encient
     Son: John
     Bro: Josiah Stallings-Exor.
     Bro-in-law: Absolum Green-Exor.
     Wit: William Green, Sr., William Kee, Shadrick Stallings

STANCIL, ELIZABETH--Dau. of James Roberts of Barnwell. Will 1802

STANSELL, ELLENOR -w- of Wm. Stansell. Illigitimate dau of Martha
     Broxton. Will 1841

STANYARN, MARY--Dau. of Charles Steed of Barnwell. Will 1807

STENSON, RACHEL--Dau. of Solomon McClain of Barnwell. Will 1814

STEPHEN, ELIZABETH--Dau. of Peter Hare of Barnwell. Will 1813

STEWART, GEORGE--Son of Elizabeth Ann Stewart--Legatee George Robson
     of Barnwell. Will 1803. Elizabeth had Dunbar Gr. Ch.

STEWART, CHARLES--Cousin of John Mysser of Barnwell. Will 1788

STIVINDEY, MARY--Dau (?) of Isaac Dyches of Barnwell. Will 1807

STOKES, NANCY--Dau. of Dixon Calhoun of Barnwell. Will 1823.
     Gr. Son: Dixon Stokes

STONE, SARAH--Formerly Gantt. See Will Mary Woodroof of Barnwell. 1822

STRINGFELLOW, RACHEL--Dau. of Adam Lard, Sen'r. Will 1828

STROMAN, JACOB--Son-in-law of Charles Milhouse. Will 1826. Barnwell

SWEAT, HARRIET T.--Dau. of Ann Trotti. Will 1833

TARVER, ELIZABETH--Legatee of Charles Beck of Barnwell. Will 1823

TAUNT, CATHERINE--Dau. of Henry Zorn of Barnwell. Will 1821 (Fant?)

TAYLOR, JOHN--Will 8 Apr. 1806. Barnwell Wills A-51
     All to Bro: Elias Taylor "son of my Mother"

TINDAL, HENSFORD D., john V., Henry F., Mary D., David O., Samuel H.,
     Martha R., Zacharia A.--Gr. Children of Magdalene Holman. Will 1842
     Dec'd Daughter: Ann Tindal

TINDAL, JOHN--Will 30 Aug. 1800. Barnwell Wills A-23
     Wife: Mary
     "Children" to be supported until of age.

TOUCHSTONE, SALLEY--Dau. of Josiah Horn, Sen'r. of Barnwell. Will 1817

TOOL, ELIZABETH--Dau. of Elizabeth Weathersbee. Will 1830. Barnwell

TUCKER, JOSEPH--Dec'd father of the wife of Samuel Patrick. Will 1847.
    His wife: Sarah I. Patrick

TURNER, JOHN--Will 2 May 1806. Barnwell Wills A-66/67
    Wife: Mary Ann--Ex'x
    Dau: Sarah Williams--Pt land pur. from Wm. Minor
    Son: James Turner
    Dau: Elizabeth Patterson--Land including her husband's improvements
    Son: William Turner Exor.
    Dau: Venity   "
    Son: Joseph   "
          John   "   Exor.
    Dau: Susannah "
          Mary   "
    Wit: Wm. Turner, Noel Turner, John Griffin

TYLER, ELSEY--Dau. of Charles Beck, Sen'r. Barnwell Will 1823

TYLER, JOSEPH--Son-in-law of Thos. Weathersbee, Sr. of Barnwell. Will
                                  Wife: Lucy   1815
TYLER, ANNA--Dau.(?) of John Blitchendon of Barnwell. Will 1803

TYLER, ELISHA--Son-in-law of Charles Milhouse. Barnwell Will 1826

TYLER, HENRY--Died before testator--Gr. son of John Hickman of Barnwell
    Will 1798. Elizabeth Tyler--a dau.

THURSTON, LYDIA--Dau. of Ruben Kirkland of Barnwell. Will 1822

THURSTON, PRISCILLA--Dau. of John Chette (or Chitty) of Barnwell. Will
                                            1805
UBANKS, ELIZA--Dau. of William Fannon. Will 1832

VAUGHN, HANNAH--Dau. of Amos Way of Barnwell. Will 1816. John Vaughn
    Seems husband.

VILLARD, DAVID--Gr. Father of John D. Hogg and Harriet Martin--Children
    of John Hogg. Will 1846

WALKER, GEORGE of Winton--Will 21 Feb. 1799 Barnwell Wills A-20
    Wife: Sarah
    Dau: Mary Cook -w- Abraham Cook
    Son: James Walker
    Dau: Pershewey Cook -w- James Cook
    Son: Israel Walker
          Jonathan Walker
    Dau: Susannah Griffin -w- Moses Griffin
    Wit: Robert Walker, et al

WALL, ELIJAH--Son-in-law of Elizabeth Weathersbee of Barnwell. Will
    1830. Gr. son: Geo. W. Wall

WALL, MARY A. E.--Dau. of Stephen Robert. Will 1836 Barnwell

WALLACE, JOSIAS "of Orangeburg Dist" (Included Barnwell) to his Dau.
    Sarah Wallace--Slaves: Primus, Ned, and Sarah--Household goods,
    Cattle, etc. and also Plt'n on "Which I now live, lying and
    being in the Dist. af'd on the Lower Three Runs Waters of the
    Savannah River. 1 May, 1785. B/S WW-116

WARD, MARTHA, Sr. and Jr.--Dau. and Gr. Dau. of Ann Golding or Ann
    Colding of Barnwell. Will 1805

WATSON, ANNA--Sister of Nancy Skipis of Barnwell Will 1816

WATERS, JONATHAN--Mentioned in Will of Samuel Reed of Barnwell. Bk ᴿ-186
    " I Will and bequeath my Plt'n on Edisto River whereon Jonathan
    T. Waters now lives unto my dau. Jane and to the heirs of her
    body". Will 24 Aug. 1823

WEATHERBY, LEWIS--J. P. for Barnwell, Promoted to J. Q. 1809-Dec. 19
    LEWIS--1813 Pg 75. Lewis W. et al apt. Com'vs. to open navigation
    of Upper Three Runs

WEATHERSBY, LINDY--Gr. Dau. of Wm. Green of Barnwell. Will 1809

WEATHERSBEE, MARTHA ANN--Dau. of Jane Thomas-widow. Will 1843.
    She came from Marion Dist.

WILLIAMS, JOHN--Will 2 Dec. 1802. Barnwell Wills A-3
    Wife: Nancy Williams
    Dau: Jenny
    Son: David
    Dau: Mary 100 Acres each.

WILLIAMS, LUCRETIA -w- Isaac W. --Dau. of Benj. Heath of Barnwell.
    Will 1805. Her ch: James, Benj., Nancy, John

WILLIAMS, NATHAN--Dec'd. Winton Co. Ct. Bk-Pg 68
    Mary Williams, Adm'x
    S: Abraham Richardson and Richard Tradaway (sp?)Ct jan. 15, 1788

WILLIAMS, SARAH -w- Martin Williams. Dau. of Wm. Kearse. Will 1838
    Also Harriet -w- Wm. G. Williams another dau. of testator.

WILLIAMSON, MARIAN--Dau. of Wm. Stringfellow of Barnwell. Will 1812

WILLIAMSON, MARY--Gr. Dau. of Amos Way of Barnwell. Will 1816

WILLS, GEORGE -w- Rebecca. Son Henry M. Legatee of Rachel Taylor.
    Barnwell Will 1829

WILSON, MARTHA--Dau. of Drusilla Turner of Barnwell. Will 1817

WIMBERLY, EDWARD--Dec'd Barnwell Ct. Min. Pg 254/5 1 Apr. 1819
    Heirs: Joseph, Marsha, Edward, Sarah, Frances, Isaac Wimberly

WIMBERLY, MARY--Formerly Mary Newman. Legatee of Patt Meckelmurray of
    Barnwell. Will 1815

WITSELL, CAROLINE GORDON--Dau. of Ann O. Hagood. Barnwell Will 1842

WOOD, MARY--Dau. of Peter Hare of Barnwell. Will 1813

WORSTER, ANDREW--Gr. 18 Oct. 1757. Passed to Henry Jackson now conv.
    by Joseph Harley -w- Elizabeth to: William Davis. 250 A.
    on W-s Main Swamp of Saltcatchers. Wit: Wm. Buford. Thos
    Crawford and Alex'r. Wood C. T. T-5 470 Barnwell File

WHALLER, BETTY--Dau. of Marbil Stone of Barnwell. Will 1788

WHEELER, JOSEPH--Wit. Will of John Bush. Apr. 4, 1802 Barnwell

WROTEN, MICHAEL--Dau and Legatee Will of Matthew Moye. Will 1829

WROTTEN, REBECCA--Dau. of John Hickman of Barnwell. Will 1798

WYATT--See Will of Benj. Tarrant of Barnwell. 1820. His son, James
    Wyatt Tarrant

YORK, ELIZABETH--Dau-in-law of Charles Steed of Barnwell. Will 1807

ZACHERY, ELIZABETH--Dister of George Odom. Barnwell Will 1830

ZEIGLER, ELIZABETH -w- Conrad Zeigler, Dec'd --Dau. of Ann Daniel.
    Barnwell Will 1827

ZEIGLER, MICHAEL-Dec'd-Part. Est.
    Widow: Mary MagdaleneZeigler Barnwell Ct. Com. Pleas 1800
    Ch: Michael, John, Conrad, Jacob, Joseph, Mary -w- Jacob Ridgdell
    Magdalene -w- James Kierson, Elizabeth -w- William Pendarvis
    Margaret -w- Thornton Cox

ZORN, MARY--Niece of John E. Steivender of Barnwell. Will 1824

ZORN, NANCE--Dau. of Avrehart Stivender of Barnwell. Will 1806

CHESTER COUNTY - SOUTH CAROLINA

Compiled by

Janie Revell

72

BALDWIN, CALEB--Wit. deed 16 Sept 1788 between John Love and James
    Lock, Jr. Pt 3 grants to John Love 1765 to 1771 at mouth of
    Broad River. Chester deed Bk-7

BARBER, ELIZABETH--Minor--Turner Jackson Pen'n Guardianship. Chester
                                                              1844
BEASLEY, MOLY--Sister of John Culp-Will 22 Aug. 1825
    Jacob Beasley a Legatee. Chester Wills

BREWAN, DANIEL--About 21 yrs. came to Carolina 8 June 1816. Cit.
    Paper 2 Nov. 1820. Native of Ireland. Took oath at Chester
    Chester File Misc. D-210

BRICE, EMELINE--Wife of Walter Brice. Dau. of Rebecca Moore-w. 1851
    Chester Wills 1845-96

CARTER, BENJAMIN--Chester Will 1788
    Children: Churchill   John   Henney
                Elizabeth   Frankey   Mourning
                Unity   Salley   Wriah (?)
    Ex: Son, Churchill, and John Terry
    Wit: Wm. Morris, Geo. Blessitt   Est. settled 1789

CARTER, JOSEPH--Dec'd. Case: Henry Carter -vs- Martha Carter et al
    Sale 4 Dec. 1843 127 A. to Henry Carter for _____? Chester

CASHEY, JAMES, JOHN, AND ROSANNAH--Niece and nephews of James Graham,
    Sr. Will 24 Sept. 1876 Chester Wills

CASHEY, JULIANNA--Will 24 Sept 1844 Chester Co. Wills A-73
    Dau: Mary Hindman   Dau: Esther Mills
          Rosannah Goosly   Elizabeth E. Cashey
    Son: John Cashey   Joannah Cashey
          James Cashes   Son: Thomas Cashey
    Nancy Cashey: Dau and legatee of Jennet Marion-Will 17 Feb 1846
    John Cashey of Chester Will 19 Sept 1785 Camden Wills A-356
        Wife: Ester
        Dau: Ezchell
             Mary
        "My 4 sons"

CHAPMAN, ALLEN--Sheriff of Chesterfield 3 Feb. 1788 Historical Com VV-
                                                             413
CLEGHORN, ELIZABETH--Niece of Mary Graham-Will 21 Jan. 1822
    Niece: Mary Adams
           Molly Peggy Boyce dau David Boyce
    Sister: Jane Boyce
    Brother: James Graham--Ch. Chester Wills

COFFEY, HUGH--Heir of Wm. Moore of Mecklenberg. Chester deeds E-162

COLVIN, MARTIN Adm'r -vs- Martha H. Colvin, et al Sale 7 Nov. 1842
                                                    Chester
COOPER, HUGH--A weaver--Will 15 Jan. 1793 Chester Wills A-128
    Sons: Tobert and John
    Daus: Elizabeth Ferguson and Jane McGarity

COOPER, JOHN--Will 6 Sept. 1827 Chester Wills J-139
    Wife: Mary
    Heirs: Jno Nisbet   John A. Cooper
           James Cooper   Robert Cooper
           Andrew Cooper   Ebenezer Cooper
    Legacy to Rusty Ch in Philadelphia $20.00

EVANS, CHARLES--Of Chester Co. dec'd Chester Misc. 3J-339
    Dau: Nancy Evans "Of Cheraw Dist Co. of Chesterfield on Lynder
    Cr. Pa 20 Sept 1797 To: Benjamin Swans of Orangeburg Dist.
    Wit: John Bush, Moses Griffin, Isaac Bush, J. P.

FANT, ABNER B. Chester Deed I I-151 Shows: Nancy H. Gregory "late
    of Chester Dist"--Dau: Lucy S. Trammell of Anderson conv. to
    her Son-in-law, Abner B. Fant all interest in estate of her
    mother, sd Nancy H. Gregory. 23 July 1850

FANT, EPHRAIM--Dec'd. Chester Prob. Bx-91 Pkg- 1497
    Let. testimony 8 July 1851 Will in File
    Sarah R. Fant, Ex'x.
    Son: Abner Fant--to his ch
             Sarah J   )
             Ephraim D.) Seem to by ch mentioned
    Son: David
    Dau: Mary Wright
          Jane Fant
          Catherine Castles
    Son: Samuel Fant
          Ephraim Fant--Will sd "Ephraim Fant" by Nicholas Colvin

FARIS, MARGARET--A dau. of David Carr -w- Margaret Will 18 Dec. 1804
    Other ch: Elizabeth Kelsey
               Agnes Kulp
               Robert Carr Chester Wills

FORD, ROBERT--No dower. To: James Clark 115 A. on Little Rocky Cr.
    Gr. to Thomas Ford 31 July 1766 Chester Deed S-311 May 22, 1816
    Bk S-386: Middleton Ford -w- Jean to Alexander Cowan--250 A.
    S. S Tinker's Cr.
    Chester Bk J-8 Sept 30 1799--John Ford to James Byrnes 24 A. in
    Chester Co. Gr. to Wm. Ford on head of Hogs Br. of Rocky Cr.
    Bd Thomas Ford and Wm. Ford, Jr.

FORD, WILLIAM--Oldest son and heir of Thomas Ford, dec'd of Chester Co.
    Dist. of Pinckney to James Clark 50 A. Gr Thos. Ford 4 Oct 1768
    on Rocky Cr. S-s Catawba R. on Hogne or Hoges? Br.
    Chester Co. Bk C-75 12 Mar 1793
    Middleton Ford--Chester Bk R-304 Dower Jennett Ford 8 Mar. 1816
    to John Westbrook 22 Dec. 1815 100 A. on Rocky Cr.
    Chester Bk A-492 Wm. Ford, Sr. to son, Wm. Ford, Jr. 200 A.
    on Little Rocky Cr.Late the property of Wm. Stormants. this
    deed 15 Feb. 1788

FRANKLIN, BARNET AND JAMES--Wit Will of James Lay of Chester Dist.
    Will 20 Dec. 1820 Chester Wills

FRANKLIN, EDMUND -w- Rachel conv. to Anderson Thomas a tract of land
    in 1768 to "a certain Edward Franklin" by mistake--intended for
    Edmund. Chester Ct. Min. Apr. 1788-Pg 206

FRANKLIN, THOMAS -w- Persley (Rendown)conv. to Wm. Trussell. Chester
    Ct. Min. Pg.-111 July 1786

FRANKLIN, THOMAS BAKER -w- Nancy conv. 5 Nov. 1791 Chester deed B-539

GASTON, WILLIAM, JOHN, JOSEPH, JR., JOSEPH, MARTHA, ALEXANDER WALKER,
    ESTHER WALKER--P. A. to Hugh Gaston, Washington Co. Ga.--To sell
    land-2 tracts- in Georgia. Gr. to Alexander Gaston and David
    Gaston

GOYER, DREWRY -w- Sarah conv. 18 Nov. 1791 Chester Deed D-250/51

GRAHAM, JAMES, JR.--Will 4 Sept. 1826 Chester Wills
    Sister: Esther -w- Alex'r Smith--land in Alabama
    Aged Mother and Father
    Niece: Mary Caskey
            Rosannah Caskey
    Nephew: John Caskey
             John Reedy
    Brother: David Graham--not of right mine.

GRICE, WILLIAM--Letter from his as wit.   Chester Equity Pg. 16/17
    WADE AND AXEY--Lived in Marion 1839   Case:
    William Lewis -w- Elizabeth -vs-_____?
    Sarah Hopkins, et al. Wade Grice offered to take $300.00 for
    his share

GRISHAM, MAJOR--Will 16 Oct. 1800 Chester Wills
    Wife: Frances
    Son: John Grisham
          Thomas B. Franklin Grisham
    Dau: Priscilla, Frances, and Sally
    Step Dau: Patty Trussel
    Wit: Wm. Wood, Mary Franklin, John Dorsay
    Exor: Thomas B. F. Grisham

HARDEN, HENRY, Dec'd--Mary Harden and George Harden Adm'rs -vs-
    Peter Harden, et al. Sale 9 Oct. 1843 Chester

HARRISON, HENRY, dec'd. Cit: Mrs. Charlotte Harrison. Chester
    Min. Bk. Sept 1797

HEAD, RICHARD--Of Chester Will Bk B-98 11 Apr. 1800
    Wife: Sarah Head--Home Plantation
    Sons: Henry and William--Lands where they live--adj.
           Richard--Plantation where he lives
           Peter Newport Head--"Hopkins Place"
           James and Thomas--Plantation home after wife's death
    Dau: Frances Tabor
          Lucinda Head
          Sarah Head

HILL, SARAH A.--Wife of George W. Hill. Dau. of Rebecca Moore w. 1851
    Chester Wills 1845 Pg. 96

HITCHCOCK, JOHN--Will June 1785 Chester
    Wife: Ester
    Dau: Elizabeth -w- John Jaggers. Son: John
    Gr. Dau: Hester -w- Daniel Jaggers
              Sarah Jeter
              Ann Davis
              Martha Hardee (Patty)
    Nephew: Wm. Hitchcock--Land on Jeffers Cr.
    July Ct. 1786 John Hitchcock -vs- David Hopkins--Slaves

HOPKINS, D.--Letter: "Orange Co. N. C. March 30, 1781--"My dear sons"
    This is to inform you that the fate of war has placed me here a
    prisoner of war xxxxxxxxxxxxx" sd. D. Hopkins Chester Bk B-445

HOPKINS, NEWTON, Dec'd--Chester Ct. Min. Jan. 1188 ? Pg-203/4
    Widow: Patience Terry Hopkins--Adm'x.
    Adm'r: Ferdinand Hopkins
    Infant Daughter: Mary Thomson Hopkins

HOWELL, ELLIS -w- Anna Pur re est Henry Smith 1846 Chester Equity 226

JOHNS, LYDDA--Dau. of Thomas Hughs-Will 3 Nov. 1794
    Chester Wills Bk F-212

KENNEDY, GEORGE--Post Master at Chester, S. C. Adv. for all who
    owed him postage for newspapers to pay up. Gazette May 1, 1800

LEE, JOHN, Dec'd Charles L. Owens, Adm'r Chester

LEONARD, THOMAS, Dec'd. Widow -m- William Dunnavant Chester min. Bk.
                                                                1797
LEWIS, ABEL -m- 27uot. Miss Catherine Tucker--Rev. John Gemmil
    All of Chester County. Laurens Equity-Scrap of newspaper Jan. 1808

LIPFORD, JOHN C. Chester June 1844
    Children: James Alex'r Lipford
               Catherine Lipford
               Henry Mitchell Lipford
    Heirs of Henry Mitchell and Nancy Mitchell

LOWRY, THOMAS--Oath of Alleg. at Chester 3 Nov. 1820 Misc. D-212

LYLES, REBECCA VALENTINE--Dau. of Newton Foote-Will 1823 Chester

MAYFIELD, ALLEN -w- Sarah-Dau of Benj. Castle-Will 23 Mar. 1852 Chester

MAYFIELD, ELISHA--Bk B--Fanny Mayfield Late widow of Isam Bond
    Chester Min. Bk-A-126 106

McALDUFF, THOMAS, SEN'r Will 23 Apr. 1808 Dau. Jean Sessions
                                              Elizabeth Durant

McCREARY, JOHN--Wit. deed from Samuel Atkins to Henry Jordan Chester
    Deed C-124. Probate Jan. 25, 1793
    Pg 237 John McCreary J. P. Prob. dec'd 1793.
    Exonerated as a Grand Juror 1791

McCREARY, JOHN--Pd. as Sheriff of Chester Co in 1806

McCLURKEN, JAMES of Chester   Chester Wills 9 Dec. 1794
    Son: Thomas McClurken
    Dau: Eleander
    Son: Samuel
    Dau: Jean
          Catherine
          Janet and her son
    Son: James McClurken's ch.
    Dau: Lilly's Ch.
    Son: James Boyd
    Son-in-Law: David Waid (Wade)
    Son or Gr. Son: John
    Gr. Son: Andrew James McClurken

McCLURKEN, JOHN Will 1813
    Wife: Elizabeth--Her will: son-in-law-Wm. Trussell
    Ch: Sarah
        Elizabeth
        Molly Gibson
        John
    Wit: Archibald McClurken

McDANIEL, PETER, JANE, JAMES--Chester 1844 John Smith ap'td Gdn.

McDONALD, HUGH, SR. Chester Wills E-272 Rocky Cr. Chester Dist
    Wife: Rebeckah   Will 2 July 1813
    Sons: John, Henry, Frances, William
    Dau: Jean Brown
         Agnes Rives (Reeves)
         Bittich Gibson's son Hugh Wit: Wm. Bond

McDONALD, MIDDLETON-Widow-Nancy dau of Wm. Dunnavant of Chester
                                         Will 1819
MEDDOR, JASON--36 A. surv. for him 31 Aug. 1796--Cheraw--on fork
    Creek--Chesterfield Co. Bd. William Reaves and Geo. Evans

MILLS, EDWIN R. et al -vs- Thomas S. Mills et al--Sale 7 Nov. 1842 to
    Dr. Thos W. Moore. Col. John Moore, Surety Chester

MITCHELL, JAMES AND DOROTHEA F.--Gr. children of Dorothy Moore
    Chester Deeds M-150 1806

MITCHELL, CLEMENTINE--Pet'n for Gdnship of Martha Ann Mitchell

MOBLEY   Bill for Par. Edward Mobley Adm'r.
    Ch: Harriet--over 12 (M. John Smith
        Samuel--under 14
        Judith and Mary--under 12 Chester Equity min. Feb 1824
    Johanne S. McDaniel--their mother, consent to aptment of gdn.

MOORE, DOROTHEA -vs- ADAM McCOOL and ADAM McCOOL, JR.
    Jean McCool, Marda McCool pg 294 Jan 1788-Will of James Mason
    Chester Min. Bk. pg-81

MOORE, DOROTHY of Chester--Dau: Dorothy Deed gift per. prop. slaves
    etc. 4 July, 1789. Chester Deed Bk B-445

MORGAN, WILLIAM -m- set 10 June 1819 Elizabeth Scott, both of Chester
Misc. D-167

NEAL, JOHN -m- set 21 Aug. 1811 Sarah Eaves, both of Chester Dist.
Misc. C-824 Samuel McCreary, Jr. Trustee

PARK, HUGH--Will 1817--Chester Wills
Wife: Jennet
Dau: Elizabeth and her son John Johnston
      Mary Glenn's son, John Park
Son-in-law: Robertson Gibson, Jr.

PARROTT, CHARLES--Apt'd. Gdn of John P. Parrott and Harriet E. Parrott
Oldest about 9 years of age. June 26, 1843 Chester

PICKETT, JAMES B. --Dec'd. Sale 2 Oct. 1843 James B. Glenn and wife
-vs- John Pickett, et al Chester

REEDY, JOHN A. adm'r. -vs- Jane Reedy, et al--Sold 3 Oct. 1842 21½ A.
to John A. Hafner. Chester
Pg-23 Ex Porte: Mary A. Reedy
                 Jane M.   "
                 Luenda   "
Dr. John A. Reedy, Gdn. Son of dec'd

ROBERTS, JOANNA--Dec'd widow John H. Roberts (or Robertson)
Son: Samuel Mobley
Dau: Mary -w- Clough S. Shelton Chester 1844

ROBINSON, JAMES--Dec'd--Intestate Bill for Part. Junt 1843 Chester
Son: Wm. M. Robinson--Had advance
Col. and Mrs. Mary Orr of Georgia--Heirs
     Andrew Orr
     Robert Robinson--A son
     Martha White--a daughter
Wit: Francis White, bro of Wm. White June 17, 1843

ROBINSON, ROBERT--Pur. land -vs- Post. sale 3 Oct. 1842 Jane Robinson

ROCK, JOHN--Will 25 Aug. 1820 Chester Wills
Son: William
      Robert
Dau: Ginny Tippins
      Cetty or Letty Wilson
      Polly
      Sally Exor: Thomas Viell

ROGERS, JOHN of Chester Will. Chester Wills A-13
To: Priscilla Franklin
     John Franklin
     Thomas B. Franklin
     Thomas Baker Franklin 10 Jan. 1789

ROGERS, WILLIAM--Will 24 Feb 1780 Camden Wills Chester File
Mother: Margaret Rogers
Brother: Ralph Rogers
          Clayton Rogers
Sister: Margaret Rogers
         Edith Woods

SANDERS, CALEY (or Catey) Dau. of James Moore Chester Wills 1779

SIBLEY, EDWARD--Dec'd Chester
    Heir: Rebecca Dye--a minor about 3 yrs old. Her father, Evan
    S. Dye apt'd Gdn. James Dye as Wit: June 27, 1843 Chester

SIMPSON, JESSE, et al -vs- Gale Simpson, et al Post. 16 Jan 1843 Sale
    282 A. to Mary Simpson and Tensy S.
    122 A. to Gale Simpson
    358 A. to Jesse Simpson. Nathan Simpson--a surety bond Chester

STARR, DR--Dec'd Chester equity Report Bk A-1843-47 A-160
    Dau: Emily S. Starr--about 2 years old. Entitled to 2/3 of
    estate $14,000.00. Jonathan J. Steele Apt'd Gdn. June 26, 1843

STEWART, JOHN Chester Deeds E-162 1793
    Heir of Wm. Moore--"Then of Co. Mecklenberg, N. C"

STEWART, THOMAS M. pet'r Chester 1844 Gdn of:
    Charles B. Stewart, Sarah J. Stewart, Harriet Stewart

STINSON, SAMUEL, Dec'd Chester
    Heirs: Elizabeth Baxter   Ezra Barton Apt'd Gdn. Eldest is
           Catherine Baxter   6 yrs old. June 26, 1843

TURNER, MARY E.--Infant--Gdn. N. R. Evans Chester June 26, 1843

WAGES, JAMES, Dec'd Jan. Ct. 1788 Chester Min. Bk. Pg-202
    Son: James--minor Philip Walker apt'd Gdn.

WEEIS, WILLIAM, Dec'd Will Chester Min. Jan. 1788
    Ex: Wm. Weeis, Sam'l Weeis

WILKS, THOMAS, dec'd Chester Box 101-1793
    Nancy Wilks, Adm'x   John W. Wilks, Adm'r
    Pd. for dresses for Martha Wilds and Mary Wilks. (wedding Dresses)
    To Son: Richard Wilks--26 Dec. 1793--Pt place where sd Thomas
    Wilks lives. Bd. "Collums" land. Wit: Francis Wilks. E-211
    Misc. M-201 Sale slaves 1842. Adm'rs Nancy Wilks and John W. W.

WILKS, REUBEN--Cit. 5 Apr 1830 Chester Box 69-1076
    Ellis Wilks, Adm'r--Had "share" Paper in File:
    Catherine was born 15 Dec 1814
    Hannah   "   "   20 Dec 1816
    Joshua   "   "   18 Mar 1819
    Harriett "   "   10 Mar 1824
    Ellen   "   "   14 Mar 1821

WILKS, WILLIAM--Dec'd d. 1839 Widow: Lydia Chester Box 69-1070
    Heirs: Ann McCollum   Nancy Johnston
           Mary Scaife   Thomas Wilks
           Sarah Land   Winney Estes
           Alsey Carter   ' Hazel Wilks
           Eliza Estes   Leah and William
    Abner Wilks and Thomas W. Adm'rs   Bond 29 Oct. 1838

WORTHY, LOUISA F.--Pet. she be apt'd Gdn of her infant dau: Margaret
    Frances Williams Worthy. June 23, 1843 Chester

FAIRFIELD COUNTY, SOUTH CAROLINA

The unusual spelling of some words, and the abbrev-
iations are those of the original copier, as are the
remarks in quotation marks and parenthesis.

F. Courtney

ADGER, JOHN, Gdn. Ex Partie   Winnsboro Equity Index. Pet-1 1836
  "   "   -vs- James Lyles and Daniel B. Kirkland Bill 17 1844
  "   "   Adv. George W. Boggs Adm. Isabella Boggs, Adm't. Bill 14
                                                                     1852

ADGER, M. R. and Mary -vs- James G. Brice, James Douglass, Chas. B.
     Douglass, and Zach'r. Gibson WinnsborroBills 4 1838

ADGER, LEWIS of St. Paul's Par., Per. Atty. Thos. Lehre. Conv. 1785
     Fairfield Deed C

AGNEW, GEORGE -w- Jane of Fairfield to Peter Wylie; gr. 1 May 1786 to
     John Johnston, 394 A. in Fairfield on Beaver Dam fork of Wateree
     Creek, bd. John Havis (et al-errors) Wit. Samuel Furgason, Wm.
     Stevenson, William Wylie. Fairfield Deed B 16 Nov. 1787

AIKEN, DAVID and James Barkley -vs- John Smith Winnsboro Bill 4 1823
  "   "   -vs- Alex Robb and Chas. Robb   "   " 3 1826
  "   "   -vs- George Hasson   "   " 10 1840
  "   "   -vs- David Elkins   "   " 14 1842
  "   "   -vs- James Wolling   "   " 11 1844
  "   "   -vs- N. B. Holly   "   " 15 1844
  "   "   and James R. Aiken Ad's Henry W. Dixon "   " 27 1845
  "   "   Jacob Blizzard, and Buckner Hagood, Adm'r. -vs- Allen R.
     Crankfield, William E. Hall, and John Rowland. Winnsboro Bill 6 1845
AIKEN, DAVID -vs- N. A. Peay and J. Cochrell, Shff. Winnsboro Bill 12 1847
  "   "   and N. A. Peay Adv. John Ford and C. D. Ford "   " 7 1850
  "   "   Adv. N. A. Peay   "   " 9 1851
  "   "   -vs- John Ford, C. D. Ford, and N. A. Peay   "   " 15 1851

AIKEN, ELIZABETH -vs- Robert Martin and Jeremiah Cockrell "   " 24 1847

AIKEN, JAMES R. and Jeremiah Cockrell Advs. Philip D. Cook "   " 20 1847
  "   "   "   -vs- Shannon McGee, Jeremiah Cockrell, Robert Ford,
     James Kennedy   Winnsboro Bills 12 1852
AIKEN, JAMES R., Jos. Kennedy, Jeremiah Cockrell Adv. John T. Hammond
     Winnsboro Bill 24 1854
AIKEN, JAMES R. -vs- John B. Walker   Winnsboro Bill 23 1855
  "   "   "   advs. John Buchanan, Com'r.   "   " 5 1824

AIKEN, WILLIAM -vs- Francis N. Taylor and Henry Head, Exor's. of Leonard
     Taylor   Winnsboro Bill 6 1823

AIRICK, THOMAS L. Per Pro Ami -vs- Lee D. Airick, John Adam Airick,
     Mary Elizabeth Airick, Wm. Airick, Lee Airick Winnsboro Bill 9 1832

ALCORN, ROBERT -w- Mary Anne Fairfield Deed A 1787

ALLCORN, ROBERT- sd Allcorn- to John and Thos. Means--100 A. N.s Broad
     R. Gr. to Francis Alcorn. 3 March 1780 To Robert Alcorn
     Fairfield Deed C 12/13 1788
     James Allcorn to Robt. Allcorn Pg. 14/15 1788

ALDER, CORNELIUS -w- Ann of Berkley Co. to Robert Hancock--150 A. N-s
     Broad R. Bd Nicholas Vansant Fairfield H-61/62 July 25, 1771

ALLEN, ANNA --by next Friend, Isaac Mothershed, Hugh R. Allen, Mahala
    Allen, Matilda Allen -vs- Turner Starke, Wyatt Starke, Starke
    Hunter, Philip E. Pearson, John Woodward, and Miles Farrer. Bill
    for Inj. and Relief. Winnsboro Bill 1 1821

ALLEN, ANNA, Hugh R., Mahala, Matilda -vs- Charlotte Starke, Jack F.
    Ross. Winnsboro Bill 10 1827

ALLEN, JOHN -vs- W.A. A. Belton and William Stephens Bill Comp. Bill 2 1819

ALLEN, MATILDA, Ex Parte Winnsboro Pet. 3 1827

ALSTON, GEORGE B. James G., Robert B., Mary E., J. Wm., E.P. G., (by
    next friend--W. H. Ellison -vs- John Alston Winnsboro Pet. 1 1859

ALSTON, JOHN --verbal will Fairfield Wills Vol. 1-1 June 16, 1787
    Oldest son: Samuel
    Wife: Not named
    Men; My Children
    Ex: James Brown, Robt Boyd
    Wit: James Mann, Wm. Boyd, Mrs. Jenny Brown

AMICK, GEORGE -w- Mary Ann Adv. Jacob Leitz, Leonard Leitz, Christian
    Leitz and Mary Ann Smith Winnsboro Bill 2 1824

ANDERSON, ELIZABETH K. and Nancy E. Kincais Adv. Winnsboro Bill 10 1860
    William A. Kincaid
    James   "
    John   "
    Nancy H.   "
    Rebecca D.   "

ANDREWS, EDWARD and Stephen Gibson, Adm's. and Sarah Ann Elizabeth
    Gibson, Mary ann Frances Gibson -vs- Elisha Scott and wife Jamima
    Jane Winnsboro Bill 7 1845

APEDARTE, JANE to Richard Gladney Fairfield Deed A-2 1786

ARCHER, JOHN -vs- William Hasson Winnsboro Bill 3 1833

ARICK, J. A., Mary E., Thos L., William, Lee, Ex Parte Winnsboro Pet 1 1832

ARICK, JOHN A. -vs- Philip D. Cook Winnsboro Bill 26 1847

ARLEDGE, AUSTIN D. -vs- James Arledge, Mary ann, Eliza, Frank, Louisiana
    (all Arledge) by next friend James H. Hughes and Wm. Robertson, Com'r.
    Winnsboro Bill 2 1853

ARLEDGE, ISAAC and Wm. R. Robertson Adv. J. B. Ulm, H. W. Hollister,
    Geo. Murphey, Jr. and Jon. Michel Winnsboro Bill 22 1856

ARLEDGE, JOHN -vs- Eliza Arledge and John Alex'r. Arledge Winnsboro Bill 1
                                                                  1853

ARLEDGE, JOSEPH, Will Fairfield Will Book 5-114 Apt 8-File 11
    Oldest Dau: Hannah) Home tract of land etc.
    Youngest "   Anns)
    Dau: Elizabeth Greyham
          Tamar Griggs
    4 March 1806--Prov. 19 Mar. 1806
    Exor's: Denny Greyham, and William Arledge
    Wit: James Arledge, Clement Arledge, Lyda Arledge

ARLEDGE, LYDIA Winnsboro Bill 3 1828, Charlotte Broom by Isiah Hinnent,
    Lucas A. Broom, William Arledge, Isaac Arledge, Eliza Hughes,
    J. H. Hughes, John Arlesge, Austin D. Arledge, Willis Arledge,
    N. C. Bailes -vs- James Arledge, William Arledge, Mary Arledge,
    James Broom, and Susan Arledge

ARLEDGE, MOSES, Samuel, Wm. Strother, and John Buchanan Avs. Thomas
    McCullough Winnsboro Bill 7 1828

ARLEDGE, SARAH and Wm. Graham and wife -vs- Mary M. Arledge, Falman J.,
    Arledge, William G. Arledge, Charlotte J. Arledge, Sarah M. Arledge
    Winnsboro Bill 15 1822

ARMSTRONG, ELIZABETH -vs- Austin F. Peay Winnsboro Bill 4 1830

ARMSTRONG, MARY M.   Winnsboro Pet. 1 1860

ARNAT, AGNES Gr 13 May 1768--100 A. to Alex'r McDowell--N-s Broad R.
    Bd. Simon Bell Fairfield Deed C-147/148 Aug. 21, 1770 (or 1771)
    149/150--Robert Jones -w- Sandra Gr. 13 July 1767 to Alexander
    McDowell--24 July 1767

ARTERBURY, NATHAN -w- Martha of Chester Co. To James McQuiston of Chester
    Co. Wit: Andrew McQuiston and Wm. McQuiston Fairfield Deed A 1787

ARTHURS, JAMES -w- Anne of Fair. To: John Watson--Gr. to Alexander
    Miller 2 Jan. 1785 To: James Arther. Pt 200 A. Bd Wm. Joiner, sd.
    Alex. Miller, John McClaws, (or McGraw), Samuel McKenney. Wit:
    Wm. Boyd, John McCombes, and Alex. Miller Fairfield C-173/174

ARTHUR, WILLIAM to Elizabeth Taylor-widow--100 A. Gr 26 Sept. 1772
    on Borcher's Mill Cr. of Broad R. Bd. Rich'd. Walker and Vac.
    Wit: James Beard, Richard Winn Fairfield H-105/106 Aug. 14, 1773
    Pg. 103 Thomas Shannon -w- Elizabeth--formerly Eliz. Taylor--To
    Leonard Taylor, Sam'l Lord 28 Feb. 1791 Wit: Ephraim Butler (X)
    Richard Head, Arch'd McQuiston, J. P.

ASHFORD, GEORGE W., Thomas Ashford, and James Broom, Exor's. Advs.
    George A. Smith, William Smith, and wife Mary. Winns. Bill 15 1844

ASHFORD, GEORGE W. -vs- Leroy J. Vaughn Winnsboro Bill 8 1852

ASHFORD, GEORGE B., Robert B. Ashford, and Jacob Feaster advs. Britton
    M. Chapman and Sevilla Chapman. Winnsboro Bill 3 1857

ASHFORD, JOEL W.. Winnsboro Pet. 1 1853

ASHFORD, JOHN H., James Morgan -w- Sarah D. -vs- George W. Ashford, William Ashford Winnsboro Bill 1 1853

ASHFORD, MARTHA -vs- James R. Ashford and Eliza Ashford Bill 4, 1853

ASHFORD, THOMAS W. -vs- James Ashford, Robert A. and John A. Bill 15
1852

ASHLEY, WILLIAM -vs- Reeve Freeman Winnsboro Bill 10 1822
   "   "   -vs- James McCants, Adm'r. "   "   2 1825
   "   "   -vs- Thomas Ashford   "   "   4 1829

AUSTIN, ELIZABETH, Sold her grant Fairfield Deed A 1784

AUSTIN, ROBERT of C. T. Fairfield Deed A 1785

BAILEY, CHARLES, orig. Will 16 July 1855 Fairfield Pro. Apt. 4-96
   Wife: Ann C. Bailey -m- J. D. Idell
   Son: James H. Bailey (or James A.)
   "my sons" "my Daughters"
   Agreement by heirs "who are of age". W. A. Bailey
   Minor children to be reared   V. M. Bowen
                                        E. A. Richlong (sp)

BAILEY, FRED 1834 Old Bood Pro. Off. Fairfield
   -vs- Wm. A. Ford, et al Receipts for shares of:
   Nancy -w- John Brown
   Robert L. Fish
   Mary Ann Love
   Sarah -w- Fred K. Bailey

BAKER, THOMAS "of Head of Jackson's Creek Fairfield Deed A 1785

BARNETT, WILLIAM -w- Agnes To James Robb Gr. 200 A. on Little River and Broad--all vac. Fairfield Deeds A

BARNES, MARIAN T. by Gdn. Thos. Lyles -vs- Robert Burns, et al.
   Shares: Frances Puckett, Marion T. Burns 1834 Fairfield Pro. Off.

BASS, JOHN To John Yarborough, Jr. Fairfield Deed A-2 1772
   Wit: Richard Yarborough, James Yarborough

BATY, SAMUEL (or Beaty?) Fairfield Deed A-2 1790

BEARD, JAMES, Dec'd Heir Archibald Beard to John Cook--100 A. N-s
   Broad R. Wit: Burrel Cook, Wm. Yarborough, James Hunt.
   1792 Fairfield H-111/112

BEARD, JONAS To William Raiford Gr. to Mathias Heinlein 21 Oct. 1775
   N-s Broad on Difficult Cr. Fairfield I 132/33 20 Aug. 1778

BEASLEY, GEORGE Will 10 Feb. 1829 Fairfield Wills
      Wife: Molly
Dau: Rachel Conder -w- John Conder
      Margaret Conder -w- Benj. Conder
      Elizabeth Beasley
      Son: Jacob Beasley
            George Beasley

BEASLEY, JACOB Will 19 Apr. 1773 Fairfield Wills Box-1 Pkg-19

```
Wife:  Margaret--Qual. Ex.
Son:   George--Qual. Ex.
       Jacob
       Peter
Dau:   Catherine
       Mary
       Madleanah
       Elizabeth
Son Adam.  Box 41 Pkg. 635  1830
George Beasley--Dec'd
```

BELL, ALEXANDER NELSON--of city of C. T. Deed A 1780's Fairfield

BELL, ALPHUS -w- Cressy Ann -vs- Asa Bell Gdn. of Elizabeth Day et al.
    Shares: Elizabeth Day
             Jennie   "
             Francis   "
             William   " all minor ch. of Wm. Day. Gdn. Aaron Powell
                 Cressy Ann -w- Alphus Bell 1832 Fairfield Pro. Off.

BELL, JOHN to William Daniel Fairfield Deed A 1778
    Gr. to Stephen Ellis 7 Feb. 1767. Wit: Barnaby Pope, Lucy Pope

BELL, WILLIAM to William David Fairfield Deeds C 212/213 Oct. 4, 1789
    200 A. on Ellis Br. of Little R., bd. Stephen Ellis and vac.--ex-
    100 A. conv. to David Montgomery by Wm. Bell, Sr. Pet. shows Ge.
    to Wm. Bell. Cert.20 Jan. 1768 by Ralph Humphreys

BLARE, ADAM (sd X) Fairfield Deeds H-39/40 1791
    To John Tidwell, 500 A. on Hog Fork of Wateree

BOYD, AGNES--dau. of James Robinson of Fairfield--sd. his will.

BOYD, DAVID Gr. 4 Oct. 1790 209 A. To Thomas Nelson--68 A. on Wateree R.
    Bd. Hugh Murdoch, John Turner and Samuel McKees, John Drenan,
    Sam'l Craig and sd. Thomas Nelson. Fairfield H 147/148 1793

BOYD, ELIZABETH, Mary, Jane, Celia, Mariah, Benj., Hester, Jackson.
    Adv--Jonathan Davis and Jas. R. Wood. Exor's--Pet'rs. Winnsboro Pet 11
                                                                      1830
BOYD, MARY, Jane M., Celia, Maria, Ex Parte Pet'r. Winnsboro Bill 3 1826

BOYD, WILLIAM--Gent'--of Winnsboro from John Winn. ¼ acre on Wash-
    ington St. Wit: Jno. Buchanan, James Craig Fairfield Deeds 66
    1786, July 11

BOYKIN, SAMUEL to John Tidwell Fairfield Deeds A or B 340/342 1788-Dec 10
    100 A. on Hog Fork of Wateree Creek. Orig. Gr. to Jane Rowan and
    by her conv. who departed this life intestate and it became pro-
    perty of her brother Samuel Boykin as heir.--12 Aug. 1768
    Wit: Peter Mathis and Ely Tidwell

BOYLE, ANN OF NANCY--dau of Robert Kerr of Philadelphia, legatee of Bro.
    Joseph Kerr--Will 20 Nov. 1821 Fairfield Wills

BOWLES, JAMES from Richard Winn--Lot 178 in Winnsboro. Fairfield
    Deed Bk. A 1787 Feb. 10

BOWLES, JAMES Gr--840 A. to Wife Ann and children. John Ellison, Tr.
    Lot in Winnsboro. Love and Affec. for Ann Bowles and her children
Land and Per. prop. Fairfield H--145/146 1793 Feb. 23

BRANNON, ROBERT, Dec'd Fairfield H 169/170 1792
    Son: James Brannon--with consent of his mother and her husband--
    Elizabeth Smithwick (sd X equals0) To: Thomas Lenks (or Lewis)
    Apprenticeship. Wit: Wm. Smithwick and Robert Brannon

BRAUSSAGER, FREDERICK -w- Elizabeth (both sd X) To: Stephen Smith
    of Richland Co. 50 A. N-s Broad R. on Cedar Cr. and vac. Gr.
    to David Braussager--father of above Frederick B.--Gr. 3 June, 1754
    Wit: Wm. Houseal, John Houseal, et al Fairfield C 167/68 Apr. 2
                                                                    1789
BRIGGS, FREDERICK To John King. Fairfield Deed A 1787

BROOM, JANE--sold horses had in William Broom's work. Fairfield Deed A2
                                                                    1789
BROOM, LEWIS A. -- of Fairfield Misc H-370 1833
    Wife: Charlotte Broom
    Tr: Moses Arledge

BROOM, GEORGE--of Camden Goodwill and affection To: Joseph Kirkland
    of same place. 50 A. on Bush Cr. of Wateree R--Orig. Gr. to John
    Single. Bd. Wm Aldredge, (Arledge?). Wit: John Means, James
    Phillips (Xhis mark) Fairfield C-172 1789 Aug. 10.

BROWN, JACOB, Dec'd. Gr. 5 March 1787 Exor: Daniel Brown of Camden
    To: John Means. 213 Acres N-s Broad River. Bd. Richard Woodward,
    Benj. Moberly, Robert Alcorn, Samuel Alcorn. Fairfield H 176/177

BROWN, JAMES To son-in-law and daughter, David Thompson and Janet
    Thompson, his wife. 115 A. on a Br. of Cedar Creek. Bd. John
    Compton, John Alston. Wit: Wm. Brown and Mary Brown
    Fairfield N-415 1802-Jan. 13.

BROWN, JANNET (sd X equals0) Deed Gift to Frances Walker--cow and calf.
    Wit: John Bull Fairfield Deed B__ 179/182 1787-Oct. 1st.
    180/183--Mary Alston To: Frances Walker and Robert Walker, Deed
    Gift--4 cattle--3 Nov. 1787. Wit: John Bull and James Man

BUCHANAN, JOHN of Little River 1785 Fairfield Deed A

BUCHANAN, ROBERT (since dec'd) Gr. 100 A. 21 Apr. 1774 Conv. by John
    Buchanan To: James Gray--100 A. on Jackson's Cr. Bd. John Rodgers
    Moses Sims. Wit: John Milling, Daniel Cochran

BUSBEE, SIMON (or Sion or Sihon) To: Alexander Brent--Gr. to John Hunt
    17 Oct. 1761. 250 A. N-s Broad who conv. to Benj. Busbee, 31 Mar.
    1767 and then to Miles Busbee. Wit: Thos. Heathcock, Hardy (x)
    Utter, and Rob't. Rayman. Fairfield C-75/76 1783

BUSBY, MARGARET (sd X) Helpless with old age To-Deed Gift- her nephew,
James Mathews. He to maintain her. Per. Prop and slaves, cows,
horses, etc. Wit: Lewis Owen, Wm. Nelson Fairfield C-205/6
1782 Oct. 31

BUSBY, MARGARET To: Zachariah Kirkland Deed A-2 1785

CALDWELL, SAMUEL 21 Jan 1788 Fairfield Deed B-128/130 To: Peter
Robinson. 150 A. on a Br. of Wateree Cr. Bd. John Huston, and
John McCombe. Wit: Alexander Johnston, Joseph Cameron, David Boner.

CALHOUN, JAMES To: Daniel Huffman, Jr. -w- Elizabeth, Land he had
par____? Wit: William Calhoun, Catherine Calhoun (X) Fairfield
Deed A 1787

CAMERON, ALEXANDER -- Gr. 6 Jan. 1773 To: Edward Holsey--100A on S Br.
of Little River. Bd. Thomas Holsey and vac. Wit: Samuel Gladin,
Rob't. Neally Fairfield H-108/109 Oct. 4, 1775

CAMERON, SIMON Gr 12 Sept. 1768. Conv. to: John Cameron-since dec'd-
passed to son: Joseph Cameron. Conv. to James Cameron in 1786
Fairfield Deed A

CAMERON, SIMON Gr. 12 Sept. 1768 on small br. Jackson's Cr. 16 May,
1770, conv. to John Cameron-since dec'd-Son and heir Joseph
Cameron.. 3 March 1786 Conv. to James Cameron 20lbs. strlg.
Winnsboro Deed A-366

CARDIN, LARKIN Fairfield Wills Vol 1-43 June 14, 1788
Wife: Not named Apt. Ex.
Son: James
      Larkin
Dau: Laodicea Cardin
      Winnifred "

CASE, HUGH of Broad River Fairfield Deed A 1754

CATES, JOSEPH Gr. 9 Jan. 1762 400 A. S-s Wateree--Conv. to Philip
Hanson--250 A. This deed to Bartlett Hanson
Fairfield H-50/51 Feb. 9, 1768

CATHCART, JOSEPH of York Co. To: James Richey of Fairfield. 100A.
on Wateree Creek. Wit: John Cameron, Jeremiah Cockrell, Samuel
Cockrell. Fairfield Deed H 132/133 1793

CATHCART, ROBERT of Winnsboro -m- set 19 May 1843. Jane Elder of
Winnsboro. Archives Dept. Misc. N-133

CHAPMAN, SAMUEL, d. intestate. Gr. 16 Jan. 1761 300 A.
Son: John Chapman--also intestate
      William Chapman To: Wm. Robb--300 A. on Little River.
sd Will Champonan (Champion and Chapman)
Fairfield Deeds A or B 231-234 Dec 11, 1783

CHAPMAN, WILLIAM Gr. to John and Thomas Means. 20 A. with a mill-seat
N-s Broad R. Conv. to John Hampton and brother-who by deed of gift
Conv. it back to sd Wm. Chapman. Wit: Robert Coleman and Hampton
Fairfield H 114/115 1799 July 13.

CLARKE, CALEB -m- set 18 Sept. 1842. Mrs. Elizabeth McKelvey.
    Fairfield File Misc. M-368

CLARKE, HENRY H. b. Nov. 28, 1813. d. Oct. 3, 1863
    James Caleb Clark, b. Oct. 4, 1839. Killed at Battle of
    Boonesboro, Md. on Sept 14, 1862 Bapt. Ch. Yd. Fairfield

COAPLING, ALEXANDER of Spartanburg and William Coapling of Abbeville,
    Bros. and heirs of Charles Coapling--dec'd. Gr. in 1774. Conv.
    to--James McMullen, 150 A. Fairfield on Sam'l McMurries Cr. Bd.
    Robert Ellison. Fairfield Deed I 137/8 1789-Jan. 15.

COCKRELL, SARAH--Dec'd Southern Times and State Gazette. Mar. 9, 1831
    Heirs: of Wm. Robuck of Fairfield
    Case: Elias Robuck -vs- Polly Robuck, Nancy Robuck
           Patrick Smith -w- Priscilla
           Joab Hill -w- Ailcey
           Copper Huppan -w- Elizabeth
           John Cockrell and sd heirs of Sarah Cockrell

COLEMAN, FRANCIS To: John Means--150 A. N-s Broad R.--orig. gr. Wm.
    Moberly 10 May 1762--who came to Benj. Moberly, and then from
    John Moberly to Francis Coleman. Fairfield C-13/14 1788

COLEMAN, KADOR of Wateree Creek--1785 To: David Evans. Gr. to George
    Reden (?) Fairfield Deed A-27 3 Aug. 1785

CONAWAY, THOMAS Gr. 12 Oct. 1762--300 A. Fairfield C-125/6 20 Oct. 1785
    Sold to: John Hunt 24/25 Nov. 1764
    19/20 March 1763 to Griffen Green--150 A. of sd. tract.
    Eldest ___?___ Heir's Son: Drury Green_____?_____.
    This deed to Burrel Cook--Reserving 50 A. as his mother's right of
    Dowry. "Where she lived". Pg. 131 Burrel Cook to Alex. Brant

CRANKFIELD, LITTLETON, Dec'd Winnsboro Pro. Box 84-225 1847
    Sons: Isaiah and Jonath'n, Allen R. Exor's.
    Wife: Lucy
    Gr. Dau: Sarah Ann Stokes
    Gr. Son: Geo. W. Stokes
    Dau: Temperance Miller, Mary, Ann, Eliza, Margaret Jane.
    a Purchaser: S. S. Hogan

CROSSWELL, HUGH Wit--1787 Fairfield Deed A

CRUMPTON, HENRY June 2, 1793 Fairfield Deed--Church Congregation
    Wit: Jno. McCoy, Thos. Poney Deed and Plat. H 171/172
    To: Benj. Boyd
         John Martin and Robert Martin
         James Gray, John Gray, Andrew Gray
         Charles Montgomery and Hugh Montgomery
         Wm. McMorris, Sr. and Wm. McMorris, Jr.
         James Kincaid and Alex'r. Kincaid
         Adam Hawthorn, William Bell, Daniel Cochran, Collon Forbes
         Thomas Lewis, William Thompson, Wm. Richardson, Sr. and Jr.
         James Wooten (sp Mooten), Robert McGill, Wm. Holmes, Wm
         Kearnaghan, H. Ronalds (Reynolds?) R. Robertson, and Hugh R.

William Kennedy and J. Kennedy, H. T. Huston, Wm. Watts, Wm.
Smithwick, and Agnes Calhoun. Members of the Am. Congregation
of the Brick Meeting House on Little R. called Ebenezer--1¼ A.
where the Meeting House stands. Orig. Gr. to Thomas May--who
conv. to sd. Henry Crumpton.

CURRY, PETER (no dower) Fairfield Deed B 90-92 Feb. 9, 1787
    To: John Elliot--Gr. 3 Sept. 1754 to John Willow 150 A. N-s
    Broad R. Bd. John Hooker (Hocker)

DALEY, JOHN to John Hampton of Orangeburg Dist. Fairfield Deed A 1783

DANSBY, DANIEL to Mother: Martha Dansby. Wit: Sarah Dansby
    Fairfield Deed A-2 1786

DAVIS, AMOS--Dec'd. Sept 1792--Will Fairfield Inv. Bk 2 1794-1800Pg 9-10
    Edward and Sandra Tillman, Adm'rs.
    Apprs. Thos. Crosby, Nath'l Harbin, Wm. Harbin, James Thomas
    Pd E: Thos. Parrot, Moses Arnold, Benj. Lindsey, Ambrose Nit,
          Nathan Jaggers, Joseph Frotti, Jesse O'Briant, George Bell
    Pd Est: John Davis, James Davis, Bond
    1791 Additional sale by Edward Tilman and -w- Sandrs. Col. re-
    ceived from Thomas Humphreys, Frizzel McTyre, Josephine Gore

DAVIS, JOHN (sd. John Doods-error) Fairfield Deed B-57 1785 Feb. 22
    To: James Davis (also James Lewis) for 100 lbs strlg. 250 A.
    on a Br. of Broad R. called Wilkinson's Cr.--Known as Engleman's
    Old Place--all vac. Wit: D. Bradford, Thos. Parrot, John Gregg

DAVIS, JOSEPH to Edward Carrol. Wit: Daniel Moore, Hannah Moore
    Fairfield Deed A-2 1785

DAVIS, THOMAS , Dec'd. Fairfield Prob. Off. old book. abt. 1830 to
    Shares: Receipts   1845 dates in bk.
        John Davis
        Thomas   "
        Jacob   " --sold his share)
        David   "   "   "   ") sold to Strother Davis
        Mary -w- Strother Davis

DAY, MATTHEW and wife Sarah of Fairfield. Fairfield Deed L-3
    To: Nathaniel Anderson. 140 A. in Fairfield Dist. 5 Nov. 1796

DELASHUNT, JOHN Gr. 150 A. 10 May 1773 Fairfield H-113/114 Feb. 5, 1793
    Conv. by Hardy Miles to Lewis Haygood (also Hiagood) Pt. 50 A.
    on Cedar Cr-Persimmon Br. Bd James Daniels. Wit: Samuel Miles
    Conrad Coon and Geo. Watts

DODDS, JONES -w- Elizabeth-otherwise Beatty, heir of Margaret Beatty,
    dec'd. To: William Daniel. Gr. 1 Sept 1765, 100 A. Bd Stephen
    Ellis. Wit: Thomas Marston Green, William Benard, James Cameron
    Fairfield Deed B-19 1779-Aug. 20.

DOUGHARTY, DANIEL -w- Barbara--now wife of Dr. Samuel Park
    Only Dau: Rebecca, d. unmarried. a minor, at home of James
    Dougharty, Sr. in Newberry Dist. in fall of year 1792.
    This is affidavit: Jane Boyd (by X)
                  Elizabeth Boyd (by X)
                  Nathan Boyd
                  Isaiah Shiver 24 Jan. 1796 in Newberry Co.
    before Arranmous Liles-J. P. Fairfield Deed K-290 1796 Jan. 4

DOUGHARTY, DANIEL -w- Barbara of Fairfield Fairfield Deed N-1 1789 Junne 5
    To: Richard Strother of Newberry Co. 150 A. land. Gr. Elizabeth
    Shiver--which Wlizabeth Shiver willed to her Dau. Barbara Shiver
    who m. Daniel Dougharty.

DRAKE, RUTLEY (Ruthy) a sister of Mosley Collin--Will 1794 Fairfield

DUBOSE, SARAH -m- James. Dau. of Roland Williamson-w- Ailcey Wyche
    Winnsboro Equity and Probate

DUFFINS, RICHARD Fairfield Wills Bk1-18 1800
    Admx: Elizabeth Duffins. Oct 2, 1800

DUGGINS, WILLIAM to William Wright Fairfield Deed A 1786

DUKE, THOMAS -w- Mary (sd X) To Robert and John Ellison. 100 A. orig.
    gr. to John Aldridge--on Wateree Creek. 15 Sept. 1750. Wit:
    Charles Pickert, Wm. Landis, Jeremiah Peason (Pearson)
    Fairfield Deed B-153-155. 1785 Dec. 7

DUNN, ALFRED, Dec'd. Fairfield Abt. 1825-1845 Prob. Off
    Shares: Charity Dunn, Eleadice, Joel, and Calvin Dunn

DURPHY, WILLIAM--Shff. of Fairfield. Suit of Michel Woolfe -vs-
    Peter Robinson To: _____ McCullock. 100 A. on Wateree Cr.
    Fairfield Deed B-142-144 1788 Aug. 20
    Deed Bk. A--John Winn to William Durphy of Rowan Co. 26/27 June 1785
    Fairfield Deed Bk A-1 Wm. Durphey, of Rowan Co. N. C. pur. lot in
    Winnsboro 26 June 1780

DUARRELL, JOSEPH of Winnsboro. Fairfield Deed Bk. A 1786

EDRINGTON, HENRY , Dec'd Fairfield Prob. Off. Old Book
    Heirs: Minors Thos. Lyles, Gdn.
      "   "   Ch. of E. Boyd. Jonathan Davis--Son
    Shares: Mary Edrington
           Frances H. and Charlotte E. minors

EFURT, ADAM -w- Mary (sd X) Gr. 500 A. 15 Oct. 1784 Fairfield Deed A or B
    To: Adam Cooper--Pt. 100A. on Beaver Cr. Bd. Andrew Feaster 215/17
    James Thomas, and Taylor's land. Wit: Peter Cooper, Wm. Robinson
    John Cooper

EFFURT, ADAM -w- Mary of Camden Dist. Conveyance--land on Beach Creek.
    Fairfield File 15 Feb. 1785--Charleston Deed N-5-537

EFFURT, ADAM Gr. 23 Nov. 1787 to William Hill. 170 A. on Veaver Cr.
    of Broad R. Fairfield H-126/127 1782

ELDER, JAMES Fairfield Wills Bk-8-105. Wit. Will of Timothy Ervin
    6 May 1821.

ELDER, JAMES Wit. Will of Leonard Kirkpatrick. 12 Feb. 1820.
    Fairfield Wills Bk-8 Pg-28

ELDER, WILLIAM and Wife, Amy (or Anna) Fairfield Co. H.H. 423 1827
    To: Joseph Caldwell --$500. 148 A. Gr. to Isaac Arledge 22 Feb. 1764
    on Crooked Creek of Catawba R. Bd. Jeptha Arledge, John Pickett.

ELKINS, JOHN Gr. 5 June 1770. 100 A. on Bear Cr. Bd. John Wilson and vac.
    To: James Randall, Sen'r. sd 100 Acres. Wit: John Wilson,
    Robert Elkins, James Wilson Fairfield C-190/191

ELLIOTT, GEORGE, Dec'd Old Book Fairfield Prob. Off. 1829
    Widow: Nancy. Receipt
            Jemima S. Elliott-minor 1832

ELLIOTT, ROBERT "gent" of Stegristown, Md. Fairfield Deed A 1787
    To: 26 Apr. 1727 Atty to sell. John Milling. Land whereon
    William Davy (Davie) late of Rutherford County, N. C. which he
    got from Samuel Kelly

ELLIOTT, ROBERT, Gent. of Hegerstown, State of Md. To John Milling of
    Winnsboro. "Where as William Davy, late of Rutherford Co. N. C.
    owned Gr. to Simon Kelly-par fr son Samuel Kelly and Aptd. Robert
    Elliott to sell it--200 - 200. ½ 400 A. gr. sd. Simon Kelly on
    Wateree Cr.--near Winnsborough. Bd Wm. Atkinson, Alex'r. Kelly
    Fairfield Deed Bk A July 1787, 21st.

ELLISON, ROBERT -w- Elizabeth--late Elizabeth Potts. Fairfield Deed C-5/6
    To: Valentine Rochell 100 A. less abt. 15 A. on Mobley's Br.
    Gr. to Elizabeth Potts--4 May 1775 Wit: Samuel Potts Ellison
    Richard Smith To: Robert Ellison and John Ellison in 1786
    Orig. Gr. to Robert Dukes S-s Wateree. Sold to John Chesnut
    Richard Smith-the father   Son: Richard Smith Pg-32

ELLISON, WILLIAM, Baptist Churchyard-Fairfield near Longtown
    Died: Sept 3, 1838, in 59th yr of age.
    Ann C. Ellison, Died May 12, 1899, 61st yr age.
    Mary B. Ellison, Died Sept 1841--22 yr age

ESTES, ZACHARAIH -w- Martha to Moses Hill Fairfield Deed A 1786

EVANS, DAVID READ, ESQ. Fairfield C-179/181   1788
    To: Elizabeth Lenox, 100 A. on Leek Cr. of Wateree Creek. Bd
    John Johnston, John Lewis, Andrew McDowle, (McDowel)

EVANS, D. Fairfield Deed Bk A-2 Pg-138 Jan. 13, 1792
    "Instructions to those who may act as my executors" "my wife and
    children".

FANT, ABNER -w- Catherine Old Book in Fairfield Prob. Off. 1834
    (receipt for share) -vs- Thos. Harrison, et al (receipt share)
    Benj. Harrison, Share, James Robertson, Share.

FANT, REV. ABNER--Trustee. Deed for Mourning Dickson of Fairfield to
    Dau. Margaret Dickson--175 A. land. 12 Aug. 1835 Archives Misc. I-310

FELLOWS, MATHIAS Fairfield Wills July 26, 1789 Vol. 1-75
    Wife: Elizabeth and her son Moses Arledge
    Heirs: Isaac Arledge
            Lydia Miller
            Hugh Maner
            Patience Ivey
    Ex: Wife Wit: John Yarborough, Geo. Peay, and John Lucas

FERRIS, JOHN -- Gr. Son. 22 Aug. 1772, both of Jacksons Creek to John
    Hamilton--100 A. on a Br. of Jackson's Cr. Wit: John Stevenson,
    Edward Martin. Fairfield H-129/130 L778-July 19

FEARIES, THOMAS -w- Janet of Chester. Gr. on Wateree. Wit: Wm. Fearis
    Fairfield Deed A 1787

FINLEY, ALEXANDER-Minor asks apt. of James Kincaid (?) as Gdn.
    Fairfield Wills Vol 1-9 Nov. 14, 1787

FLEMMINS, GEORGE Fairfield Deed A 1787

FLINTHERN (or m) JOHN--no dower Fairfield Deed B-124/126 Jan. 17, 1786
    To: Philip Pearson--200 A orig. gr. John Hick--on Br. Broad R.
    called Wilkinson's Cr. Bd John Young, Vac. Wit: Ruth (X)
    Lewelling, John Lewelling, Joseph Hartmandly (?)

FORD, JAMES--died prior to Oct. 20, 1831 Shows wife was Keziah Ford
    Adm. 1831--James E. Graham. Bond Sd. by James E. Graham.
    Austin F. Peay, Thos C. Bryant.
    Shows: In 1833 Nathaniel Ford was appt. adm. Bond sd. Nathaniel
    Ford. A. F. Peay, John Ford. Act. shows sums were pd. to James
    Ford, Wm. Ford, and Keziah Ford, the widow.
    Winnsboro Prob. Bk. L--262 Apt. 48-744

FORTE, JOHN--Pr. Est. Wm. Hill 1796   Fairfield Inv.
                        Elijah Brown 1798
                        Albert   "   1799
FORTE, NEWTON--Petit Juror 16 Jan. 1799
FORTE, WILLIAM --Grand Juror 16 Jan. 1799

FORTE, GEORGE, Junior--S. C. Probate Fairfield I Pg 409/410
    George Buchanan, Wm. Craig, Wit: Deed 16 March 1796 by Mary
    Elowine, John Elowine, Caty Elowine of Newberry Co. also Catherine.
    To: Allen de Graffenreidt of Chester. Gr. to Mary Risinger 25
    May 1774 in Fairfield

FORTUNE, JOHN Winnsboro Box 3 Pkg 82. Adm: Walter Robinson. Bond
    13 Aug. 1787. Benj. Sims, John Wilson

FOSTER, JOSIAH dec'd--Heir of Zach. Hall Fairfield 1838
    Ch: David Foster--Thos. Lyles Grsn.
         Rebecca   "
         Elizabeth "
         Lucy   "
         Susanna   "

FRANKLIN, THOMAS, SR. Gr. 22 Feb. 17__? 400A on Little Cedar Cr. on
Horsepen Br. 1774 Willed to Thomas Franklin, Jr. 200 A. Conv. by
Edmund Franklin to Wm. Kirkland. Wit: Jacob Bethany, Francis (X)
Miles, and William Dortch. Fairfield H-143/144 1787 Jan. 10

FREEMAN, PATIENCE - Dec'd Old Book in Prob. Off. Fairfield
Share: Robert Freeman--Robert Hawthorne, Gdn.
        Edward Andrews
        Elizabeth Freeman

FROST, JOHN Fairfield Wills Bk1-17 1800 Admx: Judith Frost. 15 Sept. 1800

FULGHAM, JOHN--Gr. 400 A. 13 June 1722? on Thorntree Cr. Conv. by John
Yarborough -w- Mary (X)-Joint to John Bryant. Pt. 200 A bd John
Williamson. Wit: Will Bryan and John Morrison Fairfield Deed B-64
                                                                1785

FUNDERBURGH, HENRY -w- Mary Fairfield Deed A 1786
To: "Our loving son"--Daniel Mabry

FURMAN, JAMES (or Freeman)--Gr 22 March 1769 Fairfield C-40/41 Nov. 7, 1771
To: John Willson--200 A. on Bear Cr.
Pg. 41/42--Frederick Freeman--From Aaron Loocock as Exor. of Samuel
Scott Land Gr. Samuel Scott on Beaver Cr. Wit: JamesCusart, Axdr'
Brown.
Pg. 45/46-Frederick Freeman, 21 Dec. 1789 To John Willson. Gr. to
Samuel Scott. Wit: Nimrod Mitchell, Samuel Wright

GIBSON, ABRAHAM To: Isaac Gibson Fairfield Deed A-515 1787
Wit: Jarvis Gibson, Lyah? Gibson

GIBSON, ELIZABETH--Pet'r.--Est. of John Lightner-Dec'd--Eliz. G. Dec'd
Humphrey Gibson, Adm'r. Fec't for her share. -vs- Abigail Lightner,
Shares: Barbara Kennedy, Mary Lightner, David Gable, Daniel
Lightner. Old book in Prob. Off. Fairfield

GIBSON, SAMUEL ROGER Old Family Graveyard in Fairfield Co.
        Born Jan. 19, 1792   Died Mar. 16, 1842
        Mrs. Mary Mobley -w- Maj'r. S. R. Gibson
        Born May 4, 1813   Died Nov. 20, 1839
        George Stratford -d- Apr. 24, 1856--age 78
            Wife: Jane age 63 -d- June 29, 1855
            Son: Richard -d- Sept. 11, 1898 age 71
                Son: George d. age 21

GIBSON, STEPHEN, Dec'd 1836 Old Book Prob. Off. Fairfield Co.
        Shares: Henry Gibson, Stephen Gibson, Minor Gibson, Robert Hawthorn
        Allen Gibson, Edward Gibson, Elizabeth,--Minor--Wm. Holmes, Gdn.
        James B. Gibson, Bante? Gibson, Charles Brown, Jr.

GODFRIED, JOHN, Dec'd Fairfield May 11, 1799 C-202/203
        Ext: Margaret Godfrey Suit by John Stone--Sale by Wm. Durphey--Shff.
        Fairfield to John Stone--highest bidder. Pts 3 surveys 200 A
        (1) Gr. to Margaret Godfrey 250 A. (2) 50 A. Gr. Henry Duke (3)
        Gr. to Anthony Funderburgh

GODFREY, JOHN Fairfield Deed A 1779 1786. Willed to Margaret Godfrey
24 June 1779 To: Thomas Cockrel 1786. Pg. 424: Margaret Godfrey
Widow--to George Godfrey--her son.

GODFREY, JOHN -w- Margaret Fairfield C-61/62 1787
   To: Peter Rees (Reives) 100 A. Gr. to Joseph Howard on Rocky Cr.
   N-s Broad--Gr. 19 Aug. 1774

GOODWIN, JOHN Gr. 1770 on Sawney's Cr. Fairfield H-154/155 1793
   Sold to Thomas Hide--got in debt and left state--sold the land to
   John. Now in possession of John McCants. H_____? --Shff.
   took it and sold it to John M.Cants.

GOODWIN, THOMAS Dec'd Old Book in Prob. Off Fairfield Co. 1825
   Shares receipt for: -w- Hardy Tidwell
   Susanna -w- John Cheshire
   Nancy -w- John Grant
   Thomas Goodwin. Shares sold Dr. Robert Mathews -widow-Elizabeth M.
   Jas. McCrory, Adm.

GOODWIN, REBECCA D. Baptist Church yard near Georgetown, Fairfield Co.
   Born: 18 Sept. 1813 Died 1 Sept 1825 Age 12 yrs. 11 mos.

GORDON, DAVID Fairfield Deed A 1786

GORDON, WILLIAM Fairfield Deed B-40 Feb. 7, 1785
   Gr. 21 Jan. 1780 640 A. on Waters of Fishing Cr. To: Alexander
   Miller all 640 A. on Waters of Fishing Creek--bd Catawba R.
   Bd George Halsey-James McCammon. Wit: R. Ellison, James Johnston

GLADDEN, JESSE Est. of Thomas Grafton, Dec'd. Fairfield Co. 1830 -vs-
   Thos. McCullough -wife- Elizabeth--share
   Shares to: Mary Stormant
               Wm. Grafton
               David Grafton
               Jesse Gladden
               Nancy Gladden
               Keziah Ford
               Andrew Grafton--res. Henry Co. Ga.
               Margaret Harper

GLADDEN, SAMUEL Fairfield Wills Bk 1-3 1799
   Wife: Agnes
   Sons: Richard, Hugh, Joseph, Patrick, Thomas, James
   Dau: Mary
   G-S: Samuel--son of Richard
   G-S: Samuel--Son of Thomas--Land called Howell's Land
   Date: Oct. 23, 1799. Ex: Wife and son Richard
   Will states that if Son Joseph does not claim his portion in person
   or by atty. in 7 years, it is to go to G-S Samuel, son of Patrick.
   Wit: David Cammosh(?), James McCray, H. Millings Rec'd Mar. 7, 1800

GRAHAM, ELIZABETH Legatee of Will of John Sweat 23 Jan. 1816,
   "It is my will, that Elizabeth Sweat, formerly Elizabeth Graham, do
   hold all the balance of my estate. Elisha Graham, a Wit.
   Fairfield Wills Bk. 7-227

GRAHAM, JAMES of Fairfield Dist. Winnsboro Deed KK Pg. 144/145 To Isaac
   Arledge--Division of lands Est. of Gardner's Ford, part in dispute
   divided between the two. Dated Aug. 6, 1830

GRAHAM, MARTHA Dau. of Jesse Harris Will 26 Aug. 1827 Fairfield Wills
    Elizabeth Graham--dau of Hugh Rodman, Will 5 July 1828 (probably
    Eliza. K.)
    Sarah Graham--Dau. of Burrell Hollis, Will Sept. 22, 1835
        Ch: Elizabeth Hendson
             Jane   "
             Mary Dunlap   Will Bk. 11-84 Fairfield Wills

GRAHAM, WILLIAM AND CHARLES, Wit. Will of Ephraim Pettipool dated 2 Feb.
    1793. Fairfield Wills Apt. 6-181
    John Graham--Wit. Will of Thos. Meredith Sr. 15 Sept. 1808
    Also Wit. Will of John Yarborough 1816

GRAVES, WILLIAM of Fairfield Deed A 1785

GREGG, JOHN (or Craig)Gr. 9 Sept. 1774 Fairfield Deed B 119-121 July 24.
    To: William Cato--100 A. on Bear Cr. bd John Smith. Wit: Thos.. 1787
    Parrot (X)Sr. and Jr., Nicholas Edington

GRIFFIN, JOHN --of Halifax, Colony of Va. Fairfield Deed H-70/71 1765, June 8
    To: Charles Hill Gr. 22 Jan. 1759 (or 1754) to John Griffin 200 A.
    N-prong of Wateree Cr. Bd. Samuel Griffin and Vac. Wit: Richard
    Griffin, Jr. Wm (X) Griffin, John Hill (X)

GRIFFIN, SAMUEL (X) of Halifax Va. Gr. 22 Jan. 1759 Fairfield Deed H 82/83
    200 A. N-prong Wateree Cr. Bd. John Griffin, Richard Griffin. To:
    Richard Snugs. Wit: Wm. Snugs, Meshack (X) Overbe, Charles Hill
    1765, Oct. 8
    Pg. 73/74 1778 Oct. 17 Gr. to John Griffin 22 Jan. 1754 200 A
    To: Charles Hill 7/7 June 1765
        Son: Wm. Augusta Hill
              Ely Kershaw- 12/13 May 1789 to Macajah Pickett

HAM, JOHN -w- Mary Fairfield C-91/92 1789 To: Simon Motte--500 A.
    Gr. to Adam Efort 5 Oct. 1784--on Beaver Cr.--bd. Thos. Taylor,
    Andrew Feaster

HAMILTON, JOHN (X) To John Stinson both of Jackson's Cr. Fairfield H 130/31
    100 A. on Spring Br. of Jackson's Cr. Bd. John McBride xxxx. Wit:
    Thos. Gladney, David Hamilton, David Martin 1785 May 15.
    1790-Dec. 11 H 131/132--John Stinson, Inn-Keeper To: Harvy McNeill
    Gr. to John Ferris 2 Apr. 1773

HANCOCK, ROBERT -w- Lucy Fairfield Deed H 150/151 1786 March 31
    To: William Liles--575 A. N-s Broad R. Bd. on Rt. Sd Hancock, James
    Newton, Thos. Nelson, Lewis Botner. Wit: Wm. Craig, David James,
    Zach (X) Hall
    Next: Same to Same 22 Dec. 1792. Pt. Gr. N-s Broad R.
    Gr. to Wm. Howell, Conv. to Jane Curry to Robert Hancock -w- Lucy
    Wit: Redding Ashford, David James

HARBIRT, THOMAS of Newberry Co. Fairfield 133/134 1788 Oct. 16 To:
    John Cook--100 A. Gr. 1762 Barbara Nan Levin (Vanlevin?) 50 A. Gr.
    to David Ellis 29 Apr. 1768 xxxx Wit: John Harbirt, Hardy Harbirt,
    John Cook, Jr.

HARDAGE, JOHN--of Dutchman's Creek Fairfield H-163/164 Feb. 1, 1792
   To: Bond and Mtg. land and slaves etc. Matthew McCreight and
   William Briant. 250 A. Gr. to John McDonald 7 May 1765 on S-Br.
   of Dutchman's Cr. Bd. George Payne and Vac. Sold by John McD.
   to Joseph Raines who conv. to Zachariah Williams and at his
   dec. fell to Wm. Williams who sold to Wm. Brian, "from whom I
   purchased" Wit: Edward Bryan, John Calvitt

HARRIS, JAMES Fairfield Deed H-8/9 1792 To: Bond and Mtg. per. prop.
   John Arick.

HARRISON, GEORGE (X) (sp. Harssin and Harsson). Deed B-150-153 Fairfield
   To: John Buchanan 100 A. on Br. Little R. F. Broad. Orig. Gr. to
   Oliver Dale (or Hale). Wit: John Winn, John Means. 1788-May 20

HARRISON, WILEY C. Methodist Graveyard--Fairfield Co, Near Georgetown.
   Born: Apl. 10, 1822 Died Sept. 7, 1867

HATHCOCK, JOHN to Thomas Parrott Fairfield Deed A-2 Pg-1 1785

HARVEY Fairfield
   Shares: John N. Harvey
            William   "
            Nancy -w- John Avrett
            Alexander Harvey
            Robert Harvey
            Elizabeth -w- Andrew Neil
            James N. Phillips
            Jane -w- Alex'r. Harvey
            Thos. Phillips
            William Phillips of Indiana

HAVIS, JOHN To James Workman Winnsboro Deeds H-? 1 1792

HAWTHORN, JOHN, Dec'd intestate (also shown Joseph)--Gr. 29 July 1768
   Eldest son: Adam Hawthorn To: John Pearson 350A. Bd. Gr. to Chas.
   Hill and Vac. on Waters of Broad R. Wit: Robert Hawthorn, John (X)
   Hawthorn. Fairfield C-109/110 June 20, 1777

HAWTHORN, ROBERT -w- Mary of Elbert Co. Georgia Fairfield H-69 1792 Aug28
   To: William Yarboar 75 A. Pt. 100 A. N-s Broad R. Gr. Sd Robert
   Hawthorn--5 May, 1773. Bd Wm. Mitcheson (or Richson)
   Wit: John Hawthorn, James Hunt, Joshua Fields

HAYS, DAVID Dec'd of Fairfield 1792 March 21 Fairfield Deeds H-167/68
   Adm: Mathew Tolbert (sd Tolbot) To Zachariah Kirkland.
   Sale R. E. of Dec'd: 100 A. on Cedar Cr. of Broad R.. Gr 1 Aug .
   1758 to John Lee--who sold to Jack Free 7 July 1762. Who, with his
   wife Mary, Conv. to Anthony Doeston, who sold to Benj. Sims, who
   sold to David Hays the 250 A. Gr. sd Benj. Sims in 1778.

HAYS, JOHN of Fishing Creek--Blacksmith. Pur.Lot in Winnsboro-1785
   1786--John Hays of Fishing Cr.-Blacksmith To John Heirs of Fairfield. Fairfield Deed Bk A-13

HENDRICKS, JAMES of Fairfield. Gr. May 1, 1786. 530 A. on Cedar Cr.
    To: John Woodward of Fairfield Pt 340 A. Bd. John Sibley.
    Fairfield Deed Bk-67 9 Dec. 1786

HENDRICKS, MOSES Fairfield Deed B-131-133 1788. From Clement Moberly (X)
    P. A. to Collect etc. Wit: Hance Cennemur X, George Cennemur X
    Moses Hendricks -w- Susanna (X) (145-147) To: 20 June 1788, John
    Ham. Gr. 6 Mar. 1786. 100 A. on Terrible Cr. of Broad R. Wit:
    George Cennemur, William Alexander
    Moses Hendricks -w- Susanna Gr. 191 A. on Rocky Cr. of Broad R.
    5 June, 1786. To Hance Kenemore. Pt 95½ A. Wit: George Vandiver,
    Shadrack Jacobs. Fairfield C-15/16 1789

HICHLIN, JASON--Wit. Will of Reuben Starke. 22 Oct. 1805 Fairfield Wills

HILL, CHARLES -w- Mary--Gr. 28 May 1771. Fairfield H 84/85 1772
    To: Wm. Tidwell--100 A. on Wateree Cr. St. Marks R. Bd. Wm. Hill,
    Charles Hill, Sr. and Vac.
    Next: Wm. Tidwell to Macajah Pickett--Wit: Smallwood Owen

HILL, WILLIAM -w- Agnes (X) Gr. 13 Aug. 1762 To Jane Rogers, spinster,
    and weaver. 100 A. onBowen's Mill Cr. Fairfield Deed B 113/115
    Apr. 5, 1788

HILL, WM -w- Dorcas--both (X) to Samuel Mobley Fairfield H-2 1792 200A.

HILL, WILLIAM From Wm. Mobley -w- Mary (X) Fairfield H-19/20 1792
    318 A. on Beaver Cr. of Broad R. Orig. Gr. to Jeb Meadow 12 March
    1760. Also 50 A. Gr. to John Mobley 18 May, 1771 and also 180 A.
    Gr. sd John Mobley 26 July, 1774. Wit: John F. Hill, Richard Hill,
    Wm. Alsop.
    Hill, William Fairfield Wills Vol. 1-83 1790
        Sole heir Wm. Hill, Jr. Date: June 1, 1790
        Wit: Wm. Alsup, Adam Effird, and Rich'd Odom

HODGE, BENJAMIN of Fairfield to son in law John Miller of Richland Dist.
    Deed gift, 2 Dec. 1808--Per_____? Slave. Fairfield File Misc B-522

HOGAN, CORDEL Bond--Mortg. land and per. prop. slave Jonathan Belton
    Wit: Austin F. Peay, John Calvert. John McKinney J. P.
    Fairfield H-136/137 1st Sept. 1792

HOLLIS, DANIEL W. Dec'd Old Book in Prob. Off. Fairfield Co. 1836
    Shares: Elizabeth -w- Joseph Vampkin
            Martha -w- James Sasser
            Mary -w- Jesse Hilliard
            John W., Eliza, and Nancy Hollis, minors. Jesse Hilliard,
            Gdn.

HOLSEY, THOMAS TO Margaret Holsey Fairfield Deed Bk. A 1785

HOOD, ROBERT -w- Mary (both X) Gr. 180 A. 5 March 1787 To John Dickey.
    180 A. on Lick Br. of Wateree Cr. Wit: Hez. Whitter, John Burns,
    George Hood. Fairfield H-148/149 1791

HOPKINS, DAVID of Chester Gr. 16 July 1784 to Cullen Mobley, 200 A. on
    Beaver Cr. Bd. Thomas Meadows. Wit: John Brown, Phillip (X) Hoppock
    Fairfield H-125 1792

HOWE, JOHN DE LA--of 96 Dist. His Gr. per Richard Winn, Atty. To:
   Alexander Miller. 400 A. Bt'n Wateree and Little R. Wit:
   D. Evans-David Evans in Proof, John Beckham. Fairfield Deed B-137/139
   and 141/142 May 1, 1788

HOWELL, WILLIAM Fairfield Deed H-55/56 7 Dec. 1771. To: Jane Curry,
   Fur-dealer- 200 A. on Broad R. Bd. sd River and Robert Hancock.
   Wit: Dr. Jno. Mourch, Joseph Hargrove

HUFFMAN, CHRISTOPHER and wife, Margaret--late--Margaret Patton
   Fairfield Deed A 1785

HUFFMAN, DANIEL, SR. From Daniel Huffman, Jr. Fairfield Deed A

 HUFFMAN, DANIEL, SR. -w- Mary to William Calhoun. Wit: James Calhoun,
   David Boyd, John Cameron Fairfield Deed A 1787

HUFFMAN, DANIEL, SR. -w- Mary Huffman (both X) to William Calhoun. Gr.
   to Daniel Huffman, Jr. 2 Oct. 1786. 640 A. in Fairfield on Dennis
   Fork of Little River. Bd. Christopher Huffman, Daniel Huffman, Sr.,
   and Vac. Sd. Daniel Jr. having sold 100 A. to sd. Daniel Sr. May 11/12
   1787, in Bk A. Pg. 43 Fairfield Co. Deed Bk-2 Sept 2, 1787
   Wit: John Cameron, David Boyd, James Calhoun

HUFFMAN, DANIEL (X) (no dower) Fairfield Deed B- Aug. 30, 1787. To
   James Cameron Gr. 2 Oct. 1786 640 A. on Dennis Fork of Mill Cr.
   Wit: John Milling, Wm. Boyd

HUFFMAN, DANIEL -w- Susanna (both X) Gr. 640 A. 2 Oct. 1786 on Little R.
   To William Tyner.
   Pg. 84/85 Peter Huffman of Kentucky--by Jack Huffman, his atty--
   to Margaret Beasley. 100 A. adj. Geo. Bailey, and Christopher
   Huffman. Fairfield C-20-21 Nov. 8, 1787

HUFFMAN, PETER of Kentucky by Jack Huffman his atty. Gr. 5 June 1786
   444 A Conv. to Hugh Young. Pt. 20 A. Wit: Alex'r. Miller, James
   Arthur. Fairfield Deed B-190/193 Sept. 13, 1788

HUFFMAN, PETER of Masser Co. Ky. P. A. to his Bro. Jacob Huffman to
   convey to Christopher Huffman land in Fairfield. Deed Bk A-2
   Pg-55 1780's

HUNTER, ANDREW Gr. Thomas Franklin 8 March 1775
                   Edmond Franklin 8 July 1777
                   Robert Randle 22 Aug. 1782
                   John Neil 1 Jan. 1790
                   Samuel McKinley to Samuel Cork (Cook) -w- Sarah
                     1 Jan. 1791 to
                   Robert Neil (Neel) 100 A. on a Br. Cedar Creek
                   Fairfield H 127/128 3 March 1792

HUTCHENSON, LETITIA Deed A-2 1789

HUTCHISON, JOHN of Little R. Fairfield Deed B-162/164 Feb. 20, 1774
   To Stephen Noland of Little R. Surv. for Michael Thomp___? 150 A.
   on a Br. of Little R. Bd John Waginer, Thomas Smythe, Thomas Shannon,
   Wit: Robert McCown, Hugh McCown, John Stevenson

IVEY, HENRY To: William Wimingham (also sp. Willingham) Fairfield Deed A
                                                                    1786
JAMES, THOMAS Fairfield Wills Vol. 1-29 1789. Estate: July 9, 1789
    Adm: David James

JENKINS, JOHN To: William Gladden. Wit: Jesse Gladden. Fairfield Deed A
                                                                    1786
JENKINS, RICHARD, Dec'd Fairfield Deed A-2 1787. Adm. John Moberly.
    P. A. to Thos. Jenkins of Chester Co.

JOHNSON, THOMAS, Fairfield Wills Vol. 1 1788. Appt. Ex. for John
    Williams 26 May, 1788

JOHNSTON, CHARLES To: Sibella Hall-Widow. Fairfield Deed A 1780's

JOHNSTON, JOHN of 96 Dist. Gr. 15 Oct. 1784 To: James Kincaid. 194 A.
    on Guilder's Creek--96 Dist--A Br. of Indian Creek--Bd. James Kelly,
    David Boyd, Wit: Alexander Tarver, Hugh Marshell.
    Fairfield Deed C 198/199 28 Dec. 1787

KELLY, SIMON--Gr. 8 March 1768--on Wateree Cr. Fairfield Deed A 1786
    Will: Son--Alexander Kelly
            Samuel Kelly--"of Richland Dist"
        Dau--Mary -w- Burrell Foust
    Son Samuel Conv. to Wm. Davy (Davie) of Rutherford Co. N. C.

KENNEDY, ALEXANDER, Will 10 Aug. 1824 Fairfield Wills
    Son: James
          Henry--Sons: Osburn and James
          John--His son Alex'r
          Alexander and his son Arthur
          William and his son Alex'r
          Robert
          Samuel W.
    Dau: Jane Craig

KENNEDY, CAMPBLE of Abbeville Fairfield Deed H 170/171 9 Aug. 1791
    To: To: Thomas Lewerw (or Lewis) of Fairfield. 100 A. on Wyrick's
    Br. of Little R. on Branches of Jackson's Cr. Bd. Robert Ellison
    and Vac.

KENNEDY, JOSEPH of Jackson's Cr. David Kennedy-Wit. 1785 Fairfield Bk-A

KENNEDY, WILLIAM -w- Jennett of Little River. To Wm. McMorris 1774
    Fairfield Deed Bk-A

KINKHEAD, JAMES (or Kincaid) Fairfield Deed A 1779

KIRKLAND, JOSEPH, Dau. Jane lately m. George Brown of Camden. Deed Gift
    13 Nov. 1787 Slaves. Fairfield Deed A-493 1786

KIRKLAND, JOSEPH to Henry Hunter. Fairfield Deed A 1786
    1787-13 Nov. Joseph Kirkland, Sr. to John Winn in Tr. for Dau. Jane
    Brown -w- George Brown

KIRKLAND, JOSEPH -w- Leminder of Fairfield. Fairfield Deed C-181/182
    To Richard Winn 13 Sept. 1788, 350 A. Orig. Gr. to Edward McGraw
    17 Feb. 1767 and Conv. by him to Wm. Kelly 16 Apr. 1767 and he to
    Joseph K. and party hereto 28/29 Dec. 1774.   Cont.

Also 100 A. Gr. to William Bell, on Crooked Run, 12 Sept. 1768 and
he conv. to Joseph K. 22/23 Nov. 1775. Also 100 A. Gr. to Isaac
Porcher who conv. to J. K. (Pt. 700 A. Gr)
Richard Winn -w- Priscilla to John Compty--merchant of Winnsboro,
4 Aug. 1789--Same land. C-183/184
Pg-204-5 Richard Winn to John Compty--Lots

KIRKLAND, PENELOPE--Gr. 520 A. conv. to Thos Baker. 520 A. on head of
Jackson's Creek. (Now Penelope Winn -w- John Winn)
Fairfield Deeds A 16 July, 1785

LANGHAM, SAMUEL of Richland Dist 1785 Deed-?

LAIRD, JOSEPH (sp. Lard) Gr. 6 Jan. 1774. Fairfield C-27/28 1788
Son, Henry Laird to Wm. Hughs. 100 A. on Little R. Bd. James Thomas
Wit: Burr Harrison, Benj. Harrison, Jonathan Harrison

LAND, HENRY To Leonard Hill 100 A. Gr. 28 July 1774--Bd. James Thomas,
and Land laid out to the Irish. Wit: Burr Harrison, Moses Hill
Susannah (X) Dumport (or Davenport) Fairfield B-55 8 Aug. 1785

LANGHAM, JAMES (or Laugham) to John Ham--640 A. Gr. 5 June 1786 to John
Goff and James Langham, 640 A. on Thorntree Cr. of Wateree R. and
Ford's Mill Cr. 150 A. Pt Conv. hereby. Fairfield C-185/6 1789

LAVENDER, HUGH--Wit. Deed 23 Oct. 1803 Winnsboro Deed O-322

LEE, JOHN Dec'd (1792) also Rebecca Lee, Dec'd. Fairgield Ind. P-20
Alexander Gordon--Adm. for both. Appr: Henry Moore, James Turner,
Hugh McKeown.

LEE, JOHN of Camden Dist. and wife, Mary. Deed A- Fairfield 1785

LEGGO, MADDERN to Reuben Hall Fairfield Deed A- 1786

LEGGO, MADDERN--Gr. 6 March 1786 to Leandrew Duggins--100 A.--__? Plat.
Fairfield Deed Bk B-165-169 16 Aug. 1786

LEIFTER, GEORGE (or Leister) d. intestate. Letters Gr. 4 Mar. 1800 to
Sarah Leifter. Fairfield Wills Bk-1 Pg-1 Sam. W. Youngue--Ord.

LEWELLAN, JOHN--Pur. est. James Aiken 1799 Fairfield Inv.
John and Nancy Lewellen, Wit. Conv. 19 Jan 1793
John on Petit Jury June Term 1793
" on Petit Jury--fined for failure to appear
Jonathan adv. minor W____? 1794

LEWIS, WARNER of State of Georgia to John Turner of Fairfield DeedA-90
1785
LILES, ARONAMONS-- Fairfield Deed A- 1786

LILES, EPHRAIM Archives Dept.--Mem 10-29. Eldest son Arramanes Liles. 1769

LILES, EPHRAIM--Gr. 1 Aug. 1758. Conv. by Arramanas Liles to John Means
100 A. on Rocky Creek of Broad R. Wit: Richard Winn, Wm. Roach,
Thomas Means. Fairfield H-177/178 25 July 1791

LINN, JAMES Dec'd Old Book in Prob. Off. Fairfield Co. 1837
    Shares: Grizle Linn
             Mary Jane, James A., John P. Linn Minors

LITTLE, JOHN of Fairfield Dist Gr. 3 Apr. 1786 Conv. to John Stover of
    Camden Dist. Fairfield Deed A 1787

LOT, GEORGE of Fairfield to James Neely of Fairfield 100 A. Gr. to Robert
    Owens 12 Dec. 1786 on Mill Creek and to George Lot in 1782.
    Fairfield Deed B-147-149 6 May, 1786

LOWE, ISAAC Dec'd 1792. Fairfield Inv. 2 (1794-1800 Pg. 19
    Apprs: John L. Bradford, James Rabb, Charles Bradford.

LOWRY, CONRAD of State of Va. Shoemaker Deed A-309 1787

LOWRY, PATRICK -w- Rose To Macajah Pickett 100 A. Gr. to Rose Miller on
    Br. Wateree Cr. Bd. Abraham Miller and Vac. Fairfield 79/80 1785

LOWRY, WILLIAM Dec'd Winnsboro Deed Bk II-388 1826
    Heirs: Susannah, Agnes, Joseph, James, William, Robert, John, Esther,
            Elizabeth, Alex, Thomas. John and Mary Galloway

MABRY, EPHRAIM Will (lost) Fairfield Wills Vol. 1 Sept or Oct. 1788
    Son: Joel
    Heirs: James Thomas, Daniel, Ceily, Margaret Hanchey? , Mary,
            Elizabeth, Ephraim. Wife: Mary--sole Exor. Proven by
            work of mouth. Wit: Phillip Combs, Elizabeth Duke.

MABRY, JOEL -w- Mary Fairfield Deed A 1787

MACON, HARTWELL, SR. of Fairfield Dist. Fairfield N-448 1 March, 1802
    500 lbs. sterling: To Henry J. Macon--410 A. Pts 2 tracts Gr. to
    John Martin. (1) 350 A. 13 July 1770 who sold to Francis Coleman.
    (2) 150 A. Gr. to Francis Coleman on Sandy Fork of Beaver Cr. Bd.
    Hampton, Wiers, Means

MACON, HARTWELL, SR. to Son: Hartwell Macon, Jr. of N. C. Wit: Gideon
    Macon. Fairfield Deed A-2 Pg 73 1789 (Sumter man?)

MAHAZY, JOHN-Cooper-Gr. 26 July 1774 to Samuel Boykin and Wm. Boykin.
    91 A. on Deep Fork of Wateree. Bd. Thos. Dye. Fairfield H-47/48
                                                                  1775
MAJOR, JAMES--Gr 22 Sept 1764. D. intestate Fairfield File Y5-340
    Son: John Major conv. Rebecca Bohannan and her son James Bohannan
    of Camden Dist.
    300 A. in Belfast Twp. Gr. to sd. James Major 22 Sept. 1767

MARPLE, JOHN-Planter0 Adm: Thomas Marple Jan. 30, 1789 Fairfield Wills 1-27

MARPOLE, THOMAS to James Craig Fairfield Deed A or B 218/220 Sept. 4, 1784
    3 Nov. 1762 Gr. to Jacob Reiser. 150 A. on Mill Creek of Little R.
    and J. R. conv. to T. Marpole 24/25 Feb. 1778. Wit: John Robertson,
    John Bell

MARSHAL, JANE--a sister of John Williams. Will 13 Oct. 1804 Fairfield
    Wills. (John son of Thos Williams)

MARTIN, JOHN Gr. 10 Nov. 1781. -w- Margaret xxx Fairfield C-10/11 1789
    To: Samuel Luchey 100 A. on 25-Mile Cr.. Wit: Samuel Martin,
    Goodman Hughs, Anne Perry

MATHEWS, MOSES -w- Sarah of Georgia To Wm. McGraw. 100 A. Gr. to Jacob
    Litner on Broad R. Bd. W-sd River and Vac. Gr. Bk QQ Pg. 162
    Gr. 24 May, 1756. Wit: Sanders Walker, Rev. James Mathews.
    Fairfield I-434/5 2 June, 1794

MATHIS, ISRAEL -w- Ann (joint) Fairfield Deed B-- 4 Apr. 1788
    To: William Roach. Sev. tracts. Gr. to Thomas Sanders
                                  Gr. to Isaac Hartfort
                                    " " " "

MAY, THOMAS To: Elizabeth Woodward, Spinster, Gr. to Thomas Stark, conv.
    to Thos. Woodward--since dec'd--Will to Elizabeth Woodward-to-
    Thos. May-back to E. W. 750 A. on Mill Cr. Fairfield C 8/9 1788

MAYNARD, EDWARD -w- Pherabee--dower. Fairfield H 120/121 1792
    To: Robert Eckles. 100 A. both sides of Dutchman's Cr. orig. Gr.
    to Mathias Fellers 13 Feb. 1768. Who conv. to Edward Maynard 23/22
    Feb, 1787. Wit: Hezekiah Ford, Wm. Branch, Charnel Durham.

MEADOR, THOMAS -w- Hannah of Fairfield Gr. 2 Jan. 1773, 200 A. To
    Micajah Mobley. 200 A. on N-Branch of Beaver Cr. Pt of 100 A.
    Wit: John Brown, John Lovejoy, Edward Lovejoy.
    Fairfield Deed B-34 10 Oct. 1787

MEANS, MAJ. THOMAS J. Died at res. near Buck Head, Fairfield Dist.
    Age about 45. (This is paper filed in a pkg. to show adv. notice
    of an estate in Newberry--not under Means) Newberry Prob. Pets.
    for Part. July 16, 1846

MEREDITH, THOMAS Fairfield Deed A- 1786

MEREDITH, THOMAS To Aaron Roberts--100 A. on Dutchman's Cr. Orig. Gr.
    To (?) who conv. to Reuben Hallxxxx. Wit: Wm. Cason, Jonas Knightton
    Fairfield Deed B-117/118 15 Aug. 1787

MICKLE, ELIZABETH Baptist--Fairfield Co. Near Longtown.
    Born Dec. 25, 1754 Died Oct. ___ 1895 ???

MILES, JOHN dec'd 1792. 1793 Sale at Home of Luke Rawls.
    Fairfield Inv. C19/20

MILES, FRANCIS--Gr. 6 Aug. 1774 to: David Hays--To: Mathew Talbot
    This Deed To: John Smith. Fairfield C-200/202 13 Aug. 1789

MILES, THOMAS (X) of Fairfield. Fairfield Deeds B-71 March 27, 1786
    To: John Woodward--Gr. 3 Apr. 1775 to Edmund Patrick. 200 A. on
    Cedar Cr.--Bd. James Jones, formerly conv. to Thomas Miles by
    Aaron Loocock, and Archibald Brown.

MILES, THOMAS of Fairfield. Deed Bk B-163/166 7 Jan. 1786
    To: William Summeral. Gr. 3 Apr. 1775 to Edmund Patrick on Br. of
    Cedar Cr. in Fairfield Co. Bd. James Jones and Thos. Woodward.
    Formerly conv. by Aaron Loocock and Arch'd Brown to sd Thos. Miles.

MILES, THOMAS Gr. 3 Apr. 1786 to James Hendricks. 200 A. Gr.
    Fairfield Deeds C-7/8 1789

MILLER, ALEXANDER to James Arthur. Fairfield Deed Bk A 1785

MILLER, ALEXANDER Fairfield Wills Vol.-1 54 1787
    Son: Alexander and Henry
    Dau: Susan
    Wife: Hannah
    Date: Oct. 25, 1789
    Ex: Samuel Caldwell and Hugh Milling
    Wit: Wm. Clintock, Joseph Cathcart, Geo. Kennedy

MILLING, HUGH to Alexander Johnston of Chester. Fairfield H18/19 1789
    On Brushy Fork of Little R. Bd. Burr Harrison, Wm. McMorris, Henry
    Atkinson. Wit: John Tinker and Sarah Means

MILLING, JOHN of Town of Winnsborough. Fairfield Deed B-47 7 Jan. 1788
    To: Lewis Perry 600A. to James Thomson 1 Jan. 1765? on Cowpen Br.
    of 25 Mile Cr. and Bd. _____? 27 Dec. 1767 Conv. to John Milling
    and party _____?. Pt. 150 A. Bd Nimrod Mitchell's land, James
    Wilson and sd J. Milling. Wit: Wm. Boyd and David Evans

MILLING, HUGH and John 1785. David Milling and John. Fairfield Deed A-?

MILLING, JOHN Fairfield Wills Vol. 1 16 May 1788. Hugh Milling, Adm.

MILLING, SARAH--Orphan. John Means Apt. Gdn. Aug. 13, 1788. Fairfield
    Wills Vol.-1-19 1788

MILLS, AMBROSE--Gr. 100 A. Wateree Cr. 18 May, 1773. Bd. John Lee
    Fairfield Deeds H-9/10 Dec. 10, 1784
    Wm. Mills--of Rutherford Co. N. C. to Macajah Pickett. Wit: John
    Mills, Ann Mills, and S___ls Lewis.

MILLS, SAM P. Minor--John Johnson, Gdn. -vs- James B. Pickett and John
    McCrory son of Eliza Mills. Share: Samuel P. Mills. 1832
    Old Book in Prob. Off. Fairfield Co.

MOBLY, CLEMENT--Gr. 10 June 1776 (or 1766) Conv. by Clement Mobley, Jr.
    To Aranamon Lyles. 100 A. N-s Broad R. on Beaver Cr. and Sandy
    Fork. Fairfield Deed B 93/94

MOBLEY, CULLIN (X) To Micajah Mobley--Gr. to David Hopkins 1784. 60A.
    on Beaver Cr. Wit: Thos. Mobly, Jethro Mobly, Daniel Mobly.
    Fairfield Deed H-43/44 1792

MOBLEY, ELEAZER -w- Anna Separation Fairfield Deed A-2 Pg-63 1786

MOBLEY, ELEAZER -w- Anna (X) Fairfield Deed B-73 16 July 1787 150lbs-amt.
    To: George Godfield or Godfried (both), Hannah G. and Sarah G.
    250 A. on Beaver Cr. of Broad River. Bd John Mobly, Martin Hawks,
    Robert Alcorn. Wit: Thos. Cockrill (X), John Stone (X) and
    Joseph McDanal

MONTGOMERY, DAVID-Minor-made choice of Theophlis Watson as Gdn.
    Fairfield Ct. Min. 1791-1799 17 Jan. 1793

MOORE, HENRY--Gr. 4 Sept 1786 to John Winn, Son of Wm. Winn. 200 A. on
Waters of Rocky Cr. Wit: Reuben J. Wooster (WoorsterOboth)
John Winn (X) Fairfield C-176/177 1789

MORGAN, ISAAC -w- Ann of 96 Dist. Gr. May 7, 1774 Dec. 5, 1778 87/8
To: Robert Rutherford of Chatham Co. N. C. 250 A. btn. Broad and
Saluda on Second Cr. Bd. Wm. Dawkins, Daniel Horsey

MORGAN, WILLIAM SR. Fairfield Deeds H-119/120 1793
To: Son--William Morgan 105¼ A. Pt survey for Peter Easton who Jan. 10
11,1764 gave it to sd William Morgan, Sr.--less 44 3/4 A. sold to Christian
Morgan. Wit: Adam Byerly, James Ogelvie, and Samuel Gregory

MOULTRIE, WILLIAM--Pur. lots in Winnsboro from John Winn. 1785
Henry Hampton-no dower- sold to Wm. Moultrie Plantation on head
Jack's Creek 1785. Fairfield Deed A-253 1785

MUCKLEROY, WILLIAM Fairfield Wills Vol. 1-2 1787

MUSE, JOHN Dec'd Fairfield Deed A-2 Pg 43 1762
2 orphans--Daniel and Amy Muse, and Amy Muse, Dec'd. Heir--John
Morrison released dower to Thos. Muse in 1762.

MYERS, DR. JOHN JACOB -m- Sarah E. Peay. Dau of Col. Austin Peay and
wife, Mary. Sarah E.--Born Nov. 5, 1805. Died March 1866

McCALL, FRANCIS--Inn Keeper of Winnsboro. Fairfield H-134 Dec. 14, 1792
To: Robert Craig--Per. Prop. Wit: Edward McGraw, Joseph Sims.
Jeremiah Jaggers

McCANE, SAMUEL (or McCants) Gr. Feb. 1, 1768 To Philip Walker. P. W.
To Richard Woodward. 100 A. on Beaver Mill Creek. Wit: David Cook
Samuel Caldwell, Thomas Blaire. Fairfield Deed B-- Apr. 15, 1777

McCANTS, JUDITH, share -vs- Cynthia McCants et al. Fairfield Co. Prob. 1838

McCANTS, ROBERT To Moses Wooten. 100 A. Gr. to Jane Robinson on Wateree
12 Sept. 1786--on Sawney's Cr. Wit: Benj. Sims, Joseph Sims.
Fairfiels 39/41 1784

McCARLE, THOMAS HARRIS, President of Mt. Zion College from John Winn
Several lots in Winnsboro 1787. Fairfield Deed A-353. 1787

McCARLE, THOMAS HARRIS--late of N. C. now of Winnsboro from John Winn
200 A. on Jackson's Cr. Fairfield C-73/74 1786

McCAW, JOHN "of York" Fairfield Deed A- 1785

McCLARKIN, JOHN -w- Margaret. Gr. 275 A. 6 Sept 1790 to Thomas Nelson
50 A. on Wateree Cr. Fairfield H-146/147

McCLENDON, BRYANT (x) of Orangeburg Dist. 10 June, 1771 Gr. to Frederick
Freeman on 25 Mile Cr. Gr. 100 A. 10 June 1771 on 25 Mile Cr.
Gr. 200 A. 23 June 1774 on 25 Mile Cr. (no dower)
Fairfield I-416 and 419

McCOMBS, JOHN of Fairfield--Blacksmith   Fairfield Deed B-23 Nov. 16, 1786
    To: John Huston 20 A. Pt. Gr.
    300 A. Gr. to William Winn 14 Aug. 1770 on Wateree Cr.   Fairfield.
        Rec'd in C. T. 8 Sept, 1770
    John McComb -w- Tesey 23 March 1786 to Hugh Young -w- Margaret.
    Wit: Thos. McClarkins and Wm. Bonner

McCRORY, JOHN Dec'd 1810 Apr. 16.   Winnsboro Min. Bk. Pg-93
    Exors: Jean McCrory, David Hamilton, Sam'l Clark.
    11-84   Winnsboro Original 91-39   E?-37

McCREARY, ROBERT -w- Mary of St. Marks 9 Feb. 1778 Fairfield C.T. Deed W-5-44
    Conv. to: Joseph Owen--conv. to Thos. Baker.   100 A. Granted to
    Mary Fortune at head of Jackson's Creek.   Bd. Wm. Fortune

McCREARY, SAMUEL to Robert Matthews   Winnsboro GG-128 1826

McCREARY, SAMUEL, JR. from John Grant of Chester and wife, Nancy, Dau.
    of Allen Goodman of Fairfield.   Land on Wateree.   Bd. James McCreary
    Winnsboro FF-232 1825

McCREARY, WILLIAM to Robert Young Winnsboro P-145-146 1806

McCREARY, WILLIAM--Receipt--To Simon Cameron.   "Received from S. C. the
    sum of thirty seven pounds, thirteen shillings and six pence, sterl-
    ing in full for all accounts, debts, dues or demand by me against
    the said S. C. for or concerning the estates of Adam McCreary, Dec'd.
    and I say receiving by me this 22nd day of Nov. 1796.   William
    McCreary.   Sd X and Sd X in the pres. of Arch'd McQuistan, J. P.

McCREIGHT, DAVID -w- Martha (X) to James McCreight.   Lot in Winnsboro
    Fairfield Deed A or B 213-215 Oct. 2, 1788

McCREIGHT, JAMES--Gr. 22 June 1794 to Solomon Anderson.   100 A. N-s
    Broad R. on S-fork of Little River.   Bd. John Kelly, John Waginor,
    Sam'l Mobley.   David Evan, Clerk of Ct. Fairfield H-97/98 1792

McCREIGHT, ROBERT To Joshua Harrison--100 A. Pt. 400 A. Gr. to Wm. Mc-
    Creight on Jackson's Cr. Bd. Wm. Trapp, R. McC. Wm. McCreight, Jr.
    and Wm. Owens.   Wit: Wm. Robertson, Isaac Hussey, James Hogan
    Fairfield H-174/175 1792

McCREIGHT, DAVID -w- Martha Dau. of William Orr of Ireland, Dec'd
    Fairfield Deed A-13 (A-2 Pg-13) 1786

McCRIGHT, DAVID, McCright, Margaret Fairfield Deed A 1785

McCRELESS, JOHN and Robert O'gilvie, both of Richland Dist. to Jno.
    McDowell Lowery, 6 May 1823.   Orig. Gr. sd R. O. 6 Aug 1810--on
    Wilkinson's Cr. and Terrible Cr. of Broad R.   Winnsboro Deed
    EE-253 1824

McCRELESS, JOHN OF Richland Dist. to his Dau: Hephzibah Price and her
    children.   Elias Marks, Trustee.   Deed Gift Slave.   17 March 1829
    Archives Dept--Misc. File F-401

McCRELESS, JOHN--signed as Surety--Document dated 29 Jan. 1814
in Lexington Dist. Bond of Wm. Snellgrove as Sheriff.
Archives Misc. Bk. C-Pg 101

McCRELESS, JOHN from Robert Robertson of Fairfield $30.00. 15 Acres in
Fairfield btwn. Broad and Little Rivers--Bd. Jacob Wilson, Wm.
Thompson, sd Robert Robertson and called Mount Vernon. 6 Feb. 1802
Winnsboro O-4 1802

McCRELESS, JOHN of Fairfield Dower--Ann to John Johnson 4 lots in Newberry
Village 3 March 1806. Newberry Deed H-275

McCRELESS, JOHN of Dist. Fairfield. Dower--Ann McCreless to Augustine
Williams. 15A. (same as conv. by R. R.) dated 5 Nov. 1802. Dower
13 Nov. 1802. (both signed). Winnsboro)-145 1803

McCULLOUGH, JAMES 250 A. S-s Wateree R. above Dutchman's Cr. Henry King
recovered judgment for 70lbs-6sh. Joseph Brevard, Shff. Camden
Dist--bid in by Rowland Ringeley for 100lbs. Wit: Henry Ringely,
James Atkins, Sarah Atkins. Fairfield C-214-215 June 1, 1789

McDOWELL, HUGH -w- Rebeccah Gr. 17 Feb. 1787 To William Brown--100 A.
on Little Rocky Cr.-S-s Catawba. Fairfield C-24/25 1782

McDonald, Hugh, Sr. of Camden Dist. to Hugh McDonald, Jr. Fairfield Deed-A
1786

McDOWELL, THOMAS of Fairfield %m- set 3 Nov. 1841. Martha E. Sutton,
Widow. James C. Neel, Tr. Fairfield Misc. M-18

McDOWLE, ALEXANDER--Gr 200 A. 13 May 1768 To James Smith. 100 A. on
Patrick Fork of Broad R. Wit: Sam'l Young, Robert Lindsey (x)
Fairfield C-210/211 Nov. 10, 1789

McDOWLE, ALEXANDER--Gr. 13 May 1768 Pt. 100 A. to Richard Winn N-s
Broad on Patrick's Fork Br. Fairfield H-25/26 9/10 Nov. 1781

McFADDIN, ROBERT -w- Leah of Sumter Dist. To Robert Barkley--100 A.
remaining pt. of 100 A. Gr. to Joseph Kirkland 27 Nov. 17__?
Also 143 A. Gr. Robert Ellison adj. formerly sold as prop. of
Thos. Baker and pur. by James Dickey of Black R. now dec'd.
Fairfield N-506/507

McFRYE, FRIZZEL (Frissle sp?) to Adam Free 3/4 acre adj. sd. F. McF.
Fairfield C-69/70 Nov. 9, 1789

McGILL, Share: Frances McGill--sold to Jacob Gibson.1836
Probate Records Fairfield Co.

McGRAW, EDWARD (X) to David McGraw 150 A. on Morris's Cr. of Little R.
Bd. George Straight. Wit: H. Hunter, Elisha Hunter.
Fairfield H-67/68 1784

McQUYTON, WILLIAM 9or McQueston) Fairfield Wills Bk 1-27 Aug. 12, 1800
Wife: Not named
Son: James
Dau: Jennet
Mentioned "my Daughters"
Ex: Andrew McQuyton, Alex. Chesnut and Arch'd Quyton. Wit: Jas.
Murdock? Hugh McQuyton

McKANE, JANE--Will 21 Jan. 1826   Fairfield Wills
    Son: James McKane
                Ch: John McKane
                      George   "
                      Jane   "
                      James Madison McKane
                      Mary McKane
                      Martha   "
                      Rebecca   "
    Dau: Agnes Gamble
    Son: Adam McKane
    Dau: Martha Brannen
     "   Jane Barber
    Son: Alexander McKane
    Dau: Eleanor Boyd
                Dau: Cynthia
    Gr. Dau: Martha L Smith
     "   "   Jane C. Collins
     "   "   Mary B. Collins
     "   "   Martha Weir

McKELVEY, ROBERT of Santee   Fairfield Deed A.   1786

McKOWN, JOHN Gr. to Dau: Agnes McKown. 120 Acres on Waters of Rocky Cr.
    Bd. Robert Gaston. Wit: Robert Martin, Ann McKown, Mary McDowle (X)
    Fairfield Deed A-B 339/340 Apr. 21, 1775

McKEOWN, JAMES OF C. T. to Hugh McKeown of Little River Fairfield Deed-A
                                                                    1780
McLROY (or McElroy,) William. Fairfield Deed A-2 1785

McMASTER, HUGH Fairfield Wills Vol.-1 16 Nov. 1787--Rec'd.
    "Late of the Parish of Ballymoney, the County of Antrim, Kingdom
    of Ireland, now a passenger on board the Friendship of Greenock-in
    North Brittain, Capt. Adam Cousor, bound for Charleston, S. C., last
    from Lovin in the County of Antrim, Kingdom of aforesaid" etc.
    Ex: Hugh McMillen, James Killock--passengers with him. States:
    "Whereas, on my leaving S. C. in May 1785, I empowered Wm. Dunlop
    and Arthur Morrow in 96 Dist.--Long Cane Settlement to act for me.
    Bro: Jas. McMaster of Ballymoney--if he "comes to America"
    Wife: Margaret Killock--then pregnant
    Sister: Mary McMaster
    Bro-in-l: James Killock
    Wit: Adam Cowsar, John Murray, Hugh Barclay, Thos. Kennedy.
    Rec'd 16 Nov. 1787

McMILLAN, ALEXANDER, John and Margaret -vs- Robert McMillan, et al.
    Shares to: Robert McMillen, Jemima McMillen, Martha McMillen.
    Receipt to John R. McCreight. John McMillen: Share.
    Matthew McMillen, Dec'd 1832. Fairfield Prob.

McMORRIS, WILLIAM Fairfield Deed A- 1787

McMULLAN, JAMES--Wheelwright--of Jackson's Cr. Fairfield. (no dower here)
    Survey of 30 Sept. 1784. To: John Robinson of Jackson's Cr. 100 A.
    on a Spring Br. of Jackson's Cr. Bd. Robert Neal. Wit: John
    Milling, Wm. Daniel, Robert Ellison. Fairfield Deed B-84 Nov. 1, 1787

McMURRAY, SAMUEL OF C.T. Weaver to Thomas Robinson of Camden Dist. 200 A.
    on Wateree Cr. Bd. Robert Jones, and Vac. Fairfield Deed B-181-185
    July 1, 1779

McWATERS, HUGH (X) or(Huston?) To Robert Marshall--298 A. in Richland on
    Cedar Cr. and Herman's Cr. of Broad R. Wit: Robert Ellison,
    Alex'r Owens. Fairfield Deed A 1787

NEIL, JOHN--eldest son of Grantee--to: Gen'l. Richard Winn. Wit:
    Samuel Gladen, Patrick Gladen. Fairfield H-14/15 June 24/5 1791

NELSON, HENRY to Thomas Smith. Fairfield Deed B-30 May 8, 1776
    Gr. to Thomas Nelson 19 Aug. 1768--300 A. on Little R. of Broad R.
    Bd. Thomas Woodward, Wm. Pinckney. Pt 75 Acres. Wit: Robert
    Braman, Richard Nely (Neely)
    Thomas Nelson.

NELSON, JAMES of Fairfield had grant conv. part to Wm. Moultrie.
    Fairfield Deed A 1787

NELSON, THOMAS (X) Fairfield H-168/169 1793
    To: Bond and Mortgage--Swanson Lunsford of Columbia. 300 A. head
    of Nees' Cr. Bd. James Davis, Thomas Parrot, the elder, Edward
    Going and Wm. Cato. Being a tract pur. from Thos. Parrot, the
    elder and Jacob Engleman

NETTLES, WILLIAM Fairfield Wills Bk-1-12 1800
    Adm: Zachariah Nettles
    Date: Aug. 23, 1800
    Aprs: Reuben Harrison, Joseph Cloud, Wm. Dunnavant
    2nd Apr: Samuel Douharty, Ab'n Crumpton, Moses Wooten

NEWTON, JAMES--Archives Dept. Fairfield Plat Bk 5-53. 300 A. for him-
    self and: Cert: Sept. 14, 1749
    "His Mother--Ann Hancock
    His Brother--Robert Hancock
    His Sisters--Martha, Elizabeth, Mary. N-s Broad River.

NIX, CHARLES -w- Ann. Gr. 4 Dec. 1775 to Enoch Grubs. 300 A. on Waters
    Little R. All Vac. at time of Gr. Survey. Wit: Edward Nix (X)
    Robert Nix (X) Wilson Cook, Jr. Fairfield C-193/4 July 19, 1788

OGILVIE, PRISCILLA--Dau. of George Seigler, Sr.--Will 18 Feb. 1803
    Has son Minor Seigler. Fairfield Wills

OTES, JEREMIAH of Washington Co. Ga. to Caleb Gassaway. Fairfield H-46/47
    200 A. Gr. to John Otes by N. C. 26 March 1755   N. C. Gr. 1787
    N-s Broad R. in Fairfield Co. Probate Union Co. Wit: Ben Glenn,
    Spisby Glenn, Wm. Massey

OWENS, JAMES to John Dickey--250 A. Gr. to Robert Harper on waters of
    Wateree Cr.--who conv. to James Owens Gr. 8 Dec. 1774. Wit:
    Martha Hood, Jane Dickey, Jane and Jno. Whitted
    Fairfield Deed H-110/111 1789

OWENS, JAMES SMALLWOOD of Hog Fork Br. of Wateree Cr. Bond and Mtg--
    Per. Prop. To Jonathan Belton. Fairfield H-162/63 Jan. 1, 1793

OWENS, JOHN -w- Ann (X) Gr. 3 Apr. 1772 to Samuel Owens 20 A. Pt
    250 A. on Owen's Mill Cr. Wit: Thos. and Lewis Owen's Wm. Cato
    Fairfield C 156/157 Jan 25, 1780

OWEN'S, JOHN Gr. on Jackson's Cr. of Broad R. Conv. to Thos. Baker,
    Both of Camden Dist. Fairfield File C.T.Deed W-5-46/7
    Pg. 50/51--Joseph Owen's -w- Elizabeth conv. to Thos. Baker in
    1782 land Gr. to Mary Fortune

OWEN'S, JOSEPH to William Owen's Fairfield Deed A 1785

OWEN'S, JOSEPH -w- Elizabeth to Charles I. Durham Fairfield Deed A 1787

OWEN'S, THOMAS Fairfield Wills Vol 1-80 Oct. 3, 1781
    Wife: Abigail Owens--Ex.
    Son: Samuel
    Men: "my children"
    Legacy: Baptist Society "Land in Cumberland Co. Pa."
    Date: Oct. 3, 1781
    Wit: Jonathan Lewelling, Jas. Hawthorne, Philip Pearson

PAPP, FRANCIS to Jesse Havis Recited: Jacob Holksture of City C.T.
    died intestate. Sister____Papp also died, her only son is the
    heir--sd Francis Papp. 100 A. Gr. sd J. H. 19 Feb. 1770
    Fairfield H 178/179 1793

PARROTT, THOMAS of Fairfield Dist--1/2 May, 1786 550lbs. sterl. To
    John Buchanan, orig Gr. Thos Parrott, 13 March 1772, 551 Acres on
    Little River of Broad. Bd. at time of Survey--S. W. John Robertson
    N. W. Richard Walters, Wit: John Martin C.T. Deed S-5 47/8

PATTON, MARGARET--Recites: Christopher Hoffman -w- Margaret conv. to
    John Kinnerly, 100 A. on Br. of Rocky Creek. Bd. Hugh McDonald,
    Alexander Brady, Alexander McKaine et al. Fairfield Deed A
                                            1785--Nov. 23
PAYNE, JOSEPH To James Willson 100 A. S-s Wateree--Bd. McNichols. orig.
    Gr. to John Lenoir 12 Oct. 1772. Wit: George Watts, Aaron Duke,
    Nancy Duke. Fairfield C-30/31 Jan. 13, 1788

PEARSON, JEREMIAH of Fairfield. Gr. 1 May, 1786 to Henry Haigood
    221 A. on Branch of Cedar Cr. Bd. Jacob Bethany, Wm. Dortch, John
    Swilly. Wit: Jacob Bethany, Wm. Haggood, Jno. Peirson
    Fairfield H-128/129 Aug. 14, 1787

PEARSON, MARY Widow. Deed Gift to her Gr. sons: Philip Pearson and
    William Pearson--sons of her dec'd son William Pearson. 29 Aug.
    1783. Fairfield Deed A-124

PEARSON, MARY--Will Fairfield Wills Bk-1-20 Mar. 13, 1798
    G. S: Nathaniel Cook--stock marked with John Cooks mark
    Son: John Pearson
          Philip Pearson
    G. S: Isaac Cook
    Dau: Mary Bond
    G. S: William Francis Pearson
    G. D: Mary Reddish
    D-in-L: Mary Pearson (appears -w- John)
    Exor: Sons--John and Philip
    Wit: John, William, Mary Pearson

PEARSON, MARY--Deed Gift to Gr. Ch.: Slaves 20 Aug. 1783
    Dec'd Son: William Pearson Ch: Philip and William
    Fairfield Deed A

PEARSON, MOSES--of Craven Will 10 July, 1762 Fairfield File C.T. Wills
    Son: Aaron Pearson
            Moses   "
    Dau: Ruth Aiken
           Sarah Cherry
    Son: Bradent Pearson--Home Place
    Dau: Comfort Pearson--150 A. "Walnut Bluff"
    Wife: Sarah Pearson
    Wit: Walter Folly, Wm. Cherry, John (X) Freeman
    Dedimus _? George Johnston. Prov. May 25, 1763

PEAY, AUSTIN--From old Baptist Ch. Yd. Fairfield Co. near Long Town.
    Born. Sept 10, 1844, Died Jan. 10, 1907
    Sarah E.--Dau of Col. Austin Peay and Mary E. Peay
    Born Nov. 5, 1805. Died March 1866 -m- Dr. John Jacob Myers in 1825

PEAY, EMMIA -w- Carolina--Fairfield Graveyard-Methodist- Newr LongTown
    Born Dec. 17, 1809 Died Feb. 21, 1862
    Monument: Nicholas A. Peay and Martha E. L. his wife.
        Martha E. L. Peay -w- Nicholas, B. Jan. 8, 1820 D. Apr. 9, 1851
        Nicholas A Peay--B. Feb 8, 1811 D. Feb 26, 1867
    Austin Peay D. 4 Dec. 1839 Age 70 yrs.
    Arabella E. Peay relict of John Peay, dau. of James and Margaret
    Rochell. B. Dec 29, 1793. D. Feb 17, 1869
    John Peay--B. Feb 1, 1789. D. Aug. 19, 1834

PEDGION, ISAAC--Miller--To John Wilson 250 A. Gr. to John Waight, Sr.
    12 Sept, 1768. 250 A. on 25 Mile Cr. Bd. John Waight, Jr. and Vac.
    and Samuel Waight conv. 100 A. to sd Isaac Pedgion. Wit: Joel
    Wilson, Sam'l Dougherty, Stephen Vedesto
    Fairfield C-188/189 Nov. 22, 1782

PHILLIPS, WILLIAM, John and James of Georgia Wit: deed to James Phillips
    of Fairfield 1785. Fairfield Deed Bk-A

PHILLIPS, JOHN--Adm: Jane Phillips. Aug. 13, 1788. Fairfield Wills Vol-1
                                                                         18
PICKET, CHARLES--Gr. 3 Dec. 1786 to Isaac Gibson. 150 A. on Hog Fork of
    Wateree Cr. Wit: Wm. Lewis, Jarvis Gibson (X)
    Fairfield Deed Bk B-170/173 10 Aug. 1788

PICKETT, MACAJAH to William Watts--100 A. fork of Wateree Creek. Sur.
    for John Lee--Orig. Gr. to Ambrose Miles, 16 May 1773 Fairfield C-59/60

POOLE, ADAM Pur. 1787 Fairfield Deed Bk-A

POPE, ISAAC RICKS to Benjamin Boyd--90 A. Gr. to John George Fertig for
    100 A.--22 Jan. 1759--found 10 Acres deficient. Also 75 A. Pt. 100 A.
    Gr. to Michael Easter (Feaster)22 Feb. 1771--Also 100 A. Pt 1200 A.
    Gr. to Col. Samuel Elliott 4 Dec. 1772--in its whole a plt'n of 265A.
    on Wildinson's Cr. of Broad R. Bd.--Frizzel McTier, Wm. Hughs,
    Richard Munsell, Samuel Elliott, John Elliott, Wm. McTire, heirs of
    John Holly. Plat in orig. pk. Wit: John Crawford, Thomas (X)
    Parrot. Fairfield C-160/161 1786

POPE, ISAAC RICKS to Barnaby Pope--P. A. to Collect in N. C.. 1786
    Fairfield Deed A-2 Pg-btm-7-12
    Pg 12--William Pope To Isaac Ricks Pope--1781

POTTS, JAMES of C.T. (X) to Wm. Anderson of Turkey Cr. Chester Co.
    100 A. on WWateree Cr. All Vac. Wit: Geo. Lesley, James Mitchell
    before Benj. Villemontort in C. T.

PORCHER, ISAAC Gr--? To James Andrews Sr. 29 Oct. 1775--700 A. (no Dower)
    To: Edward Andrews--Pt 200 A. Wit: William Daniel, John Pope,
    Elijah Gibson. Fairfield Deed B--? Aug. 9, 1788

POWELL, JOHN -w- Mary conv. 1795 to James Phillips of Fairfield. Wit:
    Wm. Phillips of Georgia, John and James Phillips 1785
    Fairfield Deed Bk-A-102

PRICE, WILLIAM of City of C. T.--Merchant. From Richard Winn, Sr.
    1219 Acres on Waters of Little R. of Broad R. Fairfield H-156/7 1793

QUARRELL, JOSEPH--Shoemaker of Winnsboro from John Winn of Winns. ½ A.
    on Vanderhorst St. Wit: Wm. Kirkland, D. Evans. Fairfield Deed Bk-A
    1787 Feb. 11. Pg-58 Same to same--Lot no 41 on Congress St.
    10 May 1789. Wit: Jacob Brown, D. Evans

QUARREL, JOSEPH of Winnsboro 1785 Fairfield Deed Bk-A

RABB, SAMUEL (Rawl)John, and Henry Fogler to Burrel Cook 100 A. N-s
    Broad R. Fairfield H-3/4 1790

RAIFORD, MATTHEW "son of Philip, Dec'd" Legatee of Thos. Routledge
    Will 9 Oct. 1761. Wm. Raiford, Exor. Fairfield Wills

RAIFORD, PATIENCE relict of Matthew Pearson. To--John Pearson "Colonel
    J. P." 400 A. orig. Gr. Rowland Williams and Philip Raiford-deed-
    N-s Broad R. Bd. John Adam Sumers and sd J. P. and sd R. W.
    Fairfield Deed N-357 July ? 1795

RAIFORD, PHILIP of Craven Co. -w- Judith from Rowland Williams and
    Wife Ailes of Craven Co. 223lbs 12/6. 300 A. N-s Broad R. Bd. S
    sd River--not navigable or vac. Dated 2 Aug. 1758. Prov. 7 Aug.
    1758. Wit: David Farmer and Jacob Busby Winnsboro C-98 1789

RAINS, ANTHONY , Dec'd of Fairfield Hist. Comm. Misc. Y-508
    Adm'r: John Rains Bond: 5 Nov. 1855

RANDOLPH, WILLIAM To Bond and Mtg. Jonathan Belton--200 A. on Bear Cr.
    Bd. John Wilson, Aaron Ootens (Wooten) and Per. Prop. Wit: James
    Wilson, Edmund Strange. Fairfield Deed I-46/47 July 20, 1793

REDMOND, ANDREW, "Gent". of City of C. T. 1785 Fairfield Deed A-31

REILEY, BRIANT -w- Mary of Fairfield to Margaret Richardson 150 A. Gr.·
    25 Oct. 1764 to Thomas McPhershion. Son and Heir of James McP.
    18 June 1783 to Briant and Reiley.
    Also 250 A. Gr. to David Wooten 24 Dec. 1772
    1 Jan. 1774 to Briant Reiley who sold off 60 A. to Patty Turnipseed.
    Wit: Samuel Ritcheyson (sp) Robert and Thomas R.

RICHARDSON, DAVID-no dower- To Enoch Grubbs. Gr. 6 Sept 1774--on dreans?
of Sandy River and Little R. all Vac. Wit: William Carter (Cater?)
John Moore, George Alsorn. Fairfield Deed B-32 Feb. 11, 1783

RICHARDSON, THOMAS SR. Gr. 22 Sept. 1771 200 A, to William Ball, Jr.
200 A. on Barton's Br. of Broad R. Wit: Robert Ritchardson,
Samuel Ritchardson, Rob't Bryman Fairfield Deed B-186/190
Feb. 5, 1784

RICHARDSON, WM. Fairfield Wills Bk-1-6 1800
Admx: Eleanor Richardson
Rec'd: 20 Apr. 1800
Aprs: James Davidson, William Bele, William Thomson

RICHEY, JOHN To James Grey 100 A. N-s Broad R. on Huffman's Cr. Sale
conditioned upon James Grey pay debt due by sd. Richey to Philip
Hart. Fairfield Deed B 194/197 Oct. 27, 1777

RILEY, BRYANT (sp Rayley, Rigley) To Bartholomew Turnipseed--60 A. Pt.
250 A. Gr. to Daniel Wootan 14 Jan 1774--who conv. to Bryan Reyly
31 Jan. 1774--Bd. Stephen Eleazer, John Turnipseed--Wit: Burn Pope,
David Watkins, and Jesse Frost. Plat. Fairfield Deed B-51
Jan. 27, 1785
ROBERTS AARON of Camden Dist. to Mary Henson.. Land on Taylor's Cr.
of Wateree. Wit: Isaac Gibson, Henry Sanders
Fairfield Deed A-519 Aug. 30, 1787

ROBERTS, AARON Pur. land on Dutchman's Cr. 15 Aug. 1787. Winnsboro Deeds

ROBERTSON, MARGARET FLYNN -w- of John Robertson Died March 8, 1864,
Age 69 yrs and 19 days.
Peay tombs in same square
Jane Robertson -w- Robert E. Robertson Died 19 Mar. 18__? age
69 yrs 19 days
Baptist Ch. Yard near Long Town, Fairfield Co.

ROBINSON, ALEXANDER JR. -w- Agnes to Alexander Robinson, Sr. Land Gr.
to John Stedman, 2 June 1769 sold to Alex'r. R. Jr.
Next--John Stedman -w- Ann to Alex R. Jr. 1784
Fairfield Deed Bk-A 1785

ROBINSON, HENRY -w- Mary Gr. Aug. 7, 1786-220 A. to George Vandevere
(Vandiver?) 50 A. N-s Broad R. Fairfield Co. on Waters of Rocky Cr.
Bd. Edward Vandevere, Drury Bishop, Winn's old fold, and sd H. R.
Wit: Elijah Major, Edward Vandevere, Adam Pool
Fairfield Deed B-27 Apr. 24, 1787

ROBINSON, THOMAS--Gr. 12 Sept. 1768 100 A. to John Yarborough, Sr. 100A.
on Thorntree of Wateree R. Wit: Robert Ewing, Jno. Bryant.
Fairfield H-166/167 1785

RODGERS, JAMES OF Dumpers Cr. Gr. to Susanna Rogers. Fairfield Deed A
1786

ROBUCK, WILLIAM Dec'd--Old Book Prob. Off. Fairfield Co. 1833
    Shares: Elias Robuck
            Rolley "
            Susanna -w- Thos Free
            Elizabeth -w- Cooper Haupman
            Nancy E. Robuck - Thos. Free, Gdn.
            Priscilla -w- Patrick Smith
            Ailcy -w- Joab Hill

ROCHELLE, JAMES -w- Margaret. Dau: Arabella E. -m- John Peay.
    See card Peay from tombstone Bapt. Ch. Yd. Fairfield Co.

RODLAND, NICHOLAS (or Rowland) -w- Mary Ann to Thomas Griffith--100 A.
    on both sides of 25 Mile Creek--Bd. survey for Samuel Wells and
    others. Fairfield File C. T. Deed Book B-4-312
                                              0?
ROGERS, JAMES -w- Elizabeth (X) Gr. 12 Feb. 1773 to Shadrach Wooley
    100 (160?) A. at present occupied by sd Rogers. Wit: Francis
    Coleman, Edward Moberly Fairfield Deed B-88/89 Mar. 11, 1788

ROGERS, JOHN, dec'd. David Montgomery-left state. Heir: James John
    Rodgers-minor. John Rodgers, Gdn. Winnsboro Prob. Bx 30-468 1822

ROGERS, JOHN--Gr. 15 Sept 1750 Heir Abraham Rogers conv. to Wm. Raiford
    23/24 Mar. 1761 Wm. -w- Sarah. Conv. to Wm. Tucker. 200 A. opp.
    Soxegotha. Bd. Philip Raiford, Sr. dec'd, Geo. Bosen
    Fairfield Land Mem 6-23 Archives Dept.

ROGERS, JOSEPH -w- Mary Fairfield Deed A 1784

ROGERS, HENRY -w- Elizabeth Gr. on Little R. to Joseph Cameron
    Fairfield Deed A 1786

ROTTEN, JOHN -w- Lithana to James Martin 200 A. Gr. to Richard Rotten
    11 Feb. 1756. Conv. 250 A. Wit: William Rotten, James Eades,
    Wm. Mark. Fairfield Deed A-B 233-236 Oct. 2, 1772

RUFF, CHRISTIAN of Newberry Co. to Jacob Feaster. 100 A. Gr. to Mary
    Feaster 25 May, 1774. Bd Catherine Ruff and Vac. Wit: Adam
    Cooper, Adam Keller, John Pratt, J. P Fairfield H 121-123 1791

RUFF, CHRISTIAN of Newberry Gr. 25 May, 1774 to Adam Cooper of Fairfield
    55 A. on Waters of McClures Cr. Wit: Jacob Feaster Fairfield H 13/14
                                                                    1791
RUTLAND, JAMES--his Gr. conv. -w-Sarah. Wit: Asa Rutland and John
    Robertson. Conv. to Robert Robb. Fairfield Deed A 1776

ROUTLEDGE, THOMAS Fairfield Wills Vol-1-32 29 Oct. 1761
    Dau: Rachel and Sarah "whom I left in Pensilvany".
    Heir: Mathew Raiford, son of Philip Raiford
    Wife: Margaret
    Date: Oct. 29, 1761
    Ex: Wife and Wm. Raiford
    Wit: John Edwards, Jacob Busby and John Riley
    Proven: 14 Apr. 1777

SANDERS, JAMES Gr. 8 Aug. 1772, owned by Thomas Parrott (X) to Wm.
Cato. 300 A. on a Br. of Little R. Bd. John Young, Thomas Parrott,
Thomas Nelson, Wm. Powell, Patrick Smith. Wit: Thos. Parrott, Jr.
Samuel Proctor, Nicholas Elington. Fairfield Deed B-125/127
July 24, 1787

BAPTIST CH. YD. FAIRFIELD CO. NEAR LONG TOWN.
Scott, B. R. B. Jan 6, 1827 D. Mar. 28, 1899
Pauline -w- B. R. Scott B. March 30, 1825 D. March 25, 1910
Pauline Scott -w- Rev. J. Ellison Jones B. Nov. 2, 1859 D. Nov. 16,
1885

SEMPLE, JESSE, Jr. Gr. 100 A. Conv. by Thomas McClarken of Fairfield to
John Turner, Esq. of Wateree Cr., Fairfield. 100 A. Gr. Bd. James
Cassey, Richard Friedly, John Stone, Spencer Bobo, Witaker. Wit:
David and Mary (X) Hamilton. Fairfield Deed C-169/170 July 3, 1789

SEVILLA, JOHN--Gr. 5 June 1786 to John Winn et al. 500 A. on Cedar Cr.
Bd. Jack Bethney, Mathew Raiford, and Wm. Trapp.
Fairfield Deed B-115/117 June 7, 1787

SHANNON, JOHN Fairfield Wills Bk-1-8 1800
Admrs: Creaton Buchanon and Samuel Clerk (or Clark)
Rec'd: 20 May, 1800
Aprs: David Patton, Cimson Camvion (?) Rob't Stile (?)

SHELTON, DAVID Fairfield Deed A 1787

SHIRER, ISAIAH of Camden Dist. To Daniel Dougharty of 96 Dist. 200 A.
N-s Broad R. Bd. Benj. Slutler, Martin Shirer et al. Orig. Gr.
to Martin Shirer 2 May, 1790. Heir: son-Isaiah Shirer. Wit:
James Dougharty, John Boyd, James Dougharty?
Fairfield Deed E-124 Dec. 30, 1780 200lbs sterlg.
Fairfield Deed AA-3 Sept 20, 1797
James Dougharty of Orangeburg Co. S. C. to Samuel Campbell. 100 A.
Gr. John Ewing Dec 1774. N-s Broad R. on a Br. of Little River.
Bd. Richard Nealy, Thos Wood, Earnard Elliott, Wm. Richardson.
Wit: Mary Trotti, Joseph Howell, Prob. Orangeburg Dist.

SHOEMAKER, JACOB Gr. 2 Jan. 1754--250 A. To Conrad Kinsler 25/26 March
1754. (D. intestate)Eldest son: Harmon Kinsler, Deed Gift to
John Kinsler, to John Pearson. Fairfield E-116/117 1780

SHROCK, HENRY Fairfield Wills Bk. 1-5 1800
Estate: Adm. Jonathan Belton
Rec'd 7 Mar. 1800
Aprs: David Camock, Alex Roseborough

SIBLEY, JESSE Gr. 4 Apr. 1791 To John Bagwell, 135 A. on a Br. of
Cedar Cr. of Broad R. Bd. Leonard Miles, John Woodward, James
Rutland, W. Simpson, Thos. Hall Fairfield Deed H-173/174 1793

SIBLEY, JOHN of Fairfield Gr. 3 July 1786 to John Arick--200 A. on
Dutchman's Cr. of Wateree. Wit: James Bowles, D. Evans.
Fairfield Deed B 201/204 Oct. 9, 1788
John Arick to John Sibley--169 A. Pt 640 A. Gr. sd John Arick.
3 Oct. 1785 B-205/207

SIMPSON, JOHN --Charged by Wm. McMorris. Falsely and scandalously
    maligned daughter, Ann. Acknowledged it was false, claimed he
    was drunk. Fairfield Deed A-2 Pg. 25 1787

SIMPSON, MARY AND JANE--Orphans. Capt. Wm. Robinson apt. Gdn. Nov.
    11, 1787 Fairfield Wills Vol 1-2 1787

SIMS, BENJAMIN to Son: Joseph Sims Fairfield Deed A-2 1789

SITZ, LEONARD -vs- Christian Sitz, et al Shares: Mary -w- George
    Amick. Mary Ann Smith -w- Eli Freshly. Est. Jacob Sitz, Dec'd
    Fairfield Probate 1835

SMITH, HUGH Gr. 6 Nov. 1786 to Robert Wilson 233 A. Pt. 545 A. on
    Morley's Br. of Wateree Cr. Gr. 6 Nov. 1786. Wit: Robert Erving,
    Abram Miller, Thos. Nesbit. Fairfield H-101/102 1791

SMITH, HUGH to John Shein Fairfield Deed A 1786

SMITH, JANE -- Dau James Roe Will 1839 Fairfield Wills

SMITH, JOHN, Sr. -w- Patience to John Smith Fairfield Deed A-193 1771
    John Smith, Jr. -w- Mary to Moses Cockrell-same land-1774

SMITH, JOHN Gr. 18 Aug. 1774--50 A. on Wateree Cr. Bd. John Bonner,
    Hugh Young. Conv. by Joseph Oldham -w- Perninah (X) to John Huston
    Wit: David Bonned (or Bonner-both ways) David Boyd.
    Fairfield Deed B- Jan. 3, 1783

SMITH, ROBERT (X) of Wateree Cr. to Bond and Mtg. Jonathan Belton of
    Springfield, Dutchman's Creek, Fairfield Co. 100 A. "whereon I
    now reside" on Beaver dam fork of Wateree Creek, Bd. Joseph
    Cameron, Hugh Smith-"being grant to my grand mother, Jean Smith,
    and at her death, willed to me". Also per. prop.
    Fairfield H-138/139

SMITH, STEPHEN Gr. 2 Oct. 1772--Heir: Jesse Smith--(X)--no dower.
    To Stephen Smith, Jr. 100 A. on Cedar Cr. orig. sur. for Wm. Goff.
    Fairfield Deed B-168-172 July 24, 1787

SMITH, STEPHEN -w- Sarah (both X) to Thomas Robinson, Weaver, 98 A. Gr.
    Isaac Heathcock 24 Dec. 1772 on Cedar Cr. Bd. Nightengals, Cowpens.
    Fairfield H-12/13 1792

SMITH, THOMAS of Fairfield to Handy Wooten--100 A. Gr. to John Woodward
    1 Jan. 1787 on Miley's Cr. Fairfield H-28/29 1791

STAIR, JAMES Dec'd. Share: Martha -w- Wm. Wylie, James Wright, Wm.
    White-gave receipt for, also Gdn. of Noble Wright's share.
    Old book Prob. Off Fairfield. 1836

STANTON, WILLIAM --Cit--Isaac Stanton, Adm. Heir: Martha E. Stanton,
    Minor. Charles Brown, Gdn. 1837. Sale: Joseph Stanton, John
    Stanton 1823. Widow: Rebecca -m- Gibson. Mary Ann Stanton, and
    Martha Emeline. Note: Thomas Stanton appears on deed index before
    Wills were kept. Jean must have been wife of Thomas
    Fairfield Probate Bx. 32-502

STARKE, THOMAS, SR. of Little River, Fairfield Dist.
Wife: Sarah
Son: Thomas
To: George Martin--Slave-Ann
Dau: Elizabeth King, Mary Perry, Fanny Queney
Friends: Capt. Reuben Starke and Capt. Jesse Haves, Exors.
5 July, 1806 Prov. 8 Aug. 1806 Fairfield Wills Vol 1 Bk 5-100

STARKE, WILLIAM of 96 Dist. Gr. 7 Nov. 1785 to James Kincaid--Gr 176 A.
on Patterson's Cr. of Indian Creek. Fairfield C-195/196 Dec. 28, 1787

STEVENSON, JESSE -w- Ferely (X) Gr. 3 Nov. 1770 To Martin Alkin (Elkin)
150 A. on Br. of Wateree Cr.--Fairfield Deed bk A-31. Wit: David
Read Evans, Jesse Havis

STEWART, ALEXANDER --Will not dated Winnsboro Box 31-490 Bk 6-Pg-186
Bro: James Stewart-Widow-
      Son: James Smith Stewart
            Wm. Archibald Stewart-minor
                All--
Lots in Winnsboro, Pro. of Capt. Jesse Havis. Orig. Will in File.
Provides for Widow of Bro. James--Elizabeth Stewart
File 488--James Stewart: Adm--Mrs. Elizabeth Buchanan. James
Stewart gave note and sd it on 25 Sept. 1809--1 Jan. 1812
Ret. shows--John Stewart. John Stewart-Sand Hills
Alexander Stewart of Village of Winnsboro. Prov. July 2, 1813

STEWART, JAMES S. of Winnsboro -m- set 16 Feb. 1846 Clarissa J.
Mushatt (Cl. sp. Marshall). Winnsboro File Misc P-341

STONE, JOHN Fairfield Deed A 1787

STRAUSNER, HENRY of Craven to Staffel Huffman--150 A. on Jane's Creek
Bd. Cr. and Vac. Wit: George Highley (Hiley or Bigley), Michael
Dickert, Michael Dickert, Jr. Fairfield Deed B-12 Aug. 12/13, 1783

STREET, BENJAMIN--of Fairfield Dist 1785 Fairfield Deed A

STROTHER, KEMP TALIAFERO of Fairfield. Deed Bk-B--60 July 10, 1786
To Thomas Baker:
        Gr. to Joseph Kirkland 8 March 1763
         "   "   "   "   29 Nov. 1770
         "   " John Smith   12 Nov. 1770
         "   " John Winn   25 July 1775
All on main road to Russell's Ferry. Conv. by Robert Ellison to
sd. K. T. S. 5/6 July 1786. All adj. John Winn to K. T. S.
10 May 1787, sev. lots (pg. 69)

STROTHER, KEMP TALIAFERO Fairfield Deed Bk A 1786
To John Compty--Merchant Fairfield C-207/208 1789
450 A. N-s Broad R. nearly apposite Saxagotha Twp. Orig Gr. to
Harris Michal Swagert and sold by his heir and son Jacob Swagert to
sd. K. T. S.

TAYLOR, MEREDITH to James Reiny 600 A. on Wateree Cr. 17 Apr. 1786
A or B 230/232

TIDWELL, PRISCILLA of Bush Co. Georgia to John Byrd of Bush Co. B/S
Horses. Wit: Michael Byrd. Probate Chester Co. Fairfield Deed A-2
1785
TIDWELL, ROBERT from John Winn 100 A. on Hog Fork of Wateree Creek
Fairfield H-157/158 1788

TITSHAW, STEPHEN Bd. deed Thos. Hill to John Wages S-f Little R. Gr.
to sd. Thos. Hill 1788 Fairfield I-439 Feb. 19, 1793

THOMAS, JAMES of Camden Dist. to Henry Lard (Laird?) of Camden Dist.
150 A. Pt. of 300 A. Gr. 18 May 1773 in a place called Joseph
Lard's Old Place. on little River. Wit: Anderson Thomas, Rich'd
Harris, Thomas Holsel (Holsell-also)

THOMAS, JOHN JR. Gr. 100 A. "whereon Mary Threewits-Widow now liveth--
on Mill's Cr. N-s Congaree. Mary Threewits, Sarah Williamson -w-
Roling Williamson, sisters of John Thomas. Conv. by John Threewits to Roling Williamson. Fairfield I-165 June 25, 1782

THOMPSON, ROBERT Gr. 25 Sept 1766 to Charles Picket 6/7 Apr. 1774
This day to John Ellison. Fairfield Deed B-156-158 May 16, 1788

THREEWITS, JOHN to Roling Williamson 100 A. N-s Congaree on Mill Creek
orig. Gr. to John Thomas, Jr. Fairfield H-116/117 June 23, 1782

TRAPP, JOHN -m- at home of John Andrews, Jr. Mary Colley. Jan 1, 1788
Wit: John Smith, Wm. Trapp. Deed A-2 1788

TRUE, JACOB Gr 200 A. on Beaver Cr.. Dec. 1, 1761. Conv. by Clement
Moberly to Andrew Feaster. Wit: Francis Coleman, Shadrach Wolley,
William Alsup. Fairfield Deed B-104/106 March 11, 1788

TURNER, ALEXANDER -w- Jane. Conv. Gr. to Wm. Turner 12 Sept. 1768
Fairfield Deed A- 1778

TURNER, JAMES -w- Sarah Wit: Alexander Turner Fairfield A-193 1777

TURNER, JANE --Widow of Alexander: To- John Turner Jr. and To- Wm.
McAllister Turner. Fairfield Deed A-2 Pg 5-7 1785

TURNER, JOHN -w- Margaret Gr. 6 Feb. 1773 To John Lee 100 A. Wit:
Richard Woolley, Henry McAllen. Fairfield Deed A or B 236/7
Jan. 2, 1777

TURNER, JOHN ESQ. Gr. 2 Feb. 1789 to Elizabeth McCullock-widow. 100 A.
Pt. 290 A. on Lick Br. of Wateree Cr. Bd. Robert Martin, Allen
Graffen, George Lot. Wit: Allen Graffen, Daniel McCullock.
Fairfield H-180 March 2, 1795
To: Robert Martin--100 A. Pt 290 A. on Lick Br. of Wateree Cr.
March 2, 1793. Same witnesses. H-181

VANDERHORST, JOHN Dec'd Late of C.T. Will 7 Feb. 1786
Exors: Arnoldus Vanderhorst and Thomas Waring, Sr. of C.T.
To: John Winn of Town of Winnsboro, 2 tracts--92½ A. and 31½ A.
near Town of Winnsborough. Fairfield C-177/178 May 17, 1788

VANSANT, GEORGE of Berkley Co. To William Mitcherson 500 A. N-s Broad R.
  Gr. to Nicholas Vansant. Wit: James Daniel, John Liles, Prob.
  25 Oct. 1758 before P. Raiford, J. P. Fairfield H-59/60 Oct. 21, 1758
  Apr. 9, 1782 H-64/65: Edward Mitcherson of Wilkes Co. N. C. to
  Robert Hancock--500 A. Gr. 1 Apr. 1756 to Nicholas Vansant--eldest
  son George Vansant conv. to William Mitcherson--intestate--son
  Edward Mitcherson. Wit: Jonathan Lewelling, John Pennington

WADE, DANIEL of Columbia--Gent. from John Winn--Lot in Winn. 1793
  Fairfield H-142/143

WALKER, HENRY of Fairfield Dist. Stepson, William Day, tract of land.
  Fairfield Wills Dec. 15, 1802

WALKER, JOHN Dec'd--Gr. 29 Apr. 1768--100 A. Gr. 23 March 1769
  Widow: Mary Walker
         Elizabeth -w- Wm. Walker
         Ann, Isaac, Charity, Jerusia or Busia, all of Georgia to
  Richard Winn, Esq. Bd. Gr. to Edward Walker. Wit: Benj. Mitchel,
  John Rotten. Fairfield H-20/21 May 23, 1790

WALTON, RICHARD -w- Major (X) Gr. 7 Oct. 1762 300 A. on Little R. to
  Burr Harrison. 300 A. Wit: John Roten (Rotten-both), Joseph
  Cameron, John Alton (X) Fairfield Deeds A or B 221-225 May 2, 1782

WARREN, CELENIA E. -w- John Warren B. Jan 28, 1807 D. Jan. 23, 1846
  Priscilla E. Warren dau of John Warren B. Dec. 11, 1836 D. July 16,
  From Bapt. Ch. Yd. Near Long Town, Fairfield Co.   1855

WATSON, WILLIAM to Duncan McRa and Zach'h Cantey Bond and Mtg.--slaves
  etc. Fairfield H-159 1793

WATTS, JOHN of Fairfield Co. To Nathan Sanders--Land on Wateree, orig Gr.
  to Ambrose Mills. His son, William Mills sold to Micahah Pickett.
  Wit: Henry Sanders William Tidwell (X) Fairfield A-508 Jan. 29, 1786

WATT, JOHN son in law of Alexander Kincaid--Will 1833. Wm. Watt, Exor.
  Mary Watts-dau of James Rabb. Will 1806 (James Rabb)

WATT, NANCY of Fairfield Dist. To dau. Rebecca E. Watt. Deed Gift--
  Slave 20 Dec. 1855. John Copeland, Tr. Misc. F.-316 Archives Dept.

WHITHEAD, JOHN from Minor Winn 338 A. on Wateree Cr. Fairfield H-173/4
                                                              1793
WILLY, PETER (or Wiley). Estate: Adm: John Willy, Wm. Willy, Eleanor
  Willy. Fairfield Wills Vol-1 14 May, 1788

WILLIAMS, THOMAS to Bond and Mtg. David McQuiston 170 A. N-s Broad R. on
  Turnip Patch Fork of Little R. Gr. 5 Nov. 1787. Bd. Thos. Land,
  Samuel Biggerstaff and Wm. Jones--also 30 A. Pt. 640 A. Gr. to Thos.
  Williams, 1 Aug. 1785 Fairfield H-175/6 Jan 3, 1792

WILLIAMSON, C. B. -w- Margaret Conv. to Sandy Level Church 19 Aug. 1856
  Sd C. B. Williamson, Margaret A. Williamson.
  Winnsboro Deed UU-610

WILLIAMSON, RØLING of Fairfield. Dau._____-m- Richard Hodges of
Georgia. Her ch: James Franklin Williamson Hodges, and Martha
Rebecca Hodges, minors. 5 Nov. 1818. Archives Dept. Misc. D-101

WILLIAMSON, ROLAND Dec'd Winnsboro Equity Roll Bx-68 Pkg-1037
Wife: Aily--all for life. Will 5 Mar. 1824. Prov. 25 May, 1824
Ch: Thomas T. Williamson
    Jemima A.
    Lucy R. Waring
Gr. Dau: Martha Williamson
         Sarah Dubose
         Ailey Woodward
         Martha
Don: John
     Roling
Dec'd. Dau: Mary Heath's Ch:

WILLSON, JOHN Fairfield Wills Wills Bk1-13 Dec 23, 1799
Wife: Rebeccah
Sons: James--Prop. formerly of Rich. Taylor
      Neuphilus (or Theophilus-not clear.) Orig. Gr. Jas. Freeman
      Jesse   and Louis Berry
Dau: Nancy Mitchell
     Susannah Rush
     Martha Norris or Novis
Sons: Joel and Wilson Willson
Gr. Son: Wm--sonJohn "Lawyer's tract on Bear Cr.
         James Willson
         John Norris--Land formerly of Sam'l Nipper
Dau: Mary Lanyham
Heirs: Sam'l Lanyham
       John Rush
Ex: Sons: Jas. and Theo. and Sam'l Lanaham. Wit: Geo. Watts
Randal Simmons, Patrick Marvin. Rec'd. 23 Aug. 1800

WILSON, JAMES of Horse Br. of Wateree Creek in Fairfield Co. To--Bond
and Mtg.--Horses, hogs, etc. Jonathan Belton of Springfield,
Dutchman's Cr. Fairfield H-160/161 March 1, 1793

WILSON, JAMES--Living Richland Equity Pet. 156 Fairfield Families 1820
Ch: Jacob--dec'd
    Elizabeth -w- Anthony Rains
    Judith -w- James Duke
    Lucy -w- Littleton Crankfield
    Dec'd Dau: Margaret -w- Aaron Johnson
               Ch: John, Fred, Samuel, Rhoda, Mary, Jesse,
                   Patsy, Judith, Elizabeth, Caroline

WILSON, JOHN of Richland Co. from Samuel Langhan (or langham) 310.
on Lawyers Br. of Bear Creek--Bd. J. W. and Vac. Fairfield A-?
Jan 25, 1786

WILSON, JOHN JR. Dec'd. Camden Bx 74-2640 1782
Cit: 15 Feb. 1782 Rd. by Ralph Jones, Minister
Adm'x: Dicksy Ward-m- widow of dec'd.
Bond: 19 March, 1782, Elias Ward, Moses Jordan
Appr: James Langhon, Jesse Wilson, William Jones, Charles Seal,
                                                  Robert Elkins
WILSON, LEVI -w- Isabella -vs- Jeptha Arledge-wife et al.
Shares: Thos. Loughbridge. Old Book Fairfield Prob. Off. 1832

WINN, JOHN to Richard Winn. sd. lots listed. Wit: M. Winn, John Turner
Fairfield Deed B-61 Nov. 14, 1786

WINN, JOHN of Fairfield--no dower to Ephraim Hutford, Shoemaker of
Winnsborough for Pt. 13 A. Gr. in Winnsborough. Wit: John Milly
James Bowles. Fairfield Deed B-26. Aug. 14, 1787

WINN, JOHN of Town of Winnsboro to James Douglas-Carpenter of Winns.
½ A. on Congress St. Fairfield Deed B-50 July 21, 1787

WINN, JOHN -w- Penelope To William Coleman--Gr. 21 June 1785 to John
Winn 100 A. on Beaver Cr. Bd. W. C. Wit: Robert Coleman, Richard Winn
Fairfield Deed B-83 Nov. 11, 1781

WINN, JOHN to James Brown, Hugh Milling and John Buchanan--Long list of
grants, listed on 25 Mile Creek--etc. Fairfield A or B 224/228
March 10, 1788

WINN, JOHN JR. to Dau: Love and Affec. Eliza Martha Sophia Winn.
John Winn, Sr. and David Evans, Trs. 230 A. on Wateree Cr. "whereon
sd John Winn now lives". Wit: David Reed Evans, Wm. Rees, Jr.
Fairfield H-155-156 Nov. 26, 1792

WINN, MINOR Dec'd of Va. Will. Fairfield Deed A-2 Pg-63 1780's
Son: Minor Winn of Va.
       William   "
       Richard   "   All of Fairfield, S. C.
       John   "
Pg. 64. Dau: Susannah

WITHERSPOON, WILLIAM   Gr. 13 Aug. 1756 to Thos. Williams--300 A.
13/14 Jan. 1758 to Wm. Witherspoon 150 A. to Thos. Sing -w- Joanna
14/15 Jan. 1761 to Wm. Powell and John Powell. John Powell d.
intestate. Wm. Powell d. intestate-no issue- Eldest Bro. To
Wm. Powell -w- Mary--parties here to his eldest son and heir, who
conv. to John Finley.
Pg. 250--John Witherspoon bd. Gr. to David Read Evans on Foxes Cr.
of Wateree--1794
Pg. 395--Gr. to John Witherspoon 13 Oct. 1772. To John McKinney
Fairfield Deed I-228/9 Sept. 13, 1794

WOODWARD, HENRY Deed A Fairfield 1786

WOODWARD, JOHN, Yeoman--no dower--To Thomas Smith 550 A. orig Gr. to
John Woodward 1 Jan. 1787. Wit: Thos. Parrot, Jr. Paul Wootan
Thos. Nelson. Fairfield Deed B-48 July 14, 1787

WOODWARD, THOMAS Dec'd--Will Fairfield Deed A- 1786
Dau: Elizabeth Woodward, Spinster 1786 to Thomas May.

WOODWARD, THOMAS--Will--Beq. to Son: William Woodward--125 A. Pt 450 A.
on John Marple's Br. of Broad. Orig. Gr. to Wm. McMorris who conv.
to T. W. 100 A. on Mill Cr. of Little R. Gr. John Winn. 26 A. on
Mill Cr. to John Sibley. 100 A. and 100A. both Gr. sd T. W. and
Wm. W. Sold to Kemp Taliafero Strother. To Minor Winn.
Fairfield Deed B-172/175 Jan 10, 1788

WOODWARD, THOMAS Gr. 22 Aug. 1771 to Peter Sterns. 368 A. on Mill Cr.
To: Janet Wilson "Now in her actual possession. 100 A. on N-s
To: Philip Raiford 100 A. Gr. T. W. Fairfield N-8/9 Aug. 4, 1790

WORSTER, REUBEN JUDD of Winnsborough--Tailor from John Winn, Esq. Lots.
Fairfield Deed C-50/51 1788

WOOTEN, BENJAMIN Of Wilkes Co. Ga. from Richard Winn P. A. To collect
from Nathaniel Marshall Martin of Georgia Fairfield Deed A-2 1787

WOOTAN, DANIEL Planter--Gr. 15 Oct. 1784 259 A. --no dower. To James
Daniel Gr. 259 A. Bd. Wm. Bell, Jr., Wm. Bell, Sr., James Daniel--
Conv. "all the sd 259 Acres". Wit: James Gunnels, Benjamin Scott,
John Bell. Fairfield Deed B-36 Feb. 8, 1785

WOOTIN, DANIEL--Gr. 19 Sept. 1770 to James and Edward Gregg. 150 A.
N-s Broad R. Bd. John Fraser, John Gregg. Fairfield Deed B-176/9
Dec. 5, 1787
WOOTAN, DANIEL To John Pearson 118 A. on Wilkinson's Cr. Bd. heirs of
Benj. Mathews, George Seigler, Heir of Herman Kinslen, Adam
Hawthorn, John Pearson. Wit: James Gunnell, Levi Daniel
Fairfield Deed A or B 207/209 Nov. 12, 1788

WOOTAN, HARDY -w- Jane (both X) To Samuel Clampet 65 A. Pt 250 A. Gr.
to John Woodward on 1 Jan. 1787-who conv. to Thomas Smith. and
he to John Brent 150 A. and the other pt to Hardy Wooten. 3 Sept.
1791. Wit: _____Netterville? Wm. Netterville, Wm. Russell.
Fairfield H-103/104 1792

WOOTAN, JOHN To John Kelly Gr. to Charles Seal 150 A. on Sawney's Cr.
24 Jan. 1770. Wit: Aaron Wootan, Moses Wootan. Fairfield H-41/42
1787
YARBOROUGH,"MAJOR" Rachel Yarborough apt. admx. Mar. 31, 1788
Fairfield Wills Vol. 1-12

YOUNG, ANDREW--no dower here--To William McClintock. Gr. to Charles
Spradling and Andrew Young Feb. 11, 1773--110 A. on Branches of
Wateree Cr. Bd. Hugh Young. Wit: Alexander Johnston, William
Fearys, Alexander Miller. Fairfield Deeds B-15 Mar. 1, 1787

YOUNG, HUGH -w- Margaret to John McComb--Land on Wateree Cr.
Fairfield Deed A- March 23, 1786

YOUNGE, SAMUEL M. W. Fairfield Deed A- 1787

YONGUE, SAMUEL W. To Jonathan Harrison 112½ A. Pt 450 A. Gr. to John
Phillips. Fairfield H-36/37 1792

GREENVILLE COUNTY, SOUTH CAROLINA

The unusual spelling of some words, and the abbrev-
iations are those of the original copier, as are the
remarks in Quotation marks, and parenthesis.

F. Courtney

ABBOT, Alsey--Daughter of Wm. McClanahan, Will 1802. Will Book A-175

ABNER, Paul to Aaron Kemp, 1786. Deed Book A-113

ALEXANDER, John to James Hiett, 1787. Deed Book A-31

ARMSTRONG, Matthew to James McWilliams on 21 January 1785--on Reedy
     River above the ancient boundary line. Deed Book A-7

ARNOLD, Benjamin--Will 30 January 1796. Wife--Ann. Eldest son
     William, deceased. (Sons Anderson and William to have land in
     Bedford County where William lived.) Will Book A-105
     Son: Edward
   Y Son: Benjamin
     Son: Hendrick, deceased, his son, William
     Son: John--Land where he now lives.
     Son: Thomas--Land where he now lives
     Daughter: Charity Martin
     Daughter: Temperance Hamilton

AUSTEN, Nathaniel--B/S to William Austen. 1788 Deed Book A-239

AYRES, John--To: Benjamin Bowling, a minor, son of Nancy Bowling,
     now Nancy Cooper wife of John Cooper. Sept. 1, 1808 Book A-107
     Brother: Joseph Ayres
     Brother: William Ayres
     "my brothers and sister"

BARNES, Mary to Elliott Smith. 1787. Deed Book A-35

BARNHILL, James--son in law of Hardy Roberts, 1789. Will Book A-24

BARRETT, Reuben and wife Hannah, to Benj. Ellis, 1786 Deed Book A-38

BARTON, Thomas from William Barton and wife Elizabeth, 1787, Deed Book A-73

BENSON, Wm. and wife Nelley to Joseph Benson. Also to John Evans. 1786
     Deed Book A- 80 and A-84

BISHOP, Abner and wife, Mary, to Daniel Ford. 1787. Deed Book A-26

BLACK, Hans and wife, Ann to Henry Linderman, 24 November 1786.
     Witnesses: James West, Jacob Black, Thomas Jones. Deed Book A-6

BLACKBURN, Ambrose to Joel Charles. Both of Greenville County.
     110 A. Plt. N-S Saluda R. Gr.--1st May 1786. Pres. William
     Wilson, John Ware. 3 January 1788. Deed Book A-253

BLACKBURN, J Ware from Ambrose Blackburn. East side Golden Grove
     Creek beginning on S. E. line. Said tract where Capt. Maxwell's
     line crossed the said landxxxx. Gr. said Ambrose Blackburn
     15 October, 1784. May 20, 1788. Deed Book A-256

BOWLING, Nancy "now Nancy Cooper". Son: Benjamin Bowling--heir of
     John Ayres. Will 1808. Will Book A-107

BOX, Joseph to Joseph Williams, also to Abner Norris, also to Wm.
 Woody. Wit: Wm. Young, John Young. 1788. Deed Book A-220 & 222

BRASHER, Thomas, wife Sarah. Will 27Sept. 1788. Prov. 6 Apr. 1790
 Son: Thomas   Will Book A-28
   "   Inellea (or Quilla)
   "   John
   "   Samuel--Home place
   "   Henry.

BREEDLOVE, Benjamin W. Died Nov. 1804 in Edgefield District. Adm.
 Garrett Longview. Widow: Letty, Admt. Married Julius Nichols
 prior to 1810. One son; John Watkins Breedlove. Married
 Drury Mims of Edgefield. Sister of Wm. Wade of Rutherford Co.
 N. C. (Letty was) Letty m. 3 Edward Dill Dec. 1825

BRIDWELL, Elizabeth; daughter of John Edwards, will 1799. Book A-191
 See also will of Salley Edwards 1809

BROOKS, Peter and wife, Mary and Nath'l and Benj. Perry. 1786 Book A-108

BROWN, David and wife Sarah, to David Lovell 1787. Deed Book A-193

BROWN, Isaac and wife Molly to Elias Earle 1787. Deed Book A-121

BRUCE, Mary, daughter of John Edwards. Will 1799. Will Book A-191
 See also Will of Sally Edwards 1809

CANNON, Sinecoch to Russell Cannon 1787. Deed Book A-133

CHANDLER, Jesse to Shadrack Chandler 1787. Deed Book A-130

CHANDLER, Jesse to Andrew Jones 1788. Deed Book A-181

CHILDRESS, John to George Salmon 1787. Deed Book A-58

CHILDRESS, John to Robert Nelson 1788. Deed Book A-216

CHOICE, Rebecca--daughter of Drury Sims. Will 1799. Will Book A-146

CLARK, Benjamin to Benjamin Merit 1788. Deed Book A-229

COLLINS, John of Spartenburg to Hugh Warren, Sen. Wit: Hugh Warren, Jr.
 Richard Collins. Deed Book A-168 1787

COLLINS, John Will 8 June 1792. Wife. Oldest daughter, Catherine
   Gilbert
   Son: William Collins
   Dau: Elizabeth Collins
   Son: John Collins
   Son: Abner
   Mentions small child "not named" Will Book A-54

COMBS, John, of North Carolina, Washington County to John Molin of
 Greenville. To sell land on Beaver Dam Creek-on W. side N-fork
 Saluda River. 20 Sept. 1787 Deed Book A-213

COOKSEY, Sally--daughter of Nicholas Fisher, Sen. Will 1794 Book A-62

COOPER, Nancy, formerly Nancy Bowling. Son--Benjamin Bowling--heir of John Ayres. Will 1808 Will Book A-107

COPPS, Martha # w -. Infant daughter of Charles Mone - W1814

COX, Anna--a daughter of Drury Sims. Will 1799. Book A-146

COX, Margaret w. Randal Cox. Son of John Moore-E-1857. Book A-16-48

CRAIN, Judith, Will Jan. 19, 1791 "my 5 ch" "my 3 Boys"
```
     (1)
     (2)
     (3)
     (4) Daughter-Susanna          Ment "my 5 small ch"
     (5) Daughter-Nancy            Enoch Benson and Dr. Nelson,
     Son:  Charles                 gdns.  Will Book A-47
     To:   Tolley Evans
     To:   Samuel Crain
     To:   William Crain
     To:   John Crain
```

CURETON,David--Heir of John Moore (or Moon) of Greenville, S. C. 1839

DANIEL, Nelly--A daughter of Leonard Tarrant. Will 1791 Will Book A-41

DANIEL, William Son of Nancy Hickman and John Ware. Apprenticeship. 1787 Deed Book A-234

DAVIS, Joseph--Heir of David Moore - w - 1795. (Must be son-in-law). Greenville Wills Apt 6-348

DAVIS, Thomas O. -w-. Mary of Spartanburg Co. to George Hains of Greenville Co. 1788 Deed Book A-218

DILL, John Will 7 March 1807. Wife: May Ann Dill, Gr. Dau: Peggy Randolf. Son: Renals (or Reynolds Dill). "all my children" all not named. Will Book A-198

DINING, John to Clabourn Swillivant 1788 Deed Book A-169/70

DOEG, Thomas to William Ross 1785. Deed Book A-142

DUFF, Dennis to Samuel Earle 1786. Deed Book A-125

DUNKLIN, Elizabeth, Joseph, John. Heirs of Wm. Ship. Will Book

DUTTON, Jeremiah and wife, Sarah to George Salmon 1787. Deed BookA-61

EARLE, Baylis to Joseph Whitner 1787. Wit: John Earle, Jun'r, Baylis Earle, Jun'r, Ephraim Rees. Deed Book A-114

EARLE, Baylis--J. P. Commissions. John Thomas, Jun'r. Henry White, John Ford, James Jordan, William Wood, Henry Machen Wood. Commission as J. P. under act of 24 March 1785. "An act for Est. and County Courts" Ast. of Oaths follow. Spartanburg Deed Book A-42

EARLE, John, Jr. to Samuel Earle 1787. Deed Book A-135/6

EASLEY, Daniel O, Daniel W. also Weldon Family 1760-1785 Rowan Co.

EDWARDS, John, Wife, Henrietta Will 29 Sept. 1799 Will Book A-191
 Dau: Sarah Edwards
 Son: William "
 Dau: Elizabeth Birdwell (or Bradwell) *BRIDWELL*
 Dau: Mary Bruce
 Son: Joseph Edwards
 Son: John "

EDWARDS, Sally, Will 9 March 1809. Will Book A-194
 Mother_____ a man, etc
 Sister: Betsy Birdwell
 Sister: Polly Bruce

ELDER, Thomas from Albert Robins and wife Betsy Robins of Greenville
 District. 4 January 1806. $350.00 on the low-west side of
 Reedy River, Greenville Dist. orig. gr. to Andrew Thompson.
 2 February 1789. Deed Book G-403

ELKIN, Thomas Wadsworth--a grown son of William Hunt. Will 1804
 Will Book A-178

ELLISON, Elizabeth--step daughter of Isaac Morgan. Will 1794 Book A-65

FIELD, John A. died. Bill for partition Amos L. Sutherland and wife.
 Elizabeth Field, et al Pickens Dist. Feb. 2, 1849

FISHER, Nicholas, Sen'r. Will 2 Apr. 1794. Wife: Elizabeth Book A-62
 Son: Thomas Fisher
 " : Nicholas Fisher, Jr. the youngest
 Dau: Peggy Fisher
 Dau: Anice Fisher
 Ex'rs: Thomas and John Fisher and James Tubb
 Son: John
 Son: James
 Dau: Mary Tubb
 Dau: Sally Cooksey
 Dau: Elizabeth McVay

FORD, John, Will 15 Oct. 1795. Wife Ann Will Book A-74
 Son: Isaac
 Son: William
 Dau: Leah Ford
 Dau: Linna Ford
 Dau: Polly
 Dau: Tressia
 Son: Arasmus
 To: Stacey Sibley for 10 yrs. service, mare

FORD, Mary Will 6 May 1799 Will Book A-145
 4 Bros.---   Mother: ?
 Sister: Leah   Sister: Preashey Stokes
 Sister: Salinda
 Bro: Levy

FORD, Mary--same as Polly in will of John Ford Est. 1806. Died about
      1800--(see my John Ford pkg). Admx: Ann Ford Goodlett(her mother)
      Return Aug. 1, 1808, Pd. to Isaac, Erasmus, Lin, Wm. sd. "Ann
      Goodlett late Ann Ford". Return 7 July 1806. Heirs: Lin Ford,
      Leah Ford, Tess Ford, Pressia Stokes, Erasmus Ford, Wm. Ford.
      Will: Date 26 May 1799. Wit: Zadock Ford, Mary Slazebrook.
      Prov. 1800

FORRISTER, James Will 4 July 1790. Prov. 26 May 1791 Book A-40
      Wife: Elizabeth, Sons: Hardy, Richard, John

FOSTER, John Greenville Wills Book A 1787
      Dau: Mary Hendly   Son: Josiah Foster
      Dau: Frances Hendly   Son: James Hackett Foster
      Son: John Crow Foster   Son: Robert Singleton Foster
      Son: Geo. Singleton Foster   Dau: Nance

FURGERSON, William, & W. Caty to Michael Henderson 1788 Deed Book A-225
      Wit: Frury Morris, Peggy Furgerson, John Henderson.

GILBERT, Catherine--oldest daughter of John Collins will 1792 Book A-53

GOODE, Frances N? dec'd. Greenville Probate Apt 6 Pr-397
      She seems to be dec'd daughter of Thomas Rowland and she had
      children.

GOODE, Richard and wife Rebecca to William Nelson 1786 Deed Book A-116

GOODWIN, Crofford to John Birdsong 1787 Deed Book A-69

GREEN, Joseph m set 3 Jan 1843 Frances Benson

GREGORY, Polly--heir of John Peden Will 1810. Will Book A-202.
      Seems to be his daughter.

GROGAN, David vs John Gowen. Suit over note, in file, dated dec. 7,
      1800 given by John Gowal to David Grogan. Greenville Judgement 760

GROGIN, Thomas and wife, Hannah of Greenville Co. to Jno Westfield
      397 A Golden Grove Creek. 1788 Deed Book B-82 (or Crogin? Shows
      Crogin, not signature. Also shows in body "Scrogin").

GROGAN, Elizabeth, son, David Grogan. Elizabeth, sister of George
      Wolf. Will 24 March 1812

HAINS, George of Greenville Co. from Thomas Davis and wife Mary of
      Spartanburg Co. 140 A--part of 240 A gr. to sd. Davis by Wm.
      Moultin 5 Dec. 1785--g-s Co both sides S-Tyger R. 14 Feb. 1788
      Deed Book A-218

HAINE, George and Wife Margaret of Greenville Co. to Duncan McWilkins,
of same place. 140 A Tyger River. Part grant 240 A to Thomas Deavea
(Davis) 5 Dec. 1785--for Gov. Moultine. 14 Feb. 1791. Deed Book B-272

HAMILTON, Temperance--Daughter of Benjamin Arnold Will 1796 Book A-105

HANKS, Luke Will 29 Apr. 1815. Will of Thos. Crayton directs lands
    on Hencoop Creek, Pendleton Dist. be sold to Luke Hanks.
    Abbeville Wills--Book 1, P 822. Will of Luke Hanks 21 May, 1789.
    Wife, Ann. "All my children". Will Book B-84

HARRISON, John, Will 3 July 1818. Wife. 2-Y sons: Thomas Creighton,
    James Alexander. 5 ch. not named. Will Book A-182

HARRISON, Susannah, in law of John Harrison. Will 14 Jan. 1846
    Son: Thos. C. H.   Son: John M. Harrison
    Dau: Mary Walker w Thos. Walker D-in-law: Laura Harrison
    Son: Jas. A. Harrison   "   Elleanor Harrison
    Son: Wm. Harrison   "   Sarah Harrison
    Will Book D-247 P. 244

HAWKINS, Joshua Will 16 May 1801 Will Book A-181
    Wife: Sarah Cook Hawkins
    Y-son: Pinckney Hawkins
    Grand son: Isham S. Hawkins
    Son: Eaton

HAYNES, John, "my 2 eldest daus:" Centhia and Sarah
    "Eldest son" Henry   40 A pos. of Joseph L. Beck.
    Son: John H. Haynes   200 A on Savannah R. called Point
    Dau: Mary E. Haynes   Comfort and also 200 A in Bush
    To: Elbert Corey-education ?   Co. Ga. on Savannah R. called,
    Ex: 2 sons. 11 Sept. 1830   "Williams Cider House". Bd. John
    Proven. 27 Sept. 1830. Wit: Phinizy, G. B. Pomar, and Est.
    Silas O'Neal, John M. Turner,   Richard Hankinson, Dec'd.
    John M. Turner, Jr.
    Bdl. 54 Pkg. 2 Barnwell Co. Wills Vol. 2-41

HAYNES, Hiram--a wit. will Ambrose Petty 14 Mar. 1834. Pickens Wills

HAYS, Henry to Benjamin Wharton 1786 Deed Book A-112

HEADEN, William to Anthony Beverly 1786 Deed Book A-102/3

HEEPREYS, Annas, common law wife of Charles Moore 1814

HENDERSON, James to Daniel Bush 1787. Greenville Deed Book A-44

HENDERSON, James to Isham Clayton 1787. Deed Book A-214

HENDERSON, John of Abbeville Co.to Isaac Mayfield of Greenville Co.
    1788 Deed Book A-235

HENDERSON, Robert to John Clayton 1787   Deed Book A-211

HIMMELWRIGHT, William of Philadelphia, Pa. to Thomas Lewis of
    Greenville, Co 1788 Deed Book A-205

HODGES, Elizabeth--daughter of Francis Kirby, Will 1798. Book A-114

HONE (OR HORNE), Judy--daughter of Francis Kirby (?) Will 1798 Book A-114

HOWARD, Edward Will 15 May 1808. Wife, Mary. Y-son; Edward Howard,
"7 of my daughters: Rebecca, Susannah, Priscilly, Leah, Margaret,
Sarah, Avis." Land grants to John Howard. "Ment--my wife and
12 children". Ex. son John Will Book A-189

HUDSON, Kenner and wife Sary to Hance Black. Gr. to sd Hudson of
Reedy River. 13 Oct. 1786 Deed Book A-11

HUGHES, Joseph of Union Co. to Samuel Earle 1788 Deed Book A-175

HUNT, Esli and wife, Nancy to Baylis Earle 1787 Deed Book A-93

HUNT, William. Will 20 Jan. 1807 Will Book A-178
    Wife: Mary
    Dau: Tabby (or Tolly) Proceeds of slave to be sold by Dyer
    Son: James   Talley 1 in granville Co. N. C.("Given
    Dau: Salley   me by my Uncle Jonas Hunt").
    Dau: Polly's son Thomas Wadsworth Erkin
    Dau: Nanny
    Dau: Elizabeth
    Dau: Rose
    Son: Davis

HUSH, (May be Rush) Martha Caroline (seems dec'd). Daughter of
John Moore--E 1857 Greenville Wills Apt16-48

JACKSON, Elizabeth Will 15 Nov. 1809 Will Book A-199
"my 2 daughters:" Diannah Morgin (or Morgan, and Sarah Jackson

JEFFERAS, George to John Stanford 1787 Deed Book A-146

JONES, Jans (or Jincy) wife of John W. Jones, Dau. of Elisha Moore
E-1842 Will Book Apt G.-318

JUSTINE, John to Thomas Barton 1788 Deed Book A-186

KEMP, Aaron to Moses Kemp 1786 Deed Book A-111

KILGORE, Polly Heir of John Moore (or Moon) of Greenville, S. C. 1839

KIRBY, Elizabeth, a daughter of Leonard Tarrant Will 1791 Book A-41

KIRBY, Francis Will 16 April 1798. Kirby also sp. Curby. Book A-114
    Wife: Seems to be Elizabeth
    Son: John
    Dau: Elizabeth Hodges
    Son: Jesse
    Indy Hone (or Horn)
    Ann Simson (or Simpson)
    Dau: Mary Tucker
    Dau: Susannah Curby (or Kirby)

LAND, Sarah -W- Benjamin Land, Dau. of Reuben Smith. Will 1810
Will Book A-200

LANGSTON, John Will Mar. 1, 1782 Will Book A-29
    Son: James
    Son: Solomon
    Gr. Son: Asa
    "   " : Solomon
    Son: Jechonias--the place he lives on
    Dau: Molley Smith
    Dau: Rebecca (Bekka) Williams
    Dau: Fanney Langston
    Dau: Sally Smith
    Son: Samuel
    Dau: Elizabeth Spannone (?)
    Son: Joseph
    Son: Jesse
    Gr. Son: John, son of Jesse
    Son in law: Thomas Williams
    Dau: Lusia Thompson   Dated 1st March, 1782

LEWIS, Hugh to Baylis Earle 1785 Deed Book A-57

LEWIS, Hugh and wife Elizabeth to Esli Hunt 1787. Deed Book A-96

LEWIS, Hugh--"abt to move from S. C. to Cumberland River, N. C.
    to John Sowen. 1788--Rec'd P. A. 1785. Deed Book A-215

LEWIS, Thomas, "Clerk" to William Furgerson 1787. Deed Book A-158

LEWIS, Thomas to Thomas Camp 1787. Deed Book A-100

LEWIS, Thomas of Greenville Co. to William Himmelwright of the city
    of Philadelphia, Pa. 1788. Wit: Vincent Lewis, John Lewis,
    Jesse Carter. Deed Book A201

LIGON, Nancy--Heir of John Moore (or Moon) of Greenville, S. C. 1839

LUCAS, John and wife Sarah to John Childress 1787. Deed Book A-145

MACHEN, Henry of Virginia--Prince William Co. Will 3 Apr. 1752
    Prov. pr. Wm. Ct. 24 Aug. 1752 Will Book A-55
    Wife: Grace--Preg.
    Son: Henry
    Son: John
    Son: Thomas
    Dau: Mary Machen
    Bro: Thomas Machen

MALIN, John and Wife, Elizabeth to Benj. Merit 1788. Deed Book A230

MARTIN, Charity, Daughter of Benj. Arnold. Will 1796 Book A-105

MOORE, David to John Thomas, Jun'r 1788. Deed Book A-173

MOORE, Hugh of Abbeville Co. to Robert Prince of Greenville, Co.
    1788. Deed Book A-196

MORGAN, Isaac to Paul Abner 1787. Deed Book A-174

MORGAN, Isaac. Will 12 Oct. 1794. Book A-65
    Wife: Nancy
    Son: Jesse)
    Dau: Jean) minors
    "My wife's dau: Elizabeth Ellison

MORGAN, Diannah--a daughter of Elizabeth Jackson. Will 1809 Book A-199

MOTLOW, John to Robert Laughridge 1787. Deed Book A-154/5

MULLINOX, Elizabeth, Infant daughter of Charles Moore. Will 1814

McKNEELY, Milly--a daughter of Drury Sims. Will 1799. Book A-146

McKINZIE, Sallie--a daughter of John Tarrant. Will 1799. Book A-109

McVAY, Elizabeth--daughter of Nicholas Fisher. Will 1794. Book A-7

McWILLIAMS, James and wife, Rosanna to Henry Linderman. 24 Oct. 1785
    Land on Reedy River--Gr. sd. J. Mc.

NELSON, Permelly--of Green Pond, Tuscaloosa, Ala. Heir of Charles
    Moore. W-1814

NELSON, Robert. Will 24 March 1808. Book A-196
    Wife: Rebecca Nelson
    Son: Robert Nelson
    Dau: Mary Molin
    Gr. Son: Absalom Cleyton (or Clayton)
    Dau: Jean Langford (or Gean L.?)

ODOM, John Sen'r to John Jr. 23 April 1817. Deed Book A-60
    Land on Pack's Creek, waters of South Tyger River, Greenville
    District. Pt. grant to Reuben Barrett. Sd. John Odom (X his mark)
    Wit: Peter Howard, Sarah Howard

PARSONS, Martha to her children Lucy and Sarah Parsons 1788. Book A-220
    Wit: Robert Nelson, William Nelson

PASSONS, Major and wife, Elizabeth to John Thomas 1786. Deed Book A-54

PATEES, Tobias to John Stanford 1787. Deed Book A-161

PATRICK, Melissa E.--of Green Pond, Tuscaloosa, Ala. Heir of Charles
    Moore. Will 1814. 1814-1877

PAYNE, George (or Peyn) Will 4 July 1797. Sd Thos. X Peyn-by mark.
    Wife: Ann
    Dau: Prudence
    Dau: Rachel
    Dau: Luany
    Son: Thomas)
    Son: James) Exors. Will Book A-108

PEDEN, John Sen'r. Will 13 May 1810. Will Book A-202
   Wife   Dau: Peggy
   Son: Samuel--L where he lives Dau: Polly
   Son: John   Dau: Jenny
   Son: James   Dau: Lizz (or Elizabeth)
   Son: William   To: Polly Gregory--clothing

PETTY, Jesse (or Paty. Will 9 Nov. 1795. Bx 2-23-Book A-42
   Wife: Delilah "my 5 ch"
   John Paty
   James Paty
   Son: Lora_____ (unreadable-c)
   Mary Paty
   Joshua Paty
   Son: Charles Paty 5sh
   Dau: Delilah Mullins

POTTS, Permela W. Levi Potts. 1814. Daughter of Charles Moore
   W-1814.
   Her ch: H. Powell Potts--Ch: Terrell
   Ira D. Potts   Permella Ann Cooper
   Tyre R. Potts   Charles Potts
   M. T. Potts of Ind.   Harriett Potts

POSTMAN, John Jr. and wife, Margaret to Philip Shesel 1787. Deed BookA-89

PRINCE, Patty--of Spartanburg Co-96 Dist. to Thomas Farrar. 24 Dec.
   1786. Deed Book A-1/2. 950 A on Golden Grove Creek of Reedy
   River. Pres: Robert Prince, Thos. P. Carnes.

PRINCE, Robert to John Bates 1786. Deed Book A-208

PRINCE, Robert to John Nicoll, Jun'r. 1787. Deed Book A-72

PRINCE, Robert to Joseph Logan 1787. Deed Book A-99

PRINCE, Robert to Martin Adams 1787. Deed Book A-156

PRINCE, Robert to William Tubb 1787. Deed Book A-152/3

QUEEN, Mira M. A daughter of Thos. Rowland 1835. Greenville Probate Apt-6 Pk.-397

RAINEY, Benj., Bithiah, Sarah--Wit: a deed in 1785 Book A-8

REESE, Ephraim and wife, Nancy to Thomas Barton 1787. Deed Book A-77

RILEY, Patrick from James Caldwell. 296 Dist. on small br. Reedy
   River. Dated 10/11 Jan 1784. Deed Book A-327

ROBERTS, Hardy Will 6 Mar. 1789. Wife Patience. Will Book A-24
   Son: James
   Son: Sherod
   Son in law: James Barnhill
        2 Y sons: Josiah
                 Hardin Minors

ROBINSON, Suckey--Daughter of Wm. McClanahan. Will 1822. Book A-175

RUSSEL, Jeremiah to William Lynch 1787. Deed Book A-237

SADLER, Nancy M? A daughter of Thos. Rowland. Greenville Probate Apt. 6 Pk. 397 1835

SALMON, George to James Patterson 1787. Deed Book A-129

SAMMON, John Wills Book A. Pg 210
    Wife: Betty
    Sons: John; Wm. S.; Walker; Edward;
    Daus: Jenney Sammon, Barbara Moore and her husband Robert,
           Patsy Hansel
    Son: Richard
    Dau: Suckey Wynn
    2 Daus: Polly Young and Nancy Young
    Dau: Salley Mont Gomery

SHELLEY, Moses and wife, Elizabeth to John Nicoll 1787. Deed Book A-141

SHELTON, Augustus Wills 1849 Apt 12-62, Apt 16-48
    (2) Shelton, Tabitha- W of Martin
    (3) Shelton, Jane- W John
    (1) Married half-sister of James Moore, the last infant of
         Elisha Moore,(not necessarily a Moore).
    (2) Heir of John Moore--1857 Est.
    (3) Jane W. of John Shelton, was also heir of John Moore.

SHIP, Wm., Wife: Ann Greenville Wills
    Son: William
     "   Joseph
          Harriet
    ?   Elizabeth Dunklin
          Joseph Dunklin
          John Dunklin

SHIP, Wm. Greenville Wills
    "Wife Cate's family"
    Toby
    Phillis
    Billey
    Cotts
    Jack

SIMMONS, John, Greenville Will Bk. A Page 219
    Wife: Mary
    "my 3 ch" Richard Simmons--Ex.
               James Roberts
               Shared--Ex.
    16 Nov. 1811. Wit: Jas. Horner (or Korner)
                         Wm.   "   "

SIMPSON, Anne--a daughter of Francis Kirby. Will 1798. Book A-114

SIMS, Drury Will 14 Aug. 1799. Greenville Wills A-146
    Wife: Ruth Ex.
    Son: John Sims Ex.
    Dau: Anna Cox
    Dau: Rebecca Choice
    Dau: Milly McKneely (or McNeely?)

SMITH, Alexander Will 31 May 1808. Will Book A-185

    Wife: Patty
    Son: John Smith
    Son: Drury Smith
    Dau: Nancy Smith
    Dau: Sinthy Smith (or Cyntha)

SMITH, Anna--daughter of Matthew Wynne. Will 1810 Book A-203

SMITH, Drury and wife Sarah, of Laurens Co. to James McCane. 1787
    Wit: Elliott Smith, David Ford. Deed Book A-22

SMITH, Reuben. Will 9 June 1810. Will Book A-200
    Dau: Melissa Walker -W- Nath'l Walker
    Son: Reuben Smith
    Dau: Sarah Land -W- Benj. Land
    Son: Abner Smith
    Son: William Smith
    Dau: Mary Vaughn -W- David Vaughn
    Son: John Dobson Smith--Home place

SMITH, Molly--daughter of John Langston 1782. Will Book A-29
    Sally-- "   " "   "

SPANNONE, Elizabeth--daughter of John Langston. Will 1782. Book A-29
?
SPEER, Robert, wife Ann of 96 District. 23 Nov. 1774. Land on
    Saluda River. Deed P4-41

SPEER, Robert H. to his wife, Mary C. Speer Headgl Laurens Dist.
    Emily Rowland of Greenville Dist--Trustee. Slaves. 22 Jan. 1841
    Misc. L-269

STANFORD, John to Abraham Hargiss 1787. Deed Book A232

STATLARD, McClanahan--G-ch of William McClanahan. Will 1802 Book A-175

STEGALL, Richard of Greenville Co. from John Motlow. 1787 Deed Bk D-543/2
    346 A. Saluda River. 1793 from Mary Anderson of Pendleton Co
    and Bailey Anderson, her husband, to Richard Stegall of Green-
    ville Co. C-399. Stegall, Richard of Dist. Greenville to John
    McClanahan. 346 A. on Saluda R. Dower by Elizabeth Stegall.
    G319/20. Steigall, Richard to Thos. McGrew. L - Greenville Co.
    on Checharoa R. of Saluda R. -- Pt gr to Baily Anderson. no
    dower Book E-13 1789

STEVENSON, Mary a daughter of John Young Will 1792. Book A-13

STOKELY, Ann, wife Stephen Stokely, daughter of John Moore. E 1857
     Greenville Wills Apt. 16-48

STOKES, Preashey--sister of Mary Ford. Will 1799. Book A-145

STONE, Jonathan Will 17 Dec. 1791 Will Book A-193
     Wife Mary   Dau: Polly
     Son: Stephen   "   Phany (son or dau?)
      "   Jonathan   Son: Stephen
     Dau: Sarah   Son: Jonathan
      "   Peggy   Dau: Nancy
      "   Anne
     Father: William Stone to have the place where he lives for
     joint life of himself and mother of testator. Father--Ex.
     Bro. William Stone--Ex.

STRINGER, Reuben and wife Elizabeth to Richard Briant 1787. Book A-53

SULLEVANT, Charles to Joseph Dunklin 1787. Deed Book A-50

SWILLIVANT, Hugh to William Story 1787. Deed Book A-56

SWILLIVANT, Hewlet, Stephen, Moses. Wit: Deed 1788. Book A-170

TANKERSLEY, Charles to Robert Prince 1787. Deed Book A-151

TARRANT, John of Washington Dist. Greenville Co. Will 8 Apr 1799
     Wife: Tabitha
     Dau: Sally McKinzie
     Son: Samuel Tarrant--dec'd
      "   Rowland   "
      "   Richard   "
     Dau: Nancy   "   )
     Son: John   "   ) my 3 g-ch
     Son: George   "   )
     To Edw'd Hampton Tarrant, son of Samuel, dec'd. Book A-109

TARRANT, Leonard Will 23 Feb. 1791. Will Book A-41
     Wife: Mary
     Son: Benjamin
      "   Leonard
      "   Samuel
     Dau: Nelly Daniel
      "   Elizabeth Kirby
     Son: Reuben Bible-etc
     Gr. dau: Elizabeth--daughter of Samuel Tarrant
     Son John
     Son: James

THACKSTON--Sarah A. E. child of Samuel A. Moore E 1861. Wills Apt 20-6

THOMAS, Wm. et al. Greenville Deed D-363 and 391. 1796

    363) to Edward Smith Beaver Dam, Tyger River
    391) to Joseph Davis, Beaver Dam, Tyger River
    and to many others:

Shanda Golightly	John Farmer
George Thomas	Josiah Culbertson
John Motlow	James Smith et al
Thomas Edwards	Joel Graves
Franklin Cox	etc

TINSLEY, Mary wife of Wm. Tinsley, dec'd. Wills Apt 16-48 1857
    Daughter of John Moore E-1857

TIZDELL, William to Austin Sims 1788. Deed Book A-187

TODD, Polly--daughter of Matthew Wynne Will 1810. Book A-203

TONEY, Timothy to Daniel Bush 1787. Deed Book A-41

TRIPLETT, Molly a daughter of Wm. McClanahan. Will 1802. Book A-175

TUBB, John to George Tubb 1787. Deed Book A-197

TUBB, Mary a daughter of Nicholas Fisher, Sen'r. Will 1794. Book A-62

TUCKER, Mary a daughter of Francis Kirby. Will 1798. Book A-114

VAUGHN, Mary wife David Vaughn, daughter of Reuben Smith. Will 1810
    Will Book A-200

WALKER, Melissa wife Nathan'l Walker. Daughter of Reuben Smith.
    Will 1810. Will Book A-200

WICKLIFF, Isaac, wife: Franky Will 14 July 1797. Book A-77

WHIGHT, James D. wife Ann of Spartanburg Co. to Thomas Brason 1788
    Deed Book A-184

WORD, Elizabeth: alleges she m Thos. H. Word 15 June 1823. now
    separated. She was daughter of John Bruce. She had one child
    viz: Thos. Jefferson Word. Greenville Equity Roll 96

WYNNE, Matthew. Will 8 July 1810 Book A-203
    Wife: Susanna
    "all my ch,vz": William Wynne, John Wynne, Thomas Wynne,
    Polly Todd, Mathew Wynne, Betsy, Anna Smith, Richard Wynne,
    Sloman Wynne, Clement Wynne, Robert Wynne

LAURENS COUNTY - SOUTH CAROLINA

Compiled by

Janie Revell

ABERCRUMBIE, JAMES--Laurens Deed Bk A-315 15 July 1786
"We the arbitrators chosen to determine and decide a controversy
between Charity Parker, Executrix and Andrew Rodgers, Jun'r. of
the one part--and James Abercrumbie of the other part, viz; it
is our opinion and award that the parties do Quit all amounts
on an even footing, the said Parker and Rodgers giving the said
Crumbie a Bond of Indemnity against a certain Bond now given to
Dr. John Parker for 200 lbs. old currency. John Richey,
Marmaduke Pinson, Jonathan Downs. Extended on Record 15 July 1786

ABRAHAMS, WILLIAM -w- Mary Laurens Bills 1812-1
    Nicholas Welch -w- Margaret
    John Watson, -w- Elizabeth
    Moses Duncan -w- Sarah
    Solomon Doty -w- Susannah, vs:
    Elizabeth Whitmore, Ex'x. and George Whitmore
    File contains marriage cont. between George Whitmore and widow
    of _____? And Elizabeth Gary widow of _____?m. 22 Dec. 1806
    Copy of Will of David Gary
            Wife: Susannah
            Son: Wm. Blewford Gary
            Dau: Malinda Gary
            Mother: Elizabeth Gary, Ex'x.

ADAIR, ALEX'R--Laurens Ct. Min. 50 lbs. and 3 lbs. 11 sh. fine and
    And Ann McClure admit bastardy--13 June 1786   cost
    George Barry and Nancy Terry
    Elijah Watson and Elizabeth Raburn
                    Elizabeth OBryan-refused to tell name of father
    Wm. Dean and Ann Hall
    James Harborn and _____?--Dismissed
    Christian Langston and _____?--Dismissed
    Martin Hughey and Ann Nevels

ADAIR, BEN. JR., JOSEPH, MARTHA, HEZEKIAH, ISAAC--Infant orphans of
    John Adair, Dec'd. Chose Ben. Adair, Sr. a Gdn. with Joseph
    Adair as Surety. Page 148 shows James Adair a Grand Juror.
    Page 165: James Adair, son James Adair apt. Rd. Overseer.
    Page 286--Dec. 1788--Joseph Adair--Grand Jury.
    Laurens Ct. Min. 1785. Sept 1789

ADAIR, BENJ.--John Adm. Index Record Laurens Box 1-1
    Joseph--Elisha Adm. and Exor. Box 3-6
    Hannah--James Adm. and Exor. 3-9
    John--Elisha Adm. 3-10
    Washington--3-9

ADAIR, JAMES SEN'R.--Laurens Bills
    Widow: Hannah
    Ch: Mary -m- John Prator
         Nelly Ramage
         James Adair, Jr.
         Susannah -w- Wm. Cassels
         Nancy -m- Willie Langston
         Martha -m- William Gamble
         Hannah -m- Reuben Meadows

ADAIR, JOSEPH SEN'R.--Office S. C. Historical Com. Mem 11-109
Men. of Jacob Jones--150 A. in Berkley on McCauls fork of Dun-
cans Cr. Bd. Jas. Adair, Sr., Daniel Long. Dec. 1772
JOSEPH SEN'R.--Of Duncans Creek to Benjamin Adair of Duncan's
Cr.--250 A. in Craven Co. on Duncan's Cr. Bd Benj. Killgore,
John Brotherton, Wm. Ewing, and land held by Miller. Wit:
James Adair, Benj. Killgore, Wm. Ross
Laurens Deed Bk A-189 8 Dec. 1778. Rec'd 1786

ADAIR, JOSEPH--Will. Laurens D-1-105
    Son: John--Land where Richard Hallin and John Price lives
          James--Land on Duncan's Cr.
          Robert
          Elisha and his son Joseph
    Dau: Elizabeth and her husband John Huston
          Jane -w- Thos. Holland
          Casey -w- Thos. McCrarey
          Charity -w- David Littel
    20 Jan. 1812--Inv. 19 Jan. 1813
    Wit: Richard Holland, Wm. Adair, Geo. McCrary

ADAIR, JOSEPH--"Cooper" Laurens Wills A-19 9 Jan. 1788
    Wife: Susannah
    Son: Joseph--Exor.
          James--$\frac{1}{2}$ Coopers Tools--Exor.
          Benj.--$\frac{1}{2}$ "   "
    Dau: Jean Rammage
          Sarah Adair--"Iron pot that was her Mother's"
          Mary Owens and Husband, John
    Son-in-law--Robert Long
    Wit: James Montgomery, Wm. Bowland, James Greek

AKINS, LEWIS--(Name also shown as Eakins) Laurens 1-41 A-40
    Dau: Salley Akins and Fanny Akins
    Sons: John, Ezekiel-(exor), Archer, Frank
    Son-in-law: Benjamin F"sevil" (exor)
    Gr. sons: William Petty, Thomas Petty,
    Dau: Patty Petty Prov. 16 July 1791
    Wit: Joal League, Thomas Fsevil, John Meador

ALLEN, CHARLES -w- Sukey (Susannah) Gr. 200 A. Aug. 31, 1774 to
Robert McNees--Pt 107 Acres with dwelling house. Bd. Nehemiah
Frank, Chas. Allen. Also 200 A. Bd. C. and A. on Little R.
"Acknowledged in open Ct--Lewis Saxon C. C."
Laurens Deed A-371/3 12 Sept. 1778

ALLISON, JAMES--Laurens Wills A-9 10 Nov. 1788 Prov. 9 Mar. 1789
    Wife: Nancey
    Son: James--sole exor. "Where he lives"
    Daus: Polly Allison and Elizabeth Allison
    Wit: Rolly Bowen (x), Samuel Campbell (x) Joseph Lyon
    Laurens Wills Bk D July 5 1810--Pet. for Letters by Susannah A.

ALLISON, ROBERT--Laurens Will 5 Jan. 1791 Bk A-54
    Wife: Frances
    Son: James--1 shilling
    Dau: Margaret   "
           Mary   "
    Son: Robert   "
    Dau: Janie   "
    Son: William   "
           Joseph--100 A. Land where he now lives
           Samuel--1 shilling
           Francis--50 A. whereon Wm. Stone now lives
    Dau: Ann--1 Walnut chest for life and then to her son Wm. Hellams
    Son: Watson--1 shilling
           Moses   "
    Dau: Betty
    Son: Lewis--Land where I now live N-s Beaver Dam
    Exor's: Wife and son, Joseph Prov. 5 Jan. 1791
    Wit: Wm. Turner, Emanuel York, Wm. Higgens

ANDERSON, DAVID--Of Spartanburg. Gr. Sept. 19, 1774 to Charles
    Simmons--150 A. both sides of Little R. Bd. Wm. Anderson and Vac.
    Wit: Lewis Devale, Abraham Andrews, Jesse Rice, Wm. Mitchesson
    10 June 1785 Laurens Deed A-239-241

ANDERSON, GEORGE -w- Molly (or Mary) to Miriah Goodman Dec. 15, 1786
    140 A. on both sides of North Creek. Gr. to sd. Anderson
    Laurens Deed B 96/97
    1785, Jan. 30--Deed A-158/160--George Anderson from Patrick
    Cummingham -w- Ann 50A. which was conv. to P. C. by Adam Gramaker

ANDERSON, MOLLY--Laurens Will 6 Sept. 1809 Bk-D--10
    Son: Andrew
    Dau: Molly Wit: Miner Ann Cobb

ANDERSON, DR. WADE--Dec'd Dec. 1823 int. Laurens Equity 1826-16
    Widow: Maria S.
    Ch: Jane R.
         David L.
         Maria W. All minors

ANDERSON, WILLIAM -- Of Ninety Six. to Samuel Kelly 25 May, 1785
    Gr. to Wm. Savage and James Simpson 5 May 1773 conv. to Wm. A.
    Bd. Indian line, Henry Powell and Vac. Laurens Deed B-92/94

ARCHIBALD, THOMAS and wife, Margaret--Laurens Equity--see James Parks

ARMSTRONG, CLARINDA -m- Martin Mahaffy 20 Dec. last. Rev. R. H. Babb
    See Laurens Will Herald File Issue Jan. 20, 1854   1854

ARMSTRONG, JOSEPH Laurens Will A-37 30 Jan. 1790
    Wife: Rebecca--Home on Mudlick Cr.
    Oldest Son: John--Not of full age--325 Acres
                 James
    Land to be divided between sons, "the dividing line to begin at
    John Williams and James Burnsides Corner" Spring known as Gatises
    Spring to be on west side.
    Dau: Mary Ann--112 Acres purchased from Benj. Carter.
    Exor's: Wife with Robert Gillian
    Wit: James Burnsides, Andrew Burnsides, John Butler

ARNOLD, HENDRICK--Of Laurens Co. Laurens Will 1-85 A-142
    Wife: Ruth--Exor.   Dau: Nancy
    Son: William   Son: Ira
    Dau: Mary   July 15, 1795--Prov.
    Wit: Benjamin Arnold, Thomas Hamilton

ARNOLD, JOSHUA(Also sp. Arnall) Laurens 1-36 A-34
    Wife: Leanna
    "My only Dau": Martha
    To: Joshua Millens, Joshua Arnall, and Joshua Franks--Land in
         Abbeville Co.
    Exor: Charles Smith and Samuel Franks. 5 March 1792--Prov.
    Wit: N. Franks, Robert Franks, Polly Franks

ASHLEY, JOHN SEN'R and JOHN JUN'R. to John Simpson Laurens K-248
    50 A. N-s Warrior Creek 12 Jan. 1819 Dower Elizabeth Ashley
    Wit: Stephen Garrott, James Ashley

ATTAWAY, JOHN--Dec'd Laurens Probate Bk 82 1825
    Widow: Margaret -vs-
    Elisha Attaway   Chesley Attaway
    John   "   Robert Frank and wife Elizabeth
    Isaac   "   Elizabeth widow of Ezekiel Attaway
    Jesse   "

BABB, RHODY--Widow of S. C. Will--Laurens Equity Bx-D No-6 1816
    Legacy: Rhody Merchant dau. John Merchant
    "   : Mercer Paty, son of David of Ohio 2 Sept. 1815

BABB, MERCER--Of Newberry Laurens Equity Bx-D No-6 1816
    Wife: Rhoddy
    Bro: Thomas Babb--Dec'd--Ch.
    Sis: Margaret Wadlington--Ch.
    William, James, and Warner Wadlington
    John Gary and wife, Jane
    Rachel Osborn
    - vs - John O'Neall, and Benson Jones Exor's of Rhoda Babb, Dec'd.

BAILEY, WILLIAM Laurens Will 1-49 A-48
    Wife: Ann
    Son: William--Where he now lives
          James--Where he now lives
    Gr. son: Wm. Bailey, son of David Bailey
    "my ch. viz": John, Zachariah, Marjory, Mary, William, James
                 Lucy, and Lewicy.
    Ex: Zachariah, William, and James Bailey. 27 Jan. 1787 Prov.
    Wit: A. Rodgers, Jr. Thos. Rodgers, John Rodgers

BALDWIN (OR BALDINE), MARY--Dau. of Henry Bates Dec'd. See card.
    Laurens Equity No. 12 1813

BALL, WILLIAM SR., Peter, George, Jamima.--All mentioned in will or
    as witnesses to will of Richard Griffin 1805. See Griffin card

BANTON, LEWIS -w- Jedida Gr. Nov. 22, 1775 to Wm. Goodman. Pt. -
     200 A. on Long Lick Cr. of Reedy River. Laurens Deed B-60/62
     Sept. 12, 1786

BARKSDILL, WILLIAM--Laurens Deed Bk. A-319 1786 "Whereas previous
     to my marriage with Ann Adams, the widow of Charles Adams,
     Dec'd xxxxxxxxNegro wench, Sary xxxxxxx.

BARRENTINE, NANCY--Dau. of Henry Bates, Dec'd. Laurens Eq. No. 12
                                                                1813
BARRET, THOS.--Laurens Eq. Bk. D. See card--Benj. Inman-1798

BATES, HENRY--Dec'd of Newberry Dist. Laurens Eq. No. 12 Will in
     file. 4 April 1806.
     Son: James
     Dau: ?
           Nancy Barrentine
           Mary Baldnie
           Rebecca Taylor
     Sons: Glenn William Bates, Henry, Zachariah, and James Bates
            Christopher and his sons, Henry and John

BAUGH, WILLIAM Laurens 1-25 A-21 4 May 1787
     Wife: Agnes--Ex.
     Sons: John, William David
     Daus: Elizabeth and Margaret
     Son: Jonathan
     Dau: Mary and Agnes Prov. 4 May 1787
     Wit: James Abercrombie, Wm. O'Bannon, John Pinson

BEARD, WILLIAM -vs- Frederick Paysinger. Laurens Eq. Bx. D No-13 1816

BEASLEY, LEONARD -vs- Robert Templeton--Bro in law of Robert Pucket--
     went on his security for pur. of a house for Beasley. R. Pucket
     not responsible financially. Laurens Equity 1820-3

BINGHARD, HENRY and wife Jenny. See card of John Buchanan, Sen'r.
     Laurens Eq. Bx. D 1816

BISHOP, SAMUEL -w- Mary Gr. March 19, 1773 to Thomas Duckett--100 A.
     in fork of Broad and Saluda S-s Enoree--Bd. sd Rivers, Thomas
     Fleming, Andrew Owen, Wm. Ragan's Gr. Laurens Deed B-49/51
     March 14, 1774
     Deed Bk B 44/45 Dec. 9, 1786 Samuel Bishop -w- Mary to Jacob
     Ducket--50 A S-s Enoree--Gr. to Charles King Nov. 5, 1755 and
     conv. by Charles King -w- Charity to Samuel Bishop Nov. 23, 1769
     Wit: Joel Whitten and John Odel

BLACK, JOHN -w- Sarah--Orators Laurens Equity 1817-13 Card 1
     Alleges: George McAdad Brown of Lancaster Co. Va. was, in 1790
     Apptd. Gdn. for Sarah. Took her and several of her slaves to
     the home of her godfather, Col. Edward Conway of Newberry Co.
     Since Dec'd.

BLACKERLY, JOSEPH, SEN'R.--Dec'd March 1814. Former res. Va.
   Son: Joseph, Jun'r   Laurens Equity 1819-4
   Dau: Sarah -m- Giles Cason of Pendleton Dist.
         Judah -m- Justinian Maddox
             Ch: John, Anna, Sarah, Susannah, Judah
   Son: Jedathan Blackerly of Bracken Co. Ky.
   Dau: Elizabeth -w- Charles Metcalf of Flemming Co. Ky.
         Joanna (Dec'd) -w- Samuel Pearle of Fagan Co. Va.
             Ch: Willism Pearle of Bracken Co. Ky. (Only child)

BOGAN, WILLIAM--Of Berkley Co. Will 7 Jan. 1762   C. T. Wills
   Wife: Elenor
   Son: John and James
   Daus: Elenor and Ann
   Son: Samuel and William (seem dec'd)
   Wit: Sam'l Awbrey, Joseph Garrett, John Hold and Thos Brandon

BOGAN, WILLIAM--Left with British 1782. Laurens Equity 1803-1
   Widow: Sarah--returned to S. C. and -m- Joseph Lynch
   Dau: Elizabeth--age abt. 6 yrs--died 1787
       Sarah -m- Edmond Craddock of Laurens

BOLT, ROBERT, JR. Wills Laurens 1-89 a-143
   Wife: _____? Exor.
   Sons: John and Lewis
       Unborn child--if any.
   Daus: Peggy, Sally, Polly
   Ex: Neighbor Jonathan Downs 20 Oct. 1795
   Wit: James Parker, Thomas Parker, and Susannah McHarg

BOSTICK, TOLIVER--Dec'd--Of Edgefield Laurens Equity 1819-9
   His Exor's -vs- Davis Bostick--slaves Bulkey File

BOWEN, GEORGE Laurens Equity 1820-2 -vs- Charles Pitts Land sale.

BOWLES, ELIZABETH--Widow, to Robert Bell Laurens Deed C-154
   150 A. on Duncan Cr. Gr. sd Elizabeth Bowles Aug. 10, 1768

BOWLES, RUTHERFORD -w- Elizabeth--Dau. of Oliver Towles, Dec'd. See
   Card Oliver Towles. Laurens Equity 1813 No-10

BOX, JOSIAH -vs- George W. Hodges of Charleston Dist. and Samuel
   Downs--Money. Laurens Equity 1819-12

BOYD, DAVID and -w- Margaret--Laurens Probate Bk-Pg 2 1825/6
   See card of David Ross, Dec'd.

BOYD, NANCY -w- Lard B. Boyd was widow of Maj. John Moore--1801. His
   Adm. was Sarah B. Boyd and she was also Gdn. of Anderson Moore.
   Robert Crumwell was Gdn. James Moore. Laurens Wills 1801

BRADLEY, DAVID--Laurens Will Bk-D 1808 John Meador-Pet. for Letters

BROCKMAN, JOHN--Laurens Will 27 Nov. 1800 Laurens Equity 1809-7
   Wife: Amelia
   Son: Henry
   Daus: Anney Parks, Marah Dean, Franky Mullins
   Dec'd Dau: Leucey Owens and 3 children-Becky, Amelia, John Henry
             Elizabeth -w- Wm. Ballinger (Becky)
             Amelia -w- James Crooks of Spartanburg

BROTHERTON, JOHN -w- Esther--Laurens Deed A-182/4 Aug. 4, 1774
    Gr. Aug. 10, 1766--60 A. sold to James Adair. To James Crage
    199½ A. on Br. of Duncan's Cr. Bd. Wm. Ewing--Less 60 A. sold
    to James Adair. Wit: Thomas Loggan, John Owins, John Crage

BROTHERTON, JOHN -w- Esther to James Crage: 139 A. on Spring Branch
    of Duncan's Cr. Bd. Survey of Samuel Avory and Vac. and Wm.
    Ewing. Gr. to sd John Brotherton. 10 Aug. 1766.
    Laurens Deed Bk A-181 3 Aug. 1774

BROWN, BENJAMIN--"The Legal Heir of Bartlett Brown, Dec'd of the
    State of Georgia, Berke   County to Abraham Gray of 96 Dist.
    Laurens Co. Pt. 600 A. Gr. to Bartlet Brown by Matthew Rowan,
    Gov. N. C. on S-side Enoree R. Formerly called Kings River.
    Laurens Deed Bk A-298 1785. Pg. 300--Same to John Lindsey-Pt
    same lands and same location

BRUTON, ROBERT (Brewton) See card of Ezekiel Roland Laurens Eq. Bx-D
                                                                    1815
BUCHANAN, JOHN, SEN'R.--Of Berkley Co. 96 Dist. Laurens Eq. Bx-D 1816
    Dau: Nancy Turley
    Wife: Elizabeth
    Sins: John and Micajah
    Dau: Mary Hutchinson
    Son: Wm.
    Daus: Anne Hord and Susannah. 14 June, 1785 Prov. Newberry Co.

BULOW, JOHN J.AND CHARLES W.--Merchants -vs- Creditors of Hugh O'Neal's
    Estate (Lunatic) Laurens Equity 1810-2

BUNNELS, ASA -vs Jason Platt of Greenville-Co-Partnership. Laurens
    Equity 1809-8

CALDWELL, JOHN, ESQ.--Of 96 Dist. To Gilbert Turner--200 A. pt. 1200
    Gr. John Caldwell July 8, 1774. Bd. N-Wm. Turner, near Gilbert
    Cr. all other sides part of same Gr. Laurens Deed 3-109 Mar. 1
    Laurens Deed B-108/10 Gilbert Turner 63 A.   1775

CALDWELL, SAMUEL -m- Jenny Curnall--Dau of Barnette Curnall
    Heirs: Widow: Gracey Curnall (of Barnette Curnall
                Nanny -w- Benj. Hiet (or Hilt)
                Moses Curnall
                Jenny -w- Samuel Caldwell
                Polly Curnall
                Milly -w- Stephen Mauldin Laurens Deed C-482 1802
    Deed Bk E-415: Samuel Caldwell of Va. Dec'd His Grant
                William Caldwell of 96 Dist
                Son: John Caldwell--Conv. July 15, 1793
    150 A. Fork of Broad and Saluda R. on a small Branch called
    Beaver Dam. John--Oldest brother of Samuel

CALDWELL, WILLIAM to Roger Murphey--300 A. on Long Lick Creek of
    Saluda R. Bd. Robert Woods, Robert Gills, Ebenezer Storm and
    Patrick Cunningham Laurens Deed Bk A-167 1784
    To: Jean Thompson of Laurens--200 A. on Little River. Bd. Hugh
    O'Neal, John Chesnut, Henry O'Neal and John O'Neal--Hastin Deal
    and Thos. Edgehill. Wit: Daniel Megin, Wm. McDonald, Hugh O'Neal.
    March 17, 1786 Deed Bk A-356-358

CANNON, SAMUEL--Next Friend of Sarah Pester -w- John Pester. See
    card Sarah Pester. Laurens Equity 1-1814

CARGILL, JOHN JUN'R. -w- Keziah to Thomas Dendy--300 A. in fork of
    Broad and Saluda Rivers. Wit: Samuel Powell, Sarah Tinsley,
    Laurens Deed A-129/133 March 25, 1770

CARGILL, THOMAS -w- Elizabeth to William Hall--180 A. Pt 200 Gr. to
    John Cargill, Dec'd. and willed by him to sd Thomas Cargill. Bd.
    Wm. Dendy, Samuel Powell. Laurens Deed B-65 Nov. 23, 1776

CARRITH, ADAM -vs- Henry Tandy Walker of Greenville Dist.--Slave sale
    contested. Laurens Equity 6-1813

CARRUTH, ADAM--Of Greenville Dist. Adv. Heirs of Jesse Goodwin, Dec'd
    See card J. Goodwin. Laurens Equity 1-1813
    -vs- Thomas L. McEntire of Bank Co. N. C. Box D-2
    -vs- George Maxwell--Money 1820-4

CASON JOHN -w- Sarah of Pendleton Dist. Laurens Equity 3-1814
    Joshua Smith -w- Polly
    John and William Miller of Laurens Dist.
    John Miller, Dec'd, was about to marry Sarah Cason--having lost
        his wife-conveyed his property to his children; Wm. Teague
        and wife, Elizabeth -vs- George and Sarah Miller
    Wm. Teague -w- Elizabeth
    Joseph Cason -w- Rebecca
    Zebulon Mathia -w- Jane
    James Miller, Anderson Miller, Washington Williams

CATES, AARON--Will Laurens Equity 1817-10
    Heirs: Dorothy Waddlington of Newberry
    D   Daus: Dorothy Ann
                   Polly B.
                   Sarah Susannah Frances

CATER, JESSE--Dec'd--Estate Citation: 25 Feb. 1802 Pub. at James
    Young's store by Seb. Mathia--Feb 27, 1802. Wm. Cater, Adm.
    Bond 1 March 1802. Laurens Probate 17-15
    (Shows Cato in body of most of papers. Indexed as Carter)

CHAPPEL, HENRY--Adv. James Sprowl. Laurens Equity d-10 1816

CLARK, JOHN -vs- Jennett Prather by her next Friend, Jacob Miller
    Laurens Equity 15

CLARK, ULIM--Dau. of John Ellis--1772 Laurens Eq. 12-1815

COB, SAMUEL--To William Mitcherson--300 A. on Enoree R. and Gilder's
    Cr. Orig. Gr. to Jacob Mitchell to Samuel Cob. Wit: Benj.
    Rainey and Rainey Phillips. Laurens Deed A-99/100 Oct. 27, 1783

COKER, JOSEPH--Dec'd -w- Milly, Dau. Elizabeth Coker--Grantees to:
    John Norris and John Burns--200 A. Orig. Gr. to Manoah Tindsley
    Dec'd and by him conv. to Joseph Coker. Laurens Deed B-59
    Dec. 11, 1786

COKER, JOSEPH   Laurens 1-59 A-71
    Wife:
    "Y-Son":   John
    Sons: Drury, Calvin, Thomas--Exor's.
    "All my children"--(Seems he had more)
    20 March 1792 Prov. Wit: Wm. Hellems, Thomas Coker, Martin Deal

COLE, SAMUEL--To--William Mitcherson--300 A. on Gilder's Creek of
    Enoree R. Gr. To Joab Mitchell who conv. to sd Wm. Mitchison
    who is in possession. Laurens Deed Bk A-98 1783

COLEMAN, ABSOLAM--Will Laurens Equity 1819-7
    Widow: Sarah -m- James Holt
    7 Minor children: Youngest, Deborough Ann, Elizabeth, Larken
    Polly, Alford, Alsey, Gilley

CONWAY, COL. EDWIN of Newberry, Deceased. Nov. 1801--Will
    Wife: Sarah (Sister of Martha McAdams)
    Ch: Agatha -m- Patrick McDowell (5 children)
         Jeanetta -m- Richard Watts
    Gr. Ch: Sarah -w- John Black
        5 children of Agatha McDowell
            Harriet, Charlotte, Agatha Patrick James
            16 yrs. 14 yrs.   12 yrs. 10 yrs. 7 yrs.

COOPER, REUBIN AND CHARLES--Both married daughters of James Williams
    of Laurens--Elizabeth Ann and Sarah. Will 1816

COTHRAN, SAMUEL--See card of Hugh O'Neal. Laurens Eq. No. 8 1815

COUCH, JOSEPH--Pet. by Nancy Couch for Letters. 16 Apr. 1811.
    Laurens Wills

COUNT, HENRY--Dec'd Will in File Laurens Equity Bx. D-No 6 1815
    Widow: Katherine
    Sons: Henry and Jacob
    Daus: Mary, Margaret, Elizabeth
    21 Mar. 1814. Standwin Hays in right of his wife, Catherine

CRADDOCK, JOHN--Of Orangeburg Dist. To: Sarah Craddock of 96 Dist.
    200 A. on Little R. Bd. Vinson Glass et al. Pt. Gr. to David
    Craddock Jan. 7, 1770. Father of John Craddock--Gr. 300 A.
    Wit: John Osborn, Thos. Cargill, and Tandy Walker.
    Laurens Deed A-287/89 1782

CRADDOCK, JOHN--Of Laurens Co. To: Richard Hicks--100 A. on Little R.
    Bd. Survey for James Harvey, James Ryan--Gr. to David Craddock
    Laurens Deed Bk A-276 1786

CRISSWELL, ROBERT (or Creswell)--Gdn. of James Moore. See card of
    Maj. John Moore, and James Moore, Minor. Laurens Wills 1802

CRESWELL, ROBERT AND ELIHUE -vs- James McCaa--Money Laurens Eq. 1807-2

CRESWELL, ROBERT -vs- John Garlington-Partnership--Money 1817-6

CROCKER, WLHANAN--Marriage set 11 Nov. 1815 Elizabeth Young. Josiah
    Fowler, Tr. Mixc. C-229 Laurens

CROCKER, ELHANON, Dec'd. intestate. Laurens Eq. 1826-8
    Widow: Melinda
    1 child-infant-Elizabeth--Sole heirs
    Joseph Crocker--Gdn. for child. James Crocker Adm.

CROMER, ADAM--See card of John Buchanan, Sr. Laurens Eq. Bx D 1816

CROMER, ELIZABETH -w- _____ Cromer, formerly widow of David Ruff,
    Brother of George Ruff, Jr. Dec'd. Laurens Eq. No. 11 1813

CROOK, HUGH, Lewis Duvall, et al and Elizabeth Duke--600 A. on Warriors
    Cr. Laurens Deed G-470

CROOK, JAMES AND MARGARET--To: Joseph Dean--100 A. Laurens Co. N-s
    Bratchens Cr. 3 A. enclosed on S-s sd Cr. whereon the spring is
    being ease end of two tracts orig. Gr. James and William Crooks.
    10 Feb. 1789. Wit: Wm. Crooks, Thos Dean, Joseph Hall
    Laurens Deed 502 or 602 April 1, 1794

CROOKS, JAMES AND AMELIA--Laurens Equity A 1809 Pk-7
    John Henry Owen, of Spartanburg Dist. -vs- Henry Brockman, et al
    Shows: John Brockman made will 27 Nov. 1800 (Will in file)((Died
    same date)). Heirs were: Wife, Amelia. Son, Henry
    Gr. Ch: John Henry Owen
    His two sisters: Amelia Owen now m. to James Crooks of Spartanburg
    Elizabeth now married to Wm. Ballinger
    Dau: Franke Mullins who d. without issue 20 Feb. 1809

CROOKS, MARGARET -vs- Hugh, her brother, shows James and wife, Margaret
    Ch: Hugh, Margaret, Thomas, William Laurens Eq. Bx-1 1823-4

CROOKS, THOMAS of Laurens to Willis Cheek--Laurens Deed K-304 1820
    312 A. on Warrior's Cr. Enoree R. Dower: Polly Crooks
    19 Oct. 1820 date deed.
    L-175: To Mark Noble--250 A. on Warrior's Cr. Gr. to Lewis
    Duvall who canv. to Hugh and Thos. Crooks, and by Hugh to Thos.

CROSSEN, THOMAS Laurens Equity 1826-7
    Widow: Martha -m- Thomas Quin. (Ch. name not mentioned) Suit
    by Thos. Black and Thos. Burnside as her Surety on Adm. Bond to
    foreclose indemnity mortgage on her land. Alleges Thomas Quin
    moved to Georgia

CRYMES, WILLIAM and wife, Nancy. See card John Dickie. Laurens D-4
                                                                1815

CUNNINGHAM, JOHN--"Of 96 Dist. called Cambridge Dist."
    Sons: Thomas and James   Laurens Wills A-17
    Daus: Ann Allison
           Margaret and Wm. Hall
           Dorcas and David Allison
    Sons: John, William, and George--To each a horse and saddle
    Gr. Dau: Mary Allison
    Gr. Son: Samuel Allison
    Dau: Catherine and Joseph Dean
    Son: Samuel
    Wife: Not names. 15 Oct. 1788

144

CUNNINGHAM, MATHEW Widow, Susannah--Pet. for Letters. 7 Jan. 1811
    Laurens Will Bk D 1811

CUNNINGHAM, PATRICK -w- Ann Gr. Jan. 21, 1785 To David Green, Minister
    100 A. N-s Reedy R. below the old Indian bdg. Wit: Wm. Harris
    Edward Kemp, Benjamin Turner. Laurens Deed A-125/7
    A-157--To George Anderson--50 A. N-s Reedy R. orig. Gr. to Adam
    Granaker
    B-21--To James Saxon and Samuel Saxon--about 1787 date torn off.
    Laurens Wills 1-93 A-153 Patrick Cunningham
        Wife: Ann (Exor.)
        Son: John
              Robert--to be schooled
              William--to complete school (Exor.)
    Wit: Lewis Graves, M. Walker, Sarah Clancy

CUNNINGHAM, WILLIAM, Dec'd--Laurens File. Charleston Courier Mar. 14,
    Widow: Margaret, whom he left in Nova Scocia   1806
    "Notice": To Margaret Cunningham, widow of Wm. Cunningham, late
    of this State whom he left in Nova Scocia 1788 or 1789 nee Margaret
    Brierly of Baltimore County Md. where she married sd Wm. Cunning-
    ham, now thought to be wife of David Dinsmore of Nova Scocia.

DAVIS, RICHARD, son of Frederick Davis--Apprenticeship to James Milwee
    URIAH--Apprenticeship. Laurens Deed A-317/8 1785

DAY, FRANCES--Wife of Philip--seems to have married Charles Simmons
    from Will of Jemima Day

DAY, NATHANIEL--elected sheriff of Dist. of Laurens. Bond 19 Jan. 1825
    With: John Garlington, John Dunlap, H. C. Young, William Irby, Sr.
          R. S. Simpson, J. S. James
    Nathaniel and Nancy and Willis Hill wit. Will Wm. Nugent Bk A-28
    15 Sept. 1836

DAY, PHILLIP--Of Laurens Co. 96 Dist. Blacksmith Laurens Wills 1-78
    Wife: Frances
    Ch: William, John, Arrny (or Amy), Phillip, Nancy, Daniel,
        Benjamin, Mary, Nathaniel, Elizabeth, Jemima. "Land Negroes" C
        etc, to be sold and divide proceeds. Ex: William Cason, Jr.
        of Bush River, John Watts 9 Jan. 1793
    Wit: Robert L. Smith, Thos. W. Fakes, Margaret Fakes
    Vol. 2-207--Will of Jemima Day shows heirs Charles and Pamela Simmons
                                                                1850

DEALE, ALEXANDER--Will deed gift. Laurens Deed Bk A-134 7 Apr. 1785
    to his sons: Clement and Alexander Deale, Jr.--150 A. on which
    I now live in the fork of Banks Creek and slaves. Wit: John
    Roca, John Meek and Thos. Fakes, J. P.

DEALE, CLEMENT -w- Jean to William Watson--150 A. on Spring Br. of
    Mudlick Cr. Orig. Gr. to Richard Miley. Wit: Thos. Edgewell, Jr.
    and Elijah Watson. Deed B-52/3 May 22, 1786

DEAN, JOB--Will Dec. 24, 1863--Sister, Esther Dean--His legacy of land.
    To: James E. Entrekin--all rest. Prov. Jan 21, 1864
    Laurens Deed 1862-72 Pg. 41

DEAN, SUSANNAH--Relict of Job Dean 12 March 1787 To: John Edwards
    250 A. Gr. (to Job. Dean) to John Entrekin on Indian Creek of
    Enoree. Laurens Deed B-123/125 Bd. Crawford Lewis, Allen Wilson

DENDY, THOMAS -w- Mary to Robert Hall--300 A. on North Cr. of Saluda
Wit: John Dendy, Wm. Bailey Deed A-105/8 11 Dec. 1785
Deed B-65 30 Dec. 1786 to David Burn, Jun'r--130 A. on Simmon's
Cr. Bd. on Williamson's Big Survey, Teague, George Anderson, and
Daniel Burns, Sr.
Deed A-104 To Robert Hall--300 A. Adj. Cornelius Tindley and one
Talbert. Wit: Silas Walker, Jno Dendy, Wm. Bailey
Deed B-66 To David Burn, Jr. 130 A. Gr. to sd Dendy 13 Dec. 1786
Laurens Equity 1809-6 Thomas left Will 30 Sept. 1799. Wife,
Mary d. 27 March, 1806. Thomas Dendy Jr.-Widow Mary Cert. -vs-
Wm. Dendy, Exor.

DENDY, WILLIAM d. intestate. Widow: Patsy. Sev. ch. Joshua Teague
adm. -vs- John Dendy Laurens Equity 1826-11

DENNING, JOHN 12 March 1787 to William Ray--640 A. Gr. sd J. D. 1 Jan.
1787 on Horse Cr. of Saluda. Laurens Deed B-106/8

DENNIS (OR DENNISON (both), ROBERT -w- Constant to Wm. Norris--100 A.
near Reedy R. on Beaver Dam. Bd. Peter Allen, Hugh Trimble, and
Hugh Beard. Laurens Deed A-50/52 March 15, 1785

DEVALL, LEWIS -w- Teressa to John Crumpton--200 A. on Duncan's Cr. of
Enoree S-s Broad R. Wit: Thomas Word, John Word, John Power.
Deed A-214/17 Sept 13, 1785

DEWALT, DANIEL, Dec'd--of Newberry. Will 6 Apr. 1805. Nancy Dewalt
and Edw'd Thweatt Ex. Ch: David--a minor. Laurens Eq. Bx D

DIAL, HASTINGS, SEN'R. of Laurens--Will Laurens Eq. 1811-5
Rebecca, Isaac, and Hastings Dial--Exor's. -vs- John Rodgers
over land he surveyed for dec'd.

DIAL, JAMES--Dec'd about 8 yrs ago. Land in Abbeville was sold.
Son: Joseph Dial--Gdn. for Lewis Dial a minor. Other ch.
not named in this Bill. Lewis is suing Joseph for his part.
Laurens Equity 1826-11

DICKIE, JOHN--Of Spartanburg, Dec'd father of Craddock Dickie. Widow:
Martha Vaughn--dau. of Craddock Vaughn of Lunenburg Co. Va. On
22 July 1793, sd Craddock Vaughn, John Dickie of Halifax Co. and
James Vaughn--Agreement..John Garlington and William Crymes and
his wife, Nancy. Roling Westmoreland and Susannah his wife. and
Gdns. of: Willie, Polly, Pathena, Patsey, Malinda, Mourning.
Laurens Equity Bx. D No-4 1815

DICKIE, JOHN--Of Spartanburg, died intestate. Left a number of children, among them a dau. Patsy--about 6 yrs of age. Entitled to
property from her gr-father Vaughn who made it to ch. of John
Dickie with James Vaughn, Trustee. Patsy -m- Clongh Ming-ext.
Died intestate--no issue. John Garlington also a trustee for P.

DICKSON, DAVID--Planter of Tyger River to Patrick Cunningham--150 A.
Formerly property of Hugh Brown N-s Saluda R. S-s Reedy R. sold
by conv. of forfieted estates to David Dickson. Laurens Deed
A-163/67 Nov. 11, 1785

DILLARD, JAMES -vs- John A. Elmore and Benj. H. Saxon--Money
    Laurens Equity 1812-2

DILLARD, SAMUEL -w- Ann Gr. 4 July 1785 to James Dillard 30 Dec. 1786
    440 A. S-s Enoree below the ancient boundary line. Bd. James
    James Bright, John and Joseph Whitmore, Brice Prator.
    Laurens Deed B-120/22

DOBSON, JOSEPH--Of Bunk Co. N. C. Laurens Eq. Bx D-2 1816
    See card of Adam Carruth

DOROUGH, JAMES -w- Sarah--Laurens Prob. Bk-2 1825/6 See card of David
                                                 Ross
DOYLE, MARY--Dau. of John Ellis 1772. (Dogle?) See Ellis Card. Eq.no-12

DRAKE, EDMUND--Dec'd 1797 Laurens Equity 1819-8
    Widow: Phebe--since dec'd
    4 Ch: Benjamin-of Abbeville -w- Sarah
           Sarah -w- Thos. Dalrimple
           Celia -w- James Holditch (dec'd-sev. ch)
           John Drake--Orator
    Ch. of Benjamin and Sarah -m- John Smith
        Langdon, Rebecca, John,Rachel, Josiah, Franklin
    Ch. of Sarah and Thomas Dalrimple
        John, Edmund, Celia, Phebe Ann, Sally, George

DREW, WILLIAM--Of S. C. Laurens Vol 1-1 Bk A-1
    Wife: Sarah--Ex.
    Son: Langston
    Daus: Lucy, Polly, Sarah, Elizabeth
    14 Feb. 1777--Prov. 15 March 1786 Will partly destrlyed
    Wit: A. Rogers, Jr., John Lucas, Edw. Philpot

DUMAS, FRANCES--Deed gift to following. Laurens Equity 1827-Pk-5
    Betsy -w- John Kelly
    Sally -w- Stephen Tiner
    Lucy -w- Thomas Powell
    Nehemiah, David, Polly, Matildy, Nancy, Emmaline--all minors
    In File: Notice Sale of 190 acres where Joel Tucker and wife
    formerly resided. Sale at Joshua Teague's store. Bill alleges
    by Joshua Teague that a few days after deed was made, Frances
    married Joel Tucker--he left for Georgia and left Frances on the
    land. Suit to prevent property from being removed, etc, on be-
    half of the minors.

DUNKIN, JOHN --Of Edgefield Dist. Will 5 Nov. 1805 d. Mar. 27, 1809
    Wife: Rachel--d. 11 Dec. 1805   Laurens Eq. 1811-4
    Son: Abel
    Dau: Rachel -m- Henry Hilbern 22 Jan. 1809
    Son: Jeremiah and William. Had property Newberry and ål abt.

DUNLAP, SAMUEL Laurens 1-43 A-43 5 Feb. 1791 Prov.
    Sons: John, James, Samuel
    Daus: Catherine and Suzanne
    Wife: Nancy (calls her Jeather one place)
    3 Gr. daus: Sarah, Nancy and Mary
    Wit: and Exors: Martin Dial, John Dunlap, Wm. Helams.

DUNN, WM. C. of Laurens Misc. I-558
Nat. Papers--17 Apr. 1837. Born in Parish of Dunsford, County
of Down, Ireland, 5 Aug. 1808. Sailing for Belfast on 12 May
1827--Lands in Quebec on 17 June, 1827--remarried in Canada
abt. 3 yrs--Removed to N. Y. for a year, then came to S. C.

EAKINS, LEWIS Laurens 1-57 A-60
Dau: Salley and Fanny
Sons: John, Ezekiel, Anker, Frank
Son-in-law: Benjamin Shevel (or Kevet)
Gr. sons: Wm. Petty and Thomas Petty
Dau: Patty Petty
Ex: Son, Ezekeal and s-in-1 Benj. Kevet 16 July, 1791
Joel League, Thomas Kevel, John Meddor Name also shown as Akins

EAKINS, SAMUEL -w- Jane 7 Nov. 1785 to Peter Hitt--180 A. known as
Matthias Cook's old Survey on Little R. Gr. sd Samuel Eakins on
1 Aug. 1785 Laurens Deed B-117-119

EAST, SHADRACK Laurens 1-64 A-78 12 Nov. 1792 Prov.
Wife: Mary
"my 4 ch": Thisiah (or Keziah, it seems)
            John--not of age
            Thomas
            Ann
"Oldest son: Allen. Ex: Thos. East, Sr. Bro. and James Cook
Wit: Sam'l Henderson, Wm. Young--Spartanburg, Thos. Wadsworth

EDGEHILL, THOMAS, JUN'R. 17 Sept, 1786 to Thomas McDonald--150 A. on
Little R. Gr. to Edgehill by Wm. Bull 17 May, 1774 Laurens
Deed B-110/112

EDGEHILL, THOMAS, SEN'R. --Gr. March 1775. Son: Thos. Jun'r. "For
his father, and his grant. To: Norris Merchant 23 Oct. 1786
several tracts on Little R. Gr. to John Simmons May 1758. Gr.
15 Feb. 1769. Bd. Samuel Ford, Wm. Simpson, Elizabeth Caldwell
Laurens Deed B-42

EDWARDS, CHARLES--Bill of Appraisement. Aprs: Wm. Bold, Robt. Finney,
John Coal. Sale 6 June 1788. Laurens Wills A-2

EDWARDS, ISAAC -w- Judith of Union Co. Laurens Deed B-52 Dec. 7, 1786
To: Thomas Duckett--50 A. S-s Enoree--Gr. to Isaac Edwards Feb.
6, 1786
                                                    Opal
EDWARDS, PETER--of Spartanburg Co. and wife, Opoh to Zachariah Sims
of Laurens Co. 100 A. N-s Saluda R.--Gr. to Andrew Cunningham
24 Feb. 1770. Laurens Deed A-21 1785
Pt. Gr. to Wm. Cunningham Feb. 4, 1768--200 A.
Wit: Nimrod Williams and Lewis Graves. Deed A-24/7 Sept f, 1785

ELLIOTT, THOMAS -w- Lucy Laurens Deed B-58 Dec. 12, 1786 To: David
Burn--150 A. on Simmon Cr. Laurens. Pt. of 300 A. Gr. Edward
Osborn, Dec'd. Bd. David Burns, Jr., Ambrose Hudgens, James
Henderson, Teague

148

ELLIS, JOHN of Halifax Co. N. C.1 Jan. 1772 Laurens Equity 1815-12
    Wife: Mary d. Newberry
    Dau: Jane: -m- Stephen Shell
    Ch: James
        Sarah -w- William Mills
        Mary -w- John Doyle(dec'd)
        Ann (dec'd) -w- George Clark
            Ch: Betty, Polly, John
        Susannah -w- George Elmore
        Frances -w- James Mabry--All but Jane Shell must have been
children of a first wife--suit is against her

ELLIS, JOHN Laurens Equity No-12 1815 -vs- Stephen Shell and Jane
    Shell his wife--Will of John Ellis of Halifax Co. N. C. in file.
    Wife: Mary
    Son: James
    Dau: Sarah Mills
    gr. dau: Elizabeth Fewell
    Dau:Mary Doyel, Ulin(?) Clark, Susanne Elmore, Francis Ellis,
    Jane Ellis. Son: John Ellis 21 Jan. 1772

ELMORE, GRAY, GEORGE, ELIJAH--Laurens Probate Bk-1 1825 See card
    John Shearly, dec'd.

ELMORE, JOHN A. -vs- James Dillard Laurens Eq. 1812-3

ELMORE, MATHIAS--of Berkley Co. Will 3 Apr. 1768
    Wife: Charity
    Dau: Sarah -w- James Dennis
    Gr. Son: Samuel Dennis son of James
    Son: Stephen Elmore
        William Elmore. Provincial Wills Laurens File C. T. Wills
    Wit: Joseph Wright, John Wright, William Wright

ELMORE, SUSANNA--Dau. of John Ellis-1772 Laurens Equity No 12 1815

ENTREKIN, JOHN -w- Elizabeth to Susannah Dean-widow 5/6 Feb. 1785
    Gr. 7 May, 1771 to John Entrekin 250 A. on Indian Cr. Laurens Deed
    Deed Bk B-124--250 A. in Berkley Co on   B-126/7
    Indian Cr. to Susannah Dean, Feb. 6, 1785

ENTREKIN, JOHN JR. of Laurens to Frederick Foster of Newberry 170 A.
    for $170.00. Dower by Ruth Entrekin. Laurens Deed Bk C-673
                   ^DALKYMPLE

EVELEIGH, NICHOLAS of Edgefield--Planter from Andrew Rodgers, Jr.
    Planter of Laurens--2 tracts called "The Horse Shoe". 1--200 A.
    surveyed for John and James Abernathy on N-s Saluda May 3, 1763
    2--150 A. surveyed for Michael Hunt May 4, 1764 N-s Saluda
    Wit: Daniel Webster and Absolom Babs Laurens Deed B-55/7
    20 June 1786

FARROW, SAMUEL -vs- Exors of Phillomon B. Waters. Pur. of Lot.
    Laurens Equity 1812-9

FARROW, JOHN--Late of Spartanburg, now of Laurens, and wife Mary.
    Separation--Badywine Waters of Sptg. for Mary. Alleges he took
    Emphemia Brown and left Mary. Mary had 11 children. Laurens
    Equity Bx. D-5 1815
    Laurens Equity 1820-1--John Farrow-Complainent. Wife Mary B.

Farrow--had filed Bill for Legal Separation. Alimony--her
trustees are sued for trust property settlement.
5 Ch: Thomas F. Farrow
       John F.   "
       Mary Farrow -m- _____Summer
       Sarah   "
       Hannah Farrow -m-_____Higgins

FERNANDIA, JAMES--See card Hugh Patterson Laurens Equity No-13 1815

FEWELL, ELIZABETH--Gr. dau. of John Ellis--1772 see Ellis Card 1815-12

FINDLEY, CHARLES--Gr. June 5, 1786 to Benjamin Rainey--440 A. below
    the ancient boundary on a Br. of Durbin's Cr. Bd. Wm. Young,
    John Owens, Joseph Boston--et al.
    Wit: Wm. Jackson, Elijah Findley, Sarah Rainey.
    July 10, 1786 Laurens B-34/35

FLY, RICHARD -w- Ferriby--see card Benj. Inman 1798 Laurens Eq. Bx-D

FORGUSON, NEHEMIAH, Planter. Laurens Wills A-18 9 Sept. 1789
    Sons: John, William, Thomas
           Jeremiah (Should he not "Get a home in N. C." to have one).
    Daus: Elizabeth, Margaret, Sarah
    Son: Joseph--Ex.
    Dau: Mary
    Son: James--Ex. Wit: Jos. Wood, Reubin Roland, Jno. Dalrymple

FOWLER, JOHN Laurens Wills 1-34 A-32 Bx 110 Pk-3
    Wife: Elizabeth
    "my children": Jesse, William, and James Fowler.
                    Nancy Thomas
                    Elizabeth Gowesy
                    Wade Fowler
                    Wiley Y. Fowler
                    John F. Fowler
                    Melecent, Wesley, and Louisa Fowler. Some of
    children married. Son: Wm. apt. Trustee for son Jean and his ch.
    Ex: John Henderson and son, Wm. 14 Jan. 1840 (error) (Jesse?)
    Prov. June 4, 1791
    Wit: G. Thomas, Wm. A. Boyd, Moses Williams

FOWLER, JOSIAH--Dec'd--Will Laurens Equity 1819-13
    Widow: Sarah
    7 Ch: Richard Fowler
           Elizabeth -w- Elhanon Crocker
           Polly -w- Alsa Fuller-orator (died soon after her father)
           Thomas, Ruthy, Patsy, Newton--All minors

FOWLER, RICHARD--Laurens 1-42 A-42 5 Oct. 1790--Proven
    Wife: Elizabeth
    Son: Richard--Where he lives--Durbin's Cr.
          Joshua--Land on Durbin's Cr.
          "my sons and daus: _____Barton, Rebecca Barton, Richard
          Fowler, Ann Newel, Joshua Fowler, Elizabeth Flanigan
    Wit: Hutson Berry, Joseph E. Burchfield, andJohn Armstrong

FRANKS, JOSHUA--Laurens or Newberry Will Box 102-2
    Son: Robert P.   Dau: Mary Hellams
          Miles   Nancy Bolt
          Joshua G.   Son: George Frank
          William L--Minor   Wife: Prudence
          Abner C
    Gr. Ch: Samuel Saxon, Joshua, William M., John W., Thomas L.,
             Mary Saxon. 17 Nov. 1847 Wm. Clandy, Lewis Saxon,
             Archibald Henderson. Sale 1848--Purchasers: Lewis
    Saxon, Isam Bolt, Willis Wallace, John Bolt, Yang Hellams,
    William Daynell, Martin Armstrong.

FRANKS, ROBERT -w- Elizabeth--See card of John Attaway, Dec'd.
    Laurens Probate Bk-pg 2 1825

FREEMAN, WILLIAM -w- Mary Gr. Feb. 6, 1773 To James Little--100 A.
    on a Br. of Little R. of Saluda R. Where James Little now lives.
    Wit: Robert Freeman, Richard Golding, John Hunter.
    Laurens Deed A-262/4 Dec. 20, 1785

FROST, JOHN -vs- Samuel Wells--Agreement Laurens Equity 1812-10

FULLER, ALSEA--Gdn. of children of William Glenn. Laurens Prob. Bk-1
                                                                1825
FULLER, BRITTON (also called "Fully") Laurens Wills Bk-D 1808
    Wife: Dolph--Apt. Extrix.
    Date: 10 Sept. 1808
    Wit: Zechiah Bailey, Wm. Bailey, Wm. Bailey, Jr.
    Wife petitioned for letters Dec. 25, 1810

FULLER, JONES, ISSALL, PETER, MARY ANN, ARCHIBALD, MARTHA *W* Hammond
    Miller -vs- Sarah Fuller and Henry Fuller. Papers gone or mixed
    some showed up. Isham Fuller, Dec'd.
                    Ch: Martha -w- Wm. Hammond Miller
                        Sarah -w- John Milan, Jr.
    Deed gift from Wm. Roberts of Randolph County, N. C. to his dau.
    Elizabeth -w- of Isham Fuller. She died 24 Dec. 1787
    Laurens Equity 1809-10

GARLINGTON, EDWARD--Marriage set 23 Nov. 1815--Eleanor Griffin
    Misc. C-231

GARLINGTON, JOHN--See card of John Dickie, Dec'd. Laurens Eq. D-4
                                                        1815
GARNER, THOMAS Laurens 1-45 A-44
    Son: John
    Dau: Sarah Laffold
          Molly Roberts
    Son: Benjamin, and dau: Elizabeth, 2 youngest, both minors
    Niece: Salley Garner
    Ex: David Anderson, and Joseph Downs 13 July, 1791--Proven
    Wit: Jonathan Downs, J. F. Wolff, James Floyd

GARROT, EDWARD--Verbal Will Laurens 1-75 A-102. Wife: Amy or Ann.
    John Ashley, an heir. Son: James. Pleasant Sullivan, a dau.
    now dec'd., left one child, Garrot Sullivan. Son-in-law--Stephen
    Mullins. Wm. Nelson Kelly to have charge with Stephen Mullins,
    and Stephen Garrott. "Mon., 25 inst." Supporting Wit: Ann
    Garrot, March Garrot. Proven 27 Aug. 1794

GARY, DAVID--Of Newberry. Will in File. 17 July 1806
    Wife: Susanna   Laurens Equity 1812-1
    2 Ch: Wm. Blewford Gary, and Malinda Gary
    Mother: Elizabeth Gary -widow of Wm. Gary -m- Geo. Whitmore

GARY, FRANCES--Widow of West Gary, Dec'd Laurens Equity 1815-10
    Polly, Charles, and John Gary
    Washington, Hetty Gary--minors -vs- Charles Griffin Adm. of
    West Gary, Dec'd

GARY, HARRIET JANE ELIZABETH--m-- in Cado Parish, La. 12 July by
    Elder John Bryce. John W. Smith of Shreveport, La.
    Laurensville Herald Aug. 17, 1849

GARY, JOHN -w- Jane--See card Rhody Babb. Laurens Eq. Bx D-6 1816

GARY, WEST--Of Newberry--Dec'd Laurens Equity Bill 1815-10
    Widow: Frances
    Ch: Polly, Charles, John, Washington, Hetty--Minors. Land on
    Bush River

GIBSON, JAMES "of North Carolina, Roan County, Wheelright" To
    Alexander Harper of 96 Dist. 100 A. on N-fork of Dirbin's Cr.
    of Enoree River--adj. sd Harper's land. Wit: Jacob Roberts,
    Joseph Barton Laurens Deed Bk A-84 1785
    Deed Bk A-86/93 1785--To Jacob Roberts of 96 District--100 A.
    N-s Dirbin's Cr. of Enoree R. Between Alexander Harper's and
    Ezekiel Grifiths--(Sev. Deeds)

GIBBS, JAMES--Will 8 Aug. 1793 Laurens Wills A-19
    Wife:
    Oldest Son: Zachariah Gibbs--Ex.
                 John   "
           Dau: Susannah   "
                Mary Mabry
    Exor: Jesse Connel--Land in Georgia to be sold.

GLENN, WILLIAM--Dec'd Laurens Prob. Bk Pg-1 1825
    Heirs: John Glenn
           Catherine Glenn
           Jeremiah Glenn   All Minors--Alsea Fuller, Gdn.
           Anna Glenn

GOGGEN, WILLIAM--Application Rachel Goggin, Widow, for letters of
    Administration, with Benjamin Neale. 22 Nov. 1802. Sale (26)
    Pur: Mary Goggen, James and Thomas Goggen
    Laurens Probate Bk C-1-12-26-27

GOODMAN, TABITHA--Dau. of Oliver Towles, Dec'd (see card)
    Son: Daniel Goodman
    Dau: Tabitha -m- Caleb Lindsey Laurens Equity No 10-1815

GOODMAN, WILLIAM Laurens Wills 1-77 A-86 Prov. 28 Sept. 1793
    Wife: Mary
    Bros: James and Claborn Goodman
    Wit: Samuel Sorthus, Nicholas Vaughn, Mary Goodman

GOODWIN, JESSE--Dec'd--Late of Richland Co. Laurens Eq. No-1 1813
    Heirs: James Hopkins -w- Keziah (m. James Hopkins, was dec'd.
           Ansley Hall -w- Sarah   widow)
           Mary Goodwin
           Jesse Goodwin--not 21
    Re. lamds in Greenville Dist. pur. at sale of estate of Samuel
    Saxon on Reedy River. Suit -vs- Adam Carruth of Greenville Dist.

GOODWIN, JOHN--Of ꟾLaurens Co. to Elizabeth Jones--70 Cares adj. where
    she now lives. Gr. 1 Aug. 1785. (Another card says 20 acres.*
    Wit: Robert Box, Samuel Neighbors, Bobert Box, Jr.
    Laurens Deed A-340 1786

GOODWIN, ROBERT--Of Laurens to David McDavid of Greenville, S. C.
    Pt. of Land of Wm. Gust, sold under Confiscation Act to Wm.
    Covington who sold to Robert Goodwin, July 8, 1783
    June 12, 1786 Laurens Deed A-267/69

GORDON, MAJOR THOMAS -w- Elizabeth to Thomas Duckett--184 1/16 Acres.
    Pt. 300 A. Gr. to Wm. Reagan, Apr. 20, 1763--on both sides of
    Enoree R. and bd. sd Wm. Reagan -w- Lucy conv. to Thomas Gordon.
    Wit: John Odel, Benj. Gordon, and Thomas Bishop.
    Laurens Deed B-46/48 10 Dec. 1786

GOULD, JOHN--See card of Hugh Patterson. Laurens Equity No 13 1815

GOWEN, MAJOR JOHN--Of Spartanburg Dist.--Contracted to build Court
    House etc, and died. Suit -vs- Exors. Laurens Equity 1811-1

GRANAKER, ADAM to Patrick Cunningham--50 A. Craven Co. N-s Reedy R.
    Gr. to sd Adam Granaker 4 May, 1775. Pg. 153 Bk A Laurens Deed
    Page 157--Patrick Cunningham conv. to George Anderson

GRAY, JOHN--Of Union Co. S. C. Dec'd 1806 intestate. Jesse Gray, Adm.
    Widow:_____ 9 Ch. by 1st. wife. 3 Ch. by 2nd wife, not named
    Ch: Alcy--now w. Reuben Bramlet of Franklin Co. Georgia
        John, William, Seth, Zachariah, Hezekiah,
        Elizabeth--now w. of Nathan Bramlet
        Jemima Bishop--Now a widow
    Suit -vs- Jesse Gray, son, and adm.
               (also shows son) Laurens Equity 1820-8

GARY, THOMAS, JUN'R--Dec'd 1802. Will (of Newberry Dist)
    Wife: Sarah
    2 Daus: Sarah
            Lucretia -m- Marvel Gary--orator. Unborn, if any.
    Rebecca was born shortly after his death--and she -m- Martin
    Gary, orator. Laurens Equity 1819-11

GRAY, ABRAHAM, dec'd--Case: John Taylor et al -vs- Thomas Meaders, et al
    Out of State: Thomas Meaders -w- Bathiah
              Abraham Harris -w- Louisa
              Tolotson Gray--sd David Anderson O. L. D.
    Son Times and State Gazette Dec. 23, 1830

GRAY, ROBERT -w- Jean--See card David Ross, Dec'd. Laurens Prob. 1825-6

GRAVES, ANTHONY G. -w- Elizabeth (or Eliza). Laurens Equity D-2 1816
    by Chas. Graves of City of C. T. Gdn. Thomas Evans, father of
    Elizabeth, in 1807 pardoned slaves--from John Hollingsworth.
    Robert Crenshaw, G-father of Elizabeth. Sale of slaves contested.

GRAVES, LEWIS--Laurens Bundle 29-7 1810. Adm. Wm. and Martin Graves
    Cit: 31 May, 1810 Pur: Rebecca Graves and Fanny Graves.
    Heirs: Geo. C. Madden, Fanny Graves, John Addams, Lewis Graves

GREEN, ZACHARIAH Laurens 1-63 A-73 11 Feb. 1793 Prov.
    Wife: _____?
    Nephew: Elisha Casey--Land
    "My 2 Ch": James Green and Elizabeth Eastwood
    Gr. Son: James Green and Elisha Casey
    Wit: Wm. Hallums and Elizabeth Atkins

GREER, JOSIAH -w- Margaret To: (date torn off at 1786)Gr. 1 Feb. 1786
    Thomas Murdock--On Allison's Cr. of Duncan's Cr. Laurens Deed B-43

GRIFFIN, ANTHONY--Of Laurens Co. Will 20 Aug. 1797. Laurens 1-105 A-178
    Son: Asa, James, Abia
    Dau: Betty Butler, Caty Cook, Sucky Griffin
    Wife: Mary Ann
    "My wife and 6 children" Ex: Richard Griffin, John Cole, Sr.
    Wit: Robert Russel, Robert Cleland, John Armstrong

GRIFFIN, CHARLES--See card Frances Gary, Widow. Laurens Equity 10-1818

GRIFFIN, JANE--By next friend, Thomas Teague. Husband Reuben Griffin
    They have 6 children living 4 of whom married. 1 dau. -m- James
    Young. Laurens Equity 1815-11

GRIFFIN, WILLIAM, SEN'R. Laurens 1-50 A-50 27 June, 1791--Prov.
    Wife: Rachel
    "my 3 sons": William, James and Joseph--Land on Cason's Creek
    Dau: Jane and her dau's. Peggy Griffin and Caty Griffin
    Ex: Bros. Richard and Anthony and son, James
    Wit: Charles Griffin, James Griffin, and Jane Dougharty

GRIZEL, JOHN (or Grazel) Will 6 May, 1810 Laurens Wills D-18
    Wife: Elizabeth--sole Ex.
    Dau: Julia Tary (or Gary)
        Nancy
    "All rest of my children"
    Wit: Wm. Craig, Wm. Grizzell, Stephen Gary, Jno. McClure
    Date: 6 May 1810 Prov. 6 Aug. 1810

HAGIN, ANN--Mother of Wm. O'Neale -w- Mary. Laurens Deed A-328 1786

HAIR, MATHIAS--Of Newberry Dist. Will Apr. 1, 1817 Laurens Eq. 1817-7
    Wife: Fanny
    Daus: Barbara Nichols -w- Wm. Nichols
          Sally Counts and children Peter W., and Simon P. Counts
          Elizabeth Hilan -w- Gabriel Hilan
          Rebecca Bedenbaugh -w- Jacob Bedenbaugh
          Mary McCarty -w- John McCarty (or McCartney)
    Sons: John Hair, Peter Hair

HALL, ANSLEY -w- Sarah--See card Jesse Goodwin, Dec'd. Laurens Eq 1813-1

HALL, JOHN--Grant Bk CCCC-156 To Joseph South Sept. 3, 1786--100 A.
    Laurens Deed B-821

HAMPTON, NATHAN -w- Sarah , of Greenville Co. Gr. May 21, 1772 to
    Joseph Pinson--200 A. on waters of Ready River. Bd. Lewis
    Banton's, Joseph Pinson, Wm. Anderson, John Caldwell, and vac.
    Gr. sd Nathan Hampton Laurens Deed A-241 9 Dec. 1772
    Wit: John Hughs, Rob't Middleton, and Joseph Doolittle
    Page 253-255 Joseph Pinson to Stephen Wood-June 6, 1786
    Wit: Jonathan Downs, Joseph Downs, George Anderson

HARMON, JOHN--Will 20 July 1789 Dec'd. 1794 Laurens Equity 1817-12
    Widow: Mary
    14 children: Godfrey -w- Mary d. 1811--7 ch. still living
                  Sabina -w- George Derrick
                  Mary
                  John
                  Betsy -w- John Morgan
                  Sophia -w- Daniel Taylor
                  Thomas
                  William of Bark Co. N. C.
                  Samuel
                  James
                  Jacob
                  Peggy
                  Dowd
                  George

HARPER, ALEXANDER--Laurens Deed B-36-37 Oct. 6, 1786 To: Benjamin
    Rainey--85 A. on waters of Durbin's Cr. Pt. Gr. 640 A. Gr.
    Alex'r. Harper. Oct. 15, 1784. Wit: Wm. Jackson, Samuel Cobb

HARRIS, WM -w- Frances to Michael Waldrop--Blacksmith--150 A. on
    North Cr. of Little R. Wit: Shadrach Martin, Laurens Deed A-96/7
    24 May, 1774

HARRIS, JIMMY--Apt. Gdn. for John Harris a minor of 15 years.
    Laurens Will Bk D-10 5 Mar. 1810

HARVEY, JOEL AND CHARLES--Wit: deed of Sam'l Neighbors to Joel
    Burgers. Laurens Deed Bk A-196 1779

HARVEY, LITTLE BERRY--Planter of Richmond Co. Georgia to Robert
    Goodwin, of Laurens. 100 A. late prop. of Wm. Gurt. Sold under
    Confiscation Act. to Little Berry Harvey. Wit: Joseph Downs,
    Jane Downs, and John Goodwin. Laurens Deed A-271/2 Feb. 22, 1786

HARVEY, PHILEMON -w- Sarah of Laurens 11 Dec. 1786 to Andrew Rogers, Sr.
    100 A. on Beard's Fork of Duncan's Creek. Bd. Surv. for Wm. Hanna
    Wm. Taylor, now Andrew Endsley. Laurens Deed B-56

HAYS, STANDWIN -w- Catherine (or Katherine) dau. of Henry Countz-Dec'd.
    See Countz card. Laurens Equity Bx. D-6 1815

HEAD, JOHN, John Cannon, John Campbell, George Ross Wit. deed by Mary
    Hillon and her son John Hillon--to James Adair. Dated 21 Dec. 1784
    Laurens Deed Bk A-308/9 1784

HEAD, WILLIAM SEN'R. AND JUN'R.--of Laurens Co. from Wm. and Ann
    Gunter--52 Acres on Enoree R. Laurens Deed B-262/3 1787/8

HEATH, JOHN D.--Of City of C. T. Trustee for Frances H. Tennant
    -w- Moses Tennant. F. had land in Kent. Co. Maryland.
    Laurens Equity 1812-8

HELLAMS, WILLIAM--Laurens Wills A-8 Will 1789
    Wife: Constant
    G. Son: Jonathan Hellams, son of Jonathan
    G. Ch: Ch. of son William--Jonathan, William, Nancy, Rachel
    2 July, 1788--Wit: Jno. Childress, Rich'd Owings, John Hellams
    Apr: 3 June, 1789--Robert Coke, Jno. Coke, Samuel Dunlap

HENDERSON, JOHN--Native of Ireland--Cit. papers Nov. 15, 1820.
    Archives dept. Misc. D-211

HENDERSON, NATHANIEL--of Laurens Co. to Thomas Tod--Plantation S-s
    Enoree in Laurens Co. Bd. sd River, Wm. Marchbanks, John Bakkams
    and Vac. Gr. sd Nathaniel Henderson. Wit: James Clayton and
    Stephen Wilson, Wm. Hunt. Laurens Deed A-242. 2 March 1786

HENDRICK, HANS--To Anguish Campbell--Affidavit by Wm. Caldwell that
    he drew the titles before John Satterwhite. Laurens Deed A-323

HENDRICKS, MARGARET--Of Laurens Co. 2 Jan. 1797 Laurens 1-95
    "my 2 sons": Mujah and William Win Hendricks
    Daus: Fanny Turner   May Burgess
           Peggy Forgy   Elizabeth Wright
           Rachel Hendrick   Martha Willard
    Friend Lewis Graves, sole Exor.
    Wit: John Middleton, Jacob Clemmons, Elizabeth Sims

HENDRICKS, WILLIAM--Of Tolbird Island in the Spanish Province to his
    children--Deed gift--Land in 96 District on Enoree River.
    Ch: John, Charlotte, Isaac, Thomas, Rebecca
    Charlestown Deed V5-237 1786

HILL, JOSEPH, SEN'R.--Of Abbeville. Dec'd. Will Laurens 1826-5
    Widow: Martha Hill--Oratrix
    6 ch: William Hill and Wiley Hill
           Helen -w- Isaac Bunting
           Joseph--over 14--a minor
           Isaac Mitchell--under 14
           Milton (or Melton) under 14

HILLON, MARY and her son, John Hillon--son and heir of Nathaniel
    Hillon to James Adair--Plantation formerly occupied by Elijah
    Benton--110 A. Pt. 250 A. Gr. to Nathaniel Hillon--S-side Enoree
    River. Page-313--Same to John Campbell. Laurens Deed A-308 1784

HILTON, ELIZABETH--By next friend Martin Childress. Married about
    40 years ago, Thomas Hilton-in North Carolina-Reared a large
    family together. Moved to S. C. 13 years ago. About 10 months
    ago he began to abuse her--whipped her--hit her with a lightwood
    knot, and drove her for his horse, and has married another
    woman who threatens to kill plaintiff if she enters the house.
    Laurens Equity 1826-5   No answer in file

HINTON, ROBERT--Of Laurens Co. Laurens 1-103 A-123
    Son: John Hinton--Ex.
    G. Son: Robert Anderson
    Wife: Elizabeth and "her children"
    Son: Robert Hinton
    Dau: Hanner Moore
          Elander Hinton
    Son: Thomas   "   2 Oct. 1797
    Wit: Thad. Owen, William Owen, Samuel Anderson

HITE, GEORGE--S. C. Journal of Senate 3 Feb. 1784 Page 37
    "Read the petition of George Hite in behalf of himself and others:
    Praying that a tract of sixty one thousand acres of land on the
    waters of Saluda, Enoree, and Reedy Rivers, purchased by his
    Father, may be confirmed in him, Jacob O'banion Hite, James and
    Frances Hite, Mary Manning and Elizabeth Beale. Ordered that the
    above Petition be referred to a Committee of Col. Vanderhorst,
    Col. Waters, Mr. Earle.
    Grant Bks show George Hite 500 A. Dist of 96--west of the ancient
    boundary--May 2, 1785, under act of 26 March 1784

HOGG, TALLY (or Hord)--see card of John Buchanan, Sr. Laurens Eq. D-1816

HOLCOMB, ELIAS -w- Sarah "Washington Dist" show: Wm. O'Neal, late
    Dist. of Laurens d. 1807--leaving widow and 4 children: Arthur
    John, Henry, William. Married Elias 1816 Equity Bx E-1818-4

HOLCOMB, ELISHA--Dec'd Record Book G-20 Feb. 18, 1829 Laurens
    Mary Holcomb--Widow
    Hiram   "
    John Walker -w- Sarah
        Phebe, Cossea, Nathan, Henry, John Walker--Land on Duncan's Cr.

HOLCOMB, JOSEPH--Deed from James Gibson of Roan Co. N. C. to Jacob
    Roberts of 96 Dist. conveys 100 A. on the Main fork of Dirbin's
    Creek waters of Enoree R. Bd. on vac. land lying between Mordica
    Moor's and Joseph Holcomb. Laurens Deed A-89 28 Jan. 1785

HOLCOMB, PHILIP -w- Sarah B. Dec'd--Laurens Probate Bx 43-11
    Shows: Sarah died first--Philip Apt. Gdn. her minor children.
    Bond dated 12 Aug. 1853. Minors: Mary A. Holcomb, Laura Jane
    Holcomb. Sureties on Bond: David and Robert Holcomb. Two
    minors are heirs estate of Aaron Harlan, Wm. D. Jones, Adm.
    State of Mississippi--Tippah County--"In the matter of the
    Guardianship of the person and estate of Mary A. Dazey, wife of
    Nathan Dazey, and daughter of Philip Holcomb and Sarah Holcomb,
    Dec'd.--still a minor and her husband apted Gdn. 20 Nov. 1855

HOLCOMB, RICHARD Laurens Wills 1-77 A-104
    Wife: Sarah--25 A. Mid fork Durbin's Cr. Ex: Friend Jacob
    Robards (or Roberts) to Jesse and Hays--1 heifer with increase
    from June 1, 1794. Wit: Elisha Holcomb, Rubin Higgins, Joseph
                                                              Lomas
HOLT, JAMES M. L. and ANN M. HOLT--Gift Plantation on Saluda Called
    Glasgow, slaves, cattle, etc. 10 March 1765. Old Index M. M. 248
    Page 650--Jane Holt to Jas. M. L. Holt--release of claim for
    support of his 2 children

HORD, ANNE--Dau. of John Buchanan, Sen'r. See card. Laurens Eq. D-1816

HUGGINS, WILLIAM -w- Mary--Exor. and Ex'x. of Benjamin Durbouron--To
    William Salmon--250 A. on Saluda R. Pt. Gr. to Thomas Yates,
    Dec'd, by Wm. Bull in 1774. Laurens Deed A-321 1784

HUGHES, ROBERT HENRY--Of Wake County N. C. Laurens Deed B-99/100
    To: John Newman of Laurens Co. Bond 1 Sept. 1786. Sec. by
    Mortgage 7 Sept. 1786.--200 A. and Mill on S-side Enoree. Orig.
    Gr. sd John Newman 4 July 1785

HUNTER, ANDREW--Verbal Will--By James Park--who wit. it 22 Aug. 1795
    Bro: Robert Hunter   Laurens 1-83 A-141
    Sis: Elizabeth
          Jane
    To: Andrew Hunter, son of Matthew Hunter.
    Went for Robert Hutchinson to write a Will and Andrew Hunter
    died before he returned--about 2 hours.
    Sworn to before John Hunter
    Proven by: Martha Miller, Margaret Park--25 Aug. 1795

HUNTER, JOHN--of Laurens--Will 11 Dec. 1802. Laurens Equity 1818-10
    Widow:
    Ch: Nancy Creswell (d. 4 Jan. 1812--no ch) -w- Robert Creswell
         William and John Dunlap--Trustees
         Henry Hunter, son, to be educated
         John   "
         Sarah, Elizabeth, Rachel Hunter
         To: Robert Dunlap, son of Wm. Dunlap, nephew of Nancy
    Creswell

HUNTER, JOHN, SEN'R.--Will--Laurens Equity 1819-5
    Widow: Margaret
    6 ch: Margaret -w- John McClintock
          James, John, Samuel, Nancy, and William

HUNTER, MATHEW--Will Laurens Equity 1820-11
    Widow: Margaret -m- Rev. Thos. Archibald
    5 ch: Robert, James, John, Andrew, and David
    Andrew Spears, their paternal uncle, Gdn.
    Exors: James and John Hunter--Sold lot to David Spears, Dec'd
                                       Aug. 1, 1815

HUTCHINSON, JOHN with Samuel Stedman -vs- Robert Hutchinson--was to
    go to Va. and pur. land for Glass.Laurens Equity 1809-1

HUTCHISON, MARY--Dau. of John Buchanan, Sen'r. see card. Also Thomas
    Hutchinson--same card. Laurens Equity Bx D-1816

HUTCHISON, ROBERT--Dec'd--intestate. Laurens Equity 1818-5
    Widow: Eleanor
    9 Ch: William, Robert and Jenny Hutchinson
         James Elliott Hutchinson   Name shown Hutchinson
         John S.   "   Also Hutchison
         Margaret -w- Thos. Nichols
         Other names unknown.
         Suit by John Hutchison--alleges Robert moved all goods
         from United States.

INMAN, BENJAMIN--Of Newberry Will 4 Nov. 1798 Laurens Box D
    Wife: Elizabeth

158

INMAN, BENJAMIN--Continued
My 8 ch: Ahab, Arthur, Benjamin, J**o**hn, Feneley, Charles,
    Elizabeth, and George
Bro: John Inman
Others: Joseph Thomas and wife, Elizabeth
    Richard Fly and Ferrely, his wife
    Asa Inman
    Mary Inman and Henry Steddam, Exors of John Inman

INMAN, J**O**HN--Will Son, Asa Inman--Laurens Equity 1817-**3**

IRBY, WILLIAM -w- Henrietta to Ambrose Hudgens, Sen'r.--150 A. on
Simmons Cr. of Little R. Pt. Gr. to Edward Osborn--300 A. on
6 July, 1774. Laurens Deed A-102/3 14 Dec. 1785

JACKSON, WILLIAM, School Master from Benjamin Rainey--Planter. Bond-
"Sd Wm. Jackson shall continue to teach a grammar school during
the term of 3 years". 130 A. on waters of Enoree--Pt. 440 A.
Gr. to Charles Findley, June 8, 1786, who conv. to Benj. Rainey
Laurens Deed B-41-42 Dec. 13, 1786

JAMES, JOHN--Dec'd. Of Newberry Laurens Equity 1811-7
married 6 Apr. 1780 Elizabeth Roten, only child Nancy m. William.
Gary. John James drove his wife and child off, took up with
Nancy Tucker.

JEFFRIES, THOMAS and his Mother, Elizabeth Green (or Greer) to Wm.
Fowler--300 A. Gr. T. J. Jan. 16, 1778. Wit: John Poven and
John McClintock. Deed Bk A-120/22 Jan. 18, 1785

JOELL, RATCLIF to Mark Moore or Mon--150 A. on Beaver Dam of Little
River. Wit: Peter Ragsdale, and Joel Burgess. Laurens A-43/5
Jan. 29, 1785

JOHNSON, JOHN 25 Nov. 1793 Laurens 1-70 A-84
Son: Douglas (or Duglass)
Daus: Janet, Agnes, Mary, and Margaret
Ex: Son and McClintock Charles Wilson. 25 Nov. 1793 Prov.
Wit: Wm. Fulton, James Wilson, and John Wilson

JOHNSON, MATTHEW--Dec'd. James Johnson, Exor. Laurens Equity 1827-3
Dau: _____ -w- James Scott

JONES, BENSON--See card Rhody Babb. Laurens Equity Bx. D-6 1816

JONES, CALEB To Jonathan Downs--150 A. on Saluda R.. Gr. to Henry
Neely Apr. 20, 1763. Wit: John Goodwin, Moses Tomlinson
Robert Dickinson. Laurens Deed A-18/21 March 8, 1775

JONES, JESSE -w- Ann Gr. 1769 to Daniel Williams, Jr. 100 A. on Br.
of Reedy R. called Walnut Branch. 29 Jan. 1774. C. T. Deed
Laurens File   2-5-28

JONES, THOMAS and George Brownlee--C**o**-Partners in Blacksmith. Money
Laurens Equity 1818-1

JONES, JOHN--Laurens Wills Bk D 7 Sept. 1804
    Wife: Joyce
    Niece: Joyce J. Ward, wife of Robert Ward.
    Nephew: Moses Foster
    Exor: Robert Ward, Wife, and Jones Foster
    Wife and Robert Ward qualified Mar. 11, 1811
    Wit: Thos Hill, Dinnett Hill, Samuel B. Sheperd, Chas. McGee

KELLET, JOSEPH To Harris Gilliam--Gr. to James Burges-23 Jan. 1773
    Conv. Robert Sims. Conv. James Hall. Conv. sd Joseph Kellet.
    Ester Kellet a wit. Laurens Deed A-366 1784

KELLET, JOSEPH--Planter Laurens Wills A-4
    Wife: Jennet or Jennah
    Dau: Mary
    Son: John--Where he lives along Indian Line
             William--Land on Reedy River
    Daus: Martha, Esther, and Ann
    Sons: James and Martin
    Ex: Wife and son, William 9 Oct. 1785
    Wit: Martin Mehaffy, Cornelius McMahon, Andrew McKnit

KELLET, WILLIAM--Planter of Laurens. Laurens 1-81 A-140
    Wife: Aorna--lived in Greenville Co. and Laurens Co.
    Mother: Gennet Kellet--Lived in Laurens Co
    Sister: Jennet)To get part of estate left by their Father's
             Margaret)Will
    "My Bros. and Sisters"
    Ex: Mother and Martin Kellet 13 Aug. 1795--Proven
    Wit: Edward Scarborough, Hannah Kellet, James Kellet

KERNALL, BARNETT--Laurens Wills A-22 Apr. 6 Mar. 1790
    Aprs: Alex Deal, Clement Deal, Benj. Fooshee

KERNALL, BARNETT--Of 96 Dist. Will 15 Apr. 1785. D. shortly after.
    Wife: Grace
    My Ch: Curtis Kernall
             Nancy -m- Benjamin Hitt
             Jenny -m- Samuel Caldwell
             Milly -m- Stephen Owen
             Polly Kernall
    Exors: John Turner, Patrick Kernall. Laurens Equity 1812-4

KERNS, SAMUEL S. -w- Elizabeth--Alleges Elizabeth, as Elizabeth
    Kirk, purchased 20 Feb. 1802 from James Brown -w- Jane, a tract
    of land and soon after -m- George Lowens (Lawen or Lower) who
    sold it. Suit to get land back after canv's. Laurens 1820-6

KILLGORE, JAMES to Allias Cheek 100 A. on Beaver Dam Creek--Gr. to sd
    James Killgore 21 Jan. 1785. Wit: Benj. Killgore, John McElroy
    Jane Killgore. Laurens Deed A-144 Nov. 13/14 1785
    Deed A-219/221 Dec.21, 1785 To John McElroy--500 A. of 600 A.
    Bd. Widow Dunlap's Spring Br. James Walden et al on S-s of
    Enoree R.

KIRK, JAMES--Will 1701 Laurens Equity 1817-1 To Gr. Ch.--Ch of Wm.
    Bryson. Sarah -w- John Hunter--Will
                 2nd Col. John Simpson

KIRK, JAMES--Continued from back of card
    Sarah Simpson--Ex. of John Hunter -vs-
        Jane Bryson, James, Robert and John Bryson, Jane -w-
        Hampton Bates, Sarah -w- Wm. Taylor, and Chas. Little and
        Wm. Blakely as Adm'rs Wm. Bryson, Dec'd. Wm father of
        Sarah.

KIRK, JAMES Of Laurens--Will Laurens Equity 1817-2
    Heirs: Sarah -m- Wm. Taylor
          James, Robert, and John Bryson
          Jane Bryson -m- Hampton Bates
          John Kirk--Dec'd son
             Son: James Kirk

KIRK, JOHN--Dec'd--Copy Will in File. Laurens Equity 1819-15
    Widow: Elizabeth -m- George Lowens (or Lawens)
    Son-in-law: Wm. Bryson
    Son: John Kirk and his son, James
    Gr. Dau: Sarah Bryson
    Gr. Son: James Bryson Children of Wm. Bryson, Gr. Ch. of
    Gr. Dau: Ro__? Bryson Testator.
    Gr. Son: John Bryson
    Cousin: James Kirk of N. C.

KIRK, JOHN--Dec'd Laurens Equity 1819-16
    Widow: Elizabeth -m- George Lowens
    3 ch: James Kirk
          Sarah -m- John Pharis--Orator
          John--Died a minor

KIVELL, BENJAMIN, Planter. Laurens Deed B-43/44 July 28, 1786
    To: Thomas Kivell--Carpenter and Millwright--½ of 200 A. Gr.
    to Robert Goodwin. Oct. 2, 1785 and 350 A. Gr. to Benj. Kivell
    Pt. of 640 A. Grant--On Enoree R. Wit: Martin Williams,
    Samuel P. Jones

LANG, ROBERT -w- Mellicent Laurens C. T. Deed N4-357
    Oldest son: Richard Lang -w- Sarah--To Daniel Williams of
    Halifax Co. Va.--250 A. on Reedy R. of Saluda. Orig. Gr. to
    John Reed 5 Nov. 1755. Conv. to Robert Lang 1 or 2 March 1756

LEARWOOD, EDMOND to Mark Moor--100 A. in 96 Dist. Bd. SE James Ryan
    and Augusta Hall. NE James Ryan and Vac. All other vac.
    Laurens Deed A-46 Jan. 28/29 1785

LEEK, GEORGE--Dec'd Oct. 1819--Will Laurens Equity 1820-10
    Widow: Margaret
    8 Ch: Anna and Samuel--above 14, also Jane and William
          James, Margaret, Malinda, Alzira--under 14

LEWIS, ELLINOR Laurens Wills 1-27 A-22
    Nieces: Ellinor Davis
    Bro: George Dalrymple and his dau, Elizabeth, a minor
          John Dalrymply
    Sis: Rachel Smith and dau. Ellinor
    Niece: Ellinor Dalrymple--dau. of Samuel Dalrymple and in case
          her death to her sister, Rosanna
    Nephew: Thomas Davis and his son, John Davis
    Bro: Samuel Dalrymple. Prov 11 Sept, 1789

LEWIS, JOHN, Com'r. Pub. Works -vs- Thomas Willoughby Waters-Tax
    coll. for Newberr. Laurens Equity 1796-1

LEWIS, JOHN -w- Priscilla of Gilford Co. N. C. Oct. 28, 1771 to
    Joshua Teague--200 A. on Bush R. Gr. 14 Nov. 1754 sd John Lewis
    Plat shows Surv. for Wm. Burrows. Laurens Deed B-67/69

LINN, WILLIAM of N. C. 15 Nov. 1776 to John Rodgers--100 A. Little R.
    and Reedy Fork of Saluda. Laurens Deed B-63/4

LIGON, PETER -w- Patsy, dau. of Samuel Ward, late of Va. and Thomas
    Liggon--See card of Samuel Ward. Susanna Ligon (Liggon) of Va.
    married Samuel Ward. Laurens Equity No 2 1813

LIGON, THOMAS--Dec'd Sept. 1826 intestate Laurens Equity 1827-2
    Widow:
    Heirs: William, Parmelia -w- Thos Ligon, Thomas, Jr., Virginia,
        Harriet, Woodson, Thomas

LINDLEY, JAMES of Raeburn's Cr. Settlement and son, Thomas Lindley
    -w- Elizabeth to Marmaduke Pinson--100 A. on Rayburn's Cr.--
    Orig. Gr. to Charles Quails (Quarles?) to Ralph Humphrey, to
    Lindley. Laurens Deed A-350/352 May 15, 1785

LINDSEY, ISAAC -w- Hester and Samuel Lindsey. See card Hugh Patterson
    Laurens Equity No-13 1815

LINDSEY, TABITHA -w- Caleb, dau. of Tabitha Goodman, who was dau. of
    Oliver Towles. Laurens Equity No 10 1813

LOGAN, DAVID--"of 96 Dist" Laurens Wills A-15   July 5, 1789
    Ch: Cate, David, and Polly Hannah--not 21
    Ex: Angus Campbell, James Caldwell, and Patrick Cunningham
    Wit: Reuben Pyles, Jacob Gibson, Mary Gibson
    Apr: Aug. 18, 1790
    Aprs: Richard Griffin, Jonathan Johnson, Alex. Snell
    Tract of land on Saluda sold to Gabriel Jones.

LOWRY, WILLIAM--110 A Berkley on Mudlick Cr. Cert. 14 Mar. 1769 for
    Wm. Lowry. Precept Dec. 6, 1768 Mem 10-442

LYNCH, JAMES--To Sanford Berry--40 A. on Lynch's Cr. of Enoree R.
    Orig. Gr. to Thomas Fare (or Farr). Wit: John Lynch and
    Jesse Lynch. Laurens Deed F-431 Feb. 21, 1799

MADDEN, JOHN--Dec'd Laurens Equity 1817-9
    George Madden, Exor: -vs- Moses, David, Mabry, Charles, William
    Abraham, John

MADDEN, JOHN--of Laurens Co. Laurens 1-87 A-142
    Wife: Susannah
    Ch: Charles, Abraham, William, John, David and Martha, George, Ex.
        (Might have been other children) 20 Aug. 1795--Prov.
        Wit: Richard Pugh, Ann Madden (3 more cards, same info)

MADDEN, MOSES -vs- Little Berry Sullivan of Charlotte Co. Va.
    Slave Laurens Equity 1800-1

MADDOX, JULIA--Laurens Wills Bk D Dec. 1, 1810--John and James Young
    Pet. for Letters Dec. 1, 1810

MAHAFFEY, MARTIN, SEN'R. Laurens 1-58 A-69
    Wife: Mary
    Son: Martin--Exor with wife   Prov.--no date
    Wit: John McMahan, Elisha Hunt

MANNING, LEVI--Of Newberry Dist. Will 22 March 1796 Laurens Eq. 1812-7
    Widow: Elizabeth -m- _____Grigsby
    3 sons: Luke, Levi, Jethro
    Daus: Elizabeth -m- John Thrweat (?)
          Anna -m- Wilkes B. Waters
          Margaret, Polly and Sally

MAPLES, MARMADUKE--of Lincoln Co. N. C. to John Maple of Laurens
    To sell his Warrant #657 "Granted me by the Hon. Wm. Hill,
    Sec. State of N. C. in consequence of my Rev. service" 3 Jan.
    1821--Prob. Laurens Dist. Misc. D-234

MARTIN, THOMAS--Adv. Alexander Wilkinson--see card. Laurens Eq. D-3
                                                              1816
MARTIN, EDWARD--James Davis, Adm. Laurens Prob. Bdl. 99 Pk.-12 1845

MARTIN, JOHN AND SHADRACH--Wit. deed by John Phendley--Deed Bk A-325
                                                               1786
MARTIN, REUBEN--Ex's Henry and Reuben Martin. Laurens Bdl. 48-11 1812

MARTIN, WILLIAM--Planter of Laurens--Gr. Mar. 2, 1768 to Alexander
    Hamilton--100 A. on waters of Little R. Wit: John Rodgers,
    Jefree Wicks, Edmond Learwood. Laurens Deed A-258/60 May 31, 1786

MASON, COL. JAMES--Of 96 Dist--Will Laurens Equity 1810-4 -vs-
    Exors: Archer Mason, son.
            Elihue Cresswell
            John C. Mas--
    and: Zelita Rogers, adm'x Andrew Rogers
            James Clardy
            Isaac Mitchell
            Henry Fuller -w- Sarah

MATHIS, ZEBULON -w- Jane--see card John Cason -w- Sarah. Laurens Eq. 3
                                                               1814
MAXWELL, ANDREW--Of Washington Dist. -vs- John Fletchall--Labor
    agreement contested. Laurens Equity No 9-1813

MAXWELL, GEORGE -vs- Adam Carruth--Co-Partnership-Money Laurens 1817-8

MAXWELL, ROBERT Laurens Equity 1809-?
    Widow: Mary -m- Adam Carruth. -- Bill-Missing slaves etc,
    Rowland Tankersley -vs- Adam Carruth and wife, Mary
    Thomas Tarrant
    Mary Tarrant   All rep's. of Larkin Tarrant.
    Robert Anderson

McBEE, VARDRY--Of Spartanburg to Benjamin Killgore--400 A. Gr. to
    Mertin or Martin at mouth of Gilder's Creek. Wit: Benj. Rainey
    Benj. Kevil, and Lewis Akins. Laurens Deed A-223/4 Feb. 23, 1786

McCAIN, JAMES--"Of 96 Dist, now called Oxford Dist. and Laurens Co.
    Planter". Laurens Wills A-3   5 Aug. 1786
    Son: John
    Dau: Mary Thomas (or Thurman)
         Eliz. or Eliza, Ex'x.
    Wit: Richard Pugh, Jno. Hollingsworth and Henry Hollingsworth

McCLARKIN, THOMAS--Of Camden Dist. 26 Sept. 1786 to Andrew Endsley
    Gr. to John Cunningham, 22 Feb. 1771, conv. to T. McC. on Dun-
    can's Cr.--Beard's Fork. Laurens Deed B-86

McCLERKIN, THOMAS--To Thomas Cunningham--Sadler--600 A. on Reaburn's
    Cr. of Reedy R. Gr. to David Webb 18 May, 1771--who conv. to
    James Ryan and he conv. to sd T. McC. Deed Bk A-85 1785
    Page 63--Same to John Cunningham--Gr. to Joseph Waits, 19 Nov.
    1772--who conv. to Radcliff Towell who conv. to sd T. McC.

McCLELLAND, JOHN--Next friend of Rosamond Moore. Laurens Eq. D-1

McCRARY, JOHN -w- Jane of Laurens Co. 14 Feb, 1786 to Charles Hutchings
    300 A. on Cuncan's Cr.--all vac. when gr. to Dan'l Mote, 2 Aug.
    1770. Conv. to sd John McCrary. Laurens Deed B-78
    Bk 3L-169 16 Mar. 1773--Conv. to John Coulter. On 14 July, 1774
    to J. McC. and wife Jean.

McCRARY, ROBERT -w- Mary 3 Sept. 1773 to John Pride--150 A. Surv.
    for Isaac Pennington and James Bright. Orig. gr to Richard
    Chesney on Enoree R. Laurens Deed B-97/99

McCRARY, ROBERT--Son-in-law of Sarah Penny--Will 1810 Spartanburh 72-A
                 Gr. son Robert McCrary
                 Son-in-Law of Thomas Penny--Will 1809

McCRARY, THOMAS -w- Casey (Casandra)dau. of Joseph Adair of Laurens
                                                              1812
McCRARY, THOMAS Laurens Wills 1-61 A-71 9 Jan. 1790 Prov.
    Dau: Elizabeth
    Sons: Matthew, Thomas, and Charles
    Dau: Jane -w- John Greer
    Sons: Moses and George--Land adj. Andrew McCrary
    Sons: Christopher and Andrew
    Wife: Lettie
    Daus: Mary and Catherine
    Wit: George Bush, David Bailey

McDOWALL, BENJAMIN Laurens 1-31 A-25   13 Aug. 1790--Prov.
    Wife: Elizabeth
          Wife's dau., Patsy Jinnings, Land in Georgia
          Antony Jinnings, tools etc.
    Wit: Reuben Pyles, John Gyner, Patrick Riley

McENTIRE, THOMAS L.--Of Bunk Co. N. C.--See card Adam Acrruth
    Laurens Equity D-2 1816

McGILLIVRAY, WILLIAM--Servant to Dr. Arthur Reeves. Pd. as pack-
    horseman to the Creeks, for acct of Robert Haynes--1718
    Indian Book 1-271

McKEE, MICHAEL--Dec'd. See card James Sprowl Laurens Eq. D-10 1816

McKNIGHT, ANDREW, SEN'R,--Laurens 1-16 A-15
    Wife: Abigail   8 Feb. 1789--Prov.
    Daus: Abigail, Jennet
    Sons: Andrew, Archibald
    Wit: Martin Huey, John Alexander, David Morton

McMAHAN, DAVID--Of Union -vs- Wright and James Coats of Newberry--
    Cotton. Laurens Equity 1809-2

McNEES JOHN--Cr. May 5, 1773 to Samuel Wharton--150 A. Branches of
    Cains Cr. Wit: Daniel Ozburn, Whittenhall Warner
    Laurens Deed A-141/143 Apr. 9, 1777

McNEES, ROBERT--To Andrew Endsley--Land on Duncan's Cr. Deed A-1

McNEES, SALLY (OR SARAH)--Laurens Will 17 June 1846 Box 149-17
    Dec'd husband: Lewis Saxon
    Infant son: Lewis, Dec'd
    Elizabeth Arnold -w- Lewis Arnold of Ala.
    Daus: Clarissa Downs, Polly Arnold and her dau, Ruthy, Susan
        Thurston.
    Gr. Dau: Sally Arnold
    Gr. Son: Robert Lewis Cleveland, son of Benj. F. and Tabitha
        Cleveland
    Son: Hugh Saxon, Joshua Saxon, and Lydall P..Saxon
    Gr. Dau: Isabella Weatherall, dau of son, Allen Saxon, Dec'd.
        (Seems Isabella m. Lewis Taylor

McPHERSON, WILLIAM--See card John Shealy, Dec'd. Laurens Prob. Bk-1
                                                                   1825
McVAY, HUGH --Of 96 12 Nov. 1786 to Robert Ross of 96 -w- Margaret
    100 A. on Little R. Bd. Richard Robinson, Jeremiah Franks,
    Charles Allin. Conv. by James Bird to Richard Robinson , by
    him to Robert Ross. Laurens Deed B-31/33

MEADOWS, SUSANNA--Laurens Wills Vol. 2 Bk-F Pg-20 18 July, 1823
    Dau: Anne Meadors -w- James Saxon
    Sons: Reuben, Jason, John
    Wit: Washington Meadors. Prov--7 Aug. 1826

MERCHANT, JOHN and his Dau. Rhody Merchant. Legatee of Rhody Babb
    Laurens Equity Bx-D No-6 1816

MIDDLETON, ANSWORTH-Of Co. Laurens 96 Dist. Laurens 1-79 Bk-A-119
    Wife:
    Sons: Andrew, Thomas, Hainsworth, John and James
    Daus: Margaret Hunter, and Ann Williams
          Judith
    "my 2 Y. daus: Sarah Middleton and Jane Middleton

MIDDLETON, ANSWORTH--Continued from back of card
    Exor: John Middleton and Mathew Hunter
    1 March 1795--Prov.
    Test: Will Saxon, Thos. Roberts, James Cobb

MIDOLE, WM Laurens Wills A-12
    Apr: 28 Mar. 1789
    Aprs: Wm. Hall, James McCurley, Joseph Dean, Joseph Parsons

MILAM, BARTLETT--Dau. m. James Erven. Died--2 small ch--Betsy
    Judy. Laurens Equity 1812-6

MILLER, HANSE Laurens Vol 1-6 A-7 14 April, 1788
    Y-Son: Joseph
    Wife: Susannah--Ex.
    Ch: Betsy, John, Jacob, Ellinor, Jesse, George, James
    Son-in-Law: James Gammerfine (?)
                James Huddleston
    Ex: John Brown
    Wit: Thos. Adair, Thos. Ewings, James Adair

MILLER, JACOB--Next friend of Jennet Prather. Adv. John Clarke
    Laurens Equity No-15 abt. 1818

MILLER, JOHN--Dec'd Laurens Equity No. 3 1814
    John
    William
    Elizabeth -m- Wm. Teague--See card John Cason -w- Sarah
    Card #2: John died 2 Feb. 1814. 1st wife died. Married 2nd
    wife, Sarah Cason, in 1807. Children of 1st wife:
        Elizabeth -w- Wm. Teague
        Sarah -w- John Cason
        Jane -w- Zebulon Mathis
        Anna -w- Abraham Johnston
        Rebecca -w- Joseph Cason
        George Miller
        James Miller
        Polly -w- Joshua Smith
        John, Anderson, and William Miller--Minors
    Had land Newberry, Edgefield, etc.

MILLER, SARAH--Dau. of John Ellis--See card Ellis Laurens Eq. 1815-12

MILLS, THOMAS--Advs William Summers, Sen'r--See Summer card. Laurens
    Equity Bx-D No-8 1816

MILLWEE, WILLIAM Laurens 1-7 A-7 26 Jan. 1784--Prov.
    Son: John 25 shillings
    Dau: Margaret Dunlap--2 shillings
    To: John Entrican--2 shillings
    Sons: William and James--each ½ land
    Wife: Sarah
    Gr. Son: Wm Hudgins--to be educated
    Wit: George Rose, James Henderson and Wm. Irby

MOORE, ANDERSON AND JAMES--See card Ezekiel Roland--Laurens D-3 1815

MOORE, BARBARA W--Admx. and Gdn. Robert Moore, Dec'd. 15 yrs. Ptn.
     Pd Thos Payne, Sheriff, Greenville Co. for selling land $16.56
     Minors were: Robert B., Elizabeth W., Harriett L. V., Louisa B.,
     William P., and Sarah G., Moore. Also see Feb. term Ct. min. 1817
     Laurens Gdn. Acts, also Greenville Wills 1818

MOORE, BETSY--Dau of George Mosely--See Mosely Will Laurens Will E-360

MOORE, ELEANOR--Of Newberry Dist. d. intestate Sept. 1813
     Ch: Rebecca -w- Charles Pitts
          Patsy -w- Charles Gillam--Orator Laurens Equity 1815-9

MOORE, HANNAH--Dau. of Robert Hinton of Laurens. 1797 See Hinton Will

MOORE, MORDICA AND JAMES--Laurens Deed A-89/92 Lands on Durbin's Cr.
     N-fork. Conv. James Gibson of N. C. to various persons. 1785

MOORE, TRYPARNA--Wit. Will of Wm. Hall 27 May, 1799. Laurens A-200

MOORE, WM. JR., JOHN AND ROBERT CUNNINGHAM--144 A. Raeburn's Cr.--Pt
     Gr. Richard Shirly. Feb. 15, 1796 Laurens Deed K-19 Apr. 29, 1812

MONTGOMERY, JAMES--Laurens 1-153 A-52 Aug. 17, 1791--Prov.
     Wife: Margaret
     "my 2 daus": Rebecca Adair, and Isabella Rop (or Ross)
     Son-in-Law: James Adair--Ex
                  George Ross (or Rop)
     Wit: Wm. Craig, John Craig, Isabella Craig

MURDOCK, HAMILTON--To Samuel Eakins 2 tracts 250A. and 89A. adj.
     on waters of Little River of Saluda. Bd. Thomas Edghill, and
     Matthew Cook. Sd Hamilton Murdock, John Murdock, and Jean
     Murdock. Laurens Deed A-1783

MUSGROVE, EDWARD--Of Enoree, Laurens Co. Laurens Wills 1-32 A-28
     Son: Edward Beaks Musgrove
     "my loving little son": William Musgrove
     Daus: Rebecca Cannon
            Marrey Berry
     Wife: Ann--Sole Ex.
     Wife's 7 ch: William, Margarett, Ann, Hannah, Leah, Rachel, and
          Liney--(Evidently married twice) Proven 25 Aug. 1790

MYERS, TOBIAS -w- Ann of Colleton Co. to William Dandy, 4 Nov. 1784
     150 A. on Little R. of Saluda. Laurens Deed B-28/30
     Wit: John Dunelin, Charles or Hewlett Sullivant. Prob be-
     fore Jonathan Downs, J. P.

NEELY, GEORGE--Of Liberty Spring Congregation. Laurens Co.
     Wife: Ann--Ex.   Proven--1 July, 1793
     Son: James--Ex.
     Dau: Agnes
     Wit: Joseph Hollingsworth, Henry Hitt, John McCook

NEELY, HENRY -w- Elizabeth to Caleb Jones--150 A. S-Br Bush Cr. of
    Saluda. Wit: Ralph Townsend, Wm. Neely, John Jones.
    Laurens Deed A-11 to 16 Jan. 10, 1773
    Page 18--to Jonathan Downs

NEIGHBORS, SAMUEL To Joel Burgess--75 A. on Beaver Dam of Saluda.
    Being pt of 150 A. Gr. to Agnilla Hall May 5, 1770--To Charles
    Parrott Feb. 7, 1774, and conv. ½ to Samuel Neighbors Aug. 1
    1770 (error in book) Laurens Deed A-198/6 Oct. 23, 1779

NEILY, HENRY -w- Elizabeth to Caleb Jones--Plantation where sd Caleb
    Jones now lives--on S-Branch of Brush Cr. of Great Saluda.
    Wm. Neily a wit. Laurens Deed A-10 1785

 NIBLET, SOLOMON--Laborer--Gr. March 22, 1769 to Joshua Saxon--400 A.
    on Rayburn's Cr. of Saluda. Laurens Deed B-71/2 March 2, 1787

NICHOLS, SOLOMON--Dec'd, of Newberry. Left Will. Made Deed Gift
    To Elizabeth Nichols--dated 17 May, 1784. Will dated 1790
    Elizabeth Wrenwick, "my present wife", and her children.
    Suit: Agnes Wrenwick, Jabez Gault and Solomon Royster -vs-
    John Wrenwick, William Wrenwick, alias, Miller

NORWOOD, GEORGE -w- Ann of 96 Dist. Gr 500 A. Feb. 11, 1773 to
    Joshua Teague--350 A. on waters of Little R. Wit: Robert Sims
    John Miller, and Wm. Sims. Laurens B-73/4 Dec. 11, 1773

NORWOOD, NATHANIEL of N. C. Laborer to Thomas Gafford of S. C. 96 Dist.
    Gr of 12 Aug. 1774 by Wm. Bull, Gov. to Margaret Wisman of 100 A.
    on North's Creek--Bd. George Anderson, James Burnsides, John
    Owens, Dec'd. and Joshua Roberts and Christopher Hardy.
    Laurens Deed A-304 1784
    Feb. 14, 1786 Deed A-175/6 To Wm. Hall of Laurens--100 A. on
    N-Creek. Bd. Thos Gafford, John Owins, Dec'd, and George Anderson

    O'NEAL, HUGH--A lunatic--committed by John O'Neal, Samuel Cothran
    John Caldwell. Laurens Equity 1813-3

O'NEAL, HUGH -vs- Samuel Maverick-et al--Money Laurens Bx-D-11 1816

O'NEALL, HUGH -vs- Samuel Cothran, Samuel Spleen, David Waters,--In
    re. land pur. by plaintiff from Moses Lindsey. Laurens 8-1815

O'NEALL, JOHN--See card Rhody Babb Laurens Equity 6-1816

O'NEALL, WILLIAM--Dec'd 1807 intestate Laurens Equity 1818-4
    Widow: Sarah -m- Elias Holcomb
    4 Ch: Arthur, John, Henry and William--last 3--minors
    Dec'd William was son of John O'Neall--Widow Ann Jane

O'NEALL, WILLIAM -w- Mary of Newberry to Joseph Armstrong-Blacksmith
    of Laurens--100 A. on waters of Mudlick Cr. Bd. lands of Eichart,
    Henry Conte, John Ray, Anthony Griffin--Gr. to Ann Hagin Dec. 4
    Laurens Deed A 327 to 335 Sept. 1, 1786   1776

OSBORNE, JOHN -w- Delphy--see card Ezekiel Roland Laurens D-3 1815

OSBORNE, RACHEL (or Osburn)see card Rhody Babb Laurens D-6 1816

OWENS, DANIEL Laurens Wills D-45 March 9, 1811
    Mother: Mary Owens--Home place left"by my father, Dec'd"
    Bros: Thomas and Robert
    Sisters: Martha Cabiness, Ann, Jennett, and Elizabeth Owens
    Bro. Thomas-Ex. Pet. for letters 4 June, 1811
    Wit: John and Elizabeth Owens and Mary Long

OWENS, JOSHUA--Gr 400 A. Apr. 3, 1786 to Daniel Martin--Pt 1oo A.
    Bd. James Burchfield, Isai Barton on N-fork of Durbin's Cr.
    Laurens Deed A-360/1 June 9, 1786

PARKER, JAMES "son of Catherine Allison"--Apprenticeship to Thomas
    Cunningham. Catherine Allison agreeing. Laurens Deed A-93
    Aug. 23, 1785

PARKINS, DANIEL--Dec'd Laurens Equity 1810-3
    Son: Charles Parkins and Hugh O'Neal, Admr's
    Bros: Isaac, Allen R., and Mark S., Adv: Sampson Pope of
    Edgefield

PARKS, JAMES -vs- Thomas Archibald and wife Margaret
                  Andrew Speers, Gdn for Robert Speers
                  Jane Speers
                  John, Andrew, David Speers--minors
    Plt. agreed to pur. lands from Col. John Simpson and David Speers

PARSLEY, ROBERT--Dec'd 1817 Will   Laurens Equity 1819-1
    Widow: Elizabeth
    Son: James--contested Will
    Dau: Martha -w- Isaac Mitchell
                Wm. Milam
                Daniel Cook
        Lucy Adams   Minor ch also mentioned.

PASLAY, ELIZABETH--a widow--Will shows -m-_____Byrd
    Sons: Austin Paslay, Edmund T., Henry W., and James C. and
          James daughter, Elizabeth I.
    Daus: Hannah H.Cook -w- Daniel Cook
           Eliza Coleman
           Dorothy Blum
    Will under name Elizabeth Byrd--Laurens A-42

PATY, DAVID and son, Mercer of Ohio--Legatee of Rhody Babb. See card
    Laurens Equity D-6 1816

PAYNE, THOMAS -vs- Henry Tandy Walker, Sheriff of Greenville Dist.
    In re agreement as deputy sheriff. Laurens Equity 7-1815

PAYSINGER, FREDERICK adv. William Beard Laurens Equity D-13 1816

PEARSON, BENJ. "of Bush River" Newberry Wills Pg. 25 1784
    Wife: Margaret
    7 Sons: Wm. Abel, Sam'l, Robert, Joseph, John, Enoch
    Bro: Wm. Pearson
    Dau: Rosanna Russell
         Marjory Buffington
    Cousin: Wm. Pearson--Ex. with Wm. and Enoch
    lo Dec. 1784 Prov. 6 June 1788

PEARSON, SAMUEL and Mercer Babb, Farmers of Newberry to Elisha
    Ford 12 July 1786 Laurens Deed B-90

PEEPLES, ELIJAH, WM. H., AND JOHN--Deed headed Beaufort Dist for
    estate of Jesse Peeples to Cynthis Waistcoat -w- Joel Waistcoat
    Laurens Equity 1818-11

PESTER, SARAH--By next Friend Samuel Cannon m. after 16 yrs age.
    -vs- John Pester, her husband--took up with wife of another man.
    Ch: Betsy age abt 14
        John " " 11
        Sally " " 8
        Middleton abt 2   Laurens Equity 1814-1

PERRY, THOMAS To Daus: Delilah Perry and Sarah Hunter--Deed Gift
    Laurens Equity 1817-4

PEASTER, JOHN -w- Sarah--sister of George Ruff, Jr. See Ruff card
    Laurens Equity 11-1813

PERSONS, JOSEPH -w- Alse of Craven Co. 18 Jan. 1779 to James McClintock
    550 A. Gr. James Goolsby on SW side of Warrior Creek. 3/4 Oct.
    1768 conv. to sd Joseph Pearsons (also Parsons) Laurens B-76/8

PHINDLEY, JOHN--Dec'd. His son, John Phindley to Paul Phindley. Wit.
    John Martin and Shadrach Martin. Laurens Deed A-325-327 Sept. 7
                                         1784
PINSON, AARON--"Minister of the Gospel" of Laurens Co. Laurens 1-97
    Wife: Elizabeth
    Sons: Moses and Isaac
    Daus: Jememah Kennery
         Mary Cole, Dec'd--Her heirs
    Son: John   21 Feb. 1794 Wit: John Kennery, Aaron Pinson, Jr.

PINSON, JOSEPH wife, Mary of Laurens Co to Stephen Wood--200 A.
    Laurens Co. Waters of Reedy River--Gr. to Nathan Hampton
    Laurens Deed Bk A-251 1786

PITTS, CHARLES -w- Rebecca adv. Charles Gillam -w- Patsy Laurens 9-1815

PITTS, ROBERT--Will 12 Feb. 1863 Laurens Wills 1861-1872-18
    Wife: Mary E. E. Pitts
    Son: Thomas H. Pitts of age--the Leek place, whereon he lives
    Gr. son: Preston Brooks Langston
    Dau: Margaret E. Pitts
         S. Ella
    ? M. S.
    Son: John
    Dau: Martha E. -w- Dr. Anthony Shank

PLUNKETT, ROBERT of Newberry Co 9 Jan. 1787 to Abijah O'Neal 150 A.
on Little R. and Beaver Dam, pt of 350 A. gr to Henry Stone
Pa rish and Henry Stone conv. to Wm. Pitts Feb. 1786 at C. T.
to Robert Plunkett. Laurens Deed B-89/90

POLLOCK, JAMES "Of Duncan's Creek" Laurens 1-73 A-101
  Wife: Ann   Sarah Dalrymple's son, James
  Dau: Gennet Henley   Elizabeth Gray's son, James
  Eldest Son: Wm. Pollock   Ann Scott's son, James
  Son: James and his children Ex: Pattrick Scott and Robert Long
      Samuel   26 June 1797--Prov.
  Dau: Isabella   Wit: Sam'l McConelly
      Sarah Dalrymple   Alex Adair
      Elizabeth Gray   Joseph Greir
  Gr. Dau: Ann Scott
  Son: John's son, James

POPE, SAMPSON--Of Edgefield Dist--see card John Bulow of Chas'n Dist.
Laurens Equity 3-1813

POWELL, BENJAMIN -w- Martha to Thomas Dendy--250 A. on North Cr. of
Little R. of Saluda. Bd. Wm. Dendy and vac. Deed A-172/4
Dec. 20, 1773

POWELL, SAMUEL--from John Bailey--In the fork of Little R. and North's
Cr. Bd. Wm. Bailey and Wm. Dendy. Deed burned. Affidavit by
Samuel Powell before Silvanus Walker, J. P. Also aff. by Whitten-
hall Warner, a witness

PRATHER, JENNETT--By next friend, Jacob Miller -vs- Wm. Prather
(not followed up) Laurens Equity 1809-3
1815-15--Wm. Prather esc. for good and went to East Fla. then
to Tennessee. Took wife_____and_____. 1 infant dau. Suit for
legal sep. and possession of child. John Clark who had judgement
_____moved to Clark Co. Ga.

PRATHER, WILLIAM Laurens 1-13 A-12 Prov. 3 Nov. 1788
  Wife: Mary-Ex.
  Dau: Dorcas Prather, a minor
  Wit: Abraham Gray, John Lindsey, John Wallace

PRICE, WM.--Planter to Wm. Taylor--100 A. on Todd's Cr. below the
Indian Line. Bd. Wm. Tweedy, Robert Taylor and Elines Humes.
Wit: James Cunningham, and Robert Taylor Laurens A-553-355?
                                  June 11, 1786
PUCKETT, DUGLASS--Petitions for Letters on estate of Joseph Remalett
Laurens Wills Bk-D Nov. 11, 1810

PUGH, RICHARD--Of Laurens Co 1-90 A-148 10 June 1796
  Wife: Mary
  Y-Dau: Nancy Cochran
  "my 4 Step Ch: John, William, and Samuel McClanahan
                Margaret Cochran
  Wit: Wm. Boyd, Samuel Matthews, John Cochran

PYLES, FRANCES G.--By nest Friend, Alexander Winn -m- sometime in
May 1822, Dr. Abner Pyles who had children by a former wife.
On Oct. 21, 1822--agreed to separate and she was to return to
her father in Virginia. He to furnish transportation--He
claimed the child she was ensient with would be born too soon
after their marriage. Not his child. The child, Cecelia, was
born 10 months after he married her. He alleges she stole his
property and sent it in bundles to her brother's house and that
she was in secret love meeting with Alex'r Winn--"her relative".
She also had children by a former marriage from the text of
answers. (Interesting literary document. Laurens Eq. 1826-15

RAGSDALE, PETER--Of Greenville, Dist d. 17 Sept. 1789 intestate
Widow: Sarah--oratrix   Laurens Equity 1815-14
7 Ch: Fanny -w- John Ridgeway
       Larkin, Richard, and Edmond Ragsdale
       Elizabeth -w- Abner Camp
       Elijah Ragsdale
       Frances Asberry Ragsdale

RAINEY, BENJAMIN to Benj. Kilgore Gr. to John Carmichel 8 Mar. 1768
by Gov. S. C. 100 A. on Gilder's Cr. of Enoree R.
Laurens Deed A-230 1785
A-224--100 A. on Gilder's Cr. of Enoree R. to Benj. Kilgore,
pt Gr. to William Marchbanks, 15 Oct. 1784 600 A. Bd. John
Martin. Wit: John Brown, William Little, Sarah Rainey
A-302 to Nicholas White--200 A. both sides of Durbin's Cr. Bd.
John York and vac. Surv. of John Jones

REDDIN, ROBERSON --1812 Apr. of est. Jno Creecy. Laurens Wills

REDMAN, JOHN--Of Spartanburg Co to James Barton of Greenville
28 Oct. 1786 Gr. to John Redman-640 A. on Durbin's Cr.
Laurens Deed B-102/104. Pg 106--same to Jesse Goodman

REED, JONATHAN -w- Jane (also Rud, shows both) to James Strain 89 A.
on waters of Cain Cr. bd. John Carter. Deed B-25/27 July 2, 1786

REESE, NANCY of Laurens Dist. by next friend William Pugh -m-Feb 1805
Jesse Reese of Laurens Dist. Has 3 ch. by him. Patsy age 4,
Polly age 2, and Susanna age 1, and pregnant. He beat her often
and finally ran off with Molly Fowler. Laurens Equity 1811-2

RICHARDS, WILLIAM OF Greenville -vs- Benjamin Land--Money 1811-3

RICHEY, ELENOR--Gr. May 14, 1775 to Samuel Dunlap 100 A. NW side of
Rayburn's Cr. on David's Br. Laurens Deed A-136/38 15 Dec. 1785

RILEY, FERRIL--Late of S. C. now of Georgia 5 March 1787 to William
Carson of Laurens. Adm. est of John Pursell and bid in his Gr.
Conv. his Bounty Gr. 25 June, 1765--on Little R. Laurens B-115/7

RIPLEY, JOHN -w- Elizabeth to James Sullivant 250 A. on a Br. Little
R. of Saluda--formerly owned by John Shumper who conv. to James
Ryan and he to John Ripley Deed A-210/12 Oct. 7, 1784

172

RICHEY, JOHN Laurens Wills A-20 20 June 1778
    Son: John
    Dau: Mary
          Ellinor--Cow and c-cane from Jno. McHaffy
          Martha ?
    Wife:
    Son: Robert--not 21
    Ex: Wife and Wm. McDonald and Sam'l Dunlap
    Wit: Wm. Paine and John McHaffy

RICHEY, JOHN Laurens 1-23 A-20   3 July 1819
    Wife: Margaret (or Margrett) Ex: Martin Shaw
    Son: William   Wit: David Caldwell, Jr.
    Dau: Jane Harrase   Archibald Scott
    Son-in-Law: Joseph Graves   Aven? Fuller
    ? Son: Samuel Richey

RICHEY, ROBERT--Apr. 4 Aug. 1789 Laurens Wills A-13
               Aprs: Samuel Wharton, Wm. Mitchell, Lewis Barton
               Pur: Wm. Goodman

ROBERTS, JACOB "of Laurens Dist" Laurens Wills 3 Jan. 1804
    Wife: Mary and "my Y-ch" (or Morah)
    Dau: Allemon Brown   Dau: Claresey
          Elizabeth Meadows   Copay Gilbert, Dec'd
          Sarah Gilbert   Milidey
    Son: John   Leusendey
          Morah   Ex: John Meadows, Dec'd
          Isaac
          Jacob
          Thomas

ROBERTS, JAMES--Dec'd 1816. Widow, Sarah -m- Ebenezer Starnes
    Laurens Equity See Will for Heirs

ROBERTSON, RICHARD--Gr Sept 26, 1772 to Robert Ross--150 A. on
    Beaver Dam of Little R. Wit: John McElroy, Francis Ross,
    Lewis Devall. Deed A-29/31 May 12, 1784

ROBINSON, ISABELLA and Jennet Taylor -w- William Taylor--Agree-
    ment of apprenticeship by Isabella Robinson, to bind her daughter
    Jennet White-born Dec. 3, 1781, to said Jennet Taylor--to be
    brought up to age 18 yrs. Wit: David Ross and Andrew Spear
    Laurens Deed A-316 1785

RODGERS, ANDREW, JUN'R. of Laurens 19 June, 1786 to Nicholas Everleigh
    of Edgefield--200 A. N-s Saluda. Surv. for Michael Hunt 4 May,
    1763 and John and James Abernathy Aug. 1767 Laurens B-55

RODGERS, ANDREW -w- Ann. Andrew son of Jane Rodgers. Gr July 8, 1774
    To Ambrose Hudgens 100 A. head of North Cr. Wit: James McNees,
    Wm. Rodgers, and John Rodgers. Lauresn A and B July 14, 1785

RODGERS, JOHN --Of 96 31 Mar. 1777 to William Dendy 100 A. N-s Little
    R. of Saluda on North's Creek. Orig. Gr. Thomas North. 31 Nov.
    Laurens Deed B-22/3   1757

RODGERS, JOHN -w- Margaret Aug. 31, 1774 to Lewis Saxon--10 A. near
the Ct. House on Little River of Saluda, Laurens Co. Wit: Lewiis
Saxon, and John Hunter. Laurens Deed A-233-236 1780

RODGERS, JOHN to William Dendy 100 A. N-s Little R. on North Cr.
Orig. Gr. to Thomas North. Wit: Andrew Rodgers, Thos. Dendy
Cunnl Cergill Laurens Deed B 23/25 March 31, 1777

ROGERS, LETTY--Widow of_____ Laurens Equity 1826-14
4 Daus: Letty--died
Elizabeth
Polly -m- 18 March 1818
Sarah -m- 27 March 1821
Son: Thomas Rogers--Agreement Samuel Rogers, Charles Jones to
support widow and 4 daughters in exchange for the estate lands.
Suit -vs- Nancy Jones, Widow of Charles Jones

ROLAND, EZEKIEL -w- Rebecca Laurens Equity Bx D-3 1815
John Osborne -w- Delphy
Randal Sullivan adm. of James and Robert Wade and
wife, Sarah--of Georgia
Drury, James, Walter Vaughn
Nancy Sullivan
Anderson and James Moore
Letitia, Rebecca Tolly, Edny, and Lucinda Sullivan
Robert Bruton--by Gdns

ROSS, ROBERT -w- Margaret to Hugh McVay--100 A. Little R. of Saluda
Bd. Richard Robinson and Nehemiah Franks and Charles Allen
Robinson and Allen, Dec'd. Being the land conv. by James Baird
to Richard Robinson conv. Richard Robinson, Jr. to sd Robert
Ross Laurens Deed B32-33 Nov. 13, 1786

ROSAMOND, JAMES, ADM'R, Of Abbeville Feb. 10, 1787 to Lewis Graves
100 A. on Reedy River, formerly the property of Henry Parker-
now of James Rosamond. Laurens Deed B-101/2

ROSS, DAVID, Dec'd--Settlement Robert Gray and wife, Jean. -vs-
Francis Ross   James Dorough -w- Sarah
John P. Simpson and wife, Mary   David Boyd -w- Margaret
Laurens Probate Bk-Pg 2 1825/6

ROSS, JAMES L. -vs- John Lee--Carpenters--Money Laurens Equity 1818-2

ROSS, ROBERT--Native Ireland. Cit. Papers Nov. 16, 1820 at Laurens
Misc. D-211

ROWLAND, CHRISTOPHER Laurens A-153 Will 1796 29 March 1796
Wife: Mary   Wit: Silvanus Walker
Son: Robert Rowland   Matthew Lefoy
"all my children" Not named   Mary Rowland
Adm: Wife and son, Robert   Will Prov. 17 July, 1796
Aprs: Samuel Leek, Daniel Mitchel, Joseph Hollingsworth, Wm. Strain
Nov. 9, 1815

ROWLAND, CHRISTOPHER--Continued from back of card:
Sale Bill filed 2 Jan 1816

Alex Winn	Daniel Rodgers	Abram Hall
Bart. Craddock	Wm. Winn	Rob't Rowland
Joseph Brownlee	Jonas Hares	James Paslay
John Stanfield	Menard Hares	Thos Powell
James Stanfield	James Young	Wm. Hall
Wm Fulert	Thos Wilks	Elisha Brooks
Porter Culverson	Richard Carter	John Brown
Daniel Rodgers	Youngset Dendy	James Moore
Joel Walker	Jere Conant	Sam'l Leek
Tabithea R.	Daniel Mitchel	Wm Dendy
Jos. Hollingsworth	Wm Carr	Jos Travis
Wm Walker	Wm Bailey	Wila Malam
Sam'l Rodgers	Nancy Lefoy	

RUFF, GEORGE, JR.--Dec'd of Newberry Widow, Nelly Ruff Laurens 11-1813
William Rutherford in right of his wife Elizabeth, formerly
Elizabeth Ruff, sister of sd George Ruff, Jr. -vs- Barbara
Ruff, mother of dec'd--widow of George Ruff, Sen'r. Sarah
Peaster -w- John Peaster and sister of dec'd George, Jun'r.
Elizabeth Cromer -w-_____Cromer, formerly widow of David
Ruff--brother of George, Jun'r, and ch. of sd David Ruff to wit:
Henry, George, David, Christian, John, Sally and Elizabeth

RUFF, JOHN--See card John Buchanan, Sen'r. Laurens D-1816

RUTHERFORD, WILLIAM -w- Elizabeth--sister of George Ruff, Dec'd
Laurens Equity 11-1813

SAXON, CHARLES -w- Judith to Benjamin Jones 200 A. tract on Bush R. of
Saluda. Bd. Augustia Warren and vac. Orig. Gr to Henry Neely
-w- Elizabeth to James Young -w- Ann. Charles Saxon Dec 8, 1773
Deed A-78/83 Sept 13, 1785

SAXON, ISABELLA--of Laurens Dist -m- set 17 Nov. 1845 Arnold Milner of
Cass Co. Georgia. Her son, Lewis Saxon, Tr. Her land and slaves
in Laurens Co. Misc P-110 Laurens File

SAXON, JAMES -w- Anne (also Nancy)--Tried at Laurens 1 July 1833.
Suit over slaves--Shows: Edmond Craddock conveyed to James
Yancey, in trust, for the children of sd Edmund, to wit: Mary
Anne, Edmund, Thomas John and Judith, inter alia 2 slaves,
Reuben and Dave 17 March 1789. Edmund Craddock died and his
Widow Anne married James Saxon. They had a daughter, Sarah E.
Saxon. States; James Saxon claims slaves but seems to be due to
loss of memory from old age--that in 1822 he made a schedule of
his property in order to obtain pension from U. S. and did not
list the slaves--Now is planning to leave state and take slaves
with him. Wm Clarke and wife, Judith, sue. Hill's S. C.
Equity Vol 1 and 2

SAXON, JOHN -w- Eliza A. Shows: Alfred A. Kern d. 1840--unmarried
Heirs: John F. Keen-brother
Sisters: Eliz. a Saxon, Eugenia C Byrd -w- George Byrd
            Mary A. Perry -w- _____?
            Louisa L. Kerns
Ch. dec'd bro--Paudde D. Kern (sp?) Equity Roll Laurens 1843-5

SAXON. LEWIS**Gr Jan. 21, 1785 to Joel Burges Pt 150 A. S-fork of
    Reaburn's Cr. Bd. Alex'r Marick, Thos Cahoon, John McClanahan
    Survey by Benj. Brown, Dec'd. Laurens Deed 198-200 Mar. 14, 1786

SCATTERWHITE, BARTLETT--died intestate Jan. last Laurens Eq. 1817-5
    Heirs: Dau_____ -w- Wm. Allen, Orator
              Nancy Satterwhite
    Sons: Bartlett S. John and William--above 14 yrs.
    Daus: Catherine and Elizabeth--under 12

SCOTT, SAMUEL -vs- John Ritchy--Money Laurens Eq. 1809-4

SCURLOCK, ANN Laurens 1-99 A-165
    Dau: Frankey Scurlock
          Dolly   "
    Gr. Son: Reubin Scurlock
             Joshua   "
    Friend: Lewis Banton--Sole Ex. 18 Sept, 1796

SHEALY, JOHN--Dec'd--Shubel Starnes, Petitioners -vs-
    Adam, Moses, Easter and John Shealy
    Gray and George Elmore
    Beverly, Elizabeth, Lydia, and Jean Shealy
    Wm McPherson
    Elijah Elmore
    Legatees--Joint receipt--23 March 1826 Old Probate Bk Pg-1 1825

SHELL, STEPHEN -w- Jane--see card John Ellis 1772 Laurens 12-1815

SHERMAN, SIMON T. of Newberry d. 1811 Widow Hester -m- Isaac Lindsey
    Suit over property for debts. Laurens 1815-13
SIMMONS, CHARLES Laurens 1-47 A-47
    Sons: John, Charles and William
    Dau: Sarah
    "my 2 Y-dau": Elizabeth and Jean
    Dau: Mary McCad
    Wife: Elizabeth--Ex. with son, John
    4 July 1790 Prov. Wit: Joshua Downs, John Rodgers, James Floyd

SIMMONS, CHARLES -w- Elizabeth to Samuel Bolling 168 A. on Saluda
    and Reedy R. Bd. George Martin and John Milling Deed A-202/205
    March 13, 1786

SIMMONS, JOHN deed Catey Simmons, Admx. Adm. Bond: sureties:
    Elijah Walker, James Simmons Apr. 15 Sept. 1810 Laurens D-1810

SIMMONS, JOHN Laurens Ct. Min 1782
    Nancy Simmons, Widow, Admx. Letters gr. Mar. 1788
    Charles Simmons and Robert Ross--1st Sureties
    Charles Simmons, Jr. and Wm. Simmons--2nd Sureties
    Apr. 8 May 1788
    Aprs: Joseph Downs, John Commock, Rob't Cooper

SIMPSON, JOHN P. -w- Mary--see card David Ross, Dec'd Laurens Prob.
                                                     1815
SIMPSON, JOHN -m- set 22 Jan 1811 Sarah Hunter. Wm. Dunlap, Robert
    Cresswell, John Caldwell--Trustees. Laurens Misc C-227

SIMPSON, COL. JOHN--See card James Parks Laurens Equity

SIMS, ROBERT TO Drury Boyce 100 Acres S-fork Raeburn's Cr. Orig.
     James Smith--May 13, 1768 Laurens Deed A-29 Sept. 12, 1785

SLAPPY, JACOB -w- Margaret, formerly widow of Harmon Geiger--Will
     1778 Laurens Equity D 1814

SLOAN, AGNES -w- Samuel Sloan. Dau. of James and Rosannah Moore
     of Newberry Dist. Her parents had been married 22 years so
     that she could not be above 21 yrs. Laurens Equity D-1 1816

SMITH, CHESLEY--Will 17 Dec. 1857 Laurens Wills 1854-62 A-512
     Ch: John D. Smith
          Chaney Elizabeth -w- Martin Sadler
          Martha Jane Jones widow of C. C. Jones
          Sarah Frances Smith
          Gilly Ann Smith. W. H. Langston--Ord. of Dist.

SMITH, DAVID -w- Ann of Union Co--formerly Ann Musgrove, widow of
     Edward Musgrove--to Thomas Lee of Union Co. Land on Enoree--
     known as Musgroves Mill, tract-150 Acres. Laurens Deed F-283
     Jan. 13, 1796. Page 287 T. Lee to George Gidon

SMITH, JOSHUA -w- Polly--see card John Cason Laurens Eq. 3-1814

SMITHERS, GABRIEL -w- Mary to Samuel Harris--150 A. on waters of
     Mudlick Cr. Bd. Mary Shams, Wm. Caldwell, and Nathaniel Foshea--
     being gr to Oliver Twoles--12 Apr. 1771 Laurens Deed A-341 1785

SNEED, PHILIP, SEN'R.--Son, John Sneed, had interest in slaves at
     death of his father--$\frac{1}{4}$ which slaves were sold by Sheriff for
     debts of John Sneed--as to his interest-$\frac{1}{4}$ bought by Lydall Winn-
     debt-who is sued by John Black for debt. Laurens Eq. 1820-9

SPEARMAN, EDMUND--Dec'd--of Laurens. d. intestate. Laurens Eq. 1827-1
     Widow: Susan
     Ch: Peggy -w- Chas Floyd
          Mahala -w- Robert Floyd
          Thomas, John, Edmond, Frances, Tabitha, Nancy, George
          Dec'd dau-Betsy Barrdt--her ch.
               Edmund Barret
               John   "
               Laurens   "

SPEERS, ANDREW, SEN'R. AND JUN'R.   Laurens Equity
     Robert, Jane, John, David--See card James Parks

SPEERS, DAVID--Of Laurens Dist. d. 1815 intestate Laurens Eq. 1820-5
     Widow: Margaret -m- Thomas Archibald
     5 Ch: Robert Speers, Jean, Andrew, John, and David Speers
     Andrew Speers, Uncle, aptd. Gdn. Robert Cresswell, Adm.

SPEERS, SAMUEL--See card Hugh O'Neall Laurens Equity 1815-8

SPROWL, JAMES -vs- Henry Chappel--Est. of Michael McKee, Dec'd.
     Laurens Equity 1816-10

STARNES, EBENEZER--To: Aaron Starnes Plantation Laurens Co. on Long Lick Creek. Gr to sd Ebenezer Starnes. Laurens Deed A-346 1786

STARNES, EBENEZER--4 Nov. 1789 Laurens Will 1-29 A-23
    Aaron--Where he lives (son)
    Daus: Anna, Rachel, Rebekah, Mary-(eldest),"5 shillings and what she had"
    Sons: Ebenezer and John
    Wife: Anna-Ex. with son Aaron. To support my 2 Y-ch.
    Nov. 4, 1789--Prov. Wit: Sam'l Wharton, John Field, Roger Murphey

STARNES, SHUBEL--See card John Shearly, Dec'd Laurens Prob. 1-1825

STEDDAM, HENRY--Esor's of John Inman--See card Benj. Inman 1798 Eq. D

STEEN, JAMES -w- Elinor Aug. 19, 1768 Gr. to John Lindsay of the Enoree Settlement. 300 A. on S-s Enoree. Bd. Wm. Cannon
    Wit: Peter Brooks, Wm. Moore, John Steen. Dec. 17, 1774 A-295

STEVENS, JOHN Wife: Mary Laurens Wills 1-67 A-81
    "my 2 sons": John and James
    Legacy to: John and James Stevenson
    Sons: David and Solomon--live in Maryland now in care Thos Black.
    Daus: Janey, Elizabeth, and Mary. 8 Aug. 1793--Prov.

ST. PETER'S CHURCH--Incorporated on Camping Creek of Saluda River, Orangeburg Dist. 112 Acres-Pbt. Plat Book 31-510
    Trustees: Peter Jumper
            Ulrick Mayer, Sen'r.
            Thomas Freid
            John B. Cassleman
            John Weem
            Mathias Quattlebaum
            John Shealy
            Lawrence Young
            Nicholas Henmeter

STRAIN, MARY--By next Friend Abijah Pinson. Was married 16 March 1816 to William Strain--He beat her with a "large hickory" while she was pregnant. Laurens Equity 1818-8

STUART, WILLIAM -w- Alse (Elsie) as Adm'r. Joseph Hays, dec'd of Newberry Dist. To: Samuel Akin of Laurens--Negro man-James.
    Wit: John Rainey and Wm. Rainey. Laurens Deed A-206 Jan. 16, 1786

SULLIVAN, RANDAL--Adm. of James
                   Letitia and Rebecca et al--See card
    Ezekiel Rowland. Laurens Equity D-3 1815

SUMMERS, WILLIAM, SEN'R. -vs- Thomas Mills--in re slaves pur. by Wm. Summers, Sr. and Wm. Summers, Jr. 2 Mar. 1808
    Laurens Equity Bx D-8 1816

SWINDLER, ELISHA -w- Nancy--See card John Buchanan, Sen'r. Eq. D-1816

178

TANKERSLEY, ROWLAND -vs- Adam Carruth -w- Mary Laurens Bills 1809-9
                    Thomas and Mary Tarrant
                    Robert Anderson--represented Jno Cunningham
    of Charleston. Slaves sold.

TATE, JAMES--Dec'd 14 Nov. 1795   . Laurens Equity 1817-11
    Bro: Robert Tate--Dec'd Aug. 1803 Int.
        Ch: Samuel Tate, Jr.
             Ann Tate
             Wm Bonaparte Tate
             Robert Tate
    Bro: William
         Samuel
    Sisters: Ann Burton -w- John Burton
              Margaret Speake -w- Richard Speake
              Elizabeth Thompson -w- Fasley Thompson

TATE, WILLIAM -vs- Miles Jennings, Jr.--son and heir of Miles Jennings
    Sr. agreement concerning lands made with the Senior Jennings. in
    1786. Laurens Equity - 1814-2

TAYLOR, MICHAEL--18 Apl. 1769 C. T. Wills 1767/71-412 Provincial Wills
    Wife: Sarah
    Oldest son: Thomas-Michael-Simon and George--Lands on Saluda

TAYLOR, REBECCA--Dau. Henry Bates, Dec'd. See card. Laurens Eq 1813-12

TEAGUE, THOMAS--Next friend of Jane Griffin-1818-see card. Eq. D-11

TEAGUE, WILLIAM -w- Elizabeth--Dau. of John Miller. See card John
    Cason -w- Sarah. Laurens Equity 3-1814

THOMAS, JOHN--A Schoolmaster made oath before R. Brown, J. of P.
    for Newberry Co. as to Chas. King and Levy Caisey as Gdn. of
    Pennington Children. Laurens Wills 30 Nov. 1789 A-1

THOMAS, JOSEPHUS -w- Elizabeth--see card Benj. Inman 1798. Eq Bx-D

THOMAS, NEHEMIAH--Of Newberry Dist. Will 26 May, 1786. d 12 June 1796
    Wife: Abigail--moved to Ohio
    Nephew: Edward Thomas, son of Edward of N. C.
             John Dobbins
             Thomas Johnston
             Sarah -w- George McKensey (or McKinney)
             Sarah Mills -w- Thos Mills--Orator.
    P.A. for Abigail Thomas of Warren Co. Ohio 5 May, 1808
    Laurens Equity 1812-5

THOMASON, ELIZABETH--Will Nov. 1, 1835 Prob. Bx 39-2
    Daus: Harriet and Minerva
    Sons: G. C. and A. L.
    Dau: Cynthis Cooper
    "my ch": Rebecca Tuck, Nang Prince, Wm T. Thomason, A. B.,
    Cynthis Cooper, G. C., Minerva, A. L., and Harriet

THOMASON, GEORGE--Elizabeth Thomason, Adm. 3 July 1837 Laurens Probate 70-11
  Heirs: James Thomason, George Thomason, Sarah Willis, Washington
  Thomason--minor. Aprs: B. Smith, Robert Willis, Frances Thomason

THOMASON, NANCY Laurens Vol 2-274 A-211
  Son: James Dunlap Thomason
  "Y-dau": Caty Prend   "
  Step dau: Nancy   "
  Dau: Polly   "
  "My 5 ch": Not named
  Son-in-Law: William Thomason, Exor.
  27 May 1837 Prov.
  Wit: Gidun Thomason, M. P, Evins, Wm. Studdard.

THURSTON, STREET and William--see card Jeremiah Strother 1816
  Laurens Equity D-12

TINSLEY, ABRAHAM--Will Jan. 5, 1804   Laurens Book D
  Wife: Nancy
  Son: William--to have 5 years schooling
  Dau: Sarah and Mary--3 years schooling
  Bro: James Tinsley--Exor.
  Father in Law: Henry Johnston-Ex.
  Wit: Francis Thweat, Geo. Dalrymple, Elijah Teague.
  Appraised Jan 9, 1815

TINSLEY, JAMES--See card Jeremiah Strother 1816   Laurens Bx-D-12

TOWELL, RATLIFF to Mark More--150 A. in 96 Dist on a small Br. of
  Little River called Beaver Dam Branch in Berkley Co. abt. 4
  feet broad and 4 in. deep. Bd--all vac. Prs: Peter Ragsdale
  Joel Burgess. Laurens Deed A-42 Jan 28/29 1785

TOWLES, OLIVER--Dec'd Laurens Equity 1813-10
  Widow: Jane
  Son: John--since dec'd--2 sons-James and John
       Daniel
  Dau: Tabitha--died intestate leaving Daniel Goodman and
                   Tabitha Lindsey -w- Caleb
       Elizabeth -m- Rutherford Bowles

TUCKER, LAVINIA--Laurens Vol 2-283 Univ.
  Sister: Haney and her husband Jas. B. Higgins
  Dec'd Bro: James Higgins
  Sister: Lavinia Moss (or Savinia)
  Nephew: Benj. B. Higgins--died before codicil made
  Brother: Wm Higgins, Dec'd--His children
  Sister: Nancy Fowler and her son William Fowler
          Elizabeth French -w- James
  Brother: Ezekiel Higgins
           David Higgins 17 Dec. 1842 Codicil: 24 Dec. 1845
  Wit. Will: L. Meredith, Reuben Estes, Meredith Fowler,
  Wit: Codicil: Joseph Prior (also wit. Will), Joseph Terry
                Thomas P. Gray, Wallace Thompson

LAURENSVILLE HERALD--Aug. 31, 1855--Tucker, Mrs. Lavinia, died at
    residence, Laurens Dist--16 inst. Consort of Gen. S. Tucker.
    86th year of age.

TURLEY, NANCY--Dau. of John Buchanan, Sen'r.--See card. Laurens Eq.
                                                         D-1816
UNDERWOOD, ELIZABETH--Dau. of Reuben Daniels--Will 1825--Spartan-
    burg 21-93

UNDERWOOD, WILLIAM--Will 11 Feb. 1812--Spartanburg 22

VAUGHAN, CRADDOCK AND DAUGHTER MARTHA--Of Virginia. Martha -m-
-   John Dickie--see card. Laurens Equity D-4 1815

VAUGHN, DRURY, JAMES AND WALTER--See card of Ezekiel Roland.
    Laurens Equity D-3 1815

WADE, ROBERT -w- Sarah of Georgia--see card Ezekiel Roland
    Laurens Equity d-3 1815

WADLINGTON, MARGARET--Sister of Mercer Babb and Rhody Babb. See card
    Also: Wm. Wadlington, James and Warner Wadlington.
    Laurens Equity D-6 1816

WAISTCOAT, JOEL--Of Effingham Co. Georgia to wife, Cynthia, Deed
    Gift 5 Nov. 1811--Land and per. property. Wm. S. Spencer and
    Reuben G. Taylor, Trustees. Cynthia -m- Ambrose Hudgins, Jr.
    Suit by John Dunlap. Laurens Equity 1819-10

WAISTCOAT, JOEL--D. 1816 Adm's. Ambrose Hudgins, Jun'r. -w- Cynthia
    -vs- Alijah D. Pinson--partner of dec'd. Laurens 1819-2

WAITS, JOSEPH--Gr Nov. 19, 1772 to Joell Ratclif--To Thomas McClerkin
    This deed to John Cunningham. Wit: Thomas Richardson, James
    Cunningham, James McClerkin. Laurens Deed A-63/4 Jan 8, 1780

WALDROP, JAMES--Gr to John Farrow--100 A. on Enoree S-s. Laurens Deed
                                                           B-85
WALDROP, MICHAEL--To James Farrow--both of Spartanburg Dist. 300 A.
    Orig Gr. to Rolly Bowen. Wit: Nicholas Brown, Spencer Brown
    Laurens Deed A-178/80 Nov. 21, 1785

WALKER, HENRY TANDY--Sheriff of Greenville Dist. Adv. Thos. P. Payne
    Suit for debt due as Jailor, etc. Laurens Equity 1815-7

WALKER, MOSES--Sick   Laurens 1-38 A-36 Univ.
    Wife: Elizabeth   "my child" Bro: Jatthrow (Jethro?)
    "Bees at my Father's" "Sheep I leave unto my Mother"
    Agreed to by: Elizabeth Walker. 1 June 1791--Prov
    Wit: Thos East, James Bell

WALLIS, JESSE--Convicted of Assault on Capt. Wm. Irby to stand in
    Pillory 1 hour and be imprisoned. Respite for 1 mo. by Gov.
    1 Dec. 1812 Misc C-Laurens

WARD, SAMUEL--Died in Va. 1804, Amelia County Laurens Eq. 1820-12
    Widow: Susannah--moved to S. C. Sister of Thomas Lignn
    7 Ch: Sarah -m- Benj. B. Cheshier
            Martha -m- Peter Ligon
            Susannah -m- William Wright
            Seth Ward
            Judith -m- M____Ligon
            Prudence
            Elizabeth   P____? Jeter rented the land in Va.
    Richard Ligon--a wit. states a sale of some of the property in
    Va. was made by Judith Swann, now Judith Allen--but does not
    know what she sold.

WARD, SAMUEL--Pet by Susannah Ward for Letters 9 Dec. 1810 Bk-D

WASHINGTON, ELIZABETH, Dec'd and George Washington--Real Estate
    -vs- Thomas Washington, John Washington, Lewis Christian and
    wife, Susan. H. Swindle and wife, Elizabeth, Marshall Howell
    and wife, Polly. Probate Bk. Pg-2 Laurens 1825

WATERS, DAVID--See card of Hugh O'Neall. Laurens Eq. 1815-8

WATERS, LANDON -w- Margaret--one of daus. of Edward Musgrove, Dec'd.
    Wm. Musgrove, of Laurens Co. -vs- Leah Musgrove, Rachel and Liney
    Musgrove--by Landon Waters, their next friend. Judgement A-2
    Laurens 1796

WATERS, THOMAS WILLOUGHBY--Adv. John Lewis-Gervais in re Tax Collector.
    Judgements A-1 1796. 1800--Adv. David Doylay--A-1

WELCH, DAVID -w- Frances to John Barnett--40 A. S-s Durbin's Cr. Pt Gr
    in 1773 Laurens Deed A-117/8 Oct. 28, 1785
    A-114/5 Sept 3, 1785--To Robert Shelton Pt 100 A. S-forkDur-
    bin's Cr.
    A-110/2 Nov. 19, 1785--To Michael Wallace--60 A. S-s of Durbin's
    Cr. Wit: John Barnett, Wm. Jackson, Geo. Brooks

WESTMORELAND, ROLING -w- Susanna--See card John Dickie, Dec'd
    Laurens Eq. D-4 1815

WICKEL, ANDREW--See card of John Buchanan, Sen'r. Laurens Eq. D-1816

WIER, GEORGE -w- Mary of 96 22 Sept. 1779 to William Carson, Jun'r.
    300 A. where on sd George now lives on Bush River of Saluda.
    Orig. Gr. Andrew Rodgers 22 Feb. 1771. 6 May, 1775, conv to
    George Wier. Laurens Deed B-74/6

WIER, JOHN--(wife did not ? 5 yrs) 19 Oct. 1786 to Heusting Doyal
    100 A. on Saluda. Bd. John Hellons, Patrick Cunningham
    Laurens Deed B-113/5

WILSON, ANDREW--d. intestate. Widow: Rebecca -m- John Blakeley
    Sev. children--yet minors. Whited Wilrs and widow Rebecca
    Wilson, Adm'rs. Suit by John Black and Benj. James -vs-
    John Blakeley for taking property out of state--Laurens Eq. 1828
                                                              -9

WHITMORE, GEORGE--Dec'd 1810 Laurens Equity 1812-1
    Widow: Elizabeth--formerly widow Gary
    Sisters: Martha Abrams -w- William A.
             Margaret Welch -w- Nicholas W.

Whitmore, George--Continued
    Elizabeth Watson -w- John W.
    Sarah Duncan -w- Moses D.
    Susannah Daty (Duty?) -w- Solomon D. Laurens Equity 1812-1

WHITAKER, ISAAC -w- Charity of Abbeville Dist. Advs: David Caldwell
    who had pur. shares they claimed, from Moses Madden.
    Laurens Equity 1813-8

WHITMORE, JOHN--Deceased 1780 intestate. Laurens Equity 1819-17
    Widow: Also -m- George Young
    Ch: Lydia -m- Simon Reeder
        Mary -m- Richard Duckett--orator
        Sarah -m-   Duckett
        Ann -m- David Reeder
        Margaret -m-   Pride

WRENWICK, ELIZABETH and her children; Agnes, John and William--
    See card Solomon Nichols. Laurens Equity 1813-7

WRIGHT, JOHN -vs- Sylvanus Walker Laurens Equity 1802-1

WRIGHT, SAMUEL of Laurens Will 23 Sept 1808--died soon after
    Wife: Patience C. Wright--she has died since
    Eldest son: Wm. G. Wright
                James
    Daus: Elizabeth -m- David S. Beacham
        Frances -m- Tobias Cook
        Polly -m- Henry Parsley
        Nancy -m- Dr. Elijah Watson
    Son: Samuel--Died-no issue
    Exor: Bro. William--Orator Laurens Equity 1826-1

YOUNG, JAMES--Will 25 June 1824--died soon after in 1825
    Wife: Mary Ann -m- James Hunter
    "my children"--youngest at 16 yrs. Not named
    Exors: Gallatin Young, Wm Augustive Young, Turner Richardson
    Laurens Equity 1826-6--Slaves and other property pur from
    Ann's Mother's estate, and slaves and property present wife
    had at _____?

YOUNG, JAMES -w- Ann to Charles Saxon--200 A. on Bush Creek of
    Saluda River. Bd. laid out to Augustive Warner and vac. Gr.
    to Henry Neily. Wit: Hugh Saxon, Andrew Anderson, William
    Young. Laurens Deed A-70 27 Dec. 1773

YOUNG, JAMES--Laurens May 23, 1796 1-100 A-166
    "My 2 youngest children". Wife, living, not named. Sons: Robert
    and James (Exor's with wife). Mentions the possibility moving
    west. Wit: Andrew Middleton, Abner Young

YOUNG, JOHN -vs- Joseph Camp, David Gent--Merchants--Money
    Laurens Equity 1818-6

YOUNG, JOHN -w- Mary of Rutherford Co. N. C. 12 July 1771 to George
    Anderson of Laurens Co. 200 A. on Little R. of Saluda.
    Laurens Deed B-122/23

YOUNG, ROBERT of Laurens Co. 12 March 1787 to James Cook 30 A. N-s of
    North Cr.   Laurens Deed B-106

YOUNG, SAMUEL--Of Abbeville Dist. Will 19 Apl. 1817
    Widow: Elizabeth -m- Samuel J. Hopper--Orator
    Sons: Robert, William, James
    Daus: Lucinda, Elly, Amelia   Laurens Equity 1819-3

NEWBERRY COUNTY, SOUTH CAROLINA

The unusual spelling of some words, and the abbrev-
iations are those of the original copier, as are the
remarks in quotation marks, and parenthesis.

                              F. Courtney

AARON, Jacob, of Edgefield d-1804. Owed gr. to Joseph Jay--m--
Margaret in Newberry. Margaret Aaron, widow of Jacob, m
Thomas West, Dec'd. Margaret died 1817. 1 child; Mary,
M. David Shumport.
Ch: William West
     Elizabeth West
     Thomas West
     Sarah West. all minors. Deed in file from Joseph Jay,
whose wife was Margaret. 7 Nov. 1777. To Wm. Aaron. Clerks
office, Edgefield. Bx 6, 1822-3

ABRAMS, Mary d. 23 April 1848. Newberry Probate bk. Pets. fer Part.5-91
Ch: Samuel S. Abrams
     Joseph   "
     Benjamin   "
     Nancy Narcissa W. John Whittin
     William Abrams
     John Jr. "
     Pleasant "
     Emanuel   "
     Fleming   "   dec'd son
           1 Ch. Mary Elizabeth--infant
     James   "   dec'd
           Ch. Martha W. John Golding
           Mary   )
           Adeline   ) Minors
           Lucinda   )
           Sarah Amandiss)

ANDERSON, Abraham, of Berkley Co. Will 11 July 1763. Newberry File
Wife: Ruth
To: William Gordon)
     Goven   "   ) Wife's ch.
     George   "   )
"my 4 yst. sons" 1 Abra ham
                 2 Levy
                 3 Henry
                 4 Jacob
To Jacob Brown (appears wife's son or son in law.)
Wife's son: Thomas Gordon
"my son": Abell Anderson
"all my Ch." Proven before: Edward Musgrove

ANDERSON, Jacob Newberry Wills page 33
     Estate: Adm. James Strother
     Aprs: Levi Anderson
            John Blalock
            Abel Anderson, Sr.
            Abraham Anderson, Jr.

BANKS, James T. dec'd 29 July 1838. Newberry Prob. Pet. for Par. 6-114
Widow: DrucillaBanks, Pet'r.
4 ch: Marcella--William Sheppard
Rhody-w-Henry Dominick
Randall H. Banks-d-Unmarried
James C. Banks--minor
       Marcella--also since dead--husband
                           2 ch. Rhody Frances)
                           Mary Drucilla   ) Minors

BEAM, Jesse D 20 July 1854 int. Newberry Prob. Pet. for Par. 6-118
    Widow: Martha Beam, Pet'r
    1 child: Catherine Beam, Minor

BEDENBAUGH, David d 184. Newberry Prob. Pet. for Part. 5-90 Filed 1849
    Widow: Anne Caroline-m- John Fulmer (Pet'r)
    2 ch: Simpson Kleckly Bededbaugh
    Daniel Varina Elizabeth Bededbaugh

BEDENBAUGH, Henry d 11 Feb. 1858 Newberry Prob. Pets. for Part. 6-113
    Widow: Elizabeth--Pet'r.
    7 ch. John A.
          Simon
          William P.
          E_____ -w- Frederick W. Boozer
          Rachel
          Melinda -w- Hawkins
          Rosannah -w- Allen Nichols
          Simpson C Bedenbaugh)
          Daniel V. E. Bedenbaugh) minors, children of dec'd son Daniel.

BEDSIL, Sarah d 29 Jan. 1832. Newberry Prob. Pet. for Part. Bdl. 1 Pk-6
    ch. Martha (of age) -w- Thomas Wells
    Orlando, Eliza, Jefferson Bedsil (minors)

BISHOP, John d 21 Apr. 1835. Newberry Prob. Pet. for Part. 6-112

    Widow: Louisa Bishop, Pet'r.
    4 ch: William A., Permelia A., John C., Martha H.

BISHOP, Vincent d 29 Aug. 1848. Newberry Prob. Pet for Part. 5-99
    Widow: Sarah
    4 ch: William, John, Cyrus, Nancy

BOBO, Ann, d 22 Jan 1846. Newberry Prob. Pets. for Part. 5-101
    Husband: John E. Bobo
    4 bros. and sisters: viz: Andrew Dominick, Christiana -w- Wm.
    Workman, Mary -w- B. W. Nix, Fanny -w- David N. Taylor
    Dec. **Bro**: George Dominick
        Ch: Aaron, George, Mary Ann-w- Jack Warren, Margaret -w-
        John Bowers, Henry, John, Lindsey Dominick
    Dec'd Sister: Elizabeth Taylor
        Ch: Robert Taylor, Isabella -w- Simeon Hawkins, Margaret
        Anna Taylor, George Taylor, Amanda -w- Absolam Koon, James
        Noah, and Israel Taylor
    Dec'd Bro: David Dominick
        Ch: Robert N., James J., Wesley, Jane, Thomas, Mary E.,
        William H.

BONDS, Noah (or Menoah)Newberry Wills Vol. 2 Bk-H 10
    Wife: Fanny Bonds
    Sons: James, William, Hampton, Zekiel, Beuben. Dau: Rebecca
    Some ch. minors. Exor: Wife, Barber Hancock, and James Bonds
    1 Feb. 1811   Prov. Oct. 20 1811

BONDS, Richard 1786 Newberry Wills A
    Sons: Menoah(?), Richard, William. Daus: Salley, Retter,
  Betty, Wife: Joyce. Ex. Wife and son, Menoah. 24 Sept, 1786

BONDS, Richard of Newberry Co. Newberry Wills Vol. 1 Bk A 6
    Wife: Joice
    Sons: Menoah, Richard, William. Dau: Salley, Retter.
    2 Sept., 1786. Prov. June 6 1787

BOOZER, Eliza d 2 July 1845. Newberry Prob. Pet. for Part. 4-74
    Sons: Frederick (Pet'r.) Henry, John (to Ala.) Daniel (to
  Georgia), George, David, Daus: Elizabeth -w- Daniel Senn,
  Rebecca Hendrix-widow, Sarah -w- Caperman Dec'd.
      Ch: Sarah -w- John Caperman
      Elizabeth (believed Dec'd) -w- Pete Taylor, sally, John,
      Mary Ann -m- vs. George, Margaret -w- Jack Chapman, Jacob
      Henry, Daniel, Dolly Prisby, Rebecca Pou -w- Timothy Pou
      Rebecca Dec'd. leaving 1 ch. Adam Boozer
          Ch. of Adam: Sarah -w- Ivy Lake
          John C. Boozer
          Newton N. "
          Prisby   "   (or Pressly)
          George (minor)

BOOZER, George d intest. 14 Oct. 1854 Newberry Prob. Pet. for Part.6-117
    Widow: Susannah
    5 Ch: Eliza C., Mary E., James D., Cornelius, George W., Pet'r

BOOZER, Mary E., d 17 May 1860. Newberry Prob. Pets. for Part. 6-111
    Husband: Frederick A. Boozer. 1 child: Anna R. Lake
    Pet'r. states this wife owned 40 acres when he married her.
    (Seems evidently from husband--Lake.)

BOWERS, Alexander A. d _____1825. Newberry Prob. Pet. for Part. Bdl-1
    Widow: Mary Magdalen -m- (1830) John Henry Stockman   Pkg-1
    Ch: George Washington Bowers; Levi; Nancy Caroline; Jacob
  Stephen; Andrew Michael; John

BOYD, Elizabeth 1830, Newberry Probate Office. Bdle-1 Pkg-2
    Heirs: Joshua
          Aaron
          James
          Caleb -died-
             1 ch: Jane-minor
          George D.,
             2 Ch: Elizabeth and George
          Mark
          Worthy G.
          Lewis M. Minor
          Dec'd son: John
                  Ch: Wm. Gideon, John, Nathaniel-Minors

BOYD, Elizabeth Sou. Times and State Gazette Oct 11, 1830, Dec'd
    Case: Joshua Boyd and others
          Aaron Boyd and others Newberry Dist. Out of state:
          Andrew Boyd

BOYD: John, Jr. Went to Kentucky and returned about 1862. Had
        Samuel Taylor gr. tract. He let Thomas Busby us it and T.
        B. claimed it when he came back--etc-etc. Gave the land to
        Ann Boyd's children-viz--John, Jane, Betsy, and William,-minors
        Gr-Ch-of said John Boyd, Sen'r. who made the deed to the dis▼
        land on Seneca.

BOYLES, William to Robert Rutherford 2 June 1786. Slaves. Wit:
        George Gartman, ei al. Newberry Deeds A-89/90

BOYD, George D. Dead Newberry Pro. Pet. for Part. Bdle-1 Pkg-3
        Widow: Sarah Ann-m- Wiley Dobbs, Pet'r.
        2 ch: Elizabeth
              George

BOYD, Hugh, Dec'd. Newberry Prob. Pet. for Part. Bdle-1 Pkg-4
        Widow: Frances   Son: John
        Dau: Isabella   "   Jesse
         "   Jane H.   Dau: Mary

BRADLEY, James, lately of Connecticut. 8 Sept. 1820
        Wife: Sarah
        Mother: Sarah Bradley
        Sister: Harriett Bradley
        Brother: Wm. Bradley
        Brother: Joseph Bradley Newberry Wills Vol. 2-G 81

BRASELMAN, Peter Dec'd
        Widow: Drucilla
        Dau: Maisie
             Mariah-w- Wm. Turpin
             Lara_g (Louisa) -w- Benj. Ogletree
             Wilhelmina Ann Braselman
        Son: Thomas J.
        In: Sarah S. Newberry Court Minutes Bk Pg 73. 148 to 157

             Partner of Cushman Edson

BRASWELL, William d 1816. Widow: seems to be Susan B_____.
        Ch: Rutherford and Allen (of age 1816) David, Polly
        Arthur, Betsy, James, William, Aaron, Nancy, (all minors)
        Newberry Ct. Mins. Bk-48 72 to 75

BRIDGES, Albert C. d 1855 Int. Newberry Prob. Pet. for Part. 6-115
        Father: William Bridges, Sen'r.
        Bros: Charles, William, Jr., Carville, Wiley (pet'r)
        Sis: Nancy -w- Timothy Boozer
             Temperence -w- James Kenzzy
             Dec'd sister Caroline Mosely
             Ch: Hanson C. Mosley
                 Nancy C.   "
                 William   "

BROOKS, Matthew -w- Agnes 31 May, 1786 Newberry Deeds A-55/56
        to Henry Stedham, 200 A on Beaver Dam of Saluda.
        Next: Matthew Brooks to Jonathan Taylor June 1, 1786 -w- Agnes
        Wit: Enos Elleman and Mercer Babb and Samuel Pearson (to both)

BROWN, John G. Legatee of Christine Farrow-wife- of Samuel Farrow.
"my beloved son: John G. Brown
                 Willis Brown
          dau: Sarah
               Caroline Matilda
   Newberry Wills H-141. Prov. 1815

BROWN, Joseph -w- Kezia, 23 March, 1785. Newberry Deeds A-pg. 43
   to Aaron Cates, 150 A S-s Broad R. Orig. gr. to Jack Felker,
   who con. to Joseph Brown 1st Apr. 1783. Wit: W. Malone,
   John Malone, M. Glazier

Bryan, Jonathan, 300 A Br. Little Saluda River, 8 Dec. 1749
   Plats without Grs. A-K-50 (This is a book of Plats in the
   Archives Dept. in Columbia

BUCHANNON, James D. 18 Feb, 1852 Newberry Prob. Pet. for Part. 6-116
   Heirs: Father--Joseph Buchannon
                  Margaret Buchannon, Pet'r.

BUCHANNON, John, Sen'r. Orig. will of 96 Dist., 14 June, 1785. Prov.
   6 Apr. 1793. Wife: Elizabeth
   Dau: Nancy Turley
    "   Mary Hutchinson
   Son: William Buchannon
   Dau: Anna Hoard--sd. Anna Hord
    "   Susannah Buchannon
   Son: John   "
    "   Jesse   " Receipt by Hannah Johns- In pt. 1807

BULOW, Joachim -w- Amelia of city of Charleston. 3 Feb. 1786. Newberry deeds A-pgs 61 to 65. to Samuel Pearson and Mercer Babb
   104 A. xxxx. Wit: Joshua Inman, Jacob Toland, Burr Johnston,(
   was of the city)

BURHARDT, Jacob Will 14 Jan. 1809 Newberry Ct. Min. Book24 Pg. 37
   Wife: Margaret
   Son: Jacob--"where he now lives"
   Son: Philly
   Dau: Elizabeth--20 shillings to her son Thomas Wright and his
        brothers and sisters.
   Son: Gaspar
   Dau: Ann

BUTLER, Robert of Newberry dist. Newberry Wills Box-36 Pk.-75
   Wife: Emily--all prop. that came by her and otherwise.
   "my 3 ch"--Minors Land: 100 Acres. 18 Feb. 1833

BUZARD, Anna Maria Will 13 Nov. 1790 (Burhart or Buzhardt)
   Hus: John B.
   Rebecca B.
   Anna Maria B.
   1st hus: Peter Heir and son Mathias Heir
                        John Heir. 7 daus. named.

BUZZARD, Gaspar, of Edbefield Dist. to David Wite of Newberry dist.
Mtg. Negro Beck and child sec. debt on note given to David H.
Taylor. Dated Nov. __ 1839. Newberry Dist. Misc. L-51

BUZZARD, Jacob, State grant--no. 679 John McK Alex. P8-103
150 A. in Mecklenberg Co. on waters of Dutch Buffalow Creek
7 Aug. 1787. Sd. Rd. Caswell. 10 ₺

BUZZARD, John of Mecklenberg Co, planter, John Bessinger of Meck.
Date 2 June, 1782 ₺ 180. Land on each side Buffalow Cr. Com-
monly called Dutch Buffalow in Meck. Co. Dower by Ann Buzzard
dated Oct. 12, 1782. (Same as came to him by Mitchell)

BUZZARD, John d. 1816. Newberry Prob. Pet. for Part. Bdle-1 Pkg-5
    Elizabeth -w-   Abner Buzzard
    Cyrus Buzzard   John S. "
    James   "   Ann Catherine (minor)

BUZARD--Legatee of Philip Sligh. Will 1818 Newberry Wills
"my 4 daughters, namely:
    Elizabeth -w- Jacob Buzard
    Mary -w- Philip Buzard
    Katherine Sligh
    Sarah Sligh
    Wife of Philip Sligh: Christianna

BUZARD, Rudolph. Provincial Deed in Charleston. C. T. Deed P-4 Pg.-1
Wife: Britta of Broad R. Sd. Boshart--conveyed to Joseph Fish
5/6 March 1773, land granted to Britta Steighen in 1761

BUZZARD, Rudolph--9 Nov. 1764 _____ Journal.
300 Acres on Big Bush Creek Swamp. Plat certified. 3 Oct, 1776

BUZZARD, Samuel J. Newberry Equity Bills 1857-4
Ch: DavidH., Jacob, Nancy, Josephine, Mary, John S., Daviel,
Sally, Catherine

CALDWELL, John, dec'd--Son Times and State Gazette Nov. 8, 1830
Case: Exparte Fritz et al as adm'r. Bill for sale of lands on
Caldwell's Creek. Bd. George Clark
                Allen Fritz
                Joseph Caldwell

CALDWELL, Dr. Joseph--owed est. of John Henderson--Lk-Acct ___14__
Newberry Equity--1815

CALMESS, William of Frederick Co. Va. from Capt. Chas. King-w-
Charity. Gr. to Isaac Pennington 5 Nov. 1755, by 2 sons, Jacob
and Isaac. To: Charles King. Land on Enoree or Collings R.
July 1/2 1773, c.t. T-4 Pg. 33. Provincial Deeds. Charleston
Deed Book T-4, Pg-33

CANNON, Samuel "of Craven, the northermost dist." grant 25 Sept, 1766
Conv. to: Samuel Bell "late of Tyger R" 200 A. on Br. Enoree
called Cedar Shoal Creek. Newberry File C. T. Deed R-5 157/8

COATES, John d. intestate. Widow: Mary, entitled to dower in land.
   3 ch: Mary-w- Robert Ramage
         Rebecca -w- Thomas Morgan
         Ann -w- Benj. Lake
   Newberry Ct. Minutes Bk. pg. 70 106 to 110

CASEY, Catherine, dec'd, dau. of Wm. Shell. Surv. by husband, John
   Casey. 1835. Newberry Prob. Pet. for Part. Bdle-1 Pkg.-12
   3 Ch: Thomas Casey
         William Casey
         Elizabeth -w- Lewis Hargrove

CHAPMAN, David--Died at his res. near Pomona, Newberry Dist. 36 yrs.
   of age. Wife and 5 ch. 1840's Newspaper, South Carolina
   Pets. for Part. Newberry Probate. See rolls in Newberry Probate office.

CHAPMAN, Giles d. 1 Sept. 1831, intestate. Heirs: Brothers and
   sisters. Newberry Prob. Office. Pet. for Part Bdle-1 Pkg-10
   Joseph Chapman)
   Elijah   "   ) res. Ala.
   William   "   )
   Lewis   "   res. Indiana
   Elizabeth Elmore
   Nancy Mills
   John, David, and Samuel Chapman

CHAPMAN, Mary. Newberry Prob. Pets. for Part. Bdle-1 Pkg-11
   Ch: Joseph Chapman
       Elijah
       Elizabeth
       Ellina
       Nancy Mills
       John, William, D. B., Samuel, Lewis Chapman

CHAPMAN, Samuel--d. 1 June 1795. Newberry Ct. Min. bk. 24 to 53
   did on 9 Feb 1775, at that time a widower and ch,
   Dau: Charity McCole -w- James D. B. McCole
        Abigail Collins -w- Isaac Collinw
   Charity's ch: Giles, William, Samuel, Rachel, Alse, Salley
        (by first wife) He then married Nancy_____now the
        wife of Thomas McConnell
   Nancy's Ch: Marmaduke, Robert, Joseph, Elizabeth, Jane--all
        of whom are cec'd. Archibald, Polly, and Nancy.
              William Chapman (bro. of Samuel) died prior to 1791.
              Dau: Mary -w- F. W. Grissans)
                   Lydia -w- John Douglas) all moved to distand
                   Delilah   ) lands.

CHARLES, Michael, Jr. D. int. Newberry Prob. Pet. for Part. 4-80
   Widow: Christina -m- John Prysock, Pet'r.
   5 ch: Harriet Charles, Pet'r.
         Franklin   "
         Anderson   "   All minors.
         David   "
         Elizabeth   "

CHITTY, Benjamin of N. C. 20 Oct. 1783. Newberry Deeds A-93/94
    to: James Shearer--100 A fr. to Jack Gilder who conv. to
    Benjamin Chitty--gr. dated Dec. 12, 1768, on Gilder's Creek
    between Broad and Saluda. Wit: Thomas Dugan, Anthony Parks,
    John Speaks (or Speake). James Shearer, Oct. 22, 1785 to
    John Blalock, same land.

CLARK, James d. intestate. Newberry Prob. Pets. for Part. Bdle-1 Pk.-7
    Widow: Miriam -m- _____ Sibley
    4 ch: John S. Clark, Pet'r.
          Thomas W. "
          George   " , d. 1820
          Milton H.
    Land on Broad R.--family of Thos. Clark. This file has orig.
    grant and deeds before Rev. war

CLARY, David d. Nov. 4, 1824. Newberry Pro. Pet. for Part. Bdle-1 Pk-9
    Widow: Frances -m- John Stephens, died soon after
    6 ch: William--res. Gallatin, Illinois
          Mathew W.
          Wiley S.
          Martha -m- Jordan Hunt of upson Co. Georgia
          Ivy E.
          Nancy

CLELAND, Reason d. int. 19 Jan. 1848. Newberry Pet. for Part. 5-106
    Father: John Cleland Pet'r.
    Bros: Charles S. "
         David K.   "
    Sis: Polly Cleland -w- John Sterling
         Dolly   " -w- Jesse Senn
         Frances "
         Dec'd sister: Sarah Senn
             1 ch: John Drayton Senn

COLE, Jesse (or William, Wm seems correct)Newberry Ct. Min. Bk 115
    Widow: Rachel, -w- Providence Williams d 1818
    Son: David Cole
    Dau: Betsy -w- Charley Davis
    Son: Jesse Cole
    Dau: Mary -w- William Mackle
        250 Acres--of which Providence Williams Pr. shares of David
        Cole and Charley Davis

COLE, William (or Jesse) Newberry Ct. Min. Bk. Pg. 114 184 to 186
    Widow: Rachel -m- Providence Williams, Esq. Entitled to 1/3 and
    2/3 of the rest. Providence d. 1818
    Heirs: Jesse Cole
          Wm. Mackle and wife
    Widow Rachel claims 2 shares, it seems dower by will. 275 A.
    on Indian Creek. Wit: Pendleton Page, Wm. Seymore, Thos. Davis,
    Elizabeth Williams. It was estate of Wm. Cole
        Will of Providence Williams 2 Feb. 1843. Dau: Sarah Neil,
        Elizabeth Dalrymple. Son: John Williams, (ch. of John:)
        Providence, Ephraim, Thomas, Rebecca, Stephen.) Other ch. of
        Providence Williams: Rebecca Cole, Patience McAdams, Mary
        Gary, Obedience Williams, Equilla Williams. Isaac Cole and
        Mary Cole to be pd. shares

COLEMAN, Dorcas d. 20 Mar. 1837 Int. Had no parents, bros, hus., or
child living. Heirs: Nieces and nephews.
Ch. of Wm. Summers-dec'd- listed
"   "   James   "   "   "
"   "   Eleanor -w- _____   "
"   "   Mary Wells   "
"   "   Jesse Summer   "
"   "   Col. John Summer   "
"   "   Mary Chapman   "   Some res. Alabama
Newberry Prob. Pets. for Part. Bdle-1 Pkg-11

COLLIER, Benjamin, Archives Dept. Aug. 9, 1768 Mem 8-8. 50 A. on
N. E. side Saluda R. on Mudlick Creed. Surv. Cert. 28 Oct. 1755.
Gr. L6 July 1765

COLLIER, Benjamin of Newberry Dist. Will 2 Jan. 1797 Newberry Bk-1 P-888
Wife: Elizabeth--50 Acres where I now live.
Y-Son: Benjamin
"my other 3 sons": John, Joseph, William
"my 2 Daus": Anny Collier, Cindory Collier
Execors: Friends: John Moore, James Caldwell, and Thomas
Chappell.

COLLIER, Joseph, 8 Feb. 1830 Newberry Deeds-521 to "son of Benj." "of
Newberry".. Conv. to John Simpson, Merch. of Laurens, 25 A. on
Mudlick Creek,--Little Saluda. Gr. to Benjamin Collier--in
Newberry Co. Bd. by: Samuel Harris, John Barlow "where the
widow lives" by John Collier and sd. Joseph Collier (X his mark)
Also: Book--230 William Collier to Edward Pitt 1813

COOK, Gen. P. D. of Fairfield, Sept. 14, 1847, Newberry Prob. Office
Pets. for Part. Son: J. Waring Cook, age, 21 yrs. died at
Vera Cruz, Mexico, 4 June, protracted illness. Member Palmetto Reg.

CONNALLY, Edward, wife--Mary to John Malone Aug. 18, 1784. 100 A.
Bd. Alex'r Davison, Lemuel Wilson, David Johnson, Mildred
Elivine (?). Wit: W. Malone Sr., W. Malone Jr. Benj. Hampton
Newberry Deeds A-26

COPPOCK, Harriet d. 16 Oct. 1849 Int. Newberry Pro. Pet. for Part 5-96
3 Ch: Moses M. Coppock--Pet'r.
         Emanuel   "   Minor
         Rebecca   "   "

COPPOCK, John d. int 1844 Newberry Pro. Pet. for Part. 4-73
Widow; Harriet
5 Ch. Solomon R. Coppock
        Joseph   "
        Moses   "   )
        Emanuel   "   ) Minors
        Rebecca   "   )   ,   .
Land Pur. by Sampson Coppock, Pet'r.

COTHRAN, Dempsey d. int. 1816 Newberry Equity Pet. 1816--no.-1
Rosamond: Pet. alleges they are minors and have case action vs.
David Waters Pet. Ezra Cates be Apt't. Gdn.

COTHRAN, Samuel (minor, son or Dempsey) -w- Rosa (minor, dau. of
David Waters. M-Feb. 1815. The couple sued both fathers,
claiming they promised much if they married. (Funny case).
Newberry Ct. Min. Bk pkg. 36   55-62

COULTER, John R. d. 30 Oct. 1851. Newberry Prob. Pets. for Part. 6-119
Widow: Mary L. Coulter, Pet'r.
3 ch: Eve E. Coulter
        John H.   "
        George S. "   All minors

COX, Allen d. 3 Oct. 1831, Newberry Prob. Pets. for Part. Bdle-1 Pkg-8
Widow: Polly Cox, Pet'r.
Son: Pleasant Cox--Res. Georgia
Dau: Peachy -w- Lewis Plantt. Res. Georgia
  "   Sally -w- James Bearden (Bearding)
  "   Sidney -w- James Todd
  "   Behettrene -w- Wm. Phillips
Son: Abraham Cox

CRADICK, Richard--Will 7 Apr. 1773. Newberry File, C. T. Wills
Wife: _____ 200 A Wilderson's Cr.
Ch: Richard, Christian, Randolph

CRENSHAW, Archibald --Will 22 Feb. 1818. Newberry Ct. Min. Bk. 151
Martha Crenshaw--minor under 14   242 to 248
Mary   "   "   "   "
Bros: Dr. Abner Crenshaw) Testamentary Gdns.
       Anderson Crenshaw)

CROOKS, John Sr. of Newberry Dist. Will Bk-1--58 Case 180-1806
J. A. Crooks, and J. R. Wood: Ex.
Wife: Jane
"my 2 sons" Thos. Creyton Crooks
             John Andrew Crooks
             Euphany (born before mor.) -w- James R. Wood
             Nancy Kelly-w- John Kelly
             Dec'd Dau: Elizabeth B. Graham -w- George Graham
             Dec'd Dau: Mary Duncan -w- Dabney Duncan, 2 Aug. 1838

DARBY, Rebecca d. 5 June, 1850 int. Newberry Prob. Pet. for Part. 5-109
Ch: Henry Darby   Frances
     John   Susan -w- Henry Suber
     James   Mary -w- _____?
     Nancy -w- _____ Wood   Asa
Dec'd Dau: Elizabeth Ballentine
Ch: William Ballentine
     Edward   "
     Laurens   "
     Jane   "   All minors
     Leander   "
     Warren   "

DURR, Nicholas--carpenter (or Farrer) 6 July 1751, Newberry DeedsA-26
    to Frederick Arnold: 150 A. on Wateree Cr. in Saluda Fork. Bd.
    by John Wrie Hafner. Wit: Christopher Rowe, John Abrams,
    Schwerd Fagen. St. X S X C X Orangeburg Dist. Off. Nov. 9, 1782
    He and Jacob Son (Jacobson) bargained for land which Nicholas
    Farr leased to Arnold, and from him to Grim--but no witness can
    be found to Grim XXXXX. Next--Off. by Wm. Newman that Peter
    Grim lived there in 1757 XXXX.

DAUGHERTY, James, Sen'r. Wife: Mary Newberry Wills 15 Nov. 1704
    Eldst. Son: James
            Ch: George and James
    Second Son: John
        "   George
        "   Charles--minor

DAVIDSON, Alexander, d. 10 Aug. 1842 int. Newberry Pro. Pet. for Part.
    Widow: Sarah J. Davidson, d. Oct. 9, 1843, Int.   5-102
    7 Ch: William A.
           John J.--res. Dallas Co. Ala.
           N. W.   )
           Newberry S.)
           S. J.   ) These 5 were Ch. of Sarah J.
           Jennet   )
           James W.)

DAVIS, John, d. 26 Jan. 1833. Newberry Prob. Off. Pet. for Part.
    Widow: Mary Davis--Pet'r.   Bdle-1 Pkg- 16
    Ch: Susannah "   res. Georgia
        Mary -w- Wm. Davis
        John Davis
        Dec'd son: William
             Ch: Ann E.
                 John T.
                 Mary

DAVIS, Van, Blacksmith, gr. 12 May, 1774 Newberry Deeds A-18/19
    to Wm. Tanney--150 A land of Davis Cr.   Nov. 23, 1775
    between Broad and Saluda. Wit: Robert Brooks, James Burns,
    William Willcocks

DAWKINS, William from Nancy Norman--Negro Winny--beq. to her by
    George Dawkins, Dec. Wit: Anthony Elton, James Dawkins.
    Newberry Deeds--12 Oct. 1782 A-89/90

DAY, Ambrose of Laurens Co. to Richard Johnson. Land in state of
    Georgia, Co. Washington on Williamson's Swp. 3 Oct. 1785
    Newberry Deeds E-432 Jan. 9, 1789

DAY, William "Tavern Keeper", of Laurens Co. to Rutherford Bowles,
    of Newberry Co.--88 A. situate, part in Lauren and part in New-
    berry Dist.--where Larkin Brown now lives. 23 Feb. 1796 Joint
    dower--Mary Day. Wit: I. R. Brown, Joseph Davis
    Newberry Deeds D-11, Feb. 23, 1796

DAY, William of Laurens Co. to Nathan Todd of Newberry
72½ A. Newberry Co.--on waters of Mudlick Creek and Mill Cr.   part
of grant to John Red--who conv.to Richard Griffin--who conv. to
me, whereon I now live. 22 Feb. 1797--Dower: Mary Day.
Wit: Isaac Grant and John Day. Newberry Deeds C-1044

DAY, William of Laurens Co to Thomas Chappell of Newberry Co., st, S. C.
100 A. on main rd. for Fish Dam Ford, Broad to Island Ford,
Saluda--all remainder orig. gr. to John Ray--whereon sd. Wm. Day
now lives. Dower: Mary Day Newberry Deeds D-287 Dec. 27, 1798

DeWALT, David of Newberry Dist(or Daniel)Newberry Ct. Min. Bk. Pg. 58-86
    Wife: Nancy
    Son: Daniel DeWalt
    "   David   "
    Dau: Rebecca "
    Exe'r: Edward Threatt Will not dated. Prov. Apr. 6, 1805

DICKERT, Christopher d. intestate. Newberry Ct. Min. Bk P. 41   62-68
    Widow: Christiana -m- Simon Wicker
    Ch: Elizabeth -w- Rankin Reid
         Adam Dickert
         Henry Dickert

DICKERT, Michael d. 1836 int. Newberry Prob. Pet. for Part. 4-72
    Widow: Sibl
    Ch: Henry S. Dickert, Pet'r
         John
         Nancy -w- Thomas Love
         Margaret -w- Westley Sanders
         Christina -w- Thos. Nelson
         Mary -w- Mathias Elman
         Sarah -w- John Jenkins
              Dec'd. 1 Ch.: Ann
         Catherine -w- John Jenkins (evidently after death of her
         sister Sarah

DILLARD, Thomas Jefferson d. August 1836
    Widow: Mary O. Pet'r.
    2 Ch: Margaret E. and Mary E.
    Newberry Prob. Pet. for Part. Bdle-1 Pkg.-17

DILLON, William d. 1826. Newberry Prob. Pet. for Part. Bdle-1 Pkg-18
    Widow: Esther Dillon, Pet'r.
    1 Ch: William Dillon (Minor)

DILLON, William d. 10 July 1851 Int.
    Mother: Esther Dillon, Pet'r. No wife or child.
    Newberry Prob. Pet. for Part. 6-120

DOMINICK, John d. 4 Sept. 1850 Newberry Pro. Pet. for Part. Bdl-1 Pkg-15
    Widow: Rachel Dominick, Pet'r.
    Ch: Martha -w- Bartholomew Long
         Mary Rosannah -w- Zachariah Nates
         Catherine, Elizabeth, Sophiah, John, Jesse, and Sarah

DOWKINS, George--Verbal Newberry Wills Page 22, 1788
    Legacy: Mrs. Jemima Harbett
              Nancy Barret (or Bantt or Barrott)
              Mrs. Mary Ann Lane
    Dau: Susannah Pope
          Elizabeth Pope
    G. Dau: Ellen Hampton
    Dau: "Widow" Grigsby
    Son: George Dowkins
    G. Son: Thos. Barrett and Wm. Dowkins. Ex: Son George and Nephew
    Thos. Dowkins. Prov. by Wm. Ballentine and Elizabeth Beard.
    4 June, 1788

DOWNS, David--on 5 Sept. 1801, moved to Ohio. Died 1814 Newberry Ct. Min.
    Widow: Oratrix   66-71
    Dau: Abigail -w- Samuel Hall
    Son: John Downs
    Dau: May   "
     "   Sarah
     "   Nancy, Betsy and sons: James and David all minors

DUBBER, John Frederick, Minister of gospel Newberry Deeds A-38/39 1773
    from Conrad Gallman and Herman Gallman. Wit: George Gallman
    Henry Gallman

DUGALL, John--gr. 12 Feb. 1755, 16/17 Feb. 1756 to John Pearson
    24/25 Oct. 1757 to Capt. Isaac Pennington. Provincial Deeds.
    Charleston Deed Book M-4 Pg.-113

DUNCAN, David d. intestate Newberry Prob. Pet. for Part.Bdle-1 Pkg-14
    Widow: Elizabeth -m- John Robinson
    2 Ch: Franklin Eldridge Duncan
           Narcissa Ann. Joseph Duncan, Gdn.

DUNCAN, George d. int. 8 Sept 1847. Newberry Prob. Pet. for Part. 6-121
    Widow: Rebecca
    1 Ch: Amos G. F. Duncan, Pet'r (Minor, by Gdn. Jacob Cook)

DUROT, John George Newberry Deeds P5-426, to Wm. Cannon 6 June 1764.
    100 A. on Saluda River, bd. Sd. River to Jac. Page 456 recites Wm.
    Cannon Sale same location 1764

DYSON, John d. 1825. Newberry Prob. Pet. for Part. Bdle-1 Pkg-13
    Widow: Polly -m- Stephen Jones Sr. Pet'r.
    Ch: Melinda -m- Stephen Jones, Jr.
         Abram , Peggy, Polly C., John S., James, Rebecca, Thomas Dyson

EARLE, Thompson -m- Miss Sarah Ann Herbert--dau: of Maj. Wm. Herbert.
    7 inst. Rev. E. F. Hyde, all of Newberry July 16, 1846, Newberry
    Prob. Pet. for Part.

EASTLAND, Thomas to Wm. Stripling 100 A. on wtrs. of Saluda.
    Wit: George Goggans, Wm. Irby, Wm. Blandon. Newberry Deeds
    A 42/43 Nov. 8, 1785

EDSON, Cushman R. dec'd 1790 intestateNewberry Ct. Min. Bx. 97 155-157
    Ch: Hannah R. and Casper, only children. When very young, taken
    to Miss. by their Gr. Mother. Mother having died. Edson, partner
    of Peter Braselman. (see Card, Braselman)

EDWARDS: Catherine--and her son Benj. Ketvhner to Thomas Gordon. 100 A.
    S side Enoree. Newberry Deeds A-81 May 30, 1786

EDWARDS, Obadiah, "weaver", of Berkley Co. 300₤ pd. by William Hendrix
    and Samuel Cannon. Mtg. B/S Negro girl Poll, 5 Oct. 1762. Wit:
    Issachar Willcocks, Margaret Hendrix (X her mark)
    Newberry File M. F. 22-287

EIGHBURGER, John -m- Sarah Priester--dau of Barbara Ruff. Samuel Cannon Tr.
    All of Newberry--Archives Dept. Misc. D. 367

ELLIMAN, Enos. Newberry Wills Pg. 19 1787
    Wife: Catherine
    Sons: John and William
    Daus: Elizabeth, Amey, Hannah Elliman and Mary Bonds
    Ex: Wife and Son, John, 21 Apr. 1787. Prov. June 2, 1788

EMBREE, Moses -w- Margaret of N. C. to James Wadlington of Newberry.
    150 A. Fork of Broad and Saluda on a branch of Bush Cr. Wit:
    Enos Elleman, John Elleman, and John Embree.
    Newberry Deeds A 49/50. Oct. 6, 1785

EPTING, John--died of stab wound. Newberry Clerks Off. Bx. 6 1822-5
    Widow: Caty
    Ch: all minors (not normal)

ERNEST, Johas Windall--Gr. conv. by Abraham Pennington to James Harvey
    150 A. on Little River. Sept 21, 1765 Provincial Deed Bk F-3
    Pg. 199 in Charleston
I
EVANS, Isaac Dec'd 13 Apr. 1822, Newberry Pro. Pet. for Part. Bdle-1 Pk-19
    Widow: Elizabeth Evins, Pet'r
    11 Ch: John
           Sarah -w- James Lindsey
           Elizabeth -w- Moses Whitmire   1st five adults moved
           Martha -w- Isaac Evins   out of state.
           Benjamin E. Evins
           Unity -w- John Myers
           Natty, Joseph, Huldah, Elenor, Isaac

NEWBERRY VILLAGE GRAVEYARD
FAIR, William -w- Elizabeth
    Dau: Permelia b. Aug. 28, 1816
                  d. Oct. 7, 1838 wife of Wm. T. Moore

FAIRCHILD, John -w- Rachel to Jacob Pennington 200 A. Oct. 7, 1755
    Provincial Deed B-3 Page- 89

FARRAR, Benjamin offorce River, Point Coup'ee--Prov. of Lousiana. Will
    6 Aug. 1790 at New Orleans. "pregnant wife". Son: Benjamin--to
    be ed. "my 2 daus": Ann Frances and Margaret. Ment's ch. by
    former wife.

198

FARMER, Isaac Newberry Wills Pg. 20
    Wife: Saraith (probably Sarah)
    Son: William
    "4 Daus": Not named
    Ex: Wife and Son, Wm. 31 Mar. 1787. Prov. June 2, 1788
    Wit: Wm. Hering, Robt. Brown, Catnir Ryley

FEAN, Thomas of Co. G. C. T. formerly of Newberry, Archives Dept. Misc. D
    To wife: Hannah Fean--dau of Mathias Elmore   152/3
    2 Ch: Brigit Honora Fean
           Rebecca Anna Fean. 14 June, 1819

FELKER, John A. D. int. 1848. Newberry Prob. Pet. for Part. 4-78
    Widow: Mahala -m- Wm. Low
    4 Dau: Emma -m- Barnett Fowler
            Wiley, Mary ann, Mahala (dec'd)
    John F. Glymph, gdn, Pet'r.

FIKE, Nathan from Joseph Caldwell 100 A. --X X XSept, 1785 Newberry Deeds
                                                                A-65
FINCH, Dr. Ivy d. 1815 int. Newberry Clerks Off. Bx. 6 1822-8
    Widow: Inez C. -m- James Meacham
    2 Ch: Jansey Elizabeth Finch, Edward Rush Finch--both minors
    Father: Edward Finch

FRITZMANN, Sebastian -m- 30 June, 1842 Sarah Wood. John F. Glymph, Tr.
    Newberry Dist. Misc. M-253

FROST, Mary of Pagets Creek from Charles King -w- Charity. 150 A. Gr.
    Chas. King 10 July, 1766--in fork of Broad and Saluda, on Pagets
    Cr. of Tyger River. All vac. Pg. 102 Mary Frost Widow, to Jonathan
    Frost. June 9/10, 1769. Prov. Deed Bk. Y-3 Page-98

FRASHER, John -w- Elizabeth to Jacob Pennington, 99 A. Jan 13/14, 1748
    Prov. Deed Bk-3 Pages 90-92

FULLER, John, deed gift.2 Feb.1787 .Newberry Clerk's Off. 1822-13 Bx-6
    To Dau: Catrine (died) -w- Henry County, Sen'r.
        Ch: Catherine -w- Standwix Hays
             Margaret -w- James Singleton
             Elizabeth -w- Robert Richard
             Mary Counts
             John   "
             Jacob   "
             Henry, Jr, since died, left 1 ch. Wesley County

FURGER, Jacob--alias Fulker of Faulker, Gr. 21 May, 1772, to Thomas
    Wood 350 A. fork of Broad and Saluda. Bd. Wm. Kaller, Jacob Oxner,
    draugh Eaynos. Wit: George Buchanon et al
    March 28, 1783 Newberry Deeds A 16/17

FYKE, Georga to Abraham Pennington. Mtg. 9 July 1762, to indemnify him
    as surety on a bond--cattle etc--200 A. at head of Long Br. of
    Indian Creek. 100 A. on William's Beaver Dam Cr. Wit: Erasmus
    Noble, Isachson Willcocks--a Quaker.

GALLMAN, John--Estate Adm. Gasper Peister. Newberry Pg. 28

GALLOWAY, Peter, Newberry Wills A- 1774
    Wife: Margaret
    Sons: James, Peter, John
    Daus: Mary Douglass -w- John D.
          Gean, Anna, Martha and Elizabeth Gallaway. Ex: Wm Harbison,
Robert Speer. Date: 26 Oct. 1774. Wit: Rob't. Speer, John
Douglass, Will Harbison. Proven: Sept 3, 1787

GARNER, charles G. Dec'd. 21 June, 1848 Newberry Pet. for Part. 5-108

    Widow: Mary Catherine Garner, Pet'r.
    1 Ch: Eliza Garner

GARNER, Robert Q. d. Nov. 1847, int. Newberry Prob. Pet. for Part. 5-98
    Heirs: Bro: Charles Garner, Pet'r.
             Joseph   "
             John   " (dec'd)
                Son: John M. Garner

GAUNT, Joseph d. March 4, 1816 intestate. Newberry Equity A-559
    Widow: Bathsheba -m- Benj. Stubbs
    Ch'n: Jacob, Israel, Walter, Elizabeth, Eli, Carey

GARY, Charles G. d. intestate Oct. 12, 1825
    Widow: Caroline Gary, Pet'r.
    2 Ch: Catherine Frances, (died)
          Rhoda Haseltine Gary
Newberry Prob. Pet. for Part. Bdle-1 Pg-20

GARY, Marvel and Lucretia--minors, over 14. Pet. apt. Martin Gary.
    Newberry Equity Pet. 1818-25

GARY, William D. d. abt. 1829 Will. Newberry Pet. for Part 4-75
    Widow: Jemmima
    Father: Jacob Gary- d. 1838- widow: Sarah--d. 1845
        Ch: Abigail -w- Jacob Crouch, Tuscaloosa Co. Ala
            Martha Gary--Pet'r.
            Malinda -w- Warren B. Gary, Walhen Co. Ala.
            Sarah -w- Samuel Reeder, Pet'r.
            Mary -w- James Worthington, Pet'r.

GEE, John of Craven Co Archives Dept, Newberry File B/S SS-54
    £ 1,500 to Henry Chappell of sd. Co. 5 negroes, Nov. 22, 1776
    Wit: Francis Dancy, Henry Weyly, and Prov. before Philip Pearson

GILBERT, Abram--Newberry Equity--Bills 1828-17
    LovziniKoKi Gilbert
    James Spencer
    John Holman
    David A. Crosson
    Vs: Edward Stephens and Thomas Pratt

GILBERT, Caleb of Beaver Dam Creek--Newberry Dist. 30 March 1805
    Wife: Ann
    Y Son: Caleb--a minor
    Dau: Lydda Chander
          Joseph Gilbert
          Sarah McNeary
          Syntiche Ragin
          Thos. Gilbert

GILBERT, Catherine--a daughter of John Eigelberger--will 26 Feb. 1827
    Newberry Wills

GILBERT, Carey -w- Eunice. The Son Times and S. C. State Gazette
    John Davis -w- Honey   May 25, 1832
    John C. Reagin -w- Dorothy
                    out of state
    Case: Isreal Chandler, Thomas Chandler vs Anna Case et al
    Equity Newberry Dist.

GILDER, Isaac, 12 Jan. 1799. Newberry Deed D--293, fr. Wm. Hall and
    wife Matty. $20.00 18 A. pt 118 A. Gr.--Matthew Tully, fork Broad
    and Saluda--Kings Cr. Bd: sd. Isaac G. and formerly John Wilson.
    Edw. Hill. Wit: Robt. Gowan, Obed. Parmish

GILDER, Philip d. 1808 intestate. Newberry Bk. Pg. 107 173-177
    Widow: Sarah -m- Abner Atkins
    Ch: Elia Gilder
         James Gilder
         Philip Gilder. Land on Bush River, sold

GILLUM, William to James Wadlington lo A. fork of Broad and Saluda.
    Wit: Mercer Bobb, Jacob Toland, Jane Wadlington. March 2, 1786
    Newberry Deed Bk. A-63/64

GLASGOW, James Will 17 Oct. 1775 "of Gilder's Cr." Newberry Wills A-194
    Wife: Mary
    Sons: Robert, John, Archibald, Wilson
    Daus: Margaret, Rachel

GLASGOW, John Newberry Ct. Equity AA-141
    John Kinard -w- Margaret
    Archibald Glasgow
    Wilson   "
    Robert McCrackin -m- Rachel
    Mary Glasgow
    Archibald Wilson of Ireland d. 17__. 6 sisters
        (1) Rachel
            Son: James -w- Mary
               2 Ch.

GLENN, Col. David, Dec'd, 1786 Affid. Newberry Deeds A-83
    James Blair heard Mother of Mrs. Rosannah Glenn that the Negro
    Woman Luce came into the family by her. Wm. Sparks heard Col.
    David Glenn say Luce was not his property.

GLENN, John, 1784 Newberry Wills A-
    Son: James, John, William
    Dau: Gean Glenn, Margaret, Ann. Ex: John Douglass and Thos.
    Brown. Date: 20 Sept. 1784. Proven: Sept. 3, 1787
    "Ment. my Bros. Wm. Herbison's widow, Ann". Wit: Robert Speer,
    James Douglass, James McLonin(?)

GOLDING, Thomas C. d. 21 Feb. 1845. Newberry Pet. for Part. 5-94
    Widow: Sarah
    Ch: Newman Golding--since deceased
              Widow: Jane
             1 Ch. Parmelia A. E.
                 John Foster Golding--Pet'r

GORDON, Mary--at house of Nancy Gordon, dau. of James Gordon, dec'd.
Her mother alleged of unsound mind. Legal inquiry to determine
facts as she has property--24 men examined her. "Is not a lun-
atic--but near sighted and bodily afflicted.
James Gordon, Dec'd. Widow: Nancy--abt. 55 yrs of age.
Dau: Mary Gordon--of full age
Son: James--age abt 24 yrs.
Dau: Jane -w- Loren Stewart abt 27.
" Nancy--abt 20 yrs. age
" Margaret--abt. 18 yrs. age
Son: John--abt 13 yrs. age
" David--abt. 11 yrs. age. Feb. 2, 1819

GORDON, Nancy d. int. 5 Aug. 1829, Newberry Pet. for Part. Bdle-2 Pk-21
Ch: Jane -m- Leven Stewart
James Gordon
Nancy -m- Robert Smith
Margaret -m- James Gray--res. Laurens
John Gordon

GORDON, Nathaniel of Newberry--"Stone mason and brick layer" to daughter
MaryGordon of same pl. "child"--all lands and estate being 100 acres
and 200 acres on Hunting Fork, a branch of Indian Creek. Waters
of Enoree River--mare, colt etc. 12 Sept, 1785. Pres. of James
Lindsey, James Hughes (X his mark). Prov. 16 Sept. 1785 in Newberry
County before Levy Casey, J. P. Bill of Sale Bk. XX-74

GRANT, Addison, Widow: Sarah Grant, Pet'r.
Ch: George W.
William Henderson
John Samuel
Andrew A.
Francis Marion. Newberry Pre. Pet. for Part. 5-92

GREEN, John dec'd--Will lost. Aug. 9, 1771. Newberry Deeds Bk A-84/85
Son: Edward Green--given receipt for share left will.
William Green, dec'd. (son of John).
Widow: Miltrer Liles--sd by X
Thomas Green--son of John
John Green--son of John

GREEN, Thomas, Newberry Wills 1787 A--
Bro: John Green, 30 Apr. 1787
Wit: Edward Kelsy
Edmond Kelsy
Mary Ann Smith Proven: June 6, 1787

GREEN, William, Dec'd. Widow: Miltred (or Mildred)Liles, 6 July 1782
That she does not know what became of the will of John Green, dec'd.
which her husband had last as the British had destroyed a good many of
their effects and papers. Possibly this will was destroyed. Aff.
by Daniel Green that he saw a certain will which he believes was
the will of John Green dec'd. Wherein it was specified that John
Green and Thomas Green were left heirs at law to their Father's
estate and the other three was cut off with one shilling each.
6 July, 1782. By Pre. George Ruff, J. P. for Ninety Six Dist.

Joshua or
GRIFFITH, John, Will on file 4 July 1809. Newberry Equity Off. 1822-10
    Widow: Mary -m- (1814) George McCollough
    4 Ch: Caly, John, West, Joshua (last 2 minors under 21)

GRIGSBY, Elizabeth d. int. 5 Oct. 185(2 or 4)Newberry Pro. Pet. for Part.
    4 Ch: David Payne   6-122
           Janies Payne
           Caty -w- A. L. Lark
           John W. Payne
           Dec'd Son: Edward Payne
              1 Ch: Catherine -w- David C. Boazman
           Dec'd Son Benj. Grigsby
              1 Ch: Satira -w- Stanmon Holston ofChamber Co. Ala.
                    Statira *w- Stanmon Holston Letter for Chambers
                    City, Ala Dec. 7, 1854

GRIGSBY, James, Dec'd 1783 96 Dist. Bk
    Widow_____-w- Richard Corley. Let. for him to
    Adm. 13 Mar. 1783

GRUBER, Philip to James Grayham. S. C. Gr. to John Philip Gruber.
    Oldest son: Philip Gruber. 100 A. fork of Broad and Saluda
    Sept 26, 1785 Newberry Deeds A-77/78
           b
HANCOCK, Barker, d. 1836 Newberry Prob. Pet. for Part. 4-81
    Wm. Page, Adm'r. Pet'r.
    4 Ch: Laney J. Handcock
           John   "
           Esther -w- Wm. Page
           Sarah -w- Gideon Nelson
           Dec'd Dau: Rebecca -w- John H. Gilliam
              Ch: Ann W. -w- John M. Allen

HANEY, Hiram, Union Wills Vol. 1-246
    Wife: Mary. "my ch" 12 Oct. 1808. Wit: Eliza Haney

HARRIS, Julias, dec'd. Newberry Pro. Pet. for Part. 6-123
    Widow: Elizabeth
    Infant Dau: Mahala Harris
         "Under the Act of Congress, a land warrant for 160 Acres
         was granted", to the heirs, jointly.--Bounty
         Widow Pet's sale of land warrant. Filed 16 Nov. 1855

HARRIS, Nathaniel of Ninety Six Dist. Newberry Wills Pg. 16
    Wife: Mary
    Son: Mosely
    Dau: Rebecca Ann
    Son: Richard (absent but may return)
    "my 4 Ch" Jemima -m- Gilliam (prob. David)
    Samuel, Littleberg, Clough. G, Son: Gilliam.
         Ex: Son-in-law--Samuel Harris, Littleburg Harris, Mosely Harris
         Dec. 30, 1787, Wit: Mosely Harris, Lewis Mitchell, George
         Elliott, Jamima Gilliam. Proven-?

HAYNES, Bartholomew of Mecklenberg Co. Charlotte D-3, May 22, 1815
    Wife: Sarah
    Daus: Polly, Sally, Matilda, Betsy I. C., Violet. "my 2 Sons"
        James, and David C. Ex: Friends Joseph N Haynes, and
        Moses Green. Wit: Will McKinley, Wm. Gilmer, Mag't. Greer

HAYNES, Charles, Will--_____?, 8 Nov. 1864. Anderson Wills138-93
    Sister in Law: Mrs. Betsy Reed, $240 to remain in family ____226
    pat's. All after debts. Wife: Mrs. Ann Haynes
    Wit: J. P. Caldwell, Bird Phillips, J. H. Little

HAYNIE, Maximillam of N_ Dist. Newberry Vol. 2-78 26 Sept, 1809
    Dau: Mary Harrison -w- Burr H.
        Sarah Courtney--Now in Virginia
        Susannah Shepherd
        Nancy Rutherford
        Francis Ruff
    Son: John Haynie
    Dau: Anna Haynie
    G Son: Aaron Haynie, son Peggy H., dec'd
        Ex: John Ruff, John Haynie, and Anna H. Prov. Nov. 21, 1814

HAYNIE, William, Newberry Wills 1-(?) - 49 Wife: Catherine
    Bro: John Haynie, 14 Apr. 1801--Prov. July 6, 1801
    Wit: Jesse Owen, Edmund Gaines, James Shepherd

HEAD, William and Mary Newberry Bk. C-128, to Thomas Holder £ 121
    175 A. on Enoree River. 1790

HENDERSON, David--Will 5 Dec. 1805. Newberry Wills E-75
    Wife: Hannah
    Sons: John and David S.
    Daus: Jamima, Elizabeth Littleton, Nancy Gordon.
        Dec'd Dau: Sebella Liles
                Ch: Wm. and Lacy Liles
    Dau: Sarah T. Henderson

HENDERSON, John, Will 27 Dec. 1815. Died 1 Jan. 1816 Newberry Bk 177
    Wife_____-m- Col. Benj. Maguire
    Son: David Watland Henderson d. 1816. Widow: Luch -m- John
        Ramage
    Son: Thomas--home pl. had 5 ch. Of Eloree. 1000 A.
    Son: James--Island Pl.
    "my Daughters" and my daus. by my last wife.
        Nancy -w- Andrew Thompson
        Hannah -w- Robert Pearson
        Lucy, Sarah, Caroline, and Jaime Henderson
        David Watland Henderson d. 1816. Widow Lucy -m- John Ramage
            Infant Dau: Elvira Hardin Henderson.
            Note due by John Henderson in Kentucky $36.60

HENDRIX, William d. int. 1834. Newberry Pro. Pet. for Part. Bdle-2 Pk-28
    Widow: Rebecca--Pet'r.
    7 Ch: Elizabeth, Sarah -w- David Senn, Presia, Henry, John, William,
        George. Last 5 minors.

HERNDON, Col. Benjamin, Will in file.   Newberry Clerks Off. Bx.- 1822-17
    Widow; Patience Tessy Herndon
    Ch: Mary B. -w- John M. Lewis
        Joseph
        Stephen
        Frances -w- David McKee
        Elizabeth M. -w- Samuel Farrow
        Dec'd son: Benjamin--widow: Sarah A. Herndon
        Nancy C. -w- John Rice
        Rebecca E. -w- Lachanich Reid
        Zachariah P. Herndon
        Patsy M. Harriot Herndon
        John N.
        Lucy Boswell Herndon
        _____ -w- David Johnson
        _____ -w- W. Rice
            Soilsby Glenn--oratrix

HERNDON, Col. Benjamin, dec'd. Son Times and State Gazette Dec. 4, 1830
    Case: John N. Herndon, Newberry Dist, Bill for part dec'd left
    Will. Sale of land he devised to his 2 daus: Patsey M. Herndon
    and Lucy B. Herndon--now on Duncan's Cr. Also dec'd.

HIGGINS, Dr. C. C. of Newberry. Newberry Pro. Ct. Aug. 6, 1846
    -m- 23 Alt. Miss Martha Simpson Griffin, Dau. of Capt. Anthony
    Griffin of Laurens. Rev. James C. Vaughn

HIGGINS, John J. D. Apl. 1829, int. Newberry Prob. Ct. Bdle-2 Pk-23
    Bro-whole blood: Mark M. Higgins
    Sis-- "   "   Mary E. "
    "   "   "   Sarah Ann -w- Bendett Eskridge

HIGGINS, J. J. Dec'd. Son Times and State Gazette Aug. 9, 1830
    Mark M. Higgins and Mary E. Higgins per pro ami vs: Bendett
    Eskridge and Sarah Ann, his wife.

HILL, Thomas vs Bro: John Hill. Newberry Ct. Min. 216/17 Bk-135
    States he pur. of John a tract of land--acreage found short.

HILL, William. State S. C. 96 Dist. Newberry Co. Bill Sale Bk XX-73
    Affidavit by William Hill that he saw John Green, Deceased, in
    the year 1774, sign and acknowledge a certain Will--in presents
    of Elizer Mobley and Alexander Mobley--that he left all land and
    chattels to John Green and Thomas Green, and Edward Green and
    William Green were cut off with a shilling. March 6, 1787
    Robert Rutherford, J. P.

HIPPS, Andrew d. March 1830. Newberry Prob. Bdle-2 Pk-25
    Widow: Nancy
    Son: Andrew
    Dau: Sarah -m- Joseph Ducket
         Elizabeth -m- Raif Hughes
         Juda -m- Elisha Rhodes   Some in Ga. and Ala.
         Eve -m- Hiram Rhodes
         Anna -m- John Neighbors
         Margaret -m- Laban Rhodes
         Nancy -m- Wm. Odle
         Elisha Hipps

HODGES, James Newberry Wills A- . Wife: Martha
    Son: Joseph, Dau: Christiana and Rebecca Shaw, Son: Hailey Shaw,
    Dau: Patty Shaw, Son: Jesse Hodges, Sarah Glass May 19, 1787

HOFMAN, Daniel of Craven Co. Love, good will, and affection for his
    children. Deed gift entire est. Misc. P. P.-27
    Ch: Margaret, Daniel, Christopher, Jacob, Peter, Michael, Mary.
    Wife: Mary. Dated 30 May 1771 Pres. of Alexander McQuators
    Ro: Ellison or Allison.
    Prov: 14 Aug. 1771, before Mich'l Dickert, J. P.

HOGAN, Gugiah 100 A. on Br. Saluda 1773. Newberry Plat Bk 17-1

HOGEL, John, a Tory--killed in 1783. Newberry Bk. Pk. 51. 75-86
    Land on Cannon Cr. in 1776, offered to sell to Stephen Hogel
    Son: George Hogel   Gr. Son: Frederick Hogel
    Stephen and Christopher Hogel, also Tories, moved to Nova Scotia
    John Simley -w- Rebecca claims the land by purchase.

HOGG, Maj. Lewis d 1829 Int. Newberry Prob. Bdle-2 Pk-26
    Widow: Clara Hogg
    Heirs: George Ruff and his Ch. (Minors)
           Ch: Marcella, Hannah, Patsy, Polly, Clara, Thos. S.
           Ephraim Suber and his Ch.
           Ch: John W., Lewis H., Sarah C--dec'd
           George S. Noland
           Micajah Suber -w- Elizabeth
           Hannah Noland dau. of Wm. Noland
           Sarah Noland and her ch.
           Ch: Frances and John (minors)

HOLMAN, John -w- Christian (with sd X) Newberry Deeds A-44/45 Oct. 8, 1785
    To: John Lester 55 A. Pt. 250 A. on water of Big Saluda fork of
    Broad. Wit: James Williams, Ellis Pugh, Timothy Thomas

HOPPER, Alexander -m- lately, Jane Gorden. James Gorden Tr. All of
    Newberry Sat, 9 Dec. 1813 Misc. D-3

HOPPER, John d. 5 March 1827, int. Newberry Prob. Bdle-2 Pk-24
    Widow: Mary Pet'r.
    Ch: Hugh Hopper
        Ann -w- John Boyd
        James Hopper
        Nancy -w- Jugh Boyd
        Dec'd--Willism Hopper
             Ch: James, Sarah Ann, Mary Jane

INMAN, Benjamin -w- Jemima to Mercer Babb 200 A. bd. Wm. Gillum.
    Newberry Deeds A-71/72 Jan. 4, 1772

JOHNSTON, David, blacksmith -w- Ann. Newberry Deeds A-Pg 4/5 1779 Dec. 1st.
    To: W. Malone, 100 A. on Gossels Creek--Broad and Saluda. Bd.
    Thos Johnson, and Vac. Wit: Robert Rutherford, Benj. Hampton,
    Bartholomew Johnson--Wm Melon, Clerk of Ct.

JACKSON, George--a doctor, to Nimrod Morris. July 3, 1783 Deed Bk A-73
    200 A. Gr. to Frederick Schrader, March 8, 1755, who conv. to
    Jacob Cooner Oct. 11, 1756 and he to Wm. Harris, and sd. Harris
    to sd. Jackson

JASON, John, d. int. 1854. Newberry Prob. 6-124
    Widow: Martha J. Jason, since dec'd.
    2 Ch: Mary E., and William D., Pet'rs

JOHNS, Jacob, Archives Dept. Mem 13-508. 150 A on FletchersCr.,
    Br. of Little R. of Broad R. Gr. Walner Tucker -w- Sarah
    21/22 Nov. 1770 conv. to Jacob Johns

JOHNSON, Gerard W. vs Benj. B. Cheshire, Note. Newberry Clerks Off.
    Equity 1824-1

JOHNSTON, John. Newberry Pg-13 Estate: Letters gr. John Bartow in
    right of his wife Elizabeth 7 Sept. 1787. Bond: John Bartow,
    Jeremiah Williams, Wm. Young

KIBLER, Christiana d. 1829 int. Newberry Prob. Bdle-2 Pk-30
    Husband: Adam Kibler
    Bros and Sisters: John Fellers
                       George Fellers
                       Mildred Fellers
                       Catherine -w- George M. Bowers
                       Mary -w- David Kibler
                       Polly -w- Matthew Hall
                       Elizabeth -w- Isaac Enlow

KINARD, Catherine d 22 Jan. 1861 Int. Newberry Prob. 6-127
    Ch: Mary -w- John D. Koon--Pet'r.
         Henry Kinard
         John Kinard
         Martha -w- William Boland
         Eve Kinard
         Catherine Kinard
         Cealy -w- Micheal Cromer
         Dec'd Dau: Elizabeth Suber
              Ch: Walter H. Suber--Out of State
                   Weston B.   "
                   Eustace   "
                   Effa A.   "
         Dec'd Son: David Kinard
              Ch: Jacob Kinard
                   George
                   ThomasP
                   David D.   All out of State
                   Elana
                   Caroline

KINARD, Elizabeth d. int. Newberry Prob. Bdle-2 Pk-31
    Heirs: John P., J. M., George, Samuel, Christopher, Nicholas,
            Henry (all Kinards) Geo. A. Stockman, Pet'r.

KINARD, Michael, Junior d. 1833 int. Newberry Prob. Bdle- 2 Pk-29
    Widow: Nancy -m- John N. Stockman, Pet'r.
    5 Ch: Drayton, Calvin, Jefferson, Bennett, Sparta

KOON, David, Wife: Catherine Caroline--both dec'd Newberry Prob. 6-126
    Ch: David Luther Koon abt. 14 yrs.
        Sarah E. T. Koon abt. 6 yrs.
          George H. Chapman, next friend

KOON, William Jefferson d. 18 July, 1853. Newberry Prob. 6-125
    Widow: Elizabeth Caroline Koon, Pet'r.
    2 Ch: William Solomon Koon
          John Abram Koon. (Koon deeds in File)

LANG, Maria Catherine and Michal Gromer, her husband, and George Lever,
    her son, To: James Young, wheelwright: 150 A. fork of Broad
    and Saluda on a Br. of Bush R. Wit: John Hair, Joachim Bulow,
    Wm. Blair. Newberry Deeds A-11/12 Sept, 17, 1785

LOW, Samuel, Sr.--Legator of Son: Samuel Low, Jr. Will 6 Apr. 1807.
    d. 15 Apr. 1807. Jr's Wife: Margaret Low.
    Nephew: Samuel Low Turner, son of Wm. Alex Turner
    Nieces: Elizabeth McClintock -m- James Taylor
            Acnos McClintock or Peggy or Margaret
    Nephew: John McClintock   also Nancy McClintock
    Niece: Elizabeth McTyre -m- Jesse Prater
     "   Jane McTyre
    Martha Low -w- James Low--also a legatee of Wm. McA. Turner

LESTER, Samuel of Newberry, d. 1817 intestateNewberry Bk 67 101 to 105
    Bro: Abner Lester--defendant, had the notes, etc, claimed them.
    Adm'r: Allen Lester, a nephew
    Abner L. ordered to pay debts of dec'd and costs. Notes due by:
    James D. Lester, Charles Lester, Wm. R., Lester, PeterR. Lester

LIVISTONE, Mich'l to John Wm. Hoseal: 250 A. Gr. to Hanes Peter Vernan
    on Cannon Cr. fork of Broad and Saluda. Wit: Martin Single et al.
    Newberry Deeds A-66/67/68 Sept. 15, 1774

LOWRY, Catherine _____? m. 1817--fought for about a year.
    Johnston Lowry--dept. Newberry Ct. Min. Bk-125 200 to 205

MACKLEDUFF, John -w- Feuter--(sd X) and Wm. Mackleduff and David
    Mackleduff, both of Union Co. To: David Sims of State of Virginia
    200A S-s Tyger R. Newberry Co. Wit: Thomas Gordon, Reuben Sims,
    W. Hardneigh. Newberry Deeds A-47/48 Apr. 20, 1786

MANN, Robert (or Man) Wife: Susannah Newberry Wills A- 1782
    Sons: James, John, Robert
    G-Son: Manasseh Mann
    Heir: Jean Nix (seems to be dau.)
    Ex: Wife and James (son)
    Date: 27 Mar. 1782. Prov: 6 Sept, 1787 Wit: Solomon Rees,
        Elizabeth Rees, Geo. Gogggan (3 "g")

208

LAGRONE, JOHN--Dec'd. 1831-Intestate--Newberry Prob. Bills 2-35
    Widow: Mary -m- Silas Marchant
    Ch: Susannah -m- George Boozer
        Christiana, Sarah, Ingram, Sarah, John Catherine, Elizabeth,
        and Mary.

LAKE, ELIJAH--Dec'd. 1828-Intestate--Newberry Prob. Bills 2-34
    Children: Elijah O. Lake
            Benjamin
            Ivy C. Lake--a minor
            Bensam
            Thomas
            Amy -w- Jas. S. Gillian
            Elizabeth R. Lake

LEE, ANDREW--Dec'd. Senate Journal Dec. 16, 1789 Pg.-125
    Exor's: Nancy Vaughn-later Nancy Lee Ferry over Saluda?
          Susannah Lee
          Jacob Smith

LEE, WILLIAM--Will 12 Sept. 1786 Newberry Prob. 1-52 A-49 (Or Union)
    Sons: Michael, Thomas, John, Joseph
    Daus: Catherine Breed   Jean Howell
         Olive Fraser   Sarah Bates
         Nancy Jackson

LESTER, JAMES, SR.--Dec'd. 1801-Intestate Newberry Clerk's Off.
    Children: Charles   1822-15 Bx.-6
            Samuel
            Abner-Out of State
            John
            Isaac
            Joyce -w- James Beaumont
                Child: James Beaumont
            Peter Lester
                Child: Patsy -m- George Thomas
                    Gr-child: George Thomas-a minor
            Sally -w- George Harmon
            James Lester
            Polly -w- George Moore
    Children of Peter Lester, continued:
                Willis Lester
                Rhoda -w- Julius Williamson
                Dillery
                Vincent
                Simpson
                Jinsey
                Widow: Jane Lester-widow of Peter, mother
                    of the children.
Letter in file from "Natchez" shows Edward Broughton, Parish
Judge 7th Dist. Louisiana 1821

LESTER, JANE--Of Indiana--Died Intestate Feb. 1835 Newberry Prob.
    Children: Simpson   2-36
                  Sarah -w- George Harman, Pet'rs.
                  Peter, Willis D., Vincent)
                  Mary -w- Thomas Moses?   ) All reside in Indiana
                  Jane -w- Abner Bogard   )
                  Scindilla -w- Samuel Bynum)
                  James D.--Resides in Mississippi
                  Rhody -w- Julius Williamson--Reside in Alabama
                  Dec'd. Dau: Martha Harmon (Her heirs)
    P. O. Mark, Frankfort, Indiana in file.

LEVIN, MRS. ANN -w- Jacob Levin "Of this place"
    Died 4th   Age 31   Newberry Prob. 13 Aug. 1840
    Survided by: Husband
                  4 children
                  Mother, sister and brother.

LEVY, J. BELTON -m- Miss Elizabeth Wickes 5th inst. J. P. Stockman,
    Esquire. All of Newberry. This is a piece of newspaper
    filed in a package to show adv. of Equity case. 16 July, 1840

LILES, JOHN--Dec'd. Intestate 20 Aug. 1829 Newberry Prob. 3-51
    Widow: Lydia
    Children: Drusilla -w- Richard Hilbern of Spartanburg. They
                moved to Indiana
                John
                Mary -w- Simeon B. Lestar
                Elizabeth -w- Nathan Chandler
                Mark, Bazil, Warren D., Lydia
    Gr-Children: Vashti Richardson)
                  Levi   "   ) Children of daughter, Patsy,
                  Anna   "   ) wife of James Richardson
    Lydia -m- Ledgerwood of Green Co. Indiana. Most of Heirs there.

LILES, RUTH--Newberry Vol. 2 Bk. F-34
    Dau: Dolly Liles--All 8 Aug. 1807   Prov: 26 May 1816

LINDSEY, JOHN--Newberry Wills 1783 and 1787 A-
    Wife: Else or Elsie
    Son: James (Oldest)
    Dau: Sarah Speaks
    Son: John
    Dau: Abigail Wells
    Son-in-law: Jerrard Smith
    Son: Thos. Lindsey and Samuel Lindsey
    Exor: Wife and Samuel Lindsey   9 Aug. 1783 Prov: 6 Sept. 1787
    Wit: Thos Dugan, Isaac Morgan, Moses Lindsey, Wm. Hamilton

LONGSHORE, ROBERT--Dec'd. 9 May 1832 Intestate Newberry Prob. 2-32
    Children: Martin Longshore
                Young   "
                Elizabeth "   -m- Benjamin Gregory
                David   "   -a minor

LOWRY, JOHNSTON -m- 1817 Catherine, suit by her next friend, Simon
    Cary--Separation suit. Newberry Eq. 1822-12 Bx.-6

LYLE, DRUSILLA--Cit: 25 March 1839. Col. Benj. Maybin, Adm'r.
    At the time of the deciaion "of Wilkinson Co. Miss." Paid
    to her Brother, John Sims. Rec'd. by her Adm'r--for her part
    of property of her father, Reuben Sims. Letter in file from
    Drusilla Liles to pay to her brother, John Sims.

LYLES, EPHRAEM E.--Died--unmarried, childless. Newberry Prob. 2-35
    Heirs: Nancy -w- George Red
            Mary -w- Russell Vaughn
            Susannah
            Elizabeth -w- James Pagett
            Robert, James William and John Lyles-All heirs next of
                                                            kin.

MANNING, Jethro of Saxogothic, Wife: Rosanna--Ex'r. Prov. Wills
    now in Archives Dept. Charleston. Will Proven: 1767
    Sons: Levy and Abraham
    Exor: Joseph N. Curry

MANNING, Levi of Newberry Co. Newberry Wills B-23
    Wife: Elizabeth
    Sons: Luke, Levi, Jethro
    Daus: Elizabeth, Margaret, Anna, Polly
    29 Mar. 1796. Prov: May 16, 1796

MARS, Robert, died in Newberry Dist. Will 16 Oct, 1812
    Dau: Mary -m- Wm. Carmichael
    Son: John Mars--Gra. Geo. Rye 29 Apr. 1868
    Dau: Betsy -m- John Hall of Ohio
    Gr. Son: Robert Mars
    Exor: James McMorris
    Copy will on P. 19 contested by Mary Carmichael
    Newberry Ct. Min. 17-26

MARS, Robert to Samuel Murray, 200 A on Jutting Fork of Indian Creek.
    Wit: Robert Johnson, Wm. Murray, James Murray (sd X)

MARTIN, George d. 1829 Will. Newberry Prob. Off. 5-86
    Widow: Elizabeth -m- Joseph Chupp
    2 Ch: Elizabeth Martin, Pet'r. and Noah Martin (youngest Ch.
        age 21 on 29 Mar. 1847. Pet. filed Nov. 9, 1847

MAYBIN, Elizabeth--sister of Nancy Lyles Newberry File, Misc. M-122/3
    Ch: Lucy Shelton, Caroline Pickens, Sarah Check, James Henderson,
    Benjamin R. Maybin. Deed Gift 29 Dec. 1841 to Caroline Pickens

MEANS, John of Fairfield, Will in file. 14 Aug. 1805 Newberry 1822-14
    Wife: Mary (John died 1811)   Bx. 6
    Ch: Isabella -m-   Judge
        David
        Sally -m- David Means
        Martha
        Robert A. and Mary A. born after will was made. Robert Means
            gdn. of 2 minors

Means, Thomas J.--Died at res. near Buck Head in Fairfield Dist. 8th
    inst. Age 45. July 16, 1846. Newberry Prob. Pet. for Part.

MENARY, Alexander of Ninety Six District called Oxford" To: Margaret
    Richey, widow of John Richey, Gr. to John Williams of 250 A. on a
    br. of Duncans Creek, Lamreeds fork--between Broad and Saluda
    Rivers--Bd. James Young, Rowland McCurley and vac.

METTS, Mrs. Mary A. B. L. -w- Dr. John Metts of Laurens. Died 16 Sept.
    Int. Only dau. of Mrs. Hosea Lee of Union Dist--married only six
    weeks. Newberry Prob. Oct. 24, 1844

MIDDLETON, Ainsworth--Will Laurens Equity 1826-4
    Widow: Jane
    Son: Andrew--died since, no issue
      "   Ainsworth "   "   "   "
      "   James--Since dec'd. Widow: Nancy
              Ch: Zilla
                    William
                    Jonathan   All
                    John   of
                    Angeline   Georgia
                    Penelope
      "   John--since dec'd--Widow: Margaret
              Ch: Margaret Hunter, William, John, James, Andrew,
                    Samuel, Mary, Larale
    Dau: (of Ainsworth) Elizabeth -m- James Anderson. Eliz. Dec'd
              Ch: Mary, Middleton, William. All of Missouri
      "   Anna Williams of Alabama
      "   Judith -w- James Cobb
      "   Grace Middleton (the youngest)
      "   Sally -w- Manassa Finney of Alabama

MILLER, Jonathan d. 27 Sept. 1840. Newberry Prob. Pet. for Part. 4-70
    Widow: Eliza Miller--Pet'r.
    Ch: Sarah Ann, Louisa, John Calvin--minor, died since

MILLS, John, -w- Mary and his mother, Rebeccah Mills To: Joseph Scott.
    300 A. on Young's fork between Broad and Saluda. Bd. Wm. Wm.
    Mills, Sen'r.--dec'd--orig gr. to John Mills. Wit: David Clary, Sr.
    David Clary, Jr. Jeremiah Ham. Newberry Deeds A-90 to 92.
    Sept 29, 1774

MONTGOMERY, George (sd X) -w- Ann (sd X) Newberry Deeds A-G7/8
    To: John Knox--100 A. S Broad--Bd. Wm. Johnston. Wit: William
    Johnston, Robert Johnston, Mary Johnston. May 9, 1774

MOONEY, Israel d. 1820 int. Newberry Clerk's Off. Bk. 6 1822-9
    Widow: Charlotte, Oratrix
    3 Ch: John, Joseph, Hannah--All minors

MOORE, Eleanor--Dau. of Rebecca Caldwell, Will 4 Oct. 1799. Newberry Wills
    Rebecca Moore--a grand dau. of testatrix.
    5 Ch: Margaret Richey
           Martha Calhoun
           Rebecca East
           William and David Caldwell
           James Caldwell
           Eliza Gillam

Moore, Elinor d. 1813 intestate. Newberry Bk Pg 140. 224 to 233
    2 Ch Rebecca -w- Charles Pitts-dec'd
          Patsy -w- Charles Gilliam--also dec'd. Wm. Gillam-Adm'r.
          Rebecca since died leaving one child

MOORE, Elisha -w- Susannah, dau- Martha a niece of Bartlett Saterwhite Sr.
    Bartlett's Will 15 Feb. 1803. Wife: Rebecca
          Dau: Elizabeth Bulloch (later Harris)
               Jemima Glover (later J. Lipscombe)
         A number of grand children not named

MOORE, James to Wife, Rosey--1814. Heirs of David McClellan. See
    Harry Boles of Newberry. Deed L-244

MOORE, James Den'r. dec'd. Newberry Bk 1860-1873 Pg. 111/12
    Admt--Mary Moore
    4 Ch: Ann Whaley -w- Richard Whaley
          Lucinda Crest (?) -w- David C._____
          Genia Riser -w- L. P. N. Riser
          Ellen Cromer -w- J. P. Cromer
          Dec'd Dau: Elizabeth Kiver to her Children
          Dec'd Son: John Moore to his Children   1868

MOORE, Rosamond--Will 20 Dec. 1860 Newberry Wills
    Gr-son: Thos. P. Huntington
    Gr-dau: Rose R.   "
    Dau: Jane Ann Huntington

MORGAN, Mark d. 28 Aug. 1850. Newberry Prob. 5-105
    Widow: Matilda
    2 Ch: Narcissa, Bertha (or Butler) Shields Morgan

MORGAN, Thomas--Gr. 17 Feb 1767 To: Capt. Charles King 300A.
    200A. of the 300, on King's Cr. of Enoree. Bd. John Brown and Vac.
    C. T. V. 5 pg. 5 1784

MORRIS, Samuel d. Feb 4, 1850. Newberry Prob. 5-110
    George Morris   Nancy -w- Samuel Nelson
    Sally -w- Benj. Waite   Rosannah -w- Simpson Waits
    Polly -w- John Kinard   Elizabeth -w- Jethro Harmon
    Thomas Morris

MURPHY, James Newberry Wills A-_____1787
    Wife: Sarah
    Ch: John, Dowdle,
    Dau: Jamima Murphey, Ann Mayhan, Rebecca Murphey
    Ex: Son-Dowdle and wife. Date: 27 Mar. 1787. Prov: 5 June, 17887

MCCLINTOCK FAMILY: Their mother a sister of Samuel Law, Jr.
    Elizabeth McClintock -m- James Taylor
    John   "
    Agnes   " (also called Peggy and Margaret
    Nancy   " not on all lists.
    Area of Rec. Sptg. - Chester. See card Samuel Law, Jr. and Sr.
    Newberry Equity

MCCLUNG, James d. 16 Feb. 1829. Newberry Pet. for Part. 2-40
    Widow: Mary McClung, Pet'r.
    Ch: Nancy, David, James, Jane -w- Richard Anderson, Solomon
    Martha, John, Sarah, William. Last 5 minors.

McCREARY, John, Dau: Peggy McCreary--a legatee of Wm. McAllyster Turner.
    131 A. on S-Fork of Catawba R. Newberry Equity, Will of Wm. McA.
    Turner. 1807

McCRELESS, GEORGE, d. 18_____int. Newberry Prob. Pet. for Part. Bdle 2
    Widow: Elizabeth   Pkg 37
    Dau: Mary C. -w- Thomas H. Shell
          Maria T. -w- Nathan Renwick
          Catherine and Elizabeth--Minors

McKIE, MICHAEL, d. Nov. 1, 1814 intestate. Newberry Bk. Pg. 202--303 to 305
  4 Ch: David McKie--Adm'r.
          Susanna
          Sarah
          Elizabeth--Adm'r.
               John Satterwhite--d. Sept. 1817
                 Adm'r: Michael Satterwhite
                       James Gillam
McKIE, MICHAEL, d. 1 Nov. 1814--Amended Bill Bk Pg 204. 305 to 312
    Ch: Alexander McKie--Orator
          Rebecca -w- Wm. Craig
    Dec'd: Susannah Satterwhite
    Gr. Dau: Susannah Satterwhite -w- Peter Moon
                Sarah -w- James Gillam
                Michael Satterwhite
                Elizabeth Satterwhite -w- Dr. John W. Sinpson. ?
    Dec'd Son: Michael McKie, Jr. one child
        Martha Powell -w- W. H. Powell
             By: James Gillam
                 Sarah Gillam
                 Peter.Moon
                 Susan Moon
                 John W. Simpson
                 Elizabeth Simpson
                 Michael M. Satterwhite

McLANE, JOHN, d. 1820 int. Newberry Prob. Pet. for Part. Bdle 2 Pk 38
    Ch: Frances McLane
          Margaret -m- James McDaniel
          Jane -m- James Forbes
          Jannet -m- Wm. North
          David McLane
          Mariah -m- John Penney
    Widow: Jannet McLane Orig. grants and deeds in file

McMAHAN, Daniel "of Pinckneyville" -vs- Wright Coats and James Coats--
    and Jesse Coats (Jesse--a man of color. Seems a servant of Wright
    Coats--a driver. Newberry Bk 82 129 to 140

McNEAL, JAMES d. 17 Aug. 1828. Newberry Prob. Pet. for Part. Bdle - Pk. 39
    Widow: Nancy--Pet'r.
          Jane Eliza
          Polly Ann
          Robert Neally

McNEAL, NANCY, d. Newberry Prob. Pet. for Part. 3-42
    2 Daus: Eliza McNeal
            Polly Ann McNeal
    Dominick, Mary--sister of Nancy
        Ch: Robert M. Dominick
             Jefferson   "
             Wesley   "
             Unisa   "
             Jane   "

Mc QUEEN _____? Newberry Equity Bk-6 1822-4

 Dau: Elizabeth Beard--no issue
    Susannah -w- Peter Ke___?
      Dau: Mary -w- John Johnson
         Elizabeth -w- John Caldwell
 Son: James McQueens
      Ch: Araminta Masia
        Elizabeth Caroline
        Susannah
    Alexander McQueen
    Samuel McQueen
 Dau: Esther -w- Francis Wilson
    Margaret -w- Alexander Wiley
    Elizabeth McQueens

McQUEENLING, ARTHUR -w- Elizabeth to Peter Richardson--100 A. on waters
 of Broad R. All Vac. Wit: John Gant, Joseph Smith, Thomas Cargill
 Newberry Deeds April 27, 1771 A-24/25

McTYRE FAMILY--Their mother a sister of Samuel Low, Jr. and Sr.
 Elizabeth McTyre -m- Jesse Prater
 Jane McTyre. Spartanburg Area.

NANCE, CLEMENT and wife Elizabeth -vs- John F. Gillam, et al.
 Newberry Equity Bills 1833-17

NANCE, DRAYTON * wife. Newberry Wills L 365/367
 Lucy--Dau. and Legatee of Washington Williams. Will April 9, 1829
 His 2nd wife was Ariana (or Hannah)dau: Elvira Nance, and 5 Ramage
 Children--Burr, Edward, John, Frances, and Drayton. James D. Nance
 was son of Drayton N.
 Will of Fred K. Nance:
    Ch: Robert Nance
      Sarah W. -w- Jno. K. Griffin
      Dorothy Pratt
      Drayton Nance
      Fred K.   "   , Jr.
      Alfred   "
      Laura Ann Butter
 Drayton Nance mentioned in will of Wm. Rutherford as his nephew--1842

NANCE, DRAYTON-- in his own right and as Exor. of James Williams, and
 as Adm'r. of Pamelia Williams, dec'd. -vs- John D. Williams-- Ex.
 of James Williams Et al. Newberry Equity Bills 1838-15

NANCE, DRAYTON Adm'r with will annexed of Robert Nance -vs- Robert
 Stewart, Dorothy Pratt, Fred Nance, Alfred Nance, Wm. Butter,
 Laura Ann Butter, et al. Newberry Equity Bills 1855-7

 NANCE, JAMES D. of Newberry Co. Graduate Class of 1856. Lawyer
 3rd. Reg. S. C. Vol. Made a Gl. on 1862--killed on Battle of the
 Wilderness

NANCE, ROBERT R.--Elected Tax Collector Newberry Dist. Misc. E-488
    John B. O'Neale
    Frederick Nance, Sr.
    Clement Nance
    Robert Donlop
    Drayton Nance   Bond to the State 5 Dec. 1825

NANCE, ROBERT of Newberry--Will. Widow: Sarah W. Stevens of Union--Dec'd.
    Drayton Nance, Adm'r. To: Amelia Nance, Dau. of Frederick.
    Newberry Sentinal, An Old Newspaper, Dec. 21, 1853. Will: 20 Feb.1814

NANCE, ZACHARIAH, Will 1 Aug. 1828 Union Wills
    Wife: Mary
    Son: Lowell (or Laurell)
          Zachariah
    Dau: Sarah Nance
          Elizabeth Hall
          Fanny Briant
    Son: James
    Dau: Patsy Littlefield
    Son: Fleming B. Nance
    Dau: Mary McGarity
          Peggy Hall

NEALY, ROBERT SR. d. Jan. 4, 1832. Newberry Pet for Part. 3-41
    Ch: Polly -w- David Dominick
         Robert Jr.
         Jane (d. no issue)
         Margaret (d. no issue)
         Mancy--Widow of James McNeil

NEWMAN, JOHN "of Berkley" Newberry Wills 1780 R-----
    Heirs: James Newman--not 18
    Son: Samuel Newman--not 18
           John Newmqn "youngest"
    Wife: Mine (or Mins)
    Bro: Samuel Newman
    Ex. Wife: and Joseph Johnson. Date 16 Aug. 1780. Prov. Sept 3, 1787
    Wit: Philip Phegin, Sarah Inman and Thos. Burton (or Bruton)

NOLAND, THOMAS J. d. 1833 Int. Newberry Prob. Pet. for Part. 3-42
    Widow--
    2 Ch: Frances
          John

NORRIS, JOHN, dec'd Charleston Gazette Jan. 9, 1800. Newberry File
    Only surv. child: Mary Shaw. Land to be sold--Newberry Co.
    Adj. Thos. Pearson

NORWOOD, BENJAMIN, YEOMAN, -w- Mary. Gr. S. C. June 23, 1774
    To: James Burns, 150 A. on Indian Cr. bd. James Wilson, Wm. Blackburn,
    and Dau. Newberry Deeds Aug 3, 1775 A-20/21

ODELL, RIGNAL, d. intestate Newberry Ct. Min. Bk Pg 138 221 to 224
    Widow: Mary d. Intestate
    Ch: Barnard Odell
         Mary   "   John--_____under 21. Re. land
         Rignal "   sold to James Neighbors before Part.
         Thomas "
         Margaret

O'NEAL, MARY, d. 1809 Will. Newberry Bk Pg 130 209 to 210
     Son: Thomas O'Neall
          Ch: Robert E. O'Neall)
               Polly O'Neall   ) all minors
               Rebecca O'Neall)
          John O'Neall, Jr.

OWENS, HENRY, d. int. Newberry Pro. Off. Pet. for Part. 3-44
     Heirs: Sarah Owens
             Casandra Batie -w- Moses Batie
             Daniel Owens
             Abarilla Owens
             Nancy -w- Joshua Palmer
             Sarah -w- Reuben Owens
                  Dau: Mary Ann Owens-minor(Might be dau. of dec'd
                  Reuben) John Stark-Gdn.

PATERSON, JOHN -Merchant of Berkley Co. Will 24 Jan. 1761. Newberry File
     Mother: Mary Pennington to bring up "my two daus" and 1760-1767
          Wm. Gatenbe to be with them while he lives and be maintained.
          Exors: Wm. Hendrix and Samuel Cannon
          Wit: Tobias Bright, John Duncan, and Mary Pennington Prov.
          6 June 1768
     Dedimus to Edward Musgrove
     1760-1767 Pg 119 Will of Wm. Gatenbe--March 17, 1755
          To: John Paterson "son of Mary Evans all my lands" and all
          ____ ? Wit: Wm. Daniel, John Asa, Henry Hendrickson, James
          Barnett. Dedimus to Edward Musgrove--Prov. 6 June 1761
               John Paterson's wife Mary dau. of Isaac Pennington.
               See his will.

PATTERSON, HUGH on Acct of G. Shaw and Co. -vs- Isaac Lindsey and wife
     Hester; James Fernandis; George McCreless; John Gould; and Samuel
     Lindsey. Laurens Equity 1815 No. 13

PAYSINGER, MARTIN, d. 30 Aug. 1848. Newberry Pro. Pet. for Part. 5-95
     Widow: Elizabeth Pet'r.
     1 infant dau: Mary Jane.

PEARSON, ENOCH, of 96 Dist. Provincial Wills, Charleston C. T. Wills
     Wife: Tabitha   Will--20 Apr. 1775
     Ch: Mary -w- Josiah Prother (Prothro)
          Margaret Burns
          Thomas Pearson--lived on Padgetts Creek and money left with
                         an atty. in East Jersey for Jonathan Jacobs,
                         Father of Tabitha.
     William Pearson
     Isaac   "
     Sarah   "
     Rachel   "
     Tabitha "
     CAMDEN GAZETTE JULY 4, 1816
          Mrs. Tabitha Pearson--widow--Died in Ashley, Mass. 3rd. inst.
          Age 101st year. Blind for 20 years, until the Sunday before
          the last when her sight was restored--could see without glasses
          to read.

PEARSON, SAMUEL -w- Mary (formerly Stedham) Newberry Deeds A-59/60
    To: Henry Stedham--200 A. Little R. of Saluda. Orig. gr. to
  Mary Stedham (now Pearson) May 3, 1786

PEASTER, SIMON P. d. int. 1837 Newberry Equity 3-48
    Heirs: Margaret Peaster
              Elizabeth -w- N. G. Gallman
              D. B. Peaster--et al (not named)

PETERSON, DAVID d. 7 Feb. 1848 int. Newberry Prob. Pet. for Part. 5-85
    Only heirs: Warren G. Peterson, Pet'r. Gdn: James Coleman
                Josephine   "   Gdn: John C. Stewart

PITTS, DANIEL, d. Apr. 1804 intestate Newberry Bk Pg 58 86-88
    Widow: Anna -m- Wm. Plant
    Ch: Elizabeth -w- James Stirling (m. 4 Feb. 1813)
         Jesse Pitts
         Joseph   "
         Daniel   "
         Larkin   "--d. 1816 intestate. Heirs: Mother, Bros. Sis.

PITTS, HENRY, d. 31 Dec. 1817 int. Newberry Ct. Min. Bk. 2
    Ch: Betsy -m- William Smith
        Thomas
        Rachel -m- Benj. Butler
        Jenny -m- John Johnston
        John
        Milly -m- Abram Waldrop
        Henry Pitts
        Molly Coates, Dec'd.
             Ch: Sarah Waldrop (4 children)
                    Ch: Catherine, Claibourne, Tabitha, Henry Waldrop
                  Edney -m- Christopher Hughey
                  John Coates
                  Jehn (?) Coats
        John Pitts, Cec'd
             Ch: Tabitha, Cary, Hiram, Reuben, Susan, Matthew, Belton,
             Stirling, Simpson, Drury
        Rebecca Stirling, Dec'd.
             Ch: James, Matthew, William, Betsy, John, Henry, Sarah
             Molly

PITTS, LEVI, d. int. Newberry Prob. Off. Pet. for Part. 3-47
    Widow: Sarah Pitts, Pet'r.
    Ch: Larken Pitts
        Chessly
        Jefferson--minor, abt. 15
        Huldah--minor abt 13
        Drury--died since

PLUNKETT, ROBERT, d. 1844 Newberry Prob. Pet. for Part 184/89 5-82
    Widow: Charity -m- John Cleland, Pet'r.
    Ch: Daniel S. and Charles Evans Plunkett--both minors

PLUNKETT, WILLIAM, SR. d. int. 1-gr Chas. P. 1772 Newberry Pro. Ct. 3-46
     Heirs: William Cleland, Sr.   Elizabeth Cleland
             George Cleland -w- Elizabeth   Nancy   "
             Sarah Plunkett   James   "
             Edna   "   Charles   "
             John Murdock -w- Phebe   William   "
             Jane Plunkett   Jane   "
             Nath'l   "   David   "
             Catherine P.

PRESSLY, E. E., D. D. of Abbeville, Newberry Sentinel Dec. 21, 1853
     Married Miss Mary Taylor of Laurens. Mon. Evening, 28 inst.
     By Rev. J. H. Haddon of Laurens

PRISOCK, FREDERICK d. 25 March 1817, int. Newberry Bk Pg 77 119 to 121
     Widow: Caty (Katy?)
     Ch: Margaret -m- John Legrone
          Frederick Prisock
          John   "
          Adam   "
          Sally   "
          Molly   "
          Dec'd son: George
                      His ch: Rosannah Prisock
                               David   "

REES, JOHN, Dec'd. Newberry Clerk's Off. Equity Card 2 1824-3
     David Rees, Adm'r. Adv. Benjamin Richardson
     Alleges: James Richardson -d- minor
     Bro: Benjamin Richardson
     Mother: Mary Rees formerly widow of Robert Richardson

RIESE, JOHN d. Buncombe Co. N. C. 1817. Newberry Bk Pg 116 187 to 191
     Adm. in Buncombe Co. Property in both states.
     Widow: Mary Riese
     Adm'r: David Riese--also shows Daniel (Riese also Reese?)

RICHARDSON, BENJAMIN, orator. Newberry Clerks Off. Card 1 1824-3
     Wife: Polly dec'd
     1 ch. Robert Evans Richardson. Wife owned ¼ int. in land and 1/9
     of or. tract. Isaac Evans, ¼ int. Robert Evans, Jr. His (Isaac's)
     Mother Lydia Speer. Bro: Robert Evans. Nephew: Robert Evans
     Richardson

RICHARDSON, PETER -w- Martha of 96 Dist. to David Edwards of Camden Dist.
     150 A. on waters of Broad R. Wit: John Pearson, Michael Kennamore
     Newberry Deeds A 22/23 Oct. 28, 1777   (sd X)

RICHARDSON, ROBERT d. 1798 Newberry Bk Pg 119 192-200
     Widow: Mary -m- John Rees d. 1819 N. C. Adm'r. David Rees
     2 Ch: Benjamin--Orator
            James Richardson--died minor

RODGERS, STEPHEN -w- Frances of Chatham Co. N. C. to: Aaron Cates 100A.
     S-s Enoree. Bd. by Joseph Fish and John Sterling. Wit: Thos
     Cates, Sr., Robert Cates, Thomas Cates, Jr. Newberry Deeds A-15/16
     Nov. 15, 1785

ROWLAND, JAMIMIA (Sp. Roland) --dau. of James Murphey--will March 27, 1787
    Reuben Rowland--legatee of John Blalock. Also John Blalock Rowland
    Zachariah Rowland--Exor. will of Howell Cobb--1810 -w- Abigail
    "my children". David Bozeman, also exor.

RUFF, JOHN ADAM, Sr. Newberry Prob. Off. Pet. for Part. 3-49
    Widow: Tersea -m- Fred(k Nance, Pet'r.
    1 Child: Orlando C. Ruff Pet. filed 1 Jan. 1832

RUSSELL, PHILIP M. Newberry Prob. Pet. for Part. South Carolina 13 Aug.
    1840. Officer Rev. Wife: Esther Bussell d. Philadelphia July 26th.
    9 out of 13 ch. 70 Gr. and Gr. gr. ch.

RUTHERFORD, ROBERT, SHFF. of 96 Dist. Newberry Deeds A-13/14
    To: Joachim Bulow 182 A. on gr. owned by Peter Kurr of Savannah Ga.
    Bd. Azariah Tugland, Enoch Pearson, Joseph Sommer, John Mills.
    Wit: Thos. Boyd, Henry Sommer, A. Robinson

SANSOM, SAMUEL Gr. May 18, 1773 to Wm. Anderson--100 A. N-S Saluda. Bd.
    John Lang___ Samson, James Dyson and Saluda R. and Thos. East
    Wit: Michael McKie, Thomas Norrel, John Jackson. Newberry Deed
    Bk A-9/10 June 25, 1785

SATTERWHITE, DRURY , Will 13 Oct. 1811 (Copy in Files) d. 1812
    Wife: Susannah d. 1816
    Y'st. dau: Theresa Caroline Satterwhite--not 21
    "my 5 Ch"___ ?
    Bro: Bartlett Satterwhite--Exor.--d. 1816
    Exor. James Dyson
    Dau: Elizabeth d. no issue
    Son: Thomas--a minor
          Narcissa Satterwhite
          _____? Satterwhite Newberry Ct. Min. Bk Pg 2 110-115

SATTERWHITE, JOHN d. 12 Sept 1817 int. Newberry Ct. Min. Bk Pg 59 88-96
    Ch: Sarah -w- James Gillam
         Susannah -m- Peter Moon
         Michael Satterwhite
         Elizabeth Satterwhite

SATTERWHITE, MICHAEL, d. Nov. 8, 1830. Equity Notice, Newberry File
    Case: A. L. Lark and wife -vs- John Satterwhite and others.
    Newberry Dist. Partition. Land on Mudlick Creek--Newberry Dist.
    Bd: John Williams, Dr. Peter Moon, John W. Payne

SENN, DAVID d. 8 May 1849 Newberry Prob. Pet. for Part. 5-103
    Widow: Margaret Senn, Pet'r.
    4 Ch: Rebecca L. dau. by his 1st wife, Sally
           John D. also son of Sally
           Wm. T. and Dolly C. J., ch. of Margaret. Pet'r. All infants

SENN, JOHN d. 2 May 1845 int. Newberry Prob. Pet. for Part. 5-83
    Widow: Mary d. April 1848
    Heirs: Daniel, David, Zachariah, John Martin, Jesse, William A.,
            Mary J., Frederick, also
            Salina -w- John Cromly (sd. John Crumly res. Murray Co. Ga.)

SHELL, AMY d. 9 Sept, 1830 int. Newberry Prob. Pet. for Part. 3-50
    Heirs: Patsy -w- James Abrams, Pet'r.
    Allen S. Eliza W. Casey, Thos. Casey, Wm. Casey. Ch. of Catherine
    Shell -m- John A. Casey

SHELL, LEMON (or Lemmon) Will 15 Sept. 1814 Newberry Bk Pg 151 242-248
      Wife: Nancy Shell d. 13 Oct. last Ex.
      Son: Dr. Thomas Shell, orator Ex.
            Charles Wm. Shell--minor
            Exec: Archibald Crenshaw

SHELL, MRS. PRESCIA d. 1836 int. Newberry Pet. for Part. 3-56
      Ch: Mary -w- George W. Curtis Pet'r.
           Joseph Shell
           Frances Shell

SLOAN, ARCHIBALD d. int. Newberry Prob. Pet. for Part. 3-53
      Widow: Fanny
      Ch: Rosannah -w- John Caldwell
           Jane (also Jean) -w- James J. Sloan
           Margaret -w- John Sloan, Jr.
           Martha -w- Samuel McQueens, of Ind.
           Mary, Samuel, and James Sloan

SLOAN, FANNY d. 12 Dec. 1831. Newberry Pet. for Part. 3-54(also sp. Stone)
      Heirs: John Calswell -w- Rosannah
              Samuel
              Samuel McQueens -w- Martha
              James J. Sloan --w-- Jannet
              John Sloan -w- Margaret
              Mary and James. (Sloan is correct) Some in Indiana

SLOAN, JOHN SR. Newberry Prob. Off. South Carolina, Aug. 13, 1840
      Died 30 July last. at res. Fairfield Dist. Age 8500Whig in Rev.
      War under Gen. Marion Presby.

SMITH, GERRARD Newberry Pg. 26. Estate letters to Esther Smith-Widow

SMITH, MRS. MARY of Newberry d. Oct. 1848 int. Newberry Pet. for Part 5-100
      Only heirs: Gr. Ch. John M. Sullivan
                            Warren P.   "
                            Jane D.   "   All minors of Laurens Dist.
                            James J.   "   Ch. of C. P. Sullivan. Their
            Dec'd was maternal Grandmother   Gdm. and Next friend.

SMITH, THOMAS, d. int. Newberry Prob. Pet. for Part. 3-55
      Widow: Elizabeth -m- Joshua Davis
      4 Ch: Nancy Smith
             Mary -m- Obadiah Jones
             Lucinda Smith
             William Smith

SPARKS, STEPHEN, D. 10 July 1816 Newberry Ct. Min. Bk pg 65 96 to 99
      Ch: Zachariah Sparks
           Jesse   "
           Joseph K.   "
           Isaac   "
           Phoebe Lewis
           Elizabeth Sparks
           Sarah Ann   "   Minor
           Mary   "   "

SPENCE, JAMES SR. d. 1820 int. Newberry Clerks Off. Equity Bx 6 1822/7
    Widow: Martha
    5 Ch: Elizabeth -w- Robert Calswell
          Agnes -w- Hugh Wilson
          William Spence
          John   "
          Willson   "

SPENCE, JAMES d. June 4, 1847, int. Newberry Prob. Pet. for Part. 5-89
    Father: William Spence
    3 Bros. 3 Sisters: Frances W. Spence
                  Robert C.   "
                  Martha J.   "
                  Dickson C.   " Out of State
                  Nancy H. and Margaret A., minors
SPILLERS, LEWIS d. last of 1830. Newberry Prob. Pet. for Part. 4-71
    Widow: Margaret -m- Joseph Quattlebaum
    Ch: Lewis Spillers--infant abt. 9 yrs.

STRONG, CHARLES d. int. Newberry Prob. Pet. for Part. 3-52
    Widow: Nancy, Pet'r.
    Ch: John M. H. Strong
        Martha J.   "
        Mary J.   "
        Elinor E.   "
        Nancy C.   "   Filed 1831

SUMMER, ADAM, SR. (sd X) to Adam Summer, Jr. 100 A. orig. gr. to Elizabeth
    Cobler, whereon William Summer now lives. Wit: Michael Dickert,
    John Fullmer, Henry Amigh. Newberry Deeds A-80 1784 Dec. 2

SUMMER, ELIJAH, -m- 1807--lived together abt. 10 yrs. Margaret--Oratrix.
    Formerly Margaret Peister. Newberry Ct. Min. Bk pg 78 121-128
    4 Ch: A son who died
          Susannah, abt. 9 yrs of age
          Mary Ann, abt 5 yrs of age
          Rebecca "quite an infant"
               He has left her and took the ch'n to his father's. He
               sd. he -m- her Dec. 1806

SUMMER, HELEN d. int. 4 Feb. 1836. Newberry Pet. for Part. 3-57
    Ch: Susan P. -w- James C. Chalmers
        Amanda MelvinaSummer--of age
        John Sampson   "
        Jacob Pope   "
        Elizabeth Mary   "
        Henry Hezekiah   " Last 4 minors

SUMMER, GEORGE A. of Lexington, Archives Dept Misc. D-116/7/8
    To: Wife, Mary Catherine Summer
        Dau: Mary Elizabeth Follmer
        Son: John Nichols Summer
        "   Geo. A. Summer
        "   Andrew Summer
      Dau : Susannah Margaret -w- George Hipp
      "   Maria Eve -w- Henry Ruff
      "   Magdalene -w- James Sligh (1819)(Several papers, maybe same)

SUMMERS, JAMES--Newberry Prob. Pet. for Part. Bdle 1 Pkg 11
    Ch: Ruth -m- Isaac Arnold
        Allen, Elizabeth,
        Mary -m-_____Huber
        John, William, James
        Eleanor -m- John Summers

SUMMERS, JESSE Newberry Prob. Pet. for Part. Bdle 1 Pkg 11
    Ch: John, Henry, Albert, Caleb, and 4 infants names unknown

SUMMERS, COL. JOHN Newberry Prob. Pet. for Part. Bdle 1 Pkg. 11
    Ch: Mary -m- William Griffin (2) Charles L_____(unable to read)
        Eleanor -m- Phil Waters
        Nancy -m- Peter Hair
        Caroline -m- C. Gary (2)Peter Hair
        John Summer

SUMMERS, JOSEPH of Dist of Newberry. Newberry Wills (Waters File 3 Feb.
    Wife: Eleanor Will 3 Feb. 1802 Prov. 16 Jan. 1809   1802)
    Sons: William, John, Jesse, James
    Daus: Elinor Waters dec'd to her 2 heirs
        Cassandra Rigg dec'd to her heirs
        Mary Chapman
        Ann Wells
        Dorcas Summers
    Wit: P. B. Waters, Sm'l Summers, John Summers

SUMMERS, WILLIAM, JR. Appointed gdn. of his sister-in-law: Pamela Goodman,
    a minor, who became pregnant--alleged by William Sr., gdn., who is
    about to leave state. Joseph Goodman, dec'd. Thomas Goodman, Adm.

SUMMERS, WILLIAM Newberry Prob. Off. Pet. for Part. Bdle 1 Pkg 11
    Ch: Samuel, William
        Mary -m- Robert Pitts
        Hezekiah, J. W.,
        Alsey -m- Robert Washington
        Eleanor -m- Jno. Edmundson
        E. T.,
        Tabitha -m- Allen Fuller

SWINDLER, ELISHA d. 21 Dec. 1835 int. Newberry Prob Pet. for Part. 3-58
    Widow: Nancy
    Ch: Tabitha C. over 21
        Mary -m- fielding G. Lake
        Jesse F. and Emeline J. both minors

TAYLOR, DR. A. L. -m- Elizabeth Moore--Their son, Henry Pendleton Taylor
    died at res. of Mrs. Henry Taylor in Columbia--age 2 yrs 4 mos.
    Newberry Prob. Pet. for Part. Sept. 14, 1847

TAYLOR, GEORGE d. Sept 1847. Newberry Prob. Pet. for Part. 5-87
    Widow: Julia--under 21 yrs--by her next friend--Geo. Schumpert.
    1 Ch: Nancy Taylor, Pet'r.

TAYLOR, JAMES R. d. 14 Nov. 1847. Newberry Prob. Pet. for Part. 5-84
    Widow: Mary Elizabeth Taylor, Pet'r.
    1 Ch: George Henry Taylor--under 21 yrs

TAYLOR, JOHN, Will 17 Sept. 1749 Newberry Wills Bx 1 A-
    Wife: Susannah--All and Ext.
    Exor: Moses Guyton

TAYLOR, JOHN and Wife -vs- James R. Crispin and wife--Bill for Partition
    Newberry Dist--Estate of Joseph Sibley, late of Newberry Dist. Dec'd.
    Son Times and State Gazette Aug. 16, 1830

TAYLOR, JONATHAN -w- Mary To: Son William Taylor. Newberry Deeds A-69/70
    200A. Gr. to Wm. Gillum, Feb. 15, 1769 by S. C. Wit: Richard
    Taylor, Eleanor Taylor. 1774, Dec. 3.

TAYLOR, SAMUEL D. d. 27 Jan. 1848. Newberry Prob. Pet for Part. 5-88
    Widow: Eliza Taylor, Pet'r.
    2 Ch: Susan C. Taylor and Calvin S. Taylor

LEGRONE, FREDERICK--½ Brother of Jacob Counts, Orator. d. abt 2 yrs ago.
    Wife: Elizabeth d. abt 11 mos. before her husband
    2 Ch: Elias and Jacob--minors--John Taylor apt. gdn. Gr. Ch. of
    Elizabeth Taylor
    Sisters: Catherine and Eva Taylor. Newberry Ct. Min. Bk 104 168-173

THOMAS, ABEL Newberry Bx 19-41
    Bro: Timothy's oldest dau, Sarah, to Elizabeth Comer
          Isaac
          Elizabeth Rankin
          Prudence Hawkins   March 3, 1805

THOMAS, DAVID Newberry Will Bk. M-381
    Sister: Susan Adams
             Elizabeth Jeatis
    Legacy: Mary Caroline Thomas
    "   Benton Sheppard, son John T. Sheppard
    "   David Thomas Rainey
    "   Washing Floyd Feb. 2, 1837

THOMAS, EDWARD Newberry Sentinel Dec. 21, 1853, Married Miss Mary
    Ann Enlow all of Newberry. 13 inst. By P. W. Counts, Esq.

THOMAS, JOHN, of Newberry Co. Power of Atty Greenville Deed B-111
    To: Thomas Lewis of Greenville Co. Power Atty. to recover 2 tracts
    land in Caswell Co. N. C. on Hogan's Creek--descended to sd. John
    Thomas or heir of his father, John Thomas, Sr. formerly of N. C.
    Wit: Thomas Camp and John Camp.   Newberry Deed

THOMAS, NEHEMIAH of Newberry--Newberry B-80
    Nephew: Edward, son of Edward Thomas of N. C.
    Wife: Abigail
    Legacy: Nehemiah Mills, son Thos. Mills and Wife Sarah, of Newberry
    "   Nehemiah McKinsey, son of George McKinsey and wife Sarah
    Nephew: John Dobbins
    "   James Dobbins
    "   Thomas Johnston   26 May, 1796

THOMAS, MARY   Newberry Bk. 1-100
    Son: William dec'd
          James Thomas dec'd to his Dau. Mary Frances, Legatees of
    James Thomas Sr. dec'd "in confirmity with his will" Apr. 12, 1840

TODD, DAVID d. int. 28 Jan. 1815 Newberry Prob. Pet. for Part. 3-60
    Heirs: Grizzy Todd, Pet'r.
    2 Ch: Isabella Todd and Betsy Todd, infants

TURNER, WILLIAM of Saluda--Will 1 Feb. 1774Newberry Bk Pg 155 248-278
    Wife: Elizabeth   Prov. 25 Oct. 1776
    Dau: Priscilla -m- Benj. Long
          Ch: Wm. Henry Long now dec'd
               Elizabeth--former -w- of Henry Coats, also dec'd
               Polly--present wife Henry Coats
               Sarah Gaskins -w- John Gaskins, Orator
               Benj. F. Long (MBenj. Long)
               Priscilla Long -w- Benj. Long
    Will of William Turner--Pg 160 of Bk.
    Wife: Elizabeth, Ext. Will 1811
    Son: William Turner -w- Mary (m-2 Mc?)
          John Turner widow Frances Williams
          Richard Turner and his son William. Widow Mary -m- Garrett
          Edward Turner
          Absolom Turner
          David Turner
    Dau: Mary Edwards
          Ann Abney -w- Michael Abney
          Elizabeth Stephens
          Deborah Turner -m- Cook. Land adj. Gilbert T.
          Priscilla Turner -m- Benj. Long
          Polly -w- David Peterson

TURNER, WM. McALLYSTER, 24 Oct. 1806 Newberry Bk Pg 101 163 to___
    Mother: Jean Turner
    To: Alexander Turner -w- of John Turner, lives in Fairfield
         Martha Law -w- James Law   "   "   "
         Samuel Law and Robert Bryce 500 A.
         Uncle John Turner--land in Chester Dist.
         Alexander Turner son of James Turner
         John Turner   "   "   "
         Nancy Turner Dau. of John Turner
         Wm. Hughes son of James Hughes
         Robert Bell son of John Bell lives in Winnsboro
         Samuel Yonger son of Samuel W. Yonger
         Uncle James Turner
         Peggy McCreary dau. of John McCreary 131 A. of s. fork of
             Catawba.
         Uncle John Turner--all land left to me by Benj. Wallace
VALENTINE, ZACHARIAH,dd. int. 1829 Newberry Prob. Pet. for Part. 4-61
    Ch: Thomas Jr., Sarah J. abt 19, John S. abt 17, Margaret C. abt 15
    Nathan Whitmire: Next friend

WADLINGTON, WM Newberry Wills Bk C Pg 38 1799
    Wife: Sarah
    Sons: George, James, Thomas
    Daus: Linah Littleton, Mary Eddins, Eleanor Linum
    Son-in-law John Gosery, his son John and Dau Sarah
    Ex: 3 Sons Dec. 7, 1799
    Wit: Jas Waters, John Clark, Jesse Wadlington. Rec'd June 5, 1800

WALLACE, WILLIAM d. Apr1819. Will in file Jan. 25, 1813. Newberry Equity
    Wife: Mary Wallace   1822-16
    Ch: Henry, John, Howell, Ruth, Hugh, William
        Son HenryWallace d. 8 July 1820
        Widow: Tabitha
        Ch: Sarah, Wm, Allen, Roderick, Benjamin, John, Martha Elizabeth.

WALLACE, WILLIAM d. 1816 int. Newberry Bk pg 128 205 to 208
    Widow: Frances -m- John Jamison. 1 Ch: Frances Wallace Jamison
    Ch: James Wallace
        Margaret   "
        Robert Gillum Wallace
        Mary Moore Wallace

WATERS, ELEANOR -w- Newberry Prob. Pet. for Part. Bdle 1 Pkg 11
    Ch: Eleanor -m- Henry Waite
        Prescious Lark

WATERS, PHILEMON of Newberry Co. Ninety Six Dist. To: Allen Robison
    Transfer of grant to lands 14 April 1787. Pres. of Daniel Clary and
    Jesse Griffin. Prov: 3 May 1787 by Clary before Wm. Moore, J. P.
    Archives Dept Misc X X -379

WATERS, COL PHILEMON Newberry Probate Bx 21
    Let. Adm 16 May 1796--Final1819
    "There were 4 heirs; towit"
    John Summers and wife
    William Farrow and wife
    P. B. Waters--will 26 Feb. 1808. Wife Sarahand 2 Ch. Polly and Robert
    Wilkes Berry Waters   Minors

WATERS, PHILEMON "of Orangeburg Dist" from (20 Sept 1770)
    John Sommers -w- Elizabeth of C. T. 300 A. grant N. E. Side Pee Dee
    C. T. Deed V-4 Pg-1 Philemon Waters and wife Mary of C. T. Conv.
    June 5, 1772

WATERS, PHILEMON dec'd Widow: Ruth -m- Starling Baldree 6 Feb. 1819
    Dau: Eliza Waters Newberry Dist. Misc. D--133-5

WATERS, THOMAS WILLOUGHBY of Newberry Dist to Henry Deen 6 May 1791
    Pt. gr. to Stephen Elmore on Saluda R. Dower by Fanny Waters
    Newberry Deed A-1133

WATSON, JOHN d. int. June 1849. Newberry Prob. Pet. for Part 5-107
    Widow: Nancy
    Ch: Joseph, Thomas, John, Elisha
    Dec'd Dau: Rachel Hill
            Ch: Thomas, Joseph, Martha, John, Elliott, Levi Hill.

WATTS, WILLIAM d. int. 1837 Newberry Prob. Pet. for Part. 4-77
    Widow: Temperance
    5 Ch: John, James, Eliza, Thomas, Martha Catherine (last 3 out of st)

WEBSTER, WILLIAM**His gr. 23 June, 1774 To: Gabriel Anderson, Blacksmith
    100 A. on Indian Cr. --of Fair Jurrest. Wit: John Speake, John
    Connell, Richard Speake Oct. 19, 1784 Newberry Deeds A-86

WELLS, MARY Newberry Prob. Pet. for Part. Bdle 1 Pkg 11
    Ch: Matthew Wells
        William
        Eleanor -m- John Hays
        Patsy -m- H. Martin
        Joseph and James.

WEST, WALTER will 27 Mar. 1807. Newberry Clerks Off. 1824-2
    Ex. Wife: Elizabeth
    "my Ch": Ex'rs: James Johnston, Benj. Johnston
    Ch: Benj West
        John West
        Drury West
        James West
        Caty West   James and Caty minors

WHITE, JOSEPH March 28, 1780 Newberry Deeds A-29/30 To: Nicholas
    Everleigh, 200 A. on Saluda which sd. White got from Patrick Reiley
    Feb. 25, 1767. Wit: Wm. Freeman, Wm. Sergeant
    James Mason to Nicholas Everleigh 50 A. on N-s Saluda Nov. 18, 1765

WHITMIRE, JOHN d. 1831 int. Newberry Pet. for Part. 4-76
    Heirs: Elizabeth--Florence, Lauderdale Co., Ala -w- Wm. Lovelace,out
    Frederick Whitmire   of state
    Phebe   "   d.--left will--all to John and Caroline
    Milly   "   d. no issue
    Caroline   "
    John H.   "   Pet'r.

WHITMIRE, PETER d. abt. 15 Oct. 1839. Newberry Prob. Pet. for Part. 4-79
    Widow: Sarah, Pet'r.
    3 Ch: Lucinda Elizabeth abt. 7 yrs age
           Sarah Christina   " 5 " "
           Margaret Temperance" 3 " "

WICKER, HENRY d. Sept. 1805--Will Aug. 23, 1805. Newberry Bk 75 116-118
    No wife mentioned
    Dau: Elizabeth -w- Daniel Keller, Oratrix
        Mary Wicker--minor (called Polly as well) Oratrix
    Exor: John Owen--still in charge
        David Owen--Moved to Tenn--settled before he moved

WICKER, HENRY d. Will in File 1825 Newberry Prob. Pet. for Part. 4-67
    Wife: Elizabeth--since dec'd
    Ch: Woolrod, John, Michael, Daniel, Christian, Elias, Abraham,
        Sibel -w- Christopher Singley
        Elizabeth -w- Jacob Richmond   By former wife (seems)
        Barbary -w- John Hall   Lucy Stewart
        Agatha -w- George Cromer   Rachel Mayer
        Rosanna -w- John Morris
        Uriah Wicker--since dec'd--no issue

228

WICKER, ISAAC d. 24 Aug. 1850. Newberry Prob. Pet for Part. 5-104
    4 Bros: Andrew Wicker
               Jacob   "   Pet'r.
               Samuel and Henry--minors
    2 Sis: Peggy -w- John Lominick
               Sarah Wicker

WICKER, MATHIAS, dec'd. Newberry Deeds A-82
    Widow: Mary Wicker--nee Rattlehaver, (sd X) to: Gabriel Anderson
    100 A. gr. to Mary Rattlehaver, maiden. 25 May, 1774. by S.

WICKERT, MATHIAS, JR. "of York of Broad and Saluda" Newberry Wills Pk-21
    Wife: Mary Sibla   1778
    Son: John Adam
           Simon
    Dau: Mary
           Catherine
    Exor. John Adam Yonn and Michael Dickert. 5 June, 1778 Prov: 2 June
                                            1788

WILSON, ARCHIBALD d. Ireland 1792. Newberry Bk Pg 89 141-148
    Sister: Rachel Glasgow d. 1742 intestate
    (6)   2 Ch: Ann -w- Hugh Shannon of Ireland
               James Glasgow -w- Mary (Dau. of one of sisters) Oratrix
                      Ch: John Glasgow
                           Margaret -w- John Kinard
                         Archibald Glasgow--claimed it all as debt
                         Wilson Glasgow
                         Rachel -w- Robert McCrackin

          Jane
          Margaret
          Amy
          Elizabeth
          Susannah

WILSON, FRANCIS d. 1816 Intestate Newberry Ct. Min. Bk pg 78 157-160
    Widow: Jane Wilson, oratrix
    Ch: David, Francis and John, also Hugh and William--minors
    77 A. adj. James Calswell and Robert Caldwell, et al

WILSON, SAMUEL (sd X) of Richmond Co. Ga. To: John Hampton, 200 A. on
    Second Cr. of Broad. 1784 Dec. 27. Newberry Deeds A-79

WILLIAMS, JAMES, Bro. Rignal Williams--Newberry Wills Bx 147 Pkg 1528
    Colt. to Elizabeth Snellgrove
               Baruch Snellgrove (wife)   21 June, 1823
    Wit: Wm. Whitmire, Rachel O'Dell, Nathan Whitmire

WILLIAMS, JAMES SR., Bro. Rignal Newberry Wills Bk 9-43
    Legacy: Elizabeth Snellgrove, wife of Barruch Snellgrove 21 June, 1822
    Ex. Bond: Rignal W.
              James W.
              Thos. O'Dell 27 Jan. 1823

WILLIAMSON, JOSEPH d. 1794 int. Newberry Equity 1822-1 Bx-6
    Widow: Elizabeth
    Catherine -w- Thos Walton, Pet'r   John Williamson
    Robert Williamson   Nancy -w- John Griffin
    Joseph Williamson   Rebecca Williamson

WILLIAMS, THOMAS--Will. Newberry Wills Bk F-7
    Sister: Elizabeth Teague
    Nephew: John W. Teague
    Niece: Dorothy G. Davis
    Nephew: Wm. W. Teague
    " At death of my Mother XXX, should not the above named ch. be of age"
    My Bro: Abner G. McCraw
    Step Father: Stephen McCraw
    Ex: Jas. Teague and Stephen McCraw 15 Oct. 1815
    Wit: Marten J. Gary, David Cole, Sam'l Owens Rec'd 10 Dec. 1816

WOOD, ELIZABETH d. intestate 24 Dec. 1830 Newberry Pet. for Part. 4-66
    Heirs: Anna Wood
           Nancy -w- Hector R. McCan
           William, Elizabeth, Sarah Wood, also Mary, James R., and
           Silas, minors.

WOODS, SAMUEL d. 1815 int. Newberry Pet. for Part. Bx 4 Pkg 62
    Widow: Elizabeth
    Ch: Silas Woods, Pet'r
        Anna, Ambrose
        Nancy -w- Hector R. McCann
        Elizabeth, William, Mary, and James. (last two minors)

WORTHINGTON, CHESLEY d. int. Newberry Prob. Pet. for Part. 4-64
    No wife or child
    Mother: Elizabeth Worthington. Following Bros. and Sisters.
    Frances Herbert -w- Isaac
    Margaret -w- Francis Spearman
    Elizabeth -w- Samuel Chapman
    Polly -w- George Hunter
        Ch: John, Nathan, Elizabeth, Jane, and William
    Thomas Worthington
    Samuel   "
    John   "
    Sarah -w- Joseph Griffin
    Reuben Worthington, dec'd. Only ch: Jacob A.
    Thomas Worthington--Widow: Tabitha
        Ch: Hannah, John, Emily, Marcus
    Rhoda Spearman, dec'd -w- Grover Spearman
        Ch: Elizabeth

WORTHINGTON, THOMAS d. int. 7 Nov. 1829 Newberry Prob. Off. 4-63
    Widow: Tabitha -m- Allen Fuller   (m. 16 Sept. 1832)
        Ch: Harriet B. Worthington
           John R.   "
           Amelia A.   "   Minors
           Marcus A.   "

YOUNG, JAMES m. 28 Mar. 1822 Kitty Griffin--dau. of Reuben Griffin
    Newberry Dist. Misc. D-388

YOUNG, JOSEPH d. Oct. 1820 int. Newberry Prob. Pet. for Part. 4-68
    Widow: Sarah Young, Pet'r.
    6 Ch: Jacob, James, George, Jane, Archer,Elizabeth Ann

ZEIGLER, JOHN d. int. 1820 Newberry Prob. Pet. for Part. 4-69
    Widow: Elizabeth -m- Wm. Inman
   3 Ch: Lydia
         Israel
         Margaret by John's wife. (res. Abbeville)

RICHLAND COUNTY - SOUTH CAROLINA

Compiled by

Janie Revell

ABBOT, JOHN--Richland Wills 29 January 1825
    Wife: Hannah
    Sons: Isaac, John, Jonathan
    Daus: Leby, Hannah, Rachel, Polly
    Date: 29 January 1825. Proven 29 March 1825
    Exors: Wife and son, Isaac
    Wit: Obadiah Wilson, Jos. Thornbill and Isaac Abbott

ADAMS, EPHRAIM--Richland Wills (2) 5 March 1833
    Admx: Margaret Adams
    Heirs: James Adams
            Joel Adams
            W. Killingsworth
            G. Rawlinson

ADAMS, HARRY W.--Richland Wills Bx. 1-3 Orig. Will 30 September 1815
    Wife: Martha
    Only Child: "My son" James Hopkins Adams

ADAMS, HENRY W. --Richland Probate Bx. 1-4 Orig. Will 1 July 1809
    Bros. and Sisters: Joel R. Adams
                    James W. Adams
                    Sarah and Grace
    Father: All land of "Estate of my gr-mother-Sarah Goodwyn".

ADAMS, JOEL, SEN'R.--Richland Bills 190 Filed 3 January 1821
    Vs--Joel Rawlinson, Adm. of Benj. Rawlinson--Bid to foreclose
    Bond by Benj. Rawlinson dated 25 November 1814 and mtg. con-
    veyed to deceased by Ann Johnson and heirs of Benj. Johnson.

ADAMS, JOEL--Richland Equity Bills 78--See card Clairborne Clifton

ADAMS, JOEL, SR.--Richland Wills 30 October 1829
    Sons: James, Joel, Wm. W.
    Nephews: Joel Tucker, James Tucker, and Rob't. Tucker.
    Deceased Dau: Sarah Tucker
    Gr. son: James H. Adams--not 21--son of Harry Adams, Deceased.
    Wife: Not named
    Ex: Sons; James, Joel, and Rob't.
    Wit: John W. Morgan, Edw. L. Garner, W, J. Goodwyn, James C.
          Bates. Proven 21 July 1820

ADAMS, MARGARET--Richland Probate Bx. 1-6 Orig. Will 7 March 1838
    Mary Ann Powell--50 acres not sub. to debts of Robert Powell.
    My other children

ADAMS, RICHARD--Richland Probate Bx. 1-7 Orig. Will 28 October 1787
    Wife: For life
    To: Annes Gregory--1 shilling
        John Carrill Adams and Richard Adams--Land-Beaufort Co. N.C.
        William, James, and Abraham--Land "I now live on".

ADAMS, RICHARD--Richland Probate Bx. 1-8 Orig. Will 11 January 1805
    Wife: Jane
    Bros: John Carroll Adams, William, James, Abraham
    Bro.-in-law: John Bryson--Exor.

232

ADAMS, WILLIAM W.--Richland Equity Bills 89. 1815
    Vs.--Sarah Epps Goodwyn. See card--Harry Grant

ADGER, ELIZABETH--Wife John Adger, dau. of Robert Ellison. See card
    David Ellison Dunlap. Richland Equity Bills 12

ADGER, WILLIAM--Of Dist. of Fairfield vs John Watts, Edward Walker
    and John Watts--Bill to perpetuate testimony. Richland Co. Bill 22

ADGER, WILLIAM--Richland Equity Bills Roll 22 1813--Alleges: Edward
    Walker, formerly of Fairfield, now of Ga. Suit over land he had
    in Fairfield--alleging sale.

AIKINS, SALLY--Richland Equity Bills 37 and 41 Wife of Archibald
    Aiken (?) Dau. of Brittain Spelling.

AKIN, ELIZA--Richland Co. Bills 139. Filed 5 May 1818 -vs-
    The Protestant Episcopal Church in Columbia--called Trinity
    Church alleges: Inc. 18 Dec. 1810 by Act of Legislature.
    Pltf. drew Lottery ticket #99--sold by the church--prize $500.00
    Church claimed she let 6 mos. pass which made it a donation.
    Ct. decreed church pay it.

ALEXANDER, HENRY DANA WARD AND ISAAC BROWNFIELD--Sons of Sarah
    Horton, wife of Reuben D. Horton. See card Royal Bullard, Pet'r.
    Richland Eq. Roll 123. 1819

ALLISON, ANDREW--Planter-Richland Wills 21 August 1787 (Also Ellison)
    Dau: Mary Allison, Margaret Allison
    Heir: Isaac Ross
    Gr. Dau: Martha Allison Logue
    Wife: Margaret
    Nephew: John Allison
    Date: 21 August 1787. Proven November 19, 1889
    Wit: Thos Brown, A. B. Ross, H. Beaumond

ALLEN, ANNA -vs- John Allen--Richland Bills 141 Filed 4 December 1816
    Alleges: About 26 years since Pltf. married Deft., John Allen
    of Chester and bore him seven children and about 8 years ago he
    took up with a slave--prevailed upon to sell the slave, he then
    took a white woman, wife of another man. Alleges her step-son
    John Allen, son of Deft. demanded she give up the house to him.
    Alleges Pltf. beleives Deft. is about to sell out or rent out
    and leave the state, leaving her and children in distress, with
    no home. Deft. owned large estate worth about $5000.00.

ALSTON, FRANCIS -w- James Alston, Dau. of William Kirkland. See
    Samuel Alston an Exor. Richland Eq. Bill 17. 1812

ANDREWS, HENRY and wife, Rebecca, dau. of Andrew Lester, Dec'd.
    Richland Eq. Bills 122 1816

ANSWINGER, PETER--Richland Wills (810) 16 Feb. 1789
    Adm: Frederick Answinger
    Heirs: Not shown
    Bond: Jesse Baker, Timothy Rives, Thos. Taylor, and Judges
        for Court for Richland

APPLEWHITE, HARDY--"Of Co. of Southampton, State of Va."
    Wife: Charlotte
    Mentions: "my Children". Not named-to be educated
    Ex: Wife and Bro. Thomas
    Date: 22 Dec. 1808. Proven 20 March 1809
    Wit: E. G. Blake, Geo. Belches, Mary Blake. Richland Wills #12
    Orig. on record in Va. Certified copy in Columbia. Had prop.
    in S. C. and Ga. Adm. in S. C. sold slaves to pay debt.

APPLEWHITE, WILLIAM--Minor, under 21. Richland Eq. Roll 80 1817
    Entitled small estate by Will of father. Prays apt. some fit
    person.

ARLEDGE, ELIJAH--Richland Prob. Court-Bk. 1-13 Cit. 2 Jan. 1818
    Clary Arledge--Adm'r. Bond: 8 Jan. 1818
    S: Needham Dudley and Benj. F. Harris
    Heirs not shown

ARLEDGE, ELIJAH--Dec'd. Intestate Richland-Old Book 1825
    Pet. by: Clara Arledge, Wm. Arledge, Cullen Arledge
    ¼ acre lot in ?. (Cola-probably Columbia)

ARLEDGE, WILLIAM--Cit. 18 Feb. 1831 Richland Prob. Bx. 1-14
    Mary Ann Arledge, Adm'x. Bond: 23 Feb. 1831
    S: Richard Henning
    Letter in file written by William Arledge from Greensborough,
    Ala. Jan. 1827 to Needham Dudley, Sr. Columbia, S. C.

ARTHUR, HARGROVE--Of Lexington Dist. Richland Eq. Filed 20 Dec. 1827
    Wife: Mary
    Dau: Rebecca -w- Reddich Pierce
          Sarah Glenn
          May Morgan
          Anne Arthur
    Son: William Arthur
          Joseph Arthur--resides in Columbia
          John David Arthur
    Dau: Elizabeth Caroline Arthur
          Keziah Arthur
    Will 30 August 1816

ARTHUR, SARAH--Richland Eq. Bx. 144 -m- Elisha Daniel

ATKIN, MICHAEL--Richland Wills 11 Feb. 1833
    Adm: Edith Atkins   Bond: 11 Feb. 1833
    S: R. F. Coleman and Robert Yates. Heirs not shown

ATKINSON, DAWSON AND AGNES--Richland Stray Bills Bx. 152-179
    See: Henry Zinn

ATWOOD, JOSEPH and wife Mary of Mass. Richland Eq. Bills 109
    See Joshua Benson, father of Mary

234

AUTRY, CORNELIUS--Richland Wills (17) 4 March 1808
    Adm: James McClellan Bond: 14 March 1808 Heirs not shown

AUTRY, DAVID -w- Elizabeth)Both nee McGrew. See card Alexander
    CORNELIUS -w- Mary)McGrew. Richland Eq. Bill10 1810

AVERHART, JOHN--Richland Prob. Bx. 1-16 Cit. 1 April 1831
    Adm: PaulSpigener   Bond: 11 April 1831
    S: John S. Chappell and Frederick Spigener
    Pur: Malachi Averhart--Trunk, etc.
    Pd. board for Caroline Averhart, dau. of deceased

AVERY, HENRY--Of Virginia. Richland Eq. Bills 171 1820 -m- Martha
    Greenway Dixon Hicks--dau. of Robert Hicks of Richland. See
    card Hephzekiah Watson.

BACHTER, JUDITH H.--Richland Eq. Roll 30. 12 year old dau. of
    Judith Barrett, late Judith Bachter--her father was Jacob Bachter
    who apt. his wife and Daniel Faust ex. his Will. Judith prays
    apt. Christian Bachter, Gdn. Her mother -m- Ludah (or Judah)
    Barrett.

BACOT, SAMUEL -w- Rebecca To: Richard Kirkland--567 Acres S-s
    Wateree. No Plat. (Had land on Sumter side too). Richland
    Land. C. T. Deed 00 416-23. Page 301--Gr. to John Todd, Jr.
    -w- Mary on Dutchman's Cr. Bd. by Samuel Bacot's land.

BAILEY, MRS. J. CARRIE--Dau. of Julia C. Moore and sister of H.
    Cambridge Moord. Richland Wills Bx. 138 1864

BAKER, JESSE--Richland Wills 15 Jan. 1821
    Wife: Grace
    Niece: Esther Nevill--Land near Kershaw line.
    Heir: Sarah E. Key--relation not shown
    Ex: Wife and Malachi Howell, Joseph B. Stanton, and Thos. Heath.
    Date: 15 Jan. 1821 Proven: 17 Aug. 1821
    Wit: Matthew R. Howell, John Marshall and Hiram R. Taylor

BAKER, MARGARET -m- John Wilson. Richland Eq. Bx. 152-178
    See Henry Zinn

BALDRICK, THOMAS--Richland Eq. Bx 127½. Adv--Henry McKenzie -w-
    Mariah. See McKenzie card.

BALDWIN, DAVID--Richland Prob. Bx. 1-19. Cit. 18 Dec. 1806
    Adm'r: Henry Reese Hall Bond: 3 Jan. 1807 S: David Grey

BALLARD, WILLIAM -w- Ann (Late Ann Trice, Widow Wm. Trice) -vs-
    Simon Taylor, Esq.--Mentioned slave purchased by Wm. Trice in
    Louisa Co. Va. in 1796--from Thos. Wash and let his brother,
    John Trice have said slave. Letter by Wm. Ballard in file,
    signature, etc. Richland Co. Bills 32
    Also case of Jacob Lazarus and Zachariah Florence trading as
    Lazarus & Florence.

BALLENTINE, JAMES--Dec'd intestate, prop. in Lexington. Wife,
Elizabeth, also dec'd. Richland eq. Pet. 148 1819. William
Fulmore and William Ballantine, Adm'rs. John age 17 and
Elizabeth age 13, minors, pray apt. Gdn. Pet's "of Newberry"
pray apt. their brother-William.

BANKS, AMOS--Sheriff Dits. Lexington -vs- Jacob Seitz (or Leitz)
Bill to Foreclose--Alleges: James Pen, former Sheriff of Lexington sold Plt'n. to Jacob Leitz. Orig. Grant-Henry Leitz in
Dist. Lexington on Broad River. Richland Bills 135. Filed
1 May 1817

BANKS, AMOS -w- Catherine, Zaccheus Wooley -w- Elizabeth, Jacob and
George Long, Abrahart -w- Mary, and John Rish -w- Barbera--Heirs
of George Long, Dec'd. of Lexington. Also Michael Long-Minor.
Petitioned for sale and division.

BANKS, SAMUEL--of Fairfield -m- a dau. of Alexander Robinson. See
card William Cleland. Richland Eq. Bills 39 1812
See also Emanuel Warmbezee.

BAUSKETT, JOHN--of Richland Dist. 27 May 1853 to: Dau. Susan Ann -w-
David M. Clark. Gen. James Jones, Tr. Misc. Z-791
Richland Wills 1823--Wm. Bauskett. Adm: John D. Brown.
Bond: 22 Feb. 1823

BARBER, JAMES--See Sarah Milling. Richland Eq. Bills 24 1815

BARKLEY, ROBERT--Dec'd. Richland Eq. Bills 133. Adm: Samuel Dunlop,
Wilks Caston, and Rob't. Barkley. See card S. Dunlap.

BARRETT, JACOB AND ISAAC -vs- John Russell-Bill for Foreclosure of
Mortgage. Richland Bills 167. Filed 6 January 1820

BARRETT, JOHN--Cit. 2 Dec. 1825 Richland Pro. Bx. 1-20
Adm'r: James Rowan Bond: 19 Dec. 1835 S: James Hopkins and
Green B. Rush. Pd. Emeline Broadway's Acct.

BARRETT, JUDAH--Of Town of Columbia -m- set 19 Nov. 1806 Judith
Bookter--Widow Jacob Bookter. Recites Prop. from her "former
marriage with Frost and Bookter". Seems this her 3rd. marriage.
(See card--Bachter, Judith H.)F. C.

BARRETT, JUDITH--Richland Bills 97 Filed 21 Dec. 1813 -vs- Judah
Barrett--Alleges he was merchant in Columbia. Marriage agreement
between Judah Barrett and Judith Bookter, widow, in file and recited in complaint. Marriage agreement dated 24 Nov. 1806 shows
Judith had 3 children. Wit: Herman Kinsler, John Duke, and
John Campbell. Shows Judah Barrett also had children but not
clear whether they were by Judith. Separation and suit over
property. File shows: Acct. sale of property of estate of
Jacob Bookter, Dec'd. on 27 Dec. 1805

BARRILLON, CHRISTOPHER--Richland Wills 16 Aug. 1825--"Native of
   Paris in France-Naturalized U. S. A. 8 Nov. 1802. Ct. Kershaw
   Dist. Camden, Now living in Columbia.
   Wife: Catherine
   Son: John Nandin Barrillon
          Francis Humphries Barrillon (over 12)
          Chas. Christopher Barrillon (under 12)
   Dau: Catherine
   Sister: Jane (Property in France)
   Ex: Jno. Bryce, James Young
   Date: 16 Aug. 1823 Proven: 9 Feb. 1828
   Wit: Thos. T. Willison, J. N. Hanlon, Jno. W. Arthur
   Will states wife shows signs insanity and drinks heavily and he
   wishes children taken from her.custody.

BATES, JACOB--Gdn. of George Kelly. Richland Eq. Roll 101 1818
   Shows: Jacob Kelly is infant under 14--entitled to estate of
   his father, Jacob Kelly, Dec'd. Prays apt. of Pet'r as Gdn.

BATES, JOHN--See card John Croft. Richland Eq. Bills 173

BATES, JOSEPH--Adm. John Bates. Richland Wills 18 Aug, 1823-Cit.
   Heirs: Joseph Bates, John Bates, Wm. Bates
           Mary Cain and Eliz. Fields
   Bond: 8 Sept. 1823 S: Joel A. Tucker

BATTON, JOHN -w- Nancy, dau. of Sarah Starke. See card Robert D.
   Montgomery. Richland Eq. Bills 179

BAUGHMAN, JACOB -w- Nancy and Susannah Haugabook-widow.
   Catherine, Jacob, and Barnard Haugabook--In re. estate of Jacob
   Haugabook, dec'd husband of Susannah and father of the other
   parties. Bill for partition--Lands in Lixington and Orangeburg.

BAY, ANN and children--Have personal property. Negroes, etc. Pet.
   by Thomas Waties Trustee to sell and get residences. Ann Bay
   was sister of Wm. Ransom Davis--He left her money in trust.
   Richland Eq. Roll 4 Pet. 19 June 1810

BEALE, JAMES -m- Widow Elizabeth Howell. (Widow-Wm. Howell, Jr.)
   Richland Eq. Bills 87 1814

BEARD, CHRISTOPHER--Dec'd. in Lexington. Richland Misc. D-8 1818
   Heirs: Nancy Beard   )
           Mary S. Beard) All of Lexington
           Thomas Beard)
           Mary Wolf   )
           Anne Mardney) Of Richland

BEARD, JOHN--D. intestate 16 Dec. 1863 Richland Wills Pk. 935 Bx. 38
   Widow: Martha A. Beard--Adm'x.
           Samuel Beard--Adm'r.
   Property in Spartanburg. Adm. Bond 29 Jan. 1864
   S: Henry Beard and S. G. Henry Final Dis: 30 July 1778 (Date ?)

BEARD, ULRICH--Planter Richland Wills (24) 13 March 1802
    Wife: Eave--Ex.
    Wit: Thos. Hutchinson, Rob't. Miller, John Faust
    Proven: 2 Oct. 1802 No children shown

BECKET, JAMES Richland Wills 28 May 1812. Adm: Margaret Becket
    Bond: 28 May 1812

BELLINGES, CARNOT--Of Richland Dist. Misc. Records H-28 -m- set
    1 Feb. 1832 Sarah Hails. Dr. James H. Taylor, Tr.
    Sarah Hails owned 1/5 pt. 4-acre lot in Columbia, present res.
    of Mrs. Hails, her mother and 1/5 undivided Plt'n. of Capt.
    Robert Hails, Dec'd father of said Sarah. Slaves, etc.

BELTON, JONATHAN--Dec'd. Will 17 Jan. 1804 Only child-Austin Belton.
    See card Frederick Briggs-dec'd. Richland Eq. Roll 28 1813

BELTON, WM. ADAMSON -vs- Thos. Briggs: Estate of Frederick Briggs--
    Will in file 1791--Fairfield. Wife-Elizabeth. Sons-Gray, John
    and Thomas Briggs. Richland Co. Bills 28

BELL, ALEXANDER--Dec'd. Richland Eq. Roll 106 1818. Dau: Mary,
    a minor. Abraham Geiger, Gdn. (See card A. Geiger)

BELL, ELIZABETH--Mother of Mary Bell, minor. Richland Eq. Roll 120
    Heirs of Est. of Mathias Silveah. 1818

BELL, HARRIET -vs- Thomas Taylor and John Taylor Adm'rs of James
    Taylor, Dec'd. Representatives of Daniel Tateman Alleges:
    Harriet Bell, dau. of Alex'r and Elizabeth Bell of Granby, Lex-
    ington Dist. Daniel Tate made Will 20 Nov. 1786 left slave to
    Harriet James Taylor and exor. died intestate. Richland Co.
    Bills 105. Filed 25 March 1815

BENSON, JOSHUA--Of Middleborough, Mass. A farmer and iron worker
    Son: Ichabod
          Joshua--born Middleborough. Rev. soldier-a Capt. Married
          1st: Sarah Ellis
                Ch: Joshua 3rd.
                     Elizabeth -m- Ezra Thomas
                     Mary -m- Joseph Atwood
                     Sarah -m- Wm. Kempton
          2nd: Mary ____?
                Ch: Harriet -m- Josiah Kilgore
    First wife and children of Massachusetts. Second wife and child
    of South Carolina--Both living at same time

BENTHAM, RIDER E. Richland Bills 146 1818. See card John Bryce -vs-
    Geo. C. Smith and Rider E. Bentham

BETENBURGH, URIAH--Of Lexington Dist. -vs- John Sims, Adm'r.
    Alleges: Maj. John Hampton late of Lexington Dist. on 10 Dec.
    1807 owned 100 acres in Lexington Dist. improved by Thos. Hollin-
    shed--Maj. John Hampton died leaving widow Margaret, Elizabeth
    -w- Thos. Herbert, Ann -w- John Sims and Anthony Hampton. Alleges
    Pltf. paid for land-titles not made. Richland Bills 73
    Filed 3 Jan. 1812

BIGBEA, JOHN--Highest bidder lands Est. Joel McLemore.. Richland
    Eq. Stray Deed 1802. See card Joel Adams, et al. Exor's.

BILLINGS, SAMUEL--Dec'd. Richland Bills 128 Filed 29 April 1817
    Adm'r. Henry F. Simmons -w- Elizabeth -vs- John D. Brown, Sarah
    Brown, his wife, and Children: Mary Ann Brown, Martha Brown
    Wm. H. Brown--Suit over Judgement debt.

BIRDSONG, BATIE--Comm'r. Equity for Pinckney Dist. Apt. Col. Eaton
    Walker Gdn. for James A. Walker and Frederick Walker--about
    22 Feb. 1812 Richland Co Bills 98

BLAKE, JOHN HAIG -w- Eliza Howell Blake(formerly Goodwyn) and Eliza
    D. Howell--Heirs of Malachi Howell -vs- Est. of John Howell
    His mother--Grace Howell
    Bros and Sisters: Mary -w- John A. Reese
                   Elizabeth -w- Timothy Reese
                   Sally Reese
                   Martha -w- Jesse M. Howell
    Richland Eq. Roll 267-290 Filed 3 Feb. 1827

BLAKE, MRS. MARGARET--sister of John James Haig. Richland Eq. Roll 69
    Margaret's Ch: Martha -m- Wm. Washington
                Margaret -m- Rev. Dr. Bowen
                Edward Blake
                John Haig Blake See card John J. Haig 1818

BLANCHARD, BENJAMIN--Richland Wills Bk. B-43 30 Jan. 1788
    Mother: Mary Wimberly   Proven: 18 Aug. 1788
    Brother: Noah Wimberly--Land in Washington Co. Georgia on
                     Oconee River. Gr. to Jno. Potts
  Son: Josiah Blanchard
        Wm. Blanchard
  Dau: Mary Blanchard
  Ex: Noah Wimberly and Wm. Meyers and son, Josiah
  Wit: Jesse Chandler, Arthur Thompson, David Hines.

BLANCHARD, WM.--Dec'd 1813 Richland Eq. Roll 18
    Heirs: Wm. B. Marshal--10 yrs abt.
           Elizabeth L., Mary H., Sarah W., Benj. T., John L.,
           All younger than Wm. B. All children of Martin
           and Mary Marshal

BLANCHARD, WILLIAM--A brother of Mary Marshall and 7 children.
    Richland Bills 114 1815

BLOCKER, ABNER -w- Sarah Clifton--dau of Charles Clifton. Rec't.
    for share Dec. 4, 1821. Richland Prob. Bx. 11

BOATWRIGHT, JAMES--Of Richland Dist. -vs- Asa Delozier and John
    Bostick of Richland Dist. Bill for Discovery--tract land in
    Lexington Dist. fork Broad and Saluda Rivers--Orig. Gr. to
    Farmer Dewees. Plat in file dated 16 April 1792. Richland Bills 30
    Filed 17 May, 1813

BOOKTER, JACOB--Will Richland Eq. Roll 30 1814
    Widow: Judith -w- Jacob Barrett
    Dau: Judith--minor, abt. 12 yrs.
    Son: Christian Bookter apt. Gdn.

BONEY, NICHOLAS--Intestate Richland Wills B-38 20 Aug. 1788
      Adm'r: Charles Benniker

BONSALL, ELIZABETH--Adm'x. of Samuel Bonsall -vs- Green Rives, Mary
      Ridley Rives, Adm's. Green Rives. Alleges: William Rives on
      6 March 1778 executed Bond in favor of Samuel Bonsall for pay-
      ment of $3000.00 just sum; that William Rives made a Will 26
      Aug. 1783 and apt. his son, Green Rives, since dec'd. one of
      executors and said Green Rives died intestate and Mary Ridley
      Rives and Green Rives, the younger, were apt. Adm'rs.
      Richland Bills 168 Filed 18 Jan. 1820

BOSTICK, JAMES--"Free person of Columbia" -vs- W. B. Johnson, et al,
      Trustee Alleges: John Bostick of Richland Dist. 16 Dec. 1811
      made over his property in trust for the benefits of "Judy, Henry,
      her son, and your orator, all persons of color, emancipated by
      the said John Bostick--Bill for Partition. Richland Bills 169
      Filed 15 Jan. 1820..Bill 102 Alleges John Bostick made deed
      gift of slave to William Bostick. See card Wm. Mazych, ex'r. of
      Isaac Mazych, Dec'd.

BOSTICK, CAPT. JOHN--Dec'd. Richland Eq. Roll 116 1810
      Susanna Wingate one of heirs.

BOSTICK, JOHN and Asa Delozier Adv. James Boatwright. Richland
      Bills 30 1813
      See card John Bryce -vs- Geo. C. Smith Bill 146 1818

BOUKNIGHT, DANIEL--Pet'r. Richland Eq. Roll 151 22 Feb. 1819
      Shows: Jemima Smith about 11
              Jacob Smith about 10
              Children of Thomas Smith dec'd. Part. suit pending.
              Prays apt. of Pet'r. as Gdn. Also Samuel and James
              Smith, minors, included in order.
      Roll 152: Daniel Boughnight Gdn. for ch. of Thomas Smith, dec'd.

BOWEN, NATHANIEL -m- Margaret Blake, dau. of Margaret Blake, Sr.
      Richland Eq. Bills 137 1817

BOWERS, DAVID--Dec'd. and Bros. and Sisters. See card Morris O'Hewrn.
      Richland Eq. Bills 63 1816

BOWERS, JOHN -w- Catherine, dau. Charles Leflove. Roll 11

BOYER, ADAM--Dec'd intestate Richland Eq. Roll 95 1818
      Children: Michael, Henry, John, Nancy
                 Mary Poste
                 Salina Wessinger and Mrs. Matthias Wessinger
                 Moses, Samuel, Melia, Elizabeth--Minors
                 2 children of Catherine Boyer, his gr-children.

BOYERS, RICHARD--Richland Prob. 4-84. Adm'x: Ann Boyers
      Brother: William, and William's children: Jane, Elizabeth,
                Susan, William, David, Samuel. Cit: 5 Feb. 1822
                William d. about 20 years ago.

240

BRANDY, LEWIS--Legatee Frederick Briggs 1791. See back of card
    F. Briggs. Richland Eq. Roll 28 1813

BRANHAM, RIGHARD and John Bostick--Gdn. of Susan-dau. of Edward
    Wingate, and Gdn. of his wife Sophiana and his children. Est.
    of Edward Wingate--Richland--Borrowed money from Joel Williams
    of Georgetown Dist. Misc. C-344 7 May 1816
    Misc. F-425: Richard Branham
        Wife: Sophianis E. M. (formerly widow of Edward Wingate
        Ch: William Thomas
             Mary Cecelia
    Page 430-439: Daniel House -w- Sarah, late Sarah Neil--had
                   slaves from her uncle, Micajah Hinton. To
                   Richard Branham
    Richland Eq. Roll 116 1818--Richard Branham-Step father of
    Susannah Wingate. (see Wingate)

BRANHAM, SELAH--Dec'd. Richland Prob. Bx. 3 Pk. 51 Cit: 28 Oct. 1818
    Pub. Nov. 14, 1818--at Mrs. Thompson by Capt. P. Moye.
    Pub. 7 Nov. at Jno. Blanks by Jesse House
    Show: Selah Branham, Richard Branham--app. Let. Adm. Bond
    Jesse House, one of S.

BRANTHWAITE, WILLIAM--Died 1822 intestate. Richland Eq. Roll
    Only heirs--2 infant sons: William A. and Edward. Ed. Fisher,
    Adm. Suit to foreclose and pay debts. Filed 8 Jan. 1824

BRASILMAN, PETER--Of Newberry in Dutch Fork Richland Eq. Roll 11 1815
    Widow: Drusilla
    5 Ch: Maria R. -w- Wm. Turpin, Jr.
           Louisa, Sarah, Thomas Jefferson, and Wilhelmina-all minors

BREVORD, KEZIAH--Dau. of James Hopkins of Richland. See Hopkins Will

BRIGGS, FREDERICK--Dec'd. Will in file 1781. Richland Eq. Bills 28
    Wife: Elizabeth
    Son: Gray Briggs, John Briggs, Thomas Briggs
    See card Wm. Adamson Belton -vs- Thos. Briggs.
    Alleges: Jonathan Belton, father of Austin Belton was to purchase
    land of heirs--That Jonathan made will 17 Jan. 1804. Austin only
    childof both parents. Suit over purchase of land.
    Will of Frederick Briggs of Fairfield shows:
        Wife: Elizabeth--all for life
        Legacy: Lewis Branay--not 21
        Dau: Harriet Briggs--not 21
        Sons: Gray, John, and Thomas. 24 Jan. 1791
        Ex: Samuel Boykin, Zachariah Cantey both of Kershaw

BRIGGS, JOHN--Richland Co. Bills 113. File contains a letter, dated
    15 Sept. 1812, written by him from Franklin County, Miss. to
    his brother, Thomas Briggs. Directs sale of lots in Camden at
    $80.00. Denies he authorized Caleb Clarke to bring suit -vs- his
    brother. States, Peter Knighton got killed by a rattle snake
    this summer; James Knox is about moving over here this fall on
    Fergason's place. File also shows: Franklin Co. Miss. depos-
    itions of James Knox; Gray Briggs and John Briggs by Bartlett
    Ford, Thos. Meredith, and N. King.

BRIGGS, THOMAS--Doctor. Richland Bills 120 See card J. Caldwell

BRIGGS, THOMAS and Wm. Lewis--made note favor of John Briggs 16 May
     1810 which was assigned to John Middleton at house of Gray
     Briggs in Mississippi Territory. Richland Eq. Bill 113 1817

BRIGGS, WILLIAM--Of Columbia Richland Eq. Bx. 324 and 342
     Widow: Lydia M.--Oratrix
     7 Ch: Mary -m- Neil McLean
            Sarah -m- Frank W. Green
            Ann, Elizabeth, Benjamin Franklin, William (died an infant)
            Catherine
     Had land a few miles of Phila. Penn. Pd. for Benjamin F. Briggs
     to attend Norwich School, Vermont. Boarded with Daniel F.
     Kimbell.

BRIGGS, WILLIAM--Dec'd. Son Times and State Gazette April 9, 1831
     Case: Richland Dist Lydia M. Briggs -vs- Ann Briggs, et al
     Real Estate to be sold--lots in Columbia

BROWN, ELIZABETH--Will 15 June 1813 Richland Prob.
     Sister: Mary Ellis
     Dec'd. dau: _____? -w- Simon Taylor and daus. children
     Richland Eq. Roll 71 1817 Elizabeth Brown Will
     Heirs: Edward Taylor-age 18
             Sumpter Taylor-age 17
     Considerable personal estate. William Taylor, Jr. is Exor.
     of Will of Elizabeth Brown. Prays apt. of their father, Simon
     Taylor as Gdn. Granted 1 Jan. 1818

BROWN, HENRY--Orig. Grant--Plat annexed 50 acres in Craven Co. in
     the Congaree low ground opposite to Saxagotha Township. Bd.
     N. E. Pt. on his own land; and Pt. on Est. of John Thomas, Jr.
     Dec'd. S. W. Pt on sd Estate and pt. on land of Est. of Joseph
     Hearsman, Dec'd. and S. E. on land unknown. 27 Nov. 1770
     Sherman burned Richland deeds, this is a stray Plat in Equity
     Files. Richland Co. Misc. Stray

BROWN, HENRY -m- Rosanna Boozer only child of Barbara Boozer-dau. of
     _____ Shelling. McCords Reports Vol. 1 1817

BROWN, JOHN D.--(1830
     JOHN W. and James B. (1838)
     REBECCA and John T. (1842)
     JOHN P. (1854)
     JOHN G. (1858) All minors Pet. for Gdns. Ex Parte Petitions

BROWN, JOHN B. of State of Va. Will 1830 Richland Probate
     Brother: Thomas
          Ch. of Thomas: James B.
                          Thomas M.
     Will of Mary Brown 1822 seems she might be mother of above.

BROWN, JOHN D. Richland Eq.
     Wife: Sarah
     Ch: Marry Ann, Martha, Wm. H.

BROWN, JOHN G.--Died intestate 1839. Married Rebecca A. Taylor,
    about 1820, dau. of Gov. John Taylor and wife, Sarah
    Widow: Rebecca (Did not marry again)
    Ch: John T.
         Sarah -m- J. T. Goodwyn
         Robert C.
         Manning
         Thomas
         Matilda C. Mentions land in Laurens Dist. sold to Willis
                                                              Brown
BROWN, JOHN R. -m- Gracey E. Reese, dau. of John A. Reese 1859

BROWN, JOSEPH--Of Richland Co. deed gift to wife for life in trust.
    Wife: Margaret
    3 Sons: John William, Peter Eli, Alexander Russell
    Archives Dept. Misc. H-29 10 Dec. 1829 John Cooper and
    Joseph S. Gurjnard, Trustees

BROWN, MARY, Widow and Hannah McCord, Widow, Russell P. McCord,
    David J. McCord, Hamet and Eliza McCord, Infants by Gdn. Edward
    Richardson, John McCord, Joseph McCord, Robert Weston and Mary
    his wife, and Sarah McCord--all heirs of Charles McCord who
    made his Will 12 Dec. 1773 who was son of Sophonisba McCord.
    Col. Wm. Thomson-an Exor. and his dau. -m- C. B. Cochran.
    Sophonisba died 16 Sept 1784 intestate. Filed Sept. 19, 1821
    Richland Bills 188

BROWN, SILAS AND WILLIAM--Make depositions in Twiggs Co. Georgia in
    case of Fitzsimmons -vs- Guignard. Richland Equity.

BROWN, THOMAS--Dec'd. 1836 Richland Eq. Bx. 64
    Widow: Mary Brown
    Children: William Brown
               Mary -w- Alex'r B. Fetner
               Jenny -w- Arch'd Fetner
               Nathaniel, Thomas, David, George, Leminde, John
               Daniel, and Margaret.

BROWN, THOMAS T. -vs- James H. Taylor, Trustee, et al Bills 681 1860

BROWN, RICHARD -w- Mary (sister of Wm. McCord) 1797 Hist. Com. III-246

BRYAN, JOHN--Dec'd. Richland Dist. Misc. C-320
    Widow: Lydia Bryan
    Dau: Elizabeth -w- John Ball, the younger
    Son: John Bryan

BRYAN, LYDIA--Widow of John Bryan, Esq. dec'd. Bond to John Bostick
    of Richland Dist. Shows: John Bryan, son of John Bryan, dec'd.
    joined in conveying lands, and being a minor, Bond given to
    secure titles. Orig. in file. Shows: Eliza Catherine, wife
    of John Bryan, Jr. a minor also. Richland Co. Bills 102

BRYCE, JOHN -vs- George C. Smith and Rider E. Bentham Alleges: In
    1804 Joseph Walker made Will and devised house and lots in
    Columbia to John Bostick, also now dec'd and to Andrew Wallace
    and to his 2 nephews, James Alexander Walker and Frederick Walker
    Richland Co. Bills 146 Filed 4 July 1818.

BRYSON, JOHN--Orig. Will 18 Sept. 1800 Richland Prob. Bx. 4-77
    Wife: Rachel   Son: John Bryson
    Dau: Jane--100 Acres   Dau: Rachel
    Gr. son: Wm. Bryson   Son: Henry Bryson
    Dau: Sarah--100 Acres

BULGER, PIERCE--Dec'd. Richland Prob. Bx. 4-78 Cit: 2 Oct. 1813
    Adm'r: Ann Bulger   S: John Bostick   Bond: 9 Oct. 1813

BULLARD, ROYAL--Pet'r. Richland Eq. Roll 123 1819
    Shows: Henry Dana Ward Alexander and Isaac Brownfield Alexander
    Minors--their mother, Sarah Horton, Gdn, desires to surrender
    it to Pet'r. Pet. by Reuben I. Horton and wife, Sarah also.
    (Bullard does not appear kin, but must be Atty.)

BUNCH, JOHN -m- Mary Thomas S: Jesse Bunch. Richland Co. Misc. B-51
    Aff. by Ann Carter that she knew Mary when a young woman--always
    esteemed as _____? 28 May, 1801. (second card testifies Ann
    was white woman.)

BUNCH, WILLIAM--Dec'd. Richland Prob. 4-79 1808
    Adm'r: Isaac Tucker. Bills of Dr. Samuel Jones, Pd.

BURGESS, DAVID--Richland Prob. 4-80 Cit: 15 April 1822
    Adm'r: Benj. W. Miller. Bond and Letters 25 April 1822.
    S: Wm. Hall

BURKE, STEPHEN -w- Rachel--Pet'rs Richland Roll 34 1815
    Harriet Smith and Alexander Tobias Smith--Minors under 21
    John Smith, Dec'd--Widow, Rachel now -w- Sd. Stephen Burke and
    3 children: John C. Smith, Harriet Smith and Alexander Tobias
    Smith (or Tobias Alexander).
    Richland Prob. Bx. 4-81 Cit: 15 Oct. 1822 Adm'r Widow: Rachel
    George Smith and Jacob J. Faust. Dec'd had -m- the widow Smith
    Owed Est. of John Smith.

BURNEY, JOHN--Richland Co Bills 148 Filed 5 May 1818 -vs-
    Grace Goodwyn   Uriah J. Goodwyn
    James H. Chappell   Margaret Chappell
    Sarah Weston   John S. Chappell
    Grace Howell Chappell   Ainsley Hall
    Alleges: William Goodwyn, Dec'd. 15 Nov. 1791--conv. all his
    property to Jesse Goodwyn, also, since dec'd. intestate, about
    Sept. 1792. After his death, sd William Goodwyn (then alive
    evidently) on 26 April 1794, filed suit in Ct. Court Camden on
    John Hopkins and Keziah Goodwyn; adm's of sd Jesse Goodwyn.
    Alleges: Grace -w- William Goodwyn and Uriah John; Margaret;
    Sarah W.; and Grace Howell Goodwyn--children of sd William.
    That James H. Chappell -m- Margaret
        John S. Chappell -m- Grace H.
        Sere Dubose -m- Sarah W.
        Suit over Bond given by Wm. Goodwyn.

BUSBY, JESSE--Orig. Will 2 Jan 1810 Richland Prob. Bx. 4-82
    Widow: Christina   Exor: Moses Wooten
    3 Children: Keziah, Harriet, Demeris--all minors

BUSBY, WINNIE--Orig. Will 15 Aug. 1806 Richland Prob. Bx. 4-83
    Dau: Mary Nipper   Gr. son: Turner Tarket
    Son: Wm. Tarket   "My 2 young daus:
    Dau: Alles (Alice)   Elizabeth Busby (Busbe)
    Son: Peter Turket   Rachel   "   "

BUTLER, JAMES--Of St. James Santee Died March 1814 C. T. Clerk's Off.
    Widow: Mary   1814
    Children: Thomas--orator--now of age
               James, John, and Mary

BYNUM, DRURY--Orig. Will 24 Dec. 1836 Richland Prob. Bx. 4-85
    Widow: Sally Bryson--Common Law wife
    Children: Nathaniel, Sarah, James, Gray-sometimes called John
              (All named above by Sally Bryson)
    Son: William

BYNUM, HENRY--Richland Prob. Bx. 4-86 Cit: 20 March 1793
    Adm'r: Britton Bynam   Bond: 1 April 1793
    S: Drury Bynum and John Goodwyn, Jr.

BYNUM, JOHN--Richland Prob. Bx. 4-88 Cit: 15 Oct. 1822
    Adm'r: Turner Bynum   Later: David Ewart
    Various Trails, Land--described

BYNUM, LUCY--Of Greenville Co. Va. Cit: 8 March 1804
    Adm'r: Drury Bynum   Bond: 17 Nov. 1804
    S: Clairborn Clifton and John Bynum

BYNUM, WILLIAM--Age 17--by death of gr-father, John Sexiner--Prays
    apt. of Drury Bynum

CAIN, WILLIAM--Dec'd. Richland Prob. 4-89 Cit: 8 Oct. 1824
    Adm'r: Ainsley Carrell   Bond: 6 Nov. 1824
    S: Robert Rowan

CALVERT, JOHN--Of Columbia--Orig Will 18 Dec. 1802 Richland Prob 4-91
    Dau: Elizabeth Calvert -m- Wm. Taylor
    "My daus. share and share alike.

CALVIN, WILLIAM--Orig. Will 13 Oct. 1800 Richland Prob. 4-92
    Wife: Sarah (present wife) 1/3 for life
    Son: James Calvin
    Dau: Elizabeth Clark-Clark (?)
    Son: David Calvin

CAMBRIDGE, MISS ANN E.--Richland Wills Pk. 3471 Bx. 128--Aunt of
    H. Cambridge Moore

CAMERON, JAMES--A soldier -w- Margaret. Richland Eq. Pet. 103
    See card Philip Cartwright

CAMERON, JOSEPH--Died in war. His widow-Margaret -m- 2nd, Philip
    Cartwright. Richland Eq. Roll 103 1818

CAMERON, SIMON AND JAMES--Richland Bills 104 1815--See Emanuel
    Warnbezee

CAMPBELL, JAMES--Dec'd Cit: 8 May 1801 Richland Prob. Bx 4-93
    Adm'r: Elizabeth Campbell   Bond: 22 May 1801
    Adm'r: John Taylor, Jr.   S: Malachi Howell

CAMPBELL, JANE ANN--A dau. of Maj. Samuel Wise Richland Eq. Bills 78
    Jane Ann-dec'd. No issue. See card: Charley Williamson of
    Green Co. Ga.
    Richland Co. Bills 61 Filed 13 Jan. 1813 Adm'r: Clairborne
    Clifton -vs- Executors of: Alleges Samuel Wise-Will 18 Sept.
    1799-dec'd father of Jane Ann Campbell. Mentions: Timothy
    Rives; Dr. R. Hendricks; C. E. Williamson -w- Mary; David
    Faust; Jesse M. Howell
    See Card: Clairborne Clifton and Samuel Wise
    Richland Prob. Bx. 4-94 Jane Ann Campbell Cit: 9 Feb. 1810
    Adm'r: Clairborn Clifton   Bond: 1 Jan. 1811
    S: Andrew Wallace   No return-no App.

CAMPBELL, NANCY--Dau. of James Campbell and Peter Campbell, Legatees
    of Peter Smith Will 1797. Richland Eq. Bills 115

CAMPBELL, SAMUEL -w- Jane Ann of Fairfield -vs- W. H. Harrington
    and John J. Haig. Alleges: Samuel Wise, father of Jane, made
    Will 18 Sept. 1779. Richland Bills 13. Filed 28 May 1806

CAMPBELL, THOMAS--Richland Prob. Bx. 4-95 Cit: 15 Jan. 1834
    Adm'r: James Campbell   Bond: 31 Jan. 1834
    S: A. R. Vinson and Arthur Howell

CAREW, JOHN--Of Columbia--Orig. Will 6 Sept. 1811. Prov: 7 Nov. 1811
    "My grandchildren"_____? (Also Crew)
    Son: Edward

CAREY, ANN--Orig. Will 30 Mar. 1822 wife of Lemuel Carey. (Marriage
    set 13 July 1817 to L. Carey). Formerly wife of Freeman Delane,
    who at time of marriage, had another wife. Richland Prob. 4-97
    4 gr-children: Martha Caroline LaFarge
                   Grace Ann Delane Freeman
                   Raymond Delane
                   Philip Hirons Deland
    Richland Prob. Bx. 4-98--Lemuel Carey--Orig. Will 22 April 1822
        Wife: and "Ch. of dec'd. Bros. and sisters".

CARMICHAEL, JAMES--Richland Eq. Bills 41 1811. See card Henry Young
    as Adm'r. of Hohanne Woolf

CARRELL, JACOB, SR.--Orig. Will 14 April 1815 Richland Prob. Bx. 4-99
    "My 5 sons": William, James, Jacob, Joseph, John
    2 Gr-ch": John and Eliza Collins-children of dec'd dau. Charity
    Collins.

CARRELL, JAMES--Richland Prob. Bx. 4-100 Cit: 2 Dec. 1823
    Adm'r: Ainsley Carrell   Bond: 13 Dec. 1823
    S: John Bates and Wm. Fair
    Returns show: Widow and 5 heirs
                   (1) Rebecca Carrell (or Rebena)
                   (2) Martha   "   (saddle bought for them)
                   Other 3 not named

CARRELL, JOHN--Richland Prob.5-101 Cit: 7 June 1823
    Adm'r: Daniel Keef   Bond: 21 June 1823
    S: Patrick Beleher (sp?) and Thos. Quitter

CARRELL, JOSEPH--Richland Prob. Bx. 5-102 Cit: 3 March 1823
    Adm'rs: Jacob Carrell and John Carrell
    Bond: 15 March 1823   S: Wm. Fair
    (1) Dau: Dorcas -m- Hiram Addison
    (2) Dau: Esther -m- Wm. B. Creler (Creber?)
    Return states "5 heirs".

CARRELL, THOMAS M.--Richland Prob. Bx. 5-103 Cit: 30 Nov. 1813
    Adm'r: James Carrell, Sr.   Bond: 6 Dec. 1813
    S: Wm. Carrell

CARRELL, WILLIAM--Orig Will 21 Jan. 1835 Richland Prob. 5-104
    Wife: Rebecca
    Son: Arthur B. Carrell
    Dau: Unity Gray
          Rachel Addison
          Rebecca Sowden (or Lowden)
    Son: Isaac Carrell
    Dau: Ann Carrell

CARWILE, JOHN H.--Richland Prob. Bx. 5-111 Cit: 1 April 1833
    Adm'r: John McCully and Robert Purvis

CASSIN, MICHAEL--Richland Prob. Bx. 5-112 Cit: 30 Sept. 1820
    Adm'r: Peter Maguire   Bond: 7 Oct. 1820
    S: Christopher Barrillon

CATON, ELEANOR--Richland Prob. Bx. 5-113 Cit: 14 Dec. 1793
    Adm'r: John Willis   Bond: 5 April 1794
    S: Duncan McNab and Henry Strange
    Apr: Henry Strange, Jr., Duncan McNab, Robert Duke

CARTER, BENJAMIN--C. T. Deed 3-574--Late of Amelia--d. intestate
    about 1742. Gr. 14 Feb. 1735. Eldest son-Henry Carter -w-
    Elizabeth. Conveyed lands between Watereee and Congaree.
    24/25 Feb. 1764

CARTER, DANIEL--Richland Prob. Bx. 5-105 Adm'r: Allen Gibson
    Bond: 26 Oct. 1839   S: Isom Woodward and Thos. Levy

CARTER, GEORGE--Richland Prob. Bx. 5-106 Orig. Will 21 Oct. 1802
    Widow: Sarah
    Bro: Robert Carter's children; Henry, Elizabeth, Wm. Dorcas
    Wife's sister: Mary's children -w- John Cooner
        Ch: John Cooner, Mary Cooner, and _____? Cooner.

CARTER, GRAY--Richland Prob. Bx. 5-107 Orig. Will 8 April 1824
    Son: Thomas Sturgeon Carter--74 acres "given to me by my father,
        John Carter". Thomas S. Carter-Gdn. and Exor. John S.
        Carter, Jr.
    Sister: Mary Carter and her dau. SusanCarter
    Brother: Thomas Carter
          Henry Carter
    Sister: Dorcas Hasfum Exor: Wm. Sturgeon, Jr.

CARTER, JOSEPH--Richland Prob. Bx. 5-108 Cit: 18 Jan. 1821
    Adm'x: Harriet Williams "otherwise called Harriet Justice"
            Green Williams: Wit. paper in file as J. P. 1823
    William Justice -w- Harriet "have abandoned". Formerly lived
    in Buncombe Co. N. C. where he ____? and Aunt said he had -m-
    a Miss Crockle and left her with 2 or 3 children and in 1822
    Wm. Justice stated he had a wife in Tenn. Following on back--
            Mrs. Joiner has 5 children
            Mrs. Frink   "   3   "
            Wm. Carter   "   1   "
            Rob't Carter"   2   "
            Mrs. Williams   4   "
    Heirs: 1823 sale:
            George Frink -w- Eliza
            Daniel Carter
            Absolom Joiner -w- Sophia
            Benjamin B. Carter
            Robert Carter
            William Carter
            William Justice -w- Harriet formerly Harriet Williams

CARTER, ROBERT--Richland Prob. Bx. 5-109 Cit: 15 May 1822
    Adm'x: Unity Carter   Bond: 25 March 1822
    S: Elisha Fox and David Powell

CARTER, SARAH--By her next friend, Charles Fralick -vs- Benjamin
    Carter--Alleges: In 1801 Sarah -m- sd Benjamin Carter who then
    lived with one of his slaves. Suit for Alimony etc. Filed
    1 Oct. 1817 Richland Co. Bills 145

CARTER, THOMAS S.--Richland Prob. Bx. 5-110 Bond: March 4, 1828
    Adm'r: John C. Sturgeon--sd all the property belonged to him
    having been Willed to me by Gooding Carter.
    S: Eli Kennedy and James Whitaker

CARTWRIGHT, PHILIP L. -w- Margaret--Pet'rs. Shows: Joseph Cameron
    late husband of sd Margaret died in service of U. S. at Haddrell's
    Point in War with Great Britain. Children of Joseph and Margaret
    were: John, Robert and James

CENTER, NATHAN--Richland Bills 201 Filed 9 Jan, 1822 -vs- Isaac
    Frazier--Made bond 14 Feb. 1821. Bill to foreclose Mtg. on
    house and lot in Columbia. Deft. alleges that Thomas Rives and
    Nathan Center to give good titles, alleges judgements.

CENTER, NATHAN--Richland Eq. Roll 21 1812 Will 1 Dec. 1782 in Camden
    Wife: Martha
    Dau: Elizabeth -m- Thomas Wade
    Sons: Nathan, John and William

CENTER, NATHAN--Of Richland Dist. Richland Bills 147 Filed 1 Oct. 1818
    And Thomas Rives of Georgia -vs- Harriet Rives and James Rives
    her infant son--Estate of John Turner Rives, dec'd, of Georgia--
    who owned property in Richland. Harriet Rives, the Widow and
    her son, James, the only child of dec'd. Bill for Partition.

248

CHAMBLISS, PETER--Late of Lexington-left Will Richland Eq. Roll 122
    Benjamin Nettles, Pet'r.
    Ch. of Peter Chambliss
        Sarah Lee
        Margery Caroline
        William Henry--all minors
    That by death of Dorcas, sister of Pet'r, sd children have no
    Gdn. Prays apt. as Gdn.

CHAMBLISS, POLLY--Dau. of Robert Hick of Va. Polly -m- 2nd John
    Watson, bro. of Hezekiah Watson. Her 1st husband, Peter
    Chamblis, left her and went west, still living when she -m-
    John Watson.

CHAMPAGNA, JOSEPH--Richland Prob. Bx. 5-114 Bond 8 June 1825 (J. C.
    Adm'r: David L. Wakely and Judah Barrett   Dec'd)
    S: None No return

CHANDLER, JESSE--and his dau. Mary -w- Reuben House. See card Robert
    Ogilvie. Richland Eq. Roll 84 1817

CHAPMAN, GERSHOM--Dau. Marianne -m- John Hooker. Richland Eq. 14 1812
    Mayr Ann (or Marrianne) Legatee of Claud Simon. Prop in Beaufort.

CHAPPELL, HICKS--Orig Will 17 Mar. 1836 Richland Prob. Bx. 5-117
    Wife: Elizabeth
    Sons: John J. and James H.
    Dec'd Gr-dau: Eugenia Chappell Calhoun

CHAPPELL, JAMES H. -m- Margaret Goodwyn Richland Eq. Bills 89
        JOHN S. -m- Grace Howell Goodwyn See card Harry Grant
    Also see card John Burney -vs- Est. Wm. Goodwyn

CHAPPELL, MAJ. HICKS--Had charge of Est. of John Hicks. Richland
    Eq. Bills 171. See card Hephzekiah Watson

CHAPPELL, ROBERT--Orig. Will 14 June 1794 Richland Prob. Bx. 5-118
    Bro: Hicks Chappell and Friend: John Goodman(all jointly)

CHARLETON, DOCTOR THOMAS--Richland Eq. Bills 104 1815
    Ch: Eleanor Letitia
        Ann Phoebe -m- Emanuel Warmbezee
        Thomas Usher Pulacki
        Arthur Murdock (See Warmbezee

CHARLTON, ELINOR LETITIA -m- William Cleland. Richland Eq. Roll 39
                                                             1812
CHISHOLM, THEOPHILUS WATSON--Richland Prob. Bx. 5-119 Cit: 24 Sept.
    Adm'r: William Chisholm   1800
    Bond: 26 Sept. 1800
    S: Lewis Dinkins and Robert H. Waring

CHURCH, RICHARD--Richland Prob 5-120 Orig. Will 21 June 1779
    Wife: Martha   Of Amelia Co. Va.
    Son: Robert--Home place after widow dies.
    Daus: Elizabeth Jordan, Mary Ligon, Patty Church, Judith,
        Sooky, Exor's: Joseph Legon, Jr. Robert Jordan

CLAIRBORNE, CLIFTON -vs- Timothy Rives Bills 61 before 1817

CLARK, EDMOND--Richland Prob. Bx. 5-121 Cit: 31 Oct. 1805
    Widow: Elizabeth -m- Daniel Darby Cit: 22 Oct. 1807
    Dau: Nancy Clark-minor
    S: Drury Dynum-took over Adm. after she married Darby
       John Watson
       Sterling Clark wanted to Adm. with Daniel Darby

CLARK, ISABELLA--Dec'd Cit: 23 Jan. 1808 Richland Prob. Bx. 5-124
    Adm'r: Finley Holmes

CLARK, JAMES--Richland Bills Roll 82 1817--Dec'd. U. S. Army in 1815
    Widow: Hester -m- Richard S. Manor
    Son: Middleton Clark--age 5 yrs. in 1817
    Richland Prob. 5-122 Clark, James, Dec'd Cit: 16 Nov. 1816
    Adm'x: Hetty Clark   Bond: 23 Nov. 1816
    S: Isaac Hughes

CLARK, JOHN--Richland Prob. 5-123 Orig. Will 22 April 1807
    Wife: Isabella
    Sons: Alexander, Thomas, and
    Dau: Sarah Exor's: Finley Holmes, Thomas Heggen

CLARK, JOHN -w- Mary; John Nye -w- Elizabeth; Thos. Jefferson Roach;
    James Madison Roach; and Abraham Washington Roach--children
    of Abraham Roach, Dec'd and alleges _____ Roach -m- Abel
    Muldes. Suit -vs- Abel Muldes and Samuel Roach as Exor's.
    Alleges dec'd. moved to Goose Creek. Richland Bills 130

CLARK, JOHN--Richland Eq. Roll 42 Will
    Minor ch: Sarah Clark and Thomas Clark

CLARK, RICHARD--Orig Will 12 Feb. 1808 Richland Prob. 5-125
    Wife: Elizabeth--owned farm in Ireland
    Ex: Wm. Brazier

CLARK, SARAH AND THOMAS--Minors-age 17 and 15 yrs. Pet'rs. Their
    father, John Clark died, apt'd W. Finley Holmes and Thomas H.
    Egan his Exor's. Holmes is lately dead. Prays apt. of new
    Gdn. to manage property. Richland Eq. Roll 42 1815

CLARK, STERLING--Orig. Will 13 Dec. 1804. Died 20 Nov. 1807
    Wife: All. Pet'n show Widow, Mary -m- Samuel Cobb who died
    20 Sept. 1810. 1 child. Richland Prob 6-126

CLAYTON, MRS.-Sister of Shepherd Pickett. Richland Eq. 1

CLELAND, WILLIAM -w- Elinor Letitia, late Elinor Letitia Charlton;
    Emanuel Wamburd and Phebe his wife, late Ann Phebe Charlton;
    Thomas Usher Paulaskie Charlton; Arthur Murdock Charlton; -vs-
    John Kennedy; Alexander Robinson; Simon Robinson; William
    McBright; and Samuel Miller--Bill of Account and discovery.
    Richland Bills 39 Filed 17 Jan. 1812 Slaves involved.

CLIFTON, CLAIRBORNE--Adm. of Jane Ann Campbell -vs- Joel Adams, Sr.
    Exor. of John James Haig and Charles Williamson, et al. Alleges
    Samuel Wise, dec'd father of Jane Ann Campbell made his will
    18 Sept. 1779. Exors John James Haig and Wm. Henry Harrington
    Richland Co. Bills 78 Filed 1 Jan. 1812

COBB, MARY--Richland Bills 153 Filed 13 Jan. 1819 -vs-
Ann Reynolds--Alleges on 3 March 1818 Ann Reynolds of Columbia
rented slave from Plt'n. Def't alleged purchase of slave.
Contention over the slave.

COCHRAN, C. B. -m- Dau. of Col. Wm. Thomson. Richland Eq. Bills 188
See card Mary Brown, Widow and Hannah McCord, et al.

COGDELL, MARY ANN ELIZABETH--Boarding School Mistress -vs- Grace
Goodwyn and others. Richland Bills 25

COLBEACH, GRACE--Orphan-James Kennerly, Gdn. Richland Eq. Roll 112
1818
COLE, MASON G. -m- set 6 Oct. 1816 Hariet Duke. Samuel Duke, Tr.
Richland Dist. Misc. C-442

COLLINS, ARTHUR--Of Dist of Richland -vs- Charles Oliver, et al.
Alleges: Thomas Green, dec'd. 20 Jan. 1799, late of Richland
Dist. made Will 8 Jan. 1799 and bequeathed to his wife Martha
Green, lands and slaves for life and also devised property to
his sons, Frederick W. Green and William Green and Dau. Jane
Harriet Greet and Dau. Martha Green. Marriage contract in the
file of Martha Green-widow and Charles Oliver. Copy of Thomas
Greens Will in file. Richland Co. Bills 74 Filed 29 Aug. 1816

COLLINS, ELIZABETH--a sister of Andrew Fleming, et al, also sister
of Ann Hoy -w- Robert Hoy. Richland Eq. 26 1813

COLLINS, JOHN--Dec'd. Richland Prob. Bx. 6-138/9
Sister: Elizabeth -m- Wiseman Walker and _____Phillips
Ch. of Elizabeth: Polly -w- James Fair
Cannot tell whether Walker was 1st or 2nd husband, nor whether
James Fair or Farr. Spelled both ways, Farr seems correct.

COMPTY, JOHN--Dec'd. 1790 Richland Eq. Roll 6 1811
Son: John Compty--Minor, about 17 yrs.
Pet. by Henry McGowen -w- Elizabeth, Exor's, that the minor be
apprenticed. Roll 17 shows Elizabeth McGowen late widow of
John Compty.
Richland Eq. Bill 17 shows Clairborn Clifton, Gdn. See Peter
McQuire and wife 1812

COOK, BURREL--Of Fairfield Dist. Died about Dec. 1805 Equity Roll 38
Widow: Mary -m- (Feb. 1808) Robert O'Gilvie (She died July 1808)
Dau: Elizabeth -m- George McCreless
3 sons: Thomas J., Burrell B., and Nathan P.--Minors
See card Geo. McCreless -m- Elizabeth Cook

COON, JOHN HENRY--Late of Lexington Dist. Died 3 April 1813
Left wife and several children among whom are:
Mary Ann about 17) Peters
Sarah   "   15)
John Henry   "   13
Margaret   "   9
John   "   7--Shows plainly John Henry and John
Prays apt. Mother, Mary Coon, Gdn. Richland Eq. Roll 121

CORBIN, WILLIAM P. -w- Martha--late Martha Goodwyn Richland Bills 182
-vs- Abraham D. Jones--Alleges: Wm. F. Goodwin died in 1821-
leaving widow, Martha, the oratrix and 1 child, Polly Tucker
Goodwyn--Left Will--Lived in St. Matthews Parish.

COTCHETT, GEORGE and Ephraim Lyles--Richland Eq. Bills 191 1821
See card Philip Pearson, Sen'r.

COULTER, DAVID--Richland Eq. Bills 41 1811 See card Henry Young.

COUSAR, ANN--Dau. of Thomas Dunlap. See card David Ellison Dunlap
Richland Eq. Bills 12

COX, JOHN F. -m- Jane Roach, dau. of Simeon Roach and sister of
Edmond M. Roach. See Roach card. Richland Eq. Bills 37 1811

CRADICK, RICHARD, intestate Richland Wills B-31 20 May 1788
Adm'r: Harmon Kinsler
Appr's: Jack Faust, John Geiger, Christian Kinsler

CRANKFIELD, LITTLETON -m- Lucy Wilson, dau. James Wilson Richland
Equity Pet. 156 1820

CREYON, PATRICK--Dec'd. Richland Eq. Roll 36 21 Feb. 1814
Pet's: Thomas Creyon
Sophia E. Creyon
Catherine Creyon Children of dec'd. minors under 12
Bros: John M. Creyon, Lucas Creyon

CREYON, THOMAS, Sophia E. and Catherine 1/3 each. Appears all heirs
he had. By their Gdn. Lucas Creyon -vs- John M. Creyon--Bill
for Partition of estate of Patrick Creyon. Richland Bills 36
Filed 21 Feb. 1814.

CROFT, JOHN--Richland Bills 173 Filed 8 Nov. 1820 -vs-
John Bates in re attachment suit. John Bates as Thomas H.
Harris, Harris being out of the state and Croft held responsible.
Alleges he should not be.

CULLOUGH, DANIEL, THOMAS AND WILLIAM--Richland Eq. Roll 111 1817

Adv: Reuben Pickett Dispute over ownership of land. See card
Thos. Pickett.

DAGGETT, JOHN--Filed 18 May 1820 Richland Bills 174 -vs-
Joseph May and others Alleges: John Russell, late of Columbia
was indebted to orator in several thousand dollars--and alleges
various judgements against Russell and the deft's. are the other
creditors.

DANCER, PETER--Dec'd. Richland Prob. Bx. 7-151 Cit: 24 Nov. 1789
Adm'r: Henry Duncan   Bond: 16 Feb. 1790 Rd. 14 Feb. 1790
S: Jacob Faust 72 Acres land and carpenter's tools

DANIEL, ELISHA--Of Lexington Dist Richland Bills 144 Filed 4 July 1818
    -vs- David R. Evans, Robert Means as Exors. J. J. Means, Dec'd.
    Alleges: John Means of Fairfield, dec'd--left widow, Mary Means;
    and Isabella, wife of Hilliard Judge; Sarah Means, wife of Rob't.
    Means, David Means, Martha Means and Robert Means, the younger.
    Suit over various money matters.
    Elisha Daniel -vs- Heirs of John Means--"And your orator further
    showeth unto your Honors that one, Sarah Arthur, now the wife
    of your orator, xxxx entitled to slaves in possession of Freeman
    Lewis, brought suit, and John Means purchased the debt, etc.

DANIEL, JOSE--Bx. 7-152 Cit: 6 April 1799
    Adm'rs: Dr. Robert Hendrick, Jesse Taylor, James Taylor, Jr.
    Cit: 17 May, 1799
    Adm'rs: Mathew Howell, Jesse Taylor, James Taylor
    Cit: 23 Dec. 1801
    Adm'rs: Dr. Robert Hendrick, James Taylor, Jr.

DANIEL, RICHARD--Orig Will 25 Jan. 1792 Box 7-154
    Friend: Joel Adams--Slave-Cyrus
             John Morris--Slave-Kate
             Adam Howell--Mare
             John Hiron--Slave-Wilson
             Naomi Pierce--Horse
    Wit: Christopher Tatim, John Morris, Margaret Tatim

DARBY, DANIEL -m- Widow Elizabeth Clark. Widow of Edmond Clark.
    1 child--Ann or Nancy. Green Rives, Gdn. Richland Eq. Bills 83
    Richland Bills 70 Filed 13 Feb. 1811--Daniel Darby and wife,
    Elizabeth, formerly widow of Edmond Clark -vs- Drury Bynum-
    Adm'r. of Edmond Clark--dec'd. left widow and one infant daughter.
    Bynum claims Estate owed him.

DAUGHARTY, WILLIAM Richland Prob. Bx. 7-160 Cit: 11 July 1818
    Adm'r: Pete McGuire Bond: 11 July 1818 S: John Glover

DAVIS, JAMES--Physician--Orig. Will 5 April 1837 Richland Prob. 7-155
    Wife: Catherine
    Dau: Catherine -w- Edward G. Preston
    Sons: William, James, Henry--To be educated
    Large estate Richland and Fairfield

DAVIS, JOHN--Cit: 9 Jan. 1832 Richland Prob. 7-156

DAVIS, JONATHAN AND JAMES--See card John Moore, Adm'r. John Marple

DAVIS, MARTHA MARIA--Minor under 21, Pet'r. Richland Eq. Roll 155
    Entitled to est. with her Bros. and sisters. Prays apt. Gdn.
                                                                1818
DAVIS, MARY ANN WILLIAMS--Orig. Will 10 Oct. 1820
    To: Mary Shirley--All-save per. property, bed, etc. for taking
                        care of her.
    Wit: Margaret Snead, Jane Snead Richland Prob. 7-157

DAVIS, NEEDHAM Richland Co. Bills 154 Filed 3 July 1819
-vs- William M. Simons Alleges: David Reynolds, dec'd. owned
250 Acres in Lexington Dist.-Granted sd David Reynolds--that
he died leaving Eliza Jackson, now Eliza Simons, Ann Jackson,
Rebecca Jackson, and Mary Ware (a minor) his next of kin.
The heirs executed Power of Atty. to Wm. M. Simons, in April
1813--to sell. Orator, Needham Davis agreed to purchase and
gave security for the minors part--Then Wm. M. Simons left the
state and suit was filed by Eliza Simons, Ann Jackson, now Ann
Harris, wife of Jonathan Harris and Rebecca Jackson--Alleges
illness and accident prevented filing ans. Bill for judgement.

DAVIS, WILLIAM RANSOM, et al. See card John Mayrant, Sr. Eq, Bills 151

DAVISON, WILLIAM--Will 30 Dec. 1819 Richland Prob. Bx. 7-158
Son: John and James Hall--All-includes 2 tracts land.

DAWSON, CAROLINE--Nee Pirolean Richland Eq. Bills 86 1814
Catherine Ravenel, Mary M. Ford, Martha Pirolean, Philip G. Pirolean
Elias Pirolean--children of Catherine Pirolean. See card Abraham
                                                            Blanding
DEFLORS, WILLIAM--Richland Prob. Bx. 7-161
Adm: William Rives Bond: 17 June 1815 S: Samuel Green
Letter in file to Dr. Samuel Green from Mary Joyner, headed--
"Milledgeville 25 Feb. 1819" and refers to "my son's estate."

DELAHUNT, ROBERT--Orig. Will 7 May 1819 Richland Prob. Bx. 7-162
Friend Terrence Ohanlon's daughters:
     Ann Matilda Ohanlon(
     Catherine Ohanlon) All

DELANE, ANN WOOD--Widow of Peter L. Delane -vs- Freeman Delane and
wife, Ann. (Has left state). John S. Chappell-a joint Trustee.
Shows: Complainant -m- John Yancy since filing Bill--on 24
May. Richland Bills 62 Filed 2 March 1816
Richland Bills 89 1817--Ann Delane, Pet'r entitled to certain
property settled on her before and after her marriage with
Freeman Delane. Isam Umber was Trustee and has renounced his
trust. Prays apt. of Ainsley Hall.

DELANE, FREEMAN, Physician -m- set 22 March 1803 Ann Hirons-widow
of John Hirons, intestate. Isaac Tucker, Tr. Richland Misc. B
Estate of John Hirons involved.   214

DELANE, FREEMAN--wife, Ann -vs- Lazarus and Florence--merchants of
Columbia. Shows Jacob Lazarus and Zachariah Florence.
Richland Eq. Bills 77 Filed 1 July 1812

DELANE, FREEMAN--Richland Bills 76 Filed 10 May 1813 -vs-
Minor Gladden--Alleges: On 13 Feb. 1813--Minor Gladden of Dist.
of Fairfield made agreement with Pltf. to sell lands in Fairfield Dist. Suit for compliance with contract.

DELANE, PETER L.--Will in file. Richland Eq. Roll Filed 15 May, 1824
Ch: Gracey Ann Delane, Philip H. Delane, Freeman Delane--minors
John Yancy, Gdn. Married widow of Peter D. Ann W.
Also heirs of Ann Casey Will--left land to Martha Caroline -w-
John Childs.

DELANE, PETER and Ann Wood Delane, his wife -vs- Freeman Delane and
Anne, his wife, and John Williams Heron-Alleges--Late John
Heron of town of Columbia died intestate leaving widow, sd
Anne Delane and 3 children, Anne Wood Delane, Philip Partridge
Heron and John William Heron--all minors and widow Anne Heron
-m- Freeman Delane. Bill for acct. and Partition.
Names spelled Delane, De Lane, and Delaney
Richland Bills 75 Filed 18 Feb. 1812

DELANE, PETER L.--Orig. Will 30 Dec. 1815 Richland Prob. Bx. 7-163
Wife: Ann Delane
To: Martha Caroline Lafargue
     Grace Ann Delane
     Philip Hirons Delane
     John William Delane
     Freeman Delane, Jr.

DELEON, JACOB--Orig. Will 8 July 1828 Richland Prob. Bx. 7-164
Wife: Hannah
Son: Dr. Abraham Deleon of Kershaw
      Dr. Mordecai Hendricks Deleon of Richland
4 Daus: Louisa, Harrietta, Rebecca, Adelade
Son: Uriah Deleon

DELLET, JAMES--Com'r. Ct. Equity. See card Richard Lloyd Champion
Richland Eq. Bills 118
James Dellet -vs- James Hopkins and Joel Adams, Exor's. of
James T. Goodwyn; Robert Goodwyn; Thos. G. Goodwyn; Wm. A.
Goodwyn; Albert G. Goodwyn; and Edward F. Goodwyn, children of
John Goodwyn, dec'd. Alleges James Taylor, dec'd. was indebted
to various people and a Plt'n. was sold under order of court
and bought by John Goodwyn570 acres E-s Congaree called Capt.
James Taylor's lower Plt'n. That John Goodwyn gave bond for
the money and Mortgage and died before paying in full.
Richland Eq. Bills 110 Filed 6 Sept. 1817--Suit -vs- William
Goss and Benj. F. Harris to foreclose Mtg. securing debt.
Richland Bills 116, Filed 1 Oct. 1818 Suit -vs- John J. Chappell
of Columbia in re. Bond given by Deft. to Benjamin Haile

DELOZIER, ASA and John Bostick--Adv. James Boatwright. Bills 30 1813
Richland Prob. Bx. 7-165 Orig. Will 11 July 1809
Wife: Hannah--All
Bro: Edward Delozer Friend: John Bostick

DELOZIER, HANNAH--Widow of Asa -vs- Caroline Delozier, Adeline
Delozier, and Emaline Delozier--ages 11, 9, and 6 respectively-
children of Plt'f and her dec'd husband. Dec'd had lands in
Colleton, Orangeburg and Richland counties. Estate in debt.
Richland Bills 202 Filed 25 June 1822

DENLEY, WILLIAM--Orig. Will 15 Jan. 1802 Richland Prob. Bx 7-166
Wife: Margaret--for life
Sons: William and Wright--Minors-all when of age
Ex: Friend: James Hopkins until Wm. is of age
In same Box:
William Denley Will--24 April 1824
    "My child": Mary Margaret Denly--if she lives
    Bro: Wright Denley--to rear child

DENT, HEZEKIAH--Richland Prob. Bx. 7-167 Cit: 4 Feb. 1833
      Partition lists Heirs: Adm'r: Peter Dent
            Isaac, James, Peter, Samuel, and John Dent
            Patience Duncan
            Tynah Dent
            Anna Dent -m- Thos. Brown
            Nancy Dent -m- Uriah Lee
            Widow: Elizabeth Dent

DENTON, JAMES and wife, Elizabeth--Exor's of Wm. Fitzpatrick. -vs-
      Joseph English, Adm'r. of William Fitzpatrick-a lunatic.
      Joseph English alleges 10 of the slaves had been given to Richard
      Fitzpatrick by William Fitzpatrick 2 Nov. 1799 and Wm. Gillespie
      Fitzpatrick claimed 14 slaves by gift from his natural father,
      the dec'd. Richard Fitzpatrick, lawful son, left state.
      Elizabeth Denton, formerly E. Gillespie.
      Richland Co. Bills 159 Filed 2 Sept. 1819
      James Denton and wife -vs- Joseph English--Bills 80
            File contains appeal by Plt'f. alleging error of Judge--
            on several grounds. Among exceptions: "Because his Honor
            charged the Jury that from the beauty and youth of the
            Plt'f. and age and lonliness of Fitzpatrick, they might
            presume that she had decoyed him, since there was positive
            evidence of her moral and virtuous character until destroyed
            by Fitzpatrick.

DESAUSURE, WM. F. -vs- David Coalter--Sale of lot in Columbia
      Richland Bills 181 Filed 17 Sept. 1821

DEVLIN, WILLIAM--Richland Prob. 7-169 Cit: 12 Jan. 1828
      Adm'r: James L. Clark   Bond: 3 Feb. 1828
      Had a legacy coming from estate of Samuel Scott. Bal. to heirs.

DEWEES, FARMER--Granted tract land in Lexington Dist. See card
      James Boatwright. Richland Bills 30 1813

DIMOCK, DANIEL--Richland Prob. Bx. 7-170 Bond: 19 Nov. 1811
      Adm'rs: Sophia Dimock, John Hooker, James Wheaton.
      S: John Parr, George Natting. Large estate-heirs not listed

DICKEY, JAMES--Dec'd. Exor's: Robert McFaddin and wife Leah McF.
      Richland Bills 4 See card Wm. Lenoir

DINKINS, JOHN--Richland Prob. Bx. 7-171 From N. C. No property in
      S. C. except suit for slave. Adm'r: Benj. Rawls-gave bond
      25 July 1825

DICKEY, NANCY--Dec'd Aunt of Hamiter minors. See card Hamiter.
      Richland Bills 154 1820

DOMINY, ANDREW, Dec'd. Richland Bills 176 1820
      Widow: Margaret   Dau: Susannah Dominy
      Son: Andrew--Minor   Dau: Sally -w- John Holmon
      Dau: Poly -w- John Saunders   Margaret -w- John Royser
            Catherine -w- Andrew Mohe   Elizabeth -w- Daniel Smith

256

DOMINY, SUSANNAH--See card Sally Holman--Richland Eq. 176 1820

DONAVAN, ISAAC--Dec'd. Richland Eq. 88 1817 Land in Washington
Village. Left: Widow, Mary--now wife of James Commer
Ch: John, James, Elizabeth and Ann. Died 1803
Dau: Elizabeth, 18 yrs. in 1817 Prays apt. of Adam Edgar.

DORTCH, THOMAS--Of Congaree, Will 27 Dec. 1777. C. T. Wills Pg. 617
Plt'n. bargained to Roland Williamson to go to dau. Sarah if
R. Williamson fails to purchase. Sons: Henry and Thomas

DOUBLEDAY, DOROTHA. Richland Prob. 68 Filed 5 Oct. 1808 Wm. Thorpe.
Adm'r. -vs- Casper Faust, Exor. of Casper Faust Shows: Wm.
Thorpe -m- Mary, dau. of John Henry Faust and wife, Dorotha.
Shows settlement with heirs of Casper (Gasper) Faust, Sr.
    John Henry Faust   William Faust
    Casper Faust   Burrell Faust. 17/18 Feb. 1777

DOUBLEDAY, JOHN -m- 1799 Widow of John Henry Faust, Dorothy. She
died Jan. 1809. Richland Eq. 68

DOUGLAS, JESSE--Dec'd. about 1802. Richland Eq. 1-75
Ch: Elizabeth--Roll 20 shows 14
    Nathaniel and Rebeckah--under 12
John Hughsons Pet. apt. Gdn. ad. later. 2 June 1810

DOUGLAS, NATHANIEL--Pet'r now over 14. Shows: John Hughson was Apt.
Gdn. of Pet'r. Prays John Hughson be discharged and Adam Edgar
be Apt. Richland Eq. Roll 53 1816

DREHR, JOHN--Pet'r. Shows Andrew Kayler of Lexington Dist. died
about Sept. 1815--left widow, Mary and 1 child, Ames, 1 yrs.
John Drehr, Pet'r. is gr-father. Prays Apt. Richland Eq. 141
    1819
DRAFTS, REUBEN AND JOHN--Minors--ch. of Michael Drafts, Dec'd. Prays
apt. of step-father, Andrew Farrar. Under 14 yrs. Eq. Roll 124
    1819
DRAKE, JOHN--Gdn. of Anne Kaigler-dau. of Andrew Kaigler. Richland
Eq. Roll 145. 1819

DUBOSE, SERRE(Jesse) -m- Sarah Weston Goodwyn. See card Harry Grant.
Richland Eq 89 1815

DUKE, HARRIET--17 yrs. Prays apt. of her father, Samuel Duke, as Gdn.
Richland Eq. 77 Filed 24 Feb. 1817

DUKES, JAMES -m- Judith Wilson--dau. of James Wilson (see Wilson
Card.) Richland Eq. 156 1820

DUKE, JOHN -m- Elizabeth Turner--See card James Turner, Dec'd.
Richland Eq. 40
Richland Bills--Original Deed 40
John Duke from James Turner: 300 Acres on 25 mile creek, bd.
by Elijah Jones, George Watts, and Meredith Taylor. Also 500
Acres on Bear Creek, sd. Dist, Bd. by Thomas Trap, Anak Gel (?)
and Campbell's. 16 Oct. 1808.(Cancelled by Court order.
Also: See card James and Margaret Martin and Moses Duke

DUKE, SAMUEL--Apt'd. Gdn. of his dau. Harriet Duke-age 17. Eq. Roll 77
                                                                  1817
DUNCAN, MATTHEW--(Sick) Will 1787 Richland Wills Book B-5
    Bro: Thomas Duncan--250 Acres land Berkley Co. Va.
    Bro-in-law: Wm. Wilson
    Father: Matthew Duncan
    Bro: James
          Joseph--Lands in Kentucky
          Seth
    Heirs: John Milling--releases note only
            John Copland--   "   "   "
    Sister: Sarah Greer
    Ex: Bro. Thos Duncan and Thos. Hutchinson 11 July 1787
    Wit: Leten W. Sledd and Joel McLemore Prov: 20 Aug. 1787

DURHAM, CHAMEL--Pet'r. Shows John Woodward Durham is infant under 14.
    Prays apt. of Pet'r as Gdn. Shows Pet'r. is gr-father of infant.
    Shows Gen'l. C. Strother -m- an aunt of the child. Some of
    family wish Strother to have Gdnship. Richland Eq. 96 1818

EADIE, JAMES -w- Katherine Patterson Eadie, sister of Geo. Patterson,
    dec'd. See card James Patterson. Richland Eq 201 1822

EDERINGTON, ELIZABETH -m- Capt. Minor Smith-Lived in Orangeburg.
    See card John Hampton. Richland Eq. 3

EDGAR, ADAM--Apt'd. Gdn. of Nathaniel Douglas. See card John Hughson.
    Richland Eq. 53. See also: Isaac Donavan, Dec'd.

EDWARDS, C. A. -m- Dau. of Sarah Cantey. See Cantey card. Eq. 86

EDWARDS, JAMES F.--Of City of Charleston, Adm'r. John Edwards. -vs-
    John Bruce and Harriet Benson: Alleges--John Edwards of Charles-
    ton, dec'd. made Will-James F. Edwards, Adm'r. That on 16 Feb.
    1792, Maj. Joshua Benson, now dec'd, executed a Bond in favor of
    sd John Edwards for payment of 160 pounds, Just sum, and sd
    Joshua Benson died intestate and leaving widow, Mary and Harriet
    his only child. Owned Real Estate in Richland Dist. and then
    the Widow, Mary Benson -m- John Bruce and then sd Mary died,
    leaving her 2nd husband and her daughter Harriet Benson as owners
    of the property. Harried -m- Josiah (?) Kilgore. Suit over
    Bond. Richland Eq. Bills 106 Filed 5 May, 1815

EDWARDS, JOHN--Of Charleston, dec'd. Left Will and appointed:
    John B. Holmes)
    James Fisher   ) Renounced the Executorship
    Philip Gadsin   )
    Alexander Edwards, who died, and James Fisher Edwards were
    appointed on 24 April 1812. Richland Co. Bills 106
    Richland Bills 105 shows letter from A. Edwards, brother of
    John in re Bond given by Joshua Benson to John Edwards--letter
    dated 18 Nov. 1802 and appears handwriting of Alexander Edwards.

EDWARDS, THOMAS -m- Widow of Geo. Robinson. See Robinson card. 1813

ELDER, JOHN--Of Congaree. Will 30 Oct. 1770 C. T. Wills 1771-74
    Son: Thomas--Land   5 Mar. 1771
    Dau: Elinor
    All the rest of my children.
    Exor's: Friends-Peter Smith, and Wm. Scott
    Wit: Henry Banks and Wm. Scott

ELDER, JOHN--Richland Bills 10 Filed 14 Nov. 1811 -vs-
    Cornelius H. Vanters--Alexander McGrew, dec'd. owned 500 Acres
    on Congaree River in Richland Dist. Made Will. Left wife and
    children; James, Peter aldo called Alex'r. William, Mary and
    Margaret. Peter, also called Alex'r McGrew died intestate
    previous to 1791, leaving widow, Margaret and one son, John,
    also died-no issue-since 1791 and dau. Anna now wife of Corn-
    elius H. Vanters. Elizabeth -m- Cornelius Autry-died leaving
    2 children; David Autry and Mary Ann Autry. Hugh McLain-bro.
    of Margaret McGrew.

ELDERS, JOHN--Of Richland Dist. Benj. Everitt--Deed in trust for
    his 2 children; James and Martha Elders. Misc. C-306 13 Aug.
                                                 1816
ELDERS, MARY--Of Dist. of Richland to son: Thos. Wescott and her
    gr-children: Nancy D. Cooper -w- Jesse Cooper
                       Mary Ann Wescott
                       Robert Wescott
    4 negroes--sd Mary Elders (1s)
    Pres: G. Louden and F. M. Drennan Trust Deed M-13 25 Jan. 1824

ELDERS, WILLIAM--Of Richland Dist. Misc. C-222 23 Jan. 1813
    Mary Boucher-Each to keep own property.
    Wit: sd MaryBoucher (1s), John Elders, William Elders, Thomas
           Wescott
    Also: William Elders -m- set 13 Jan. 1815 Mary Boucher.

ELLIS, SARAH--Of Mass. -m- Joshua Benson. His 1st wife. 2nd wife,
    Mary. Richland Eq. 129. See Benson card.

ELLISON, JANE--Relict of Robert Ellison-had Will-died in Fairfield
    Dist. Robert Ellison left Will and Apt.
           William Allison, Samuel Johnston, and Robert Ellison-Ex's.
    Suit against Wm. Ellison for keeping money himself.
    Richland Eq. 3 1809

ELLISON, MAJOR ROBERT, SR.--Miss Sarah Elizabeth, William, John,
    Robert, Jr. Joseph--called sister-in law and brothers-in-law by
    Rev. David Ellison Dunlap in his Will and his wife, Susanna
    Potts Dunlap, and mentions no children. Appears that Robert
    Ellison, Sr. was father-in-law
    Richland Co. Family-1804 Stray bills Bx. 126/151

ELLISON, ROBERT--Richland Eq. Bills 12
    Widow: Jane Ellison
    Ch: William, John, James, Joseph, and
        Sarah Elizabeth -w- John Adger. See card David E. Dunlap

ELLISON, SARAH ELIZABETH--Sister-in-law Samuel Dunlap Bills 12 1812

ELLISON, WILLIAM, JOHN, ROBERT, JOSEPH--see card Rev. David E. Dunlap

ENGLISH, JOSEPH -m- Harriet Fitzpatrick--dau. of William and Elizabeth
    Fitzpatrick, parents separated and Wm. G. Fitzpatrick was ill-
    egitimate son by Elizabeth Gillespie-after death of Fitzpatrick
    she married James Denton and they sued for part of Fitzpatrick
    estate. Richland Co. Stray Bills 159 1819

EVANS, DAVID R.--Richland Eq. 144. See card Elisha Daniel

EVERINGHAM, JOHN--Richland Co. Bills 127½--A Witness--testified John
    Jon of Richland Dist. was trustee names in a Deed of Joseph Smith
    of Orangeburg Dist. to his infant dau. Mariah Smith, for a slave
    in 1794 or 1795. Made at Mr. Swanson Lunsford's house.
    File also contains copy of Ct. proceeding of Henry Dana Wood
    -vs- Joseph Smith-on note Filed 12 March 1810, in Orangeburg.

FARRANT, GEORGE -m- Polly Walker, dau. Edward Walker. Richland Pet.
    111 (Or Tarrant)

FARRAR, ANDREW--Stepfather of Reuben Drafts. Richland Pet. 124

FAUST, CASPER--Of Craven Co. Richland Will. Bills 68
    Wife:
    Dau: Elizabeth
    Son: Burrell
          William00land on Crane Creek, near Widow Hunter
          Casper   )
          John Henry Faust) Exor's 13 Jan. 1776
    Wit: Wm. Strother; Casper Coonz, Richard Adams. Rec'd in C. T.

FAUST, HENRY--Or Richland Co. Richland Wills B-11 1787
    Sons: Jesse and Moses   Date: 8 Feb. 1787
    Wife: Dorothy   Prov: 19 Nov. 1787
    Wit: Nicholas Gubb, Samuel Kelley, Wm. Allen Tharp

FAUST, JOHN--Dec'd Richland Prob. Bx. 9-224 1807
    Children: Balser (Belser)
               Henry
               John
               Christian
               Peggy -w- Aaron Duke
               Mary -w- Moses Duke
               Kate -w- Dempsey Hunter
               Elizabeth -w- Dr. Robert Miller
               Charlotte -w- Thos. Smith
               Harriet -w- Wm. Motte
               Selina Faust

FERRAND, ALEXANDER--Of City of Charleston. Richland Bills 69
    Alleges: That on 19 Jan. 1808, Thomas Parrott of Fairfield
    Dist. and John G. Brown of State of Penn. entered into agree-
    ment general business together--had creditors in Miss.
    Wm. Dansby, Surety. Filed 1 Feb. 1811

FISHER, DR. EDWARD--Gdn. of ch. of Samuel Stanley.   9 Sept. 1809

FITZPATRICK, WILLIAM--Dec'd--Will null and void. Elizabeth Gillespie,
    Exor. Dau. Harriet -w- Joseph English. Richland Co. Ct. Min.
    9 Sept. 1809
    Richland Eq. Bills 159--Fitzpatrick, William--dec'd. Scandal
    See card James Denton and Wife.

FITZSIMMONS, THOMAS -w- Catherine-of Philadelphia, Pa. to Louis de
    Noailles, of Phila. Pa. 52 tracts land--1000 acres--on Saluda
    River, Ninety Six Dist. Greenville Co. South Carolina. Gr. of
    Robert Middleton-1796-who conv. 18 July 1785-to Thos. Fitz-
    simmons on thickety Creek, Bulloch's Fork. 1 Sept. 1802.

FLEMING, ANDREW -vs- Joseph Fleming--Bill for Partition. Ann Hoy,
    wife of Robert Hoy, lately died in Columbia. Sister of Andrew
    Fleming, Nancy Fleming a sister; Rebecca Walls-Joseph Fleming,
    Caroline Fleming, dau. of a dec'd. brother and Thomas Fleming
    ch of a dec'd bro. Mentions: Margaret O'Hanlon, Samuel Heron
    Matilda O'Hanlon, Catherine O'Hanlon, Lawrence O'Hanlon.
    Richland Bills 26   Filed 26 Feb. 1813
    Richland Eq. Roll 61   Filed 12 July 1816--Pet'r. shows that at
    Feb. term 1814 he was apt'd Gdn to Caroline Fleming, abt 13 yrs.
    and Thomas Fleming, abt. 9 yrs. to defend them in their partition
    of lot of land in Columbia. The lot was sold--money in hands
    of Comm'rs. Prays apt. Gdn.

FOOTE, ISABELLA--Widow of John Foote, dec'd. and exec'x. of his
    Will, and Burr Johnson and Harriet his wife, late Harriet Foote,
    dau. sd John. Isabella Harper Foote; Sarah R. Foote; and Mary
    Louisa Foote, minors, under 21. By Gdn. David Holladay, ch. of
    sd John Foote, dec'd. and Thomas Means, Ex. Will of sd John
    Foote shows: sd. John Foote dec'd. Left Will. Late of Fair-
    field. Pray for Writ of Part. Daniel H. Means, Gdn. for the
    Minors. Copy John Foot'es Will in file.

FOOTE, ISABELLA HARPER--Under 21, Mary Louisa and Sarah R.--under 14
    ch. of John Foote. David H. Means, Gdn. Eq. Roll 111 1818

FOOT, JOHN, SR.--Of Fairfield Dist. Will Richland Eq. Roll 118
    Father:--Land on Sandy River where his father now lives, re-
    leased to him. 100 A. Pt. of James Dillard Gr.
    Wife: Isabella
    Children:
    Thomas Means and William Foote, Exor's. Date: 13 Apr. 1806

FORD, DANIEL--Will Richland Bx. 10-244 1800
    Wife: Rachel--Home Place
    Step dau: Rachel Lansdon
    Gr-son: William Morris
    Dau: Fanny Geiger
          Sally Hoof -w- James Hoff, Sr. (Sp?)
          Molly Morris -w- John Morris, Sr. 13 April 1800

FORD, MALACHI -m- Sat. 25 March, 1823 Sarah A. Edwards. Henry A.
Deasussus, Trustee. Letter in file by Jas. S. Guignard, dated,
15 May 1834--used as cover for W. D. D. Lindsay file--shows
as all one. Richland Prob. 18-442

FORD, MARY M.--Nee Priolean Richland Eq. Bills 86 1814
Caroline Dawson; Catherine Ravenel; Martha Priolean; Philip
G. Priolean; Elizabeth Priolean--children of Catherine Priolean
See card Abraham Blanding

FORTUNE, ANN--Of Wateree Creek--Widow Richland Bills 24
To: John Milling--Bond 3 Nov. 1777 original in file. Plat to
John Fortune 1767--350 acres. Deed-8 Feb. 1802. William
Fortune, son of John Fortune, dec'd. to John Woodward, Sr.
Planter; James Barkley and James Barber of Winnsborough.

FORTUNE, JOHN of Jackson's Cr. Fairfield Dist. left Will. Widow-
Ann. Oldest son-William. Richland Eq. Roll 24 1803
See card Sarah Milliny.

FOSTER, DAVID -m- Widow Harriet Snyder. Widow of Col. Geo. Snyder
of Lexington Dist. Richland Eq. Roll 144 1817

FOSTER, ANDREW--Heir of Samuel Dunlap. See Will 9 Sept. 1804
Richland Eq. Roll 12

FOX, WILLIAM--Will Richland Bx. 10-245
Son: Henry Fox
Dec'd. dau: Ann Scott's children
Dau: Unity Carter
Mary Powell
Dec'd. dau: Elizabeth Killingsworth's children (2)
Son: Elisha and Elijah
Ex: Robert Carter   Date: 13 April 1828

FRALICK, CHARLES--Richland Eq. Bills 145. See card Sarah Carter -vs-
Benj. Carter

FRASER, CAROLINE--Dec'd. intestate Richland Eq. Roll 65 1816
Heirs: Mary -w- Henry Richardson
Sarah -w- John Richardson
John Frazer   Harriet Frazer
Alexander Frazer   Eugenia Frazer

FRAZIER, ISAAC--Of town of Columbia -vs- John W. Wilkins--Suit to
foreclose Mtg. House and lot in Columbia on cor. of Richardson
and Walnut streets. Richland Bills 165
See card Nathan Center Bills 206

FREEMAN, ANN--Mother of the children of_____Shepherd. See Shepherd
card. Richland Eq. 15 1813

FRIDAY, JOHN--Dec'd. Intestate Oct. 1821
Wife: Barbara
Ch: John Jacob, Emanuel, and Nancy. Land in Lexington sold
under executions. Nancy dec'd. was wife of James Cayce.
Her ch: Harriet M., John A., Sarah R.

FROST, JOHN--Dec'd 1798 Intestate Richland Eq. Roll 15 1812
Leaving Widow, Judith, mother of Mary Kinsler, now wife of
John Kinsler, orator and oratrix. Said Mary and John, a
minor son. Alleges the widow, Judith took out letters of
Administration and since married Judah Barrett. Part of slaves.

FULMER, ABRAHAM and wife, Mary--Heirs of George Long. See card Amos
Bank and wife, Catherine. Richland Eq. Pet-149

FULMER, LUCY ANN AND JOHN WILLIAM--Ch. of William Fulmer 1820.
Richland Eq. Roll 155. See card David Montgomery.

FULMER, WILLIAM--Dec'd. Land in Lexington Dist. on Hollow Creek
Saluda River. Richland Eq. Pet. Roll 98 1818
Widow: Margaret
2 ch: Ann Fulmer
William Fulmer.
The widow, Margaret has married Theophilas Wilson of Fairfield.
Pray order of sale.

GARDINER, SAMUEL COTTON, MARY GARDINER--See Henry Zinn Stray 152

GARNER, GILBERT -w- Elizabeth--Heirs of George Rawlinson.
Plat 1838-div. Rawlinson Est.
Gideon Garner -m- Mary R. Widow of Wm. H. Killingsworth
Richland Eq. Part. Bx. 324/42 1837
Gilbert Garner -w- Elizabeth -vs- Joel, Franklin, John and
Charles--Minors--A. B. Joyner, Gdn.

GARVEY, ELEANOR -widow of Joseph Garvey--Shows Joseph Garvey died in
Service of U. S. leaving Martha Matilda and Elizabeth Garvey,
his daughters, ages 8 and 5--and they are entitled to Bounty
Lands. Prays apt. Pet'r as Gdn. Richland Eq. Roll 99 1818

GAHAGAN, JOHN--Dec'd. Richland File Misc. C-46
Widow: Elizabeth -m- Dr. John Hughs. Separated 29 Aug. 1810
4 Gahagan children mentioned.

GAHAGAN, PHILIP; John Hughs -w- Elizabeth; William Goss -w- Eliza;
-vs- John Gahagan and Bridgett. Gahagen Alleges: John Gahagan
dec'd in 1807 intestate owned lands in Kershaw Dist--adj.
Burwell Boykin on Swift Creek--survived by his widow, Elizabeth.,
who married John Hughes and his daus. Eliza who -m- Wm. Goss;
and Bridgett, and sons, Philip and John Gahagan. Bill for
Partition. Richland Bills 85 1814

GIBSON, JACOB, JR.--otherwise called Jacob Hortin, acknowledged by
Joseph Gibson of Fairfield as son. Richland Eq. Bills 65

GIBSON, JOSEPH--Richland Wills Bk. B-28 1788
Adm. James May and Gilbert Gibson Letters: 20 May 1788

GIBSON, ROGER--Gr. 19 Oct. 1748 Wateree River Land Richland File
Mem. 8-119/20 500 Acres--owned and conveyed by Isaac Ross and
wife, Mary 1765. Also 250 Acres conveyed by Samuel Gibson to
Isaac Ross

GRILL, HUGH -vs- Jonas Bradly and Walter Ledbetter--Alleges: On
20 Nov. 1819 the 2 deft's. Citizens of North Carolina--owned
beef cattle which they brought to Columbia for sale and that
Wm. O. Walton, also of N. C. and neighbor of deft's. sd note
of plt'f for bal. of purchase price, as security--Fraud.
Richland Bills 193 Filed 20 May 1822

GILL, JOHN--Of Messer County, State of Virginia, Kentucky Dist.
Wife: Margaret (May have another child)"Home place at Head of
Quirk's Run".
"My children"   26 Sept. 1788
Exor's: Wm. Gill (Bro.) John and Thos Pitman as Ex. in Kentucky
Exor's: Bishop and Richard Ellis and Robert Lithgow in S. C.
Richland Prob. Bx. 11-261 1788 (Card #2--Mercer Co.)

GILLESPIE, ELIZABETH -m- James Denton--Richland Bills 159 1819
She was a legatee of Wm. Fitzpatrick by reason of being the
mother of Wm. G. Fitzpatrick, an illigitimate son of Dec'd.

GILMORE, ROBERT, ROBERT, JR. WILLIAM-"Robert Gilmor & Sons" -vs-
John Maitland and Thomas Mailtand--Promissory note of Thomas
Fitzsimons of Philadelphia, to Louis de Noailles of Phila-
delphia. Maitlands were purchasers of lands. Richland Bills 124
Filed 11 Sept. 1826

GLADNEY, JAMES -w- Ann--See card James and Margaret Martin Eq. 40
Gladney, James -m- Ann Turner. 1811

GLOVER, SANDERS--married dau. of Mr. Lestergette. Richland Roll 70
                                                              1818
GOFF, ELIAS -m- Widow Mary Patterson, widow of Matthew Patterson.
Richland Bills 170 1819

GOODWYN, ALBERT G.: EDWARD F.: AND ADELLA--Who held by descent from
John Goodwyn, dec'd; and Henry Adams and James Adams, the
younger, who held by descent from Mary H. Adams, wife of sd
Henry; which sd mary held by descent from Jesse Goodwyn, dec'd.
who held by devise from Howell Goodwyn, Keziah Hopkins, wife
of James Hopkins; Sarah C. Hall, wife of Ainsley Hall and Jesse
Goodwyn who hold by descent from Jesse Goodwyn, Dec'd--who held
by devise from Howell Goodwyn--Shows: Keziah Hopkins, late
widow of Jesse Goodwyn. Richland Bills 89

GOODWYN, GRACE--Widow Wm. Goodwyn -vs- Uriah John Goodwyn--Alleges:
Wm. Goodwyn dec'd in Nov. 1791 having previously deeded his
property in Trust to Jesse Goodwyn--for himself, wife and children.
Richland Bills 95 1812
Richland Bills 60 Filed 30 Jan. 1812 shows: Grace Goodwyn--
Relict of Col. Wm. Goodwyn -vs- James Hopkins and Joel Adams
Exor's of John Goodwyn--shows; Margaret Goodwyn -m- James H.
Chappell and Grace H. Goodwyn -m- John S. Chappell--daus. of
Wm. Goodwyn
See card--Mary Ann E. Cogdell Richland Bills 25

GOODWYN, JAMES--Of Richland Dist -vs- Chastain E. Williamson and wife,
and John Howell Alleges: Wm. Howell died intestate on 1st April
1799 leaving widow, Mary and 2 daus. Sarah and Mary Howell.
Widow married Robert Hendricks--died 1805 and the widow Mary
then married C. E. Williamson.

GOODWYN, JAMES T.--Richland Bills 204 1822
Sarah Epps -w- Wm. Adams
Robert Goodwyn
Martha T. -w- Benj. R. Waring   All children of Sarah
Thomas J. Goodwyn   Goodwyn--heir of James
William A.)   Simon Taylor
Albert G.) Minors
Edward F)

GOODWYN, JAMES--Pet'r. -w- Jane, Dec'd. Shows Jane, lately Jane
Green, entitled to estate in what is called the Yazoo Claims.
Jane died leaving 2 children by Goodwyn marriage. Eliza Howell
Goodwyn and Jane Harris Goodwyn--minors. Prays apt. of Gdn.
Richland Roll 33 25 Nov. 1814

GOODWYN, JESSE--Of Congaree--Will 11 May 1764 Richland File
Wife: Martha--Land of Wm. Mazyck
Dau: Martha Epps Goodwyn--not 14 yrs. old
To: Wm. Goodwyn--oldest son of Robert
Bros: Thomas, Joseph, Bozwell, Robert, James, Francis.

GOODWYN, JOHN--Dec'd Richland Bills 101 1815
Widow: Sarah   See card Samuel Watkins
Ch: Robert
     Martha Taylor

GOODWYN, JOHN --Of Craven Bk. 1774-1779 Pg. 343
Wife: Lucy--Pt. Gr. to Robert G. 5 Oct. 1775
Son: William
Gr-son: Howell Goodwyn
Son: Joseph L.--Lived in Va.
     Boswell, Robert, James and Francis

GOODWYN, JOHN -m- Mary Rontz about 1793 Richland Bills 55

GOODWYN, MARTHA -m- Wm. P. Corbin. Richland Bills 182. See Card.
Also Polly Tucker Goodwyn, her dau. by Wm. Goodwyn.

GOODWYN, ROBERT--Dec'd. Will Richland Bills 89 1815
Heirs: Grace Goodwyn   Jesse Goodwyn, sole Exor.
        Uriah J. Goodwyn
        Margaret -w- Jas. H. Chappell
        Sarah Weston -w- Serre Dubose
        Grace Howell -w- John S. Chappell.
All heirs of Wm. Goodwyn, dec'd son of Robert.

GOODWYN, SARAH, THOMAS TAYLOR AND JESSE M. HOWELL, Pet's. Show
That James Taylor died intestate and John Taylor obtained letters
of Adm. That sd James Taylor was also survived by 3 children.
Sarah -w-____Goodwyn, Mary -w- Thomas Taylor and Martha -w-
Jesse M. Howell and also gr-son, James Taylor abt. 18. and son
of Jesse Taylor, dec'd. Martha d. Apr. 1811 leaving 2 children
James M. age 8 and Martha age 5.

GOODWYN, WILLIAM--The elder--Richland Bills 1. Bro. John Goodwyn, Pet'r.
being in debt jointly with sd brother-conv. his property to his
cousin, Jesse Goodwyn for nominal consideration of 10,000 lbs.
in year 1791 to be held in trust until debts paid. Jesse dec'd.
5 Sept. 1792 leaving Kezia Goodwyn, widow, who with William
Goodwyn, the younger, and John Hopkins apt. Adm. Left 3 children
    Mary Howell Hart Goodwyn
    Sarah Cook Goodwyb
    Jesse Goodwyn. Prays protection of court.

GOODWYN, COL. WILLIAM, Dec'd--Richland Bills 95
    Wife: Gracey
    Ch: Uriah--a minor
John Goodwyn and James Goodwyn, Trustees
Deed in file 1 Nov. 1802 Wit: Henry Brown, John Lucius

GOODWYN, WILLIAM F.--Dec'd. Abraham D. Jones and John Howell, Exor's.
Left widow, Martha Goodwyn and 1 child--Pollu Tucker Goodwyn.
Wife: Whole of Plt'n in St. Matthews Par. Dau: Plt'n on
Congaree where Tyson lives. Date: 6 June 1821

GOODWYN, WILLIAM F.--Dec'd. Widow, Martha -m- Wm. P. Corbin.
Only child, Polly Tucker Goodwyn -m- Thos J. Augustine before 1830
Filed 7 May, 1832 Richland Eq.

GOSS, WILLIAM -m- Eliza (or Elizabeth) Gehagan--dau. of Philip and
Elizabeth Gehagan. Richland Bills 85 1814

GRANT, HARRY--Dec'd. -vs- James F. Goodwyn, et al Alleges: Robert
Goodwyn, dec'd. had made Bond 26 Aug. 1779 to Christopher
Williman for just sum of 24,371 pounds 10 shillings which Bond
was assigned to Harry Grant and then Robert Goodwyn made a
Will--Jesse Goodwyn, sole exor.--Suit was entered on the Bond -vs-
the Estate of Robert Goodwyn and judgement entered, then Jesse
Goodwyn died. Lands now owned by Grace Goodwyn, Uriah J. Goodwyn,
Margaret Chappell, wife of James H. Chappell, Sarah Weston Debose,
Grace Howell Chappell, wife of John S. Chappell--who held by de-
cent from William Goodwyn, dec'd. son of sd Robert and Sarah
Goodwyn, James T. Goodwyn, John J. Goodwyn, Sarah Epps Adams,
wife of William W. Adams, Robert H. Goodwyn, Martha Waring -w-
Benj. R. Warring, Thos. Jefferson Goodwyn, William C. Goodwyn.

GRAY, DAVID--Dec'd. Will Richland Eq. Roll ? Filed 20 May 1823
    Wife: Sarah Gray--Ex.
3 children: Robert Hendricks Gray--minor
              John Lewis Gray--died infancy
              David Larmer Gray--minor

GRAY, WILLIAM -m- set 9 June 1821 Harriet Green Misc. D-364

GREEN, JANE--m--James Goodwyn. Richland Eq. Roll 33 25 Nov. 1814
2 children: Eliza Howell Goodwyn
           Jane Harris Goodwyn.

GREEN, MRS. SALINA--Will Richland Eq. Filed 3 Sept. 1864
    To: Martha Wilkerson--maiden name--now Martha Williamson -w-
        James C. Williamson, dec'd.
        Her children: James W. Williamson--in Confed. Army
                George C.   "   --"   "   "   17 yrs.
                John P   "   Nearly 15
                Thomas C.   "   Abt. 13
                Roland T.   "   Age 11
                Elizabeth J. "   Age 10
                Arthur E.   "   Abt. 8

GREEN, SAMUEL. See Samuel Warnbezee. Richland Bills 104

GREEN, THOMAS, Dec'd. Richland Bills 74
    Wife: Martha -m- Chas. Oliver
    Ch: Frederick W. Green
        William Green
        Jane Harriet Green
        Martha Green See card Arthur Collins

GUIGNARD, MARGARET -m- Peter Horry. Richland Eq. Bills 121 1815

HAIG, JOHN JAMES--Dec'd. Left Will. Late of Orangeburg. Owned
    "Bacon Hill. Richland Eq. Roll 69   4 May 1806 (Bills 137)
    Wife: Mary -m- Henry Dana Ward
    Sister: Margaret Blake
            Son: John Haig Blake--"Bacon Hill"
            Dau: Elizabeth Blake
                  Martha -w- Wm. Washington
                  Margaret -w- Dr. Nathaniel Bowen
                  Harriet and Mary Blake
                  Edward Blake
    Apt'd: John Blake-also dec'd. Fily Warley, John Alexander
    Cuthbert, James Elliott McPherson, and Joel Adams (Roll 61)
    See card Samuel Campbell and wife. (Bills 13)
    See card Clairborne Clifton (Bills 78)

HAILE, BENJAMIN--Comm'r. of Town of Columbia Richland Bills 8
    Bill to foreclose Mtg. -vs- James Bolan, Thomas Egan; Filed
    27 Feb. 1809. Mentioned previous executors in favor of Mary
    Tucker, and Charles Stone and wife.

HALL, AINSLY--See Ann Delaine (Delane) Richland Eq. Pet. 89

HALL, AINSLEY -w- Sarah--late Sarah Goodwin -vs- Grace Goodwyn and
    Jos. H. Chappell and wife.--Jesse Goodwyn, dec'd intestate.
    Wife, Keziah--now wife of James Hopkins. 3 children; Sarah
    -w- Ainsley Hall, Mary H. Goodwyn, and Jesse Goodwyn.
    Richland Bills 21
    Richland Eq. Bills 148 1818. See card John Burney.
        Ainsley Hall owned the house he had Robert Mills design.
        Recently bought and preserved by people of Columbia, S. C.
        as being of Architectural value.
    Richland Eq. Bills 191 1821--Ainsley and William Hall, et al,
    Adv. Philip Pearson, Sr. See Pearson card.
    Richland Eq. Bills 195 1822--Ainsley Hall -vs- Jos. Martin.
    Agreement to purchase lot in dispute.

HALL, AINSLEY and William. John and George Kirkpatrick -vs- Pet'rs.
Marriage set. of Louisa M. Hendricks of Columbia and Michael
J. Rudolph--of same place. Jacob J. Faust, Tr. Alleges note
and debt. Richland Bills 198 Filed 1822
Richland Bills 197 Filed 12 Jan. 1822--Ainsley Hall and William
-vs- Robert E. Russell--Bill to foreclose
Richland Eq. Rolls 259 - 261--Ainsley Hall--Est.--Left Will 1822
        Wife: Sarah C. Hall (C probably Cotchett)
        Ex: Wm. Hall and George Cotchett
        Eliza D. Howell and Eliza D. McCord are made parties.
Richland Eq. Filed 20 Jan. 1825--Ainsley Hall-dec'd 1823. Widow
        Sarah C. Hall, Oratrix.

HALL, HENRY REES--Richland Eq. Roll 27 1813. Conv. property in
trust for Sarah Wolf and her children--widow and children of
Henry Wolf. See card H. Wolf.

HALL, JAMES--Richland Eq. Roll 153 1820--Owns land in Columbia
through which canal is to be cut--Board of Public Works requests
apt-ment of 5 persons to fix value of land.

HALL, JAMES--Of Town of Columbia--Will 4 Jan. 1822. Prov. 1824
        Wife: Sarah
        Ch: Celina McSwain to have property coming to "her mother from
        her gr-father-Wm. Kelly".
        Polly, Sarah, Prudence, and Jane Hall
Richland Eq. Filed 21 Dec. 1825

HALL, THOMAS--Sheriff of Fairfield -vs- Henry Moore, John Barkley,
James Barkley, William Martin, James Bryant,Obediah Kirkland,
Jesse Harris, William McMorris--Concerning transactions with
Minor Winn and John Winn and mentions John Watson's estate.
Richland Eq. Bills 64 Filed 1813

HAMILTON, JOHN--Dec'd 1809. Richland Eq. 5--Left several children.
Moses Hamilton--17 yrs. 1811) Wm. Pauling and Jas. Hamilton
Pet. to be apt. Gdn.

HAMILTON, DAVID--See card Emanuel Warnbezee. Richland Bills 104

HAMPTON, JOHN -vs- Richard Winn. Answer of R. Winn filed 24 Aug.
1803 admits owing William Lindsey and Co. Estate of Minor
Smith in action. Will Gen'l Richard Winn- Elizabeth Smith
widow. Richland Bills 13. Sale of Est. of Capt. Minor Smith
20 Jan. 1785 Purchasers; John Winn, Gen'l. Richard Winn, James
Davis, Abraham Marpile, Maj. John Liles, William Liles, Capt.
D. Duff, Thorogood Chambers, Capt. Robert Hancock, Christian
Ederington, James Ogilvie, Mrs. Smith.

HAMPTON, WADE -vs- John Francis Delorme and Elizabeth Dinkins--widow
of John Dinkins--in re sale lots in Columbia and Bond given by
John Francis Delorme to Wade Hampton--23 Aug. 1810 in file.
And Bond of John Dinkins to Wade Hampton 30 Mar. 1807
Richland Bills 84 Filed 11 Jan. 1814

HAMPTON, WADE -vs- Thomas H. Egan, Chastine C. Williamson and wife,
Mary and Louisa Hendricks. In re lot in Columbia which Robert
Hendricks, now dec'd. sold to Thomas H. Egan. Filed 19 May 1814
-Richland Bills Roll 34 1814--Wade Hampton--Alleges: Robert Hendricks (dec'd.) of Columbia owned Lot 34 on Lady St.--which he
agreed to sell to Thomas H. Egan. Alleges: Robert Hendricks
left Will. Wife, Mary Hendricks -m- Chastine C. Williamson.
Dau: Louisa Hendricks--an infant.
-Richland Bills 127 Filed May 1816. Wade Hampton -vs- John K.
Davis, et al--heirs of Capt. Wm. Ransom Davis. File contains
testimony of Major Pierce Butler, Esq. of Philadelphia who was
acquainted with Capt. Wm. Ransom Davis in S. C. and states he
paid an account of Wm. R. Davis to Thomas Fitzsimmons--for which
Gen'l. Wade Hampton should be re-imbursed--Hampton having re-
imbursed him for the amount. Diposition taken in Philadelphia
-Richland Bills 2 1806--Col. Wade Hampton, Henry Hampton -vs-
Gideon Dennison of Philadelphia, Alexander Bolling Stark of
Lexington Dist.--Dispute over surveying of land. Mentions land
on Edisto River.
-Richland Bills 35 1817--Gen. Wade Hampton Adv's James S. Guignard
as Com. of Town of Columbia--Suit over property

HAMMITER, FREDERICK -m- Elizabeth Scott Richland Bills 120 1816

HAMMITER, JACOB, Dec'd. Richland Eq. 101/2 1818. See card George
Kelly

HAMITER, FANNY, JOHN, DAVID--above 14. Richland Eq 154 Filed 17 July
Entitled to Est. from dec'd. Aunt, Nancy Dickey. Pray apt. 1820
of Gdn. Thomas Shuler.

HARPER, ESTHER -vs- James Ward--Alleges: Esther Harper on 20th Sept.
1814--conv. to James Ward of Town of Columbia a lot in Columbia.
Gave Bond and Mtg. Bill to foreclose. File contains agreement
or Bond from James Ward. Esther Harper and James Ward of Dist.
of Newberry-late of Columbia. Richland Bills 119 Filed 30 April
1817
HARPER, LUCY--A dau. of Wood Tucker. See Tucker card. Roll 7 1810

HARRINGTON, W. H.--Richland Bills 13. See Samuel Campbell and wife
see, also Clairborne Clifton.

HARRIS, BARTON--Will 13 May 1823 Richland Prob. Prov. 31 July 1823
Wife: Mary Wright Harris--To have all land on Colonel's A.
Dau: Epsey McVay--$200. (or $2.00)
Son-in-law: John McVay--$200. (or $2.00)
Gr-dau: Elizabeth McVay--to have all land after death of widow.

HARRIS, JONATHAN -w- Ann--See Needham Davis. Richland Bills 154

HARRIS, THOMAS H.--See card John Croft. Richland Bills 173

HARRISON, JOHN -m- Lucy W. Rives, dau. Green Rives. Richland Eq. 47

HARRISON, BENJAMIN--(living 1815) Richland Roll 36 1815
      Ch: James Burr Harrison-under 6
           Ann Rebecca Harrison-under 4 Father apt. Gdn. 1815
      Richland File Misc. E-100 Benjamin Harrison -w- Anna--Separation
      27 April 1823. Sterling C. Williamson, Tr.

HARRISON, WILLABY -m- Rachel Rives, dau. Wm. Rives-d. 1804
      Rachel also called Elizabeth. John Harrison -m- Lucy W. Rives,
      dau. of Green Rives-d. 1812

HART, BENJAMIN -w- Harriett, Pet'rs. Shows: Edward M. Herron and
      Eliza Ann Herron, children of Harriet are entitled to Est.
      Ch. are minors. Pray apt. of Edward Mortimer as Gdn. Eq. 150

HARTIN, JACOB, otherwise called Jacob Gibson, Jr. of Fairfield Dist.
      acknowledged by Joseph Gibson of Fairfield as his son. Mentions
      David McGraw and Henry Jones, Samuel Clamp in Est. of Joseph
      Gibson. Richland Bills 45.

HARTLEY, JAMES--Pet'r. Shows: His son, Thomas Ladson Hartley is a
      minor, not 20, entitled to Est. by wife. Pet. apt. Gdn. (Seems
      to refer to wife of the minor). Richland Roll 23 1813

HARTLEY, THOS. LADSON -m- Sarah Howell, dau. of Wm. Howell. Bills 90
      Wm. Howell, Dec'd.   1815
           Widow: Mary -m- Dr. Robert Hendricks
           Dau: Sarah -m- James Dozier Zimmerman
                 Mary -m- Thos. Ladson Hartley

HARVEL, JOHN--Richland Bills 55 Filed 3 Oct. 1807 -vs-
      Augustine Williams, of Fairfield, a purchaser--Alleges: Jacob
      Rontz, resident of Congaree R. died about 1776 leaving widow,
      Sarah Rontz and one child, Mary. The widow, Sarah, -m- John
      Harvel, the Orator and died about 1779. That soon after death
      of Sarah, the daughter, Mary Rontz went away under Guardianship
      of Martin Stadler and about 1793 she married John Goodwin. Bill
      for division of slaves. Alleges: John Harvel -m- widow of
      Jacob Conch or Rontz?

HARVEY--Sarah Brown--of Richland Dist. to her gr-children: Misc. J-119
      Wm. Henry Harvey   )
      Sarah F. Harvey   ) Children of "my daughter" Mary A. Harvey and
      Charles E. Harvey   ) her husband, Wm. E. Harvey. $500.00 with
      Elizabeth B.   ) their father, Trustee. 22 Jan. 1835

HATFIELD, FRANCIS--Dau. of Andrew McElmurray--Will 1843

HAUGABOOK, JACOB--about 16 and Bernard, about 15--Infant or minor
      children of Jacob Haugabook, dec'd. 1812. At request of their
      mother, minors apply for aptment of Abraham Geyer (?) as Gdn.
      Bill for Part. between above minors and their mother and sisters.

HAUGABOOK, JACOB--Dec'd Richland Bills 150 Filed 13 Feb. 1819
      Widow: Susannah Haugabook
              Catherine, Jacob, and Barnard Haugabook
              Nancy -w- Jacob Baughman--see Baughman card.
      Lands in Lexington and Orangeburg. Bill for Partition.

HAUGABOOK, JACOB--from Joseph Pike and wife, Margaret. Deed dated 4 Oct. 1774. Richland Bills 150. See Pike card.

HAY, PETER--Of Craven--Will 28 June 1767 Richland File C. T. Wills
Wife: Elizabeth
"My son and daughters in law, the children of Gilbert Gibson"
To: Bartholomew Vawter
Ex: David Hay
Wit: Joel Threewits, Jemima Threewits, Richard Strother

HEARSMAN, JOSEPH--Dec'd. Est. Bds-Gr. to Henry Brown. Misc. Stray

HEATH, BETSEY--Of Dinwiddie Co. Va. Legacy from her brother, Ethel
Heath of Richland. P. A. to her friend, James Lewis of Dinwiddie Co. Va. to receive her part. 16 Jan. 1809. Prov. before Braddock Goodwyn of Dinwiddie Co. P. A. from James Jackson
in right of his wife, Drusilla--sister of Ethel Heath of Dinwiddie Co.

HEATH, ETHEL--Will July 19, 1796 Richland Prob. 14-327
Wife: Mary--formerly wife of John Thomas
God-son: Thomas Heath--Overseer on Gill's Creek Plantation
Sister: Bridget Jones
Legatees: Harris Heath
          Bridget Jones   (All appear bros. and sisters)
          Drusilla Jackson
          Elizabeth Heath (sister)

HEATH, HARRIS--Will 4 Dec. 1807 Richland Prob. 13-323
Wife: Nancy -m- 2nd. James Hay
Ch: Sarah Heath -w- James Hall
    Nancy, Judith, Ethel, and William Heath
Exor: Thomas Heath
Pet. shows that Harris Heath's Estate entitled to share of
estate of Ethel Heath, dec'd. To be paid 4 yrs after death of
Mary Heath

HEATH, JOHN--Of Richland--Will 10 Sept. 1798 Richland Prob.
Sister: Elizabeth Heath--100 lbs. sterling
Bro: William, Thomas, and James.
Thomas to have "my share" of crop on Mary Heath's Bluff Plt'n.

HEATH, MARY--Will 15 Aug. 1807. Prov. 8 Nov. 1807 Richland Box 13-324
Gr-son: John Thomas Heath--son of Thomas Heath
Gr-gr-son: Thomas
Gr-gr-dau: Mary Taylor Heath   (Mary owned Bluff Plt'n)
"   "   Rebecca Heath
"   " son: Ethel Heath
Gr-dau: Mary Heath
Exor: Joel Threewits, Thos. Heath, Sr. and his son John T. Heath.

HEATH, THOMAS--"The younger"--Will 18 Aug. 1828 Richland Prob. 14-376
Father: Thomas Heath--All
Box 46 Pkg. 01136
Thomas Heath Will--15 Aug. 1847   Gr-son: Thomas Heath Owens
    Son: Ethel Heath   Gr-dau: Mary Heath Owens -w-
    Dau: Eliza -w- Wm. Owens   Samuel H. Owens
    Son: John T. Heath   Dau: Rebecca Kirkland
    Gr-dau: Sally W. Nott

HEATH, WILLIAM -w- Mary Richard Tucker -w- Sarah -vs- Mary Taylor,
John Veal and wife, Rebecca; Henry Taylor; William Taylor;
Martha Taylor and William Taylor, Adm'r. John Taylor, dec'd.
Alleges: 19 Nov. 1805, Daniel Gurr conv. to John Taylor, land
in Richland Dist. 580 acres, orig. Gr. sd. Daniel Gurr. That
sd John Taylor was the father of complainants--Mary Heath and
Sarah Tucker--that he died intestate leaving widow, Mary and
children: Mary Heath, Sarah Tucker; Rebecca Veal; Henry Taylor;
William Taylor; and Martha Taylor--who are now tenants in common
of the 80 acres. Bill for partition.

HENDRICKS, LOUISA--Marriage agreement with Michael J. Rudolph. 1813
Richland Eq. Roll 166. Roll 9--Robert Hendricks widow, Mary
-m- Chastain C. Williamson. Dau. Louisa-a minor.

HENDRIX, JOHN--Dec'd.--Richland Eq Roll 68. 1816
Ch: William and Elizabeth Hendrix-iver 14- Pet. John Harris
be apt'd. Gdn.

HERRON, EDWARD M. AND ELIZA ANN--Minor children of Harriet -w- of
Benj. Hart. See Hart card. Richland Pet. 150

HERRON, GEORGE--Dec'd. Richland Eq. Filed 25 Sept, 1830
Widow -m- Chas. Beck. Samuel Herron, Dec'd. Partnership div.

HERRON, JOHN, et al. See Peter Delane card. Richland Bills 75

HICKS, JOHN--Richland Prob. 897. "He is Guardian for Henry and Lucy
Hicks, his brother and sister living in Mecklenburg.--had in
his possession in the month of Dec. last, a certain note of hand
drawn by Wm. R. Tucker, payable to him, the sd John Hicks in
trust and in behalf of his brother and sister, Henry and Lucy
Hicks who reside in Mecklenburgh County, State of Virginia. That
on the 2nd day of said month of December, Mr. Tucker paid him
sixty dollars on amount of said note, and which sum was duly
credited on the back of said note

HICKS, ROBERT--Of Greenville, County, Va. Richland Wills C-199 1796
Dau: Mary--"Dau. of my 1st wife, Angeline Hicks, Dec'd. Mary
is wife of John Watson of Fairfield.
Martha Greenway Hicks
Wife: Mary--now pregnant

HICK, ROBERT--Late of Va. Dec'd. Richland Eq. Bills 171 1820
Dau: Polly, widow Chambless. Polly -m- John Watson, only
bro. of Hephzekiah Watson. See card. Mary (or Polly) -w-
of Peter Chambliss. Married in Aug. 1793 in Va. to John
Watson. Richland Bills 171 1827

HILEY, JACOB--Richland Co. Bx. 14-343. Adm: Fred K. Spigner and
Mary Magdalana Hiley. Adm. Bond: Fred K. Spigner; Mary M.
Hiley. 5 Oct. 1799 John Patridge and Henry Brown Appr's. apt'd.
19 May, 1800. Conrad Myers, Wm. Goodwyn, Wm. Hopkins.

HINTON, MICAJAH -vs- Edward Croft, Esq. Bill for debt--secured by
    Bond, Note, Slaves, etc. File contains testimony by William
    Hinton. Richland Bills 140 Filed 11 May 1818

HIRON, JOHN--Dec'd. Richland Misc. D-433
    Widow: Ann--otherwise Ann Delane -m- set. Lemuel Cary 30 July 1807
    She had 350 acres on Cedar Creek. Former res. of sd John Hirons
    -Richland Co. Extra Bills 142 John Hirons -w- Ann -m- 2nd Freeman
    Delane. Philip Patricge Hirons and John William Hirons, sons of
    John Hirons--dec'd. without issue. Shows: Freeman Delane came
    from Baltimore to Charleston and stated he had a wife and child
    in Charleston, and later said she and the child, a son, had re-
    turned to Baltimore. Ann filed answer as Ann Carey.

HOGAN,WILLIAM, SEN'R. and Lewis Hogan with George Croft appr. Est. of
    Mason Wood. Abigail Wood, Adm'x. 20 April 1822 Richland Bk-Pg129

HOLDER, JESSE--Not 5 yrs age. Pet'r. Alleges his father, Jesse
    Holder died in Service of U. S. in Jan. 1814 and Pet'r is only
    legitimate child. Entitled to Bounty land or commutation money.
    Prays apt. Gdn. Richland Eq. Roll 132 1819

HOLMAN, JOHN -m- Sally, dau. of Andrew Dominy. Richland Bills 176
                                                                1820
HOLMAN, SALLY--Widow of John Holman, and John Royser -w- Margaret,
    Susannah Dominy and Andrew Hohe -w- Catherine--all out of state
    and Sally did live in Georgia. Faa'd. by Daniel Smith 1 Jan. 1820
    Richland Extra Bills 176

HOLMES, FINLEY--Died 4 Junt 1815. Richland Eq. Roll 67 1815
    Ch: Catherine   16 yrs   Robert   10 Yrs.
         Finley   14 "   William   5 "
    James Holmes refuses Guardianship--and Gen. Jacob J. Faust,
    Daniel Faust, Sr.; and Dr. Samuel Green were sppointed.
    -Richland Probate 16-383 1814/15 Finley Holmes--
         Widow: Jane
         5 heirs: William Holmes
                   Finley Holmes
                   Robert Holmes
                   James Holmes
                   David Bryan
    -Finley W. Holmes--See card of Sarah Clark and Thos Clark, minors

HOOD, JOHN--See card Mary McAdams Richland Eq. Bills 33

HOOKER, J--This file contains a letter from J. Hooker to Mr. Guignard
    written from Yorkville, 9 March 1811--Appears Hooker's hand-
    writing. Also appears John Hooker-a lawyer. Extra Bills 105
    -Richland Bills 14 Filed 27 Feb. 1812 John Hooker -w- Mary
    Ann Hooker -vs- Gersham Chapman and Paul H. Perrault--Claude
    Simon of Columbia, late, of Beaufort, bequeathed that house and
    lot to Marianne, dau. of Gersham Chapman.

HOPKINS, EMMA T.--Of Richland to David T. Hopkins 30 May 1833--slaves
    Misc. H-463

HOPKINS, JAMES -w- Keziah--formerly relict of James Goodwyn of
Richland Co. See card Jesse Goodwyn-1813. Laurens Eq. No. 1

HOPKINS, JOHN--Of Craven Richland People. C. T. Wills, Richland file.
    Wife: Sarah--Ensient   Dau: Mary Hopkins
    Son: David Hopkins   Sarah   "
          John   "   Son: James   "
          William "   To: Anna and Mary Strother
    Will dated 29 Oct. 1771. Will Bk. 1774-79

HOPKINS, JOHN and Keziah Goodwyn--See card John Burney -vs- Est.
Wm. Goodwyn. Richland Bills 148 1818

HOPKINS, JOHN and Joel Adams and Clairborne Clifton--Exor. Will of
Joel McLemore. See card Joel Adams. Richland Eq. Stray 1802

HORRY, PETER--Dec'd. Widow: Margaret Richland Eq. Bills 121 1816
Exor: Elias Horry, Wm. A. Trapier, James S. Guignard.
Peter and Margaret Horry -m- in 1793

HORTON, REUBEN -w- Sarah--See card Royal Bullard, Pet'r. Roll 123
                                             1819

HOUSE, JESSE--Son-in-law of Sarah Weston. See Weston card. Roll 134
                                           1819

HOUSE, JOHN--Mem 10-143 and 271. 92 Acres N-s Wateree River. Bd.
N. W. Chas. Russells, N. E. Wateree, S. W. Beach Creek. Cert.
24 Nov. 1769. Gr. 2 May 1770 Isham Moore, D. S.
100 Acres S-s Wateree in Wateree fork--all vac. Cert. 6 Feb.
1770. Gr. 12 Oct. 1770

HOUSE, MILLY--Dau. of Thos House--Legatee of Gabriel Parker. Bills 66

HOUSE, REUBEN--Dec'd. Richland Roll 74 1817
Ch: Mary Linna and Esther House--minors. Pet. apt. Jesse House
as Gdn. 1817. Relationship not shown.
-Richland Roll 84 1817 Reuben House -w- Mary.
Ch: Elizabeth Ann -m- Robert Ogilvie
    John, Jesse, Mary, Herter, and Reuben, Jr.
See card Robert Ogilvie

HOUSEAL, WM. F. -m- Mary Elizabeth Setzler. Richland Roll 114 1818

HOWE, MARY -w- Samuel Richland Eq. Bills 12
Joseph, David, Robert, Sarah
Sarah -w- David Howe, and son John
See card David Ellison Dunlap. Heirs. Will 9 Sept. 1804

HOWELL, ADAM--Buried 12 Nov. 1766--Reg. St. Phillip's Par. Pg. 315

HOWELL, ANN--Gr. on Wingaw River. Son, William conv. to Robert Jones,
His (or her) brother--then of Philadelphia, a yeoman. Sd deed
6 Sept 1718. Wit: Thos. Williams and James Howell. Mem. 27

HOWELL, ARTHUR--Of Craven County Charleston Wills 1752-56 Pg. 87
    Wife: Sarah--Home Place
    Son: John--150 Acres in neck between Santee and Wateree. Gr.
      to me.
      Matthew--200 Acres on Santee
      William--20 Acres Low ground N-s Congaree. Gr. Hans Bothers
    Exor: William Howell, Martha Howell, and Wm. Hay
    Proven: 9 March 1753
    Wit: John Hamilton, Wm. Hart, John Lester
    -Stub Cont. (Salley) Pg. 236 Arthur Howell
        Entry 139 - 222 days militia duty 1781/82
               32 - For provisions and supplies LN 254 Continentals
                                                        1783

HOWELL, ARTHUR--Richland Wills Bk. B-235
    Son: John
    Wife:
    "All my children"
    Bro: William and Martha Howell with Jose Daniel apt. Exor's.
    Date: 22 March 1792 Wit: Robert Howell, John Howell, Wm. Moyer
    -Richland Prob. Bk. D-72 Arthur Howell. Cit: 16 Dec. 1801
        Mary Howell applied for letters
    Apprs: John Hopkins, John Hamilton, Robert Howell. 20 Feb. 1802

HOWELL, ARTHUR--Dec'd. Richland Prob. Bx 6-139
    Widow: Margaret Howell-Adm'x.
    Dau: _____ -w- Isaac Roy (or Ross)(Ross seems correct)
    Cit: 11 Oct. 1806 Margaret Howell said it was intended for
    Mary Howell. Seems to have been Mary Collins, Wm. Collins dau.

HOWELL, ARTHUR--Misc. Rec. J-556 Arthur Howell recites: Wheras
    Arthur Howell, on 1st April, 1834--purchased negro--Jane.
    Heirs: M..R. Howell, M. H. Tyson, J. A. Oliver, Samuel Oliver.
    To: Mary Ann Prescott--a slave.
    -Richland Prob. Bk. K-126 and 342 Inventory 13 July 1836

HOWELL, CALEB--Rev. Rec. AA7773 Shows: Hudsons Ferry on Sav. River.
    Shows: He with Daniel Howell, and James Smart signed cert. appr.
    of Rice _____. Capt. John Garvin's Co. of Granville Co. dated
    29 March 1779. Names James Hudson, John Looper, Butt'n Williams
    Wm. Stafford, J. P.

HOWELL, CATHERINE--Wit. Will of Sedgewick Lewis of St. James, Goose
    Creek. Sarah Simons dau. S. Lewis. Wills 1774-79 Pg-218

HOWELL, CELIA--Gdn. minors. Anderson County Roll 838 1827

HOWELL, DANIEL--Will proven in open Court 2 June 1797. Union Ct.
    Min. 1797 Union Co.

HOWELL, DANIEL G. and Jane Eliza Howell (formerly Jane Eliza Lyall,
    dau. David Lyall, Dec'd. of South Carolina). of Hamilton Co.
    State of Ohio. Apt. Alice Orr -w- Arthur Orr to collect Jane's
    share of the Lyall property in South Carolina. 21 Sept. 1819
    Misc. 4R-357.

HOWELL, ELIZABETH--Buried at private burial ground 22 June 1774.
    St. Phillip's Par. Reg.

HOWELL, ELIZABETH -vs- Stephen Richardson 3 Feb. 1796 Salisbury, N. C.

HOWELL, ELLIOTT -w- Matilda--Court of Ordinary--Sale of R. E. of Benj. Shavey, Dec'd. Camden Journal 21 Dec. 1842

HOWELL, ELLIS--To John A. Reedy in Trust for Elizabeth McDaniel, wife of Samuel McDaniel as set forth in Will Capt. John Reedy. Dec'd. Dower--Ann Howell. York Deed 1 Nov. 1851 P-413

HOWELL, FRANCIS--S. C. Hist. & Gen. May 25-151 List Pay Roll Capt. Wm. Caldwell's Co. for Aug., Sept., and Oct., 1779. 3rd Reg't. Continental Line.

HOWELL, FRED--Gen'l Indents--Sale of lands. 80 Acres. 18 May 1789

HOWELL, GEORGE -vs- George Jubb, et al. Charleston Bills 1792-23

HOWELL, GILLILAND--Suit over money--Camden Equity 2093 Pg. 84 1856

HOWELL, MRS. GRACE--Widow of Thomas Howell -m- Agreement with Capt. Charles Russell. 11 May 1762 C. T. Prob. Misc. 1758-63 Pg. 490 -Richland Bills 148 1818--Grace Howell--see card John Burney -Richland Book K-90 Grace Howell 19 Dec. 1835
  Nephew: Arthur H. Reese
  Sister: Sarah Reese, Mary Reese, and Elizabeth Reese
  Niece: Sarah Howell, widow of John R. Howell
  Dec'd. Bro: John Howell
  Sister: Martha Howell
  Legacy: "Old Mrs. Mary Higgins
  Ex: Col. Wade Hampton, B. F. Taylor, Dr. John Fisher, and Arthur H. Reese. Prov: 27 Jan. 1836
  Wit: Jas. L. Clark, M. M. R. Howell and E. Brenin

HOWELL, MISS GRACE--Richland Will Bk. L-569
  Bro: Jesse Malachi Howell--All 12 Aug. 1857
-Page 117--Harriett Howell
  Bro: William Howell
  Sister: Mrs. Epps G. Trezevant
  Sister: Jesse M. Howell
    Grace Howell
  Mother: Mrs. Martha Howell June 1850

HOWELL, HARDY AND JOSEPH--Listed 1st Council Safety-Capt. Andrew Cummings Co. Vol. Militia. S. C. Hist. and Gen. Mag. V-3 127

HOWELL, HARRIETT--Will Richland Co. Bx 45-1125 Date: 18 June 1850
  Bro: William
  Mother: Mrs. Martha Howell
  Sisters: Mrs. Epps, Mrs. Trezevant, Jesse M. Howell (a girl) and Grace Howell
  Bro: Jesse Malachi Howell

HOWELL, HOPKINS--"Of Craven" to Gracie Howell, Widow. Mar. 26, 1760 Charleston Bk. 1758-1763-pg. 260

HOWELL, JAMES--Seaman Buried 5 Sept. 1750 St. Phillip's Par. Reg.
                                                          Pg. 216
HOWELL, JAMES -w- Elizabeth - Parents of:
     James--born 13 Oct. 1736 Bap. 9 Feb. 1736 Pg. 124
     John--born 14 Feb. 1739 Bap. 2 April 1739 Pg. 81 and 128
     Thomas--born 11 Aug. 1742 Bap. 8 April 1743 Pg. 85 and 133
     Buried Elizabeth Howell--Private Burial Place 22 June 1746 Pg. 203
     Information from St. Phillip's Par. Reg. Pg. 76

HOWELL, JAMES and Elizabeth--Son, John born 14 Feb. 1739. Son,
     Thomas born 11 Aug. 1742

HOWELL, JAMES--To Henry Middleton Bond and Mtg. 24 Dec. 1748 Slave-
     Bellah. Pg. 249--To Judith West, negro woman Scipio. 1 Dec.
     1746. Pg. 293: Joseph Wragg of St. Phillip's Parish, as Att'y.
     for Mrs. Sophia Hume, widow, now residing in London to Capt.
     James Howell of sd Parish, Negro woman Scipio. 2 Sept. 1746.

HOWELL, JEREMIAH--Of St. Phillip's Parish, to Thomas Baldrick of St.
     James-Goose Creek-Parish--Negro man, Emanuel in trust for Wm.
     Alexander Arthur, a minor, and to allow Dorcas Perry -w- Philip
     Perry, mother sd minor, to have use--Should Wm. Alex'r Arthur
     die, to Allen Dorman Perry--half brother Wm. Alex'r Perry.
     7 Jan. 1811--Wit: Alexander F. White. Prov. Charleston Dist.
     -S. C. Rep. (Mill) Vol 1 1814. Jeremiah Howell -vs- Wm. D.
     Hunt and Jno. Roche before Justice Colcock at Charleston May
     Term 1814. Bail in case of Thos. G. Wait.
     -Chester Deed Bk II-294--Jeremiah Howell of Chester Dist. from
     William Aiken of Charleston--$1200--33½ Acres W-s Catawba River
     on Fishing Creek, formerly property of James Wood, Dec'd. Bd.
     Samuel Stinson; A. I. Green; H. A. Darri; Henry Culp; et al.
     9 Dec. 1830 Wit: James F. Woods, Matthew Williams
     -Chester Bx. 81-1273--Jeremiah Howell Will Prov. 4 Oct. 1841
     Heirs: "The 3 children of John G. Howell-Nephew"
              William Christie
              Zachariah Jordon
              Mary Ann.
     Mentioned land Wm. and Agnes Wood now live on.
     -Chester-1840-Pg. 68--Jeremiah Howell Est. H. A. Davie, Ex.
     -Mrs. Wallace's card data:--Jeremiah and John Howell-Mary Christie,
     Jan. 1839-1810 (?), buried in old graveyard two miles from
     Lenedrs Ferry, six miles south of Land's Ford, near crossing of
     Chester and Lancaster R. R. John Howell 1845-1800, buried in
     Columbia, S. C. Zachariah Jordon Howell, living 1908, said he
     had seen grave of Mary Christie many times.

HOWELL, JESSE M.--Pet'r. Shows Petitioner is father of 2 children--
     a son and a daughter--the eldest about 6 yrs. of age, and the
     youngest about 4 yrs. who own estate independent of their father.
     Prays his apt. as Gdn. 28 Feb. 1815 Richland Roll 35
     -Richland Co. Bx. 74-1833--Jesse M. Howell, father of James
     Malachi and Martha Sarah Howell-minors. Appointed Gdn. 28 Feb.
     1815. James Goodwyn surety on Gdn. Bond. Bx. 75-1861 shows
     James Malachi died while a minor-leaving his father, one whole
     sister, and 2 sisters and 1 brother of half blood. 1 Jan. 1827

HOWELL, JESSE M.--Richland Roll 175 11 Jan. 1820--Suit by Comm. for
payment of property sold to Jesse M. Howell.
-Misc. Record I-106--Jesse M. Howell-"Love and affection to my
sons William Howell and Malachi Howell-Jewelry, silver plate, etc.
-Richland Eq. 1835--Jesse M. Howell -m- Martha Taylor, dau   1834
James Taylor, the elder.
-Richland Prob. Bk. K-33 Will (Very long)--Jesse Malachi Howell
      Wife:
      Dau: Mary Howell Epps
           Mrs. Martha Means
      Son: Goodwyn Howell
           Jesse Malachi Howell
      Dau: Grace Howell
           Harriett Howell
           Lucy Howell
           And unborn, if any. 1 May 1834. Prov: 27 Feb. 1835
-Misc. J-197--Jesse M. Howell--Deed of gift to "my beloved
friends and relatives, Sarah H. Howell and her two sons, Joseph
R. Howell and John R. Howell-(should all above die, to his rel-
atives-Reeses) 6 Feb. 1835 Wit: Peter Gaffney, Grace Howell
Catherine M. Robertson.
-S. C. Hist. and Gen. Mag. V-3--Jesse Howell -w- Martha, parents
of Epps Goodwyn Howell, born 1819, daughter. Married Daniel H.
Trezevant, 1841

HOWELL, JNO.--Lieut. of Bahama--Memorial in re distress of sd Garrison.
11 July 1721. Council Journal 1-135
-Stubs Ent. (Salley) Pg. 120--John Howell, Ent. 3213 for duty in
Roebuck's Regt.
-St. Phillip's Par. Reg. 99--John Howell -w- Elizabeth--Son
born 11 June 1753. Bapt. 20 June, Rev. M. A. G.
Page 195--On 29 July 1751, were -m- John Howell and Elizabeth
Phillips. License by M. A. Garden, Rector
-Charleston Will Book 1757-60 Pg. 307--John Howell (or Thomas)
      Wife: Gracey--Home Place
      "my 5 ch.": Thomas
              William--Where I now live on the lake.
              Robert
              Malachi--adj. where I now live
              Gracey (dau.)--On the Savannah near Gills Cr.
    Ex: Wife and Son, William
    Wit: John Hamilton, Ann Bourget and Wm. York.
    Dated: 13 March 1760-   Prov: 9 Aug. 1760
-Reg. St. Phillip's Par. (Smith and Salley) Pg. 9--John Howell
and wife, Martha--parents of John, born 15 Sept. 1763. Pg. 153
shows John Howell -m- Martha Edwards, widow, 17 Jan. 1759
-Provincial Bk. 1774-1779 Pg. 620 and 804--John Howell, of Craven.
      Wife: Patience   8 April 1777
      Bros: Arthur Howell, Matthew Howell, and Wm. Howell
      (Shows: Family-John, Matthew, William, and Arthur)
      Wit: Richard Bell, Wm. Smith, James Proctor
      Widow Brackwell's son, John Brackwell
-Old Index Misc. S. S.-282--John Howell-infant-Wm. Axson, Jr.
Apt. Gdn. 13 Nov. 1778.
Pg. 272--Sarah Howell and Wm. Starke, Gdn. 16 Oct. 1778

HOWELL, JOHN, Capt.--133 days duty as a horseman in Capt. Moses
Woods Company. Col. Roebuck's Reg't. from 15 July 1780 (no
memtion to when)..Wm. Axson, Adm'r. in 1778. Rev. Act.
-1796 Camden A-208--John Joseph Howell to Joseph Payne (shows
Joshua Joseph) slave, Toby, about 16 yrs age. 14 Feb. 1796
-Bill Sale Misc. 3L-332--John Howell -w- Catherine of Savannah,
Georgia to Daniel Mazyck, of S. C., Capt. in the late 3rd. Reg't.
of S. C. Slave for $500.00, named Abraham, 20 Nov. 1798
-Richland Bills Bx. 16-Greensboro Record--John Howell, Jr. Gdn.
for Mary and Sarah Howell 1810 return; Cash pd for 2 yds lace in
Greensboro, $1.50. In re Est. Wm. Howell-widow, Mary -m- Hendricks
and Williamson
-Roll 61 Filed 13 Jan. 1813--John R. Howell (could not locate name
in file-might be John Rives Howell) and Claiborne Clifton, Pet.
as Gdn. for Jane Ann Campbell. Shows: Samuel Wise made Will
18th Sept. 1779, and died same year. His dau., Jane Ann Wise,
-m- Samuel Campbell. Mentions his 1st wife, Betsy Wise-pro-
ceeds of sale of her clothes to go to Jane Ann, with all land
in Parish of St. David's. John James Haig was Exor. Alleges:
Jane Ann was infant at time of death of her father, Samuel Wise.
Jane Ann Wise -m- Campbell and she died 1810. Lt. Adm. Gr. Pet'r.
Ans. of Joel Adams Alleges: Small tract, about 25 acres, of the
land of sd Maj. Wise which was occupied by his brother, Jonathan
Wise, who was very poor and who was brought over from England
by the said Maj. Wise. Which, after death of Jonathan was planted
by sd Ball and wife and a small part by Rives J. Howell for one
year. (Also written Howell J. Rives)

HOWELL, JOHN, SENR. Richland Bx. 15 Pk. 367 Cit: 9 Dec. 1814
Robert Weston, Jr. Adm'r. and Wm. R. Howell. Papers show-Lived
on Corbin Br. Congaree River.
Wife: Mary
Dau: Gracey Arrington Howell
Son: John--Died 1825
Inventory: 14 Jan. 1815 Appr's: J. Howell, Thos. Howell
Green Rives and Richard Smith

HOWELL, JOHN--Late of State of Georgia--owned slaves in Ga. Robert
Watson -w- Mary, Joseph Whetstone -w- Sarah, Thomas Buldrick -w-
Elizabeth, Joseph Howell and Robert Howell, Pet'rs.--Ask permiss-
ion to bring slaves to S. C. Richland Roll 115 23 Feb. 1818

HOWELL, JOHN R.--Of Richland Dist. to John Howell $5,090.00--Mtg.
slaves, Frank, John and Henry. 8 March 1822. Wit: B. R. Waring
John D. Brown. Misc. Rec. Archives D-381

HOWELL, JOHN and Abraham D. Jones--Exor's: Will William F. Goodwyn
Alleges: Wm. F. Goodwyn, died in Oct. 1820, left widow, Martha
and an only child, Polly Tucker Goodwyn. Dr. Robert Goodwyn, Gdn.
Appr's Est. in Orangeburg Dist. Alleges that dec'd, Wm. F.
Goodwyn, was entitled to 1/3 bluff land of Mrs. Lucy D. Howell.
Bill of Part. filed. The widow Martha -m- Wm. P. Corbin.

HOWELL, JOHN--"Of Richland Dist" 28 Nov. 1825 at Cabbin Branch 2
inventories, one for Richland and one for Fairfield. Show very
large estate. A 3rd inventory shows him joint owner with Mary
and Gracey Howell, property being in Richland. Mary was his
mother and Gracey his sister. All living in same house at Mill
Creek

HOWELL, JOHN--Dec'd Oct. 1825 Richland Eq. Roll 284 1827
    Eliza D. Howell and Eliza Howell Blake -w- John Haig Blake--
    Suit over property. (Eliza H. Blake formerly Goodwyn)
    Left: Mary Howell, his mother
           Grace Howell
           Mary Reese -w- John A. Reese
           Elizabeth -w- Timothy Reese
           Sally Reese
           Martha Howell -w- Jesse M. Howell.

HOWELL, JOHN--Of Lincoln. Lincolnton Will N. C. Record 30 Mar. 1828
    Wife: Mary
           James (son Billy)
           William   )Land N-end Cheny Place
           Joshua   )
           John
           Elizabeth
           Polly
           Thomas and children, Billy and Hetty

HOWELL, JOHN--died intestate in 1825 Richland Eq. 371 1836
    No wife or child
    Kin: Mrs. Sarah Reese (sister)
          Elizabeth -w- Timothy Reese (sister)
          Mary -w- John A. Reese (sister)
          Grace Howell and another sister Martha -w- Jesse M. Howell

HOWELL, JOHN J.--Chester Drawer 99 Est. 1856 Adm: Reuben Crawford
    1 Jan. 1856. J. L. Howell and R. Crawford-Gdns.

HOWELL, JOSEPH--Of Craven Co, N. C. Halifax, N. C. 3-195
    To: John Fenny of Brunswick Co. 26 Feb. 1747
    20 pounds. 150 Acres Co. of Johnston, both sides of Tyces R.
    ½ 300 acre. 27 Feb. 1747. Wit: Wm. Whitehead, Nath'l Cooper

HOWELL, JOSEPH--Stub Ent. (Salley) Pg. 75.
    Ent. No. 2881 for duty in Brandon's Reg't.
    Ent. No. 3557 for duty in Roebuck's Reg't.

HOWELL, JOSEPH and Malla.--a debtor to estate of Swanson Lunsford
    Richland C-267 1798

HOWELL, JOSEPH, SR.--Of S. C. to Mary Patrick--Slave 28 May, 1803
    Archives Misc. 4-H 135

HOWELL, JOSEPH to James Plaxco--100 A. on Broad River. Bd. Thompson
    Dower: Lucy Howell 20 Mar. 1806 York Deed G-87

HOWELL, JOSEPH--"Aged about 27" Late of Chester, of England, a mer-
    chant. Made application to be made citizen of U. S. Declared
    enrolled a citizen by Thos. Hall, Federal Clerk, Register of
    S. C. Dist. 18 May, 1807. Ct. at Charleston

HOWELL, JOSEPH HALSEY -w- Ann to John Adamson--All of Kershaw Dist.
347 Acres below Chesnut Ferry, Wateree River. Ann was widow
of Wm. Bond. Kershaw Deed F-10 1808
-Book F-83 1809--Joseph H. Howell to Israel Scranton-Lot in Camden
-Book F-141--Joseph H. Howell to Henry H. Dickinson-several tracts.
-Kershaw Deed E-490 1808--Joseph H. Howell from Drury Jones Camp-
bell 200 Acres on Daniel's Branch of Granny's Quarter. Conv.
to grantor by Nathan Campbell in 1805. Dower by Mary Ann Campbell
-Camden F-83 1809--Joseph H. Howell of Kershaw Dist. to Israel
Scranton-Lots in Camden on King Street
-Camden F-503--Joseph H. Howell -w- Ann to Mary and Bond English
(also shows Margaret)--All claim of Ann in Estate of Joshua
English, dec'd. 3rd April 1812
-Camden G-168 1814--Joseph H. Howell from Henry Hinson Dickinson
Land surveyed for John Cha (?) 2 Jan. 1787 Gr. to Daniel Brown
1 Dec. 1788 in Kershaw Dist. on Daniel's Branch E-s Wateree R.
on Br. Granny's Quarter Cr.
-Camden Deed G-130/1 1814--Joseph H. Howell to James S. Smith
Lots in Camden. Dower by Ann   Smyth
-Archives Misc. 2D-270--Joseph Howell--living in 1857. Dau.
Mary Eliza -m- Thos. Dickson. Set. 8 Dec. 1857. Mary Eliza
is gr-dau. of Moses Simmons of N. C.
-Camden Deeds G-339/40/41/42--Joseph H. Howell of Kershaw Dist.
to John Nelson Lenoir, land on Granny's Quarter Creek, Daniel
Br. Kershaw Dist. Dower by Ann

HOWELL, JOSEPH T.--Dec'd. Richland Eq. Roll 1104 1859
Robert H. and Michael Christopher H.--minors, alleges: 12
March 1835, Jesse Reese for $1.00 and good will conv. to Joseph
Howell,Charles--died 9 Aug. 1848-2 ch. Olin and Chas.
              Elizabeth-now -w- John J. Chaplin
              Robert-Orator
              Sarah--now -w- Robert M. McCollum
              Jesse Malachi, Michael Christopher, Catherine Postell H.
              Daniel Reese H. Children of Joseph T. born since 12 Mar.
              1835. Mary Howell, widow, mother of all.

HOWELL, JOSEPH--J. M. Smarr, Adm-   Letters: 2 July 1864
Order for sale of property at late residence of Williamson
Howell. Dec'd 6 Aug. 1864.

HOWELL, JOSEPH--York Will Bk. 56 Pg. 261 8 Nov. 1865
Wife: Sarah Ann, Ex.   Prov. 24 Nov. 1865
"my 3 young children; Jane, John and George
Attached to orig. Will: 3 receipts, each showing "Rec'd of
Jos. H" for estate of Moses Simmons, 1858, 1859, 1860. All
said Mary E. Dickson and a fourth said M. E. Howell. Jos.
Howell was her administrator.

HOWELL, JOSIAH--Of Edgefield to wife, Martha Golphin Howell--Deed
Trust to Property which she owned, when married. Wit: Catherine
Green, and John J. Gray. Hist. Com. Misc. Rec. F-435 30 Jan. 1829

HOWELL, LOUISA E. AND WILLIAM H.--Pet'rs. minors 17 yrs. and 14 yrs.
    by friend John K. Witherspoon. Shows: Their father, William
    Howell died in Liberty County, Ga.--leaving estate worth some
    $1500.00 subject of distribution between Pet'rs. and a sister
    of a former marriage, Julia Clarke. Pet'rs. mother predeceased
    their father and 3 named are the only children of Wm. Howell.
    Pet'rs. are living here in Camden with their grandmother and
    Aunt. Pray apt. of Gdn. and John K. Witherspoon apt'd. 5 June
    Camden Equity 2744   1863

HOWELL, LUCY--Of Dist. of Richland Richland Prob. Bk. G-220 Will
    Son: Malachi Howell   Date: 30 Nov. 1831 Prov: Feb. 1822
    Dau: Grace Baker (in trust)
    Gr-dau: Lucy Stanton -w- Joseph B. Stanton)Share to which their
            Elizabeth Ware -w- Thompson Ware)mother was entitled.
    Gr-Niece: Rebecca May
    Codicil shows son, Malachi died without issue.
    Wit: James Goodwyn, Wm. F. Goodwyn, Abraham D. Jones
    Wit. to Codicil: Thos Long, Thos. Taylor, W. J. Taylor
    -York Probate Case 78-1164 1844 Lucy Howell--Williamson Howell
    Adm'r. Sale 23 April, 1844. Pur. Susan Howell and Williamson
    Howell, John Howell, and Isam Howell. Pet. shows 10 heirs-one
    died. Small per. est. only.

HOWELL, MALACHY--Salley's History Orangeburg. Pg 159 and 204
    Baptized--son of Thos. and Race Howell, born 20 May, 1755
    Howell, Wm. died 4 Feb. 1757--"A settler for many years on
    Santee or Congaree. Craven Co.
    -Archives Men 12-168--Malachi Howell--300 Acres Craven Co. St.
    Mark's Par. on Cedar Creek 6 miles from Russell's Ferry on
    Congaree River. Bd. N. W. land laid out. S. and W. by Jesse
    Goodwyn and Frances Goodwyn. Gr. 17 Dec. 1772
    -Stub Ent. (Salley) YZ-177
        Howell, Malachi
          "   , Martha Epps (or Epsey. Index shows Epps, Entry shows
                              Epsey)
        Ent. 1227--to Wade Hampton, Adm'r. Est. Malachi Howell,
        dec'd. for provisions he supplied the Light Dragoons and
        for a horse.
        Ent. 1226--To Wade Hampton, Adm'r. Est. Epsey Howell, Prov.
        and supplies-the southern army
    -Camden Prob. Apt. 33 Pk. 1186--Malachi Howell-Cit: 5 April 1782
        Widow: Martha Epps Howell
        Bond surety: Thomas Howell
        Wit: Rachel Hamilton
        "At High Hills of Santee, sale of slaves; 7 Jan. 1783--by
        Wade Hampton "in right of Martha Epps, his wife".
        Wade Hampton bought entire estate.

HOWELL, MALACHI and Thomas Howell --Bills 87 1811 -vs-
    James C. Beal -w- Elizabeth, Thompson Ware -w- Elizabeth, Joseph
    Stanton -w- Lucy Shows: Thomas Howell, the elder, Bro. of your
    orator, Malachi Howell and father of your orator, Thomas Howell
    owned several tracts which Thomas Howell, the elder, claimed by
    descent from his father, William Howell. Wm. died leaving widow,
    Elizabeth who -m- James Beal.

HOWELL, MALACHI--Of Richland to Thomas J. Howell for love and affection towards my beloved wife, Eliza D. Howell and my adopted
dau., Eliza Howell Goodwy, Slaves. 14 Oct. 1816 Misc. C-314
-Richland Prob. Bk. G-209 Will--Malachi Howell of Richland
     Wife: Eliza D.
     Adopted dau: Eliza Howell Goodwyn
     "my nieces and nephews, the ch. of Lucy Stanton and Eliz-
     abeth Ware.
     Ex: Wife, Adopted dau., Thos. Heath, John Howell, John
         J. Chappell 20 Nov. 1821
     Wit: Bryan Gunter, Richard M. Todd, Wm. L. Patridge

HOWELL, MARGARET--Of Richland Dist. Richland Prob. Will Bk. E-341
     Dau: Polly Oliver   )
     Sons: Mathew, Arthur and Thomas)All children she had.
     Dau: Margaret Tyson   )
     16 Jan. 1816   Proven: 30 Jan. 1816
     Wit: Grace Baker, Gilbert May

HOWELL, MARTHA--Stub Indents (Salley) Pg. 69
     Ent. 475--for fodder and corn supplied the Continentals in 1781
     Ent. 508--524 Bu. Corn for Cont. use in 1781
    -S. C. Hist. and Gen. Mag. V-7 208--Martha Sarah Howell -m-
    Wm. Burney Means 24 May, 1831

HOWELL, MARTHA Richland Bk. L-145
     Son: Jesse Malachi--Home place called Ridgeway on the Camden Rd.
         William
     Dau: Jesse
         Grace 15 Sept. 1851   Proven: 15 Oct. 1851

HOWELL, MARY--Dau. of Matthew and Margaret Howell -m- Samuel Oliver
     prior to 1813. All of Richland Co. Agreement as to property
     of estate of Matthew Howell, Margaret Howell, widow Misc. C-55

HOWELL, MARY ANN--Wife of Rev. Joseph Howell, died 6 Ult. in Barn-
     well Dist. Left husband, 4 small children, 3 step-children.
     19 May 1821 Carolina Gazette

HOWELL, MARY--Widow of Robert Howell of Richland Dist. Will
     Son: Wm. Robert Howell
         John Howell, Jr. Dec'd
     Dau: Mary Weston
     Gr- dau: Sarah Howell McCord
     Dau: Sarah White
     Gr-son: Thomas Richard Baldrick, son of Elizabeth and Thomas
         Robert Howell Baldrick.
     Nov. 1820   Proven: 22 Mar. 1829
     Dec'd son John had property in Ga.

HOWELL, MARY -w- Samuel Howell to Miles Howell. Mary dau. of Robert
     _____? Union Dist. Misc. P-241 1845

HOWELL, MARY C.--Pet. of Jeremiah Howell Apt. R Est. dated 1 Dec. 1854
     Shows: Mary C. Neely owned 113 A. on Tailore Cr. Bd. John Neely,
     dec'd, A. Shiles, Jno. McCullough and S. W. Moore. That she -m-
     1st____Neely by whom she had Alex'r A. and Hyder A. D. Neely,
     minors--she then married Jeremiah Howell, Pet'r, who prays divis-
     ion.

HOWELL, MARY ELIZA -m- agreement with Thomas Dickson both of York
Dist. S. C.--Dau. of Joseph Howell. She owns inheritance from
Est. of Moses Simmons, formerly of N. C. and sd Joseph Howell
is her Gdn. 8 Dec. 1857 Archives Misc. A A-270

HOWELL, MATTHEW--Rev. Record 3813 "For service rendered at the Congaree
as saddler, and for service at Orangeburg under command of Capt.
James Shaffer, Private on horse. Affidavit-Camden Dist. before
Wm. Meyer. Receipted for by Frederick Meyer 22 June 1785
-Stub Ent (Salley) Pg-204
Ent. #628 for 43 days as Saddler and 31 days duty in 1781/82

HOWELL, MATTHEW -w- Margaret Will Richland Bx. 15-374 1803
Ch: Mary Ann -w- Samuel Oliver
               -w- Isaac Roy
     Peggy Howell-(Margaret Tyson -w- of_____)

     Matthew R. Howell
     Arthur and Thomas.
     Mentions 500 pounds received from the Daniel Estate.
Bk. H-475--Will of Mary Ann Oliver
     Ch: Matthew H. a nd Samuel W.
     Bro: Matthew R. Howell

HOWELL, MATTHEW--Richland Roll 83 Feb. 1818. Pet'n. shows that he,
together with Arthur and Thomas Howell, his 2 brothers, by Will
of Martha Howell, their Dec'd mother, entitled to 116 Acres in
sd Dist. (Richland). Pray for order of sale.
-Richland Probate Bk. C-81--Matthew Howell. Adm'x: Margaret H.
Surety: Alexander McDaniel and Thomas Heath
Bond: 22 Feb. 1802
-Archives Misc. C-55 Richland--Matthew Howell-Dec'd of Richland
Widow and Adm'x: Margaret Howell
Dau: Mary -m- Samuel Oliver-Agreement 22 April 1813

HOWELL, MATTHEW R.--Richland Will Bx. 46-1132 1852
     Wife: Mary Ann
     4 ch: Thomas Ann Howell
            Charles Robert
            William Arthur
            Mary Elizabeth   Date: 8 Aug. 1852

HOWELL, NATHANIEL--Stub Ent. (Salley) R. T. 257
Ent. 350--For militia duty as Lieutenant and also prov. and
supplies for Continentals.

HOWELL, PATRICK--Kershaw Deed E-155 6 Nov. 1805
Release to Wm. Hickson 100 A. on Waters of Great Flat Rock,
Kershaw Dist. granted to Patrick Layton (or Fayton) reserving
life estate to Mary Howell

HOWELL, PHILLIP--Council Journal 32 Pg. 441 8 Feb. 1765 S. C.
Philip Howell of St. Mark's Parish being called to support his
Caveat against a grant to Jacob Lampley of the same Parish for
200 Acres of land on Cedar Creek and he not appearing. Ordered
the Caveat be dismissed.

HOWELL, PHILLIP--To Joseph Brown of Georgetown--50 A. on Little
    Cedar Cr.--Old Mill. 100 A. on Big Cedar Cr.--New Mill.
    20 Mar. 1765 Wit: Thomas Harnson, Joseph Huggins
    Archives Misc. 1762-1766 Pg. 220

HOWELL, ROBERT--Charleston Deeds A3-614 3 Feb. 1764--A son of Thos.
    Howell died 1760. See card Wm. Howell
    -Archives Men. Vol. 11-39--Robert Howell--300 A. Craven, on Br.
    Cedar Creek called Vabin Branch. Waters of Congaree R. All
    sides vac. Gr. 30 July 1771 to Men. 23 Aug. 1771
    -Stub Ent. (Salley) O. 2-Pg.-198 and 235--Robert Howell
        Ent. 545--Sundries for Continental and State Troops 1781/2
    -Camden Dist. Rev. Record.--Robert Howell--Rich Brown, J. D.
    #2 Col. Thomas Taylor's Reg't.

HOWELL, ROBERT, SR.--Of Richland Dist. Richland Wills Bk. D-178
    Wife: Mary--Plt'n.   14 May 1804
    Sons: John and Robert   Prov: 16 Oct. 1804
    Dau: Mary Weston   Owned land in Georgia
          Elizabeth Baldrick
    Son: Joseph
    Dau: Sarah Smith

HOWELL, ROBERT--Richland Prob. Bk. D-243/45 Est.
    Aprs Warrant to: Joel Adams, Isaac Tucker, James Adams, Green
    Rives, John Howell, Jr.
    Ex: Mary Howell, John, Joseph, and Robert Howell
    16 Oct. 1804   Inv. and Appr.: 2 Jan. 1805

HOWELL, SAMUEL--To Manol Antonia--Mtg. over sorrell mare--secure
    $100.00 6 Jan. 1721 Wit: Wm. T. Little. Misc. D-230
    -Hist. Com. (Old Index) W W 553--Samuel Howell to John Footman-a
    slave-freedom.
    -Elapse Book 1784--Samuel Howell, survey, 193 A. elapsed by
    John Ott.
    -York Deed I-211 30 Aug. 1819--Samuel Howell of State of Tennessee
    Knox County--"All my part of land of Joseph Howell. Gr. owned
    on Broad River, including the Ferry.

HOWELL, SARAH--Hist. Comm. (Old Index) SS-272 1778
    Wm. Starke appt'd. her Gdn. 16 Oct. 1778.
    SS-282 13 Nov. 1778--John Howell and Wm. Axson, Jr. Apt. Gdn.
    -Elapse Bk-1784--Sarah Howell--500 A. Surveyed for James Berry

HOWELL, SARAH A.--Of Camden from Wm. and Rebecca Nixon of Camden
    Lot in Camden #1098 2 Feb. 1836 Camden N-378

HOWELL, SARAH H.--Will 30 Dec. 1867 Richland Bx. 87-2169
    Son: Joseph R.

HOWELL, SARAH--Misc. E-71 "South Carolina, Town of Columbia, I,
    Sarah Howell, of the town of Columbia,--love and affection for
    daughter, Sarah Daniel. 26 June 1821

HOWELL, SARAH "Miss"--Camden Prob. Bx. 33-1187 1860
    John K. Witherspoon, Adm.

HOWELL, STEPHEN -m- Fanny Festerman. S: Lewis Howell 9 Aug. 1829
    Howell, Stephen -m- Jincy Mitchell. S: Sam'l Paul 9 Nov. 1843
    Meck M. B. at Raleigh

HOWELL, THOMAS--Pet. he desires making settlement of some of his
    family on Santee--Pet'n. for 100 Acres. Council Journal 20-458
    Council Journal 20-226--Howell, Thomas, 100 Acres 1753
    -Archives Mem. 14-60- Thomas Howell--150 Acres appo. Saxegotha
    below mouth of Broad River. Bd. S. on Congaree, S. E. Richard
    Jackson, N. E. Vac. N. W. by heirs of Thos. Brown. Gr. 4 June
    1755 to men. Men. 7 May 1761.

HOWELL, THOMAS, Est 800 A. in Craven. Archives 13 Apr. 1765 pg.-152
    -Smith and Sally Reg. St. Phillip's Par. Pg.-326-Thomas Howell
    buried 21 Nov. 1768
    -Halifax, N. C. Will 1777 Will Bk. 2-65--Thomas Howell
    Wife: Ann
    Sons: William and Thomas
    30 Oct. 1777   Proven: Nov. Ct. 1777
    -Richland Co. Bk. B-53 Thomas Howell--Will
        Wife: Mary--Ferry tract of 150 A. and Home Place
        Son: Thomas James Howell--lands from est. of my father,
            William Howell, dec'd.
        "My father's land to be equally divided between my son,
        Thomas James Howell and William Howell, Jr. and Malachi
        Howell, being my two brothers.
        Date: 29 Oct. 1788   Prov: 18 Nov. 1788

HOWELL, THOMAS J. --Richland Bills 125 Filed 17 June 1815 -vs-
    Malachi Howell, Alleges: Thomas Howell, father of Thomas J.
    Howell, orator, died 1788 and made will--devised to his wife
    and son, Thomas James Howell, Bros. William Howell, Jr. and
    Malachi. Were sons of William, Sr. Orators uncle, William
    Howell, dec'd. Widow, Elizabeth now wife of James Beal and
    in State of Georgia. Wm. died 28 June 1811. Shows (definitely)
    that Malachi Howell, son of William and Lucy, came of age in
    the year 1794.

HOWELL, THOMAS W. and ARTHUR B. (or P) Pet'rs.--both minors, above
    14 yrs. Entitled to share estate of their father. Pray apt.
    of their Brother, Matthew R. Howell. Richland Roll 77 Filed:
    23 June 1818

HOWELL, THOMAS--Of Richland--Mtg. and Loan Office 193 1825
    Land "Gr. to my gr-father", Thomas Howell, who bequeathed the
    same to his son, Thomas H., who died during his minority and
    which my father, Wm. Howell inherited as heir at law. Sd tract
    given to me by Will of my father--Howell's Ferry.

HOWELL, THOMAS WEBB -m- Mary Ann Holland Mar. Bk. 10 Pg. 54 1828

HOWELL, THOMAS W.--A Doctor. Richland Bx. 16-376 1833
    Arthur Howell, Adm'r. Small per. estate. 1 bed, 2 blankets,
    negro woman, Harriett, boy, George. Appr's: Timothy Reese
    James Rowan, John L. Chappell

HOWELL, WILLIAM, THOS. CARY AND JAS. BLAKE to Capt. James Moor-1698
    Archives Dept. Last resort. Plat Bk. or Memorial 96/97

HOWELL, WILLIAM--Archives Dept. Mem 5-246--500 A. on Wingaw butting
    on Sea Marsh and Thomas Clard. Gr. to Ann Howell of Berkley,
    a widow 13 Jan. 1711. Sd Ann died intestate 1719. It came
    to William as eldest son and heir of Anne. Men. 24 Mar. 1732.
    Test: Charles Pinckney
    -Salley Reg. St. Phillip's Par. Pg. 26 and 244--Wm. Howell
    buried 28 Sept. 1734

HOWELL, WILLIAM -m- Almay Vickers 24 Mar. 1738 by Nathan Bassett
    S. C. Hist. and Gen. Mag. V-12-140

HOWELL, WILLIAM--Of Craven Co. to Joseph Parker of Edgecombe Co.
    Land S-s Tar River-N. C. 20 Aug. 1742 Halifax N. C. 5-160
    -S. C. Hist. and Gen. Mag. V-20-253--William Howell died
    1 Jan. 1745/6. Reg. of Christ Church Parish

HOWELL, WILLIAM --Of Craven Will 2 Feb. 1757 Charleston Bk. 1757/60
    Wife: Martha--Home place-slaves   Pg. 44
    Dau: Sarah--Minor--In case death of Sarah without issue, all
          to go to Arthur Howell and the children of Thomas Howell.
    To: William Howell, son of Arthur Howell, dec'd., land on Br.
          Broad River, called Little River.
    To: Robert, son of Arthur, dec'd., 100 Acres on S-s Great Lake
          where James Anderson family lived. States Arthur had
          five children.
    Ex: Wife, Thos Howell and John Hamilton
    Date: 2 Feb. 1757   Proven: 6 May 1757
    Wit: Benj. Farah, Evan Reese, Francis Carnie (or Currie)
    - Gessendanner Papers 1757--William Howell
          "On Friday morning, Feb'y 4th, died and on Saturday evening
          Feb'y 6th, was interred at the Plantation of William Howell.
          The body of the sd William Howell, a settler for many years
          over Santee or Congaree River in Craven County. Richland
          Co. Government workers building the new Airport near
          Eastover, S. C. opened the old Howell graveyard and found
          a metal casket with name of William Howell on it. The
          name ran through the family and I do not know date of the
          one found--but very early.

HOWELL, WILLIAM--Of Craven Co. S. C. Charleston Deeds R-3 Pg. 614
    To Robert Howell--Hill and Hartfield Plantations
        Malachi Howell--Home Place
        Gracey--Near Gill's Creek, Savannah
        All children of Thos. Howell who died leaving Will dated
        13 March 1760. He also had an "eldest son" Thomas, who died
        without issue. 3 Feb. 1764
    -Quit Rents 1764, Feb. 21st. Pg. 138--William Howell Estate.
        Pd. on 700 A. in Craven, Pd. by Martha Goodwyn
    -Archives Dept Mem. 9-91--William Howell--400 Acres N. E. side
    -Santee nearly opposite to lower part of Saxegotha Township.
    Bd. N. W. on William Moore and Mark Chants. N. E. post by
    heirs of Thomas Howell and vac. S. E. by Wm. Howell, Jr.
    10 July 1766.

HOWELL, WILLIAM--Archives Dept. Mem 10-197--700 Acres Craven at
Congaree on Hays Mill Cr. Bd. S. Joseph Curry, Robert Goodwyn
and David Rumph. S. E., by Wm. Hay and vac. N. E. John Thomas
Est. and vac. N. W. Benj. Farrar and vac. Gr. 13 July 1770
Men. 21 Aug. 1770

HOWELL, WM--Of Craven, Planter to Jane Curry of Berkley Co. Province
aforesaid freedealer. 200 A. Craven Co.-Broad R.- Bd. Robert
Hancock. No dower. Winnsboro Deed H-54 7 Dec. 1771

HOWELL, WILLIAM--Archives Dept. Men. 11-74--200 A. N-s Broad R.
Bd. S. E. Robert Hencocke. N. E. by R. H. 14 Sept. 1771

HOWELL, WILLIAM--S. C. Hist. and Gen. Mag. V-7-108 William Howell
elected delegate for Dist. between Broad and Catawba Rivers.
to Colony Congress. Journal 1st session 1 Nov. 1775

HOWELL, WILLIAM--Camden Will Bk. A-68 (Owner of Howell's Ferry)
Wife: Lucy-1/6 stock, slaves, and household furniture
Mother: Living at Howell's Ferry
Sons: Thomas, William, Malachi, James
      Robert-born after Will made
Dau: Grace Howell-land bought of John Howell
Date: 20 June 1776

HOWELL, WM. AND NATHANIEL CENTER--Of St. Mark's Par. Planters of
Winnsboro--Bill of Sale Deed A-34 11 March 1787 to Philip
E. Raiford--slaves--2 women 4 children. Wit: J. Baker, Capt.
3rd Reg't. S, C. and Wm. Howell. Proven Camden Dist. before
James Craig-J. P. (Think this is Charleston record.

HOWELL, WILLIAM--Dec'd. intestate. Of Richland. Prob. Bk. C-114
Adm: Elizabeth Howell
     Malachi Howell
     Ethel Heath (a man--see his will on pg. 141. Wife was Mary
Letters: 6 July 1795

HOWELL, WILLIAM--Of town of Columbia. Richland Prob. Bk. C-244
Adm'x: Polly Howell (also Mary) Cit: 6 Aug. 1799
Surety: Thos. Heath and James Goodwyn. Bond 5 July 1799
Sale: 15 Feb. 1800   Purchaser: Polly Howell-household goods

HOWELL, WILLIAM, JR. Richland Bx. 16-377 1795-1800
2 Ch: Sarah and Mary--minors
Wife: Mary (called Polly) or Elizabeth
John Howell, Jr. Adm. Joseph B. Stanton, Arb.
Seems this file has papers for 2 Wm. Howells

HOWELL, WILLIAM, JR.--Bro. of Malachi Howell. Richland Prob. E-138
Dau: Elizabeth -m- Thompson Ware
Arbitrators: Thos. Taylor Lenoir, Joel Adams, John Hopkins,
     Isaac Tucker, James Adams.
Thomas James Howell, a witness
Thompson Ware got $293.00 as his wife's part. No other heirs
mentioned. 9 May 1808

288

HOWELL, WILLIAM--Richland Bills 91 and 93 1814
    Dau: Lucy T. -m- Joseph B. Stanton
          Elizabeth D. -m- Thompson Ware
    Son: William, Jr. died intestate
    Widow: Elizabeth -m- James Beal of Ga.
    Grace A. died intestate

HOWELL, WILLIAM--Dec'd. Est. Richland or Darlington-both show heirs.
    Pet'rs: James Dozier Zimmerman -w- Sarah
          Thomas Ladson Hartley -w- Mary. Said Sarah and Mary
          being daus of Wm. Howell, dec'd. -vs- Chastine Williamson
          -w- who was widow of Wm. Howell. States the widow -m-
          Dr. Robert Hendricks of Town of Columbia in 1799 or
          1800. He died, and she then -m- Chastine E. Williamson
          in 1805. That John Howell, Gdn. of Sarah and Mary

HOWELL, WILLIAM --Camden-Kershaw County Equity 2684 Pg. 111
    Shows: Wm. Howell -m- Louisa M. Mickle, dau. of Robert and
    Catherine Mickle, late of Town of Camden, both now dead. Pet'rs
    resided in Alabama, Perry Co., the wife, Louisa died in Alabama
    Oct. 1839. Left one infant, Eugene R. Howell now a lettle over
    3 yrs. old. Wife intitled--shows estate of her father, John
    B. Mickle. Adm.

HOWELL, WILLIAM ROBERT--Richland Bx. 16-378
    Heirs: Joseph White
          Robert Weston
          Thomas Baldrick
          Charles R. Howell 1825(?)

HOWELL, WILLIAMSON--York Deed N-381 10 Jan. 1843
    John, Isham, Joseph, Elizabeth, and Susan Howell to Richard
    Thomson of Spartanburg, Land Joseph Howell, Sr. owned on E.
    Bank Broad River, including ½ Howell's Ferry and flat.
    -York Deed C-176 1 March 1847--Williamson Howell-Love and affection
    and $250.00 to Wm. C. Howell 863/4 A. on Bullocks Cr.

HOWELL, WILLIAMSON AND SAMUEL to H. H. Thomson of Spartanburg. On
    Broad River, York Dist. York Deed P-192 19 Dec. 1850

HOWELL, ZACHARIAH--S. C. Hist. Mag. V-1-185--Member Company Commanded
    by Capt. Matthew Singleton, Isham Moore, John Singleton, in
    Parish of St. Mark's. "We the subscribersxxxdo voluntarilyxxx
    we have hereinto set our hands 26 Aug. 1775.

HOWELL--S. C. Hist. and Gen. Mag. V-5-70/71--Letter from Hon. Henry
    Laurens to his son John: Charles Town, S. C. 18 July 1775--
    "Eb. Simons told me last week he had received a letter from a
    school fellow at Winson Green informing him of Mr. Howell's total
    Paralytic Stroke--admitting this intelligence to be true, I con-
    clude the Good Old Man did not long survive. Consequently, I
    am anxious to learn how you sidposed of my little James. I take
    it for granted that in case of Mr. Howell's death you had re-
    moved your youngest brother from Winsor Green-not to Geneve, I
    supposexxprobably to Westminster.

HOY, ANN -w- Robert, sister of Andrew Fleming. Richland Bills 26
    Filed 26 Feb. 1813. See Fleming card. Richland Equity.
    Heirs: Andrew Fleming-Brother
            Elizabeth Collins-Sister
            Alexander Fleming-Brother
            Rebecca Wells-Sister
            Nancy Fleming-Sister
            Joseph Fleming-Brother
            Caroline and Thomas Fleming-infants-children of Dec'd
            Husband also heir   brother, John
            Andrew B. Fleming, Gdn. of infants
            Joseph, Caroline and Thomas out of State

HUBBARD, LEVERETT--Adv. Ephraim Peck--Contract for business.
    Richland Eq. Bills 164

HUGHES, ELIZABETH--Richland Eq. Roll 14 1813--Pet. her apt. as Gdn.
    2 children of her former husband, Bridget Gehagen and John
    Gehagen--under 12 yrs. (1810)
    -Elizabeth Hughes was the widow Elizabeth Gehagen, widow of
    John. Their dau. Elizabeth -m- Wm. Goss

HUGHES, ISAAC--Pet'r. Shows: His infant son, George Washington
    Hughes, about 3 yrs, is entitled to property. Prays apt.
    Pet'r. as Gdn. Richland Roll 136 1819

HUTCHINSON, COL. THOMAS--Richland Co. Bills 58 Filed 4 July 1807
    -vs- John Vanmeter Alleges: orator enlisted in a Rifle Com-
    pany in Virginia in 1775 in the Revolutionary War. Col.
    Bailor of 3rd Reg't. Va. Line later commanded by Gen'l. Wm.
    Washington (then Col) and later came to S. C. and served under
    Col. Wade Hampton as a Corp'l and Lieut.

HUGHSON, JOHN--Richland Eq. Roll 53 1816--Apt. Gdn. of Nathaniel
    Douglas. See Douglas card and Adam Edgar card. Also apt'd.
    Gdn. Elizabeth Douglas. See James Douglas, her father. Also
    Rebecca Douglas

HUTCHINSON, BURREL B., pet'r. Richland Eq. Roll 142 1819
    Shows: That his father, the late Col. Thomas Hutchinson died
    1st Nov. 1818--left Will, widow Mary, and several children,
    other than Pet'r. Prays apt. of his Mother. Money etc.

HUTCHINSON, THOMAS--Richland Bills 58 Filed 1807/8 -vs- Maurice
    Kain, John Van Metree--Suit over contract.

HUTCHINSON, COL. THOMAS--Richland Eq. Bills 38 1811--See card
    George McCrelers.

IRONS, SIMON--Dec'd. Prob. Office Gdn. Bk-Pg.-14
    Widow: Sarah -m- _____ Williams
    Ch: Hannah and Mary
    James Thomson apt. Gdn. 12 July 1784

INGRAM, SAMUEL,--Richland Co. Bills 51 Filed 4 Oct. 1809 -vs- Lewis
    Dinkins in re lands sold by Gabriel Rawles -w- Elizabeth to
    Sam'l Ingram in 1796. Lewis Dinkins -w- Elizabeth. Ch: Samuel,
    William, and Eliza Scott Dinkins. Mentions Wm. Scott

INGRAM, SAMUEL--Continued--Roll 92 mentions Brothers: Micajah,
    Jeremiah, and Samuel Dinkins.
    Roll 292-B mentions: Paul Dinkins-minor, Samuel Dinkins, and
    Elizabeth S. Dinkins -w- Reuben House
    -Richland Equity Roll Filed 28 Dec. 1827--Samuel Ingram in 1806
    conv. Plantation to Wm. Scott in trust for Elizabeth -w- Lewis
    Dinkins (Lewis died many yrs ago). Elizabeth -m- 2nd Jesse
    Killingsworth--separated. Children were:
            Samuel C. Dinkins
            Elizabeth S. Dinkins -w- Reuben House
            Paul S.--now about 13 yrs.

JACKSON, ELIZA, ANN, AND REBECCA--Richland Bills 154--See card
    Needham Davis

JACKSON, JAMES--Richland Bills 178--Married Rachel Rawlinson, dau. of
    Benj. Rawlinson. See card.

JACKSON, JOHN AQUILLA--about 8 yrs. has neither father or mother.
    Pet. by Jesse M. Howell that he be apt. Gdn. 25 June 1816. Minor
    also called "John E" Jackson. Richland Roll 90
    -Richland Roll 90 1817--John Equilla Jackson, orphan, about
    8 yrs old owned small tract land which his father had bought.
    Jesse M. Howell, Gdn. Pet. sale. Sold to James R. Fritz

JAMES, WILLIAM DOBEEN, waddy Thompson, Thomas Waters, Henry William
    de Saussune. Judges of St. of Equity for Columbia Dist. 1820

JENKINS, HENRY -w- NANCY (nee) Parker, niece of Gabriel Parker.
    Richland Roll 66

JENNINGS, GIDEON--See Henry Young as Adm. of Johanna Wolf. 1811 Bills
                                                                    41
JERMAN, SALLY (or Sarah)--A gr-dau. of Sam'l Stanley. See Stanley
    card. Richland Bills 156 1815

JOHNSON, AARON--Richland Pet. 156 1820 -m- Margaret Wilson, dau. of
    James Wilson. Childrenwere: John, Frederick, Samuel, Rhonda,
    Mary, Jenny, Patsy, Judith, Elizabeth, Caroline--all Johnson

JOHNSON, BENJAMIN--Dec'd.--and Ann and heirs of. See card Joel
    Adams -vs- Joel Rawlinson--foreclosure. Richland Bills 190 1821

JOHNSON, BURR -m- Harriet Foote, dau. of Isabella and John Foote.
    Richland Roll 118 Feb. 1818

JOHNSON, JOHN, JR.--Sold land near Town of Columbia to Zachariah
    Phillips. Dower: Wife, Catherine Johnson 1813. Richland Eq.

JOHNSON, SAMUEL -w- Rebecca, late Rebecca Surginer, William Surginer,
    William Bryan (or Bynum). John Surginer, Dec'd.--heirs. Pray
    writ of Partition. Richland Roll 91 1817
    -Richland Roll 86 Filed 25 Feb. 1817 Shows: Surginer spelled
    Saxiner. John Saxiner lately died. Rebecca and William only
    children. William Bynum, a gr-child.

JONES, TOBIAS -w- Sarah, formerly Sarah Wolf. See card Oliver Lonus.
Richland Roll 9 1812

JONES, WALLIS, SEN'R. --Of Congaree, Mortgaged 20 Jan. 1765, Woman,
Jenny and girl, Cate. Wit: John Chapman and John Randal Thews
Archives Dept. Mtg. Bk. 1762-66 Pg. 212

JUDGE, HILLIARD -m- Isabella Means. See card Elisha Daniel, also
Rowland letter in file. Richland Bills 144
-Richland Bills 88 Filed 1814--Hilliard Judge -w- Isabella
David, Sarah, Martha, Robert Means--Infants by their next friend
Hilliard Judge, also Mary Aranana Means, all heirs of estate of
John Means, dec'd. -vs- Mary Means, David R. Evans, and Robert
Means, Exor's.
-Roll 144 Shows: Hilliard Judge -m- Isabella Means, dau. of
John Means.

KAGLER, ANDREW--See John Drehr, Pet'r. Richland Pet. 141

KAIGLER, ANDREW--Dec'd. Est. Richland Roll 145 1819
Widow: Mary Kaigler, Pet'r.
Dau: Ann--her Gdn. John Drehr.
Andrew had ½ interest in land of his father, John Kaigler. His
mother was Margaret Kaigler. Brother, James.

KAIGLER, ANN--about 19 Richland Equity Roll 45 1815
Harriet about 17
Lavinia about 15
David, of age
Elizabeth, (wife and mother, it seems)
Drusilla about 12
Henry about 10.
Father, Michael, dec'd. Est. David and Elizabeth apt. Gdn's.

KAIGLER, JOHN--Dec'd. Richland Roll 44 or 45
Ch: Andrew--apt'd. Gdn. of minors
John James--about 16
Ann about 14
Reuben? about 10
Thomas about 7
William about 2
Margaret--wife and mother--apt. Gdn.
Back of card states Michael Kaigler, brother, died August last.

KEITH, JOHN, Adm'r. of Thomas Young, dec'd. -vs- William Purvis and
Burridge Purvis.--In re sale of property under judgement. Bill
missing from file. File contains orig. affidavit by Malachi
Howell, showing his sign. Richland Bills 82 Filed June 1810

KELLY, GEORGE--Pet'r. above 14--Entitled to money from estate of his
father, Jacob Kelly, dec'd. now in hands of Exor's. of Estate.
of Jacob Hamiter, dec'd., who was adm'r. of estate of Jacob
Kelly dec'd. Prays apt. of Jacob Bates as Gdn. Roll 101 1818

292

KELLY, JOHN--Of Newberry Dist. Richland Roll. Will 21 Nov. 1836
     Heirs: Ann E. Kelly
             Langston H. Kelly
     Son: John T. Kelly
           Wm. Z. Kelly--son of 1st. wife.
     Dau: Harriet C. Kelly
     Date: 21 Nov. 1836--Proven
     Ex: Dau. Harriet, and George Graham
     Wit: James Liles, Henry Adams, B. G. Durrett
     Note: Will does not seem to mention all children. Deed in file
     from John Kelly to "my 2 sons", James Z. and Milton H. Kelly,
     minors. Dated 29 Aug. 1836

KELLY, JULIA--Pet'r. age 14 yrs.--Entitled to money from estate of
     her father, Jacob Kelly--now in hands of Jacob Hamiter's Exor's.
     who was adm'r. of her father's estate. Pray apt. of James
     Langford as Gdn. Richland Roll 102 1818

KEMPTON, WILLIAM -w- Sarah of Massachusetts, dau. of Joshua Benson.
     Richland Bills 109. See Benson card.

KENNERLY, JAMES, Pet'r. Shows: Grace Colbach (Colbeach) an orphan,
     no father of mother prays pet'r. be apt. Richland Roll 112 1818

KENNEDY, JOHN--Of Chester Dist. -m- a dau. of Alexander Robinson.
     See card William Cleland. Richland Rolls 39 1812

KENNERLY, RACHEL CAROLINE--Minor about 11 vrs, pet. apt. her mother
     Susannah Kennerly--1815 Equity Roll 39
     -Susannah Kennerly apt. Gdn. for dau. Rachel age 11. 1815

KILGORE, JOSIAH--Richland Bills 109 Filed 31 Jan. 1817 -vs-
     Thomas Briggs, Joshua Benson, et al Alleges: Maj. Joshua A.
     Benson of Columbia, died intestate, leaving widow, mary who -m-
     John Bruce. Said Mary died intestate leaving her husband, John
     Bruce and her dau. Harriet Benson who is now wife of orator,
     Josiah Kilgore, who has since learned that Maj. Joshua Benson
     formerly resided in the town of Middleboro, Mass. and before
     coming to S. C. had -m- Sarah Ellis, by whom he had several
     children and said Sarah was living at the time of his death and
     also the following children by sd Sarah: Joshua Benson,
     Elizabeth Thomas -w- Ezra Thomas, Mary Atwood -w- Joshua Atwood
     and Sarah Kempton -w- Wm. Kempton who have come forward claim-
     ing the property. File contains letter from Joshua Benson of
     Charleston to his brother, Ichabod Benson in Massachusetts in
     1789, Oct. 14th.

KILLER, MARY--A niece of Robert Latta. See Latta card. Roll 635-46
                                                              1852
KILLINGSWORTH, CAROLINE--Of Richland -m- 30 Jan. 1761 (check year
     Gilbert Garner, Tr. Misc. BB-275   854-A)

KILLINGSWORTH, ELIZABETH--A sister of Wm. Scott, purchased at sale of
     Lewis Dinkin's estate. Richland Misc. E-184

KILLINGSWORTH, JAMES--Of Richland--name changed to James Kenilworth.
     Misc. I-141 14 Feb. 1835

KILLINGSWORTH, JESSE--Will 17 June, 1818, died soon after. Gr 1798
   Ch: Nancy--Dau, Ex.   Proven 3 July 1818   sold.
      Elizabeth
      Mary
      Jesse, Jenny (or Jane) Martha--minors
      Son-in-law, John McLean, Exor. Dau., Nancy, did not act.
      Richland Roll. Filed 3 April 1823

KILLINGSWORTH, JESSE, et al -vs- William Killingsworth. Bill for
   Part. Richland Dist. To sell land "whereon Mrs. Mary Woodward,
   lately resided. Slaves, etc. Son Times and State Gazette
   8 Dec. 1830

KILLINGSWORTH, JOSEPH--About 18 yrs. Father: John Killingsworth,
   Dec'd. Property in hands of Mary Killingsworth and Wm. Kill-
   ingsworth, Adm'rs. Pray apt. of friend Eli Williams. No order
   in file. Richland Roll 128 1819
   -Roll 129 Richland Equity--Mary and Sarah Killingsworth, age 19
   Same as above. Pray Apt. Andrew Wallace. No order.   and 16

KINSLER, CHRISTIAN--Will 8 Feb. 1789. Richland Bx-106
   Wife: Susanna   Proven: 18 May, 1789
   Ch: Daniel, John Jacob, Jeremiah, Andrew, Dorothy
   Exor's: Adam Coon and Jasper Faust

KINSLER, DANIEL--Will Richland Wills C-33
   Br: John Conslow Kinsler
      Jary (Jeremiah)
      Andrew
   Exor: Adam Koon (Coon)   Proven 2 Jan. 1793
   Land on Broad R. left to me by my father. 28 Dec. 1792(Will dated)

KINSLER, ELIZABETH--Widow--Richland Wills G-130 Will 4 April 1817
   Son: Herman Kinsler--Exor.
   Dau: Mary Coon
      Elizabeth Smith -w- John Smith (Their son-John)
      Sophia Rawls and Christiana Mitchell--In Western Country
   Date: 4 July 1817   Proven: 17 March 1820

KINSLER, HERMAN--Will Richland Wills F-291
   Wife: Sarah
   Dau: Barbara Hollenshead--Land at Ruff's Ferry, Fairfield Co.
   Dau: Margaret Mary Ann--Sandy Level--the patrimony of my wife,
      Sarah, one half.
   Dau: Mary Rigsby-other half
   Son: Junius Alfred and John Herman Kinsler. Prov. 11 Dec. 1828

KINSLER, JOHN -m- Mary, dau of Judith, widow of John Frost. See
   Frost card. Judith -m- 2nd Judah Barrett. Richland Bills 15 1812

KINSLER, JOHN J.--Will Richland Bk. M-1 12 Oct. 1864
   Wife: Amelia
   Bro: David, William, Edward, Henry
   To: Children of Col. Daniel D. Finley.
   -Richland Bk. L-408 John J. Kinsler
   Gr-children: John Kinsler Davis and Julia C. Davis
   Family graveyard reserved 20 Aug. 1851
   Wit: Harriet Davis, Jno. H. Kinsler, D. D. Finley

KINSLER, MRS. SALOME--Of Lexington Dist. Div. Estate 18 Dec. 1859
    Children: Mary A. Arthur   Catherine Kaigler
             David Kinsler   Henry O. Kinsler
             Edward Kinsler   John J. Kinsler
             Elizabeth Kinsler   William Kinsler

KINSLER, WILLIAM--Dec'd. 8 children--estate to be divided between
    them. Value about $20,000.00. Edward Kinsler a minor.
    Mary Ann Arthur apt. Gdn. Copy Will in file. Land in Georgia
    Wife: Sarah
    Children: John J. Kinsler, William K., Mary Arthur, Daniel K.,
    Elizabeth K., Catherine, Ed, Henry O.--last 3 minors
    Mentions father and mother

KIRKLAND, WILLIAM--Will. Of Fairfield Dist. 4 Dec. 1806
    Minor ch: Mary Honor
             John DeBell
             Martha Maria Will in file Richland Bills 16
  -Richland Eq. Roll 17 1812--William Kirkland Will in file
    Shows: "my 3 beloved children"-Mary, John, and Martha--also
        Dau: Sarah Taylor and her children
        Son: Archy
        Dau: Frances Alston -w- James Alston, exor.
        Son: William and his children.
        Son: Joseph
        Friend: William Strother and Samuel Alston-both exor's.

KIRKLAND, ZACHARIAH TUCKER--17 yrs.--his gr-father was Isaac Raiford,
    dec'd. His father, Zachariah Kirkland, resides in Louisiana.
    Ex. Will: Isaac Raiford; Joel Adams; James Adams; and John
    Howell. Richland Roll 56 1816

KIRKPATRICK, JOHN--See card Philip Pearson, Sr. Richland Bills 191

KNIGHT, BENJAMIN -m- Nancy Spelling, dau. Brittain Spelling.
    Richland Eq. Roll 37 1811

KNIGHTSON, PETER--Killed in Mississippi by rattlesnake. See card
    John Briggs. Richland Eq. Bills 113 1812

KNOX, DR. JAMES--Had infant son, James Knox, by a former wife.
    Ch. by Susannah: Eliza Knox and Matilda Knox.
    Susannah -m- Shepherd Pickett--see card
                2nd-Reuben Stark Richland Eq. 1 1808
  -Richland Eq. Bk. 113 1812--James Knox--moved to Miss. See
    card-John Briggs

KUNZLER, CONRAD--Will Of Craven Co. Richland File C. T. Wills
    Wife: Dorothea
    Sons: Herman and John
    Son: Christian--The home place
    20 March 1767   Proven: 19 Jan. 1770

LAFTON, CHARLES--Dec'd. Richland Roll 11 also 50 1812
   Children: Charles about 21
               Nancy about 18
               Edward about 17
               John about 14
               James died age 2
   Jacob Bowers apt'd. Gdn. Their mother wants land part. (Ann)
   Dau: Catherine-of age-m- John Bowers
   -Roll 50 filed 1815--Edward Lafton about 20 and John about 17.
   Pet. their mother, Ann Lafton, be apt'd. Gdn.

LATTA, ROBERT--Will Richland Rolls 635-46 15 May 1852
   Son: Wm. Albert Latta
         James Theodore Latta lived in York Dist.
   Wife: Elvira D.--Ext'x.
   Daus: Jane and Cicelia
   Niece: Mary Killer   Nephew: Albert Latta

LAZARUS, JACOB,JR., of Columbia--born in Groningen, Holland, has no
   family. Citizenship papers 23 Nov. 1809 Misc. B-616/617

LEE, FRANCIS--A sister of Sarah Cantey. See Cantey card. Bills 86

LEDINGHAM, WILLIAM, SR.--Died 6 March 1826 Richland Roll 292 Will
   Ch: William, Jr.--died intestate--no issue
       James D.--Died intestate--no issue
       Catherine
       Sarah Ann -w- John Sanders
       John -m- Frances Catherine
       Jacob H.   Filed 18 March 1832

LESTAGETTE _____ of Orangeburg, Dec'd. Dau:_____-m-
Sanders Glover. Richland Roll 70 1817

LESTER, ANDREW, John Lester, Thomas Lester, Rebecca Lester -w- Henry
   Andrews, William Lester, Catherine Dargan, widow of William
   Dargan and Francis Lester -vs- Samuel Nelson. Alleges: Plt's.
   are children and heirs of Andrew Lester, dec'd. and that William
   Strother was their grand-father--that Wm. Strother made Will
   16 May, 1779 and bequeathed to his daughter, Catherine, a slave
   girl. That Col. Thos. Taylor refused to act as Exor. and Kemp
   Strother the other exor. qualified. That in 1783 Catherine
   Strother married Andrew Lester-father and mother of the complainants and Andrew Lester died in Nov. 1795 and then Catherine
   married Samuel Nelson--Alleges slave has increased by 3 children.
   Suit for slaves. Richland Co. Bills 122 Filed 31 July 1816

LILES, MILLTRET--formerly the lawful wife of William Green, Dec'd.
   Affidavit that she does not know what became of the Will of
   John Green, dec'd. which her husband had, but as the British
   has destroyed a good many of their affects and papers, possibly
   the Will was destroyed. 6 July 1782. Before Geo. Ruff, J.P.
   Affidavit by Daniel Gore that he saw a certain Will which he believes was Will of John Green, dec'd. wherein it was specified
   that John and Thomas Green were left heirs at law to their
   Father's estate and all the rest of the other three was cut off
   with one shilling each. 6 July 1782. Geo. Ruff J. P.

LINDSAY, WILLIAM--Dec'd. Richland Eq. Bills 56 1809
    Exor's: Robert Lindsay, Wm. Thompson, William Milligan

LOCKHART, THOMAS B.--Of Laurens -m- set. 30 March 1843 Emily Henrietta
    Kimble, of Columbia. Adam Edgar, Tr. Richland Misc. N-15

LONG, GEORGE--Dec'd. Richland Eq. Pet. 149 (stray 1819)
    Jacob and George Long--see card Amos Banks -w- Catherine

LONUS?, OLIVER--Trustee for Sarah Wolf, now Sarah Jones -w- Tobias
    Jones. Her children are:
        Rosanna -m- Malachi Ott
        Eliza -m- Sylvester Brunson (about 19)
        Levi
        William-10, Pamelia-11, Louise-9--all minors
    Richland Eq. Roll 9 1812

LOWERMAN, JOHN--Of Lexington--Dec'd. 1800. Widow-Elizabeth-Pet'r.
    Ch: William, George, Jacob, Joseph, and Catherine.
    Land on Ridge between Sandy Run and Beaver Creek.
    Pray writ for sale and division. Richland Roll 146 1819

LYKES, GEORGE--Will 17 July 1775 C. T. Wills Richland File
    Wife: Susannah
    Son: Frederick
    Daus: Barbara and Catherine Lykes
    Son: George

LYLES, EPHRAIM--Richland Bill 191 1821 See card Philip Pearson, Sr.

LYNCH, MISS ESTHER--Dec'd. and Mrs. E. A. Gadsden, Dec'd.
    Their heirs: Sabrina Lynch over 14 under 21 in 1820
               John under 14
               Ann, Thomas and Esther, under 14
    Gdn: John Bowman Lynch S: Mary H. Bowman
    Bond: 27 Dec. 1826 Return by Dr. John Bowman Lynch of Mont-
    gomery Co. Tenn. 20 Jan. 1830. Property of minor Pet'r, "Duck
    Pond" in Pr. George Winyan and 2 negro children. Also ¼ of
    30 or 40 negroes of Miss Lynch's estate.

LYNCH, THOMAS--Dec'd. Cit: 13 May 1837 Adm. John Lynch
    Richland Bx. 19 Roll 454.

MAGARGILL, ALLEN -w- Jane, Elizabeth Marple, Co-heirs of John Marple,
    dec'd. and John Northrup Marple, Admore de bonis non of John
    Marple, dec'd. -vs- James Rabb and Robert Rabb Exor's Thomas
    Marple, dec'd. and Philip Raiford. Shows: Jane and Elizabeth
    daughters of Richard Marple, dec'd--oldest bro. of John Marple,
    late of Fairfield Co. S. C. and also heirs of sd John. Elizabeth
    and Allen -w- Ann reside in state of Pennsylvania. John Marple
    never married. Allen Margargill -m- Jane in 1792. Thomas Marple
    a brother, took property of John after he died, including land
    of Jacob Reizer, which he later cancelled and delivered to Jacob
    Reizer, Jr. heir of Jacob, Sr.

MAITLAND, JOHN AND THOMAS--Purchasers of lands. See cards Robert
    Gilmore, Thomas Fitzsimmons. Richland Eq. Bills 124 1816

MANNING, JETHRO--Of Saxagotha--C. T. Wills Richland File
    Wife: Rosanna   Will-Proven 18 Jan. 1767
    Son: Levy Manning "if he should come into province"
    2nd son: Abraham Manning   Exor: Joseph Carey

MANOR, RICHARD S. -w- Hester--Pet'rs. Shows: James Clark lately
    died in U. S. Army, in 1815. Entitled to arrears of pay.
    Left Pet'r., Hester, and infant child. Named Middleton Clark
    Prays apt. of Pet'r. as Gdn. Hester was evidently the mother
    of the minor. Richland Roll 82 Filed 23 June, 1817

MARKS, DR. ELIAS -vs- Michael J. Rudolph -w- Louisa M. and Jacob J.
    Faust--Suit for Doctor's bills. Alleges, marriage agreement of
    Michael J. Rudolph and Louisa M. Hendricks, with Jacob J. Faust
    as Trustee-1 Oct. 1816 and alleges marriage same month and have
    since had several children.

MARPLE, EDWARD AND DAVID--Adm'r. John Marple--reside without State.
    Affidavit by Michael Moore. See card John Moore. Bond of
    David and Ann Marple to James Davis in file. Dated 28 Feb. 1806

MARPLE, JOHN--never married. Richard, his oldest brother. Richard's
    daughter: Jane -m- in 1792 Allen Magargill. Daughter: Elizabeth
    and sons: John, Thomas, David, Northrup. Eq. Roll 2? See Allen
    Magargill. Name also spelled McGargle
    -Richland Eq. Bills Card #2-A--Thomas Marple, Dec'd. Died in
    1790 leaving Will--at Fairfield. James Rabb and Robert Rabb
    were Exor's. Shows Richard Marple, dec'd. Children listed as
    above. Philip Raiford a surety on Bond. Shows: a David
    Marple, "the younger".

MARSHALL, MARTIN, JR. -w- Mary Richland Roll 19 1813
    Ch: William B.   Sarah W.
         Elizabeth L.   Benjamin F.
         Mary H.   John L.
    Legatees of Wm. Blanchard, dec'd. See card

MARSHALL, JOHN, Adm'r of Joseph Neal, dec'd. See Neal card. Bills 134
                                                                1819
MARSHALL, JOHN--Dec'd. Richland Roll 29 1814
    Son: William--also dec'd. (1814)
         Ch. of William: Frances, Rebecca, Thomas, Sarah
    James Hopkins and David Myers apt. Gdn's. 1814
                                                     Voy?
MARSHALL, CAPT. JOHN--Apt. Gdn. of Lewis McVay. See McVay Card
    Richland Roll 158 1820

MARSHALL, WILLIAM--Dec'd. Richland Eq. Bills 134
    Heirs: Ann, John, William, Green, Francis, Rebecca, Thomas and
        Sarah. -vs- Martin Marshall, Sen'r., Adm'r. File con-
        tains inventory estate of William Marshall 31 May 1810.
        Also, inventory estate John Marshall, dec'd 13 Nov. 1801

MARSHALL, WILLIAM--Of Fairfield dec'd. 23 Feb. 1800 Richland Roll 76
    Son: William--since deceased   1817
          Thomas, John and Francis
    Dau: Rebecca Marshall
          Mary Murph
          Green Marshall
          Nancy or Ann Marshall
          Sarah Marshall, a minor.
          Conrad Murph -m- Margaret?--Gdns.

MARSHALL, WILLIA (or William) Richland Roll 29 1814
    Ch: Francis A. Marshall about 20
          Rebecca Marshall about 18
          Thomas Marshall about 16
          Sarah Marshall about 15
          And their gr-father, John Marshall, dec'd.

MARTIN, EDWARD--died about 25 Dec. 1813--intestate. Richland Roll 117
    Leaving widow: Mary Martin   1818
                Children: John, Edward I., Agnes W., and Mary A. all
                minors except Pet'r. Entitled to land in Fairfield Dist.
                on Jackson's Creek. Pet. of James Martin, Jane Martin,
                and Henrietta Martin, infants under 21, show same fact.
                Pray apt. of Brother John as Gdn. Pet. of Mary Martin,
                Robert Bell, John A. Robertson, John Sloan, Thomas Bell,
                Robert Martin, William Montgomery, and James Martin,
                Jane Martin and Henrietta Martin--infants under 21, by
                John Martin and Edward Martin, Agnes W. Martin, Mary
                A. Martin under 14 yrs. alleges Edward Martin d. 25 Dec.
                1813 intestate. Pray Part.

MARTIN, ELISHA--Of Richland Dist. -vs- George Rawlinson--Bill to
    Redeem. Richland Bills 18 Filed 28 July 1812

MARTIN, JAMES -w- Margaret, late Margaret Turner; James Gladney -w-
    Ann, late Ann Turner, William Turner, John Turner -vs- John
    Duke--Pltf's. are daughters and sons of James Turner, dec'd.
    John Duke, def't, also -m- Elizabeth, dau. of James Turner. Bills
                                                              40
MARTIN, JAMES -m- Margaret Turner. Richland Roll 40 1811 See card
    James Turner, Dec'd.

MARTIN, JOEL -w- Sarah, Joseph Martin -w-. -vs- Thomas McPherson and
    Reuben Gill alleges the widow Sarah Smith, legatee of her hus-
    band Peter Smith died. That Nancy, dau. of Peter Smith, had 2
    children living when her mother, sd Sarah Smith, died--who were
    entitled to 2 slaves which Thomas McPherson had sold to Reubin
    Gill. That the 2 children of Nancy are the oratrixes of this
    Bill. Richland Co. Bills 115

MAY, JAMES--Will 15 April 1767 Richland File C. T. Wills
    Wife: Elizabeth   Proven 11 May 1767
    Sons: John, James   Exor: John Thomas, Jr.
    Dau: Lucy   Wit: Thomas Taylor
                                 Martha Mills
                                 Martha Taylor

MAY, JAMES--Dec'd. Richland Eq. Bills 187 Filed 24 Dec. 1821
    Widow: Elizabeth
    Ch: Gilbert, Elizabeth, Mary Ann,
        Lucy Wallace -m- Thos. Flowers
        James May
        John Thomas May
    Will dated 26 Nov. 1807--in file

MAZYCK, WILLIAM, Exor. of Isaac Mazyck, dec'd. -vs- John Bostick--
    debtor of the estate. Suit over Bonds or notes secured by Mtg.
    of lands and slaves. Alleges: John Bostick made Deed Gift of
    one of Mtg'd. slaves to William Bostick.

McADAMS, MARY--By next friend--John Hood. Richland Roll 33 1814
    Alleges: Her husband, Joseph McAdams, is untrue, uses her
    property, etc. Separation suit.
    -Filed June 11, 1814--Alleges: Joseph is husband of Mary. Were
    married 1st Aug. 1806--she owned property in her own right--
    that Joseph is running through with it--beat his wife, etc.

McBRIGHT, WILLIAM--Seems to have married a dau. of Alexander Robinson.
    See card William Cleland. Richland Roll 39 1812

McCARTER, JOHN and Elizabeth--Wit. Will of Benj. Harrison dated 23
    April 1837. Richland Bx. 13-309

McCORD, CHARLES--Salley's Hist. Orangeburg Co. Pg. 140 and 185
    S. C. Gazette--29 Aug. 1768: To be sold at public auction,
    all the personal estate of Capt. John McCord, late of St. Mark's
    Parish. Dec'd. sd Sophonisba McCord, Adm'x. and Charles
    McCord, Adm'r.
    -Charleston Wills Pg. 495--Charles McCord--Mother: Sophia Nisby
    names brothers and sisters. 12 Dec. 1773 Prov: 17 Dec. 1773

McCORD, COL. DAVID J.--Richland Prob. Bx. 52-1280 Will
    Wife: Louisa S. McCord
    Son: Russell
         Turguard?--Minor
    Dau: Julia--Minor
    Son: Junius--at school in Alabama Pet. shows: Henry Junius
    Dau: Mary E.
    Son-in-law: Edward L. Parker for widow
    Gr-dau: Anna Parker
    Dau: Charlotte Cheers?
    "My Aunt": Mrs. Richardson--Dec'd.
    "Children of my first wife"
        Emma McCord, dec'd. (or Emma Parker, dec'd.)
        Emma Parker 24 Feby. 1856

McCORD, DAVID--Salley's Hist. Orangeburg. Pg.-185
    David McCord, Baptized, Son of John and Sophinisba McCord.
    Born 12 March 1759. Sureties; Wm. Thomson, John Russell, and
    Rachel -w- John Lloyd. His entire family lived in SaxeGotha

McCORD, DAVID, JOSEPH AND RUSSELL--Of Richland Co. and Richard Brown
-w- Mary, brothers and sister of late Wm. McCord who died intestate leaving Catherine McCord, his widow. Wit: Rob't.
Weston and Wm. Clarkson. Misc. Rec. III-246 29 April 1797

McCORD, DAVID--Richland Prob. Bx. D-15 Will 17 May 1801
    Wife: Mary--Ex.   Proven: 23 Nov. 1801
    "My 3 daus": Mary, Maria, and Sarah Howell McCord
    Ex: Friend, John Bostick
    Wit: Joseph McCord, Henry Fox Appr: 2 Jan. 1802

McCORD, HANNAH, et al. See card Mary Brown, widow. Richland Bills
                                                    1821   188
McCORD, JOHN -m- Sophianisba Russell, dau. of Capt. Charles and Mrs.
    Mary Russell, of Amelia Township. Pg. 23 Salley's Hist. Orange-
    burg. Pg. 113--Married at home of Mrs. Mary Russell in Amelia
    John McCord of SaxaGotha and Sophinisba Russell--Tuesday 5th
    Feb. 1750. Pg. 130: Baptized--Charles, son of above-born 7th
    Nov. 1751. Pg. 143: Baptized--Mary, dau. of above, born 11th
    Dec. 1753. Pg. 169: Baptized--John, son of above, born 26th
    Jan. 1757. Pg. 185: Baptized--David, son of above, born 12th
    March 1759

McCORD, JOHN--Of the Fork of Wateree River--Bond 5 Jan. 1758
    Mtg. slaves--31 Jan. 1760 Richland Mtg. YY 1769 Pg. 240(Grey Bk)

McCORD, RUSSELL P. -w- Elvira (or Eliza)--Assignment of Right of
    Elvira in estate of Ainsley Hall, dec'd. to John Thomas and
    John McIven. Excepts Real Estate owned by Ainsley Hall in En-
    gland-if any. Orangeburg Dist. Wit: J. R. McCord. Misc. F-310
    Hist. Com. Records. 20 June 1828

McCORD, MRS. SOPHIA NISBA--Of McCord's Ferry on the Congaree, died
    1784. Issue S. C. Weekly Gazette, Sat. Sept. 25, 1784
    S. C. Hist. and Gen. Mag. V-19-108

McCORD, WILLIAM--Richland Probate Bx. 20-485 Cit: 3 Dec. 1796
    Catherine McCord, Adm'x   Bond: John Bostick and John Brown
    Appr's: Russell McCord, Joseph McCord, Wm. Clarkson, Henry Fox
    5 Jan. 1797
    -Archives Dept. Richland File Misc. 3J-26 William McCord, Dec'd
    Widow: Catherine
    Brothers and Sisters heirs: Mary -w- Richard Brown
                                 David McCord
                                 Joseph   "
                                 Russell "
    Quit Claim in favor of widow. 29 April 1797

McCRELESS, GEORGE -m- Elizabeth Cook, dau. of Burrell Cook. See
    Cook card. Richland Eq. Bills 38 1811
    -Richland Bills 38 Filed 26 Feb. 1811--George McCreless-for
    himself and wife and as Gdn. for Thos. J. Cook, Burrell B. Cook,
    and Nathan P. Cook -vs- Robert O'Gilvie and Col. Thos. Hutch-
    inson. Estate of Burrell Cook of Fairfield, died 1803. Widow,
    Mary. Elizabeth who has married George McCreless, and 3 sons
    (minors). Widow Mary -m- Robert O'Gilvie 1808 and died in July
    same year.

McCRELESS, JAMES--Dec'd. Estate sales 14 Dec. 1799. Purchasers:
    John McCreless and Effamy McCrelan Deed Bk. A-87

McCRELESS, JOHN--Ordinary for Lexington Dist.--Certificate in re
 Estate of Maj. John Hampton, dec'd. 23 June 1817 Richland Bills
 138

McCRORY, JOHN--Pet'r.--Richland Eq. Roll 13 1813
 Dau: Peggy--age about 9 yrs. legatee of Wm. M. Turner. Land
 Fork of Catawba.

McCULLOUGH, THOMAS and William of Fairfield to Reuben Picket--100A.
 where Mary Hill formerly lived, orig. gr. Thomas Shirley on
 Walnut Creek adj. Dan'l McCullough and Edmond Tidwell. 24 Jan.
 1810. Pres of: Daniel McCullough and Daniel Grafton Extra
 Bills 111 Richland Co. Deed

McDONALD, MIDDLETON--Gr-father of the children of George Wade.
 Richland Pet. 46 1815

McDONALD, WILLIAM--Will 2 July 1838 Richland Prob. Bx. 50-1244
 Wife: Mary Ann and children by her:-
     Oldest: John A. Martin McDonald
     Minors ?
 Shows: Tuition for John and Frances (Fanny)

McDOWELL, ALEXANDER--Of city of Charleston. Richland Bills 72
 Suit over purchase of lots in Columbia from John Harper of
 Columbia in 1805 -vs- Thomas Parker--in Baltimore
                     Thomas Haly) Out of state. Residents
                     George Luckly) of England
 Filed 8 June 1812
 ?
McDOWELL ALEXANDER--Dec'd. Will in file. Died 1817 Filed 5 Feb.
                 Richland Roll 289 Bx. 267-270   1827
 Children: Peter McDonald
           Catherine -w- Jethro Raiford--moved to Alabama
           William McD.--Moved to Ala.
           Sarah McD.--died unmarried
           Daniel McD.--moved to Ala.
           Margaret -w- Needham Howell, moved to Ala.
           Roderick, John, James-age 18 and Mary Ann--age 15
           Land on Sandy Run. (Spelling of name is as written
                          on card. F. C.)

McFADDIN, ROBERT -w- Leah, exor's. of James Dickey. See card Wm.
 Lenoir. Richland Bills 4

McGARGLE, ALLEN -w- Jane, John McKenny -w- Elizabeth--daus. of
 Richard Marple, dec'd. Richland Equity.

McGOWEN, HENRY--Dec'd. Of Columbia. Richland Filed 28 Dec. 1832
 Widow: Eliza
 Children: Henra M. and Sarah A. M. McGowen
 -See card John Compty, dec'e.
 -Henry -w- Elizabeth apt'd. Gdns. of John Compty, minor 1790
 -Richland Equity Roll 17 1812--Elizabeth McGowen -w- Henry
 McGown, late widow of John Compty. See card Wm. Kirkland
 -Richland Bills 156 1815--Elizabeth McGowen, a dau. of Samuel
 Stanley. See Stanley card.

McGOWEN -w- Betsy and Sally Trapp. Richland Bills 156 Filed 20 May
    Alleges: Samuel Stanley, died, left Will dated 29 June 1815
    devising to his wife, Martha, and children, that his wife pre-
    deceased him. Will proved 7 Sept. 1818 and Edward Fisher qual-
    ified as Exor. (See card showing abstract Wills in file)Alleges:
    Orators, together with C. E. Williamson -w- Mary, James Waddel
    -w- Lucy, Robert Hendrick Stanley, William B. Stanley and Martha
    Stanley are tenants in common.

McGREW,ALEXANDER,--Dec'd. Had 500 Acres on Congaree, Richland
    Dist. Left Will, Apt'd. James McGrew, William McGrew, and
    Alexander, "otherwise called Peter" McGrew, Exor's. Copy
    Will in file shows: Will of Alexander McGrew of Province of S.C.
    Craven County--sick--Dau. Margaret, and wife, Margaret, son,
    William, son, John. Apt's 3 sons, James, Pet'r. and Wm. ad
    Exor's. Mentions definitely "my wife" and children now residing
    in the Province. Bill show children residing in the Province,
    were: James, Peter "otherwise called Alexander", (Alexander
    died previous to 1791-leaving widow, Margaret and one son, John,
    who died since without issue; and 3 daughters towit: A Anna
    now married to Cornelius H. Vanters; Elizabeth -w- David Autry;
    and Mary who married one, Cornelius Autry, and died in 17__?
    leaving two minor children, David Autry and Mary Ann Autry.
    Richland Bills Roll 10 Filed 8 June 1810

McGUIRE, PETER -w- Rebecca, John Compty by Clairborn Clifton his
    Gdn. -w- H. T. McGowen -w- Richland Bills 17 6 Jan. 1812
    -Richland Equity Filed 30 Dec. 1830--Peter McGuire -w- Rebecca--
    Bill for Alimony. Large family. Elizabeth made affidavit of
    father's _____?. 3 youngest--Harriet-7, Rebecca-5, Rosanna-2.
    Charles Compty, next friend.

McHUGH, MATTHEW--Of Beaufort Dist. and James S. Guignard -w-
    Elizabeth Dinkins and William Scott. Pltf's. are creditors of
    Lewis Dinkins, dec'd.--late of Richland Dist. Alleges:
    Elizabeth Dinkins, widow, and Wm. Scott took possession. Suit
    for payment of debts. Richland Bills 162 Filed 4·Jan. 1820

McILWAIN, CHARLES--Dec'd. Richland Eq. Roll 26, 27, 78 and 79 1813
    Minor children under 14: Charles, died before Feb. 1817.
    Johnson, and William, over 14. John McIlwain, brother of minors,
    Plt. he be apt'd. Gdn. Sarah McIlwain, widow, died before 1817.
    consented

McILWAIN, JANE -w- Johnston McIlwain; Robert Yates, and Samuel
    Herron, Exor's of Will of John McIlwain, dec'd. Will-7 May 1818
    and devised to his sister Jane McIlwain and brother Johnston
    McIlwain, equally. And he died in 1818. Lands in Richland Co.
    part devised from estate of Charles McIlwain, father of Jane,
    Johnston, and the dec'd brother John. Pet. for Gdn. by Johnston
    McIlwain, a minor of 14 years--brother of Jane. Robert Yates
    apt'd. Gdn. Richland Bills 155 Filed 3 Feb. 1817

McKINNEY, JANE -w- Benjamin McKinney--Suit for alimony for support
    for herself and one child. Richland Roll 107 1818

McKINZIE, HENRY -w- Mariah -vs- Thomas Baldrick; Joseph B. White,
-w- Sarah, Robert Weston, and William R. Howell. Alleges
Oratrix, Mariah, is the only child of the late Joseph Smith,
dec'd. of Orangeburg Dist., who made a Will and appointed
his wife, Sarah (now Sarah White), Thomas Baldrick, and John
Howell, Executors. Thomas Baldrick, qualified, took possession with the widow and John Howell--That sd John Howell died
intestate in 18__? and Adm'r of his estate was granted to Robert Weston and William R. Howell and the widow Sarah -m- Joseph
White. Alleges: Emanuel Pooser, Sheriff of Orangeburg Dist.
levied on all estate of Joseph Smith except the property which
he derived from Will of Robert Howell, dec'd. Alleges: Joseph
Smith made B/S gift to his daughter, Mariah, in 1794 or 1795.
Richland Bills 127½ Filed 5 April 1817

McKINZIE, JOHN -w- Ann--Deed to Simeon Roach in file. Plat of
Alex'r. McKinzie. See card Edmund M. Roach Bills-57

McKUNE, MARGARET--formerly widow of Alex'r Robinson Bills 104 1815

McLEMORE, JOEL--Of Richland Co. Planter to: John Bigbea, Cabinet
Maker--137 Acres. Pt. of 434 Acres granted sd Joel McLemore.
Bd. Congaree R. Heirs of John Hopkins, Robert Goodwyn, Green
Rives. Pres: Frederick Meyer and Wm. Meyer. Richland Deeds.
Filed 22 May 1787
-Richland File-Camden Apt. A 1798/99--Joel McLemore's widow -m-
Charles Clifton. Allotment 1799--1/3 part. lands to the widow
129 Acres on Raiford's Creek
261 "   " Back Swamp
241 "   " Gill's Creek--Plats in file.

McMILLAN, MRS. M. E.--Aunt of H. Cambridge Moore. See Will Julia
C. Moore. Richland Wills Bx. 138-3 and 71 1864

McPHERSON, THOMAS--See card Joel Martin -w- Sarah. Bills 115
-Richland Bills 115-Will in File.--Thomas and James McPherson
Their children legatees of Peter Smith-Will 1794

McVOY, JOSEPH--Apt'd. Gdn. of his brother and sister, Elizabeth-18
and Lewis-15. James Dallet, Com'r has their money. Roll 73 1817

McVOY, LEWIS, Pet'r.--Now about 17 yrs. His father died about 5
yrs ago, intestate. Left widow and several children. Prays
apt. Capt. John Marshall. Roll 73 shows in 1817, Lewis age 15
and his sister, Elizabeth age 18. Petitioned the appointment
of Joseph McVoy. Richland Roll 158 1820

ME, ELIZA (or Mey)--See card Mary Brown. Richland Bills 188 1821

MEANS, JOHN--Dec'd. Will Richland Roll 31,32,43, 62 1814
Widow: Mary A. Means, Pet'r.
Ch: Isabella, David, Sarah, Martha, Robert, Mary Arenana.
Sarah -m- Robert Means
Isabella -m- Hilliard Judge--See Judge card.
Robert and Mary A. born after Will was made.
-Richland Roll 75 1817--Mary Means apt'd. Gdn. for David, Martha,
Robert and Mary. Rob't Means and David R. Evean, Exor's. Will
of John Means Dec'd. 1817.

MEANS, ROBERT--Ov Beaugort Dist. Pet'r.: Alleges: James Craig,
Henry Hunter, and John Milling got orig. gr. for 1200 acres
on Cedar Creek-Broad River. Minor Winn conv. to Thomas Means
who conv. to Pet'r. Partition suit of partnership property.
Richland Bills Roll 29 1813
-Richland Equity 144--Robert Means, et al. See card Elisha Daniel
-Richland Bills 172 Filed 28 Jan, 1820--Robert Means -vs-
William Branthwaite Alleges: 6 Jan. 1818 def't claimed inheri-
tance in property--applied to David H. Means for a loan $2,299.00
and Mtg'd the lands to secure it. Fill to foreclose.

MEANS, WILLIAM B. -m- Martha Howell--dau. of Jesse M. and Martha
Taylor Howell. Richland Equity 1835

MEYER, FREDERICK--Dec'd. Richland Roll 402 1840
   Children:((Frederick   Benjamin F.) All seven minors,
         (Rebecca W.   Martha   ) all gr-children
         (Lucy A.   Robert   ) of Wm. Meyer
         (Green R.
         Wm. M. Meyer
         Mary -m- Samuel H. Addison
         Frederick Meyer's widow -m- Thomas Howell
         That Frederick had land in Ala. and had moved hands
         and property there.
         Robert Rives, Uncle of Pet'r.

MEYER, FREDERICK -m- Mary Rives, dau. of Green Rives. Roll 47

MIDDLETON, JOHN -vs- Thomas Briggs and Wm. Lewis--Suit over note
made by Thomas Briggs and Wm. Lewis in favor of John Briggs.
16 May 1810 and assigned to John Middleton and at the house of
Gray Briggs in Miss. Territory. Orator informed of transfer.
Richland Bills 113 Filed 4 Jan. 1817

MILES, SARAH ELLEN--Age 19 yrs. -m- ____? Procter 12 June 1854
Charles Riley, age 16 yrs. on 1 Nov. 1854--Children of Thomas
and Rebecca Riley. Adm'r. Robert C. Miles. Gdn. Rebecca Miles
Wit: Geo. Worthington Miles and Wm. H. Miles.

MILLER, SAMUEL--See Emanuel Warnbezee--Richland Bills 104
See also, William Cleland (Richland Bills 39)
-Richland Bills 39 1812--Samuel Miller seems to have married
a daughter of Alex'r Robinson.

MILLING, DAVID--Dec'd. Estate. Richland Roll 24 1813
   Widow: Sarah, Pet'r
   Margaret Milling
   Jane Wright Milling
   John Patterson Milling
   "The youngest child of sd David"
   Alleges: John Fortune of Jackson's Creek, Fairfield Dist. Left
Will devising to his widow, Ann, who, on 28 Nov. 1777 gave Bond
for title simple to John Milling, father of sd David Milling (
(the dec'd.) That William Fortune, oldest son of sd John, be-
ing cut off from Will of his father stole it and disappeared.
That Ann died, leaving sd William as her oldest son and heir.
That sd William made title to James Barber, J. Barkley, and J.
Woodward, Sr. who knew of the missing Will. Alleges David oldest
son of John Milling.

MILLING, SARAH--Widow of David, Margaret Milling, Jane Wright
    Milling, John Patterson Milling -vs- James Barber, John
    Fortune dec'd. wife Ann--Suit to force estate of John
    Fortune to comply with promise to sell. Bills 24
    Filed 10 May 1813

MILLS, JOHN -w- Mary of Richland Dist. Richland Co. 17 Sept. 1785
    To: Uriah Goodwyn of sd County 1000 pounds sterling--640
    acres on Gill's Creek, Camden Dist. Co. afsd--Waters of Con-
    garee River. Bd. S. W. Mary Hay and Gill's Creek. N. E. on
    Bette land. Pres. of John Moore and John Taylor. (Stray Bills)

MOAK, ANDREW--Son, Jacob Moak (or Mock, sp. both ways)--Est. in
    Richland Prob. Ct. Archives Dept. Mem 9-198 1767

MOAK, JACOB--Dec'd. 1804 Richland Co.
    Widow
    8 Ch: Jacob Moak
           Sarah -w- Wm. Perry
           Susannah -w- Thos. Hunter
           Elizabeth -w- Wm. Prue (or Price)
           Andrew Moak
           Mary -w- Wm. Prue   (or Price)
           Emanuel Moak
           John Moak

MOAK, JOHN -w- Anna Richland Bk. 1832
    Robert Price-dec'd
           Heirs: Speer Price
                   John Price
                   Wade Moak
                   John Moke -w- Ann
                   Jonah Etheridge
                   Benjamin Corley -w- Sarah
                   John Partin -w- Lucy
                   Andrew Sanders -w- Mary
                   William, Robert and Joseph Price

MOHE, ANDREW -w- Catherine--See card Sally Holman. Bills 176 1820
    Catherine, dau. of Andrew Dominy

MONTGOMERY, DAVID-Pet'r. Shows: Lucy Ann Fulmer abt. 11 yrs. and
    John William Fulmer, abt. 9 yrs. Their father, William Fulmer
    Deceased. They are entitled to estate in hands of Ordinary
    of Lexington Co. Their mother, Margaret Wilson. Father died
    intestate. Prays pat. Pet'r. as Gdn. Richland Roll 155
    Filed 2 Feb. 1820

MONTGOMERY, ROBERT D. and Archibald Hagood and wife -vs- Sarah
    Starke, Douglas Starke, and others. Pet. by Turner Starke
    showing his brother, Douglas Starke and his niece, Caroline
    Starke are minors and entitled to share in estate of Turner
    Starke, dec'd. father of Pet'rs. File shows plat of 1206
    acre orig. gr. to Moses Duke, E-s Catawba R. on branches of
    Singleton's Creek. Orig. called 1,000 acres. ½ to Robert
    Montgomery and ½ to Heirs of Turner Starke.

MONTGOMERY, DAVID--Continued:
Plat certified 2 Jan. 1824. Widow of Turner Starke, Sarah Starke
Children: Philemon, Lewis, Turner, Douglas, Elizabeth -m- to
Archibald Hagood, Nancy -m- to John Batton and Jane Starke. And
since death of sd Turner Starke, his son, Philemon died leaving
widow, Margaret and children: Baldwin, and Caroline. Also shows
Jane Starke, dau. of dec'd. Turner has also died intestate, no
husband or child. Also shows: Nancy Batton, wife of John Batton,
has died intestate leaving her mother, sd Sarah and her husband.
Bill for partition. Shows Robert Montgomery purchased ½ of the
land from Duke and Turner Starke purchased the other ½.

MOORE, JACOB -w- Christiana--Of the Congarees conveyed to Grace Russell
in 1765 250 acres in Amelia--Gr. to Frederick Reese (or Neese)
Eldest son: John Rees or Reise. John sold to Jacob Moore.
C. T. Deed. F 3-405 Richland File

MOORE, JAMES C.--Richland Dist. Misc. L207--Debt due E. C. Kleckley
Elizabeth Ann Moore and James Moore, Sr. Mtg. 7 Jan. 1841

MOORE, JOHN--Adm'r of John Marple. -vs- James Davis, Joshua Durham,
Edward Marple, David Marple. Alleges: On 24 Jan. 1803 David
Marple obtained letters of Administration on Estate of John
Marple, dec'd. and James Davis, Joshua Durham, and Edward Marple
were sureties on theBond. Alleges: David Marple as Adm'r sold
off property and used funds, then the Ordinary of Fairfield Dist.
revoked the Letters of Administration, and sd David left the
state. Then the Ordinary of Fairfield Dist. apt'd John Moore,
Adm'r. Alleges Thomas Moore, brother of John Moore had purchased
all interest of the heirs of John Marple. File contains Bond
and Mortgage by David and Ann Marple to James Davis. Witnessed
by Jonathan Davis, and John Boyde dated 28 Feb. 1806-original-
covers slaves.

MOORE, MARK--1805 June 4--"Paid Mark Moore" Per Bill
            1803 Feb. 15-" " Michael" "   "   "
Estate of John Compty, dec'd. Richland Prob. Bx. 6-140
-Richland Probate 1805--Mark Moore-read citation for Estate of
Joshua Benson on 30 Oct. 1805

MOORE, MAURICE A.--Gdn. apt'd. In file. See Roul, John L. de C.
Richland Eq. 119 1837

MOORE, MICHAEL--Of Columbia -m- set. Rebecca Lunsford-widow of Swanson
Lunsford. Robert Stark and Simon Taylor, Tr. She owned ¼ pt.
2 lots next the Mary Wales lot which Rebecca Wade now Lunsford
had purchased from David Wade. Archives Misc. B-239 28 May 1803

MOORE, MORRIS--Acct. William Goodwyn, Sr. to Ext. of Jesse Goodwyn.
1792. "To Morris Moore's part of Crop-1791" Richland Bills 95

MOORE, REBECCA--Columbia-Washington St. M. E. Church--Tombstone
Rebecca Moore-B. 25 Aug. 1805 d. 8 July 1846

MORGAN, AARON -w- Mary--Adm'rs. Estate of John Morris. See Morris
card. Richland Eq. Roll 7

MORPHY, MARY -w- Neal Morphy, dau. of Sarah Howe. Sarah, sister of
David Ellison Dunlap. See Dunlap card. Bills 12

MORRIS, JOHN--Richland Eq. Roll 7 Pet: 15 Feb. 1811
    Wife: Mary--owned land in N. C.
    Ch: Martha, Harriett, and John--all minors
         Other children not named.
    Adm'r: Aaron Morgan -w- Mary.

MOUNTZ, GEORGE--Gdn. children of Godfrey Roof. See Roof card.
    Richland Eq. Roll 139 1819

MULDES, ABEL--See card John Clark -w- Mary Bills 130

MUMFORD, JAMES--Deed Gift to children of Dr. Thos. Charleton. See
    card Emanuel Warmbezee. Richland Bills 104

MURPH, CONRAD -m- Widow Mary Hampton, widow of Gayle Hampton. See
    Rebecca Hampton card. Richland Eq. Roll 93
    -Richland Eq. Roll 93 1818--Mary Murph, mother of Rebecca Hampton,
    John T. J. Hampton, and James G. Hampton, children of Gayle

MURFF, JOHN -w- Catherine--See card Morris O'Hewrn. Richland Bills
    # 63 1816

MURPH, MARY--Dau. of Wm. Marshall. Gr-dau. of John Marshall. See
    cards both names. Richland Eq. Roll 76

NEAL, JOSEPH--Dec'd. Richland Co. Extra Bills 134
    John Marshal, Adm'r. File contains Acct's. for 1818 and 1819
    Certificate by Sanders Glover, Ordinary, for Orangeburg Dist.
            Paid to: Dr. R. Murchison   Wm. Clarkson
                      Dr. Wm. Dicks   Samuel P. Jones, Ordinary
                      Samuel Felder   Rec'd from. D. D. H. Treaevant
                      Thomas Barton-

NEILSON, JARED AND DAVID--See card John Mayrant, Sr. Bills 151
    Jared Neilson--Dec'd.--Land he purchased of Mrs. Still, subject
    to life estate of Mrs. Sumter and devised by sd Jared Neilson to
    his niece, Isabella Maysant (formerly Isabella Norvell) and to
    Wm. Ransom Davis, and David Neilson--in equal shares.

NEILSON, SARAH--Legatee of Wm. Trice. See Trice card. Bills 32 1802

NELSON, SAMUEL -m- Widow Catherine Lester. Widow Andrew Lester, Sr.
    See card Andrew Lester, Jr. et al. Richland Bills 122 1816

NETTLES, BENJAMIN--A brother of Dorcas Rix, dec'd. See card Peter
    Chambliss, dec'd. Eq. Roll 122

NETTLES, ZACHARIAH -vs- Anderson Rochell--Alleges Gardner Ford on
    7 Nov. 1803 sold plt'n in Fairfield. Bills ?
    -Richland Eq. Bills 19? 1812--Zachariah Nettles, Pet'r. Shows:
    Gardner Ford, late of Fairfield Dist. died, widow Magdalena
    and Mary -w- Wm. Love, Sarah -w- William Arledge, Jane -w- John
    Middleton, Keziah Ford, Gardner Ford, Donald Ford, Spencer Ford,
    LeRoy Ford, Robert Ford, William Ford, and Nancy Magdalena Ford--
    Alleges: Gardner Ford died while option in land existed.

NORTH, JOHN--Trustee for Sarah Smith. Richland Eq. Roll 157 1820

NORTON, CATHERINE--Will 25 March 1856 Richland Wills 390
    Gr-dau: Mary Elizabeth Boland. Wm. McGinnis, Tr.

NORRIS, JOHN--Of Columbia, Dec'd. 1816 Intestate Richland Eq. Roll
    Heirs: Bro: Elick Norris   Filed: 9 Jan. 1823
            Sis: Esther Avery -w- Jonathan Avery--res. in Ala.
                  Polly Walton -w- John Walton
                  Elizabeth Davis -w- Needham Davis

NORVILLE, ISABELLA--See John Mayrant, Sr. 1819 Richland Eq. 151

NOTT, HON. ABRAHAM--Richland Co. Bills 92 -vs-
    John Richardson -w- Sarah
    Henry Richardson -w- Mary
    John Fraser, Alex'r L. Fraser, Harriet Fraser, Eugenia Fraser,
    and Caroline Fraser, now dec'd.--Lots 31 and 32 in Columbia.
    Agreement to purchase in litigation.

NOYLE, SAMPSON--Res. of Georgia Richland Prob. Bx. 14-330
    Ch: Mary Bryan Noyle   Charlotte Noyle
         Eliza Hester Noyle   Emily Noyle
    Sister: Caroline Harbeinont. Will Prov: 27 Sept. 1836

NYE, JOHN -w- Eliza--Pet'rs. Richland Eq. Roll 60 Filed 25 Feb. 1816
    Shows: James Madison Roach, age 6 yrs. by death of his father,
    late Abraham Roach of Columbia, is entitled to considerable
    Real Estate, and personal property. That Eliza Nye is sister
    of the minor. Prays apt. of 2 Pet'rs as Gdns. June 5, 1819.
    John Nye asks to be relieved of Guardianship.

NYE, JOHN -w- Elizabeth, dau. Abraham Roach. See card John Clark
    -w- Mary. Richland Bills 130

O'GILVIE, MARY ANN--Age 4 yrs in 1813. Pet. of Robert O'Gilvie that
    he be apt. Gdn. Richland Eq. Roll 24

O'GILVIE, ROBERT -m- Mary Cook, widow of Burrell Cook. See Cook
    Card. Richland Eq. Bills 38 1811. Also card Geo. McCreless.

O'HANLON, MARGARET, Samuel, Matilda, Catherine, and Lawrence. See
    card of Andrew Fleming. Richland Bills 26 Filed 26 Feb. 1813

O'HEWRN, MORRIS -w- Catherine (also Hearn) -vs- Adam Bowers, John
    Bowers, John Murff -w- Catherine, brothers and sisters of David
    Bowers, dec'd. and husband of the oretrix. David Bowers left
    1 child. Land in Lexington Dist. Richland Bills 63
    Filed 16 Sept. 1811

OLIVER, CHARLES-m- Set. 29 Sept. 1814 Martha Green. Richland Misc.
    Martha is widow. See card Arthur Collins.
    -Richland Eq. Bills 74 1816--Martha, widow Thomas Green

O'NEAL, JOHN -m- Widow Romedy (or Rummy (See Romedy card. Bills 149

OSTMAN, GEORGE--100 Acre Gr. Richland Co. Richland File Misc. B-659
   Sister: Barbara Ostman -m- 1st: Cappepower
                              1 dau: Katy Cappepower
                         2nd: George Weator
   Katy Cappepower -m- Andrew Kaigler.
   Aff. by Elizabeth Bayliss as to Barbara's being his sister.

OTT, JACOB--See Henry Young as Adm. of Johanna Woolf. Bills 44 1811

OTT, MALACHI -w- Rosanna, dau. of Sarah Wolf. See card Oliver Lomas, Tr.
   Richland Eq. Roll 9 1812. Richland Roll shows 1813 (Roll 27)

OWENS, HENRY--Gdn. for Ann Scott, age 13. Richland Pet. 55 1816

OWENS, SALLY--Pet'r. Claims: Bill of complaint has been filed against
   her minor son, Benjamin Owens Leonard by Benjamin Owens, et al.
   Prays apt. Gdn. Richland Pet. 143 1819

PARISH, SHEROD--Richland Prob. Bk. E-194 Bill of Apr: 27 Oct. 1809
   Sale: 15 Dec. 1809
   Pur: David Sharp, John W. Stevens, Daniel Boyer

PARKER, GABRIEL--Will--Richland Co. Extra Bills 66
   Wife: Lucy--All the property that came by her originally, be-
   longing to Estate of William Rives, dec'd.
   To: Miss Milly House, dau. of Thos. House, two feather beds,
   Remainder to wife for life, then to heirs at law. 19 March 1789
   File shows: Lucy Parker the mother of Green Rives and that she
   had a sister in Columbia
   -Richland Bills 66 Filed 24 Dec. 1810--Gabriel Parker, Dec'd.
   Widow, Lucy Green Rives, Adm.--Land in Edgefield.
        Joseph and John Parker
        Demsey Jones -w- Sarah, late Sarah Parker
        Nathaniel Jones -w- Elizabeth, late Elizabeth Parker
        Mary Farilisa, late Mary Parker
        Henry Jenkins -w- Nancy, late Nancy Parker, of the County
   of Gates, State of North Carolina -vs- Lucy Parker, widow and
   Green Rives, the Adm'r. Alleges: Gabriel Parker of Edgefield
   Dist. S. C. was full uncle to orators. Made Will 20 March 1789
   Exhibit A--leaving legacies to the children of Joseph Parker,
   dec'd, his brother of full blood, and apt. Thos. Hutchinson
   and Joel McLemore Exor's. Lived many years. Died in 1808,
   left widow, Lucy, no lineal descendants. Joel McLemore had
   died and Thomas Hutchinson refused to serve, and Lucy Parker,
   the widow of Green Rives, Adm'r.

PARTRIDGE, WILLIAM--Richland Wills Bk. B-35 1787
   Bro: Philip and John--All and apt. Ex.
   19 Nov. 1787   Proven: 21 Nov. 1787
   Wit: John Cook, Thos. Hutchinson, Burrell Cook

PAULASKIE--See card Wm. Cleland. Richland Eq. Bills 39

PEARSON, PHILIP, SR.--Of Fairfield Richland Bills 191 29 Sept. 1821
   -vs- Ainsley Hall, William Hall, John Kirkpatrick, George Catchett,
   and Ephraim Lyles. Indebtedness to Bank-secured by slaves over
   which there is a dispute of ownership.

PECK, EPHRAIM--Formerly of New Haven, Conn. -vs- Leverett Hubbard
and D. L. Wakely--Leverett Hubband files ans. setting forth that
in 1815, lived in City of New Haven, Conn. and entered into a
verbal agreement with Pltf. to carry on business as Merchant
Taylors. Later, assignment was made to Gad. Peck and Leonard
E. Wales, both of New Haven.--Partnership in business, etc.
Richland Bills 164   Filed 29 June, 1820
-Richland Bills 184   Filed 4 Dec. 1821--Ephraim Peck -vs- Samuel
Percival and David L. Wakeley--Co-Partnership affairs of Pltf.
and Deft.

PERIN, GEORGE--Dec'd. Richland Eq. Filed 3 Feb. 1823
Mother: Christiana Perin, Adm'x.

PERRIN, JOSEPH--Pet'r. Over 14--By death of his father, Joseph
Perrin, dec'd.- entitled to estate. Prays apt. of his mother,
Christine Perrin as Gdn. Richland Eq. Roll 138 1818
-Richland Bills 143 1818--Joseph Perrin, Dec'd. April 1816.
          Widow: Christiana
          Children: Jane, Joseph, and Ann, who married Philip Yancy.

PHILLIPS, REBECCA and Robert Yates as Adm'rs. of Zachariah Phillips
-vs- John M. Creyon--Bill for performance-sale of property of
estate. Richland Bills 185 Filed 27 Nov. 1821

PHILLIPS, ZACHARIAH--Dec'd. 1821 Intestate Filed Dec. 1826 Roll 297
Widow: Rebecca
Children: Ann, Elizabeth, Zachariah, and Martin
Lands in Abbeville, Pendleton, Lancaster, Sumter, and Barnwell .
Pickens, etc. Dist. of Washington. See also Box 324 and 342
Final settlement in 1832 shows:
          Rebecca -w- Lemuel Casey
          Nancy -w- Thomas Brenan
          Elizabeth -w- A. Carter
          Zachariah Phillips
          Dr. Martin Phillips
File contains various deeds:
          Peter Maguire -w- Rebecca Maguire
          John Johnson -w- Catherine

PICKET, REUBEN--From Thomas McCullough-land. See McC. card. Richland
Eq. Bills 111 1810

PICKET, SHEPHERD -w- Susannah, formerly wife of Dr. James Knox, late
of Chester Dist. Dec'd.--Hugh Knox and Gen'l. Edward Lacy, Adm'rs.
Heirs: James Knox--infant son of sd Dr. James Knox by a former
          wife, James (#2), Eliza Knox, and Matilda Knox, all
          minor children of oratrix, Susannah. Susannah -m- 2nd.
          Reuben Stark, 4 March 1797. Reuben Stark left Will.
          Legatees: Oratrix and two brothers, Samuel and Thomas
          Starke. David R. Evans and Sam'l Starke, Orators and
          Adm'r. Will of Shepherd Picket in file.
          Heirs: Wife and 2 little sisters and the rest of my
          brothers and sisters, Mrs. Clayton giving to my 2 little
          sisters, fifty dollars each. 21 Sept. 1813

PICKLEY, MARY ANN--Gr-mother of Wingard Children. Richland Pet. 57/8

PICKREN, SAMUEL -m- set 16 May 1804--Elizabeth Nelson. Wm. Trice, TR.
    Archives--Richland File Misc. B-365

PIERCE, JOHN--Dec'd. 1813 Will Filed 27 Feb. 1824 Roll 238
    Widow: Jerusha-m- Green Rives
    Sons: James
            William-died a minor
            John-born after death of father

PIKE, JOSEPH -w- Margaret of Lexington Dist. Richland Bills 150
    Deed dated Oct. 1794 To: Jacob Haugabook of sd Dist. Con-
    sideration 18 pounds. 449 Acres in Dist. of Orangeburg on
    Cernies Br. N-Fork Edisto River. Bd. Wm. Jones, George Stiddoms,
    Thos. Wadsworth. Wit: Wm. Pool, Henry Baughman, and John
    Wainwright. Orig. Plat in file.

POOSER, EMANUEL--Sheriff of Orangeburg Dist. See Henry McKinzie.
    Richland Eq. Bills 127½

POINDEXTER, REUBEN--Dec'd. Richland Eq. Roll 133 1819
    Widow: Sarah
    Children: Benjamin-under 12, Mary-8 yrs., Robert-6 yrs.
    Thomas Poindexter, Pet'r. Prays his apt. as Gdn.
    Owned land on Saluda River

PRICE, JOHN -m- Widow, Mary Trapp (Widow of John Trapp) Roll 104 1818

PRIOLEAN, CATHERINE--Family card. Richland Bills 86
    Children: Elias -m- Martha Rebecca, sister of Sarah Cantey.
               Catherine -m- _____? Ravanel
               Mary M. -m- _____? Ford
               Martha Pirolean
               Philip G. Pirolean
    See cards Sarah Cantey and Abraham Blanding

PURVIS, WILLIAM AND BURRIDGE--Adv. John Keith, Adm. of Thomas Younge.
    See Keith card. Richland Eq. Bills 82 1810
    -Richland Bills 94 Filed 14 Dec. 1816--Wm. Purvis, Burridge
    Purvis and Ainsley Hall--trading as William Purvis & Co. -vs-
    Mrs. Ann Bay and J. F. Quirke. File contains orig. agreement
    by J. H. Quirke with E. M. Bay as a witness 1814. Also agree-
    ment by P. H. Perrault. Ans. of Thos. Waties, Trustee for Mrs.
    Ann Bay and her children.
    See card Rev. David E. Dunlap.

RABB, JAMES AND ROBERT--See Thomas Marple, Dec'd. 1780

RAIFORD, ISAAC--Gr-father of Zachariah Tucker Kirkland. See Kirk-
    land card. Richland Roll 56 1816
    -Zachariah T. Kirkland, age 17, resides in Louisiana. Pet. to
    move property to La.

RAINSBURGH, JOHN--Intestate. William Howell Adm'r.
    Apprs: Jacob Faust, Christian Kinsler, John Geiger.
    Richland Wills B-41 20 Aug. 1788

RAOUL, DR. LEWIS -w- Harriet--See card Mary Brown, widow, Hannah
McCord, et al. Richland Bills 188 1821

RAWLINSON, SILAS, Moses Rawlinson, James Jackson -w- Rachel, Abraham
Rowlinson, age 15, Rebecca Rawlinson, age 13, and Tempe, widow
of Benjamin Rawlinson, dec'd. are tenants in common. Bill for
Partition. Widow and children of Benjamin Rawlinson--Lands
on Cedar Creek and Carter's Creek, Wateree River.
Richland Bills 178 Filed 10 April 1820

RAWLS, GABRIEL -w- Elizabeth sold lands to Samuel Ingram in 1796.
See Ingram card. Richland Roll 51 1809

RAVENEL, CATHERINE--Nee Priolean--Richland Bills 86 1814
Mary M. Ford, Caroline Dawson, Martha Priolean, Philip G.
Priolean--Children of Catherine Priolean and sisters and broth-
ers of Elias Priolean. See card Abraham Blanding

RAYSER, JOHN -m- Margaret, dau. of Andrew Dominy Eq. Bills 176 1820

REA, WILLIAM--Richland Eq. Filed 25 Dec. 1827
Heirs: Agnes -w- James Rives
        Elizabeth -w- James Casey

REES, EVANS -w- Margaret, sister of Hopkins Price. Evans Reese resident of Great Britain. See Will Hopkins Price 1781
Archives Dept. C. T. Will Richland File 13-281

REES, SARAH -w- Evan Rees, Gr▾dau. Sarah Humy -m- 1-Thos. Allison
2-James Herlock (or Heilack, Henlock) C. T. Deed

REESE, JESSE--Dec'd. 1820 Intestate Roll 227 Filed 24 Feb. 1823
No wife or child.
Heirs: John A Reese 1/7   Catherine Wells 1/7
        Timothy Reese 1/7   Joseph Reese   )
        Mary Arthur 1/7   Sarah Reese   ) 1/7
        Ephraim Reese 1/7   Ann -w-Chas Kester)
        Ann Tucker1/7   Mary Reese-minor)

REESE, MRS. SARAH, ELIZABETH, MARY--All sisters of John Howell.
See Howell card. 1836

REYNOLDS, ANNE--See Mary Cobb. Richland Bills 153

REYNOLDS, DAVID--Dec'd. See Needham David Richland Bills 154

RHODAWITZ, JOHN -m- set 27 April 1820. Barbara Vass. John J. Myers, Tr.
Filed About 1820 to 1830. Richland Eq.

RICHARDSON, HENRY -m- Mary Fraser, dau. of Caroline Fraser. John
Richardson-m- Sarah Fraser, dau. of above. Richland Eq. Roll 65
Filed 2 March 1816
-Richland Eq. Bills 92--See Hon. Abraham Nott

RISH, JOHN -w- Barbara, heirs of George Long. See card Amos Bank
-w- Catherine. Richland Pet. Roll 149

RIVES, GREEN--Gdn. Nancy Clark -vs- Daniel Darby -w- and Drury Bynum--
Alleges: Edmond Clark, dec'd. of Dist. of Richland died in 1803

RIVES, GREEN--Continued:
He left widow, Elizabeth and only child, Nancy or Ann. Widow,
Elizabeth, married Daniel Darby. Green Rives apt'd. Gdn. for
Ann-1810. John Watson and Drury Bynum were sureties on Ad'm.
Bond for Elizabeth Clark, widow. Mentioned: Sterling Clark,
Morris Clark. Also--amount collected from Daniel Colvin who
received it from James Clark, the Exor. of Peter Clark, of
Virginia. 25 Dec. 1803

RIVES, GREEN--Died 1812--Richland Eq.
Heirs: Green Rives, Jr.
Lucy W. -m- John Harrison
Mary -m- Frederick Meyer
Robert Rives-minor.
-Richland Eq. Roll 47 1815--Shows widow: Mary R.
-Richland Prob. 26-623--Green Rives, Dec'd Cit: 13 Nov. 1812
Adm't: Mary Ridley Rives   Adm'r: Green Rives
-Richland Extra Bills 83 1815--Green Rives, Sen'r. Dec'd--
"Ordered that Green Rives be appointed Guardian for Robert
Rives, a minor under the age of 21 years, upon his giving the
Comm'r. of the Ct. the usual security.

RIVES, GREEN -m- Jerusha Pierce, late widow of John Pierce. John
and James Pierce, sons of John Pierce, dec'd. 1824 Equity.

RIVES, HARRIETT--Of Washington Co. Ga. Pet'r.--Shows: She is widow
of Turner Rives, late of S. C. Columbia, Dist. He died on
or about 11 July 1818 in Georgia. Had property in Richland
County, S. C. Left an only child, James Turner Rives, about
3 yrs. old. Prays apt. Gdn. Richland Eq. 147 1819

RIVES, JAMES -m- Agnes Rea, Dau. of Wm. Rea. Richland Eq. 1807

RIVES, LAZRUS -vs- Sampson Russell--Bill to foreclose Mtg. 200 A.
on Crain Creek-Richland Dist. called Dry Fork of Broad River.
Pt. of Gr. to Alexander Kennedy sold by pltf. to deft. 29 Jan.
1811. Part of Pur. price secured by mortgage. Orig. bond in
file. Richland Bills 136 Filed 8 Jan. 1817

RIVES, LEWIS--As Gdn. of the orphans of Jonathan Davis. 28 July 1831
To: Joseph Jackson--Lot #270--containing 202½ acres.
Bk. C-338 Lovett Reaves of Jones Co. to John French of Jones
County. 23 Jan. 1837. This is a Georgia card but Richland
family name.

RIVES, ROBERT--Will 8 Oct. 1790 Prov: 3 Jan. 1793 Prob. 26-636
Wife: Priscilla
Ch: William, Simon, Robert, John Turner, Patience.
Bro: Timothy Rives--Exor.
Friend: Thos. Taylor--Exor.
Richland Bx. 26-635
Priscilla Rives Will 10 June 1796 Prov: 12 Nov. 1800
James Rives-son of Timothy
Charlotte Rives-dau. of Timothy
Turner-son of Timothy
William-son of Robert
To: Miss Priscilla Rives and her 2 daughters--
Mrs. Polly Williamson
Charlotte Rives
Timothy Rives, Exor.

RIVES, STERLING WILLIAMSON -w- Louisa, dau. Harris Turner, dec'd.
1800. Richland Eq.

RIVES, THOMAS--Of Georgia and Harriet, and James et al. See 2 cards
Nathan Center. Timothy Rives--see card Jane Ann Campbell #61.
Richland Eq. Bills 147

RIVES, TIMOTHY--Will 19 May 1821. Codicil 3 Feb. 1820 (reverse dates)
Proven: 16 June 1821 Richland Bx. 26-637
Dec'd son: John Turner Rives, widow Harriet of Washington Co.
    Son: Thomas   Ga.
Gr. Son: James Rives, only son John Turner age 3
            Sterling Williamson Rives
Son-in-law: James T. Wade -m- Martha
     Dau: Mary -w- Sterling C. Williamson
           Charlotte -w- Nathan Center

RIVES, WILLIAM--Died 1804 Richland Eq.
Son: Silas Jesse Rives, age 13
     Wm. Henry Rives, of age
     John Green Rives, of age
     Rachel -w- Willaby Harrison (called Elizabeth on one paper)

RIVES, WILLIAM, JR. Richland Prob. 26-638 Bond: 19 Oct. 1804
Cit: 14 Oct. 1804
Adm'r: Green Rives and James Adams
S: Timothy Rives and Clairborne Clifton.
Pd: Hat for Wm. H. Rives
    Shoes for Eliza and Betsy
    For children's board and schooling.
-Richland Equity Bills 66 Shows: Lucy Parker -w- Gabriel Parker
an heir of Wm. Rives. See card Gabriel Parker

RIVERS, WILLIAM (or Rives) Will 27 Aug. 1814. Prov: 28 Nov. 1818
To: Mrs. Sarah Weston -w- Malachi Weston
    William Clarkson, Jr. of Charlestown Prob. 26-632

RIX, DORCAS--Dec'd. sister of Benjamin Nettles. See card Peter
Chambliss, Dec'd. Richland Eq. Roll 122 1819

ROACHE, ABRAM -vs- James Rutherford Alleges: Abraham Roach, cec'd.
on or about 17 June 1806, purchased a house and lot in Columbia
from James Rutherford. Suit over titles. Richland Bills 79
Filed 24 Sept. 1810
-Richland Pet. Roll 60--Abraham Roach-Son, James Madison Roach,
minor. John Nye, Gdn. Dau. Eliza -w- John Nye

ROACH, EDMOND MORGAN -vs- Jane Roach Richland Bills 57 Alleges:
Simeon Roach, copy of Will in file, father of Edmond Morgan
Roach, the orator made a Will 27 Nov. 1807. Widow: Jane
Daughter: Jane -m- John Cox. File contains orig. grant and
Plat to John McWilliams 1765, also a Deed from James Ruther-
ford of Rutherford Co. N. C. for lots in Columbia. to Abraham
Roach in 1810. Also Deed from John McKinzie and wife, Ann to
Simeon Roach and Plat to Alex'r. McKinzie.

ROACH, THOS. JEFFERSON-age 19, Abraham Washington Roach-age 14,
James Madison Roach-age 10. Pet. apt. of their eldest brother
Samuel Roach as Gdn. Alleges their father Abraham Roach, died
intestate. Richland Co. Extra Bills 130
-Thos. Jefferson Roach, et al,--See card John Clark -w- Mary.

ROBINSON, ALEXANDER, JOSEPH AND SIMON--See card William Cleland.
Richland Eq. Bills 89

ROBINSON, ALEXANDER--His dau. -m- John Kennedy of Chester Dist.
Another dau. -m- Samuel Banks of Fairfield. Sons: Joseph and
Simon Robinson. See card William Cleland. Richland Eq. 39 1812
-Richland Eq. Bills 104 1815 Shows widow, Margaret -m- 2nd
_____? McKane.

ROBINSON, GEORGE--Died several yrs ago. Widow -m- Thomas Edwards,
Pet'r. Several children among whom--Anne Jane about 12 yrs.
Eleanor about 8 yrs. Richland Roll 22 1813

ROCHELL, ANDERSON--Advs. Zachariah Nettles (see Nettles card)--Sale
Plt'n in Fairfield by Gardner Frost to Plt'f. Richland Eq.

ROMEDY, JOSEPH (Also spelled Rumney) -vs- John Chappell, Adm'r. of
Andrew Romedy, who died intestate. Alleges: Joseph Romedy,
Orator is gr-son and sole heir of dec'd. Ans. Alleges:
Father of Plt'f died before the gr-father and left a widow who
married John O'Neal, who refused to let Plt'f remain with his
mother unless the Adm'r. paid his board, etc. and therefore,
def't paid 10 year Board at $20.00 per year. File contains
Act. Estate of Andrew and Catherine Rumney, dec'd. Andrew
R. left Will. Catherine R. survived her husband by a few
months. Acct by John Kaigler, for services rendered.
Richland Bills 149 Filed 6 Feb. 1818

ROOF, GODFREY--Dec'd. Left 4 children: Nancy about 17
                                        Reuben "   15
                                        John   "   11
Mother also dead. Benj. Roof   Andrew "   7
and George Mountz, Adm'r.

ROSS, ISAAC -w- Mary Richland File Mem 8-119/20 1 Oct. 1765
500 Acres land. Orig. Gr. to Roger Gibson. 250 A. conv. by
Samuel Gibson to Isaac Ross.
-C. T. Wills--Richland File--Isaac Ross of Wateree Will 17 March
        Sons: Isaac--Home place on Wateree   1775
              Samuel--Land on Tyger River
        Daus: Elizabeth, Jane, Mary, Euphemia
        Bro: Arthur Brown Ross

ROUL, JOHN LOUIS de CHAMPOINORS--a citizen U. S. Resident of Dedville,
Orangeburg Dist. Being about to embark for France.
Wife: Caroline--Exe'x.
Ch: Louis, Alfred, Caroline -m- Dr. Thos Starke, Frederick
    Harriett, and other lawful issue.
Wit: Mary Gaillard, A. Godefrey, Z. Perry.
Will date: 4 May 1824 Prov: 22 Aug. 1827
File contains apt. Gdn. ad. liten. for Maurice A. Moore-1842

ROUTZ, JACOB--A resident of Congaree. Died about 1776. Widow,
Sarah -m- John Harve. One child, Mary -m- John Goodwyn.
Richland Eq. Bills 55 Filed 30 Oct. 1807

ROYSER, JOHN -w- Margaret--See card Sally Holman. Extra Bills 176
1820

RUSH, JOHN -w- Barbara. Heirs of George Long. See card Amos Banks
-w- Catherine. Richland Eq. Bills 1849

RUDOLPH, MICHELL J. and Louisa M. Hendricks--both of Columbia, marriage
agreement 1 Oct. 1816. Jacob J. Faust, Trustee. James Gregg, Wit.
Richland Co. Extra Bills 166

RUDOLPH, ZEBULON--See card Abraham Blanding. Richland Eq. 86 1814

RUFF, SEVELAH (Susannah) -m- Benjamin Scott. Richland Eq. Bills 123
Ch: Susannah, Mary, Jane, James Scott   1816
Sevelah is 2nd wife.

RUSSELL, ALEXANDER -vs- James Douglass--Bill for settlement of Co-
partnership affairs. 1804 or 1805. Sawmill or Millers.
Richland Eq. Bills 199 Filed 13 May 1823

RUSSELL, CHARLES--Will 1 Jan. 1736 Richland Mem. 4-19
Wife: Mary Russell and her children
        Rachel Heatley
        William Heatley   Wit: Henry Sp___? and
        Charles Russell   John Pearson
        Sophianisbia Russell
        John Russell
        Eugenia Russell
        Joseph Russell

RUSSELL, ROBERT E. of Richland -m- set 16 May 1821 Martha Taylor,
dau. of Mary Taylor. Richland File Misc. D-363

RUTLEDGE, HUGH, William James, Waddy Thompson, Henry W. DeSaussure,
Theodore Gaillard--Comm'rs in Equity for Columbia Dist.

RYAN, DR. DANIEL--Pet. by John Hooker that Comm. be Apt'd. to in-
vestigate lunacy of Dr. Ryan--alleges he is unable to attend
a business. 26 June, 1812 Richland Eq. Roll 25 1813

SARGENER, JOHN--Planter -vs- Martin and Mary Marshall and their children. Land bequeathed to Mary Marshall by Will of Wm. Blanchard,
her dec'd. brother, for life and then to her children--of whom
7 are living-all minors--Suit for titles. Answered by:
        Wm. B. Marshall   Benjamin F. Marshall
        Elizabeth L. Marshall   John L. Marshall
        Gary H. Marshall   Green B. Marshall
        Sarah W. Marshall   By: James Goodwyn, Gdn.
Copy Will of J. W. Blanchard in file.
Heirs: Cousin, Joseph Neal, son of Lewis and Penny Neal--a
        slave, and a judgement -vs- James Blanchard in Mont-
        gomery Dist. Georgia. Sister Mary Marshall -w- J.
        Martin Marshall 28 May 1800
Richland Bills 114 1815 Filed 26 June 1815

SARGINER, JOHN--Dec'd.   Richalnd Eq. Bills 81 1817
    Gr-son: William Bynum age 17 Pet. Drury Bynum, Gdn.
    Roll 86--Rebecca -w- Samuel Johnson. Late Rebecca Sarginer.
    Only 2 children.
    -Richland Equity Roll Filed 15 May 1826--John Sarginer of Rich-
    land died 1817. Widow: Elizabeth Sarginer, married March 1815
    Son: William Sarginer, by former wife. William's widow -m-
    Joseph Scott after his death in 1821.

SAUNDERS, JOHN--Richland Bills 176 1820 -m- Polly, dau. of Andrew
    Dominy

SCOTT, ANN--Richland Equity #55 1816--About 13 yrs.--both parents
    dec'd. Pet. apt. Henry Owens as Gdn. 1816

SCOTT, BENJAMIN--Richland Eq. Roll 54/5 1815
    Wife: Mary--Legatee of Philip Shaver
    Ch: Daniel Scott
         Francis Scott--both minors. Also Fanny
    Pet. Henry Owens Apt. Gdn.
    Pet. Ann Scott, about 13 yrs. Henry Owens, Gdn.

SCOTT, JOSEPH--Richland Bills 207 Filed 25 June 1822
    John, age 20,
    Samuel, age 19
    Sarah, age 16
    William, Adm'r.
    Mary, Jane, and James--All children of Samuel Scott, dec'd.
    Land in Richland Co. on Tom's Creek
    Jane Scott, widow. Mary age 11, Jane, age 9, and James, age 6

SCOTT, SAMUEL -vs- Thomas Woodsides--Alleges shortage in acreage
    of lands sold to Plt'f. by Def't. Richland Bills 131
    Filed 23 Sept. 1817
    -Richland Equity Roll 339 Filed 5 Jan. 1832--Samuel Scott-Will
        Heirs: Francis Killingsworth--All Real Estate
                Mary R. Reese--All slaves (Mary is dau. of Joseph)
                William H. Killingsworth--$2000.00
                William Devlin
                Jesse Reese
    Brothers: William Scott and John Scott--had charge of property

SCOTT, WILLIAM--Richland Eq. Bills 51 1809--See card Samuel Ingram.
    See card Matthew McHugh 1820 Bills 162
    -Richland Equity Roll 292 Filed 22 Dec. 1827 Will 20 April 1806
        Wife: _____ and all my children
        Son: William Scott
              Samuel Scott
        Mentions amounts paid to Elizabeth Dinkins, his daughter.
        He held her trust property from Samuel Ingram. Nephews:
        Joseph Scott and Wm. Scott. James L. Clark -w- Martha
        Adm'r.

SCOTT, WILLIAM, SEN'R. --Dec'd. Conv. 1805 Will 20 Jan. 1810
    Dau: Hester -w- Hezekiah Thomson
          Children: William A. Thomson
                     Sarah Thomson
                     Joseph Thomson
                     Mary Rebecca Thomson
    Son: Wm. Scott, Jr. Will 20 June 1820 Filed 20 Jan. 1830

318

SEABROOK, WILLIAM -vs- William Robertson, et al.   Bill to foreclose
    Richland Bills 203   Filed 25 June 1822

SEIBELS, JACOB -vs- Drusilla Brasilman--Alleges Jacob Seibels and
    Peter Brasilman, late of Dist. of Newberry, were jointly
    seized of several tracts in Lexington--originally granted
    jointly. Peter died leaving widow, Drusilla and 5 children-
        Maria R. H. Turpin -w- William Turpin, Jr.
        Louisa Turpin   Filed May 12, 1812
        Sarah Turpin   Richland Bills 11
        Thomas Jefferson
        Wilhelmena
Land situated in the Dutch Fork of Broad and Saluda Rivers.
7820 acres.

SEABELS, SARAH--Rob't Stark apt. her Trustee, 1815. Mentions Wm.
    Seabels. Richland Eq. Roll 37 1815

SETZLER, JOHN--Dec'd. About 1813 Richland Eq. Roll 113 1818
    Widow: ? -m- Honorius Sheppard
    Shows: George Setzler, and his children:
            Jacob-died 1813--3 children-John, Wm. and Mary
            William-19
            George-17
            Mary Elizabeth -m- William F. Howell

SEXINER, JOHN--Dec'd. Gr-father of William Bynum. See Bynum card.
    Richland Eq. Roll 81 1817

SEXINER, REBECCA -m- Samuel Johnson. See Johnson card.
    Family: John Sexiner -w- Rebecca   Richland Eq. Roll 86 1817
             Only child: William
             Gr-child: William Bynum

SHARPE, J. M. E.--Of Richland Dist. Deed Bk 00-577 26 Dec. 1853
    To: Andrew J. Moses of Sumter Dist.--Lot in Sumterville.
    Bd: N-Thos McGee, E-Broad St. S-Jas. H. Dingle, W-Sumter St.

SHAVER, PHILIP--Will 1793--Richland Eq. Bills 123 1816
    Widow: Margaret
    Dau: Mary Scott -w- Benjamin Scott who -m- 2nd- Sevelah Ruff
    Ch: Hiram,
          Margaret -m- Daniel Turnipseed
          Elizabeth -m- Frederick Harminter
          Danniel, Francis and Ann
    Children of Sevelah Ruff: Susannah, Mary, Jane, Tames (or Fanny)

    -Richland Eq. Roll 54 1816--Philip Shaver devised property to
    Mary Scott, wife of Benj. Scott. Both dec'd. Their children:
    Daniel and Francis Scott, also called Fanny Scott.

SHEPHERD,   ? Dec'd. Richland Eq. Roll 15 1813
    Widow: Ann -m-   Freeman
    Son: George James about 16 yrs.
          Lewis about 14
    Land in Laurens Dist. Pet. Mother be apt'd. Gdn.

SHEPHERD, STEPHEN -vs- Wm. Sherlock In re Co-partnership agreement
    Bill for discovery shows invoice for 39 lbs. Shad and other
    Fish sold by J. Darmeduitt of Richmond Va. Pur: Job. Green
    Tarlton Sanders, et al. Richland Bills 52 Filed 18 May 1809

SHEPPARD, ABRAHAM -m- Elizabeth Garner, dau. Presley Garner of
    Richland Dist. Elizabeth now dec'd. Left 3children:
    Jeremiah, Rebecca and Elizabeth Ann Sheppard.
    Deed gift 1812 Richland File Archives Misc. B-734

SHEPPARD, HONORIUS--Pet'r.--Married widow of Jacob Setzler, died
    about 1813. Jacob left 3 children:
    John Adam about 9, William about 7 and Mary about 5. Jacob
    owned ¼ of 2/3 of estate with George Setzler, his father, and
    Wm. Setzler. George Setzler and Mary Elizabeth Setzler were
    brother and sister. Receiving 1/4 of 2/3 share were; Jacob,
    George, Wm. and Mary Elizabeth who married Wm. F. Hu_____?
    Richland Pet. Roll 113   1818

SHEPPARD, JAMES, WILLIAM, JAMETHY?, SARAH--Children of George
    Sheppard, died about 1798--by Joseph Strother, their next friend.
    Leaving Widow Mary, daughter now married to Wm. Lee and the
    complainants. Mary widow of Henry Alimons. Richland Bills 44
    Filed 28 Jan. 1810

SHEPPARD, JOHN E.--Dec'd. Will--Richland Will Bk. K-265
    "An inventory taken of the Estate of John E. Sheppard after
    the death of his father, Abraham Sheppard and of his mother
    Susannah Sheppard, dated 9 Feb. 1838 Value: $8,796.00

SHEPPARD, MRS. MARY--Richland File Archives Misc.QQ-367
    Ch: Catherine and Mary. Henry Pooser purchased slaves on
    their behalf from Benj. Waring as Exor. of George Evans.
    4 Feb. 1780

SHIRLING, JAMES (sick) Richland Wills Bk. B-45 Will 1785
    My brother's son: John Shirling
    John's dau: Becky
    Heir in case of death of above: Wm. Shirling.
    Ex: John Shirling and Thos. Taylor   30 May 1785
    Wit: Benj. Gubb, John Dortch, Allen Hunter

SHIRLEY, THOMAS--Had grant on Wateree Creek. See card Thomas
    McCullough. Richland Eq. Bills 111

SILVEAH, MATTHIAS--Dec'd. Estate. Richland Roll 120 Filed Feb. 1818
    Elizabeth Bell, Pet'r,--Mother of Mary Bell-minor heir. age
    not shown. Prays apt. Abraham Geiger.

SIMONS, CHARLES DEWAR--Richland Wills Bx. 28-176 (or 676)--Shows
    he was the son of James Simon, of Charleston. Died in Columbia
    and sent to Charleston for burial-1812. Thomas Barksdale, Adm.
    Also, Robert Dewar, and Peter Croft. And Mrs. Sarah Simmons

SIMMONS, CLAUD--Richland Prob. Bk. E-90 Will 30 Dec. 1807
    Heir: Miss Marianne Chapman, "Eldest dau. of Mr Gersham
             Chapman of this city, my house and lot in Town of
             Beaufort".
    Exor: Mr. Perrault and Mr. Gersham Chapman
    Wit: John Dubose, Geo. Paterson, P. H. Perrault.
    Proven: 4 Jan. 1808
    -Richland Eq. Bills 14 1812--Claude Simon, See card John
    Hooker and wife.

SIMMONS, HENRY F. -w- Elizabeth--Richland Eq. Bills 128 1817
    Adm'r: Samuel Billings, Dec'd. See Billings card.

SIMMONS, WILLIAM M. and Eliza--See card Needham Davis. Richland
    Equity Bills 154

SIMS, JOHN -m- Nancy Hampton, dau. of Maj. John Hampton.
    Maj. John Hampton's widow, Peggy
                  son: Anthony
    See Herbert card.   dau: Elizabeth -w- Thomas Herbert
    Richland Eq. Bills 47 1810

SISTRUNK, MARGARET AND JOHN--Of Orangeburg to John Weanwright of
    Orangeburg, Planter, ½ of 100 acres Gr. to Anthony Stack.
    Richland Bills 150 24 Dec. 1798

SMITH, GEORGE C.--See card John Bryce. Richland Eq. Bills 146 1818

SMITH, JOHN--Dec'd. 1801 Richland Eq. Roll 34 1791
    "Came to Richland in 1791"
    Wife: Rachel -m- Stephen Burke
    Son: John C. Smith
          Harriet Smith not yet 14 yrs.
          Tobias Alexander Smith not 14 yrs.

SMITH, JOHN--Dec'd. Richland Eq. Roll 157 1820
    Sarah Smith--by her Trustee, John North--Pray for Partition
    of lands.

SMITH, JEMIMA--about 11   SAMUEL-minor
    JACOB--about 10   JAMES-minor
    Children of Thomas Smith, dec'd. See Daniel Bouknight, Pet.
    Richland Eq. Roll 151 1819

SMITH, JOSEPH--Dec'd. Richland Eq. Bills 127½ 1817
    Widow: Sarah -m- Joseph B. White
    Dau: Mariah McKinzie -w- Henry McKinzie. See McKinzie card.

SMITH, CAPT. MINOR -m- Elizabeth Ederington in 1784 and lived in
    Orangeburg. See card John Hampton. Roll 3 Richland Eq.

SMITH, PETER--Of Richland. Richland Extra Bills 115--Copy in file/
    Wife: Sarah   Will: 24 March 1797 Prov: 7 July 1797
    Dau: Catey's children
          Nancy
    Legacy: Thomas McPherson's children
              James McPherson, Jr. son of J. McP. Sr. dec'd.
              Nancy Campbell dau. James Campbell
              Peter Campbell

SMITH, RICHARD--Left Will--Richland Eq. Filed 21 Jan. 1832
Case: John Feltmetz otherwise called John Smith
    Margaret "   "   "   M-   "
    Martha "   "   "   M-   "
    Sarah   "   "   "   S-   "
    Children of Sarah Feltmetz and Richard Smith, the testator.
    Evidently 2 died, Christian F. and Mary F.
    Sarah -w- Christian Feltmetz

SNYDER, COL. GEORGE--Of Lexington Dist. died 1811. Roll 144 1819
    Widow: Harriet -m- David Foster, Pet'r.
    Ch: Mary Rebecca and Margaret. Pray apt. Pet'r. Gdn.

SOMARSALL, WILLIAM AND SON, THOMAS--Assignees. See card William
    Lenoir. Richland Bills

SPANN, JAMES -m- Leonora Davis, Dau. Wm. Ransome Davis. See card
    Warren R. Davis. Richland Bills 152

SPELLING, BRITTAIN--Of Columbia Dist. Land on Cedar Creek, Congaree
    River. Richland Eq. Bills 37 1811
    Wife: Nancy
    6 Children: Rebecca, Jesse, William, Brittain
                Nancy -w- Benjamin Night
                Sally -m- Aikins
    Alleges some of heirs sold their share to Simon Roach-father
    of Edmond M. Roach and Jane Cox, wife of John F. Cox.
    See card Edmond M. Roach

STACK, ANTHONY--Gr 100 Acres conv. by Margaret and John Sistrunk
    of Orangeburg. to John Wainwright. Richland Bills 150 1798

STANLEY, SAMUEL--Of Town of Columbia Will 29 June 1815 Bills 156
    Dau: Polly Williamson
          Betsy McGowen (also called Elizabeth)
          Lucy Waddell--after death of her husband--20 yds. home-
                  spun annually for herself and her children.
    Gr-dau: Sally Jerman
    Dau: Sally Trapp
    Wife: Martha
    "My four Y-children": Robert Hendrick, William Bird, Martha
                      and Samuel.
    Exor's: Wife and Dr. Edward Fisher
  -See card Henry McGowen 1819

STANLEY, WILLIAM, ROBERT, AND MARTHA--Minors. Dr. Edward Fisher
    apt'd. Gdn. to sup't division of estate of their father,
    Samuel Stanley Richland Extra Bills 126 1819

STANTON, JOSEPH B -w- Lucy T. late Lucy Howell -vs- Malachi Howell,
    and James Deale and wife Allegea: William Howell, late of
    Richland Dist. died 1795, leaving widow, Elizabeth and Wm.
    Howell, the younger. Elizabeth, now -w- Thompson Ware, Grace
    A. Howell, oratrix, Lucy T. Howell Ware, alleges the widow,
    Elizabeth -m- James Beal of Ga. Wm. the younger died intestate.
    Grace A. Howell Died intestate. Richland Bills 91 27 June 1814

322

STARK, ALEXANDER B. -vs- Henry McGowen--Bill for Injunction. Alleges
John Compty was authorized to build a bridge across Broad R.
about confluence of Broad and Saluda by act of Gen. Assembly.
19 Feb. 1791 Richland Bills 157 Filed 14 Jan. 1819
-Richland Eq. Roll 251 Filed 30 June 1823--Alex'r Stark died
1822. Of Lexington
Widow: Sarah--oratrix
Only child: Sarah Ann Stark about 5 yrs.

STARKE, REUBEN--Richland Eq. 1 1808 -m- Widow Susannah Knox.
Widow of Dr. James Knox. She married 3rd Shepherd Pickett.
See Pickett card. Bros: Samuel and Thomas

STARKE, DR. THOMAS -m- Caroline Roul, dau. of John Louis de
Champoinois Roul. See Roul Will Richland Bills 119 1837

STARKE, TURNER, et al--See card Robert D. Montgomery Eq. Bills 179
-General Turner Starke--Mentioned as a purchaser of lands
and negroes from John Allen in or about 1814. Extra Bills 141

STEEL, DAVID -w-Applicants -vs- Frances Blythe and Mary Ann Blythe,
Heirs and representatives of Samuel Blythe, Dec'd.
July 12, 1830 Son Times and State Gazette

STEVENSON, ELIZABETH--See card Rev. David ElliSon Dunlap. Stray Bills
-Elizabeth is sister of David Dunlap. Bills 12

STITT, AGNES--Sister of William Jamerson. See Jamerson card. Bills
151

STONE, CHARLES -W- SARAH--Charles Smitten of C. T. Trustee.
Sam'l Herron and Dan'l Ewar, Pet. for confirmation of sale of
property. Richland Eq. Roll 63 Filed 27 Feb. 1816
-Both Charles and Sarah between 50 and 60 yrs. No children.
Owned lot in C. T. Charles Smitten, Tr. 1816

STONE, ENOCH--Richland File Archives Dept. Misc. D-207
Wife: Massey
Dau: Elizabeth -w- Micajah Dinkins
Deed Gift 30 Sept. 1820--personal property, horse, etc.

STROTHER, GEN'L. C -m- an aunt of John Woodward Durham. See
card Chamel Durham Richland Eq. #96

STROTHER, JOSEPH--Next friend to the children of George Shepard,
dec'd. Richland Bills 44 1810

SURGINER, JOHN -m- set 18 March 1815 Elizabeth Randol   widow of
John Bond Randol. Robert Weston and James Adams, Trustees
Archives Dept, Richland File Misc. C-171.
Page 177--Receipt by Elizabeth Randol for her part of her
father's estate. Delivered to her by Wm. Sarginer. 4 April 1815
Page 271--John Surginer to son, Wm. Surginer--Plat land on
Wateree R. 50 Acres.

SURGINER, WILLIAM--Dec'd. Will Filed 25 Dec. 1827 Richland
Heirs: _____? -m- Samuel Johnston.

TATE, DANIEL--Dec'd. See card Harriet Bell. Richland Bills 59
                                                              1807
TAYLOR, EDWARD AND SUMTER--sons of Simon Taylor, Dec'd. Heirs of
    Elizabeth Brown. See Brown card. Eq. Roll 71 1817

TAYLOR, JAMES--Dec'd. Adm'rs. Thomas and John Taylor. Bills 59
                                                              1807
TAYLOR--Richland Eq. Roll 40 1815
    Son, James Simon, age about 17, pet's his uncle, Thos. Taylor
    be Guardian.
    Son, Simon Taylor, Equity Bill 41, Pet's to exchange slaves.

TAYLOR, JAMES--Dau. Sarah -m- John Goodwyn. See Goodwyn cards.

TAYLOR, JAMES, The Elder, died about 1809 Richland Roll 343 1835
    Dau: Sarah Goodwyn -w- Maj. John Goodwyn
          Mary Taylor -w- Maj. Thomas Taylor
          Martha Howell -w- Jesse M. Howell
          Gr-son: James Simon Taylor--only heir.
    That Martha Howell died intestate about 1812, leaving Mrs. Jesse
    M. Howell and her 2 children.
    Martha T. Means -w- Wm. B. Means, Complainant, and James M.
    Howell. Jesse Malachi died 1835.

TAYLOR, JAMES SIMON--a minor about 14 yrs. Pet. that his uncle,
    Thomas Taylor, the younger, be apt'd. Gdn. Pet. Roll 40 1815
    Pet. Roll 41--Simon Taylor -w- Eliza Pet. to sell or exchange
    slaves.
    Bills 43--Simon Taylor -w- Eliza -vs- Martha Davis, John H.
    Davis, et al--Suit over slaves.

TAYLOR, JOHN--Will 29 July 1766 Richland File C. T. Wills
    Wife: Mary
    Son: John Taylor--Land adj. Jno. Thomas, Jr. Formerly Dr.
           Farmer's.
           James and William--Land formerly of John Hopkins
    Dau: Elizabeth
    Son: Thomas Taylor--Exor.--300 A. formerly Jno. Pearson
    Wit: Joel Threewits, Jemima Threewits, Samuel Strother

TAYLOR, JOHN--Intestate. Richland Eq. Bills 117 1817
    Widow: Mary
    Children: Mary -w- Wm. Heath
               Sarah -w- Richard Tucker
               Rebecca -w- John Veal
               Henry Taylor
               William Taylor
               Martha Taylor
    See card Wm. Heath -w- Mary.

TAYLOR, JOHN --Of Columbia--Richland File Misc. H-383 Archives
    Heirs: Sarah Taylor, Adm'x. (widow)
            James H.
            William
            Rebecca -w- John G. Brown
            Harriet C. -w- Franklin H. Elmore
            Sarah Cantey
            George Taylor
            Alexander Taylor.

324

TAYLOR, JOHN C.--Son Times and State Gazette 9 April 1831
    Widow: Jane Taylor, also dec'd. Case--Richland Chancery
    Andrew Wallace and James K. Taylor, Adm'rs. Real Estate
    to be sold.

TAYLOR, MARY--Of Richland. Will Filed 5 July 1788
    "my 3 cousins": Elizabeth Brazele, Mary Howell, Ann Strowman
    Mary Howell, dau. Arthur Howell
    Mary Howell, wife Arthur Howell
    Sarah Howell
    Friend: John Bostick.

TAYLOR, SARAH--Dau. of William Kirkland. See Kirkland card.
    Richland Bills 17 1812

TAYLOR, SIMON -w- Eliza Maria--only daughter of Gen'l. William
    Henderson, dec'd. Alleges: Prior to June 1791, Douglas
    Starke, one of Exor's of Will of William Henderson, placed
    in hands of William Ransom Davis, funds to purchase negroes.
    Bill for Discovery and Acc't. Richland Bills 42

TAYLOR, SIMON--Apt. Gdn. Richland Eq. Roll 71 1817
    Ch: Edward Taylor age 18 Heirs of Elizabeth Brown, dec'd.
    Sumter Taylor age 17 Wm. Taylor, her exor.

TAYLOR, WILLIAM -w- Margaret -vs- William McGrew Alleges: Alex'r
    McGrew, father of Margaret Taylor, left a Will. His children
    were: James
           William Peter, cllled Alexander
           Margaret--Died in 1786
           Mary -m- Grove Young--both died, leaving 2 children
               who also died without heirs.
           Peter or Alexander died 1791--left 1 son, John who
               died intestate, no issue.
           Richland Bills 67 Filed 5 Nov. 1810

TERRY, THOMAS -m- Widow Martha Hopkins, dau. of Bird Booker.
    Widow of Geo. W. Hopkins, dau. Mrs. Glenn. Hills Eq. V-1 Pg.-1

THERON, SAMUEL--Trustee for Margaret O'Hanlon and 2 children. See
    O'Hanlon card. Richland Roll 38

THOMAS, CECELIA--Of Craven--C. T. Wills Richland File 13 Feb. 1768
    Mother: Slaves
    Brother: James, and John Thomas, Jr.
    Exor: John Hopkins
    Wit: Peter Hay, David Hay, and Mary White Prov: 10 Sept. 1768

THOMAS, JOHN -m- Eleanor Threewits-widow of LLewllan Threewits.
    Richland Bills 46

THOMAS, EZRA -w- Elizabeth of Mass. Dau. of Joshua Benson. See
    Benson card. Richland Eq.

THOMAS, JOHN, JR.--Dec'd. Estate. See card Henry Brown. Stray Bill

THOMAS, JOHN, JR.--Of Craven. C. T. Will Richland File
   Wife: Mary   Will 27 June 1767
   Son: John Thomas
   Dau: Mary and Sarah-Land adj. Neese's Old Place
   Exor: John Thomas, Sr., Thos. Taylor, John Hopkins
   Wit: John Elders, John Taylor and Martha A. Thomas
-Card #2--John Thomas, Jr.
        Widow, Mary -m- again and died many yrs ago.
        John Thomas died while still a minor
        1 dau. -m- Roland Williamson and died about 1786. Left
           2 daughters. 1 died. 1 -m- Thomas Heath
        1 dau. -m- Maj. John Threewits. Left no children
        Thomas Heath married gr-dau. of John Thomas, Jr.
           Ch: John T. Heath
               Ethel
               Rebecca Kirkland
               Alice Owens
               Eliza Owens
               Mary Whitaker, dec'd.
                  1 child: Sally W. Nott

THOMAS, JOHN--Of Lexington to Wife: Eleanor. Deed gift--4 slaves
   6 April 1811 Richland - Lexington File Misc. B-461 Archives

THOMAS, HEZEKIAH--Richland Eq. Filed 20 Jan. 1830--On 24 May 1815
   Made Trust Deed--Land on Tom's Creek.
   Wife: Hester
   Children: Wm. A., Sarah, Joseph, Mary Rebecca.

THOMSON, COL. WM.--Dec'd. Had been Exor. Will Chas. McCord.
   His daughter -m- C. B. Cochran
   See card Mary Brown, widow and Hannah McCord, et al.

THORP, WILLIAM -m- Mary Faust. Richland Bills 68 See card
   Dorothea Doubleday

THREEWITS, JOEL--Of Newberry Dist. Richland Wills K-172
   Wife: Lucretia--dau. of legatee of Mrs. Mary Phelps
   Son: John Hawkins Threewits
          Joel Thomas Threewits
          Lewellan Williamson Threewits
   Dau: Emma Eliza Threewits
          Lucretia Silvia Threewits
          Jemima Williamson Threewits
          Epsey Davis Threewits
          Keziah Ann Rose Threewits
   Will: 1 Jan. 1818 Wit: John and Mary Threewits, John Thomas

THREEWITS, MAJ. JOHN--Late of Lexington Dist. Richland Eq. #38
   Sister: Mrs. Martha Tucker
          Children: Joel T. Tucker
                   Martha J. Jumper
                   Ann R. Williams
   Sister: Mrs. Elizabeth Chappell
          Children: James H. Chappell
                   John J. Chappell
   Brother: Joel Threewits

THREEWITS, MAJ. JOHN--Continued:-
Children of Joel Threewits:
  John H. Threewits
  Lewellyn W. Threewits
  Jemima W. Poole
  Eppes (Epsey) D. Geiger -w- William Geiger
  Keziah A. R. Butler -w- Henry Butler
  Mary A. Jones -w- Henry Jones
  Emma E. Rivers -w- James Rivers
  Lucretia S. Cason -w- William Cason

THREEWITS, LLEWLLEN--Of Lexington. Richland Bills 46 Filed 8 Jan. 1810
-vs- John Thomas -w- Eleanor--Alleges: Complainant is only
child of Llewellen Threewits, late of sd Dist. That he died
about 14 yrs. since, leaving widow, Eleanor, Complainants
mother, who about 1800 -m- John Thomas. Bill to Acc't. for
property of dec'd. Shows Lewellan Threewits, the elder,
died in the summer of 1796.
Shows: Llewellen Williamson Threewits -m- a sister of
_____ ? Daniel. Lewellen a drunkard, separated from wife.
-Richland Co. Bills 71 Filed 24 Jan. 1811--Llewellan Threewits
and wife, Catherine of Lexington Dist. -vs- John Daniel--
Alleges: William Daniel, late of Edgefield Dist. owned 1000
Acres in Fairfield Dist. on Broad River. Left Will. Apt'd.
John Daniel, James Daniel, and Philip Raiford of Dist of
Edgefield, Exor's. Devised to daughters, Catherine (oratrix)
and Mary Daniel, son John.

TIMMERMAN, JAS. DOZIER -m- Sarah Howell, dau. of Wm. Howell
Richland Eq. Roll 10
-Richland Eq. Bills 90 Filed 2 March 1815--Jas. Dozier
Zimmerman -w- Sarah; Thos. Ladson Hartley -w- Mary -vs-
Chestine C. Williamson -w- Mary (late widow of Wm. Howell)
Allege: Sarah and Mary, daughters of Wm. Howell, dec'd. who
died intestate. John Howell apt'd. Gdn. of Sarah and Mary.
Alleges: Mary Howell, widow, -m- Dr. Robert Hendrick. in 1799

TRAPP, JOHN--Dec'd. Estate--Owned land orig. gr. David Moore.
3rd. Oct. 1769 and Gr. to James Craig 8 Dec. 1774.
Heirs: Sarah Trapp   Elizabeth Trapp
   William Trapp Mary Trapp
   John L. Trapp Thomas Trapp-a minor
   Widow, Mary, since -m- John Price.
Richland Eq. Roll 104 1818

TRAPP, SALLY (or Sarah)--a dau. of Samuel Stanley. See Stanley card.
Richland Bills 1815. See also, card Henry McGowen

TRAPP, THOMAS--Pet'r. a minor about 14 yrs. Pray apt. Aaron Trapp
as Gdn. Richland Pet. Roll 110 1818

TRICE, ANN -m- William Ballard. Was widow of William Trice.
Husband left all to Ann and Creditors came in to claim it.
Richland Eq. Bills 32 1814

TRICE, WILLIAM--Of Richland Dist.   Richland Bills 32 Copy in File
     Wife: Ann--13 slaves, etc
     To: Sarah Neilson--3 slaves
     9 Oct. 1802   Prov: 3 Jan. 1807
     Wit: John Surginer, Wm. Blanchard
     Widow -m- William Ballard

TUCKER, ISAAC--Of Richland Dist. 30 April 1811 Misc. Rec. B-695
     To: Capt. D. R. Prowell $50.00--All right, title and interest
     to lands from Richard Allen and wife, and from Aaron Morgan and
     wife on which Rachel Ford now lives. Wit: James Adams, John
     Pierce
     -Richland Bills 142--Isaac Tucker, Trustee for Marriage agree-
     ment of Dr. Freeman Delan and Anne Hirons, widow. See card
     Freeman Delane (sp)

TUCKER, JOEL E.--Et al. -vs- Emma E. Rives, James Rives. Bills 475
                                                       1847

TUCKER, RICHARD -w- Sarah, Dau. of John Taylor. See card William
     Heath -w- Mary. Richland Eq. Bills 117 1817

TUCKER, WOOD--Will in file. Richland Co. Bills 7
     Wife: Milley   Dated: 18 Feb. 1783
     2 sons: David and Robert   Proven: 1804 7th May
     Son: Wood
     Dau: Lucy Harper
     Wit: Ludwell Evans, Jno. Dickey
     Suit by Robert Tucker of Kershaw Dist. -vs- Wood Tucker
     Shows: Mother, Milly, has dec'd. Also Brother, David.

TURNER, HARRIS--Died in 1810 -Richland Roll 8 1800
     Four minors taken to Virginia to live with James Gee, Pet'r.
     Ch: Louisa -m- Sterling W. Rives
          John
          Frances -m- Thomas Branch
          Rebecca -m- Chas. Williamson
     Filed 22 Dec. 1824
     Henry Vos had purchased the house and lot and had not paid for
     it.
     P. A. for Thomas Branch -w- Frances at North Hampton Co. N. C.
     Case: Sterling W. Rives -w- -vs- Dabney Duncan and wife, and
     John D. Brown.

TURNER, JAMES--To John Duke--Orig. Deed tract land. See John Duke
     Card. Richland Eq. Bills 40 (stray)

TURNER, WM. M.--Richland Eq. Rolls 1813--(13)--Devised lands on
     S-fork Catawba R. to Peggy McCrory, dau. John McCrory. Peggy
     age 8 yrs. 1813.
     (17)--Left land near Wm's Brother to Samuel Young--8 yr. old
     son of S. W. Young, who pet. Apt. as Gdn.

TURNIPSEED, DANIEL-m- Margaret Scott--Richland Eq. Bills 123 1816

TURPIN, WILLIAM -m- Maria R. Brasilman, dau. of Peter Brasilman
     Richland Equity Roll 11

TYSON, WRIGHT C., ESQ.--Shff. Richland Dist. Died Sunday night,
last. Camden Gazette, June 13, 1816. Issue of June 27th.
Eli Kennedy appointed to take his place as Sheriff of
Richland. See card Samuel Dunlap.

VANTERS, CORNELIUS H. -w- Mary Ann, dau. of Alexander (or Peter)
McGrew, dec'd. -vs- Wm. McGrew and Col. Thomas Taylor--David
Autry -w- Elizabeth, dau. of Alexander of Peter McGrew,
Cornelious Autry -w- Mary, also dau. of Alexander or Peter
McGrew in re settlement Estate of Alexander McGrew, Sr.
Richland Bills 53   Filed 29 Dec. 1809

VANTERS, CORNELIUS H. -m- Ann McGrew. See card Alexander McGrew.
Richland Eq. Bills lo 1810

VOS, HENRY--Lived at Granby 1811-1819. Widow: Barbara -m- John
Redwits April 1820. No children. Then married Dabney Duncan
in May 1824. Suit over purchase price of Vos House and lot
from estate of Harris Turner. Filed 22 Dec. 1824 Richland Eq.

WADE, JAMES T. -m- Martha Rives, dau. of Timothy Rives. See T.
Rives Will 5 Feb. 1820

WALKER, EDWARD--Now of Georgia, formerly of Fairfield. See Wm.
Adger -vs- John Watts. Richland Bills 22

WALKER, EDWARD--Dec'd. Estate Richland Eq. Roll 119 23 Feb. 1819
Alexander Walker and Frederick Walker, Pet'rs-under 21- by
Gdn. Eaton Walker. 614 Acres in Richland about 16 miles below
Columbia. Gr. of Wm. Meyer who sold to Walker. Died intestate
Heirs: Francis Walker, Elizabeth Walker, Polly Walker, now
Polly Farrant, wife of George Farrant.

WALKER, JAMES ALEXANDER and FREDERICK--By Guardian, Eaton Walker,
called "Col." -vs-John Bynum and Andrew Wallace, Exor's. of
Joseph Walker--Alleges Edward Walker, dec'd. father of the
minor orators, died intestate leaving widow and five children.
Green Rives, Joseph Walker, and Lucy Walker , Adm'rs. and said
Joseph Walker then had himself appt'd Gdn. of the minor orators
in Pinckney Dist. Alleges Frederick Walker, Uncle of the minor
orators, brother of their father, also died intestate, without
wife or child. Leaving his mother, 3 brothers, and 4 sisters,
and orators as heirs. That Joseph Walker the Gdn. died in 1812
Left a Will--Andrew Wallace, and John Bynum Exor's. and then
Eaton Walker was apt'd by the Court of Equity for Pinckney
Dist. as Gdns. Richland Bills 98 Filed 12 May, 1814

WALKER, JOSEPH--and his nephews, James Alexander Walker and Frederick
Walker. See card John Bryce. Richland Eq. Bills 146 1818
-Richland Roll 31--Joseph Walker--Suit over the freeing of slaves.
Very interesting papers on slavery.

WALLACE, ANDREW--Richland Eq. Bills 146 1818--See card John Bryce
-vs- George C. Smith, et al

WALTON, ENOCH -w- Nancy--Heirs of Philip Jennings. See card.
Edgefield Receipt Bk. B-185 1850

WARD, HON. HENRY D. ESQ. -m- Mrs. Mary Haig--John James Haig's
widow. See Haig card. Richland Roll 69 1816

WARD, HENRY DANA -m- Mary Haig, widow of John Haig. Richland Bills
#137 1817
-Richland Bills 163 1820--Henry Ward--Only heir Henry Dana
Artimus Ward.

WARE, MARY--Minor--See Needham Davis Richland Bills 154

WARE, THOMPSON -m- Elizabeth Howell, dau. of Wm. Howell. Richland
Bills 91 1814

WARING, BENJAMIN R. -m- Martha Goodwyn. See card Harry Grant.
Richland Bills 89 1815
-Richland Equity Pet. Roll 127--Benjamin Waring--Claims land
and crop damaged by canal opened by Public. 80 Acres between
Broad and Saluda Rivers.

WASHINGTON, WILLIAM -m- Martha Blake, dau. of Margaret Blake, sister
Of John J. Haig. See Haig card. Pet. Roll 69 1816
-Richland Bills 137 Filed 14 June 1817--William Washington -w-
Martha F., Nathaniel Bowen -w- Margaret -vs- Edward Blake, et al.
Alleges, John James Haig made Will 4 May 1806 whereby he be-
queathed negroes to his wife in lieu of dower and all for life
with remainder to his sister, Margaret Blake's children, ex-
cept Plantation on Congaree called Bacon Hill, purchased of
Exor's. of my late Brother's estate, which I give and bequeath
unto my nephew, John Haig Blake. Alleges children of Mrs.
Margaret Blake are:
Martha F. Washington
Margaret W. Bowen
Harriet Haig Blake
Edward Blake
John Haig Blake-a minor-Margaret Blake, Gdn.
That Mary Haig, widow of John James Haig, has married Henry
Dana Ward and has since died.

WATKINS, SAMUEL--Richland Bills 101 Filed 7 May 1815 -vs-
Sarah Goodwyn, widow of John Goodwyn who died Jan. 1810
Martha Taylor
William Taylor
Abbott Gallatin Goodwyn
Robert Goodwyn
Thomas Jefferson
Adella Frances
William Adams -w- Sarah Epps Adams, late Sarah E. Goodwyn
John Jesse Goodwyn
Robert Howell Goodwyn
Martha Taylor Goodwyn--Samuel Watkins alleges he bargained to
purchase, etc. Part of the children are minors.

WATSON, HEPHZEBIAH--Oratrix--sister of John Watson. -vs- Nancy Avery
    Alleges: Robert Hick, dec'd. late of Virginin, owned about
    48 acres in Richland Dist. That sd Robert Hicks was father of
    Polly Chambless who entered -m- agreement with John Watson,
    only brother of oratrix and sd John Hicks agreed to give John
    Watson sd Plantation as a marriage portion with his daughter,
    Polly Chambless, and they married, about Aug. 1795, and sd
    Robert Hicks addressed several letters to Maj. Hicks Chappell,
    "Then and now, resident in the Dist. of Richland, who had
    charge of the Plantation" and directed him to turn the place
    "New Market" over to John Watson -w- Polly who came to settle
    it in Jan. 1797 and continued there until July 1807. That sd
    Robert Hicks died, left widow who is also dec'd. and one child,
    Martha Greenway Dixon Hicks who -m- Henry Avery of Virginia.
    That Plt'f brother, John Watson, died shortly after death of
    Robert Hicks, leaving plt'f as only heir and oratrix sold the
    Plantation to Richard Crawford. Answer by Col. David Meyer
    alleges Peter Chambless, husband of sd Polly was living when
    she married John Watson, and def't. is informed, is still
    living in the west. That the land was to revert to the estate
    of Hicks after death of John Watson and Polly, if no children
    by Polly.

WATTS, JOHN--Richland Bills 22. See Wm. Adger -vs- John Watts.

WAYNE, RICHARD, SR.--Will made in Georgia--in File. 1080
    Son: Richard Wayne
        Ch: Mary Wayne -m- Robert Poole
            Eliza Clifford Wayne
            Michael Wayne
            Thomas Wayne
    Dau: Elizabeth Clifford Anderson -w- George Anderson
        Mary Stiles -w- Richard M. Stiles
    Son: James Moon Wayne
        William Clifford Wayne
    Children of Mary Stiles: Richard Stiles
                             Eliza Clifford Anderson -w- Geo. A.
                             Sarah Anderson Stiles of Chatham, Ga.
    Richland Eq. Roll 253 Filed 3 Aug. 1825

WELLS, REBECCA--A sister of Andrew Fleming. Also sister of Ann
    Hoy. Richland Eq. Roll 26 1813

WESTCOTT, DAVID--Will Richland Wills B-15 19 July 1787
    Wife: Hannah
    Son: Ebenezer, James, and Samuel
    Dau: Elizabeth and Mary
    Bros: Samuel, Ebenezer and John--All Exors.

WESTCOT, JAMES and present wife Archives Dept. Richland File B-597
    5 children: Cynthia Ju___? Wescot
                Mary, Martha, David and Rachel-All by pres. wife.
    Deed gift--slaves--from Green Rives 1 Nov. 1809

WESTON, MALACHI--Of St. Mark's Par. C. T. Deed B-5-385 16 May 1777
    To: John Dawson, of C. T., Merchant. 1/7 undivided part of
    450 acres in St. Mark's Parish--orig. gr. to Mary Russell on
    29 Nov. 1751--Bd. by Santee River on the west and Wateree
    River on the east. Which 1/7 became vested in William Heatley
    by -m- with dau. of sd Mary Russell. Conv. to sd Malachi
    Weston 30/31 Dec. 1774. Richland File. No dower.
    -Richland File C. T. Deed E-5-94 16 May 1777--Malachi Weston
    To: Aaron Lovelock of C. T., Merchant. Orig. gr. Camden
    Dist. 23 Dec. 1771. No dower. 300 acres in Craven, fork of
    Congaree and Wateree Rivers. on both sides road from McCord's
    Ferry to Can____?. Bd. N. E. Richard Singleton and John
    Russell, S. E. Richard Tucker and Jno. McCord, N. W. by Wood
    Tucker and vac,

WESTON, ROBERT -w- Mary--Heirs of Charles McCord--Will 1773. See
    card Mary Brown, widow. Richland Bills 188. 1821
    see also, card Henry McKinzie -w-. Bills 127½

WESTON, SARAH--Estate Wm. Goodwyn. See card John Burney. Bills 148
                                                                1818

WESTON, SARAH--Pet'r. Richland Eq. Roll 134 1819 Shows:
    William Rivers, Will dated 7 Aug. 1814, by Will bequeathed to
    her $500.00 and made William Clarkson, Sr. her Trustee. Pet'r,
    being about to move to the Western Country and for other good
    causes, desires to change Trusteeship to her son-in-law, Jesse
    House.

WESSINGER, SELINA and her husband, Matthias. Heirs of Adam Boyer.
    See Boyer card. Richland Eq. Roll 95. 1816

WHITAKER, WILLIAM, JR.--Will not dated. Proven: 21 Aug. 1787
    Sister: Martha Belton--1/8
            Elizabeth-½
            Catherine Baker-1/8
    Brother: Thomas and Samuel-1/8 each
    Sisters: Winefert, Peggy and Polly--1/8 each
    Honored Father, William Whitaker, the elde . Exor.
    Wit: Alex'r. Irvin, Martha Whitaker, Will LaCont
    -Richland Bills 4 1789--William Whitaker moved to West Florida
    near the Mississippi River. See card William Lenoir.

WHITE, JOSEPH B. -m- Widow, Sarah Smith. See card Henry McKinzie
    Richland Bills 127½ 1817

WHITTEN, SARAH--Miss, sister of Elizabeth -w- James Hunt Taylor.
    Richland Bills 205 1822

WICKOR, JOHN--Dec'd. Richland Eq. Roll 59 1816
    Ch: Daniel about 18
         Andrew about 14
    Pet: Margaret Wickor--first, her name struck out--John
    Wickor, apt'd.

WICKER, JOHN--Late of Lexington Dist. Died about 8 yrs. ago.
    Heirs: Margaret Wicker--Widow
           Matthias, and John
           Daniel and Adam--minors. Richland Roll 94 1818

WILKINS, JOHN W.--Bills 160 Filed 16 Dec. 1817 Richland Co.
    -vs- James McCalla, John Hanrahan--Suit over notes, partnership
    -Bills 189-1821--John Wilkins -vs- Ainsley Hall and Wm. Hall &
    Co.--Indebtedness

WILLIAMS, ELY--Will June 1829. Died June 1829 Richland Eq.
    Eldest dau.: Mary Ann -m- Allen Gibson (Set. in file-7 Apr. 1830
        Next : Charlotte Jane Williams
    Youngest D.: Caroline Elizabeth Williams
    Only son: John Ely--Had property from his uncle Joel Williams.
    Appr's: Isom Woodward, E. Adams, Thos. Seay, Wm. Killingsworth

WILLIAMS, GREEN--Died March 1840--Intestate--Richland Eq.
    No widow: Filed 29 April, 1841
    Children: Green Williams
           Joel Williams
           Nathan--a minor
           Sarah -m- John E. Williams

WILLIAMSON, C., et al -vs- James and Thomas Rives. Bills 311 1835

WILLIAMSON, C. B.--Richland Deed C-390--To: John H. Kinsler 24 March
    1857--Mtg. 207 acres--orig. gr. to Zachariah Kirkland and Alex'r
    Kennedy and conv. to C. B. Williamson by David H. Ruff. Part
    in Fairfield and part in Richland--on streams of Crane Creek of
    Broad River. No dower.

WILLIAMSON, CHARLES--See card Clairborne Clifton. Richland Bills 78
    Richland Probate. Bx. 31--Charles Williamson -w- Rebecca and
    Sterling Rives -w- Louisa--Heirs of Harris Turner.
    -Misc. 3R-582--Charles Williamson--Apt'd Sheriff Richland Dist.
    21 May 1803. Misc. 30-242--Sterling Williamson com. as Sheriff
    of Richland Dist. 12 Feb. 1800

WILLIAMSON, CHESTAIN E. -w- Mary -vs- Louisa Hendrick--Est. of Dr.
    Robert Hendrick-late of Columbia. Heirs: Wife, Mary, who
    later married Chestain Williamson. Daughter, Louisa-now a minor.
    Rihland Bills 9 Filed 8 June 1809

WILLIAMSON, CHASTINE C. -m- Widow, Mary Howell. Widow of Wm.
    Howell. See Wm. Howell card. Roll 10 Richland Co.
    -Richland Wills H-20--Chastian C. Williamson--Wife-Mary-All
    23 Oct. 1822

WILLIAMSON, JAMES--Richland Will D-33
    Wife: Rebecca--All 11 July 1801 Prov: 22 Sept. 1801

WILLIAMSON, JAMES C.--Richland Deeds A-495 2 Nov. 1857
    Foreclosure sale of his lands--1800 acres. The Elkins Mill
    tract on Crane Creek

WILLIAMSON, POLLY--Dau. of Samuel Stanley. See Stanley card.
    Richland Bills 156 1815

WILLIAMSON, ROBERT--Richland Wills D-141
    Brother, Charles Williamson--All 11 Jan. 1803
    Proven: 5 Mar. 1803.   Wit: Sterling C. Williamson

WILSON, SAMUEL, Reubin Picket, Needham Davis -vs- Freeman Delane -w-
    Anne; Ainsley Hall; and Dr. Samuel Green, Adm'rs Peter L. De-
    lane--Sets forth Peter Delane had judgement -vs- Greeman Delane
    also that Freeman Delane owed Thos. B. Creagh and Reuben
    Pucket. Ainsley Hall substituted Trustee in place of Isaac
    Tucker who was Trustee of Ann Hirons, widow in her marriage
    settlement with Freeman Delane. Shows: Freeman Delane left
    State and ans. filed by his wife as Ann Carey who alleged she
    learned he had a previous wife living which nullifies her mar-
    riage. Richland Bills 142

WILSON, THEOPHILUS--Of Fairfield -m- Widow Margaret Fulmer. She was
    widow of William Fulmer. See Fulmer card. Roll 88 1818

WILLSSON, THOMAS--Comm'r. of Ct. Equity -vs- Jesse M. Howell--
    Suit to foreclose Mtg. for purchase price of property.
    Richland Equity Bills 175. Filed 11 Jan. 1820

WINGARD, MICHAEL--Richland Eq. Roll 57 and 58 1816. Daughter, Mary
    Wingard, age 18, Pet'r. She is gr-dau. of Mrs. Ann Mary Pick-
    ley, dec'd.
    -Roll 58 shows minor children of Michael Wingard:
        Jacob, Michael, and Juliana--all under 14.
    All Petition their father as Gdn.

WINGATE, SOPHINISHA E. M.--Richland Eq. Roll 21
    Dau: Susannah Wingate age 5 yrs. Mother Pet. apt. as Gdn.

WITHERSPOON, ELIZABETH--Sister of Sarah Cantey--Bills 86.
    See Cantey card.

WOOLEY, ZACCHEUS -w- Elizabeth--Heirs of George Lang. See card
    Amos Bank and wife, Catherine. Equity Bills (Stray) 1819

WOOLF, JOHANNES--Of St. Matthews--Dec'd. Richland Bills 41 1811
    John Francis and John--See Henry Young, Adm'r. of Johannes
    Woolf.

WOLF, HENRY--Of Columbia, Dec'd. Richland Roll 27 1813
    Widow: Sarah
    6 Ch: Rosanna -m- Malachi Ott
           Levi
           Eliza -m- Sylvester Brunson
           William, Pamelia and Louisa--Yet minors
    In 1808 widow -m- Tobias Jones. Pet'r. alleges 18 July 1806,
    Henry Rees Hall, conv. to Oliver L_____? in Trust for Sarah
    Wolf and her children. Lots in Columbia

WOOD, JAMES, SR.--Will 25 June 1751 Grimes N. C. Wills Richland
    Dau: Sarah Outlaw   File
    Sis: Sarah Killingsworth James Wood of Northampton Co,

WYCHE, JOHN--Dec'd. 1821--Intestate. Richland Eq. Bills
    Adm'r: Sterling G. Williamson
    Heirs: Ann Wyche-otherwise Ann Harrison
           Mrs. Judith Tucker
           Thomas, Rebecca, Ainsley, and William Wyche--Infants
   by next friend, Samuel Willson, Tr.

YANCEY, JOHN -m- Anne Wood Delane, widow of Peter Delane. See
   card Anne Wood Delane. Equity Bills, Richland Co.

YANCY, PHILIP -w- Ann -vs- Joseph Perrin, Jane Perrin, widow
   Christiana Perrin, heirs of Joseph Perrin, Dec'd. April 1816.
   Alleges: Joseph Perrin died leaving widow, Christiana and
   children: Jane, Joseph and Anne and that Anne married Philip
   Yancy. Bill for Partition. Bills 143 Filed 12 Jan. 1818

YATES, ROBERT--Gdn. of Johnston McIlwain. See card Jane McIlwain.
   Richland Bills 1819 155

YOUNG, HENRY--Adm'r. of Johannes Woolf of St. Matthew's Parish -vs-
   James Carmichael, David Coulter, Henry Jones, Gideon Jenning,
   Jacob Ott, John Francis Woolf and John Woolf.--Bill to discover
   and account. Richland Bills 41 Filed 8 Oct. 1811

YOUNG, SAMUEL--Age 8 yrs. and son of S. W. Young. Legatee of Wm.
   M. Turner. Richland Eq. Roll 13 and 17 1813

YOUNG, THOMAS, DEC'D. John Keith Adm'r. Bills 82 1810

SPARTANBURG COUNTY, SOUTH CAROLINA

FRENCH IMMIGRANTS--C. J. Photo Pg. 519/20 1755-1756
On board the Sloop Endeavor, James Nichols, Master. "Late in
____ ? of Arcadia" 126 in all. 67 men and sons, 64 wives and
daughters.

Line Ongan and sons, wife and daughter..4				
Peter Ongan	4	"	"	"	3
James Ongan	2	"	"	"	2
Peter Ongan	1	"	"	"	2
John Corme	4	"	"	"	5
Michael Corme	2	"	"	"	1
John Multon	2	"	"	"	3
John Jerns	1	"	"	"	1
Glad Toaden	2	"	"	"	3
Paul Morton	4	"	"	"	1
John Morton	1	"	"	"	1
Innes Woirt	3	"	"	"	3
Jeremiah Duset	5	"	"	"	2
Joseph Care	2	"	"	"	4
Charles Benn	2	"	"	"	2

ACKER, NAOMI--6th Dau. of George Brewton. Will 1815. Spartanburg-60

ALLEN, JAMES--Will 2 Jan. 1824 Sptg. (2)-66

ALLEN, JOHN--Will 3 June 1822. Sptg. (2)-26

ALLEN, POLLY--Dau. of Joseph Woodruff. Will 1817. Sptg.-110

ALLEN, SPARTAN--Nephew of Hannah Timmons, who was sister of Dolly Allen
Timmons Will 1817. Sptg.-103

ALEXANDER, ALEXANDER--Dec'd. Sptg. Div. of Per. and R. S. Bk.
Widow: Ester Alexander
Children: John, Alexander, William, Nancy, James, Anne, Salley.
Part. Oct. Term 1806. Plats

ALEXANDER, ALICE--Dau. of Richard Chesney. Will 1816. Sptg.-87

ALEXANDER, ELIZABETH--Dau. of Thomas Williamson. Will 1813. Her 3
children: Thomas, James, and Ann Alexander. Sptg.-25

ANDERSON, DAVID--Will 18 April 1825. Sptg. (2)-99

ANDERSON, JAMES--Son in law of Michael Miller. Will 1815. Sptg. 54

ARENDALE, MARY--Heir of Thomas Cole. Will 1816. (Seems dau.) Sptg. 74

ARMSTRONG, MARTIN--To Richard Harrison 200 A. on both sides of Fairforest Creek. Granted by N. C. as being in Tryon Co.--to Thomas
Case who conv. to sd. Martin Armstrong. Sptg. Deed Bk. A-82

ARNOLD, CHARLOTTE--Niece of Samuel Farrow. Will 1824. Sptg. (2)-57

ARNOLD, JOHN--19 July 1813 Sptg. 35

AUSTELL, JOSEPH--Will 5 Oct. 1823. Sptg. (2)-33

BAGWELL, HAYS--Dec'd. Sept. 1819 Intestate. Sptg. Box 2 Bill 6
    Widow: Margarette
    6 minor children: Milly, Harriet, Littleberry, Mary, Cynthia
    and Willis. Filed 4 June 1821

BALLENGER, EDWARD--Will 23 July 1823. Sptg. (2)-30

BALLENGER, JAMES, SEN'R.--Will 19 July 1813 Sptg. 31

BALLENGER, POLLY--Dau. of Obediah Wingo. Will 1824 Sptg. (2)-115

BARNETT, ELIJAH--Dec'd. Pendleton Messenger Equity--Aug. 7, 1846
    Heirs: Nathaniel Duncan
           David Harris -w- Luraney
           Riley Corbin -w- Melina
           Thomas Barnett
           Ann, Riol, and Mary Barnett
           Melinda Barnett, widow of J. J. Barnett--All -vs- Wm.
    Wilson in right of wife and heirs of J. J. Barnett, Dec'd. Deft's
    out of state. Sale of Real Estate

BARRY, ANDREW--Will 1854 Sptg. 16

BARRY, JAMES H.--Son in law of Gen. Moore York Ct. 1830 Vol. 1-504

BARRY, MARGARET--Will 24 Sept. 1823 Sptg. (2)-44

BARRY, RICHARD--Will 16 May 1816. Sptg. 82

BARRY, VIOLET--Dau. of Thomas Moore-Will 1817. Sptg. Wills Bx. 19/20

BARTON, WILLIAM--Son in law of Edward Smith. Sptg. 58

BATES, ELIZABETH--Dau. of Benjamin Howard-Will 1817. B. Howard was
    son in law of Anthony Bates. Wit: Nancy Bates, Mathias Bates,
    and James Pool. Sptg. 126

BEARDIN, ELIZABETH--Dau. of Sarah Moore-Will 1853. Sptg. Wills Bx. 40

BELL, SAMUEL, Planter of Sptg. To Samson Bobo, Planter of Sptg. 200 A.
    on Cedar Shoal Creek of Enoree River. Gr. 23 Sept. 1763 to Samuel
    Cannon who with his wife, Lide Cannon, conv. on 16 Aug. 1776 to
    Samuel Bell. Sptg. Deed Bk. A-63 1785

BENNETT, JAMES--Will 11 Dec. 1816 Sptg. (2)-62

BENSON, JOSHUE--Son in law of Samuel Nesbitt-Will 1816 Sptg. 96

BENSON, PATSY--Dau. of Thomas Moore-Will 1817 Sptg. (2)-21

BENSON, ROBERT--Will 15 May 1813 Sptg. 33

BENSON, WILLIAM--Sptg. Deed Bk. A-85 1785. To Richard Harrison, Gr.
    to Archibald Robinson of 200 A. Grant by S. C. on Fairforest Cr.

BENSON, WILLIAM, ESQ.--Dec'd. 20 July 1796 Sptg. Div. Per. and R. E.
    Widow: Nelly--since dec'd.   Page 1
    13 children: Rebecca -m- Ignatius Stokes
                Gabriel, Willin, James, Abner, Elizabeth, Nancy
                Robert, Elias, Thirza, Patience, Nimrod, Polly
    Writ Part. 1 Nov. 1799. Plats on pg. 18--but pgs. not numbered

BISHOP, ISAAC--Will 13 July, 1819 Sptg. (2)-13

BLASSINGAME, JOHNES--Son in law of John Gowan-Will 1809 Sptg. 2

BOBO, JANE--Sister of Samuel Farrow--Will 1824 Sptg. (2)-57

BOBO, SALLY--Will 20 Jan. 1813. Sptg. 69

BOBO, SAMPSON--Dec'd. Sptg. Div. Per. and R. E. Bk.--Pgs. not num.
    Sally Bobo seems dau.
    Children: Rev. Spencer Bobo, Burrell, Birum, Absolem, Chaney
           Hryam, Willin
           Elizabeth -w- Anthony Foster
           Polly -w- Absolem Bobo
           Nancy -w- Matthew Patton
           Jeremiah Bobo
           Dec'd. son: Sampson Bobo whose children are;
                John, Polly, Nancy, Elizabeth, Sally, George
                Roebuck, Leviniah
    Part. March ct. 1809. Plats in Book.

BOBO, SPENCER --Will 1816. Sptg. Box 11-Bill 5 Filed 2 May 1829
    Wife: Jane Bobo
         Barious children

BOMAR, ELIZABETH--Dau. of Benjamin High-Will 1816 Sptg. 92
    Wit: Edward Bomar and John Bomar

BONNER, ANNA--Dau. of Thomas Harrison-Will 1819 Sptg. 132

BONNER, BENJAMIN--Will 29 July 1814 Sptg. 48

BRAGG, CHANEY--Gr. child of George Devine-Will Rec'd. 1825 Sptg. 53

BRAGG, DANIEL--Mentioned in Will of David Bruton 1815 Sptg. 71

BRAGG, ELIZABETH--Eldest dau. of George Brewton-Will 1815. 3rd. dau.
    Abigail Bragg--Land where Peter Bragg now lives. Sptg. 60

BRAGG, ROSANNAH--Niece of Samuel Farrow--Will 1824 Sptg. (2)-57

BRANDON, WILLIAM--Dec'd. Sptg. Div. Per. and R. E. Bk.
    Heirs: Saxaby Brandon--widow--1/3
           Edmond Bishop -w- Polly
           Dudley Brandon
           John Bobbet -w- Ester
           James, John, Betsy (Elizabeth), William, Willmouth, Sally
           Rhody.
    Part. March Term 1803 Plats in Book

338

BREWTON, GEORGE--Will 6 July 1815 Sptg. 60

BRIANT, NANCY--Dec'd dau. of John Tolleson-Will 1820 Sptg. (2)-6

BRIGGS, ROBERT--Archives Dept. Sptg. file. Vol. 8 Bk. 279
        100 A. on a Branch of Raybournes Creek. Bd. N. E. John Turk.
        Cert. 30 June 1768. Gr. 12 Sept. 1768. Men. 15 Oct. 1768

BRIGGS, THOMAS -w- Katherine to Thomas Tod--100 A. Sptg. Co. N-s
        Enoree. Conv. to John Briggs by Wm. Cox, dec'd. late of Enoree.
        The tract on which John Briggs did live. Thomas Briggs-son of
        John Briggs of Edgecomb Co. N. C. and heir of sd. John Briggs
        late of Enoree. Sptg. Deed Bk A-104 1785

BRIGHT, ELIZABETH--Dau. of James Reynolds-Will 1826. Sptg. (2)-87

BROCKMAN, JENNY--Legatee and seems dau. of Charles McClain-Will 1821
        Sptg. (2)-14

 BROWN, WILEY S.--Will 7 Oct. 1825 Sptg. (2)-108

BROWN, PATSY--Legatee and seems dau. of Isham Foster-Will 1816 Sptg. 112

BENTON, JAMES--To Thomas Williamson-Gr. 12 Jan. 1770 by S. C. to James
        Bruton--200 A. in Craven Co. on Ferguson's Creek of Tyger River.
        Bd. David Bruton and vac. Sptg. Deed Bk. A-89 1785

BUFFINGTON, JOSEPH--His dau. Mrs. Matilda Wood-a Legatee of Samuel
        Farrow-Will 1824 Sptg. (2)-57

BURNETT, EDWARD--vs--John J. Jenkins--Money Sptg. Box 11-Bill 4

BURRES, ELIZABETH--Dau. of James Wofford-Will 1815. Sptg. 64

BURTON, DAVID--Will 17 Mar. 1815. Sptg. 71 (Bruton?)

BURTON, ESTHER--Dau. of Jane Thomson-Will 1816 Sptg. 133

CALLICOT, ASA--Will 21 Aug. 1820.. Sptg. 139

CALWELL, WILLIAM -w- Peggy and son, Patrick--Mentioned in Will of
        Samuel Stewart. Patrick a legatee. Will 1814. Sptg. 126

CAMP, JAMES--Will 28 Jan. 1817. Sptg. 94

CAMP, MARGARET JORDAN--Legatee of Margaret Jordan-Will 1825 Sptg. 64

CANTRELL, ISAAC, Dec'd.--Will. Sptg. Div. Per. and R. E. Book.
        Widow: Mary
        Ch: Peter, Mary, John, Enoch, Abraham, Elijah, Jacob, Richard
             Sarah Purtle and grand son, Isaac Purtle
             CalebCantrell and Nimrod, Mark, Daniel, Isaac, Benjamin,
             Charles, Reuben, Thomas, Lunsford Cantrell
        Part. Oct. Ct. 1807. Plats in Book

CARNOL, POLLY--Son, James-a minor. Deed gift-slave. Sptg. Box 2 Bk. 3

CASEY, JOHN--Will 5 Dec. 1815. Sptg. 81

CASEY, RANDALL--His sons, Hiram and Matthew, legatees of Matthew
    Couch-Will 1816. Sptg. (2)-11

CASEY, SARAH--Will 15 Aug. 1828. Sptg. (2)-113

CATHCART, SAMUEL--Will 29 May 1820. Sptg. 142

CHAMBERS, EDMOND--Will 1 April 1819. Sptg. (2)-8

CHAMBLISS, HENNRIETTA -w- of James Chambliss. Dau. of David Anderson-
    Will 1825. Gr-son, Wyatt Chambliss. Sptg. (2)-99

CHAPMAN, SALLY--Dau. of William Foster-Will 1817. Sptg. 118

CHESNEY, RICHARD--Will 18 July 1816 Sptg. 37

CLARK, BESSY--Legatee of Robert Page-Will 1817. Sptg. (2)-90

CLARK, JOHN--Brother in law of John Lewis-Will 1813. Sptg. 43

CLARKE, MARTHA--Dau. of Samuel Cathcart-Will 1820. Sptg. 142

CLAYTON, WILLIAM--Archives Dept-Rev. Rec. 1783-1281 Also for Roebuck's
    Reg't. Stub Ent: 3478. 26 May 1782--Received of Wm. Clayton
    one beef valued at twelve pounds for which he is entitled to
    receive pay from the public for the use of _____?. Henderson's
    Brigade.
    Messrs. Boquit and Mitchell--Treasury Keepers. Gentlemen: Please
    to deliver to Mr. Sam'l Favor my indents and my special indents
    and this my order shall be your receipt for the same--Witness my
    hand this 17 of July 1786. Spencer Bobo Wit. William Clayton

CLAYTON, WILLIAM AND ELIZABETH to Joseph Wofford--497 A. on Two mile
    Branch. Gr. sd. Wm. Clayton 1 Jan. 1785. Wit. 4 April 1787
    Joshua Smith and Thos. Todd. Sptg. A-254 1787

CLAYTON, WILLIAM--To Joseph Wofford--Acknowledged Deed and Ct. ordered
    it recorded. Sept. Ct. 1787. States: Wm. Clayton came into Ct.
    Sptg. Oldest Min. Bk. Pg. 131

CLAYTON, WILLIAM--Tr. Jane Bobo of Sptg. "to my nephew, William Clayton"
    50 A. on Ferguson's Branch Tyger R. Part tract Spencer Bobo pur-
    chased from James Wofford. Between Tyger and Enoree (Laurens line-
    not over f miles of Laurens line.) Sptg. Deed M-119 1818

CLAYTON, WILLIAM--To Benjamin Wofford. 100 A. on Fort Shoals-Enoree
    River. Bd. John Farrow, James Clayton, Willis Bobo and John
    Bagden. No dower Sptg. R-387 1820

COLBERT, NANCY--Dau. of Zachariah Leatherwood-Will 1814. Sptg. 45
    Also spelled Coldbert.

COLLYER, JOHN--Wit. deed for Jacob Earnst, Sr. and wife, Agnes, to
    Robert Harmon. 25 Dec. 1789 Sptg. Deed B-361

COLE, THOMAS--Of Sptg. Orig. Will Bk. A-86 Box 7 Pkg. 28
    Son: Obediah Cole   Nancy Guyton
    Dau: Patsy   Elizabeth Dubarry
    Heirs: Mary Arendale   John Cole
        Sarah Fondren   Patsy Kennedy
        Grove Cole   Thomas Cole
        Susannah Cooper
    20 Feb. 1816. Rec'd. 19 April 1816
    Exor's: Wm. Dubarry and Thomas Cole
    Wit: Thomas D. Wendale, Silas Cooper, James Cooper

COLE, THOMAS--Will 20 Feb. 1816 Sptg. 74

COLE, THOMAS, SR.--to Thomas Cole, Jr. 150 A. on Beaverdam Creek.
    Sptg. Deed O-236 1814

COMPTON, BARBARA--Dau. of Sarah Moore-Will 1853 Sptg. Wills Bx. 40-38

COMPTON, THOMAS--Will 8 Mar. 1817. Sptg. 109

CONNELL, JESSE -w- Anne to George Connell--Gr. 24 Dec. 1770 by Wm.
    Tryon, Gov. N. C. to Jesse Connell--500 A. E-s Fairforest Creek.
    Sptg. Deed Bk. A-51 1786

CONNELL, MARY--Widow of Capt. Connell, Pet'r. as Mary Turner. Pet.
    for equal distribution of property of her former husband, Capt.
    Connell because the eldest son claims all--the father dying in-
    testate. Archives Dept. Sptg. file. Senate Journal 1789 Pg.-77

CONNER, PHEBY--Legatee of Isaac Bishop-Will 1816. Sptg. (2)-13

COOK, DAVID--To Michael Sprinkle--135 A. land on Fairforest and Buffalo
    Lick Creek. Formerly belonging to John Gibbs, Sr., Dec'd. Orig,
    Grant to Giles Tillet by N. C. Sptg. Deed Bk A-11 1785

COOK, WILIE--Dec'd. No wife or children. Sptg. Div. Per. and R. E. Bk
    3 Bros: John, William and 3rd not listed
    2 sisters: Mary Cook
               Catherine -w- Owen Sullivan
    1 Niece: Elizabeth Cook) Children of dec'd. Brother, Gicon Cook
    1 Nephew: William Cook)
    Part. Oct. Ct. 1806

COOPER, ADAM--Will Sptg. Book D-11   12 June 1838
    Brother: William Cooper of Mecklenberg Co. N. C.
      "   Thomas Cooper for his three children:
             Nancy Elizabeth Cooper
             Mary Adeline Cooper
             John Jeremiah Cooper.

COOPER, CAPT.--Bdg. Gr. to Jasper Dubose's-7 Aug. 1735--500 A. at
    Fairforest in Craven Co. Bd. S. E. land held by Capt. Cooper.
    N. E. land of James Sinclair. N. W. on widow Palmer's; S. W. pt.
    on land of William Newman, and pt. vac. John Hentie D. S.
    Archives Dept. Plat Book 2-233. (Fairforest was in Sptg. Co.)

COOPER, CYNTHIA--Dau. of Elizabeth Thomason of Sptg.-Will 1853

COOPER, ELIZABETH--Widow of David Cooper, Sen'r. to Daniel Amos--
217 A. on Thickety Cree. Same land she got from Bremar. Wit:
William Amos, Sarah Amos. Sptg. Deed K-181 1805

COOPER, ELIJAH HARRISON--on Fairforest and Tyger 1784-1794
JEREMIAH--Same Archives Dept. Plats

COOPER, MATTHEW of Sptg. Will Bk. D-469
Wife: Elizabeth
Children: John, Caleb, William, Benson, Dillard
Nancy -w- William Cole
Elizabeth Missouri -w- Marion Amos
Ann -w- Daniel Arendale
Polly Fondren, Dec'd.--Her children
Laura Henny. 25 Jan. 1854

COOPER, SUSANNAH--Heir of Thomas Cole-Will 1816. Seems dau. Sptg. 74

COOPER, WILLIAM--Of 96 District. Sptg. File C. T. Wills Pg. 401
Wife: Lidy--200 A. Home Place. Will 23 June 1775
Sons: Jacob--100 A. bought of James White
William--100 A. bought of Isaac Young
Stacey--45 A. etcs.
Nathan and Samuel--Home place after wife's death
Jeremiah, Jonathan and David--Money-not 21
Joseph--not 1
Daus: Sarah and Hannah
Wit: Henry Clark, Henry Trueman Hill, Mary Peckett

COOPER, WILLIAM--Will 8 Aug. 1808 Sptg. Orig. Will Bk. A-15
Wife: Frances
Sons: Micajah, Matthew, William, Sherward, James
Daus: Mary, Phebe
Exor's: Joshua Richards and Daniel Amos
8 April 1808. Rec'd. Nov. 19, 1810
Wit: Cion Cooper, Charles Amos, Benj. Stanley

COUCH, MATTHEW--Will-7 Sept. 1816. Sptg. (2)-11

COUCH, BENJAMIN--Will Rec'd. 1817 Sptg. 91

COX, ELIZABETH--Dau. of James Allen-Will 1824. Sptg. 66

CROCKER, MARTHA--Gr. dau. of Benj. Howard-Will 1817. Sptg. 126

CROOK, JESSE--"Major" Will 9 Mar. 1841 Sptg. Bx-16 Pk-31
Wife: Elizabeth--"Left me"
Children: A. B. Crook
Margaret B. Dickie
James
Martha W. Bragg
Tiolette L. Woodruff
Jesse W. Crook
Catherine M. Crook
John M. Crook
Wit: B. E. Wofford, Levi H. Wofford, Jacob R. Frey

CROOK, JOSEPH -w- Jane, Wm. Crook -w- Sarah with: Mather Evans, Samuel Evans, James G. Evans, Ephram M. Evans, John P. Evans, Alex'r.
Evans, Mary Evans -vs- Dr. Jno. P. Evans, Alex Evans d. 31 May 1815
1823 Heirs of Alex'r. Evans, Dec'd. Sptg. Equity Bx-2 Pk-5

DANCLER, DAVID--Son in law of Michael Miller-Willer 1815. Sptg. 54

DANIEL, REUBEN--Will 12 Aug. 1825 Sptg. (2)-92

DARE, THOMAS--Of Sptg. Sons in law: Mose Tollison and Wm. Ross
Deed gift in file. 1 April 1821 Bx-6 Bill 10

DAVIS, JESS--Will 11 Feb. 1812. Negro wife-Suckey, sole heir. Sptg. 20

DEAVOURS, RACHEL--Legatee of Isaac Bishop. Sptg. 13

DEMSY, LUCRETIA--Will 10 June 1826 Sptg. 81

DICKSON, DAVID of Tyger River, Sptg. Dist. Laurens Deed bk. A-161
To Patrick Cunningham--100 A. formerly property of Hugh Brown
on S. side Saluda River. Bd. W. on Reedy R. E. sd P. C. and N.
formerly of John Willard. Also another tract. Sarah Cunningham
a witness.

DICKSON, EDWARD--Of N. C. to Bozel Lee of Sptg. Co. 100 A. land Sptg.
S-s Lawson's Fork, adj. grantor's land, formerly Alexander Dickson.
land. Spartanburg Deed Bk. A-109 1786.

DICKSON, WILLIAM OF N. C. to Thomas Farrar of Sptg. 300 A. land on
Fairforest Creek of Tyger River adj. John Prince's Survey. Gr.
to William Dickson 26 Oct. 1767. Gr. on Pg. 37 Rec'd. at Wilming-
ton. Sptg. Deed Bk. A-35 1785

DIVINE, GEORGE--Will Rec'd. 1825 Sptg. 53

DODD, BETSY--Dau. of Matthew McBee-Will 1817. Sptg. 105. James Dodd
                                                           mentioned
DRAPER, NANCY--Dau. of William Wilkins-Will 1807. Sptg. 155

DUBERRY, ELIZABETH--Heir of Thomas Cole-Will 1816. Seems dau. William
Duberry, Exor. Also spelled Dewberry. Sptg. 74

DUBERRY, MARY--Legatee and seems dau. of John Law-Will 1822. Sptg. 78

DUNNAWAY, SAMUEL--Will 9 May, 1810 Sptg. 99

EARLE, THERON--Son in law of Michael Miller-Will 1815. Sptg. 54

EDWARDS, ELIZABETH--Dau. of James Bennett-Will 1816. Sptg. 62

EDWARD, FRANCIS--Dau. of Zachariah Leatherwood-Will 1814 Sptg. 45

EDWARDS, MARY--Dau. of Elsworth Moore-Will 1854. Sptg. Wills Bx-40-1

EISON, JOHN--Will 15 Jan. 1826. Sptg. (2)-68

ELDER, ALEXANDER--Archives Dept. Rev. Rec. #2182
Horseman 15 Dec. 1780 to 8 Sept. 1781 in Capt. John Elder's Co.
36 P. 14 Sh. 3 Pen.
Horseman in Col. Roebuck's Reg't. sd Rec't 12 Feb. 1787 and on
20 Feb. 1790 Thomas Heany also sd. Rec't. 5 Feb. 1789. And'r
Mayes--cd Acct. 19 Jan. 1790. Also in Co. of Capt. Wm. Elder.
For 194 days duty as horseman from 15 Dec. 1780 to 8 Sept. 1781
in Capt. Jno. Elder's Co. for 63 days do an do from 10 Bec. 1781
to 10th Feb. both days inclusive at 20 P. per day. Roebucks Reg't.
-Alexander Elder, planter of 96 Dist. from John Elder 110 Guines.
Horses, cows, household goods. 10 May 1780. Wit: Robert Elder
Thomas Clary. Sptg. Deed Bk. A-167
-Alexander Elder -w- Mary of Sptg. Co. to Zopher Smith 151 A. N-s
Tyger River, Dutchman's Creek. Wit: Jonathan Smith, Robert
Elder, John Elder. Sptg. E-48 23 May 1795
-Alexander Elder--Dower by Mary Elder to Burgess West. Sptg. F-79

ELDER, D. H. et al -vs- La. and I. L. Green--Debt case. Sptg. 9974
-D. H. and L. C. Elder-Judgement 10141 Sptg. 1891   1890

ELDER, ELIZABETH AND JOSEPH--Judgement 7444. Sptg. 1880

ELDER, EPHRAIM--Of Sptg. From John Gibbs and Wife Anne Gibbs of Sptg.
20 A. on Lick Br. of Buffalo Creek of Fairforest. Wit: Peter
Elder, Caty Smith. Sptg. Deed B-525 20 Aug. 1791
-Ephraim to Mark Swadley--100 A. on Buffalo Lick Creek. Sd. Ephraim
Elder and Sally Elder. Sptg. D-101 7 May 1794
-Ephraim Elder from Jesse Laxton. Sptg. Deed D-169 11 Sept. 1794
-Ephraim Elder from John Kirkland. Sptg. Deed E-73 14 July 1796
-Ephraim Elder from Sampson Trammell. Sptg. Deed F-368 28 Feb. 1799
-Ephraim Elder from Abraham Markly. Sptg. F-378 16 Mar. 1799
-Ephraim Elder -vs- Wm. Dermed-Confess before Clerk. Amt. of Judg't.
$162. Int. 15 Sept. 1829. Judg't. Confessed 15 Sept. 1829

ELDER, HAMMON--Owed the note. Adv. James Nesbitt. Note: $106.48
Due James Nesbitt one hundred six and 483/9/100 dollars with interest from the 1st January last for value rec'd. Witness my hand
and seal March 13, 1843. Sig. Hammon Elder. Sptg. Judgement 2857
Filed 13 March 1843.

ELDER, JAMES--Estate of: 17 pounds 25 sh. 10 pence for thirty days
hire of waggon and team in 1788 and horse lost. Note by Rob't
Stirling to pay indent due James Elder, Dec'd. to James Purvis
7 June 1786. 96 Dist. Rev. Rec. Archives Dept. #2183

ELDER, CAPT. JAMES--Archives Dept. Rev. Rec. 2183--133 Pounds 10 sh.
for Militia duty in Roebuck's Reg't. since the fall of Charleston.
Pr. Anderson Ret. Rec'ts by James Elder; Wm. Smith, Peter Braselman. Allowed Bounty Bonds

ELDER, JAMES--Dec'd. Intestate. Chester Book G-32 1817
Adm: Joseph Robinson   Let. Adm: 2 Feb. 1817
Chester Bk. 1-39 1843--William Elder, Dec'd. Adm: Margaret
Ann Elder, Widow. Cit: 20 Sept. 1843
-James Elder to Edward Shrewsbury B/5 1 slave. 22 April 1822
Archives Dept. Misc. Vol 4X-105
-James Elder to James Buckham-Bond for payment money 1 July 1822
Misc. Vol. 4Y-32
-James Elder to Jas. Buckham-Mtg. Slaves 1 July 1822. Misc. 3R-473

344

ELDER, JAMES to Thomas S. Grimke-Mtg. Slaves 4 March 1830 Archives
    Dept. Mtg. 3V-152

ELDER, JOHN to Mary (his daughter) gift of 1 slave. 23 Aug. 1728
    to Eleanor Muncrief-Gift 1 slave 10 May 1750. Old Index H. H. 239
    -John Elder--50 A. Congaree 30 Jan. 1761 Mem7-343   242
    -John Elder--200 A. Craven 3 April 1764 Mem. 6-245
    -John Elder--500 A. Craven 3 April 1775 Mem. 2-463
    -John Elder--"Of Settlement of Tyger River" -w- Mary to Samuel
      Farrow of Settlement of Enoree--Land on Brown Creek-Br. Broad
      River 450 A. Gr. of 14 Aug. 1775 to sd John Elder. Bd. Daniel
      Huger and Wm. Williams. Wit: Andrew Thomson, sd John Elder,
      Philemon Waites, Sr., Mary Elder. Sptg. Deed A-14 22/23
      June 1784
    -John Elder--sd name by mark one place, sd John Elder another.
      8 pounds 11 sh. 5 pence for 120 days duty in militia in 1782
      in Col. Thomas Taylor's Reg't. Certificate Camden Dist be-
      fore Timothy Rives, J. P. Rec't 22 Sept. 1785 by Hugh Means.
      Archives Dept. Rev. Rec. 2184 Ret. #61
    -John Elder--Of Ninety Six Dist Sptg. Co. to Robert Elder, Planter
      300 A. half of tract which said John Elder bought from Robert
      Cowden under date 16 Jan. 1765. Recorded in N. C. at Ct.
      held for Mecklenberg County 4 Monday July 1789 on S-s Broad
      River on Cowden's Creek. N. C. Gr. to 1753 3 Sept. Wit:
      Alexander Elder, Thos. Carey

ELDER, CAPT. JOHN--Alexander Elder allowed pay for duty in Capt. John
    Elder's Company, Col. Benj. Roebuck's Reg't. Also allowed
    pay for services in Capt. Wm. Elder's Co. Benj. Roebuck Reg't.
    Archives Dept. Rev. Rec. #2182

ELDER, JOHN--Farmer Pinckney Dist. Sptg. Co. to Thomas Bearden, farmer.
    200 A. Pinckney Dist. W-s Cowden's Cr. Bd. Robert Elder, Ephraim
    Hill. Plat on page 208. Wit: Samuel Morrow, Alexander Elder
    Isaac Bearden. Sptg. Deed 206 15 May 1793
    -John Elder to Thos Bearden 200 A. on Cowden Creek. Sptg. Deed
    C-206 1793/4
    -John Elder of Sptg. Dist. to Samuel Morrow Jr. Gr. to Robert Cowden
    by N. C. and conv. by him to sd John Elder 16 Jan. 1765
    Sptg. Deed D-330 4 May 1795
    -John Elder -w- Elizabeth nee Smith (see note book) Sptg. Equity
    Bill Box 2 Pg-8 1821

ELDER, MATTHEW--Notice of Ireland Pet. for citizenship 1 Nov. 1810.
    States has been in America since 1798. Granted. Chester Nat.
    Book Page 129
    -Will Book A-14--Matthew Elder-Will 5 Feb. 1840
        Wife:
        Sons: Matthew and Robert

ELDER, PATIENCE and Abigail Smith--Note: Due James Nesbitt-one hun-
    dred and fifteen and 59½ dollars, with interest from the 1st Jan.
    last for value rec'd. Wit: our hands and seals on 13 March 1843
    Test: James McLurkam. Patience Elder, Abigail Smith--their mark
    Letter from James Nesbitt headed "Mountain Shoals, S. C. 30 Oct.
    1845" Directs property be sold to pay his debt. The property of
    Patience Elder "that John B. Page has lived on".

ELDER, PETER--From Richard Hampton, Jr. of Sptg. Co. Gr. 4 July
1785 to Richard Hampton 296 A. on small Br. of Fair forest Creek
called Reedy Branch. Wit: John Watson and George Connell.
Sptg. Deed B-171 29 Jan. 1787
-Peter Elder from James Gibbs -w- Anna of Union Co. on both sides
of Lick Brance about a mile below Miller's Waggon Road. Wit:
Ephraim Elder and Thomas Rees 21 Sept. 1790 before Wm. Smith J.P.
Sptg. Deed B-494 5 June 179-
-Peter Elder -w- Elizabeth to Alexander Autry 222 A. on Fairforest
Creek. Gr. to Richard Hampton. Sptg. Deed C-236 1793
-Peter Elder to Ephraim Elder 48 A. on Buffalo Lick Creek 30 Pounds.
on W-s Buffalo Cr. Sptg. Deed C-144 25 Feb. 1793
-Peter Elder and wife, Elizabeth of Sptg. Co. to William Lancaster
50 A. on Buffalo Creek 30 Pounds sterling. "Where sd Lancaster
now lives" Gr. to Thos Bullion-from him to Zach. Gibbs and from
him to Jas. Gibbs and from him to Peter Elder. Sptg. Deed C-127
26 Feb. 1793
-Peter Elder to Robert Sprinkle. 12 A. on Buffalo Creek. Sptg.
Deed C-193 22 Feb. 1793
-Peter Elder Adv. Fielding Turner--Suit on note dated 11 Sept.
1832 "One day after date I promise to pay Fielding Turner or
bearer the sum of one hundred and eleven dollars thirty nine $\frac{1}{4}$
cents for value rec'd of him. Witness my hand and seal this 11
of Sept. 1832. Test. M. Turner (sig) Peter Elder. Sptg. Judgement Filed 19 Sept 1832. Judgement #1740

ELDER, ROBERT--Archives Dept. Rev. Rec. 2185--267 days duty as Pvt.
Horseman in Capt. James Elder's Co. from 15 Dec. 1780 to 8 Sept.
1781. 63 days in Capt. Wm. Elder's Co. 10 Dec. 1781 to Feb. 1782.
Both Col. Roebuck's Reg't. Rev. Rec. #2185
-Robert Elder--Sole Legatee of Samuel Morrow-Will 9 Feb. 1796
Sptg. 150
-Robert Elder -w- Sarah of Sptg. Co. to James Crowder. Sptg. F-4
25 April 1797

ELDER, SAMUEL--Archives Dept. Rev. Rec. #2186--Militia duty Roebuck's
Reg't. since the fall of Charleston. 14 pounds 11 sh. 5 pence.
"Please deliver to Sam'l Lancaster the whole of the indents due.
xxxxto Samuel Elder, Dec'd.xxxxAlexander Elder, Exor. 14 Mar. 1787
-Samuel Elder of Sptg. from Drew Smith of Georgia. Sptg. F-229
14 Aug. 1787
-Samuel Elder to James Hickey 100 A. on Dutchman's Cr. of Tyger R.
Wit: Wm. Roberts, Jacob Isam. Sptg. Deed C-179 5 Feb. 1793
-Samuel Elder -w- Patience to Thomas Moore. Sptg. Deed G-267
8 July 1794
-Samuel Elder -w- Patience of Pinckney Dist to Thomas Moore of
Sptg. Dist. 35 A. on Vice's Springs, Ward's Br. Tyger River.
Sptg. Deed 1794
-Samuel Elder to James Moore 150 A. on Ward's Creek. Gr. to Thos.
Moore 11 Aug. 1774 and by sd Thos. Moore conv. to sd Samuel Elder.
Wit: William Otts, Samuel Otts, Samuel Elder, Jr. Sptg. Deed D-280
9 May 1795
-Samuel Elder to James Moore 50 A. W-s Ward's Creek orig. Gr. to
Thomas Moore-who conv. to sd Samuel Elder on 11 Aug. 1774

ELDER, SAMUEL--Will 5 March 1797. Sptg. Probate Box 9 Pg. 18
   Wife: Anne--"Absented from me--1 shilling sterling
   Dau: Catherine--1 Shilling
   Son: Hammon--1 shilling   ) Had already received their shares
   Dau: Lucy   )
   Son: Samuel
   Exor's: Thomas Moore and Samuel Otts
   Wit: John Otts, Wm. Otts, Hammon Elder
  -Hammon Elder estate--Box 9 Pkg. 19 Cit. 15 March 1821
   Adm'r: Wm. Rogers   Bond: 22 March 1821
   S: Elisha Jennings, John Meaden, Wm. Golightly
   Another Bond: 4 March 1822 for Abigail Elder, Gdn. of Hammon
   Elder. Shows as heirs or part of them:
        Elizabeth Elder   Patience Elder
        Alice Elder   Hammon Elder
        William Jinnings

ELDER, SAMUEL--No dower. To Samuel Otts Sptg. Deed F-345 18 Jan 1799

ELDER, SAMUEL--Adv. Thomson and Trimmier for Wm. Trimmier--Note: One
   day after date I promise to pay Thomson and Trimmier on order,
   fifty dollars value received. 14 Nov. 1828. Test: Sam. A. Elder
   Judgement about 27 Oct. 1842 Sptg. Judgement 2942 1843
   Filed 26 Sept. 1842

ELDER, SMITH--Of Sptg.--To his children: Jane Ann Elder, John Elder
   Elizabeth Elder, Martin Elder "my tract of land where I now live--
   200 A. on Buck Creek. 25 June 1844. Sptg. Deed Y-422 Deed Gift
  -Smith Elder -vs- Henry Parris. Sptg. Judgement 10130 1891

ELDER, THOMAS--Archives Dept. Misc. Mtg. 3D-213 305
   (1) Mtg. to Richard Wade 16 Sept. 1772 Slave
   (2) Mtg. to H. Simonson, et al 13 Nov. 1772 Slaves 13 Nov. 1772
  -Thomas Elder to Wm. McKinney B/S 2 slaves. 13 Nov. 1779
   Archives Dept. Misc. Vol. RR-206
  -Thomas Elder--Archives Dept. Rev. Rec. Ret. #94--38 pounds 5 sh.
   8 pence ½ penny for 267 days as private horseman in Capt. James
   Elder's Co. from 15 Dec. 1780 to 8 Sept. 1781. Roebuck's Reg't.
   Order on Treasurer by William Elder "next of Kin" and Adm'r. to
   pay to Hugh Means. Nov. 20, 1785

ELDER, DOCTOR THOMAS--Archives Dept. Rev. Rec. 2187 Ret. #114. For
   a loan to the state--2000 pounds. Thomas Elder for Militia duty
   in Roebuck's Reg't.--since the fall of Charleston. 14 pounds
   11 sh. 5 pence.

ELDER, THOMAS--Of Greenville Dist. to Eli Baldwin 115 A. S-W-side
   Reedy River. Orig. Gr. to Andrew Johnson 2 Feb. 1789. 18 April
   1807. Wit: John Cureton, John M. Cureton. No dower
   Greenville Deed Bk. H-208

ELDER, WILLIAM--Archives Dept. Misc. Rec. 1736-1740C. T. pg. 94
   "Know all men by these presents that I, John Amory of the Province
   of South Carolina, Indian Trader, have bargained, sold and deliv-
   ered and by these presents do bargain, sell and deliver unto Wm.
   Elder all these geldings and mares hereafter mentioned. Vizxxxx
   (Brands etc) 4 May 1744. Wit: John Watts, Wm. Winsmore
   Prov. before Stephen Crell, J. P. for Berkley County 12 May 1744

ELDER, WILLIAM--Trader. From Henry Shackly of the Cherokees--de-
   livered "in the Cherokee nation" (list horses.) Wit: Bryant
   Salmon, John Gillespie. Page 404.
   -William Elder-Indian Trader from Andrew Brown of Berkley Co.
   Horses, Cows etc. 5 June 1745. Wit: Jas. Francis. Archives
   Dept. Misc. 1736-1740
   -William Elder, Indian Trader, Dec'd. Inv. and Appr. 13 July 1748
   Appr's: Charles Russell, William Sewright, John McCord. Archives
   Dept. Misc. 1748-1751
   -William Elder--Archives Dept. Rev. Rec. 2188--267 days duty as
   Private horseman in Capt. James Elder's Co. form 15 Dec. 1780 to
   8 Sept. 1781 and 63 days duty as Capt. of Horse from 10 Dec. 1781
   to 10 Feb. 1782 and 42 days as Capt. of Fort from 14 July to 24
   Aug. 1782. Order to pay to Hugh Means. Order to pay James Martin
   2 Nov. 1790
   -William Elder--Sptg. Judgement Roll 3864 Filed 22 March 1854
   Adv. Dr. R. E. Cleveland. Note-Printed form: "$42.90 Spartanburg,
   S. C. 8 Dec. 1840" "One day after date I promise to pay Jesse
   Cleveland on order forty two dollars and 90/100 for value re-
   ceived as witness my hand and seal. William Elder. Jesse
   Cleveland had died intestate. John B. Cleveland, Adm'r.

FANNING, JAMES -w- Elizabeth of Sptg. to William Lipscomb--Gr. to
   James Fanning 8 March 1763 by Gov. Bell on Thickety Creek.
   Sptg. Deed Bk A-61 1786

FARLEY, AARON AND ARTHUR--Gr-sons of James Bennett. Sptg. (2)-62

FARRAR, THOMAS--Of Sptg. from William Dickson of S. C. Co. of Duplin.
   300 A. land on head branch of Fairforest Creek-on Tyger River.
   Middle ground-gr. to sd Wm. Dickson. Sptg. Deed A-35 4 Oct. 1785

FARRAR, THOMAS--Sheriff of 96 to Thomas Farrar, Esq.--Whereas James
   Brown and Jesse Brown were lately seized--300 A. on waters of
   Lawson's Fork xxxx and whereas Thomas Farrar did in November term
   1784 commence an action out of Ct. Com. Pleas at Charleston. xxx
   sd Thomas Farrar. Sptg. Deed B-278 21 Sept. 1789

FARROW, CHANEY--Of Sptg. -vs- Wm. B. Mays of Edgefield--Suit on note
   Nov. Term 1818.
   -Recites sale lands--Farrow to Mays--Land on Horn's Creek, Bd. John
   Gray, John Ryan, Wm. Hill. Formerly land of Samuel Walker, Dec'd.
   and on which Mrs. Martha J. Walker now lives.
   -Recites Chaney Farrow -m- dau. of Samuel Walker
            Joseph Eddins -m- "   "   "   "
   _____? Beams -m- Rebecca, dau. of Samuel Walker
   Printed Law Book-McCords Reports-Vol. 1 Law Library

FARROW, JAMES--Of Sptg. -m- 8 Sept. 1868 Susan Savage of Henrico Co.
   Va. Archives Dept. Misc. 7-K-3

FARROW, LANDON -w- Rachel to John Farrow 100 pounds--167 A. N-s Enoree
   River. Pt tract conv. by Mr. Brown to Benj. Wofford who conv. to
   Henry Meredith-who conv. to Landon Farrow. Sptg. B-249 12 March
                                                              1789

FARROW, LANDON--From Henry Meredith -w- Milly 333 A. Part gr. 26 March
1755 to Thomas Ervine--both sides of Enoree. Gr. by N. C. as
being in Anson Co. Sptg. B-174/5 20 Aug. 1788

FARROW, SAMUEL--Will 9 Jan. 1824 Sptg. (2)-57

FARROW, THOMAS--Of 96 Dist. to "My well beloved brothers" Samuel
Farrow and Wm. Farrow "All my right and title to a certain tract
of land containing 300 A. on the waters of Cedar Shoal Creek. A
branch of the N-s of Enoree--Orig. gr. to Henry Hamilton-who conv.
to John Farrow, late of sd Dist. Dec'd. and he, the sd John Farrow,
dying without a Will. I the sd Thomas Farrow, son of the sd John
Farrow, became heir at law. Not to molest, intrude my mother,,
Rosannah Farrow. Sptg. A-10 12 Jan. 1784

FINLEY, MARY--Dau. of George McCarter-Will 1815 Sptg. 65

FONDREN, SARAH--Heir of Thomas Cole-Will 1816 (seems dau.) Sptg. 74

FORD, JOHN--"Heir at law of Estate of Philip Ford of Montgomery Co.
Tenn. to James Ford, Jr. of Montgomery Co. Tenn. 200 A. on Fair
Forest Cr. adj. Giles Connell. Orig. Gr. to John Ford 7 June 1767
Wit: Ed. Lacy, Richard Miles, James Ford. Sptg. Deed F-99
-John Ford of 96 Dist. and his son in law, Philip Ford--Land in
Fairforest where sd John Ford formerly lived-gr. sd John Ford
1 June 1767. This deed Dec. 21, 1773 Sptg. Deed B-242
-John Ford of Tyger River from Robert Miller, Jr. -w- Rachel,form-
erly of Anson, now of Tyger River-Land on Little River, gr. 3
Sept. 1773, Little River now called Tyger River--adj. Robert
Lawson's land. This deed 17 Aug. 1771. C. T. Misc.-5 Pg. 30

FORD, JOHN -w- Catherine of Mecklenburg to John Robinette--Land Meck-
lenburg-McCorppins Creek. Pt. land from Selwyn to Ford 1767.
Wit: Wm. Smith, John Hall. Mecklenburg Co. N. C. 14 Oct. 1771
Harris-Deed Bk. 14-82

FORD, POLLY--Her children legatees of Isaac Bishop-Will 1816. Sptg. 13

FOSTER, ANTHONY--Will 26 Nov. 1804. Sptg. 153

FOSTER, BETSY--Dau. of Joel Traylor-Will 1807 Sptg. 1

FOSTER, HENRY--Will 1 Jan. 1821 Sptg. (2)-3

FOSTER, ISHAM--Will 5 Aug. 1816 Sptg. 112

FOSTER, JOHN C. SEN'R.--Dec'd. in 1816 Intestate Sptg. Bx-10 Bill-5
Wife: Since dec'd. 1822 Intestate
Children: Moses Foster
          Mary B. -w- John Harmon
          Elizabeth, Isaac N. and Sarah M. Foster--all minors
          John C. Foster, Jr. Def't. Filed 22 May 1829

FOSTER, JOHN--Will 14 Feb. 1817 Sptg. 107

FOSTER, MOSES--Will 15 Nov. 1809. Sptg. 39

FOSTER, NANCY--Dau. of Samuel Cathcart-Will 1820 Sptg. 142

FOSTER, SIMPSON--Will March 4, 1824 Sptg. 39

FOSTER, TABITHA--Dau. of James Ballenger-Will 1813. Richard Foster
    mentioned-$1.00. Sptg. 31

FOSTER, THOMAS--Dec'd. Intestate. Sptg. Div. Per. and R. E. Bk.
    Widow: Sally Foster
    Children: Oney -w- Thomas Tinsley
               Nancy -w- John Foster
               William Foster
               Stephen Foster
               Polly Pollard, Dec'd. Her children:
                   Benjamin Pollard
                   William   "
                   _____   "
                   James   "
    Part. March term 1804. Plats in Book

FOSTER, WILLIAM--Will 1 March 1817. Sptg. 118

FRAZER, POLLY--Wife of William Frazer. Dau. of Samuel Stewart-Will
    1814. Sptg. 126

FRIE, PETER--Will 11 Jan. 1813. Sptg. 28

FRYER, RICHARD--Will 3 Feb. 1821. Sptg. (2)-1
    U?
FORGISON, JANE--Dau. of William McWilliams--Will 1824. Sptg. (2)-37

GAMBRELL, CATHERINE--4th dau. of George Brewton-Will 1815 Sptg. 60

GAMBRELL, NANCY--Legatee and seems dau. of Sarah Carey-Will 1828
    Son in law, Washing Gambrell. Sptg. (2)-113

GARVIN, THOMAS -w- Jean to Thomas Wadsworth and Wm. Turpin of Charles-
    ton, Merchants. 196 A. on Cary's Br. of Lawson's Fork below
    ancient boundary. Bd. Edward Bishop, Robert McMardy, and vac.
    Gr. sd Thos. Garvin by Benj. Guerard 21 Jan. 1785. Sptg. A-122
                                                       Deed Bk. 1786
GILKY, WALTER--Son in law of Joseph Austell-Will 1823. Sptg. (2)-33

GILLENWATERS, MARY--Dau. of William Wilkins-Will 1807 Sptg. 156

GILLERLAND, REV. JAMES--Son in law of Samuel Nesbitt-Will 1816. Sptg. 96

GOLIGHTLY, AMERY--Will 1812. Sptg. 50

GOODLETT, ANN--Will 14 Mar. 1818. Sptg. 127

GOODLETT, ROBERT--Of Sptg. Co. Dec'd. Will in file. 5 Aug. 1796
    Widow: Nancy   Sptg. Box-6 Bill-3 1825
    Son: James Goodlett
    Dau: Jean -w- Thomas Grisham
          Peggy
          Catherine -w- Francis Powers
          Anna -w- Henry Jameison
          Margaret -w- Jesse Waddle
          Ruth -w- Robert Conner
    Son: John, William, David of Greenville Dist. and Robert

350

GOODLETT, ROBERT--Will 5 Aug. 1796 Sptg. (2) 35

GOSSETT, ANNY--Dau. of John Tolleson-Will 1820 Sptg. (2)-6

GOWEN, JOHN--Will 20 Aug. 1809 Sptg. 2

GRACE, POLLY--2nd dau. of George Brewton-Will 1815. Sptg. 60

GRAMLING, ANDREW--Gr. son in law of John Foster-Will 1817. Sptg. 107

GRAMLING, PATSY--Dau. of Benjamin High-Will 1816. Sptg. 92

GRANT, DANIEL--Will 20 Sept. 1819. Sptg. (2) 95

GRAY, ALEXANDER--Son in law of Absolom Lancaster-Will 1814 Sptg. 67

GREENDEL, JOHN -w- Esther of Mecklenburg Co. N. C. to Alexander Love
    21 Nov. 1766--400 A. N-s Broad River and S-s Fishing Creek, in-
    cluding the Sand Creek above Wm. Ratchford's and above the Beaver
    Dams. Gr. to Blaney Mills 3 Feb. 1754 who conv. to Jas. Milliken
    on 29 Jan. 1767 and conv. by sd Jas. Millikin and his wife Jean
    to sd John Greendel on 12 Jan. 1765. Harris Deed Bk. 10-288 for
    Mecklenburg Co. Pres: Wm. Sharp, George Dickey.
    Note: This was before State line between North and South Caro-
    lina. The land is Chester-Spartanburg section--Greendel moved
    about.

GRICE, ANN--Dau. of Samuel Cathcart-Will 1820

GRIFFIN, HANNAH--Legatee and seems dau. of John Law-Will 1822. Sptg. 78

GRIST, JOHN--Will 17 Oct. 1793 Sptg. 79-A
       John--Will 19 Jan. 1816 Sptg. 79-B

GRIZEL, ELIZABETH--Dau. of Christopher Rhodes--Will 15 March 1806
    Sptg. 24

GROGEN, BARTHOLOMEW--384 A. in Rowan Co. Buffalo Island Creek-Dan
    River. 2 Aug. 1760. Raleigh Land Grants Bk. 6-153 Books 1730/31
    -Bartholomew Grogin--From John Gowan 18 March 1794--Land on Beaver
    Dam S Pacolet. Gr. to Abigail Tennif by N. C. Trans. to sd Gowan
    as by reference to rewards of Ct. at Cambridge. Sptg. Deed D-9
    -Bartholomew Grogan, Sr. to Bartholomew Grogan, Jr. $500.00 Land
    S-s Pacolet R. Wit: Thomas Grogan, Willey S. Brown. 14 Dec. 1819
    Sptg. Deed R-48
    -R-221 1820 to Henry Grogan

GROGAN, JOHN--To Benj. Hammett and James Hammett land on head waters
    of Easleys Creek. 11 Oct. 1838. Sptg. Deed Y-182
    -John Grogan to Andrew M. Walker 14 Dec. 1844. Pg. 537 Walker of N. C.
    Land on Pacolet R. Dower by Mourning Grogan 22 Jan. 1845

GROGAN, RICHARD--Of Sptg. from Lawrence Brock and Henry Brock of Green-
    ville land in Sptg. Co. on Motlow's Cr. Sptg. Deed V-305 and 306
    -Grogan, John Jr. 150 A. Sptg. Dist.--Gr. to Wm.D. Thomas. Wit:
    Augustus Clayton, J. L. Holcombe. (306)

GUYTON, NANCY--Heir of Thomas Cole-Will 1816 Seems dau. Sptg. 74

HAM, JAMES--Will 25 Feb. 1804 Sptg. 135

HAMES, JOHN--Father in law of John Eison-Will 1826. Sptg (2) 68

HAMILTON, HENRY -w- Agnese of Enoree Settlement to John Farrow of
     Enoree Settlement 300 A. Cedar Shoal Creek of Enoree R. Bd. John
     Stone's Survey and vac. Sptg. Deed A-17 29 Oct. 1776

HANNA, LUCINDA--Dau. of Sarah Moore-Will 1853 Sptg. Wills 40-38 1853

HANNA, VIOLET--Dau. of Margaret Barry-Will 1823. Sptg. (2) 44

HARRALSON, ELIZABETH--Dau. of William Meaders-Will 1814. Sptg. (2) 18

HARRIS, ANN--Dau. of John Jones-Will 1812. Sptg. 116

HARRISON, THOMAS--Will 23 April 1819 Sptg. 132

HART, JANE--Dau. of John Foster-Will 1817. Sptg. 107

HATCHETT, JOSIAH--Will 18 Dec. 1824. Sptg. (2) 45

HAWKINS, ARMEN--Dau. of Isham Foster-Will 1816. Sptg. 112
     -Page 119-Armin Hawkins and Herbert Hawkins witnesses Will of Wm.
     Foster. Jane Jones other witness.

HAWKINS, PRUDY--Sister of John Lewis-Will 1813. Sptg. 43

HAYS, SALLY--Dau. of Obadiah Wingo-Will 1824. Sptg. (2) 115

HEAD, JAMES--From John Hillen and Mary Hillen, his mother, 300 A.
     on Fulses Branch. Wit: Moses Casey, Abigail Casey, Wm. Head.
     Sptg. Deed B-58/9 14 Jan. 1785
     -James Head -w- Ann of Sptg. Yeoman, to David Vinson, of State of
     Georgia, Richmond County, 300 A. Gr. to Eleazer Benton in Co.
     Sptg. on Fulses Branch, waters of Cedar Shoal Creek. Sd. Berton
     conv. to Nathaniel Hillim and his heirs and Exor. Mary Hillin
     and John Hillin conv. to James Head on 15 Jan. 1787. Sptg. Deed
     A-265. 27 June 1787 Wit: Ralph Jackson, Lucretia Head, Charity
     Smith (Their mark x)
     -Robin Head wit. deed in 1785 (pg. 11)
     James Head wit. deed in 1776 (pg. 18)

HEAD, JOHN -w- Sarah to Samuel Farrow, 375 A. on Enoree R. Gr. to
     Robert Howard. Wit: Stephen Head, Wm. Easley, Josiah N. Kennedy
     Dower-Greenville Co.Sptg. Deed F-92 7 Feb. 1797

HEAD, SARAH--Aunt of Samuel Farrow-Will 1824. Sptg. (2) 57

HENDRICKS, JOHN et al -vs- John Grissel, et al. Sptg. Judgement 97
                                                                  1804
HENDRIX, NANCY--Dau. of Christopher Rhodes-Will 1806 Sptg. 24

HENDRIX, SALLEY--Dau. of Joseph Woodruff-Will 1817. John B. Hendrix
     a wit. Sptg. 110

HENRY, JAMES EDWARD--Of Sptg. Dist.--Bond to John M. Roberts of Green-
     ville Dist. Sec. by Mtg. Cotton Mfg. Co. stock. 8 Feb. 1840
     Archives Dept. Misc. L-81

HERING, EDWARD--Will 26 July 1811. Sptg. 27

HEWATT, JOHN--Will 3 Nov. 1811. Sptg. 21

HIGH, BENJAMIN--Will 4 May 1816. Sptg. 92

HIGH, BENJAMIN--Dec'd. Intestate 1816 Sptg. Box 2 Bill 4
    Widow: Sarah--since dec'd.   Filed 31 May 1821
    Children: Elizabeth -w- Thomas Bomar
              Richard R. High
              Burwell High
              Rebecca -w- Jeremiah Russell
              Benjamin High
              Patsy -w- Reuben Gramblin
              Pascal High
              Charity -w- Jesse Dodson
              Nancy -w- Thomas Underwood
              Swepston and David High--minors-over 14
              Polly, dec'd. -w- Edward Martin, her children:
                Thomas and John Martin-over 14 yrs.

HIGH, NANCY--Dau. of Reuben Daniel-Will 1825. Sptg. (2) 93

HINDMAN, PEGGY--Dau. of William Meadors-Will 1814. Gr-son-Wm.
    Hindman. Sptg. (2) 18

HINDMON, JOHN--Will 10 April 1819 Sptg. 146

HINDMON, SALLY--Dau. of Samuel Cathcart-Will 1820. Sptg. 142

HINDS, ANNA--Dau. of James Allen-Will 1824. Sptg. (2) 66

HOBBY, ELIZABETH--Dau. of Zachariah Leatherwood-Will 1814. Sptg. 45

HOBBY, JOHN--Will 30 Dec. 1826. Sptg. (2) 96

HOGAN, JOHN--Of Orange Co. Hillsboro Dist. to Verdry McBee of 96 Dist.
    300 A. on Thickety Creek, Sptg. Co. Orig. Gr. to sd John Hogan
    by N. C. 3 May 1785. C. T. Deed Q-5-440

HOLCOMB, HOSEA--"Son" of Phebe Wilbanks-Will 1820. Appears other
    sons: Elijah?, and Warren. Daus: Susannah and Manoh. She
    was probably widow Holcomb. Sptg. (2) 71

HOLCOM, JOHN--Wit. Deed with Thos. Wingo. Made by Wm. Benson to
    Richard Harrison for land on Fairforest. Sptg. Deed A-89 1785

HOWARD, BENJAMIN--Will 20 Feb. 1817. Sptg. 126

HOWELL, OBEDIAH--Bd land of John Bogan on Fair Forrest-1774. Sptg.
    Stream. Archives Dept. Mem. 13-96

HOUSE, THOMAS--Will 9 Aug. 1811. Sptg. 15

HOY, ALBERT--Gr-son of Andrew Barry-Will 1854?. Sptg. 16

HUFF, ROSANNAH--And her daughter, Ginsy Smith--Legatees of Samuel
    Farrow-Will 1824. Sptg. (2) 57

HUNT, SARAH--Sister of Simpson Foster-Will 1824. Sptg. (2) 39

HUNT, WILLIAM--Wife, Asameth-dau. of Richard Daniel, Sr. of Sptg.
    Robert M. Daniel, Adm'r. Archives Dept. Misc. H-480 1833

JACKSON, THOMAS--Will 14 Jan. 1820. Sptg. (2) 74

JAMES, CHARLES--Will 23 May 1821. Sptg. (2) 15

JAMES, JOHN--Will 14 April 1817. Sptg. (2) 28

JAMES, REBECCA--Dau. of Thomas Harrison-Will 1819. Sptg. 132

JOHNSON, CHRISTOPHER--Will 22 May 1804. Sptg. 4

JOHNSON, DIDAMA--Dau. of Catherine Wofford-Will 1824. Sptg. (2) 70

JOHNSTON, FANNEY--Dau. of Zachariah Leatherwood-Will 1814. Sptg. 45

JONES, JOHN--Will 22 Mar. 1812. Sptg. 116

JORDAN, JAMES--To George Debor--½Grant to Robert Henderson-4 May 1769
    by N. C. Conv. James Jordan 1778e. Land in Mecklenburg Co. on N-s
    of Pacolet River. J. Jordan conv. to heirs of Robert Bishop, Dec'd.
    Seems Geo. Debor represented the heirs. Sptg. Deed A-98 1786

JORDAN, JOHN--Dec'd. Intestate. Sptg. Box 2 Bill 9 Filed 8 Feb. 1821
    Widow: Lucy -m- Robert Jameison
    5 minor children: Sarah, over 14; Elizabeth, James, Samuel, and
                            John, under 14.
    John Crawford, Gdn. with James Hunt

JOURDAN, MARGARET--Will Rec'd. 1825. Sptg. (2) 64

KIRBY, LEVICEY--Dau. of John Tolleson-Will 1820. Sptg. (2) 6

KIRBY, RICHARD--Dec'd. Intestate. Sptg. Box 10 File 7/8
    Widow: Lovicey Kirby
            James Kirby
            Nancey -w- Charles Liles
            Green Kirby
            Polly -w- Thomas Burgess
            John Kirby
            Catherine -w- John Garrett
            Stephen Kirby
            Ity -w- Samuel White
            Fenilty -w- Daniel White
            Tolleson, Angus, and Ecender Kirby by Gdn. Louvicy Kirby
    Bill of Part. filed 4 May 1829. Receipt in file from all.

KELLY, ELIZABETH--Dau. of Josiah Hatchett-Will 1824. Sptg. (2) 45

KELSO, JOHN AND JOSEPH--Sons in law of Moses Foster. Gr. dau-Elizabeth
    Foster Kelso and her mother, Margaret. Sptg. 39

KENNEDY, PATSY--Heir of Thomas Cole-Will 1816. Sptg. 74
Kenady?

LANCASTER, ABSOLOM--Will 3 May 1814. Sptg. 67

LANCASTER, CLEREMONT--Dau. of Amey Golightly-Will 1812. Sptg. 50

LANCASTER, RICHARD--Will 5 Dec. 1824. Sptg. (2) 54

LANCASTER, SAMUEL--Will 9 Aug. 1797. Sptg. 5

LANCASTER, WILLIAM--Will 2 July 1824. Sptg. (2) 40

LANGFORD, LIDDEY--Dau. of Zachariah Leatherwood-Will 1814. Sptg. 45
    Also: Ginney Langford, Ruthey Langford and _____ Langford.

LAW, JOHN--Will 25 Nov. 1822. Sptg. (2) 78

LAWRENCE, LYDIA--Legatee of Isaac Bishop.-Will 1816. Sptg. (2) 13

LAWSON, POLLY--Dec'd. dau. of Margaret Barry-Will 1823. Sptg. (2) 44

LEATHERWOOD, JOHN--Will 14 June 1820. Sptg. 140

LEATHERWOOD, ZACHARIAH--Will 28 June 1814. Sptg. 45

LEE, LEVI--_____? Will 26 Sept. 1822. Sptg. (2) 25

LEGON, ROBERT--Dec'd. Sptg. Div. Per. And R. E. Bk.
    Heirs: Edith Legon-Widow   Part. Oct. Ct. Plats in Book
            Robert and Peter Legon
            Susannah -w- Henry Brown
            Nancy -w- Walter West
            Obedience -w- Obediah Wingo
            Polly, Elizabeth, John W., Abner W., James Legon
            Sally -w- John Cook

LEONARD, NANCY--Legatee and seems dau. of Charles McClain-Will 1821
    Sptg. (2) 14

LEWIS, BENJAMIN--Appointed Overseer of Island Ford Road, that part
    from West Harris to Ephraim's Branch and Drury Matthews and from
    thence to Burton's old place. March Ct. 1795. Joseph Lewis--
    warned. Rd defaultors--to testify of default. Edgefield Ct. Min.
    October 1794.

LEWIS, DAVID--200 A. on Indian Creek. Surv. for David Lewis by John
    Pearson, D. S. 11 Nov. 1754 and Cert. 3 May 1757. Gr. 17 April
    1764 to Ment. Men. 22 May 1764. William Cannon. Archives
    Dept. Mem. 6-274
    -David Lewis--Mem. 10-22 Sptg. File, Archives Dept. 500 A. on head
    of Kelso Branch. Fairforest Richland Creek of Pacolet R. Bd.-all
    vac. Cert. 1 Aug. 1769. Gr. 31 Oct. 1769. Mem. 28 Dec. 1769

LEWIS, GEORGE--Will 21 March 1818. Sptg. Wills Orig. A-138 Bx-17 Pkg-8
    Wife: Mary--Exec.
    Brother: Ephraim
    Property to be divided at death of widow between his brother and
    sister and her heirs.
    -George Lewis--Sptg. Box 6 Bill 4--Brother, Ephraim Lewis-1000 A.
    N-s Tennessee River. N. C. Grant. Brothers: Isaac, Abel, Isiah
    all out of state. Sisters Mrs. Polly Boley and Mrs. Peggy Elison

LEWIS, JOEL--Of Sptg. Will 14 Jan. 1815. Sptg. Wills Orig. A-64
    Wife: Polly
    "My 2 Ch.": Frances-to have Plt'n "I purchased from David Lewis"
                 John-th have Plt'n "I purchased from James Lewis.
    Ex: John Chapman. Rec'd: 15 Aug. 1815

LEWIS, JOHN--Of Gilford Co. N. C. -w- Priscilla. Gr. 14 Nov. 1754
    To Joshua Teague--200 A. on Bush River. sd John Lewis -w-
    Priscilla Lewis. Wit: Elijah Teague, Thos. Welborn and James
    Hilley. Laurens Deed B-68/69 29 Oct. 1771

LEWIS, COL. JOHN--Of Granville Co. N. C. -w- Catherine to Thomas
    Smith, Esq.--5000 A. in Dist. 96. Bd. John Murray, Dec'd. John
    Rutledge, James Parsons, Wm. Brown, Wm. Simpson-now James Simpson
    C. T. D-5-322 4 June 1777

LEWIS, JOHN--Will 2 Dec. 1813. Sptg. 43
    -John Lewis of Sptg. Dist. Sptg. Will A-47 Box 18 Pkg. 6
        Wife: Frances   Will not dated
        Son: Joel--should he die without issue, land to go to my
                     brothers and sisters.
        Brother in law: John Clark
        Wit: Alex'r. Roddy, Joel Lewis, Mary Lewis. Rec'd. 14 May
                                                              1814

LEWIS, MARGARET--Dau. of William Wood--Will 1793. Sptg. 149-B

LEWIS, PEGGY--Of Sptg. Co. to Thomas Wadsworth and Wm. Turpin of
    Charleston, Merchants. 400 A. above ancient boundary. Bd. N-Moore's
    land. W-Smith's land, and all vac. Gr. sd Peggy Lewis by Wm.
    Moultrie, Gov. 7 Nov. 1785. Sptg. Deed A-125. 1786
    -Peggy Lewis--Dau. of James Ballenger-Will 1813. Sptg. 31

LEWIS, RICHARD--Will 1st May 1838. Edgefield

LIGGON, POLLY--Dau. of Josiah Hatchett-Will 1824. Sptg. (2) 45

LINN, NANCY--Her heirs. Legatees of Isaac Bishop-Will 1816. Sptg. 13

LIPSCOMB, DAVID--Dec'd. Intestate. Sptg. Equity Bills
    Heirs: Sally -w- Peter Peterson
            Elizabeth -w- James Peterson
            Minor Lipscomb
            Amity -w- John Patterson
    6 Minor children: Patsey (near 14 yrs), Marcena, Hopson, Caty,
                       Dolly, Avena

LIPSCOMB, DAVID--Will 3 June 1816. Sptg. 85

LIPSCOMB, JOHN--Will 1 Oct. 1827. Sptg. (2) 101

LIPSCOMB, JOHN AND DAVID--Sons in law of Edward Smith.-Will 1815.
    Sptg. 58

LIPSCOMB, JULIET--Dau. of William Lancaster-Will 1824. Sptg. 40

LIPSCOMB, WILLIAM--Will 17 July 1808. Sptg. 10

LIPSCOMB, WILLIAM--Dec'd. Intestate. Late of Abbeville Dist.
   6 children: Nancy -w- William Wood
              Thomas, David S., John H., Sally, Elizabeth
   William Lipscomb, Sr. of Sptg. Dist. also since dec'd.--left slaves
   to above children. Part. March 1811. Personal property.

LITTLEJOHN, ELIZABETH--Dau. of John Lipscomb-Will 1827. Sptg. 101

LITTLEJOHN, MARY--Dau. of William Lipscomb-Will 1808. Land where
   Thos. Littlejohn now lives. Sptg. 10

LIVELY, JOHN--Will 18 March 1825. Sptg. (2) 84

LOVE, NANCY--Dau. of Henry O'Neill-Will 1815. Sptg. 51

LOVET, ELIZABETH--Dau. of Joseph Austell-Will 1823. Sptg. (2) 33

MARTIN, THOMAS AND JOHN--Gr-sons of Benj. High.-Will 1816. Sptg. 93

MASON, FRANCIS--Will 4 Nov. 1825. Sptg. (2) 63

MAYER, THOMAS--Will 19 April 1814. Sptg. 131 (or Mayes)

MAYFIELD, JANE--Dau. of John Jones-Will 1812. Sptg. 116

MAYFIELD, POLLY--Legatee and seems dau. of Charles McClain-Will 1821
   Geo. Mayfield an exor. Sptg. (2) 14

MEADOWS, JOSEPH--Dec'd. Sptg. Box 6 Bill 2
   Widow: Sela
   5 children: John, Lettice, Vancy, Nozinth, Edgbert--all minors
   Hardy Williford and Henry Golightly, Gdn's. John Meadows, Adm.

MEADOWS, THOMAS--Will 8 Feb. 1816 Sptg. 70

MEADERS, WILLIAM--Will 4 March 1814. Sptg. (2) 18

MEANS, JOHN--Son in law of Thos. Williamson. Will 1813. Sptg. 25

MELLICAN, WILLIAM--Dec'd. Intestate Sptg. Div. Per. and R. E. Bk.
   Widow: Mary -m--Pleasant Brannon
   4 children: Jenney, Moses S., Washington, Nancy. Part. March
   1809. Plats in Book.

MERRIMAN, DELITHA--Dau. of Benjamin Bonner-Will 1814. Sptg. 48

MILES, ISAAC--Nephew of Samuel Farrow-Will 1824. Sptg. (2) 57

MILLER, JAMES--Dec'd. Will. Sptg. Div. Per. and R. E. Bk.
   Children: Nathaniel, Jane, Joshua, James, Samuel, John, Thomas
          Charles. 3 Plt'ns on Tyger River. Part. Oct. Term
          1801. Plats in Book.

MILLER, MARGARET JORDAN--Legatee of Margaret Jordan-Will 1825. "son"
   Samuel Miller. Sptg. (2) 64

MILLER, MICHAEL--Will 8 Feb. 1815. Sptg. 54

MILLER, NATHANIEL--Farmer of 96 Dist. Sptg. Deed A-46 1779
    To John Miller-late of Cumberland County, Pennsylvania, now re-
    siding in S. C. 116 A. Pt. Gr. to Robert Miller 30 May 1763 by
    Thomas Boone, Gov. S. C. On Lawson's Creek N-s of N Fork of Tyger R.
    -Nathaniel Miller to Robert Miller--150 A. on Middle and N. Fork
    Tyger R. Gr. to. Robert Miller 13 May 1763 who bequeathed to his
    son, sd Nathaniel Miller. Sptg. Deed A-66 1782. Page 76-Another
    conv. same to same.

MILLER, ROBERT--Dec'd. 1813 Intestate. Widow Jennett Miller, Oratrix.
    Married in 1792. .Children: John -m- Cassey Nicholls. Son-John N.
    Sptg. Box 7 Bill 5 1826

MILLER, SARAH--Dau. of Thomas Harrison-Will 1819 Sptg. 132

MONTGOMERY, ANNA--Dau. of James Reynolds-Will 1826. Son in law-Hugh
    Montgomery. Sptg. (2) 87

MONTGOMERY, JOHN--Son in law of Michael Miller-Will 1815. Sptg. 54

MOORE, BETSY--Dau. of John Law-Will 1822. Sptg. (2) 78

MOORE, CHARLES to Thomas Moore--Gr. to sd Charles Moore 11 Aug. 1784
    Sptg. Deed A-1 1785

MOORE, NANCY--Dau. of William Meaders-Will 1814. Sptg. (2) 18

MOORE, PEGGY--Dau. of James Wofford-Will 1815. Catee Moore another
    dau. Sptg. 63

MOORE, THOMAS--Weaver of the State of S. C. County of Spartanburg.
    To: Thomas Moore, farmer and Thomas Moore, Junior of this State
    and Co. aforesaid. P. A. to convey unto Jonathan Hamilton of
    Maryland formerly of the County ofBaltimore, a certain parcel of
    land which he, the said Hamilton, hath my bond for the conveyance.
    Also, P. A. to collect from James Norris, Bonds or Accts--Also
    to collect from William Fisher of Md. 7 Nov. 1788. Pres. of
    Wm. Ford, Jason Moore and Proven Sptg. Dist. 7 Nov. 1788.

MORNINGSTAR, RHODA--Dau. of John Voinset-Will 1822. Sptg. 144

MORRIS, JOSEPH -w- Jemima to William Morris, Sen'r. Gr. 22 May 1772
    by N. C. to John Kirconnell--200 A. Tryon Co. now in S. C. both
    sides of Beech Creek of Pacolet River. Bd. Robert Nelson and
    vac. and conv. by Kirconnell to sd Joseph Morris. Sptg. Deed A-117
                                                                    1785
MORROW, SAMUEL--Will 9 Feb. 1796. Sptg. 150
    -Samuel Morrow "Of Dutchman's Creek" Will 8 Feb. 1842
    Wife: Jennet
    Son: Samuel, Jr.
    Niece: Nancy Morrow
    Gr-son: Samuel M. Smith
    Son: David--Land in Livingston Co. Ky.
    Son in law: Henry M. Story. Prov. Feb. 1842 Sptg.

MUSGROVE, EDWARD--Will 25 Aug. 1790. Sptg. 1823 Box 4 Bill 1
    Wife: Ann -m- David Smith
    7 Children: Margaret, William, Ann, Hannah, Leah, Liny
                Rachell -m- Geo. R. Adair

McBEE, MATTHEW--Will 9 Jan. 1817. Sptg. 105

McCARTER, GEORGE--Will 11 Oct. 1815. Sptg. 65

McCLAIN, CHARLES--Will July 16, 1821. Sptg. (2) 14

McCLANAHAN, MARY AND SARAH--Daus. of James Reynolds.-Will 1826 Sptg. 87

McDANIEL, MARY--Dau. of Amey Golightly-Will 1812. Sptg. 50

McDOWALL, JAMES -w- Mary of Laurens Co. to Richard Fryar of Sptg.
    Gr. of 20 May 1768 to James McDowall-150 A. on Branch Enoree R.
    Cedar Shoals Creek. Sptg. Deed A-110. 1786

McDOWELL, DORCAS--Dau. of Henry Foster-Will 1821. Henry McDowell
    an Exor. Sptg. (2) 3

McELLHENNY, WILLIAM--"Of 96 Dist. Tyger River" and Wm. Steel of C. T.
    Merchant, B/S 26 April 1785. Misc. 22-427

McELRATH, JOHN--Will 9 Feb. 1825. Sptg. (2) 47

McHUGH, POLLY--Legatee of Michael Moore-Will 1826. Sptg. (2) 72

McKIE, ALEXANDER--Orig. Deed gift of slaves in file 16 Nov. 1811
    Daus: Sally, Narcissa, and Nancy McKie. Sptg. Box 1-Bill 1

McKOWN, WILLIAM -w- Martha of Union Co. S. C. To William Tate, Sen'r.
    Gr. 21 April 1775 by S. C. to Wm. McKown-250 A. in Sptg. on
    Cherokee Creek S-s Main Broad River. Sptg. Deed A-113. 1786

McMAKIN, BENJAMIN P.--Dec'd. Sptg. Div. Per. and R. E. Bk.
    Widow: Mary
    7 Children: John, Peter, Alexander, Rachel, Andrew, Elizabeth
              Jane. Part. Oct. Ct. 1807. Plats in Book

McWILLIAMS, WILLIAM--Will 4 Dec. 1824. Sptg. (2) 37

NANCE, NANCY L.--Dau. of John Lipscomb-Will 1827. Sptg. (2) 101

NEEL, WILLIAM--Slave-to Daniel Jackson. Sptg. Deed A-45 1785

NESBITT, SAMUEL--Will 3 Sept. 1816. Sptg. 96

O'NEILL, HENRY--Will 18 Jan. 1815. Sptg. 51

ORBEY, CENETH (?)--Dau. of Josiah Hatchett-Will 1824. Sptg. 45

OTT, DELILAH--5th dau. of George Brewton-Will 1815. Land where Wm.
    Ott now lives. Sptg. 60

OTTS, SAMUEL--Will 10 July 1813. Wife and children not named.
    Sptg. 73

OWEN, WILLIAM--Will 7 June 1817. Sptg. 114

OWENS, JOHN--Will 2 July 1821. Sptg. (2) 16

PACE, SUSANNAH--Legatee and seems dau. of John Allen-Will 1822
    Sptg. (2) 26

PADEN, THOMAS--Dec'd. 6 March 1825. Filed 3 Oct. 1825. Sptg. Bx-10 Bill2
    Widow: Elizabeth
    Children: James, Mary, Margaret, Elinder, Andrew
               Elizabeth -w- John T. Paden
               Jane -w- Robert Paden
               John
               Moses W.
               Sarah -w- Anthony Pearson
               Agnes -w- John Fowler
    Name also spelled Peden and Peaden. Peden seems correct.

PADEN, THOMAS--Will 25 Nov. 1822. Sptg. (2) 50

PAGE, RACHEL--Wife of Robert Page. Sptg. (2) 90

PAGE, ROBERT--Will 6 July 1817. Sptg. (2) 90

PALMER, JOHN D.--Will Rec'd. 1819. Bro: Elias Palmer sole legatee
    Sptg. 134

PATTON, JOHN--Of York Dist. to Zadock Ford of Sptg. Dist. 600 A. S-s
    Broad River on both sides of King's River-conveyed by Samuel
    Gilkey to John Dickinson and he conv. to sd John Patton. Sptg.
    Deed A-6/7 1785

PEARSON, BETSY--Wife of Samuel Pearson. Dau. of Samuel Stewart.
    Sptg. 126

PENNY, SARAH--Will 16 May 1810. Sptg. 72A

PENNY, THOMAS--Will 28 May 1809. Sptg. 72B

PERSON, MARY--Dau. of Sarah Penny-Will 1810. and of Thomas Penny
    Will 1809. Sptg. 72A and B

PETERSON, SARAH AND ELIZABETH--Daus. of David Lipscomb-Will 1816
    Sptg. 85

PETTIT, JOSHUA--Will 15 Dec. 1826. Sptg. (2) 104

PHENNIX, GREEN A. (or Pennix)--Son in law of Joseph Austell-Will 1823
    Sptg. (2) 33

PHILLIPS, NANCY--Dau. of Thomas Harrison-Will 1819. Sptg. 132

POPE, THOMAS--Will 17 May 1822. Sptg. (2) 43

PORTER, SAMUEL -w- Anne of Sptg. to Uriah Conner-Gr. 21 Jan. 1785 by
    S. C. to Samuel Porter-313 A. N-s Saluda on waters of Golden Grove
    Creek. Bd. Capt. Wm. Wood, Maj. Bowie, and vac. Wit: Maximillian
    and John Conner. Sptg. Deed A-24 13 Nov. 1785

PREWITT, PETER--Will 2 July 1823. Sptg. (2) 32

PRICE, THOMAS--Dec'd. Of Sptg. Born a British subject, never natur-
     alized. Came to S. C. after Rev. War and married Ann Grant,
     Widow, of Charles Town about 1796. She was native born South
     Carolinian. Accumulated large estate including land on Tyger
     River. Land in Greenville and Spartanburg. Widow Ann, only
     heir. She has since, also died, intestate. Her heirs were
     children of deceased sister, Mrs. Elizabeth Combee:-
          Paul Combee
          Ann -w- David P. Wilmot*
          Rachel -w- Frederick Steading
     * Left county under circumstances which forbade expectations of
     his return. Sptg. Box 10 Bill 9. Filed 20 March 1826

PRICE, THOMAS--Will 17 May 1820. Sptg. 138
                    Box 3 Pkg. 1 shows Will filed 28 Jan. 1822 by heirs

PRINCE, RICHARD--Will 28 March 1811. Sptg. 19

PROCTOR, ELIZABETH--Legatee and seems dau. 1f Samuel Dunaway-Will 1810
     Sptg. 99

RAINWATER, NANCY--Niece of Samuel Farrow-Will 1824. Sptg. (2) 57

RAINWATER, POLLY--Dau. of Francis Mason-Will 1825. Sptg. (2) 63

RED, JOHN--Will 12 Feb. 1825. Sptg. (2) 48

REYNOLDS, JAMES, SR.--Will 17 Jan. 1826. Sptg. (2) 87

REYNOLDS, JUSTICE -w- Mary of Sptg. Co. Conv. to Alexander Alexander
     29 June 1797 Land on Pacolet and Lawson's Fork. Pt. Gr. to James
     Hammett. Sptg. Box 1 Bill 1

RHODES, CHRISTOPHER--Will 15 March 1806. Sptg. 24

RHODES, REBECCA--Dau. of James Wofford-Will 1815. Exor: William
     Rhodes. Sptg. 64

RHODES, REBEKAH--Dau. of Catharine Wofford-Will 1824. William Rhodes,
     Sen'r. Exor. Sptg. (2) 70

RICE, WILLIAM and his son, Samuel Farrow Rice. See Will of Samuel
     Farrow-1824. Sptg. (2) 57

ROBERTSON, NANCEY--Dau. of Reddick Rutland-Will 1824. Sptg. (2) 85

RODDY, MARGARET -w- John Roddy. Dau. of Thomas Moore-Will 1817
     Sptg. Wills Bx-19-20 1817

ROSS, JOHN--Dec'd. Widow: Sarah -m- _____Trimmier
                    3 Children: John, Sarah, and William
     Part. March Ct. 1810. Plats in Book. Sptg. Div. Per. and R. E.

ROWLAND, GEORGE--Will 23 April 1817. Sptg. 128

RUSSELL, REBEKAH--Dau. of Benjamin High-Will 1816. Sptg. 92

RUTLAND, REDDICK--Will 10 Mar. 1824. Sptg. (2) 85

SANDERS, POLLY and daughters--Legatees John Gowan-Will 1809. Sptg. 2-3

SAYE, ANN-Her heirs--Legatees of Josiah Hatchett-Will 1824. Sptg. 2-46

SEAY, JAMES M.--Son in law of Henry Walding-Will 1826. Sptg. 2-79

SELMAN, FIELDING -m- Patsy Rutland, dau. Reddick Rutland 4 March 1821.
    Had 1 child, separated. The child, a boy, to be given the father
    at age 7 years. Sptg. 1822-bx-3 Bill-4 Larkin Selman a party.

SELMAN, JEREMIAH--Dec'd. Partition: To
    James Selman
    Larkin Selman
    Frederick Williams -w- Martha
    John Selman
    William Selman
    William Covington -w- Nancy
    Elizabeth Selman   Sptg. Will Bk. 2. Pg. 93

SHERLEY, THADDIUS--From John Robertson, Jr. -w- Sarah 100 lbs. Sterl.
    100 A. Fork of Enoree and Broad Rivers. Pt. Gr. to John Robertson
    Sr. of 400 A. Assigned by Thaddeus Sherley to Wm. Thomas Linton
    on 4 Jan. 1793. Newberry Deed E-542 27 Feb. 1791

SHIRLEY, EDWARD--Dec'd. Cit. 1 Aug. 1815. Thomas Shirley, Adm'r.
    Robert Shirley, Wit. Sptg. Bx-26 Pg-1

SHIRLEY, JAMES--Of C. T.--Gentleman. Mtg. A. B. 432. 1736

SHIRLEY, SAMUEL--Pendleton Messenger March 9, 1838 -vs-
    Elizabeth Shirley, Widow
    Stephen Shirley and George Shirley, et al.
    Ch. and gr-ch. of John Shirley, dec'd. Anderson Dist. Out of State.
    Richard Shirley; James Brackenridge -w- Fanny; Enoch Bell; Margaret
    Bell; James Bell; Letty Bell; Frederick Bell;

SHIRLEY, THOMAS--Of C. T. Merchant. P. A. to: Wm. Price, John Smith
    and Joshua Ward, Merchants of C. T. To sell Plt'n 9 Aug. 1774
    B/S 1776-8 Pg. 147

SHUBERT, DICEY--Legatee and seems dau. of John Law.-Will 1822. Sptg. 78

SIMMONS, JOSEPH--Of Sptg. Dist.   Will   Sptg. Book B-147
    Wife: Ammy (or Annis)   27 Sept. 1825
    Children: Jesse, Payton, John, Carpenter, Nathaniel, Nancy
               Sally, Dec'd.-Her share to her children.

SIMMONS, JOSEPH--Will 27 Sept. 1825. Sptg. 2-111

SIMMONS, RICHARD--Son in law of Edward Smith-Will 1815. Sptg. 58

SLOAN, JOHN, ADAM AND ANDREW--Gr-sons of Richard Barry-Will 1816.
    Dau: Catherine Sloan. Son in law: Adam Sloan. Sptg. 82

SMITH, CHARLES--Will 14 Dec. 1822. Sptg. 2-55

SMITH, EDWARD--Dec'd. No wife or children. Filed 1 Jan. 1821
    Sister: Polly -w- Wm. Burton
           Ch: Charles, John, Elizabeth, Sarah, Nancy, Dolly, Drury
    Sister: Sarah -w- John Lipscomb
    Sister: Catherine -widow- David Lipscomb
    Brother: Thomas Smith, Dec'd.
           Ch: Reuben, William, Thomas, Nancy
    Sister: Frankey -w- Richard Simmons
    Sister: Patsy -w- John Willis
    Brother: Reuben Of Pittsylvania Co. Va. in 1817
    Brother: Charles
    Brother: William, dec'd.-Widow, Anna
           Ch: Holman
               Elizabeth -w- John Elder
               Sarah
               Anna Bunch late Anna Smith
               Mary, Patsy, John W., Rebecca, James J., Charles
Sparta nburg Equity Box 2 Pkg. 8 Edward Smith died 1801

SMITH, EDWARD--Will 17 April 1815. Sptg. 58

SMITH, ESTHER -w- Joseph Smith. Dau. of Zachariah Moore-Will 1829
    Sptg. Wills Box 20-8 1829

SMITH, FRANKLIN--Son of Sarah Moore-Will 1853. Might have been
    Franklin Smith Moore or might be son of former husband. Sptg.
    Wills 40-38 1853

SMITH, GINSY--Dau. of Rosannah Huff. Both legatees of Samuel Farrow
    Will 1824. Sptg. 2-57

SMITH , CAPT. JAMES--Dec'd. Sptg. Div. Per. and R. E. Book.
    Jane Smith, Adm'x.
    10 Children: Cynthis, James, Jr., Hancock (or Hannah) Susannah,
                 Matilda, Rutha, Catherine
                 Martha Lovina -w- Capt. Wm. S. Golightly
                 Lettuce -w- David Lynch
                 John Cantrell, Jr. (Ment. relation, not shown.
                 William Ross Smith-a son.
    Part. Nov. 1811. Plats in Book

SMITH, JANE--Dau. of William Meaders-Will 1814. Sptg. 2-18

SMITH, JOHN--Will 1816-Rec'd. Sptg. 76A

SMITH, MAIDON?--Dau. of William Foster-Will 1817. Sptg. 118

SMITH, MARGOT (or Margaret)--Dau. of Richard Chesney-Will 1816.
    Sptg. 87

SMITH, PATSEY--Niece of Samuel Farrow-Will 1824. Sptg. 2-57

SMITH, POLLY--Wife Isaac Smith. Dau. of Richard Barry.-Will 1816
    Sptg. 82

SMITH, POLLY--Dec'd. Dau. of Thomas Moore-Will 1817. Sptg. Wills 19-20

SMITH, SARAH--Dau. of Francis Mason-Will 1825. Sptg. 2-63

SMITH, SOPHIA--Dau. of Reuben Daniel-Will 1825. Sptg. 2-92

SMITH, WILLIAM--Of Fairfax County, Va. Son: James Smith of Orange
     Co. N. C. Hancock Smith and William Smith of 96 Dist. S. C.
     P. A. to James Smith 19 May 1773. Pro. before Wm. Wofford.
     Archives Dept. Sptg. File PP-501

SMITH, WILLIAM R.--Dec'd. 1818 Intestate. Filed 30 Sept. 1828
     Heirs: Mother-Jane Smith
               Brother: James Smith, Orator
               Sister: Lovenia -w- Wm. J. Golightly
                        Lettice -w- David Lynch
                        Cynthia Bradford, Dec'd. Minor children?
                        Susannah -w- Richard Barrett
                        Matilda -w- Ambrose Stone
                        Ruth -w- Joseph Willis
                        Catherine -w- Moses Stone
                        Hannah Smith.
     Sptg. Box 11 Bill 3

SNODDY, SAMUEL--Will 6 April 1817. Sptg. 98

SPARKS, EUNICE--Dau. of Joseph Woodruff-Will 1817. Sptg. 110

SPARKS, LYDIA--Dau. of John Tolleson-Will 1820. Sptg. 2-6

STEWART, SAMUEL--Will 13 Sept. 1814. Sptg. 126

STONE, LEVI--Legatee of Matthew Couch-Will 1816 Sptg. 2-11

STONE, SAMUEL--Will 23 Dec. 1826. Sptg. 2-89

SARRATT, THOMAS--Will 12 Aug. 1817. Sptg. 115

STONE, WILLIAM--Will 2 July 1814. Sptg. 47

STROUD, HANNAH--Dau. of Christopher Rhodes-Will 1806. Sptg. 24

SYMMS, DANIEL--To Thos. Wadsworth and Wm. Turpin of Charleston,
     Merchants. Gr. to sd Daniel By Gov. Moultrie 2 May 1785. In
     Sptg. Dist. east of ancient Boundary line on Lawson's Fork of
     Pacolet River. Sptg. Deed A-39 1785

WADE, JOSEPH--Of Sptg. to his grandson, William Thomas, the minor son
     of Richard Thomas of Sptg. Dist. On Fairforest 16 March 1802.
     Sptg. Deed H-196. 1802
     -On next page--Zachariah Robinson-of Montgomery Co. Tenn. to
     John Robinson of Sptg. Co. S. C. Slave. B/S 19 Aug. 1802

WALDEN, ASA--Will 5 Oct. 1827. Sptg 2-107

WALDING, HENRY--Will 14 March 1826. Sptg. 2-79

WALDRUP, RACHEL--Dau. of Christopher Rhodes-Will 1806. Sptg. 24

WALKER, ELIZABETH--Dau. of Joshua Pettit-Will 1826. Sptg. 2-104

WALKER, HARRIET--Dau. of George Rowland.-Will 1817. Sptg. A-142

WALKER, JOHN--To Jesse Connell--Upper half of tract called McClure's
     tract. Orig. Gr. to Arthur McClure by N. C. Sptg. Deed A-29 1784

WALKER, JOHN--Will 16 Dec. 1813. Sptg. 41

WALKER, NANCY--Sister of Robert Benson-Will 1813. Sptg. 33

WALKER, SAMUEL--Of Edgefield. McCord's Rev. Vol. 1-313 1818
     Widow: Martha J.
     Dau: _____ -m- Joseph Eddins
     Dau: _____ -m- Cheney Farrow of Sptg.
     Dau: Rebecca -m-_____ Beam
     See card Cheney Farrow

WALLING, DANIEL--Will 30 June 1812. Sptg. 23

WALLING, URIAH--Legatee of William Owen-Will 1817. Sptg. 114

WARD, ELIZABETH--Legatee and seems dau. of Charles McClain.-Will 1821
     Sptg. 2-14

WARD, SAMUEL--Son in law of Henry Walding-Will 1826. Sptg. 2-79

WATERS, CHARLES -w- Mary of Sptg. Co. to Samuel Farrow--150 A. Gr. sd
     Charles Waters on Enoree R. 2 Oct. 1786. Wit: Mary and Polly
     Blassingame, Betsy Ham. Sptg. Deed B-479. 25 Dec. 1786

WATERS, MARY GILLEN--Dau. of William Wilkins-Will 1807. Sptg. 156
     (or Gillenwaters)

WATERS, WESTWOOD -w- Abby and Elizabeth Waters and her heirs, all of
     Enoree--100 A. in Fork of Broad and Saluda Rivers on the Cedar
     Shoal Creek. a branch of Enoree. Bd. Rosanna Farrow, Thomas
     Saurie. -vs- Landon, Rosanna, Boardwin, and Thomas Waters.
     Sptg. Deed B-152/3 3 June 1786

WATERS, PHILEMON -w- Mary of Charleston to Henry Rugeley. 25 Aug. 1772
     P4-321 1777

WATERS, PHILEMON, SEN'R. --Dec'd. Widow-Ruth -m- Sterling Boldree
     Set. 6 Feb. 1819. Dau.-Eliza Waters. Misc. D-133

WATSON, VIOLET--Dec'd. See Will of Margaret Barry 1823. Sptg. 2-44

WEAVER, THOMAS J.**Will 13 April 1813. Sptg. 38

WEST, DORCAS--Will 31 Aug. 1804. Sptg. 44

WEST, JANE -w- David West. Niece of Samuel Farrow-Will 1824. Sptg. 2-57

WIGGINGTON, MILLY--Dau. of Lucretia Demsy-Will 1826. Sptg. 2-81

WILBANKS, PHEBE--Will 24 Aug. 1825. Sptg. 2-71

WILBANKS, WILLIAM--Will 2 Feb. 1816. Sptg. 89

WILKINS, MARTHA--Dau. of Thomas Jackson-Will 1820. Sptg. 2-74

WILKINS, POLLY H.--Dau. of John Lipscomb-Will 1827. Sally Wilkins
    another daughter. Sptg. 2-101

WILKINS, WILLIAM--Will 30 March 1807. Sptg. 155

WILLS, JINCEY--Dau. of Reuben Daniel-Will 1825. Sptg. 2-92
    (Name possibly Wells) John Wells an Exor.

WILLIAMS, EDWARD--Sptg. Will Book (?) 125
    Sons: Wilson and Austin--to be schooled
    Daus: Charlotte, Mary, Jane--to be schooled
    Son: Perry (seems to be Oliver Perry)
    Exor's: Sons and friend, Drury Willing.
    Date: 17 Oct. 1844   Proven: 3 May, 1847
    Wit: W. B. Turner, Robert Scruggs, Drury Willing

WILLIAMS, GARRISON AND JOHN--Of York. Money. Equity Sptg. 1824
                                                Box 5 Bill 3
WILLIAMS, ISAAC--Sptg. Will Book C-105
    Wife:
    Son: Thomas Anderson "my younger son"
          Drury
    Dau: Tilda
    Exor: Son Drury and Edward Williams
    Legacy: Pelea Reynolds wife
    Date: 23 Nov. 1836   Proven: 16 Jan. 1839
    Wit: Robert Wyatt, Jackson Scruggs, Elizabeth Scruggs.

WILLIAMS, JOHN--Son in law of David Bruton-Will 1815. Sptg. 71

WILLIAMS, JOHN--Sptg. Will Book 339   1 March 1851
    Wife: Margaret   Proven: 7 June 1852
    Son: Dr. Thomas Williams--Bounty tract
          R. R. Williams
          James L. Williams
          Ralph Williams
    Dau: Rebecca A. E. Alexander

WILLIAMS, RICHARD--Will Sptg. Will Book 142 23 March 1846
    Wife: Sarah   Proven: 7 April 1848
    "my 5 children: Silona, James, Tinny(or Linny) Sarah Ann, John
    All children-minors.

WILLIAMS, ROBERT--Will Sptg. Will Book 1857. Page 353
    Wife: Alice   Feb. 20, 1879
    "my 3 sons": Whitner, T. J. Lanier, James M. and Robert W.
    "my 3 daus": Mildred, Melissa McArthur, and Ann. Feb. 20, 1879

WILLIAMSON, HENRY--Will 25 May 1801. Sptg. 151

WILLIAMSON, THOMAS--Will 2 April 1813. Sptg. 25

WILLIS, JOHN--Son in law of Edward Smith-Will 1815. Sptg. 58

WILSON, HANNAH--Dau. of Henry O'Neill-Will 1815. Sptg. 52

WINGO, ABNER--Will 4 Feb. 1812. Sptg. 49

WINGO, MARIAN AND CATY--Nieces of Hannah Thomas-Will 1817. Sptg. 103

WINGO, MARY--Dau. of Henry O'Neill-Will 1815. Sptg. 52

WINGO, OBADIAH--Will 30 April 1824. Sptg. 2-115

WINGO, WILLIS--Dec'd. some years ago. Widow, Mary married Joshua
    Hammond. Notes due Estate. Sptg. 1826 Box 7 Bill 3

WHITE, ANNA--Wife of Robert. Dau. of Samuel Stewart-Will 1814.
    Sptg. 126

WHITE, JOHN--Will 13 March 1822. Sptg. 2-19

WHITE, MARTHA--Dau. of Joseph Wofford-Will 1825. Sptg. 2-109

WHITENER, SARAH--Dau. of Peter Frie-Will 1813. Sptg. 29

WOFFORD, BENJAMIN -w- Mary and Burwell Thomson -w- Ann to Henry
    Meredith--500 A. Pt. Gr. to Thomas Irwin by Arthur Dobbs, Gov.
    N. C. 26 Mar. 1755 and conv. to Bartlett Brown, sr. dec'd. on
    11 May 1755. 100 A. sold to Matthew Couch. The North part in
    Sptg. Co and South in Laurens Co. Sptg. Deed Bk. A-53

WOFFORD, CATHERINE--Will 21 Jan. 1824. Wife of James Wofford, Dec'd
    Sptg. 2-70

WOFFORD, JAMES--Will 22 June 1815. Sptg. 63

WOFFORD, JAMES--Dec'd. D July 1815. Filed 1821. Bx-2 Bill-7
    Widow: Catherine, oratrix. Will in file. Called caty in Will
    Son: John
    Suit by mother claiming her son John, has taken slave left her by
    dec'd.
    Will shows 4 sons: Nathaniel, John, Jesse, Isaac
    Dau: Diadamin Johnson
         Peggy Moore
         Elizabeth Burrow
         Rebecca Rhodes
         Caty Moore.
    Ex: Son, Nathaniel, Wm. Rhodes. 12 June 1815

WOFFORD, JOHN, SEN'R.--Will 3 May 1808. Sptg. 37

WOFFORD, JOSEPH--To William Linch--Gr. 21 Jan. 1785 by S. C. to Joseph
    Wofford 100 A. on Patterson's Branch of N. fork of Saluda River.
    Bd. Robert Henderson's survey and vacant. Sptg. Deed A-27 1786

WOFFORD, JOSEPH--Will 25 Aug. 1825. Sptg. 2-109

WOFFORD, WILLIAM--a deserter from 6th Regt. Apprehended. 1778 6th
                                                 Reg't. Pg-1
WOFFORD, WILLIAM--To Wells Griffith--N. C. Gr. to James Hammett-200
    A. both sides of Lawson's fork, including a Mill seat. Then in
    Tryon Co. N. C. Sptg. Deed A-101 1783

WOOD, AGNES R.--Dau. of John Lipscomb-Will 1827. Sptg. 2-101

WOOD, ELIZABETH--Dau. of Lucretia Demsy-Will 1826. Sptg. 2-81
    Gr-son: Solomon Powers Wood
             James Tate Wood
    Gr-dau: Milly McDaniel Wood

WOOD, JAMES--Dec'd. Bro. of George Wood of Va. who died without Ch.
    6 children?: William, Drury, George, Polly, John, James, Betsy?
    Sptg. Div. Per. and R. E. Bk.

WOOD, JOHN--Will 28 Dec. 1802. Wife-Maden Wood. Sptg. 136

WOOD, MRS. MATILDA--Dau. of Joseph Buffington. Legatee of Samuel
    Farrow-Will 1824. Mrs. Wood of Georgia. Sptg. 2-57

WOOD, NANCY--Dau. of William Lipscomb-Will 1808. Sptg. 11

WOOD, PENNUEL--Will 3 June 1809. Sptg. 8

WOOD, REBEKAH--Dau. of Joel Traylor-Will 1809. Sptg. 1

WOOD, WILLIAM to Thomas Williamson--440 A. 96 Dist. where sd Williamson
    now lives. Wit: Moses Wood. Sptg. Deed Bk. A-3 1785

WOOD, WILLIAM--Will 22 Jan. 1787. Sptg. 149A
               Will 6 Aug. 1793. Sptg. 149B

WOODRUFF, JOSEPH--Will 22 Sept. 1817. Sptg. 110

WOODRUFF, MARY--Legatee and seems dau. of John Allen-Will 1822.
    Sptg. 2-26

WOODSON, ELIZABETH--Dau. of John Gowan-Will 1809. Sptg. 2

WRIGHT, ANTHE AND MARGARET--Nieces of John Owens-Will 1821. Hannah
    Wright a grand daughter of John Owens. Sptg. 2-16

WRIGHT, JOSEPH--Will 24 Feb. 1827. Sptg. 2-97

YOUNG, MARGARET -w- John Young. Dau. of William Wood-Will 1787.
    Wit: Sally Young. Sptg. 149A

YOUNG, WILLIAM--Bond as Sheriff of Sptg. Co. S. John Young. Sptg.
    Deed Bk. A-45 19 Sept. 1785

YOUNGER, JAMES--Will 7 Feb. 1827. Sptg. 2-98

UNION COUNTY, SOUTH CAROLINA

ADAIR, --ADAIR of Union H-59 to James Nogher--85 A. Hughs Creek.
   23 Mar. 1802 Dower: Mary Adair

ASHBY, JOHN and Bro. Stephen. Adv: John McClure, et al. Union
   Equity 1854-1867 June 1854

BAILEY, JOHN and wife, et al--claimed the land -vs- Wm. Cole, et al
   "Wife of Old John Cole"--Mary Cole
   Rhoda Yerby -w- John Yerby
   Nancy -w- Absolom Bailey
   Dau: Mrs. Kendrick, and Mrs. Cannon Union Bk Pg-144 June 1837

BAILEY, SUSANNAH--Will 13 Nov. 1796 Union Prob. Bx 2-26 A-58
   Dau: Unity Bailey, Reacey Bailey, Frances Tomlin, Renald,
   Rachel Redmon

BAKER, LEONARD--Will 22 Feb. 1845 Union Wills
   Wife: Nancy
   Dau: Rhody Lay
   Gr-dau: Sally Jane Leach
   Sons: Amos, Ferdinan, Ivy
   Daus: Polly Posy
          Elizabeth B. Grubb
          Charlotte Baker, and Elmira Baker
   To: Julianna Susannah Frances Skains, Gr. ch. of Wm. I. Eaves
   Exor: Capt. L. B. Jeter, Isaac Gregory

BALDWIN, THOMAS of Laurens Co. to Walker Roberds. 1 Feb. 1793
   mare, 2 colts, 8 cattle, ___?, and plantation whereon I now
   live. Wit: Jas. Roberds, John Roberds, Isaac Baldwin
   Prob. 9 Apr. 1794 Union Prob.

BISHOP, THOMAS -w- Mary to William Martindale--184 1/6 A. "now in
   possession of Thomas Ducket --on Enoree R. and Saluda.
   Pt. 300 A. Gr. to Wm. Ragan Apl. 20, 1763. He conv. to Thomas
   Gordon, who conv. to Thos Bishop. Union Prob. 24/25 Oct. 1785

BOWLES, JOHN Of Va. Will--Union Bk-B-227 26 Dec. 1830
   Sons: Charles K. and Thomas
   Daus: Sally W. Glenn
          Betty Bowles
          Nancy Johnson's neice
   Son: Benjamin
   Mentions land in Va. and agreement with his son Charles K.
   Son: John, dec'd.

BRADLEY, SARAH A.--Heir ofWm. Reid estate--generations down. Also
   Nanny Davidson, Lizzie DeLoach, Mrs. Eliza Alexander, et al
   Union--33 1866

BRANDON, THOMAS--Union Cty. Rec. Pg-23 24 Sept, 1787--1 Guinea
   To: James Adams McCool--negro boy abraham abt. 4 yrs. old
   Wit: William Johnson, Joseph Howard, William Hughes
   To: Daniel White--negro girl 2½ yrs old. Union Rec. 30/31
   Wit: Jeremiah Gregory 8 Nov. 1787

BRANDON, JOHN -w- Mary to Wm. Kennedy 1 Sept. 1785--Upper end on land
   where I now live. Wit: Thomas Vance, et al

BRANDON, GEN. THOMAS   Union A-33 14 Dec. 1801
    "I Thos. Brandon, General of the United States of America, and
    living at this time in state of S. C., Union Dist"
    Wife: Rebecca: Prop. left her by her last husband, Geo.
        Harland
    "My 3 sons": Thomas, William and James
    Geo Brandon (son my brother John) Browns Cr. and Geo. Young of
    Duncan Cr. Exor's.   2 Feb. 1802
    Codicil: My 5 daus: Mary, Jane, Elizabeth, Martha, Annd

BRIGGS, JOHN of Union Co. to Thomas Todd of Spartanburg--Bond for
    title 15 Mar. 1787. The plantation which sd John Briggs now
    lives--pur. of John Martindale. Wit: Peter Chastain, R. Burger
    Union Co. Rec. Pg. 34

BROOKS, ISAAC of Chatham Co. N. C. P. A. to William Birdsong to collect
    from Jack Terrell--a slave. Wit: John Murrell, Sam'l Murrell
    Union Rec. Pg-52 2 Nov. 1787

BROWN, GABRIEL, SR. of Camden Dist Apl. 23, 1785 to Col. Wm. Farr of
    96--Slaves. Wit: SamuelOtterson. Union Rec. Pg-1
    Pg-15--Hannah Brown to Wm. Farr--Quit Claim 14 Sept. 1786

BROWN, JACOB -w- Ruth--both of Berkeley Co. to John Mayfield--300 A.
    in Tryon Co. N. C. on both sides of Browns Cr. of Broad River.
    Union Rec. Pg 134 2 Aug. 1790

BUCHANAN, MICAJAH--Dec'd Union Bk pg-86 1834 June
    Heirs: Thos. G. Buchanan
           Clary Buchanan
           Elizabeth -w- George Souter
           Mildred -w- Thomas C. Crooks
           Drusilla -w- James Fant   Land in Newberry also

BULLOCK, ZACHARIAH of Union Co. Will 10 Feb. 1791 Union Prob Pg-8
    Bro: Len Hinley Bullock's 4 youngest daughters--namely:
        Fanny Lyne, Lucey, Agnes, and Nancey B.--each 250 sterling
    Bro: Len Henley Bullock of Warren Co. N. C. Exor.--All rest
    Nephew: Richard Bullock-son of Len Henley. one of Exor's.
    Exor: James Lyne of Granville Co
    Wit: Adam Potter, John Lipscombe, Wm. Lipscombe, Jr.

BULLOCK, WILLIAM of Union Co. Will 16 March 1787 Union Rec. Pg-75
    Bro-in-law: Nicholas Waters--all and exor.
    Wit: Wm. Williams, John Pulmore, Ephraim Puckett sd X

BURNS, THOMAS--Dec'd Union Rec. pg-87 1834
    Widow: Barsheba Burns--oratrix
    Son: John--Orator
    1st wife: Mary Thorne--by whom sev. children(dau. of Mrs. Mary
        Jemema--w-- Lewis Fant   Thorne)
              -W- Thomas Owen
        Alva Burns

BURSON, JOSEPH -w- Mary of Georgia gr. 29 Apl. 1768--150 A. on Branch
    of Fairforest called Buffalo Cr. Wit: Isaac Burson, Wm. Nit
    Wm. Little. Union Rec. Pg-118 18 Dec. 1793

BRYANT, ELIZABETH Mar. set 26 Jan. 1830 to Wm. Rountree Misc. G-99
Union Dist. "This agreement to be of three parts" William
Rountree of 1st part; Elizabeth Bryant of 2nd part; Adam Little
of 3rd part. Wm. and Eliz. to be married. Elizabeth owned
land on Buffalo Creek, Union Dist. 65 A. Wm. owned 700 A.
same dist. Wit: Willis Walker, William Little, Joshua Little

CAINE, ALEXANDER to Son: Isaac Caine--per. prop, horses, etc.
Union Rec. Pg-11 13 Aug. 1787

CAMPBELL, JAMES -w- Martha to Hohn Hope--200 A. both sides thicket.
Gr. to James Fanning 26 Oct. 1767.. Wit: Robert Mayfield,
Edmond Mayfield, Wm. Casey. Union Rec. Pg-84/85 6 March 1779

CANNON--Bd owner land on Sandy Creek, Pitsylvania Co. Va. conv. by
John Kirby, Sr. of Union Dist. S. C. to John Kirby, Jr. of
Pittsylvania Co. Va. 11 May 1799 Union Prob. Pg-62

CAROTHERS, JOHN--Will--d. 13 May, 1854 Union June 1855
Wife: Rachel T.
Son: William E. d. July 1854--no children
John d 1853 before testator--no issue
3 daughters.
Formerly married to Miss Hope--d. 1826 or 1827. Leaving 6 child-
ren. Claimed the "Hope Land."

CARROLL, WILLIAM--Heir estate of Edward Moore--Union Deeds G-372

CHESNEY, ROBERT To son: John Chesney, lands and property, the same
to support him for life. Union Prob. Pg-19 2 March 1793

CHISHOLM, DAVID--Will 27 Dec. 1791 Union Co. Bx-1 Pk-34 Bk A-1
Father: ? All cash
Brothers
Sister
Ex: Bro: William
Bro Samuel not yet 10 yrs old.
Exor: John Henderson, Obadiah Trimmer

CLANTON, CHARLES to Absolom Petty--100 A. on ridge between Thickety
Cr. and Gilkin's Cr--Pt. Gr. Francis McNamar who conv. to sd C. C.
Union Deed Pg 59/60 2 Mar. 1786

CLANTON, CHARLES--Will 15 Nov. 1783 Union Prob. Bx-1-50 A-191
Wife:
2 Sons: Sion and Stephen

CLARK, HENRY--Will 8 Aug. 1793 Union Prob. A-62
Son: John Clark--To pay "to his 5 daus" or 5 daus of Wm. Henry
for whom land pur. not clear.
Dau: Hester Campbell
Gr-Son: Henry Clark
Henry Clark -w- Sarah 1 Sept 1773 to John Foster 180 A. Pg-56

CLARK, JOHN--N. C. Gr. Sept. 3, 1753--Pt 400 A. S-s Broad R. conv.
by Caleb Gassaway -w- Nancy as ext of Wm. Moore, dec'd and
Savannah Moore

CLARK, JOHN--Will 9 Sept. 1796 Union Prob.
Wife: Mary--Land bequest--"My father's Will" 22 Aug. 1793
Sons: John, Thomas, Henry, and Jonathan
Daus: Elizabeth, Rachel, Hester, Mary, and Rebukah

CLARK, PATRICK--100 A. Berkley--between Broad and Saluda. On
_____ ? of John's Creek of Enoree. Bd James Parnell and John
McCrory. Gr. 10 Feb. 1775 Union Min 14-2

CLARK, RYDARUS of Gilkie's Cr--from James Love of Camden Dist.
Union Deeds Pg-53 19 Apl. 1784
Pg-63 2 Jan. 1779--Rydarus Clark -w- Anna of Camden Dist. to
John Foster--200 A. W-s Broad River

CLAYTON, WILLIAM--To Mtg. Thomas Blasingame, Esq. Negro named Cambridge
Wit: D. B. Rowne. Union Rec. Pg-44/45 27 Mar. 1789

COLLINS, CAROLINE AND BARLOW--Children of Joseph Collins--see card of
Gordon Moore--Union Deeds Bk R-421 1822

COMMER, DANIEL--Will 14 Feb. 1793 Union Prob. Bx-1-40 Bk-A
"My surviving heirs, towit:
John, Thomas, Daniel, Samuel, Anis, Joseph Flechal
Mary -w- Thomas Commer

COOPER, ELIJAH H.--Will 8 Aug. 1796 Union Prob. Bx-2-28 A-60
Wife: Susannah
3 sons: James (2)_____? (3)_____?
All his children

COOPER, SAMUEL--Will 14 Feb. 1781 Union Prob. Bx-1-51 A-24
Wife: Elizabeth--Land on Fairforest
David Cooper

CROSLEY, GEORGE--Will 7 June, 179? Union Co. Wills
Wife: Lydda--All for life--widowhood
"my children"

DABNEY, JAMES of Louise Co. Va. -- on 18 Dec. 1789--loaned to his
daughter, Eliza Johnson, wife of Christopher Johnson, a negro
girl Isobel. Moved to Union Court House-gave mtg. of slave.
Union 49 Feb. term 1815

DARBY, WILLIAM Union Prob. Pg-6 19 Feb. 1781 from James Bennet--
Horse. Wit: James Darby, John Hanse, Wm. Smith.
Page 56--Elizabeth Darby, age 11 and Jane Darby, age 12--Wm.
Rowe Apt'd. Gdn. 5 July, 1797

DAVIS, NATHANIEL--Will 18 Jan. 1793 Union Bx-2-30 R-61
Wife: Elizabeth
Dau: Margaret
Son: Joseph
Dau: Sarah
Sons: Nathaniel, Ephraim, James
Dau: Elizabeth Wit: John Davis

372

DENHAM, ROBERT of Abbeville Bond for Title to John Buchanan of Fair-
field--200 A. on Pacolet River. Orig. Gr. to James Campbell,
sd. Robert Denham being the heir of sd James Campbell. Wit:
Creighton Buchanan. Union Prob. Pg-58/59 23 Nov. 1793

DODD, JESSE of "Arrensberg" Dist (Orangeburg) bond for title to
Peter Renfroe of 96 Dist. 300 A. on Tyger River. Wit: Lewis
Golson, J. P., Jno. Golson, Lewis Bobs. 7 Feb. 1784
Next: Peter Renfroe assigned to Andrew Torrance the same 300 A.
Pg-73/73 23 Jan. 1790 Bond and Mtg. to Andrew Torrance "In Penal
sum of 40,000 pounds of inspected tobacco". "First sum of 28,000
pounds"--300 A. on a ridge between Tyger and Enoree. Gr. to Wm.
Rhoads 24 Aug. 1770. Also 5 slaves. Wit: Archer and Nancey Howard
1?

DRAKE, FRANCIS--Will 18 Mar. 1794 Prov. 2 June 1794 Union Bxl-52 A-24
Wife: Joyce
Son: William Drake
Dau: Martha Hinton
Gr-son: Cilas (Silas) Drake
         Francis Drake
?   John Parham
?   Wm. Wallace
         Martha Hinton
         Joseph Hinton
Gr-Dau: Margaret Drake--dau. of Britton Drake
Bro: Richard Drake--Exor.

DUNCAN, ROBERT dec'd--Will 2 Aug. 1823 Bk Pg 46-130 1831 Aug
Wife: Susannah Duncan d. 1830

DUNN, MARY -w- H. E. Dunn (living) -vs- W. C. Dunn--Trustee for Mrs.
Dunn's 2 daughters, both married.--Negroes sold--Confederate
money no good. Union Equity Pg-6 1869

EDMONDSON, CALEB--Will 4 Jan. 1791 Union Rec. Bk Pg-1
Wife: Jude--Home Plantation
Son: Thomas
      Joseph
      Caleb)
      William) to their children
      Isaac)
Exor: John Clark   Rec'd. 6 Apl. 1791
Wit: Ralph Hunt, Caleb Smith, Ann Smith

EDMONDSON, ISAAC of Union Indemnity Bond and Mtg. to Jacob Duckett of
Laurens Co. Surety for Isaac on bond to Caleb Edmondson "Father
of him, the said Isaac Edmondson for the support and maintaining
of him, the said Caleb Edmondson during his natural life".
Wit: John Pearson, Jno. Townsend, James Townser.nd.
Pg-63/64 15 Feb. 1790
Pg 65/66 26 Feb. 1790 To: Jesse Dodd of Union Co--P. A. to col-
lect and also to "prosecute a suit now commenced against me by
Robert Murrell of the State of Pennsylvania". Wit: William Ray
Caleb Edmondson, John Birdsong
Pg-46/47 12 May 1784--Bond for Titles to Bro. Caleb Edmondson
½ interest in 700 A. N-s Enoree. Wit: John Needeman, Edward
Musgrove and by Caleb Edmondson, Jr. to John Fincher 12 Sept.
1789--Wit: Jas. Woodson; Thos Bishop, Jno. Nit.

EWART, JOHN of Union Co. Will 31 Aug. 1788 Union Rec. Pg-41/42
    Bro: Robert Ewart-Living in Scotland 524 A. on Broad River
        Mathew Ewart- "   "   "   150 A. adj. Union Court
                               House bought of Joseph
                               Jones. Also 300 A.
        William Ewart- "   "   "   923 A. on Brown's Creek of
                               Broad River
    Friends: Thos. Blasingame and Andrew Torrance--a negro woman
    now living at Thomas Nance's, and Negro Charles in possession of
    Througood Chambers to be sold--money to be used by exor's-Thos.
    Blasingame, Esq. and Andrew Torrance. Wit: William Morgan
    Isaac Bogan, Moses Collyer

FAIN, W. D., ELIZA R., ELIZABETH A. J.,--Union Prob. 1854
    See estate of Wm. Moore

FANT, JAMES Union Equity June 1855. Case: Eleanor Martin -w- Samuel
    Martin -vs- James Fant--Suit over sale of slave

FANT, WILLIAM Will 12 Aug. 1852 Union Wills
    Wife: Mildred
    Heirs: James B., Joseph C., Permelia I.A.Fant, Oliver H. P.
        Fant--already provided for.
    Son: Dr. Francis M. E. Fant:)Share alike in residue and should
        Samuel F. Fant   :)either die-no issue-other to have
                        all and apt'd. exor's.

FARR, WILLIAM of Union Co. to Elias Hollingsworth of Newberry Co.--
    Quit Claim to 99 A. S-s Broad River being pt Gr. to Thomas
    Tramel by S. C. in Nov. 1764. Bd. David Tramel. Wit: Bernard
    Glenn, Joseph Coleman, and Henry Bates. Union Prob- Pg-68
    10 Nov. 1789
    Pg-71/72 Elias Hollingsworth to William Farr--46 A. Pt Gr. to
    William Love by N. C. 3 Sept. 1753. Wit: Bernard Glenn, Joseph
    Coleman, Humphrey Bates

FARR, WILLIAM Will 30 July 1792 Union Wills Bx1-53 A-16
    Wife: Eliza Toliaforro Farr
    Dau: Hannah Green McDuff
    Son: Richard
    Step dau: Betty Brown Ellis) Seems 1 person only
              Betty Jeter   )
    Son: William Black Farr
         James Farr
         Thomas Farr
         John Poloskie Farr
         Titus Greene Farr
    Dau: ‾Elenor Thomas Farr
         Ann Keneheloe Farr
         Eliza Frances Farr

FARR, COL. WILLIAM --Dec'd Union County 1810-1819 Very long
    Widow: Elizabeth
    Dhildren: William B., John P., Titus Green,
    Elizabeth -w- David A. Thomas
    Robert G. H. Farr

FARROW, SAMUEL to William Buchanan--450 A. Gr. To John Elder 14 Aug.
    1775 on Brown's Creek. To: Samuel Farrow 20 Nov. 1775

FINCHER, AARON Will 23 Mar. 1802 Union Wills Bx-2-2 A-157
    Mother: Mary Fincher
    Bro: John Fincher
    "My Gr-Father--Jonathan Parker's grant"
    Bro: Jesse Fincher
         Jonathan P. Fincher
         Timothy R. Fincher
    Sis: Hannah, Mary, and Sarah
    Ex: Cousin-Francis Fincher
    Wit: Aaron Compton, Elizabeth Fincher, Wm. Morgan
    Pg-177 24 March 1786 A-702 Aaron Fincher -w- Mary to Moses
    Collier--100 A. on a br. of Fairforest. Orig. Gr. to Archibald
    Gilliand--To John Irvin To Jonathan Parker-now dec'd. Adm--
    Aaron Fincher

FLINTON, JOHN of the State of N. C. Orangeburg County, heir at law to
    Edward Flinton, Dec'd--Quit Claim to Thomas Flinton, Richard
    Jenkins, Daniel Price, and Daniel Comer--by all claims against
    them. Wit: Thos. Brandon, Richard Powell Pg-61 28 Nov. 1789

FOSTER, JOHN--Will Union Pg-142-294 June 1830
    Widow: Hannah
    Dau: _____? -w- Wm. Blakely
    Son: Edmond--an idiot
         Nathaniel--Exor.
         George B.
         Pleasant
    Pg-53-56 John Foster from George Gowan-1777
    Also from Henry Clark -w- Sarah 1773

FRANKLIN, JOSEPH -w- Marry Ann to James Beauford 75 A. on Tyger River
    "Where said James Beauford now lifes". Union 4 Nov. 1785

FROST, MARY--Will 25 Dec. 1796 Union Prob. Bx-7-32 A-52
    Bro: James Benson--Exor.
    Dau: Rebecca Frost
    Son: John
    Dau: Sarah Williams
         Mary Frost
    "My youngest children": Barnet, Elizabeth, Rachel, William
    Exor: Jesse Young, James Townsend

GAGE, JOHN, SEN'R.--Native of Ireland. Has resided in Union Dist.
    4 years. Citizenship 2 Oct. 1808 Union Misc. B-517

GASSAWAY, NANCY -w- Caleb Gassaway Ex. Will of Wm. Moore with
    Susannah Moore--(seems to be dau.) Union Deeds Bk B-33 1785

GEORGE, JOHN--Will 16 Mar. 1791 Union Prob. Pg 8/9 24 June 1789
    Wife:
    Son: John--The plantation whereon he lives
    Dau: Mary--200 A. N-s Pacolet R.
    Son: Thomas--The plantation whereon I now live
    Bro-in-law: John Jasper--one of exor's
    Wit: John Jasper, John McWhorter, and Charles Hames

GILBERT, BENJAMIN**of Newberry to: Bond B/S James Bell of Union--
horses, etc. for "special bail for Jonathan Gilbert to Wm.
Shaw, esq. Wit: Daniel Jackson, Thos. Brandon Pg-31/32
24 June 1789

GILLAM, CHARLES and wife Patsey -vs- Charles Pitts and wife, Rebecca.
Laurens Equity No. 9 1815

GOLIGHTLY, JOHN--Gr. S. C. 150 A. on Fairforest to William Heald.
Wit: Anna Hollaway, James Green, Frederick Crowder. Feb. 2, 1786

GOOD, ROBERT of Union Co. Union Wills A-98 Will 19 Jan. 1799
Wife: Elizabeth--all until youngest child is of age. sd Robert
Good. Exor: John Bankhead, John Mitchell

GOODE, EDWARD of Rutherford Co. N. C. P. A. to friend Herman Howard
of Union Co. S. C. to collect from Mark Jackson of S. C. Wit:
Thos. Brandon, Thomas Crosby. Pg 20/21 17 Dec. 1789

GONDYLOCK, ADAM--Will 24 Dec. 1793 Union Prob. Bx2-3 A-44
Sons: Davis and William
Daus: Sarah, Susannah, Anna Saffold, Elizabeth Johnston
Prudence Stockton, Hannah Blakey
Gr-dau: Hannah Stockton
Exor: Adam Potter, Thomas Stockden
Deed Bk 1786-1787 pg-42 Adam Gondylock -w- Hannah N. C. Gr. on
Thickety Cr. Pt. to Robert Lusk. Pt to Maj. Charles Miles.

GOSS, JOHN W.--Dec'd Adm'r James H. Goss Union Prob. 34 1866

GREER, _____? Dec'd--Will Union June 1861
"Testator's children removed from his plantation and escaped the
evils of low associations and restored to position they had prior
to their father's last marriage. The widow with her natural
children has now exclusive possession of the plantation. Case:
Sarah A. E. Greer, et al -vs- Robert Macbeth and Nancy Greer.

GREER, ROBERT To William Greer--Bond for titles to 200 A. in Greene
Co. N. C. "Known by the name of Robert's Place". Wit: Benjamin
Savage, Joseph Hughes, Benjamin Woodson, J. P. Pg-20 17 Aug. 1788

GREER, WILLIAM--Dec'd--Inv. and Appl. per. prop. Dec. 17, 1789. Appr's
Thomas Vance, and Wm. McJunkin. Wm. Kennedy, J. P. Union Pg-21/22

GREGORY, ISAAC--Will 13 Aug. 1796 Union Wills Bx2 Pk-34
Wife: Alse
Son: Jarred--to have the land
Dec'd son-Benjamin: -m- Margaret _____?
Ch: Sally, Gordon and Wm.
Ch: John, Robert, Elizabeth, Isaac, Jarred, and Jeremiah

GRINDEL, JOHN of Pendleton -w- Esther (also sp Crindle) Quit claim and
dower 11 May, 1780 to John Watson and Aaron Chisholm
Union Will Bk-A

GYTON, MOSES (or Guyton) to John Lick--Gr. to Jacob Gardiner--1771 Dec.
to Robert Whitley July 23, 1772 to Moses Guyton. 100 A. on
Abington's Cr--Union Co. Union Deed Pg 73/74 12 May, 1785

HAILES, JOHN--Dec'd Will Union Co. Rec. 1838
    Widow: Ruth
    Sons: Samuel, John, Thomas, Hampton

HAMES, CHARLES Union Wills Vol 1-224
    Wife: Catherine
    Sons: William, Charles, John, Edmond
    My 4 daughters 26 May, 1802

HARRIS, THOMAS--Will 2 Apl. 1796 Union Wills Bx2-62 A-46
    Wife: Salley   Ex: James Townsend
    My Children   Wit: James Benson, Richard Haeris
                         Thomas Harris

HARRINGTON, JOHN--Will 12 Nov. 1792   Union Wills
    Wife: Fanny
    My children as they come of age.
    Son-in-law: Nicholas Corry

HART, AARON--Miller--S. C. Gr. on Fairforest Bd. Wm. Wofford-Dep
    Surv. Chas. King, Benj. Gist, John Littel--To Col. Thos Brandon
    Pg-94 1 March, 1786

HAWKINS, JAMES--Will 24 Dec. 1790 Union Wills Bx1-45 A-8
    Wife: Martha
    Son: Isaac--Land-Gr Jonathan Hawkins
          Nathan--Land-Gr Amos Tims 1774
          John, Benjamin, Amos, William, James
    Dau: Martha Cook

HAWKINS, JOHN Union Deeds Bk G-372
    Heir estate Edward Moore--See card Dinah Moore

HAYS, EDMOND -w- Jemima--To or From? John Thomas on Buffalo Br. of
    Fairforest bd. John Hays, Jesse Fore, Joseph Thomas. Wit:
    Evan Thomas, Uriah Paulk, Elijah Palmer and John Palmer
    14 Feb. 1786 Union 97

HENDERSON, JOHN Of Union Co. as exor. of Est. of Solomon Alston, Dec'd.
    Receipt and discharge from Lemuel James Alston for money. Pg-44
    John Henderson app'd Sheriff. Bond 7 Apl. 1795. S: Adam Potter
    Hugh Means 30 Jan. 1794

HENDERSON, THOMAS of York Co. S. C. To Bond for Title John McCooll of
    Union Co. 227 A. in Camden Dist. on N-s Broad R. in Chester Co.
    being a tract conv. by John Montgomery to sd T. H. Wit: Seth
    Alday, John Lackature. Pg 61/62 25 Mar. 1789

HENDLEY, WILLIAM--Will 27 Oct. 1793 Union Wills A-15
    Wife: Mary
    Sons: John Foster, George, and Wm. Herrod

HARDWICK, GARLAND of Union Pg 28/29 10 Oct. 1787--Love and Affection
    Nancy Hardwick Taylor infant daughter of my sister Nancy Taylor.
    Negro girl: Mariah. Wit: William Hardwick, Nancy David,
    Molly Hardwick.

HARDWICK, JAMES to Francis Possey--100 A. Gr. to Isaac Simonson bd
    N. C. Gr. to John Clark. between Broad and Saluda Rivers on
    Lower Fish Dam Cr. Union Pg 24/25 9 Dec. 1778

HENDRICKS, WILLIAM of East Florida Col. Thomas Blandon and Margaret
Hendricks. P. A. Wit: John Hendricks--Union 27 May 1785

HENRY, JAMES of Amelia Twp.-Berkley Co. Bond for Title to Richard
Hughes--250 A. in Craven Co.. Wit: David George, William Hard-
Wick. (Where sd _____ _____did formerly live. Union 26/27
14 Feb. 1772

HILL, DEMPSEY -w- Patsy-out of state. Chancery Case: Henry Gibbs
-vs- Dempsey Hill and wife Patsey. Union Dist. June 4, 1838
The Columbia Telegraph

HODGE, JOHN and John Grindel, sen'r.--Aff.--That they saw John Beckham in 1775 or 1776 sign L. and RE 1. to William Hodge of Pic-
olet for the tract of land "whereon said William Hodge now lives"
Union Pg-16 27 Aug. 1784

HOLBORT, JAMES -w- Elizabeth--Out of state--Chancery case: Henry
Gibbs -vs- James Holbort -w- Elizabeth Union Dist. Columbia
Telescope 2 June, 1838

HOLCOMB, BENJAMIN--Will 12 Aug. 1789 Union Wills Bk-A-40
Wife: Ailsy
    Rachel Holcomb, Isaac Holcomb, Solomon Holcomb
Gr-dau: Frankey Comer

HOLCOMB, PHILIP of Union Co. from Seycily Prince and her son Edward
Prince, both of Union Co. $200.00 150 A. on Tyger River--Gr
to Solomon Smith--who conv. to Ralph Jackson, who conv. to
Thomas Scales, who conv. to James Prince and from him to Seycily
Prince, his wife, and Edward Prince, her son. Union Deed E-258
22 Nov. 1797. Wit: Solomon Holcomb, Robert Bowtman

HOLLINGSWORTH, LEVI--Heir estate Edward Moore. See card Dinah Moore
Union Deeds Bk G-372

HOPE, JOHN--Will 2 July 1791 Union Wills Pg-67 2 July 1791
Wife: Jean
"my six daughters to be reared and educated, namely:
    Catherine, Agnes, Mary, Margaret, Rebecca, Jean
Exor: Moses Meek and Chester Rogers
Wit: James Thompson, William McCollock, Nathaniel Thompson

HOPKINS, DAVID of Camden Dist. Union Rec. Pg. 54/46 12 Sept. 1783
Bond for Title to Nathan Glenn of Cumberland Co. Va. 250 A. tract
above and below Fish Dam Ford on Broad River called "Feemster's
Land" Also 1000 A. adj. above bd. Isaac Simpson, George Bell
Wm. Moore, Widow Hollingsworth, Thos Shockley, Jno. Armstrong
etc. Wit: Elias Hollingsworth, Daniel McKee, Wm. W. Smith

HOWELL, JEAN Union S. C. A-Pg-61--Named as dau. in Will of William
Lee. Ch: Michael Lee, William Lee, Thomas Lee, Joseph Lee,
John Lee. Wife. Dau: Catherine Breed, Jean Howell, and Oliviah
Frazer and Sarah Bates and Nancy Jackson--1796

INLAW,JOHN, of 96 Dist to John Jinkins-of Union. Cattle, beds, etc.
Wit: David Hudson. Union Ct. Rec. Pg-18 15 Aug. 1786

IVEY, LUCY--Will 20 July 1848 Union Wills 2 (B) 487
   W. W. Glenn   Mary Briggs
   Bro: Thomas A. Glenn   Sarah C. Thomas
        Nathan Glenn   James S. Glenn
        Patsy Glenn   Elizabeth Coleman, dec'd--was
                           ch. of Nathan Coleman, Tr.

IVEY, SAMUEL--a minor--his grandmother, Mrs. Glenn, to have care of
   him. Thomas Bowker former gdn. Union Equity May 1826

JACKSON, DANIEL--Mtg. Bonds to secure debt--also to secure a debt to
   Wm. Shaw--To Col. Thomas Brandon--personal property, horses, bee-
   hives, etc. Wit: John Brandon, Christopher Brandon Union pg 58/59
   13 July, 1789

JACKSON, DANIEL--of Wilkes Co. Georgia to Thomas Brandon-Slaves.
   Pg 19/20 Union Prob. 1791

JACKSON, MARK -w- Elizabeth Gr. by S. C. 1774 To Patrick Shaw of Union.
   200 A. bd. Avery Breed, et al. 23 Feb. 1786 377-Union

JEFFERIES, NATHANIEL to John Jefferies--Both of Gilkie's Cr. 280 A.
   Gr. to Zach'h Bullock. Wit: John Ewart, Jonathan Jones, Sarah
   Jefferies. Union Rec. Pg 135/6 4 Jan. 1786

JOHNSON, ALEXANDER--Carpenter and Joiner -w- Margaret all of Camden
   Dist. to Joseph Guyton 200 A. Gr. to Robert Wilson by N. C.
   6 Dec. 1771 on Arlington's Cr.--then deemed in Tryon Co. Wit:
   John Barnett, Hugh Rogers, Alex'r Brown. Prov. before John
   Drennan, J. P. Union Rec. Pg-100 23 Oct. 1778

JOLLY, JOSEPH--"Capt. of 96 Dist. living on Brown's Creek--being sick
   xxxxWill 15 Apl. 1770 Union Rec. Pg-67
   Wife: Mary--her full thirds "and land for life".
   Son: John--the land when he is of age, etc.
   The rest of my children
   Ex: Wife, maj. Thomas Brandon, Benj. Jolly, John Brandon,
   James Bogan

JOLLY, WILSON -w- Mary to Moses Meck--150 A. on Dick's Br. of Thickety
   Cr. Union Deed 66/67 29 Dec. 1785
   Pg. 67 29 Dec. 1785--Joseph Jolly, Sr. to John Hope 73 A. S-s
   Thickety Cr.

JOURNEY, JOHN--Of 96 Dist. Planter Union Rec. Pg-43/44 22 Oct. 1782
   Bond for Titles to Joseph East. 300 A. Wit: Alex'r. MacDougal
   James Crawford

KAYSER, CAPT. JOHN HENRY--Of Union Co. Will 8 Jan. 1789 Pg 11 U. Rec.
   Son: Henricas Mauretas Keiser--2 Horses, 1 desk and working tools,
   hby. and clothing. Exor: Friend Daniel Wooden
   Codicil: To Herman Nederman--pt. tools
            To Mary Caldwell--for services
   Wit: W. Wadlington, James Caldwell, Mark Littleton.

KELLY, WM. of Union Dist 5 Dec. 1839 to Mary Ann Louise Thomas--his
   dau.--wife of William A. Thomas--Deed gift-Thomas Bowker, Tr.
   Misc. Rec. L-49 1839

KELLY, WILLIAM of Union Dist. 29 Nov. 1843 Trust Deed Misc. Rec. N-224
    To Thomas Bowker in trust for Kelly's dau.--Frances Emeline
    Thomas. Wit: George B. Tucker, Wm. H. Clowney.
    Same to same--Mtg. 12 Jan. 1842 M-97 in trust for dau.--Susan
    E. Hopkins

KENNERLY, THOMAS of Broad River--Will Apl. 6, 1771 C. T. Wills Union
    Wife: Mary   File
    4 -m- ch: Mary Holenshed is oldest dau. --her 3 girls
               John Kennerly
               Ellen Strother -w- George Strother
               James Kennerly--500 A.--Amelia Co.
    Son: Thomas--Grist and Saw Mill
          Joseph
          Samuel-or Samewell
    Dau: Elizabeth Kennerly
    Bro: James Kennerly of Augusta Co. Va.

KIRBY, JOHN, SR. of Union Co. S. C. and John Kirby Jr. of Pitsylvania
    Co. Va. 50 A. tract of land in Pitsylvania Co. on Sandy Cr. Bd.
    Cannon's line and running to Mathew Orender's line. Union Pro.
    pg-62 11 May 1799 pg-34

KNIGHT, ROBERT of Union Dist -w- Mary--dau. of Messer Fuller--abt. 8
    yrs. old 21 July 1836. M. 10 June 1856. She had slave from
    her father, now settled on her. 31 Oct. 1856. Silas Knight, Tr.
    Union File Misc. z-356

LANDRIM, REUBEN of Union Co to Obadiah Pruett--Negro girl 12 yrs old.
    Wit: Nicholas Keating, Dan'l Palmer. Union Rec. Pg 75/76
    6 Feb. 1790

LANDRING, SHADRICK--Planter to Aaron Fincher--both of Union--per.
    prop--horses, cows, hogs. Union Deed Pg-6/7 1786

LATTA, JOHN -w- Sarah of Chester Co. to Robert Walker of Chatham Co.
    N. C. 278 A. both sides Sugar Cr. a br. of Fairforest--orig.
    Gr. to James Means nov. 18, 1752 Union pg 132 29 Oct. 1785

LAYTON, THOMAS--Will 8 July 1795 Union Wills Bx Z-6 A-38 To: Humphrey
    Bates. To: Elizabeth -w- Lewis Wells

LEDBETTER, LEWIS -w- Sarah to James Petty 200 A. on Abbington's Cr.--
    orig. Gr. to Samuel Gelkie. Wit: George Petty, et al. Union 86
    23 Mar. 1786

LEE, HORACE dec'd 1854 Union 35
    Widow: Mary A. -m- Sebastian Kraft
    1 child--D. Sheldon Lee

LINDSAY, JANE Union Wills A-298 4 Oct. 1813 (or 7th)
    Dau: Elizabeth Lindsay--Home place
    Gr-dau: Jennet Scott Martin
    Dau: Ann Norman
          Mary, Jane, and Sarah De hay (sp)

LITTLEFIELD, WILLIAM and Absolom -vs- John Clark--dif. over par. of
    land. Union 43 Feb. 1811

LUNY (LOONY), ROBERT--son of Adam Loony-Grantee-by N. C. to George
    Marchbanks --tract where G. M. now lives. Wit: John Nichols
    Wm. Marchbanks Union Deed 2 June 1774 Pg-10
    Deed Bk Pg-71 Robert Looney of York to John Jefferies. 600 A.
    gr. by N. C. to Adam Dickison who conv. to Robert Loony

LUSK, ROBERT--pur. in 1784-1786 3 tracts on Thickety Cr.
    1-from Hugh Moore N. C. Grant $1768.00
    2- Adam Gondelock-N. C. Gtant $1770.00
    3-Edmond Kennedy   C. T. Deed Union File S-5-Pg 49-50-53

MARTIN, GEORGE--Will 8 July 1785 Pg-20
    Wife: Susanna--440 A. on Gilkie's Cr. etc. etc.for life
    Son: (Wyly--½ of above 440 A. to each after death of wife.
        (Randolph--
    "My reputed son--Joseph John--400 A. "Reubens Pond"
    Dau: Anne
    Exor: Bro: Philomen Martin
    Wit: John Herrington, Richmond Terrell, George Petty, Thomas
                                                            Pettey
McCOOLL,ADAM of Chester Co. -m- Mary Love (Senior-see Probate)
    To friend: John McCooll of Union Co. P. A. to collect from
    estate of his father-in-law, James Love, father of "my wife
    Mary". Wit: Thos. Brandon, James Barron. Pg-62/63 Union Rec.
    19 Nov. 1788

McDOWELL, MARGARET--Gr. sept 12, 1768 by Wm. Bull of S. C. 100 A.
    fork of Fairforest and Sugar Cr. conv. to Philip Bryon. Heir:
    Wm. Bryon to Jonathan Penall Union Pg 36/37 26 Jan. 1785

McELDUFF, DAVID -w- Hannah to Robert Crenshaw tract on Tyger R. Bd.
    Wm. Hill and Wm. Hardwick. Wit: David George, John Crenshaw,
    Edward Ragsdale, Joseph Tucker Union Pg 137 10 May, 1785

McELLDUFF, THOMAS--Grant by S. C. 1754 200 A. on Tyger R. conv. to
    Gr. son David McEllduff and John McEllduff--to Stephen Crenshaw.
    Union Pg-83 9 Mar. 1786

McKEE, NANCY--See card Gordon Moore--Union Deed Bk R-421 1822

McMILLEN, WILLIAM--N. C. Gr. sept. 26, 1766 conv. by Robert Montgomery
    to James Kennedy. Wit: Thomas Kennedy et al. Union Deed Pg-87
    25 Sept. 1785

McNAMAR, FRANCISof Rutherford Co. N. C. --also sd by Hannah McNamar
    to Charles Clanton of Union--100 A. on Thickety Cr. by. Edmond
    Kennedy. Chas. Thompson, et al. Union Deed 8 2 Dec. 1785

McWHIRTER, BELTON--Thomas McWhirter-Adm'r. -vs- Oliver P. White
    Mary McWhirter, et al. Union Equity 13 1854

McWHORTER, JOHN to John George 800 A. Pacolet which was conv. by
    John Portman to John McWhorter 20 Sept. 1773. Wit: Adam Potter
    Nicholas Jasper. Union A-703-1786 12 Feb. 1778

MERCHANT, WILLIAM -w- Hannah Deed Gift--Affection and good will to
    George Harling--Hatter. cattle, hogs, ___?, etc. Wit: Thomas
    Palmer, Sr. Duncan McCreven. Union Rec. Pg-45 8 June 1789

MERRICK, ROBERT of Buck's Co. state of Penn. to Bond for Titles-
John Taylor of Union. Pg 13/14 19 Mar. 1791
Orig Pg 43: Robert Merrick, Sen'r. of Bristol Borough in
Bucks Co. Penn. to son: Robert Merrick, Jr. P. A. 22 Dec.
1794

MILLER, ELIZABETH Union Co. Bx 1-58 A-23 14 Dec. 1794
Son: Dinnos Miller--land-all else
Exor: John Gregory, Jeremiah Gregory

MITCHELL, JOAB -w- Mary Gr. by S. C. 1775 to Richard Hawkins--300 A.
on Br. of Pacolet. Bd. Robert Coleman, Wit: Christopher Coleman
Isham Sofold, Zach'h Bullock Union 22/23 13 May, 1775

MOORE, ANNA DORATHEA to John Jefferies--Slave girl-Jean 2 Apl. 1792
Union Prob. 9/10

NANCE, THOMAS--Will 25 Aug 1841 Union Wills
Wife: Elizabeth
Son: Andrew J. Nance
Dau: Martha Matilda Nance Minor ch. mentioned

NANCE, ZACHARIAH of Union Dist. to his daughter Patsy Littlefield--
a loan of $389.00 being amount of an execution against her hus-
band, Philip Littlefield--Lowell Nance of Union Dist. Trustee-
After her death to her children. 20 Sept. 1825 Misc E-422

NORMAN, GEORGE--Will 28 Jan. 1794 Union Wills A-47
Wife: Margaret
Son: Robert Norman, Thomas, John, George, Jonathan, David.
Daus: Elizabeth, Irene, Lydia

NORRIS, WILLIAM -w- Mellica--See card of Gordon Moore Union Deed Bk R-44
1822
NUCKOLS, JOHN--App'd by Legis. as Sheriff of Union Dist.--Bond
S: Davis Gondylock, Wm. Gondylock, charles Littlejohn
Wit: Benj. Haile, James Davis, Wm. Rice

NUCKLES--Wm. T.--see card of Gordon Moore. Union Deed Bk R-44 1822

OLLIPHANT, JAMES of Union Co. Formerly Silversmith--Bond to Wm. Shaw
for money. Pg 10 28 March 1791
Pg-18 James Oliphant to John Moncrief-slaves etc.
pg-49 James Oliphant dec'd 5 Oct. 1796 a slave sold by Wm.
Bratton, Shff. to pay a deby.

OTTERSON, DR. SAMUEL -w- Narcissa--Relative Gordon Moore -w- Sarah
See card-G. Moore. Union Deed Bk-R-421 1822

OLIVANT, JESSE--Heir estate of Edward Moore. Card Dinah Moore
Union Deed Bk G-372

PALMER, ELIS -w- Ann to John White 150 A. Gr. To Wm. Akeridge on
Brown's Cr. of Broad R. Union Deed Pg-61 28 Feb. 1780

PEARSON, WILLIAM -w- Sarah all of Union to Tabitha Pearson--Pet'rs
devised to sd Wm. P. by his father Enoch Pearson- on Padgetts Cr.
Union Co. Pg 115/116 27 Mar. 1786

PLUMMER, DANIEL of St. John's River, East Florida to William Plummer
of 96, S. C. Gr. 520 A. from S. C. on Fairforest. Pt 220 A.
Pg 142/3   2 Jan 1785

PLUMMER, WILLIAM--Will 8 Aug. 1781   Union Prob. Bx-1-36 A-3Wills
Wife: Christen--her Bro: Moses Collyer
To: Melvon Wood--son Peggy Wood
Sis: Rebekah Moore
Bro: Thomas Plummer
Daniel Plummer--his dau: Elenor Pritchett
Nephew: Allin Cox

POAG, HARRIET E.--Minor   Charles S. Cline appt. Gdn.   Union

PORTER, EDWARD SANDERS--Will 1 Dec. 1791   Union Wills Bx 7 A-6
Wife: --All for life or widowhood
Son: Calvin Porter
Ephroditus Porter
2 eldest: Lancelot and Hancock

POWELL, MARK of Spartanburg to Sarah Gist of Union (Girt.) 3 Aug. 1791
Slaves--Soll in hands of James Miller of Rutherford Co. N. C.
Pat, Eve and Jack--in hands of Andrew Hampton of Rutherford, Co.
Wit: Margaret Holden

POYTRESS, THOMAS--late of Georgia to Wm. Farr--slaves Union pg-16
19 Jan. 1782 Wit: Wm. Beckham, Gilsone Foote, Richard Farr

PRICE, JOHN of Chester--His dau. was wife of Gen. Thos. Moore.
See card Rachel Moore-Union   1824 Union Deeds S-8 1824

PRINCE, DANIEL--Will 25 July 1791   Union Prob. Bx1-33 A-11
Wife: Lydia   Dau: Elizabeth
Son: William   Sarah
Joseph   Celia
Eldest son: John
Son: Richard
Edward
Isom

PRINCE, JAMES--Will 14 Aug. 1789   Union Rec. Pg-32 14 Aug. 1789
Wife: Susey (or Suzehy) Plantation, etc, home
Son: Edward Prince--all other land
All rest to be equally divided between my respective children
namely: John, Elizabeth, Baney, Secily, Jories, Mary, Ruthy,
Esther, and Edward
Exor: Thomas Greer, Sen'r,
Wit: Elijah Cooper, Thomas Winn

PRINCE, JOHN Dec'd Union equity June 1835 Pg-114 244
Widow: Elizabeth Prince "old and not educated"
Adm'r: Isaac Pearson
Son: Edward   Daniel Prince a witness

PUCKETT, JAMES D.-Merchant-of Pinckneyville store and stock to Alex'r.
Morrison-Merchant. Union Prob. pg-47 4 May 1795
Wit: Douglass Puckett, John McGirt

REID, WILLIAM, Dec'd Will Union 33 1866
    6 ch'n: Jeremiah
            Nancy -w- James F. Walker-ch: A. O., Y Falin, Samuel S.
            William   S. S.,
            John   Frances E. A. -w- Dr. M. A.
            James   Moore
            Eliza -w- James H. Alexander

ROBINSON, JAMES of Green Co. Georgia d. Oct. or Nov. 1821--Will
    Bro: Bro: Joseph Robinson--sole legatee   (date ?)
    Exor's: Thomas Green and David Sanford. Union Bk pg-157

ROBINSON, JOSEPH--Dec'd Thomas Wilks, Exor. -vs- Hiram Davis -w- Ann
    John Waren -w- Sarah and Elizabeth Robinson. Union Pg-123 June
                                                                 1831
RIDER, THOMAS of Union Co, To John McCullough--Mtg--per. prop.
    Wit: Samuel Clowney Union Prob. Pg-14/15 15 May, 1793

ROGERS, RALPH to Henry Smith--200 A. on Gilkie's Cr. Orig. gr. to
    Archibald Robison 26 Sept. 1766. Wit: Solomon Mangham, John
    Hyndman. Union 1786-1787-92 13 Nov. 1784

SAFOLD, TEMPERANCE--receipt from Thomas Wright-price of 3 slaves.
    Wit: Adam Thomson and Matilday Wright. Union Pg 15 7 Mar. 1795

SANDERS, JOHN--Carpenter of Union Co. To Lewis Sanders--Bond--Per.
    prop. Wit: Jas Terrell, Henry Gibson (Gipson) Nathaniel Gibson
    Union Rec's. Pg 23 30 Nov. 1789

SARTOR, WILLIAM--Will Union Wills Pg-27
    Dau: Nancy d. 15 Jan. 1856 -w- Joseph McJunkin--d. 1855
        Ch: Emaline -w- Wm. Wilson
             Frances -w- P. A. Davis
             Amanda -w- David A. Fant
             Sarah J. -w-_____Thomas
                       (2) John Fant
             Wm. S. McJunkin
             Robert D. McJunkin
             Harriet -w- Wm. Jeter
             Mary -w- Thomas Wilson (Mary born after death of Wm.
                                     Sartor)
    Recites-- Sarah J. Thomas -m- (2) John Fant
               Harriett McJunkin -w- Gilliam Jeter

SCALES, MARY--Widow--Pet's her son, John Scales--apprentice to
    Luzeann Parler--widow--for education. Union Deed Pg-4 12 Dec. 1785

SHARP, WILLIAM--Dec'd. Will Union 6 June 1857
    Widow: Sarah--Tenant for life is dec'd.
    pg-14 Nimrod Sharp and John Sharp 1857 -vs- Joseph Cantell et al,
    Post. ex. Wm. Sharp -w- Sarah

SIMONSON, MAGNUS Union Co. Prob. Bx 2 Pkg 7 A-40
    Wife: Elizabeth   Son: Isaac Simonson
    Dau: Mary Hollingsworth   Dau: Grace
          Lydia Simonson   Son: Magnus
          Eleanor Teague   Dau: Maryann
          Hannah Bisshop   Nancy
          Phebe Bishop   Ex: Arthur Thomas, Richard Cox

SIMS, CHARLES-- A J. P. etc, etc. Josh Sims--usually as a wit. On record many times. Union Co. Records

SIMS, JAMES--Will 20 Nov. 1794 Union Wills
    Wife: Elizabeth
    To: Wm. Gilliam -w- Nancy
          Jeter Brasellman -w- Drusilla
    Dau: Anne Glenn Sims
    Sons: Mathew, John, Nathan, Reuben, James

SIMS, WILLIAM and James Fanning--Gr. 400 A. by N. C. pt. 200 A. Conv. by James Fanning to Charles Thompson of Gilkie's Cr. Union Deeds 1786-1787 28 Oct. 1785

SMITH, ABRAHAM C. T. Court Co, Pleas Pg 39. Union Co.
    Exors: Joseph Smith and Mary Smith -vs- John Martin, dec'd. Widow, Elizabeth, Adm'x. Joseph Palmer, Adm'r. James Martin-heir

SMITH, ADAM--Dec'd Union Equity June Term 1810 pg-39
    Exors: Mary Smith and Joseph Smith -vs- James Martin--in own right and John Martin, dec'd heir. Elizabeth Martin (aunt of John Martin) and Joseph Palmer and James Martin. res. York Dist. Abraham Smith--an heir

SMITH, ARCHER--S. C. Grant 1774 to Nehemiah Howard Union Pg 126/7 21 July 1785

SOUTER, MARGARET--Dec'd May 9, 1849 -w- George Souter Union 19
    To: Dau-Dolly Ivey -w- James Ivy Sept. 5, 1844
        Son-in-law: Henry Koon

SPIVA, DAVID--"Died in the west some two years since". Ch. by a previous marriage.
    Rebecca Spiva--formerly Rebecca Lee--had ch'n. -w- David Spiva sept. 26, 1844. Dau: Paulina Lee a wit.
    Singleton Jeter, son of A. O. Jeter
    Wm. C. Lee, a wit. to Marriage set Sept. and he left for west Nov. 1846. He moved her to house of Joseph Shuttleswaits.
    Adeline Spive--dau. of David Spiva Union June 1856/7 7

STEEN, JOHN of Union Co. to Charles Miles . Bond for Title. Wit: Frances Lattimore, Philip Shavour. Union Rec pg-24 10 Nov. 1786

STEPHENS, EDWARD--Will Union Bk pg 85 194 July 183_
    Widow: Sarah W. Stephens--denied her dower. Adm'r, Jane Gordon--Will annexed

STEVENS, HENRY--Dec'd Union Wills Pg 36 57 June 1814
    Widow: Elizabeth--sister of Thomas Davis--claimed the mtg'd slave was her own as a gift from Thomas Davis. Deed rec'd in County of Caroline, Va. Negroes entailed to the ch'n. of Elizabeth

SUMNER, HOLLAND of 96 Dist to Col. Thomas Brandon--slaves, cattle, etc. Wit: James Woodson. Union Rec's pg 18/19 5 Aug. 1784

TERRELL, JAMES--Gr. 21 Jan. 1785 to Moses Quals-134 A. on Broad R. Union Co. Union Deeds Pg-81 12 Dec. 1785

385

THOMAS, COL. DAVID--dower--Mary O. Thomas 15 Jan. 1829 to Richard G.
    Hobson 70 A. on Neal's Creek   Union Deeds T-167
    Bk 1785-1800 pg-3--Daniel Thomas--son of Daniel and Catherine T.
    after their decease to sister Sarah Thomas-Slave-Bea- 29 Dec. 1777

THOMSON, THOMAS HOBSON from John Elliot--100 A. Gr. to John Grindell
    1 Mar. 1775 by Wm. Bull of S. C. on both sides of Pacolet and Gr.
    to Joab Mitchell. 1888 a pt. 200 A. both tracts--? Union pg-123
    3 Feb. 1786

THOMSON, WILLIAM-of Spartanburg for 50 pounds sterling to William
    Hendley--Negro gild about 8 yrs old named suza. Wit: William
    Bostwick, Richard Thomson. Union Rec. Pg 5 26 1st Dec. 1787

TRAMMEL DANIEL--Dec'd. Union Rec. Pg 21 24 Sept. 1787
    Eldest son: Daniel Trammel to Charles Sims, Esq. 7 slaves. Wit:
    John Ewart, Wm. Birdsong

TUCKER, FANNY--Dec'd. 1857 Union Equity 594
    Ch: George B.
         James A.
         Nancy -w- Edmond Oxinon (sp)
         Mary -w- Thomas C. Jeter

WAFFORD, WILLIAM--Will 28 Mar. 1787 Pg-30 Union Rec's.
    Wife: Abigail--all rest for life
    Son: Absolom--1 sh. sterling
    Dau: Elizabeth Rhodes--1 shilling
          Hannah Merchant--   "   "
          Mary Brian--   "   "
          Rebeckah--residue after wife's death
    Wit: Jeremiah Wilson, Ambrose Yarborough, Thos. Todd.

WATERS, JOHN-of Union Co. Will 10 Aug. 1786 Pg 22 Union Rec's.
    Bro: Moses Waters 133 A. land on Thickety Cr. whereon sd Moses
    now lives.
    Sister's son: Thomas Ownbey--1 slave-Lewis.
    Wit: James Terrell, Thomas Wright, Samuel Shippey

WEEDINGHAM, JOHN of Newberry Co.--Planter to William Hendley slave girl
    --Lucy. Wit: Ezekiel Stone, John D. Morris. Union Rec. Pg-39
    20 Feb. 1788

WELLS, ELIJAH--Dec'd Union Rec. Pg-9 10 Apl. 1788
    Widow: Phebe
    Son: Larkin Wells--Heir
    To: George McWhorter--100 A. S-s Pacolet R. Bd. bank of River
    and per. title from John Steen 18 yrs. past.
    Wit: John McWhorter, Abner Wells, George Wells

WHITE, JOHN -w- Margaret (Peggy) Gr. by S. C. 12 Feb. 1773 to Wm.
    Mays--250 A. Lick Br. of Tyger R. Union Deeds 89 27 Mar. 1786

WHITE, WILLIAM of Union Adm'r. of estate of Christopher Coleman, dec'd.
    To Thomas Stribling, Jr. P. A. to receive or recover 3 negroes-
    Phebe, Dick, and Ned. Wit: Clayton Stribling pg 36/37
    6 Sept. 1788

WHITLOCK, WILLIAM--Bond to Cushman R. Edson who is to stop a suit
brought exor's and adm'rs of the late John M. McPhearson, dec'd.
for tobacco and sugar. Union Prob. Pg 13/14 23 Dec. 1791

WILKS, THOMAS--Exor of Joseph Robinson, dec'd. states J. R. filed
bill 10 Sept. 1828 vs Hiram Davis -w- Anne, John Warren -w-
Sarah, Elizabeth Robinson in re. Acct. Wm. Robinson Union
Ct. Com. Pleas-123 June 1831

WILSON, JOHN--Will 7 May, 1794 Union Prob.
    Wife: Dinah
    Son: John
    My 5 daus: Mary Spray, Phebe Hawkins, Esther Turner, Sarah
              Hawkins, Hannah Wilson
    Son: Seth Wilson
         Cristopher Wilson

WILSON, LETTY--Union Deed Pg-13 11 Sept. 1785
    Son: William Wilson apprenticed to John Young-tailor- of Union

WRIGHT, THOMAS--Will 1 Dec. 1787 Union Prob. Bk Pg A-28
    Wife: Sole possession for widowhood
    2 youngest ch: Elizabeth and Joannah Morris Wright
    Son: Wm. Wright
    Son-in-law: Abraham Gosel(sp?)
    Dau: Mary, Matilda, Nancy, Dellèe
    Son: Abner
    Dau: Sally

YARBOROUGH, AMBROSE--Will Union Co. Rec. Pg-40/41 27 Aug. 1788
    Wife: Mary--All for life
    Ch: Ann Pinnell
        Jeremiah Yarborough
        Humphrey
        John
        Mary
    Lands to be sold to John Bailer, Thos. Scales, and Jonathan
    Pennell--agreeable to bonds
    Ex: Stephen Layton, Peter Pinnell
    Wit: William Hendley, Elijah Alverson, Thos Tod.

YOUNG, THOMAS of Brown's Creek Will 14 May, 1777 Union Rec. Pg-3
    Wife: Catherine
    Son: William
         George
         Christopher
    Wit: Thomas Brandon, Wm. Kennedy, John Brannon. Prov 3 Feb. 1791

YOUNG, WILLIAM of 96 Dist. Will 13 Oct. 1787 Union Rec. Pg 34/5
    My wife and seven children--Plantation on Enoree where I now
    live, till youngest son, Thomas, comes of age. Lane in Laurens
    to be sold.
    Wife: Margaret
    "my 7 sons": Samuel, Adam, William, James, John, Joseph, Thomas
    Wit: Hugh McWilliams
         Jeremiah Moore
         Joseph Vines

ADAIR, JAMES--of Mecklenberg, and Mary his wife. Mecklenberg Deed 12-69
    To: Absolom Waters--same. Aug. 10, 1768. Land in Mecklenberg
    W-s Catawba River--where he (Waters) now lives--by the river near
    the upper end of the Island. Wit: Andrew Hampton, Benjamin Haden,
    and Sam'l McComsley

ADAIR, MAJOR JOHN York Minutes Pk-54 Oct. Ct. 1786
    and Joseph Dickson -vs- James M. Randles--Referred to Col. Wm.
    Hill and Maj. John Adair and their award to be returned to Ct.
    and be the judgement of the ct.

ADAIR, WM. and Mary, his wife of Anson Co. Mecklenberg Deed 4-137
    To: Wm. Moore--same. 95 pounds. 300 A. land in Anson Co. S-s
    Catawba River, joining Judith Coburn's survey--including Tudk-
    alige Path--Gr. Fred K. Hambright 30 Aug. 1753--conv. sd Hambright
    and Sarah, his wife 25 Sept. 1758. Wit: John Price, Ben Lacey
    and John Thomas. 14 Dec. 1762 N. C.

ADAIR, WM. --of Mecklenberg--Planter. Mecklenberg Deed 12-36 24 Aug.
    To: Mich'l Rudinell--400 A. both sides Long Creek and S 1768
    side S-J-Catawba River about a mile above Jacob Hoyls Plantation
    Gr. sd Wm. Adair 27 Mar. 1755. Wit: John and Sam'l Moore and
    James Williamson

ADAIR, WILLIAM--and his wife Mary--Tryon Ct. Min. Spring 1767
    Deed sale to David Sturat 25 July 1769 for 205 A.

ADAIR, WILLIAM--York Deed B-105 22 Jan. 1771 from Wm. Watson and
    Violet his wife of Tryon Co. Land in Province of N. C. on Waters
    of Fishing Cr. Wit: John Price, Robert Adams, and John Thompson

ADAIR, WILLIAM of Lincoln Co. N. C. Planter--York Deed B-108 To:
    John McCaw 260 A. land S. C. Co York. N fork of Fishing Creek.
    Bd. Watson--Gr. Wm. Watson by N. C. 4 May, 1769. Who conv. by
    sd Wm. Watson to Violet his wife. 22 Jan. 1771. No dower.
    Wit: Francis Curry, John Rowe, Wm. McCaw

ADAIR, WILLIAM York Deed B-139 16 July, 1778 To: James Hemphill
    Land S-s Catawba River. S fork Fiching Cr. Joining Robert
    Kerr. Wit: Mames Adair, Wm. Adair.
    Page 141 Wm. Adair to James Hemphill--Land S-s Catawba River on
    Waters S-fork Fishing Cr. Adj. Robert Kerr, Wit: James Adair
    Wm. Adair. No dower

ADICKS, SARAH--Niece of James Moore-w 1845. Her dau: Dorcas
    Antionette Adicks. York 1845

ALEXANDER, ROBERT and his wife, Aylse to John and Joseph Gabie.
    York Deed Bk A-24 1772

ARNOLD, JOSEPHUS--Will 17 May, 1802 York Wills A-93
    Wife: Delphy
    Son: William
          John
    Dau: Polly
          Rebecca Lovens

YORK COUNTY - SOUTH CAROLINA

Compiled by

Janie Revell

ASH, JOHN--Of Camden Dist. York Will Bk A-12 Pg 2 14 Feb. 1785
    Son: Robert
            William Exor.
    Dau: Isobel Patterson's oldest son, John
            Mary--Bond due by Wm. Burris
            Elizabeth
    Wife: Isobel

ASHMORE, WALTER--York Wills A-12-59 23 Nov. 1790
    Wife: Cleranah
    Dau: Margaret and Mary
    Son: William and Walter
    Dau: Elleoneer

BEARD, JAMES--Of Fishing Creek, York Co. York Will A-12-29 21 Sept,
    Wife: Mary--Ex'x.   1788
    Son: John
    Dau: Jean Beard and Catherine Beard
    Exor's: Robert House, John Murphey, Sr. Rec'd June 17, 1789

BERRY, CATHERINE--sd Keathin (X) Barry York Wills A-12-28 10 Jan 1784
    Dau: Violet Simsil
    Son: Hugh Berry
    Dau: Catherine Barron
    Son: John Berry   Roger Berry
            Andrew Berry   Richard Berry
            William Berry

BIGGER, JOSEPH of York Co. York Wills A-12-8 22 July 1786
    Wife: Sarah, Ex'x.
    Daus: Margaret, Agness, Sarah, Elinor
    Son: Robert--a minor
            Joseph   Exor: James Ramsey

BIGGER, MATHEW York Wills A-12-34 5 Dec, 1788
    Wife: Ann
    Bro: Moses son James Bigger
    To: Ann Drennan
    Bro: James son Mathew Bigger
    Friend: John Drennan

BLACK, JAME--Dau. of Thomas Clendinen. Will 20 Jan. 1817. Lot in
    Columbia. York Wills D-169

BLACK, ROBERT, SR.--"Of the New Acquisition-Camden District".
    Wife: Agnes--"remainder of the orphan Sarah's time"
    Son: George   York Wills A-12-52 9 Oct. 1779
    Dau: Elizabeth
    Son: Robert
    Dau: Agness
    Son: John
            Jacob
    Ex'x: Wife, George, and James Blankhead.
    Wit: Thomas Woods, Edith Woods, Andrew Woods

BLANTON, GEORGE To John Barrow. York Deed A-14 1778

BOYLS, MARY--York Wills A-12-83 4 May, 1793
    Dau: Jean Allcorn
           Sarah Clark -w- Wm. Clark--Exor.
           Mary, Margaret, and Ann
    Son: John and Ebenezer--Minors
    Ex: Son-in-law: Wm. Clark Rec'd 7 Jan. 1794

BROWN, THOMAS and wife, Frances Anne to Godfrey Adams. York Deed A-21
                                                                                     1783

BULLOCK, ZACHARIAH--to Peter Quinn York Deed Bk A-35 1784

BUZZARD, JOHN--Of Mecklenberg Co. from John Mitchel and wife, Eliz-
    abeth of Salisbury, Rowan Co. $150.00   3 Sept 1786 202 A.
    Mecklenberg, formerly Anson, on both sides Dutch Buffellow Cr.
    Wit: Sam'l Patton, _____Cinder. sd. John Mitchell and
    Elizabeth Mitchell   Harris 14-15

BYARS, CAPT. WM. and wife, Elizabeth. York Deed A-42 1780-1786
    Aff. in re Nathaniel Porter and David Porter.
    Pg. 43 Aff. by Sarah Porter
    Pg. 44 "   " John McNabb and Wm. Wallace

CAMPBELL, ABIGAIL--Wit. Will of Mary Boyles 4 May 1793 York Wills A-12-83

CAMPBELL, JANE A.--Dau. of James Moore of Indian Land York 1849

CARNAHAN, JOHN York Wills A-12-62 12 Dec. 1790
    Wife: Mary--Ex.
    To: George Patterson--1 slave
          James McCallen--1 slave
          William Stevenson--1 slave--Exor.
          James Jameson--1 slave
          Frances Gutterey   sd. Jno. Cernehen

CARREL, JOSEPH--"Of Allison's Creek, Craven Co. York Wills Case 55
    File 101. Codecil 17 May, 1777
    Son: Thomas and John
    Dau: Mary -w- Wm. Rachford
          Elizabeth -w- Nathaniel Henderson
          Jane -w- David Neel
          Ann -w- James Alexander
          Hannah -w- Richard Venable
    Wife: Jane
    Son: Joseph
          Samuel--"To take care of his mother"
    "My bound boy": Matthew Carrel
    Ex: Samuel and Samuel Young   of Rowan Co. N. C.
    Wit: Sam'l Young, William Young, Janet Yound Codicil

CARREL, JOSEPH York Wills Bk A-12-113 2 Jan, 1784
    Wife: Jennet Cary
    Son: Joseph
    Gr. Sons: Joseph and Samuel--sons of dec'd son Samuel
    Dau: Mary -w- Wm. Ratchford
          Ann -w- James Alexander
    Son: Thomas
    Dau: Hannah -w- Richard Venable
    Gr. Dau: Mary and Elizabeth--daus. of dec'd son, Samuel
    Gr. Dau: Jennet Ratchford

CARUTHERS, JAS.--Abbeville Wills Bk-2--100 11 Dec. 1823
      Sister: Margarette Caruthers
      Bro: Samuel Caruthers and his son James
      Ex: Benj. Levy and Francis Young
      Wit: Geo. Whitfield, Benj. Levy.   Prov: 9 Apr. 1824

CAROTHERS, JOHN--Will 26 Mar. 1848   Union Wills C-Bx-39 Pkg-13
      Wife: Rachel   York Wills
      Her 5 children: Elizabeth A.
                       Amanda E.
                       Arimintha
                       William
                       John
      Son: Thomas L.
            W. W.
            Jane Pilcher '
            Margaret Parker

CARRUTHERS, MARTHA--Of Abbeville Abbeville Bk-1-143 5 Dec. 1791
      Son: James--Exor.
            Francis Young--1 shilling
            Benjamin Terry--1 shilling
      Son: John Carruthers--1 shilling
      Dau: Margaret Carruthers--3 pounds
            Martha
      Ch. of Sam'l Caruthers
      Son James to be paid for going to N. C. to collect debts

CAROTHERS, WILLIAM--Will York Wills 3-59   2 Feb. 1843
      Wife: Dorcas
      Sons: Thomas and Samuel D.
      Son-in-law: Dawson N. Mitchell   Prov. Mar 6, 1845

CLARK, PEGGY---w- Wm. Clark. Dau. of Ruth and John Moore York 1835

COOK, JOHN M.--d. 1823--13 yrs. Flint Hill Cemetary York Co.
      Son James and Sara h
      Charles--left widow 1 child 1821
      Elizabeth -w- Robert, Sr. d. 1829 age 72
      Robert, Sr. d. 8 Oct. 1832--b. 18 Dec. 1763
      Austin Cook

COOPER, ISLER--Will made in Halifax Co. N. C. 5 Feb. 1813
      Wife: Nancy   York Wills A-349
      Bro-in-law: Thomas Willey
      Residue to all of my surviving children

COOPER, JACOB--Of Craven--Will 9 Feb. 1769   C. T. Wills
      Wife: Mary   (also spelled Copper)
      Son: Jacob--400 A. on Catawba River
      Dau: Elizabeth Cooper

COOPER, JOHN--Will 17 Sept 1812 York Wills G-146
      Wife: Elizabeth
      Dau: Margaret
      Sons: Robert and John
      Daus: Elizabeth Davidson and Mary Wallace
      Son: William. Mentions his legacy for father in York Co. Pa.

COOPER, MARGARET--Will 10 July 1824 York Co
    Bros: Robert, William and James Cooper
    Sister: Elizabeth Davison--her dau. Eliza Mary
             Mary Wallace
    Bro: John Cooper's dau. Margaret

COOPER, ROBERT--Will Prov: Nov. 18, 1842 York Probate P-46
    Wife: Mary
    Bro: John Cooper of Kentucky and his dau. Jane Ferguson
         James Cooper--Of Georgia
         William Cooper of Tennessee and his son John
    Sister: Elizabeth Davison--of York Village
         Mary Wallace--of Virginia and dau. Elizabeth Powell
    Nephew: Robert-son of Wm. of Tenn.
    Niece: Mary Eliza Alston
    Legatees of "my wife, Mary Cooper, dec'd-viz: the children
        Nancy Wallace of Alabama
        Jane S. Davison of Alabama

COULTER, JEBIDIAH -m- set 28 Nov. 1828 Rachel Moore--owns 3 slaves
    John Moore--Trustee. Wit: Alfred Moore, Wm. Mangle
    York Dist. Misc. F-403

COULTER, RACHEL--Heir of John Moore W. May 7 1831 York

CROSBY, DENNIS--Of St. Mark Par. C. T. Wills York File
    Wife: Hannah Crosby--Home Plantation--Will 5 Aug. 1771
    Son: Richard--Land at mouth of Sandy Run   Prov: 11 Oct. 1771
         Thomas--Land where he now lives
    Dau: Lydia Dove
    Son: William
         John--Land on Broad River
    Dau: Mary

DICKY, JOHN --"Of the new Acquisition" York Wills A-12-9
    Wife: Martha   Son: George
    Son: David   Robert
    Dau: Susannah   Dau: Mary
         Jane   Martha
    Son: John   Elinor
    Wit: Robert Kennedy, William Dickey, James Dickey

DICKEY, ROBERT to John McNabb York Deed Bk A-32 1785

DICKEY, ROBERT to Robert Kennedy York Deed Bk A-19 1785

DENTON, SAMUEL--Of York Dist. York Wills A-12-Pg-1
    Wife: Elizabeth   12 Apr. 1786 Rec'd: 9 Apr. 1789
    Sons: John, Benjamin, and Joshua
    Ex: Wife and Joshua
    Wit: Peter Aiken, George Hoge, James Riley

ELDER, DAVID from David Dickson York Deed E-88 11 Feb. 1792
    So-side Crowder's Creek whereon the said David Elder now lives--
    at head of the Long Branch near James Alexander's land. Pres:
    John Henry, Wm. Price
    York Deed C-370 18 Feb. 1792--from William Henderson of Meck-
    lenburgh Co. N. C.--200 A. in York Co. on both sides of Beaver
    Dam Creek--Bd beginning at Gordon's corner, thence along Gordon's
    line to David Dickson's Line.

392

ELDER, DAVID from John McCaw-Clerk of Co. Ct. York --York Deed D-48
     On waters of Crowder's Creek--Gr. to sd John McCaw by Chas .
     Pinckney 1 Oct. 1792. This deed 7 Feb. 1795. Wit: Thomas
     Nelson, John McCaw, Mary Gordon-no dower
     York Deed E-89 1797--David Elder and wife, Margaret to Francis
     Ray of Chester Co. 500 A. including 3 old surveys on Crowder's
     Creek in York County. Wit: John Barnwell, William Ray, David
     Elder, Margaret Elder (X)
     York Deed H-537 from Anthony Kendrick 87 A. S-s Crowder's Cr.
                                                               1802
ELDER, MARGARET--Legatee--Will dated 12 Oct 1791 York Wills A-12-71
     Will of Nancy Gorden of York Co.
               Son: James Gorden
               Dau: Elinor Henry -w- P. Henry
               Sons: Samuel and Hugh Gorden
               "Oldest Dau." Nancy Floid
               Son: Robert's dau. Mary Gorden
                     William
               "My 7 Ch": Samuel, John, James, Hugh, Nanny Floid
               Elinor Henry, Margaret Elder
     Wit: Robert Faries, John Gordon, Nelly Henry

ELDER, MARY J.--E. B. Mendenhall York Deed Bk-22-17 1895

ELDER, MATTHEW--To Robert Patterson 87 A. on Crowder's Cr. York Deed
                                               H-538 1804
ELDER, MATTHEW from J. G. Love--Lots in Yorkville York Deed J-10-731
                                                               1859
ENLOW, MARY--Of Craven Co. S. C. York Wills A-12-16 28 Aug. 1774
     Younger Dau: Christen Enlow
     "all my children"--not named   ⟩

EVANS, MARIA--Niece of James Moore w. 1845

FARIS, REBECCA AMANDA--Dau. James A. Moore 1867

FARRIS, WILLIAM--Will 18 Apr. 1805 York Wills A-215 Prov. 15 Nov. 1805
     Wife: Nancy
     Son: David
     Dau: Margaret and Mary
     Sons: John, James, Joshua, Isaac
     Dau: Sarah

FARRIS, WILLIAM--Will 5 Oct. 1842 Bk 3-50 Prov: 2 Jan, 1843
     Wife: Susan
     Son: Wm. I. Farris, Exor.
     Daus: Margaret, Jane, Mary, Nancy

FERGUSON, JAMES--York Wills A-12-77 7 Jan. 1793
     Wife: Annaritta
     Sons: Richard, Thomas, James Hamblet (or Hambley)
     Dau: Margaret
     To: Rebecca Long--Cow   Rec'd Apr. 30, 1793

FERGUSON, MOSES and wife Martha of New Acquisition to John Gabie
     York Deed B-25 10 July 1786
     Wit: James Ferguson, Roger, Barry, Jas. Gelse

GILLHAM, THOMAS, SEN'R. to Thomas Jr. York Deed A-9 1780

GORDEN, NANNY York Wills A-12-71 12 Oct. 1791
    Sons: John and James Gorden
    Dau: Eliner Henry
    Son: Samuel
    Y-son: Hugh
    Oldest dau: Nancy Gordon-dau. of Robert Gordon
    Dau: Margaret Elder
    Son: Hugh Gordon
    Son: William Gordon

GRAHAM, JEAN--York Wills A-12-69 16 Aug. 1790 Rec'd: 30 Apr. 1792
    Dau: Margaret Templeton--Ex.
        Nancy
    Ex: Hugh Berry

GREEN, PETER A. of York Dist. S. C. -vs- Sarah Walton--Legatee of
    Joseph Chower of C. T. 30 Jan. 1811 Misc. 4G-214

HAGGANS, WILLIAM and wife, Mary to John Drennan--York Deed A-29 1765

HALL, JOHN--from Ireland, of York Co. Will 30 Oct. 1796 York Wills A-157
    1 son: William
    Daus: Betsy, Nancy, Ann(My 3 youngest daus.), Martha, Sarah
    Margaret, and Jean. Legacy from my dead father in Ireland

HEMPHILL, ALEXANDER of York Co. York Wills A-12-65 8 July 1788
    Wife: Mary--Ex'x.
    Eldest son: Robert
    Son: John--a minor
    Dau: Janet
    Sons: James and Samuel Exor: Andrew Love

HEMPHILL, JAMES -m- 17inst. in Chesterville Miss Rachel E. Brawley
    by Rev. John Douglas. South Carolinian 1 June 1840.
    Died in C. T.--Ellen Chapman Black, wife of Francis Blace age 32

HENDERSON, ESTHER of York Co. York Will Bk A12-44 7 Nov. 1789
    Son: Robert Henderson
    ? Mary Henderson
    Dau: Mary Todd
    Gr. dau: Esther Henderson
    Son: Samuel--Bible
    Ex: Robert Patrick and Joseph Howe
    Wit: John Howe, James Howe, Martha McCown. Rec'd 17 Feb. 1790

HOWELL, JOSEPH, SR. Cit: 20 Nov. 1818 York Case 24-378 Bk F-310
    Gordon Moore--Adm. 3 Mar. 1819. Sale: Mar. 20, 1819
    Pur: Lucy Howell--nearly all
        Smith Howell
    Adm. Bd: S. Williamson Howell and Miles Smith.
    Williamson Howell appeared with Gordon Smith Howell, Sam Howell,
    Williamson Howell pd. amts as creditors of est.
    Receipts: Lucy Howell 1/3 of per. est. and $35.45 1 Jan. 1829
            MilesHowell--#11.35   Elliott Howell--$11.35
            Williamson Howell--$11.35 Joseph Howell--$11.35
            Elizabeth Howell--$11.35   Susan Howell--$11.35
            Gehu Howell--$11.35   Isam Howell--$11.35
            All same date-- 1 Jan, 1829

HOWELL, SARAH -m- James Stuart or Stewart Dec. 6, 1789. Wit: James
    M. **Feeters** at Salisbury, N. C.

HOWELL, WILLIAMSON--York Wills Case 52-172 29 Nov. 1860 Prov: 4 Aug.
    Son: Samuel Howell, Ex.   1864
    Wife: Elizabeth
    "All my children, male and female".
    List in file shows apparent heirs:

Joseph Howell	Elizabeth Howell Burns
Sarah Howell Black	Mary A. Howell (J. G. Alexander)
Lucinda Wilkerson	Crocker Howell
Smith Howell	Matilda Howell Broxtster (sp?)
John D. Howell	W. C. Howell
Samuel Howell	Jane E. Howell Brandon

IRWIN, NATHANIEL York Wills A12-91 13 Dec. 1793
    "Son-by-law and dau": Abraham and Mary Roach
    Dau: Abigail Irwin
    Sons: Alexander, William, Nathaniel, James
    Daus: Susanna and Soffia
    Wife: Leah Ex: Bro.-in-law: Jacob Julan

KING, GEORGE Of York Co. Pinckney Dist. York Wills A12-121 26 Nov. 1792
    Eldest son: George
    Sons: Samuel, Benjamin, and John-not 18
    Wife: Mary Rec'd: 26 Feb. 1796

LANEY, JOSEPH Of York Co. York Wills A-12-27 18 July, 1788
    Wife: Elizabeth
    Dau: Elinor McCown or McQuown
    Other children mentioned but not named
    Ex: David Leech, Esq., and Moses Leathern

LEECH, WILLIAM--"Late of Pennsylvania, now of York Co. S. C.
    Wife: Margaret Leech--All York Wills A-12-68 31 Aug. 1791
    Mentions "the children"--not named
    Ex: Richard Sadler, Sr.

LEWIS, JAMES York Wills A-12-60 27 July, 1786
    Wife: Margaret
    Gr. Children: "then living" excepts Jinson Clark who is to have
    10 pounds more.
    Dau: Margaret Clark -w- John Clark
    Son: John Lewis

LOVE, ALEXANDER Of New Acquisition York Wills A-12-48 21 Mar. 1781
    Son: Andrew
          James--Land adj. Michael McGarity
    Dau: Elizabeth
    Son: William
    Wife: Margaret
    Son: Alexander
    Dau: Margaret

LUSK, ELIZABETH--Widow--of Tryon. York Wills A-12-176 7 Oct. 1770
    Sons: Robert and Samuel Lusk
    Son-in-law: Hugh McCleland
    Dau: Elizabeth McCleland
    Son-in-law: Hugh Whitside
    Dau: Margaret Whitside
    Son: James

MARGRAVE, JESSE Of York Co. York Deed C-358 9 Sept. 1793
    To: Catherine Penny of York Co.--Land in York Co. on a branch
    of Allison's Creek--Pt. tract conv. by Wm. McLmurry (sp) to
    grantor. no dower

McADORRY, THOMAS Of York Co. York Wills A-12-46 14 Nov. 1789
    Wife: Ann--Ex'x
    Daus: Elisabeth, Martha, Mary, and Ann
    Sons: James, Robert and Thomas
    Ex: James Mitchell, Robert Howie and Jas. Williamson of Chester

McCORD, JAMES Of York Co. York Wills A-12-90 31 July, 1793
    Wife: Jean
    Sons: John and William

McDONALD, JOHA "Laborer" of York Co. to his dau. in law, Nancy Pee.
    Cows, etc. York Deed C-539 23 May, 1794

McGARITY, MICHAEL of York Co. York Wills A-12-19 18 Oct. 1787
    Wife: Elizabeth--2/3
    "Nephew": Katrine Williams--1/3

McKNIGHT, JOHN York Wills A-12-13 20 June 1785
    Wife: ?
    Son: Robert
    Daus: Mary, Sarah, Eloneer, Isabella, Betsy

McWHORTER, _____ ? York Deed B-303
    Sons: John McWhorter
          Benjamin McWhorter
          Moses Winsley McWhorter
          Hance McWhorter
  They conveyed to Shadrach Rawls 8 March, 1791

MELTON, SARAH THOMPSON--Wife of Samuel Melton b. 18 Sept. 1796 -
    d. 15 Sept. 1854
    Her youngest dau: Elizabeth R. b. Aug. 1, 1838 d. Sept. 4, 1850
    Rose Hill Cemetary--York Co.

MISCELLY, FRANCES--Single woman York Wills A-12-127 26 Aug. 1786
    Mother: Jean Miscelly
    Brother: James "
    Sister: Jean Garoin
    Brother: William Miscelley

MISKELLY, JAMES York Wills Case 60 File 295 5 Oct. 1778
    Wife: Jean
    "My 3 children": James, William and Frances

MOORE, JAMES -w- Dorothy--Gr. 4 Nov. 1762 C. T. Y-5-24
    Son: Thomas Moore conv. to Col. David Hopkins 7 Dec. 1784 Land
    on Sandy River

MOORE, JANE Of York Co. York Wills A-81 21 May, 1791
    Dau: Margaret
    Sons: Robert, Jesse, John, Samuel's Dau. Jane, William's son
          Joseph
    Dau: Rosannah Bell
    Ex: James Hemphill, Samuel Moore

MOORE, MARTHA--Dau. of John Price--Will 17 Nov. 1792 Chester Wills B-13
    Gr. Dau: Margaret Moore
    "   "   Mary Moore
    Son-in-law: Thos. Moore of Spartanburg.
        Mary Moore--sister of Isabell Findley Will 1818 (Maiden it
                                     seems)

MOORE, RACHEL Of York Dist to John Moore, Trustee. Mar. agreement
    between Rachel and Jebediah Coulter. Wit: Alford Moore
    Wm. Nangle. Hist. Com. Misc. Rec. York File F-403 28 Nov. 1828

MURPHEY, DORCAS E.--Dau. of James Moore of Indian Land. York 1849

MURPHEY, JAMES Of Fishing Creek, York Co. York Wills A-12-94 18 July
    Son: John Murphey--Ex.   1787
    Gr. Son: James Murphey, Robert Murphey, and Alexander Murphey
    Dau: Susana Sadler and her dau: Mary Miles
        Rachel Sadler and her son Isaac Sadler
        Mary Sadler
        Exor: Richard Sadler

NEEL, DAVID to John McCaw--York Deed A-5 1780

NEELY, JACKSON, SR. Of Indian Lands York Wills A-12-17 21 Jan. 1785
    Wife: Ann
    Son: Samuel Neely
    Son-in-law: Matthew Brown
    Son: David Neely
    Son-in-law: Henry Carswel
               James Henry
    Son: Thomas Neely
    Dau: Hannah Neely
        Jane Neely
    Sons: Matthew and Robert Neely

NESBITT, SAMUEL Of Spartanburg by P. A. from His brother John Nesbitt
    of Cumberland Co. Pennsylvania to John Waters of York--Carpenter
    Gr. 19 Dec. 1777 this deed 1 Nov. 1785. Formerly in tryon Co.
    N. C. on S-s Catawba River. York Deed A-169

PATRICK, BETSY--Dau. of Ealeanor Moore d. 1814 York Will

PATRICK, MARY LUCINDA w.? J. P. Pattrick. Dau. of James O. Moore
    See Will 1867

PENICK, WILLIAM C. York Deed M-522 28 Oct. 1825 Dower: Elizabeth N.
    $500.00 to Jas. S. Hemphill 74 A. on Broad River--Bullock's Cr.
    Wit: John T. Plaxico and Robert Hays
    K-418 1826--From John Gill--Dower by Nancy Gill $2000.00 180 A.
    on Bullock's Creek--sold at a sheriffs sale as property of
    Jonathan Minter. 2 Nov. 1825

PENICK, WILLIAM C. M. D. of Va. -m- Miss Elizabeth Narcissa Byers
    24inst. Rev. Cyrus Johnston. In this district. York Encyclo-
    pedia Nov. 5, 1825

PETTUS, GEORGA of York to Stephen Pettus, Sr. 26 Oct. 1842
    $1400.00--All personal estate "now in possession of my mother,
    Mary Pettus, wife of Wm. Pettus, Dec'd Misc. M-337

PORTER, SAMUEL Of Camden Dist.   York Wills A-12-12   28 July
    Oldest son: Mathew Porter   Son: James
    Dau: Agness   Son: Nathaniel
    Son: David   Wife: Sara
    Dau: Violet   Dau: Ann
    Dau: Ruth and her dau. Rebecca
    Ex: William Byers, Sr., and David Porter

1788

PURSLEY, JAMES Of York.   York Wills A-12-22 14 Aug. 1788 Codicil 14 Aug.
    Wife: Jean   Second Dau: Margaret Nickelle
    Son: Robert   Gr. son: David N.
    Eldest Son: John   Third Dau: Agness Fiechet
    2nd Son: James   Y-Dau: Elizabeth Stevenson
    Y-son: David   Dau: Mary Hemphill
    Eldest Dau: Jean Ridley   Son: Ephraim Pursley

RAY, HENRY, SEN'R. Of York. Will Bk A-12-41 26 Aug. 1789
    Wife: Agness Ray
    Dau: Isabell and Sarah
    Son: Henry--Exor. with Alex Galaway. Rec'd Dec. 28, 1789

ROBINSON, PATRICK York Wills A-12-117 12 Mar. 1793
    Wife: Sarah
    Daus: Elizabeth Gillom, Cetura, Sarah, Agness, Jean
    Ex: Wife and Samuel Robinson. Rec'd: 7 Jan. 1794

ROOKER, JOHN "Elder" Flint Hill Cemetary York Co.
    b. 12 Mar. 1755 in Va. d. 24 June 1810 or 1840 86 yr age
    Joined Baptist 1782. Entered Ministry 1783. 1792 became pastor
    Sugar Creek Church where he remained until death.

ROSS, RACHEL York Wills A-12-54 1 April 1790
    Sons: James, Alexander, William
    Niece: Rachel Murphey--dau. of John Murphey
    Ex: Geo. Ross and Andrew Levi

SHEARER, HUGH York Wills 15 Oct. 1789
    Wife: Lydia
    Son: William--Dec'd?
    Gr-son: Thos. Shearer
    "   "   Hugh   "

STALLINGS, JOHN TO DEMAY WINBORNE--York Deed A-28 1779
    Jesse Winborn and Josiah Stallings--Wit.

STEARN, ROBERT -m- set 15 Dec. 1821 to Sarah Fewell, York Dist.
    Misc. D-411

STEWARD, MARGARET York Wills A-12-55 1790
    To: James Young's children
        Alexander McWhorter's children
    Son-in-law: James Young
    Dau: Mary
    Son: Alexander McWhorter
    No date. Prov. 6 July 1791

398

STURGES, DANIEL Of York Co. York Wills A-12-31 22 Oct. 1787
    Wife: Jean
    Son: Leban Sturges--oldest
    Son: John--third son
          Daniel
    Dau: Mary
    Son: Joshua
          James Armstrong Sturges

THOMASON, NATHANIEL York Wills Bk 2-Pg-44 Aug. 2, 1838
    Wife: Elizabeth
    Son: Lemuel and Thomas
    Also had other children. Prov. Sept. 24, 1838

THOMASON, WILLIAM Of York Dist. Misc. Rec. E-119 15 May 1824
    To: Wm. Barron, Sen'r. $2442.00 Mtg. "Tract land whereon I
    now live--in the Indian Boundary 100 A. Bounday shown
    Wit: James Thomason 23 May 1825 Pg. 438 G. T. Snowden and Co.
    Gets ont. notes proof of signature of Wm. Thomason of York.

TIPPING, JAMES Of Camden Dist. York Will A-12-72
    Wife: Rosannah Tipping--Ex.
    Son: Henry
    Dau: Jane Rainey -w- Wm. Rainey--Ex.
          Elizabeth Tipping
    Exor: David Gordon
    Dated 19 Aug. 1783 Rec'd Apr. 30, 1792

WADDLE, JOSEPH Of York. York Wills A-12-6
    Wife: Lydia--Ex.
    Sons: David and John--both minors
    Daus: Ann, Lydia, Susannah, Margaret, Elizabeth
    Ex: John Drennan

WALKER, JOHN TO JAMES McNair Deed Bk A-41 1781 York Co.

WALLACE, OLIVER, JR. of York. York Wills A-12-42 1789
    Wife: Judith
    My 3 daus: Not named
    Son: Oliver Berry Wallace
    Exor: Friend Thomas Wallace and Andrew Love Rec'd Dec. 28, 1789

WILLIAMS, MICCIJAH--Mecklenberg Wills A-161
    Wife: Fanie W.
    My 2 Daus: Sarah Kelly and Elizabeth Cowan
    All my G-children. Date: Apr 6, 1826

WILLIAMS, COL. THOMAS Of York is elected Lt. Governor of this
    State. Camden Journal Dec. 20, 1828

WILSON, JOHN York Wills A-12-66 3 July, 1791
    Wife: Sarah--Ex'x.
    Dau: Elizabeth
    Sons: Joseph and Elijah
    Dau: Mary
    Sons: Robert and Hezekiah
    Exor: Joseph Steel and Elijah Wilson

ANDERSON, Jacob,184
, James G.,027
, James,001,212,286,335
, Jane R.,136
, Jane,213
, Levi,184
, Levy,184
, Lucinda Matilda,027
, Margaret,036
, Maria S.,136
, Maria W.,136
, Martha,020
, Mary,027 ,131,212
, Middleton,212
, Molly(Mary),136
, Molly,136
, Nathaniel,087
, Rebecca,001
, Richard,213
, Robert,002,027,156,162
,178
, Ruth,184
, Samuel,156
, Sarah Mary,036
, Sarah,001
, Solomon,103
, Stephen,001
, Susan,024
, Wade(Dr.),136
, Walter,024
, William,001 ,005,030,
136,212
, Wm.,020 ,056,109,154,
220
, Wm.Gordon,184
ANDRES, Harriot,057
, Israel,057
, James,057
, Juliet,057
, Nancy,057
, Sidney,057
ANDREWS, Abraham,136
, Edward,080,091,109
, Henry,232,295
, James Sr.,109
, John Jr.,115
, R.B.(Q?),040
, Rebecca,232,295
ANGLIN, John W.,024
, Polly,024
ANSTEAD, J.(Miss),046
ANSWINGER, Frederick,232
, Peter,232
ANTHONY, Joel,046
, John,036
APEDARTE, Jane,080
APPLETON, Thomas,001
APPLEWHITE, Charlotte,233
, Hardy,233
, Thomas,233
, William,233
ARCHER, John,080
ARCHIBALD, Margaret,136,157,168,
176
, Thomas,136 ,168,176
, Thos.(Rev),157
ARDIA, Christian,001
ARENDALE, Ann,341
, Daniel,341
, Mary,335 ,340
ARGO, David,030
, Polly,030
ARICK, J.A.,080
, John A.,080
, John,094,112
, Lee,080
, Mary E.,080
, Thos.L.,080
, William,080
ARINGTON, Burel,036
ARLEDGE, Anns,081
, Austin D.,080 ,081
, Cullen,233
, Charlotte J.,081
, Clara,233
, Clary,233
, Clement,081
, Elijah,233
, Eliza,080
, Falman J.,081
, Frank,080
, Hannah,081
, Isaac,080 ,081,089,090,
092
, James,080 ,081
, Jeptha,089,117
, John Alex'r,080
, John Buchanan,081
, John,080 ,081
, Joseph,081
, Louisiana,080
, Lyda,081
, Lydia,081
, Mary Ann,080 ,233
, Mary M.,081
, Mary,081
, Moses,081 ,084,090
, Samuel,081
, Sarah M.,081
, Sarah,081 ,307
, Susan,081
, WIlliam G.,081
, William,081,233,307
, Willis,081
, Wm.,233
, Wm.Strother,081

ARMSTRONG, (Col.),065
, Andrew G.,027
, Archibald P.,027
, Archibald,027
, Arty E.,027
, C.C.,028

ARMSTRONG, Charles,028
, Clarinda,136
, Daniel B.,027
, Eliz.Shirley,027
, Elizabeth,027,028,081
, George,028
, Isabella,028
, James Sr.,028
, James,027,036,136
, John A.,027
, John R.,028
, John,028,136,149,153
, Joseph,136 ,167
, Lucinda,028
, Margaret S.,028
, Martin,150 ,335
, Mary Ann,027,136
, Mary M.,081
, Mary,027,028
, Matthew,027
, Minerva,027
, N.H.,028
, Narcissa,027
, Palestine,027
, Polly A.E.,028
, Polly,028
, Rachel R.,027
, Rebecca,136
, Sarah,028
, Tabitha,036
, William B.,028
, William C.,027
ARNALL, Joshua,137
ARNAT, Agnes,081
ARNOLD, Anderson,120
, Ann,120
, Benj.,127
, Benjamin,120,124,137
, Charity,127
, Charlotte,335
, Delphy,387
, Edward,120
, Elizabeth,164
, Frederick,194
, Hendrick,120,137
, Ira,137
, Isaac,223
, John P.,008
, John,008,120,335,387
, Josephus,387
, Joshua,137
, Leanna,137
, Lewis,164
, Martha,036 ,137
, Mary,137
, Moses,087
, Nancy,137
, Polly,164 ,387
, Rebecca,387
, Ruth,137,223
, Ruthy,164
, Sally,164
, Temperance,124
, Thomas,120
, William,120,137,387
, Wm.P.,008
ARRINGTON, Arthur,036
ARTERBURY, Martha,081
, Nathan,081
ARTHER, James,081
ARTHUR, Alexander,276
, Anne,233
, Eliz.Caroline,233
, Hargrove,233
, James,096 ,101
, Jno.W.,236
, John David,233
, Joseph,233
, Keziah,233
, Mary A.,294
, Mary,233,312
, Rebecca,233
, Sarah,233 ,252
, William,081,233
ARTHURS, Anne,081
, James,081
ASA, John,217
ASH, Cato,036
, Elizabeth,388
, Isobel,388
, John,388
, Mary,388
, Richard,036
, Robert,388
, William,388
ASHBY, John,368
, Stephen,368
ASHFORD, Eliza,082
, George B.,081
, George W.,081 ,082
, James R.,082
, James,082
, Joel W.,081
, John A.,082
, John H.,082
, Martha,082
, Redding,093
, Robert A.,082
, Robert B.,082
, Thomas W.,082
, Thomas,081,082
, William,082
ASHLEY, Ann,036
, Ausabel,036
, Charles,036
, Elizabeth,036 ,137
, James,036 ,137
, John Jr.,137
, John Sr.,137
, John,036,150
, Joshua,036
, Nathaniel,036
, Polly,036

ASHLEY, Sally,036
, William,036,082
, Wilson,036
, Wm.,061
ASHMORE, Cleranah,388
, Elleoneer,388
, Margaret,388
, Mary,388
, Walter,388
, William,388
ASKINS, Elizabeth,001 ,019
, George,001 ,019
, Sarah,001 ,019
ASTON, Elizabeth,001
, James,001
, John,001
, Mary,001
, Samuel,001
, Sarah,001
, William,001
ATKIN, Edith,233
, Michael,233
ATKINS, Abner,200
, Elizabeth,153
, James,104
, Jean,002,026
, Samuel,075
, Sarah,104 ,200
ATKINSON, Agnes,233
, Dawson,233
, Henry,101
, M.D.,028
, Tabitha,022
, Thomas,022
, Wm.,089
ATTAWAY, Chesley,137
, Elisha,137
, Elizabeth,137
, Ezekiel,137
, Isaac,137
, Jesse,137
, John,137 ,150
, Margaret,137
ATWOOD, Joseph,233 ,237
, Joshua,292
, Mary,233,237,292
AUGUSTINE, Polly T.,265
, Thos.J.,265
AUSTELL, Elizabeth,356
, Joseph,335,349,356,359
AUSTEN, Nathaniel,120
, William,120
AUSTIN, (Land),030
, Elizabeth,082
, Robert,082
AUTRY, Alexander,345
, Cornelious,328
, Cornelius,234,258,302
, David,234,258,302,328
, Elizabeth,234,258,302,328
,345
, Mary Ann,258,302
, Mary,302,328
AVERHART, Caroline,234
, John,234
AVERY, Elizabeth,035
, Esther,308
, Henry,234,330
, Jesse,035
, Jonathan,308
, Nancy,330
, Sarah,035
AVORY, Samuel,140
AVRETT, John,094
, Nancy,094
AWBRAY, Sam'l,139
AXSON, Wm.,278 ,284
, Wm.Jr.,277
AYER, Henry,037
, Rebecca,037
AYRES, John,120,122
, Joseph,120
, William,120
BABB, Mercer,137,169,187,188,205
, R.H.(Rev.),136
, Rhoda,137
, Rhoddy,137
, Rhody,137,151,158,164,167,
168
, Thomas,137
BABS, Absalom,148
BACHTER, Jacob,234
, Judith H.,235
, Judith,234
BACON, Edward,037
BACOT, Rebecca,234
, Samuel,234
BADGER, Delia Ann,048
, Nathaniel,048
BAGDEN, John,339
BAGWELL, Cynthia,336
, Harriet,336
, Hays,336
, John,112
, Littleberry,336
, Margarette,336
, Mary,336
, Milly,336
, Willis,336
BAILER, John,386
BAILES, N.C.,234
BAILEY, Absolom,368
, Ann C.,082
, Ann,137
, Charles,082
, David,137 ,163
, Frances,368
, Fred K.,082
, Fred,082
, Geo.,096
, J.Carrie(Mrs),234
, James H.(A?),082
, James,137

BEDENBAUGH, Jacob,153
, John A.,185
, Melinda,185
, Rachel,185
, Rebecca,153
, Rosannah,185
, Simon,185
, Simpson C.,185
, Simpson K.,185
, Wm.P.,185
BEDSIL, Eliza,185
, Jefferson,185
, Martha,185
, Orlando,185
, Sarah,185
BELCHER, Patrick,246
BELCHES, Geo.,233
BELE, William,110
BELL (?) ,024
BELL, (Gov),347
, Alex'r,237
, Alexander Nelson,083
, Alexander,237
, Alphus,083
, Asa,083
, Cressy Ann,083
, Delany,048
, Elizabeth,237,319
, Enoch,361
, Frederick,361
, George,087,377
, Hannah,037,048
, Harriet,237 ,323
, James,180,361,375
, John,083 ,099,119,225
, Letty,361
, Margaret,361
, Mary,037 ,048,237,319
, Rhody,037
, Richard,277
, Robert,139,225,298
, Rosannah,395
, Samuel,189,336
, Simon,081
, Thomas,298
, William,086 ,098
, Wm.Jr.,119
, Wm.Sr.,083,119
BELLINGER, Edmund,044
, John S.,044
, Mary,045,058,060,064
BELLINGES, Carnot,237
BELTON, Austin,237 ,240
, Jonathan,095,106,109,112
113,117,237,240
, Martha,331
, W.A.A.,080
BENARD, Wm.Adamson,237 ,240
BENN, Charles,335
BENNET, James,371
, Mary,066
BENNETT, Elizabeth,342
, James,336,342,347
BENNIKER, Charles,239
BENNIT, John,002
BENSON, Abner,337
, Elias,337
, Elizabeth,237 ,292,337
, Enoch,122
, Frances,124
, Gabriel,337
, Harriet,237,257,292
, Ichabod,237,292
, James,337 ,374,376
, Joseph,120
, Joshua A.,292
, Joshua III,237
, Joshua(Maj),237
, Joshua,233 ,237,257,258,
292,306,324
, Joshue,336
, Mary,233,237,257,258,292
, Nancy,337
, Nelley,120
, Nelly,337
, Nimrod,337
, Patience,337
, Patsy,336
, Polly,337
, Rebecca,337
, Robert,336 ,337,364
, Sarah,237 ,258,292
, Thirza,337
, William,336,337
, Wm.,120,352
BENTHAM, Rider E.,237 ,242
BENTLEY, Elizabeth,037
, Henry,002
BENTON, Eleazer,351
, Elijah,155
, James,338
BERRY, Andrew,388
, Catherine,388
, Hugh,388,393
, Hutson,149
, James,284
, John,388
, Marrey,166
, Richard,388
, Roger,388
, Sanford,161
, Violet,388
, William,002 ,388
BERT, Benajah,062
BESSELIEN, Elizabeth,037
BESSINGER, John,189
BEST, John A.,037
, John B.,037 ,038
BETENBURGH, Uriah,237
BETHANY, Jack,112
, Jacob,091 ,107
BEVERLY, Anthony,125

BIBB, Patsy,014,018
BIBLE, Richard,002
BIGBEA, John,238,303
BIGGER, Agness,388
, Ann,388
, Elinor,388
, James,388
, Joseph,388
, Margaret,388
, Mathew,388
, Moses,388
, Robert,388
, Sarah,388
BIGGERSTAFF, Samuel,116
BIGHAM, James,025
, Mary,025
BIGLEY, George,114
BILLINGS, Samuel,238,320
BINGHARD, Henry,138
, Jenny,138
BIRD, William,321
BIRDSONG, Batie,238
, John,124 ,372
, William,369
, Wm.,385
BIRDWELL, Eliz.,123
BISHOP, Abner,120
, Cyrus,185
, Drury,110
, Edmond,337
, Edward,349
, George W.,064
, Isaac,337 ,340,342,348,
354,355
, Jemima(Wid),152
, John C.,185
, John,185
, Louisa,185
, Lydia,354
, Martha H.,185
, Mary,064 ,120,138,368
, Nancy,185
, Permelia A.,185
, Phebe,383
, Polly,337
, Robert,353
, Samuel,138
, Sarah,185
, Thomas,152 ,368
, Thos.,368 ,372
, Vincent,185
, William A.,185
, William,185
BISSHOP, Hannah,383
BLACHARD, James,316
BLACK, Agnes,388
, Agness,388
, Ann,120
, Archibald,002
, David,019
, Elizabeth,029
, Ellen Chapman,393
, Emmerson,029
, Francis,393
, George,388
, Hance,126
, Hans,120
, Hardin,058
, Jacob,120,388
, Jame,388
, James,019
, John,138,142,176,181,388
, Martha,058
, Mason,058
, Richard,058
, Robert Sr.,388
, Robert,388
, Sarah,038,138,142,394
, Thos.,143,177
, Wm.,018
BLACKBURN, Ambrose,120
, J.Ware,120
, Wm.,216
BLACKERLY, Elizabeth,139
, Jedathan,139
, Joanna,139
, Joseph Jr.,139
, Joseph Sr.,139
, Judah,139
, Sarah,139
BLACKMAN, Winifred,038
, Zelpha,038
BLACKWELL, Maria,025
, Stephen J.,025
BLAIR, James,200
, William,007
, Wm.,207
BLAIRE, Thomas,102
BLAKE, Adam,083
, E.G.,233
, Edward,238 ,266,329
, Eliza H.,279
, Eliza Howell,238
, Elizabeth,266
, Harriet Haig,329
, Harriet,266
, Jas.,286
, John Haig,238,266,279,329
, John,266
, Margaret Sr.,239
, Margaret(Mrs),238
, Margaret,239,266,329
, Martha,238 ,266,329
, Mary,233,266
, Rebecca,181
BLAKELEY, John,181
BLAKELY, Wm.,160,374
BLAKEY, Hannah,375
BLALOCK, John,184 ,191,220
, Sarah,038
BLANCHARD, Benjamin,238
, J.W.,316
, Josiah,238

BLANCHARD, Mary,238
, William,238
, Wm.,238 ,297,316,327
BLAND, Ann,002
, Elisha,002
, James,002
, John,002
, Lividey,002
, Mary,002,038
, Micajah,002
, Payton,002
, Pressly,002
, Robert,002
, Sophia,038
, Wormley,002
BLANDING, Abraham,261 ,311,312,
316
BLANDON, Thomas,377
, Wm.,196
BLANKHEAD, George,388
, James,388
BLANKS, Jno.,240
BLASINGAME, Thomas,195
, Thos.,373
BLASSINGAME, Johnes,337
, Mary,364
, Polly,364
BLESSITT, Geo.,072
BLICHENDON, John,043,049
BLITCHENDON, Anna(?),069
, John,038 ,069
, William,038
BLIZZARD, Jacob,079
BLOCKER, Abner,238
BLOOM, Darling,037
BLUM, Darling(son),061
, Dorothy,168
, John Sr.,061
, Sarah,061
BLUME, Darling(Son),038
, J.B.Sr.,038
, John Sr.,038
, Sarah B.Jr.,038
, Sarah,038
BLYTHE, Frances,322
, Mary Ann,322
, Samuel,322
BOATWRIGHT, James,238 ,239,254,
255
BOAZMAN, Catherine,202
, David C.,202
BOBB, Mercer,200
BOBBETT, Ester,337
, John,337
BOBO, Absolem,337
, Ann,185
, Birum,337
, Burrell,337
, Chaney,337
, Elizabeth,337
, George,337
, Hyram,337
, Jane,337 ,339
, Jeremiah,337
, John E.,185
, John,337
, Leviniah,337
, Nancy,337
, Polly,337
, Roebuck,337
, Sally,337
, Sampson,337
, Samson,336
, Spencer,112 ,337,339
, William,337
, Willis,339
BOBS, Lewis,372
BOGAN, Ann,139
, Elenor,139
, Elizabeth,139
, Isaac,373
, James,139,378
, John,139,352
, Samuel,139
, Sarah,139
, William,139
BOGARD, Abner,209
, Jane,209
BOGGS, George W.,079
, Isabella,079
BOHANNON, James,099
, Rebecca,099
BOLAN, James,266
BOLAND, Martha,206
, Mary Eliz.,308
, William,206
BOLD, Wm.,147
BOLDREE, Ruth,364
, Sterling,364
BOLE, John,003
BOLES, Harry,213
BOLEY, Polly,354
BOLLING, Samuel,175
BOLT, Isam,150
, John,139 ,150
, Lewis,139
, Nancy,032,150
, Peggy,139
, Polly,139
, Robert Jr.,139
, Sally,139
BOMAR, Edward,337
, Elizabeth,337,352
, John,337
, Thomas,352
BONCHILLON, Elizabeth,003
, Jean,003
, John,003
, Joseph,003
BOND, Ann,280
, Isham,075
, Mary,107
, Robert,003

BRAUSSAGER, Elizabeth,084
, Frederick B.,084
, Frederick,084
BRAWLEY, Rachel E.,393
BRAZELE, Elizabeth,324
BRAZIER, Wm.,249
BREADIN, James,004
BREAZEALE, Drury,004
, Elijah,004
, Enoch,004
, Henry,004
, Joel,004
, John,004
, Mary,029
, Patty,004
, William,004
, Willis,004
BREED, Catherine,208,377
BREEDLOVE, Benj.W.,121
, John Watkins,121
, Letty,121
BRELAND, Abraham,038
, Elizabeth,038
, James,038
, Jinsy,047
, Mary,038
, Nancy,038
, Wm.,038,047
BRENAN, Nancy,310
, Thomas,310
BRENIN, E.,275
BRENT, Alexander,084
, John,119
BREORD, Keziah,240
BREVARD, Joseph,104
BREWAN, Daniel,072
BREWTON, Catherine,349
, Delilah,358
, Elizabeth,337
, George,335,337,338,349,350,358
, Naomi,335
, Polly,350
, Rebecca,061
, Robert,140
BREWTPM, Rebecca,038
BRIAN, Mary,385
, Wm.,094
BRIANT, Fanny,216
, Nancy,338
, Richard,132
, William,094
BRICE, Emeline,072
, James G.,079
, Walter,072
BRIDGES, Albert C.,187
, Carville,187
, Charles,187
, Nancy,187
, Temperence,187
, Wiley,187
, William Jr.,187
, William Sr.,187
BRIDWELL, Eliz.,123
, Elizabeth,121
BRIERLY, Margaret,144
BRIGGS, Ann,241
, Benjamin F.,241
, Catherine,241
, Elizabeth,237 ,240,241
, F.,240
, Frederick,084 ,237,240
, Gray,237,240,241,304
, Harriet,240
, John,237,240,241,294,338,369
, Katherine,338
, Lydia M.,241
, Mary,241,378
, Robert,338
, Sarah,241
, Thomas(Dr.),241
, Thomas,237 ,241,292,304,338
, Thos.,237 ,240
, William,241
BRIGHT, Elizabeth,338
, James,146 ,163
, Mary Ann,031
, Tobias,217
, William B.,031
BRIGHTWELL, Sarah,038
BRISBANE, William,038
BRISKY, Elizabeth,004 ,013
, Nicolaus B.,004
, Nicolaus,013
BROADWAY, Emeline,235
BROCK, Henry,350
BROCKMAN, Amelia,139,143
, Henry,139,143
, Jenny,338
, John,139 ,143
BROOKER, Leah,054
, Mary,038
BROOKS, Agnes,187
, Christopher,004
, Elisha,004 ,174
, Geo.,181
, Isaac,369
, Mary,121
, Matthew,187
, Peter,121 ,177
, Robert,194
BROOM, Charlotte,081,084
, George,084
, James,081
, Jane,084
, Lewis A.,084
, Lucas A.,081
, William,084
BROTHERTON, Esther,140
, John,135,140
BROUGHTON, Edward,208

BROUGHTON, Willoughby,030
BROWDWAY, Lydia,038
BROWN, (Mr),347
, Albert,090
, Alex'd Russell,242
, Alex'r,091
, Alex'r.,378
, Allemon,172
, Almedia,050
, Amanda,018
, Amelia,039
, Andrew,347
, Anna,255
, Arch'd,100
, Archibald,100
, Austin B.,039
, Barnett H.,038
, Barrett,062
, Bartlett Sr.,039
, Bartlett,038,039,062,063,140,366
, Benj.,175
, Benj.B.,038
, Benjamin,039,140
, Caroline Matilda,188
, Charles I.,039
, Charles J.,052
, Charles Jr.,091
, Charles,067 ,113
, Chas.I.,063
, Cornelius,004
, Cynthia W.,063
, Cynthis W.,038
, Daniel,084 ,242,280
, David,121,242
, Elias G.,032
, Elijah,029 ,090
, Eliza,039
, Elizabeth,016,019,241,323,324
, Emphemia,148
, Experience,038
, Frances Ann,389
, Frances,019
, Gabriel Sr.,369
, Geo.McAdad,138
, George,097 ,242
, Hannah,369
, Henry,241,265,270,271,324,354
, Hugh,145,342
, I.R.,194
, Isaac,121
, Isabel,019
, Jabez G.,063
, Jacob G.,038
, Jacob,084,109,184,369
, James B.,241
, James,039,080,084,118,159,347
, Jane,021,039,097,159
, Jannet,084
, Jean,076
, Jenny(Mrs.),080
, Jenny,242
, Jesse,347
, John D.,235 ,238,241,278,327
, John G.,188 ,241,242,259,323
, John P.,241
, John R.,242
, John T.,241 ,242
, John W.,241
, John Wm.,242
, John,018,019,021,082,095,100,165,171,174,213,242,300
, Joseph,188 ,242,284
, Joshua,016
, Josiah E.,063
, Josiah,039
, Kezia,188
, Larkin,194
, Leminde,242
, Lewis M.,039
, Lucinda,032
, Manning,242
, Margaret,019,242
, Marry Ann,241
, Martha,019 ,049,238,241
, Mary Ann,238
, Mary,019,039,084,241,242,250,300,303,312,325,331
, Matilda C.,242
, Matthew,396
, Michael,038
, Molly,121
, Nancy,082
, Nathaniel,242
, Nicholas,180
, Patsy,338
, Peter E.,039
, Peter Eli,242
, R.,178
, Randolph,032
, Rebecca,011 ,032,241,242,323
, Rich,284
, Richard,242 ,300
, Robert C.,242
, Robert,061
, Robt.,198
, Ruth,369
, Sarah,019,121,188,238,241,242,269
, Silas,242
, Spencer,180
, Susan E.,039,059
, Susannah,354
, Tarlton(Col.),039

BROWN, Tarlton,039 ,043,050,051,052,063
, Thomas M.,241
, Thomas T.,242
, Thomas,242 ,389
, Thos.,200,232,255,285
, Wiley S.,338
, Wiley,029
, Willey S.,350
, William,004 ,104,242
, Willis,188 ,242
, Winny,039
, Wm.,039 ,062,084,355
, Wm.D.,039
, Wm.H.,238,241
, Wm.Sr.,019
BROWNFIELD, Isaac,232
BROWNLEE, George,158
, John,004 ,012
, Joseph,174
, Mary,004
, Sarah,004
BROXTON, Eliza,064
, Martha,068
, Spires,064
BROXTSTER, Matilda,394
BROYLES, Cain,034
, Lucinda,034
BRUCE, C.C.M.,028
, Elizabeth L.,028
, Elizabeth,133
, George(Maj.),039
, James A.,028
, John,133,257,292
, Jonathan,028
, Mary,028,121,123,292
, P.S.F.,028
, S.P.,028
, Vancy,028
BRUNSON, Eliza,296 ,333
, Sylvester,296 ,333
BRUNTON, Jacob,056
, Margaret,056
, Reuben,056
BRUTON, David,337 ,338,365
, James,338
, Robert,140 ,173
, Thos.,216
BRYAN, Anderson,039,043
, Ann,039
, David,272
, E.M.,065
, Edward,094
, Eliza Cath.,242
, Elizabeth,242
, Fortunatuc,039
, Fortunatus,043
, John Jr.,242
, John,242
, Jonathan,188
, Josiah D.,039
, Lydia,242
, Rebecca,039
, Robert,004
, Will,091
, William,290
, Wm.W.,065
BRYANT, Elizabeth,039 ,370
, Evan,039
, James,267
, Jno.,110
, John,039,091
, Mary,039
, Robert,004
, Thos.C.,090
, William,039
BRYCE, Jno.,236
, John,151,237,239,242,320,328
, Robert,225
BRYMAN, Rob't,110
BRYON, Philip,380
, Wm.,380
BRYSON, Henry,243
, James,160
, Jane,160,243
, John,160,231,243
, Rachel,243
, Ro-(?),160
, Robert,160
, Sally,244
, Sarah,160 ,243
, Wm.,159,160,243
BUCHANAN, Anne,156
, Clary,369
, Creighton,372
, Drusilla,369
, Elizabeth(Mrs),114
, Elizabeth,140,369
, George,090
, Jenny,009
, Jno.,083
, John Sr.,138 ,140,143,156,157,174,177,180,181
, John,009 ,079,084,094,107,118,140,372
, Micajah,140 ,369
, Mildred,369
, Nancy,180
, Robert,084
, Susannah,140
, Thos G.,369
, William,374
, Wm.,140
BUCHANNON, Elizabeth,188
, James D.,188
, Jesse,188
, John Sr.,188
, John,188
, Joseph,188
, Margaret,188

BUCHANNON, Susannah,188
, William,188
BUCHANON, Creaton,112
, George,198
BUCHLEY, Edward,039
BUCKHAM, James,343
BUFFINGTON, Joseph,338 ,367
, Marjory,169
, Matilda,367
BUFORD, William,004,067
, Wm.,052,071
BULDRICK, Elizabeth,278
, Thomas,278
BULGER, Ann,243
, Pierce,243
BULL, John,084
, Wm.(Gov),167
, Wm.,147 ,157,380,385
BULLARD, Royal,232 ,243
BULLION, Thos.,345
BULLOCH, Elihu,004
, Elizabeth,212
BULLOCK, Agnes,369
, Fanny L.,369
, Len Hinley,369
, Lucey,369
, Nancey B.,369
, Richard,369
, William,004,369
, Zach'h.,381
, Zachariah,369
BULLOCk, Zach'h.,378
BULOCK, Luther M.,004
, Wm.,004
BULOW, Amelia,188
, Charles W.,140
, Joachim,188 ,207,220
, John J.,140
, John,170
BUMLEY, John,059
BUNCH, Jesse,243
, John,243
, William,243
BUNNELS, Asa,140
BUNTING, Helen,155
, Isaac,155
BURCHFIELD, James,168
, Joseph E.,149
BURDEN, Abraham,004
, John,004
, Wm.,004
BURDINE, Regional,004
BURDIT, Averilla,004
, Giles,004
BURDITT, Giles,004
, James,004
BURDSHAW, John,005
BURFORD, J'n.,029
BURGER, R.,369
BURGERS, Joel,154
BURGES, James,159
, Joel,175
BURGESS, David,243
, Joel,158 ,167,179
, May,155
, Polly,353
, Thomas,353
BURHARDT, Ann,188
, Elizabeth,188
, Gaspar,188
, Jacob,188
, Margaret,188
, Philly,188
BURHART, ,188
BURKE, Rachel,243 ,320
, Stephen,243 ,320
BURKHALTERS, James,038
, William,038
BURN, David Jr.,145
BURNETT, Edward,338
BURNEY, Andrew,005
, John,243,248,266,273,275
,331
BURNLEY, John,044 ,057
BURNS, Alva,369
, Barsheba,369
, Daniel Sr.,145
, David Jr.,147
, Elizabeth,005,394
, George,005
, James,194,216
, Jemema,369
, John,005,095,141,369
, Luke,005
, Lula,005
, Marion T.,082
, Mary,369
, Robert,005 ,082
, Thomas,369
, William,005
BURNSIDE, Thos.,143
BURNSIDES, Andrew,136
, James,136,167
BURRES, Elizabeth,338
BURRIS, Wm.,388
BURROW, Elizabeth,366
BURROWS, Wm.,161
BURSON, Isaac,369
, Joseph,369
, Mary,369
BURTON, ,354
, Ann,178
, Caroline C.,005
, Charles,362
, David,338
, Dolly,362
, Drury,362
, Elizabeth,362
, Esther,338
, James,005
, John A.,005
, John,005,178,362

BURTON, Joseph,005
, Margaret,005
, Mariah,005
, Mary Ann,005
, Mary,005
, Nancy,362
, Polly,362
, Sarah,362
, Thos.,216
, William,005
, Wm.,362
BUSBEE, Benj.,084
, Miles,084
, Simon(Sion-Sihon),084
BUSBY, Alles(Alice),244
, Christina,243
, Demeris,243
, Harriet,243
, Jacob,109,111
, Jesse,243
, Keziah,243
, Margaret,085
, Thomas,187
, Winnie,244
BUSH, Daniel,125,133
, Esaac,039
, George,163
, Isaac,040,058,060,073
, John,040 ,071,073
, Mary,040
, Sarah(Sary),058
BUSTION, Patsy,048
BUSY(BUSBE), Elizabeth,244
, Rachel,244
BUTLER, Benj.,218
, Betty,153
, Emily,188
, Ephraim,081
, Francis,038
, Henry,326
, James,005 ,244
, John,136,244
, Keziah,326
, Louisa A.,038
, Mary,244
, Penelope,040
, Pierce(Maj),268
, Rachel,218
, Robert,188
, Thomas,244
BUTTER, Laura Ann,215
, Wm.,215
BUWTON, George,050
BUZARD, Anna Maria,188
, Elizabeth,189
, Jacob,189
, John B.,188
, Mary,189
, Philip,189
, Rebecca B.,188
BUZARDT, ,188
BUZZARD, Abner,189
, Ann Catherine,189
, Ann,189
, Catherine,189
, Cyrus,189
, David H.,189
, Daviel,189
, Elizaeth,189
, Gaspar,189
, James,189
, John S.,189
, John,189 ,389
, Josephine,189
, Mary,189
, Nancy,189
, Rudolph,189
, Sally,189
, Samuel J.,189
BYARS, Elizabeth,389
, Wm.(Capt),389
BYERLY, Adam,102
BYERS, Elizabeth N.,396
, William Sr.,397
BYNOM, Mary,005
BYNUM, Britton,244
, Drury,244,252,312,313,317
, Gray(John),244
, Henry,244
, James,244
, John,244,328
, Lucy,244
, Nathaniel,244
, Samuel,209
, Sarah,244
, Scindilla,209
, Turner,244
, William,244 ,290,317,318
BYRD, Dudley,023
, Elizabeth,019,168
, Eugenia C.,174
, Frances,023
, George,174
, John B.,019
, John B.Sr.,019
, John,115
, Michael,115
, Thos.B.,023
BYRNES, James,073
CABINESS, Martha,168
CAHOON, Thos.,175
CAIN, Edward,040
, Mary,236
, Sarah Ann,040
, William,244
CAINE, Alexander,370
, Isaac,370
, Richard,005
CAISEY, Levy,178
CALAHAN, Dempsey,015
, Hannah,015
CALDWELL, David Jr.,172

CALDWELL, David R.,023
, David,182,212
, Elizabeth,023,147,215
, Ezekiel,005
, Geo.F.,021
, J.,241
, J.P.,203
, James,014,129,161,192,
212,378
, Jenny,140,159
, John,005 ,140,154,167,
175,189,215,221
, Joseph(Dr.),189
, Joseph,005,089,189,198
, Mary,378
, Rebecca,212
, Robert,228
, Rosannah,221
, Samuel,085,101,102,140
,159
, William,005 ,140,212
, Wm.,155 ,176,275
, Wm.T.,005
CALHOUN, ,038
, Agnes,087
, Catherine,085
, Cynthis W.,038
, Dixon,059 ,068
, Elizabeth,040
, Eugenia,248
, James,005 ,006,011,085,
096
, Jemima,045
, Jennet,005
, John Ewing,040
, John,005
, Martha,005,212
, Micajah,040,045
, Patrick,004
, William,005,085,096
, Wm.,005
CALLICOT, Asa,338
CALMESS, William,189
CALSWELL, Elizabeth,222
, James,228
, John,221
, Robert,222
, Rosannah,221
CALVERT, Elizabeth,244
, Hugh H.,023
, Jesse,015 ,023
, John,011 ,023,095,244
, Lucinda,005
, Lucy,023
, Mary,023
CALVIN, David,244
, James,244
, Sarah,244
, William,244
CALVITT, John,094
CALWELL, Patrick,338
, Peggy,338
, William,338
CAMBRIDGE, Ann E.,244
CAMERON, Alexander,085
, Angus,005
, Archibald W.,005
, James,085 ,087,244,247
, John,005 ,022,085,096,
247
, Joseph,085,111,113,116,
244,247
, Margaret,244 ,247
, Robert,247
, Sam'l.,005
, Simon,085 ,103,244
CAMMOSH(?), David,092
CAMOCK, David,112
CAMP, Abner,171
, Elizabeth,171
, James,338
, John,244
, Joseph,182
, Margaret J.,338
, Thomas,127,224
CAMPBELL, ,256
, Abigail,389
, Anguish,155
, Angus,161
, Arabella,006
, Archibald,042,057
, Charlotte,006
, Drury J.,280
, Duncan,005
, Easter,006
, Elinor,006
, Elizabeth,006,245
, Enos,006
, Hester,370
, Isabella,006
, James,006,245,320,370,
372
, Jane A.,389
, Jane Ann,245 ,249,278,
314
, Jean,008
, Jesse,006
, John,006 ,154,155,235
, Josiah,010
, Lydda,006
, Margaret,006
, Martha,370
, Martin,055
, Mary Ann,280
, Mary,005 ,006,055
, Nancy,245,320
, Nathan,280
, Peggy,006
, Peter,245,320
, Polly,006
, Robert,008
, Samuel,112,135,245,266
,268,278

CHAPMAN, Gersham,272,320
, Gershom,248
, Giles,190
, Jack,186
, John,085 ,190,291,355
, Joseph,190
, Lewis,190
, Lydia,190
, Margaret,186
, Marianne,248 ,272,320
, Mary,190 ,192,223
, Sally,339
, Samuel,085,190,229
, Sevilla,081
, William,085,190
, Wm.,085
CHAPPEL, Henry,141 ,176
, John S.,234
CHAPPELL, Eliz.(Mrs),325
, Elizabeth,248
, Eugenia,248
, Grace H.,263 ,265
, Grace Howell,243
, Grace,264
, Henry,199
, Hicks(Maj),248,330
, Hicks,248
, James H.,243 ,248,263, 265,325
, Jas.H.,264
, John J.,248 ,254,282, 325
, John L.,285
, John S.,243 ,248,253, 263,264
, John s.,265
, John,315
, Jos.H.,266
, Margaret,243 ,264,265
, Robert,248
, Thomas,192,195
CHARLES, Anderson,190
, Christina,190
, David,190
, Elizabeth,190
, Franklin,190
, Harriet,190
, Joel,120
, Michael Jr.,190
CHARLETON, Ann Pheobe,248
, Arthur,248
, Eleanor,248
, Thomas U.P.,248
, Thomas(Dr),248
, Thos.(Dr),307
CHARLTON, Ann Phebe,249
, Arthur M.,249
, Elinor L.,248,249
, Thos.U.P.,249
CHARNOCK, John,055
CHASPINGS, J.H.,011
CHASTIAN, Peter,369
CHAVOUS, Elisha,038
CHECK, Sarah,211
CHEEK, Allias,159
CHEERS(?), Charlotte,299
CHERRY, Elizabeth,040
, James,040
, Jesse,040
, Joel,040
, Sarah,108
, Wm.,108
CHESHIER, Benj.B.,181
, Sarah,181
CHESHIRE, Benj.B.,206
, John,092
, Susanna,092
CHESNEY, Alice,335
, John,370
, Margot,362
, Richard,163,335,339,362
, Robert,370
CHESNUT, Alex.,104
, John,089 ,140
CHESTER, Henry J.,075
CHETTE(CHITTY), John,058,069
, Wineford,058
CHETTE, John,066
, Polly,066
, Priscilla,069
CHEVAS, Thomas,006
CHEVELLETTE, Louisa,040,065
CHILDRESS, Jno.,155
, John,121,127
, Martin,155
CHILDS, John,253
, Martha C.,253
CHILES, Bluford,006
, Elizabeth,006
, Emily(Minor),006
, Garland,006
, Thos.,017
CHISHOLM, Aaron,375
, David,370
, Samuel,370
, Theo.Watson,248
, William,248 ,370
CHITTE, Edward,041
, Frances,041
, James,041
, Jephey,041
, John,041
, Robert,041
, William,041
, Willis,041
CHITTY, Benjamin,191
, Cynthia,041
, Elizabeth M.,041
, Mary,041
, Regina,041
CHOICE, Rebecca,121,131
CHOWER, Joseph,393

CHRISTIAN, Lewis,181
, Susan,181
CHRISTIE, Mary,276
CHUPP, Joseph,211
CHURCH, Judith,248
, Martha,248
, Patty,248
, Richard,248
, Robert,248
, Sooky,248
CLAHOUN, James Sr.,001
CLAIN, James,011
CLAIRBORNE, Clifton,249
CLAMP, Samuel,269
CLAMPET, Samuel,119
CLANCY, Sarah,144
CLANDY, Wm.,150
CLANTON, Charles,370,380
, Sion,370
, Stephen,370
CLARD, Thomas,286
CLARDY, Benj.,034
, James,162
CLARK, (Rev.Dr.),006
, Alexander,249
, Ann,148
, Anna,371
, Benjamin,121
, Bessy,339
, Betty,148
, David M.,235
, David,034
, Edmond,041 ,249,252,312
, Elizabeth,041,244,249,252, 313,371
, George,148 ,189,191
, Henry,341,370,371,374
, Hester,249 ,371
, Hetty,249
, Isabella,249
, James Caleb,086
, James L.,255,317
, James,073,191,249,297,313
, Jas.L.,275
, Jinson,394
, John S.,191
, John,141,148,170,226,249, 307,308,315,339,355, 370,371,372,376,379, 394
, Jonathan,371
, Margaret,394
, Martha,317
, Mary,249,308,315,371
, Middleton,249,297
, Milton H.,191
, Miriam,191
, Morris,313
, Nancy,249,312
, Patrick,371
, Peggy,390
, Peter,313
, Polly,148
, Rachel,371
, Rebukah,371
, Richard,249
, Rydarus,371
, Sam'l,103
, Sarah,249,272,370,374,389
, Sterling,249,313
, Susan Ann,235
, Thomas W.,191
, Thomas,249 ,371
, Thos.,191,272
, Ulim,141
, Ulin(?),148
, Wm.,389,390
CLARKE, (Mrs.),022
, Caleb,086 ,240
, Henry H.,086
, John,165
, Judith,174
, Julia,281
, Martha,339
, Wm.,174
CLARKSON, William Jr.,314
, William,331
, Wm.,300 ,307
CLARY, Daniel,226
, David Jr.,212
, David Sr.,212
, David,191
, Frances,191
, Ivy E.,191
, Martha,191
, Mathew W.,191
, Nancy,191
, Thomas,343
, Wiley S.,191
, William,191
CLAYTON, (Graveyard),033
, (Mrs),249 ,310
, Absalom,128
, Anna,041
, Augustus,350
, Carter,033
, Elizabeth,055 ,339
, George,041
, Isham,041 ,125
, James,041 ,155,339
, Jene,041
, John,043 ,055,125
, Joseph,041
, Louisa E.,033
, Mary,041
, Rebecca,041
, Sarah,041
, William,339,371
, Wm.,339
CLEGHORN, Elizabeth,072
CLELAND, Charity,218
, Charles S.,191
, Charles,219

CLELAND, David K.,191
, David,219
, Dolly,191
, Elinor L.,249
, Elizabeth,219
, Frances,191
, George,219
, James,219
, Jane,219
, John,191 ,218
, Nancy,219
, Polly,191
, Reason,191
, Robert,153
, William Sr.,219
, William,219,235,248,249, 272,299,304,315
, Wm.,309
CLEM, John,006
CLEMENT, Polly,028
CLEMENTS, James,020
, Reuben,029
, Sarah,020
CLEMMONS, Jacob,155
CLENDINEN, Jame,388
, Thomas,388
CLENDOL, Winnifred M.C.,041
CLERK(CLARK), Saml.,112
CLEVELAND, Benj.F.,164
, Jesse,347
, John B.,347
, R.E.(Dr),347
, Robt.Lewis,164
, Tabitha,164
CLEYTON, Absalom,128
CLIFTON, Charles,238,303
, Claiborne,278
, Clairborn,244 ,250,302
, Clairborne,231,245,249, 266,268,273,314,332
, Hannah,041,043
, Jonathan,041
, Levina,041
, Sarah,238
CLINE, Charles S.,382
CLINKSCALES, Asa,028
, Berry,028
, Polly,033
, Stephen,028
, William F.,028
CLINTOCK, Wm.,101
CLOSSENS, Edward,055
CLOUD, Joseph,106
CLOWNEY, Samuel,383
, Wm.H.,379
COAL, John,147
COALTER, David,255
COAPLING, Alexander,086
, Charles,086
, William,086
COATES, Ann,190
, Edny,218
, John,190
, Mary,190
, Molly,218
, Rebecca,190
, Sarah,218
COATS, Elizabeth,225
, Emelia,041
, Helena,041
, James,164,214
, Jehn(?),218
, Jesse(Negro),214
, John,218
, Pollard,041
, Polly,225
, Wright,214
COB, Samuel,141
COBB, Abigail,220
, H.A.,028
, Howell,220
, James,006,014,018,165,212
, Judith,212
, Mary,249 ,250,312
, Miner Ann,136
, Polly A.E.,028
, Samuel,154,249
, Thomas,014,018
COBLER, Elizabeth,222
COBURN, Judith,387
COCHRAN, Andrew,010
, C.B.,242 ,325
, Daniel,084,086
, James,006 ,016
, John,016 ,037,170
, Margaret,170
, Mary,041 ,057
, Nancy,170
, S.C.,250
COCHRELL, J.,079
COCKRAN, Elizabeth,001
COCKREL, Thomas,091
COCKRELL, Jeremiah,079 ,085
, John,086
, Moses,113
, Samuel,085
, Sarah,086
COCKRILL, Thos.,101
COFFEE, Maria Jane,031
COFFEY, Hugh,072
COGDELL, Mary Ann E.,250
, Mary Ann,263
COHEN, Barnett A.,041
, Catherine Eliz.,041
, Cochia,041
, Eleaser H.,041
, Elsa,041
, Isaac,041
, Isabella,041
, Jacob G.,041
, Michael,041
, Moses A.,041
, Samuel,041

DANIEL, Wm.,105,217
DANIELS, James,087
        , Reuben,180
DANSBY, Daniel,087
        , Martha,087
        , Sarah,087
        , Wm.,259
DANSLEY, Isaac,012
        , Jane,012
DARBY, Ann,252
        , Asa,193
        , Daniel,041 ,249,252,312,
          313
        , Elizabeth,041,249,252,313
          ,371
        , Frances,193
        , Henry,193
        , James,193,371
        , Jane,371
        , Jeremiah,066
        , John,193
        , Mary,193
        , Nancy,193,252
        , Rebecca,193
        , Susan,193
        , William,371
DARE, Thomas,342
DARGAN, Catherine,295
        , William,295
DARLINGTON, Eleanor,064
        , Elizabeth,064
        , James,043 ,059
        , Job,064
        , John,064
        , Mary H.,043,059
DARRI, H.A.,276
DATY(DUTY?), Solomon D.,182
        , Susannah,182
DAUGHARTY, William,252
DAUGHERTY, Charles,194
        , George,194
        , James Sr.,194
        , James,194
        , John,194
        , Mary,194
DAVENPORT, Charles,008
        , Jane,007
        , John,008
        , Patty,008
        , Peggy,008
        , Richard,008
        , Susannah,098
DAVID, Nancy,376
        , Needham,253
        , William,083
DAVIDSON, Alexander,194
        , Elizabeth,390,391
        , James W.,194
        , James,110
        , Jennet,194
        , John J.,194
        , N.W.,194
        , Nanny,368
        , Newberry S.,194
        , S.J.,194
        , Sarah J.,194
        , William A.,194
DAVIE, H.A.,276
DAVIES, Mary,021
DAVIS, Amos,087
        , Ann E.,194
        , Ann R.,043
        , Ann,075 ,383
        , Anne,386
        , Betsy,191
        , Catharine,252
        , Charity,043
        , Charley,191
        , David,087
        , Dorothy G.,229
        , Elizabeth,043,221,308,371
        , Ellinor,160
        , Ephraim,371
        , Frances,383
        , Frederick,144
        , Harriet,293
        , Henry,252
        , Hepsibeth(Mrs),046
        , Hiram,383,386
        , Honey,200
        , Jacob,087
        , James,043,087,106,162,252
          ,267,297,306,371,381
        , Jess,342
        , John H.,323
        , John K.,268 ,293
        , John T.,194
        , John,087,160,194,200,252,
          371
        , Jonathan,083,088,252,306,
          313
        , Joseph,021 ,087,122,133,
          194,371
        , Joshua,221
        , Julia C.,293
        , Leonora,321
        , Margaret,371
        , Martha M.,252
        , Martha,323
        , Mary Ann W.,252
        , Mary,043,087,122,124,194
        , Nathaniel,371
        , Needham,268 ,290,308,329,
          333
        , Neeham,320
        , P.A.,383
        , Peter,252
        , Richard,144
        , Sam'l,053
        , Samuel,052
        , Sarah,371
        , Strother,087
        , Suckey(Negro),342

DAVIS, Susannah,194
        , Thomas O.,122
        , Thomas,087 ,124,160,384
        , Thos.,191
        , Uriah,144
        , Van,194
        , Warren R.,321
        , William R.,324
        , William,008 ,043,071,194,
          252
        , Wm.(Col.),043
        , Wm.,041 ,052,055,194
        , Wm.Brewster,041
        , Wm.Ransom,236,253,268,307
        , Wm.Ransome,321
DAVISON, Alex'r,192
        , Eliza Mary,391
        , Elizabeth,391
        , James Hall,253
        , Jane S.,391
        , John,253
        , Patience,043
        , William,253
DAVY(DAVIE), Wm.,089,097
DAVY, William,089
DAWKINS, George,194
        , James,194
        , William,194
        , Wm.,102
DAWSON, Caroline,253,261,312
        , John,331
DAY, Ambrose,194
        , Arrny(Amy),144
        , Ballard Sr.,029
        , Benjamin,144
        , Daniel,144
        , Edmond,008
        , Elizabeth,083 ,144
        , Frances,144
        , Francis,083
        , Jemima,144
        , Jennie,083
        , John,008 ,144,195
        , Johnson,029
        , Luke,008
        , Mary,043 ,144,194,195
        , Matthew,087
        , Middleton,029
        , Nancy,144
        , Nathaniel,144
        , Philip,008,144
        , Phillip,144
        , Sarah,087
        , Silvey,029
        , Silvy,031
        , William,008,083,116,144,194
          ,195
        , Wm.(Dr),049
        , Wm.,083
DAYNELL, William,150
DAZEY, Mary A.,156
        , Nathan,156
DAZYCK, Daniel,278

DE GRAFFENREID(T), Allen,090
DE HAY, Sarah,379
DE LA HOWE, John(Dr.),025
DE LANE, ,254
DE NOAILLES, Louis,260 ,263
DE SAUSSUNE, Henry Wm.,290
DEAHAM, Robert,372
DEAL, Alex,159
        , Clement,159
        , Hastin,140
        , Martin,142
DEALE, Alexander Jr.,144
        , Alexander,144
        , Allegea,321
        , Clement,144
        , James,321
        , Jean,144
DEAN, Esther,144
        , Job,144
        , Joseph,143,165
        , Marah,139
        , Susannah,144 ,148
        , Thos.,143
        , Wm.,134
DEASUSSUS, Henry,261
DEAVEA(DAVIS), Thos.,124
DEAVOURS, Rachel,342
DEBOR, George,353
DEBOSE, Sarah W.,265
DEEN, Henry,226
DEFLORS, William,253
DELAHUNT, Robert,253
DELAINE, Ann,266
DELAND, Philip H.,245
DELANE, ,254
        , Ann W.,253
        , Ann Wood,253,254
        , Ann,245,253,254,272
        , Anne W.,
        , Anne,333
        , Freeman Jr.,254
        , Freeman,245,253,254,272,
          327,333
        , Grace Ann,245 ,254
        , Gracey Ann,253
        , Greeman,333
        , John Wm.,254
        , Peter L.,253,333
        , Peter,254 ,271,334
        , Philip H.,253
        , Philip Hirons,254
DELANEY, ,254
        , Peter L.,254
DELASHUNI, John,087
DELECHAUX, Elizabeth,008
        , Jacob,008
        , James,008
        , Peter,008
        , Sarah,008

DELECHAUX, Suzanna,008
DELEON, Abraham,254
        , Adelade,254
        , Hannah,254
        , Harrietta,254
        , Jacob,254
        , Louisa,254
        , Mordecai H.,254
        , Rebecca,254
        , Uriah,254
DELK, Kinched,047
        , Winnefred,047
DELLET, James,254
DELOACH, Lizzie,368
        , Sarah Smith,043
DELORME, John F.,267
DELOTH, Nancy,061
DELOZIER, Adeline,254
        , Asa,238 ,239,254
        , Caroline,254
        , Edward,254
        , Emaline,254
        , Hannah,254
DEMSY, Lucreita,367
        , Lucreita,342,364
DENDY, Jno.,145
        , John,145
        , Mary,145
        , Patsy,145
        , Thomas Jr.,145
        , Thomas,141 ,145,170
        , Thos.,173
        , William,145 ,172,173
        , Wm.,141 ,170,174
        , Youngset,174
DENLEY, Mary Marg.,254
        , William,254
        , Wright,254
DENNING, John,145
DENNIS, (Maj.),065
        , James,148
        , Joseph,008 ,026
        , Robert,145
        , Samuel,148
        , Sarah,148
DENNISON, Constant,145
        , Gideon,268
        , Robert,145
DENT, Anna,255
        , Elizabeth,255
        , Hezekiah,255
        , Isaac,255
        , James,255
        , John,255
        , Nancy,255
        , Peter,255
        , Samuel,255
        , Tynah,255
DENTON, Benjamin,391
        , Elizabeth,255 ,263,391
        , James,255 ,259,260,263
        , John,391
        , Joshua,391
        , Samuel,391
DEPONT, Abraham,043
DEFRONG, Abraham,039
DERMED, Wm.,343
DERRICK, George,154
        , Sabina,154
DESAUSSURE, Henry W.,316
DESAUSURE, Wm.F.,255
DEVALE, Lewis,136
DEVALL, Lewis,145 ,172
        , Teressa,145
DEVEAUS, Andrew,036
DEVEAUX, Andrew,038,057
DEVINE, George,337
DEVLIN, James,024
        , John,024
        , William,255,317
DEWALT, Daniel,145 ,195
        , David,145 ,195
        , Nancy,145 ,195
        , Rebecca,195
DEWAR, Robert,319
DEWEEN, Sarah,037
DEWEES, Farmer,238 ,255
        , Margaret,059
        , Sarah,036 ,039,059
DEWITT, Charles,050
        , Matthew(Capt.),048
DIAL, Hastings Sr.,145
        , Isaac,145
        , James,145
        , Joseph,145
        , Lewis,145
        , Martin,146
        , Rebecca,145
DICKEE, Susanna,023
DICKERT, Adam,195
        , Catherine,195
        , Christina,195
        , Christopher,195
        , Elizabeth,195
        , Henry S.,195
        , Henry,195
        , John,195
        , Margaret,195
        , Mary,195
        , Mich'l,205
        , Michael Jr.,114
        , Michael,114,195,222,228
        , Nancy,195
        , Sarah,195
        , Sibl,195
DICKEY, George,350
        , James,104 ,255,301,391
        , Jane,106
        , Jno.,327
        , John,095,106
        , Nancy,255 ,268
        , Robert,391
        , William,391

GOODWYN, Martha Epps,264
, Martha T.,264 ,329
, Martha,251,264,265,278,
286,329
, Mary H.,265,266
, Mary,264 ,316
, Polly I.,264 ,278
, Polly Tucker,265
, Polly,251
, Robert G.,264
, Robert H.,265 ,329
, Robert (Dr),278
, Robert,254,264,265,287,
303,329
, Sarah Cook,265
, Sarah E.,329
, Sarah Epps,232,264
, Sarah W.,243 ,256,264
, Sarah,231 ,242,264,265,
323,329
, Thomas J.,264
, Thomas,264
, Thos.G.,254
, Thos.G.,265
, Uriah J.,243 ,264,265
, Uriah John,243,263
, Uriah,265 ,305
, W.J.,231
, William (Col),265
, William A.,264
, William C.,265
, William F.,265,278
, William Sr.,306
, William,243,264,265
, Wm.,248,263,264,271,273
331
, Wm.A.,254
, Wm.F.,278 ,281
GOOLSBY, James,169
GOORLEY(GORLEY), James,010
GOUSLY, Rosannah,072
GORDEN, Eliner,393
, Elinor,392
, Hugh,392,393
, James,205 ,392,393
, Jane,205
, John,392,393
, Mary,392
, Nancy,392 ,393
, Nanny,393
, Robert,392 ,393
, Samuel,392 ,393
, William,393
GORDON, Alexander,098
, Benj.,055 ,152
, David,092 ,201,398
, Elizabeth,152
, James,201
, Jane,201,384
, John,201
, Margaret,201
, Mary,201,392
, Nancy,201 ,203
, Nathaniel,201
, Thomas(Maj.),152
, Thomas,014 ,184,197,207,
368
, William,092
, Wm.,042
GORE, Daniel,295
, Josephine,087
, Thomas,295
GORLEY, Hugh,010
, James,012
, Robert,010
, Thomas,010
GORMY, Wm.,019
GOSEL, Abraham,386
GOSFRY, John,226
, Sarah,226
GOSS, Eliza,262,265
, Elizabeth,289
, James H.,375
, John W.,375
, William,254 ,262,265
, Wm.,262 ,289
GOSSETT, Anny,350
GOUGH, Thos.,042
GOULD, John,152,217
GOVAN, Andrew,047 ,065
, Eliz.Ann,047,065
GOWAL, John,124
GOWAN, Elizabeth,367
, George,374
, John,350,361,367
, Robt.,200
GOWEDY, James,010
, Krianaque(Indian),010
, Mary,010
, Nancy(Indian),010
, Peggy(Indian),010
, Robert,010
, Sarah,010
GOWEN, John(Maj.),152
, John,124,350
GOWSEY, Elizabeth,149
GOYER, Drewry,074
, Sarah,074
GRACE, Polly,074
GRAFFEN, Allen,115
GRAFTON, Andrew,092
, Daniel,301
, David,092
, Wm.,092
GRAHAM, Charles,093
, David,074
, Elisha,092
, Eliza K.,093
, Elizabeth B.,193
, Elizabeth,092 ,093
, Esther,074
, George,193 ,292
, J.W.,010

GRAHAM, James E.,090
, James Jr.,010 ,074
, James,072 ,092
, Jean,393
, John,093
, M.,010
, Martha,093
, Mary,072
, Sarah,093
, Tusday,010
, William,093
, Zachariah,047
GRAM, Moley(Ch.),043
GRAMAKER, Adam,136
GRAMBLIN, Patsy,352
, Reuben,352
GRAMLING, Andrew,350
, Patsy,352
GRANAKER, Adam,144 ,152
GRANT, Addison,201
, Andrew A.,201
, Ann,360
, Daniel,350
, Francis Marion,201
, George W.,201
, Harry,232,248,256,265,329
, Isaac,195
, John Samuel,201
, John,092,103
, Nancy,092,103
, R.H.,032
, Sarah,201
, Wm.Henderson,201
GRAVES, Anthony G.,153
, Chas.,153
, Elizabeth(Eliza),153
, Fanny,153
, George,010
, Joel,133
, Joseph,172
, Lewis,144 ,147,153,155,
173
, Martin,153
, Rebecca,153
, Selly(Sally?),006
, Thomas,006
, William,093
, Wm.,153
GRAY, Abraham,140 ,152,170
, Alcy,152
, Alexander,350
, Andrew,086
, Arthur A.,001
, Bathiah,152
, David Larmer,265
, David,265
, Elizabeth,152,170
, Hannah,001
, Harriet,265
, Henry,004
, Hezekiah,152
, James,084,086,170,201
, Jean,153 ,173
, Jesse,152
, John F.,005
, John J.,280
, John L.,265
, John,001 ,025,086,152,347
, Louisa,152
, Lucinda,010
, Margaret,201
, Robert H.,265
, Robert,153,173
, Sarah,265
, Seth,152
, Thomas P.,179
, Tolotson,152
, Unity,246
, Washington R.,010
, William,152 ,265
, Zachariah,152
GRAYHAM, Caroline(Mrs.),010
, James,202
GREEK, James,135
GREEN(GREER), Eliz.,158
GREEN, A.I.,276
, Absolem,047
, Absolum,068
, Ann,313
, Catherine,280
, Civil,063
, Daniel,067 ,201
, David,144
, Drury,086
, Edey,047
, Edward,201 ,204
, Eliza,059
, Elizabeth,313
, Ethel,021
, Francis M.,047
, Frederick W.,250,266
, G.H.,047
, Griffen,086
, Harriet,265
, I.L.,343
, James,153,375
, Jane H.,250
, Jane Harriet,266
, Jane,264,265
, Job,,319
, John F.,021
, John,201,204,295
, Joseph,124
, L.a.,343
, Martha,018 ,250,266,308
, Mary,047
, Milltret,295
, Moses,203
, Nancy,313
, Needham,059
, Peter A.,393
, Peter,018

GREEN, Rives,313
, Salina,266
, Samuel(Dr),272 ,333
, Samuel,253 ,266
, Sarah,047
, Stephen,054
, Thomas,201 ,204,250,266,
308,383
, Thos.Marston,087
, William Sr.,068
, William,201 ,204,250,266,
295
, Wm.,047 ,063,070
, Zachariah,153
GREENDEL, Esther,350
, John,350
GREENE, (Gen'l),065,067
GREENWAY, Martha,234
GREER, ,375
, Jane,163
, John,163
, Josiah,153
, Mag't,203
, Margaret,153
, Nancy,375
, Robert,375
, Sarah,257,375
, Thomas Sr.,382
, William,375
GREGG, Edward,119
, James,119,316
, John,087,093,119
GREGORY, Alse,375
, Annos,231
, Benjamin,209 ,375
, Elizabeth,209 ,375
, Gordon,375
, Isaac,368 ,375
, Jarred,375
, Jeremiah,368 ,375,381
, John,375 ,381
, Margaret,375
, Nancy H.,073
, Polly,124 ,129
, Sally,375
, Samuel,102
, Wm.,375
GREIR, Joseph,170
GREY, David,234
, James,110
GREYHAM, Denny,081
, Elizabeth,081
GRICE, Ann,350
, Axey,074
, Wade,074
, William,074
GRIDEL, John,377
GRIFFIN, Abia,153
, Agnes,004
, Anthony(Capt),204
, Anthony,153,167
, Asa,153
, Caty,153
, Charles,151,153
, Eleanor,150
, Hannah,350
, James,153
, Jane,153 ,178
, Jesse,226
, Jno.K.,215
, John,069 ,093,228
, Joseph,153,229
, Kitty,229
, Martha Simpson,204
, Mary Ann,153
, Mary,223
, Moses,047 ,069,073
, Nancy,228
, Peggy,153
, Rachel,153
, Reuben,153,229
, Richard Jr.,093
, Richard,137,153,161,195
, Samuel,093
, Sarah W.,215
, Sarah,229
, Sucky,153
, Susannah,047 ,069
, Vincent,004
, William Sr.,153
, William,153,223
, Wm.,093
GRIFFITH, Caly,202
, John,202
, Joshua,202
, Mary,202
, Thomas,111
, West,202
GRIFITHS, Ezekiel,151
GRIGGS, Tamar,081
GRIGSBY, (Widow),196
, Benj.,202
, Elizabeth,162 ,202
, James,202
, Satira,202
GRILL, Hugh,263
GRIM, ,194
, Peter,194
GRIMBLE, Elizabeth,039
, Robert,039
GRIMES, Jinsy,047
, John D.,047,061
, Polly,047 ,061
GRIMKE, Thomas S.,344
GRINDEL, Esther,375
, John,029
GRINDELL, John,365
GRINDWELL, John,029
GRISHAM, Frances,074
, Jean,349
, John,074
, Major,074

MILES, Isaac,356
, John,100
, Leonard,112
, Mary,396
, Rebecca,304
, Richard,348
, Robert C.,304
, Samuel,087
, Sarah E.,304
, Thomas,100 ,101
, Thos.,100
, William,022
, Wm.H.,304
MILEY, Daniel,059
, Elizabeth,059
, Richard,144
MILHOUSE, Charles,068 ,069
MILLEDGE, John,046 ,056
, Mary,046
, Susan G.,059
MILLENS, Joshua,137
MILLER, ,135
, Abraham,099
, Abram,113
, Alex'r,096
, Alex,081
, Alexander,081 ,092,096,
101,119
, Anderson,141,165
, Andrew,010 ,016,017
, Anna,165
, Archibald,016
, Benj.W.,243
, Betsy,165
, Cassey,357
, Charles,356
, Cornelia G.,058
, David,059
, Dinnos,381
, Eliza,212
, Elizabeth,165 ,259,381
, Ellinor,165
, Esther,016 ,017
, George,006 ,016,141,165
, Gilbert,016
, Giles,042
, Hammond,150
, Hannah,101
, Hanse,165
, Henry,101
, Jacob,016 ,141,165,170
, James S.,016
, James,141 ,165,356,382
, Jane,058,059,165,356
, Jennett,357
, Jesse,165
, John Calvin,212
, John Franklin,031
, John Jr.,016,017
, John,022,095,141,165,167
,178,356,357
, Jonathan,212
, Joseph,165
, Joshua,356
, Louisa,212
, Lydia,090
, Margaret J.,356
, Margaret,016,017
, Martha M.,059
, Martha,016 ,150,157
, Mary,008
, Michael,335,342,357
, Nathaniel,356 ,357
, Nicholas,008
, Polly,165
, Rachel,348
, Rebecca,165
, Rob't,237
, Robert Jr.,348
, Robert,016 ,259,357
, Rose,099
, Samuel,249 ,304,356
, Sarah Ann,212
, Sarah,031 ,141,165,357
, Susan,101
, Susannah,165
, Temperance,086
, Thomas,356
, William,141,165
, Wm.Hammond,150
MILLIGAN, Andrew,021
, William,296
MILLIKEN, James(Capt.),067
, Jas.,350
, Jean,350
MILLING, David,101 ,304,305
, Hugh,101 ,118
, Jane Wright,304,305
, John P.,304,305
, John,084 ,089,096,101,
105,175,257,261,304
, Margaret,304 ,305
, Sarah,101 ,235,304,305
MILLINGS, H.,092
MILLINY, Sarah,261
MILLS, Alexander,016
, Ambrose,101 ,116
, Ann,101
, Edwin R.,076
, Eliza,101
, Elizabeth,022
, Esther,072
, Henry,043
, John,212,220,305
, Martha,298
, Mary,212,305
, Matthew,016
, Nancy,190
, Nehemiah,224
, Rebeccah,212
, Robert,266
, Sam P.,101
, Samuel P.,101

MILLS, Sarah,059,065,148,178,224
, Thomas S.,076
, Thomas,165 ,177
, Thos.,178,224
, William,016 ,116,148
, Wm.,101
, Wm.C.,022
, Wm.Sr.,212
MILLWEE, James,030 ,165
, John,165
, Sarah,165
, William,165
MILLY, John,118
MILNER, Arnold,174
MILWEE, James,144
MIMS, Drury,121
, Letty,121
MING, Clough,145
, Patsy,145
MINOR, Elizabeth,059
, Robert,059
, William,057
, Wm.,069
MINIER, Jonathan,396
MIRICK, Elizabeth,047
, James,047 ,054
, Mary,054
MISCAMPBLE, Ann,016
, James,016
, John,016
, Robert,016
MISCELLY, Frances,395
, James,395
, Jean,395
, William,395
MISKELLY, Frances,395
, James,395
, Jean,395
, William,395
MITCHEL, Benj.,116
, Daniel,173,174
, Elizabeth,059 ,389
, John,389
, Mary,066
MITCHELL, ,189 ,339
, Catherine,017
, Christiana,293
, Clementine,076
, Daniel Cook,168
, Dawson N.,390
, Dorothea F.,076
, Henry,075
, Isaac,017,162,168
, Jacob,141
, James,076,109,395
, Jincy,285
, Joab,142 ,381,385
, John,009 ,016,375
, Lewis,202
, Lucy B.,011
, Martha ann,076
, Martha,009 ,016,168
, Mary,017 ,381
, Nancy,075,117
, Nimrod,091 ,101
, Samuel,011
, Sarah Ann Eliz.,011
, Sarah,017
, Ursula,017
, Wm.,172
, Wm.Milam,168
MITCHERSON, Edward,116
, William,116,141,142
MITCHESON, Wm.,094
MITCHESSON, Wm.,136
MITCHISON, Wm.,142
MIXON, A.K.,059
, Chas.J.,059
, Edward M.,059
, J.,059
, James J.,059
, John,059
, Lavorice,059
, Mary H.,059
, Mary,040,043,045,056,059
, Susan E.,059
, Wm.,059

MOAK, Andrew,305
, Ann,305
, Anna,305
, Elizabeth,305
, Emanuel,305
, Jacob,305
, John,305
, Mary,305
, Sarah,305
, Susannah,305
MOAT, Andrew,017
, Elizabeth,017
MOBERLY, Benj.,084 ,086
, Clement,095,115
, Edward,111
, John,086 ,097
MOBLEY, Alexander,204
, Anna,101
, Clement Jr.,101
, Cullen,095
, Cullin,101
, Edward,076
, Eleazer,101
, Elizer,204
, Hannah G.,101
, Harriet,076
, John,095
, Judith,076
, Mary(Mrs),091
, Mary,076,095
, Micajah,100,101
, Sam'l,103
, Samuel,076 ,077,095
, Sarah G.,101
, Wm.,095

MOBLY, Clement,101
, Daniel,101
, Jethro,101
, John,101
, Thos.,101
MOCK, Jacob,305
MOHE, Andrew,255,305
, Catherine,255,305
MOLIN, John,121
, Mary,128
MONCRIEF, John,381
MONE, Charles,122
MONOR, John D.,066
MONTGOMERY, Ann,212
, Anna,357
, Charles,086
, David,083 ,101,111,
262,305,306
, George,212
, Hugh,086,357
, James,135 ,166
, John,381,395
, Margaret,166
, Robert D.,236 ,305,
322
, Robert,306 ,380
, Salley,130
MOODY, James,043,066
MOON, Peter(Dr),220
, Peter,214,220
, Susan,214
, Susannah,214 ,220
MOONEY, Charlotte,212
, Hannah,212
, Israel,212
, John,212
, Joseph,212
MOOR, James(Capt),286
, Mark,160
, Mordica,156
MOORD, H.Cambridge,234
MOORE(MON), Mark,158
MOORE(MOON), John,122 ,126,127
MOORE, (?),017
, (Gen),336
, ,029
, Agness,031
, Alford,396
, Alfred,391
, Amanda,018
, Anderson,139,166,173
, Ann,017 ,132
, Anna D.,381
, Anne,017
, Barbara W.,166
, Barbara,130
, Betsy,034,166,357,396
, Catee,357
, Catey,078
, Caty,366
, Charity,033
, Charles,125 ,128,357
, Christiana,306
, Daniel,087
, David,028,122,127,326
, Davis,012,017
, Dinah,376,377,381
, Dorcas E.,396
, Dorothea,076
, Dorothy,076 ,395
, Ealeanor,396
, Edward,017 ,370,376,377,
381
, Eleanor,166 ,212
, Elinor,212
, Elisha,126 ,130,212
, Elizabeth Ann,306
, Elizabeth W.,166
, Elizabeth,059,223
, Elsworth,342
, Emeline,072
, Frances Louisa,017
, Frances,017 ,383
, Franklin S.,362
, George B.,018
, George,017 ,208
, Gordon,371 ,380,381,393
, Grant A.,034
, H.Cambridge,244 ,303
, Hannah,087 ,166
, Hanner,156
, Harriet,017
, Harriett L.V.,166
, Harriet,018
, Henry,098,102,267
, Hugh,127,380
, Isham,273,288
, Jacob,306
, James C.,306
, James Den'r,213
, James O.,396
, James(Dr.),001 ,017
, James,017,032,078,130,139
,142,166,173,174,176
,213,306,345,387
,392,395,396
, Jane,031,059,395
, Jans(Jincy),126
, Jason,357
, Jeremiah,386
, Jesse,395
, John A.,034
, John W.,033
, John Morgan,028 ,029,032,
033,035
, John(Col.),076
, John(Maj),139
, John(Maj.),142
, John,002,017,110,122,126,
130,132,133,192,213,
252,297,305,306,387,
390,391,395,396
, Jonathan,017

NEELY, Elizabeth,167,174
  , George,166
  , Hannah,396
  , Henry,158,167,174
  , Hyder A.D.,282
  , Jackson Sr.,396
  , James,099,166
  , Jane,396
  , John,009,282
  , Mary C.,282
  , Matthew,396
  , Rebecca,009
  , Robert,396
  , Samuel,396
  , Thomas,396
  , Wm.,167
NEESE, ,325
NEESSE, Frederick,306
NEIGHBORS, Anna,204
  , James,216
  , John,204
  , Sam'l,154
  , Samuel,152 ,167
NEIL(NEEL), Robert,096
NEIL, Andrew,094
  , Elizabeth,094
  , John,096,106
  , Sarah,191,240
NEILSON, Cornelius,060
  , David,307
  , Elizabeth,060
  , Jared,307
  , John,060
  , Sarah,307 ,327
NEILY, Elizabeth,167
  , Henry,167,182
  , Wm.,167
NELSON, (Dr.),122
  , Catherine,295 ,307
  , Christina,195
  , Elizabeth,311
  , Fanny,008
  , Gideon,202
  , Henry,106
  , James,106
  , Nancy,213
  , Permelly,128
  , Rebecca,128
  , Regt.Col,048
  , Robert,121 ,128,357
  , Samuel,213 ,295,307
  , Sarah,008 ,202
  , Thomas,083 ,102,106,112,392
  , Thos,093 ,118,195
  , William,124,128
  , Wm.,085
NELY(NEELY?), Richard,106
NESBIT, Thos.,113
NESBITT, Allen,022
  , Hugh,022
  , James,343 ,344
  , John,396
  , Samuel,336,349,358,396
NETTERVILLE, Wm.,119
NETTLES, Benjamin,248 ,307,314
  , William,106
  , Zachariah,106 ,307,315
NEVELS, Ann,134
NEVILL, Esther,234
NEWEL, Ann,149
NEWMAN, Alex'r,050
  , Alger,060
  , Charles,017
  , Eliza,060
  , George,060
  , Isaac,060
  , James,060
  , John,060,157,216
  , Letty,060
  , Mary,017,060,070
  , Mine(Mins),216
  , Patrick,060
  , Rich'd,058
  , Richard,060,063
  , Samuel,216
  , Susannah,060
  , Thomas,040 ,060
  , William,060,340
  , Wm.,060,194
NEWSOM, Eleanor,036,045
NEWSOME, Eleanor,067
NEWSON, Eleanor,036
NEWTON, Elizabeth,106
  , James,093 ,106
  , Martha,106
  , Mary,106
NIBLET, Solomon,167
NICHOLS, Allen,185
  , Barbara,153
  , Elizabeth,167
  , James,335
  , John,380
  , Julius Jr.,018
  , Julius,018,019,121
  , Letty,121
  , Margaret,157
  , Patty,018
  , Rosannah,185
  , Salley,014,018
  , Sally,018
  , Solomon,167,182
  , Thomas,018
  , Thos.,157
  , William,018
  , Wm.,163
NICKELLE, David N.,397
  , Margaret,397
NICOLL, John Jr.,129
  , John,130
NICOLLS, Cassey,357
NIGHT, Benjamin,321
  , Nancy,321

NIGHT, Thos.,061
NIGHTENGALS, ,113
NIGHTINGALE, Thos.,065
NIMMONS, William,062
NIPPER, Mary,244
  , Sam'l,117
NISBET, Jno.,073
NISBY, Sophia,299
NIT, Ambrose,087
  , Jno.,372
  , Wm.,369
NIX, Ann,106
  , B.W.,185
  , Charles,106
  , Edward,106
  , Elizabeth,060
  , Jean,207
  , Mary,185
  , Robert,106
NIXON, Rebecca,284
  , Wm.,284
NOBLE, Erasmus,198
  , Mark,143
NOBLES, Elizabeth,060
  , Gideon,051
  , James,060
  , Julia,060
  , Mahala,060
  , Mary A.,060
  , Nicholas,060
NOLAND, Frances,205,216
  , George S.,205
  , Hannah,205
  , John,205,216
  , Sarah,205
  , Stephen,096
  , Thomas J.,216
  , William,205
NORMAN, Ann,379
  , David,381
  , Elizabeth,381
  , George,381
  , Irene,381
  , John,381
  , Jonathan,381
  , Lydia,381
  , Margaret,381
  , Nancy,194
  , Robert,381
  , Thomas,381
NORREL, Thomas,220
NORRIS, Abner,121
  , Elick,308
  , James,357
  , John,117,141,216,308
  , Martha,117
  , Mellica,381
  , Nancy,013
  , William,381
  , Wm.,145
NORTH, Jannet,214
  , John,308,320
  , Thomas,172 ,173
  , Wm.,214
NORTON, Catherine,308
  , Ezekiel,031
  , Hannah,031
NORVELL, Isabella,307
NORVILLE, Isabella,308
NORWAY, Blakely,019
  , Elizabeth,019
  , John,019
  , Joseph,019
  , Robert,019
  , Samuel,019
  , Theophelus,019
  , Thomas,019
  , William,019
NORWOOD, Ann,167
  , Benjamin,216
  , Elizabeth,019 ,025
  , George,167
  , John,010 ,019
  , Mary,216
  , Nathaniel,167
  , Phebe,019
  , Richard,019
  , Samuel,019,024
  , Theophilos,019
  , Theophilus,025
NOTT, Abraham,308
  , Sally W.,325
NOVIS, Martha,117
NOYLE, Charlotte,308
  , Eliza Hester,308
  , Emily,308
  , Mary Bryan,308
  , Sampson,308
NUCKLES, Wm.T.,381
NUCKOLS, John,381
NUGENT, Wm.,144
NYE, Eliza,308 ,314
  , Elizabeth,249
  , John,249 ,308,314

O'HEAR, Ann,062
O'HEWRN, Catherine,308
  , Mary,307
  , Morris,239,307,308
O'NEAL, Aijah,170
  , Arthur,156
  , Henry,140 ,156
  , Hugh,140,142,167,168
  , John,140,156,167,308,315
  , Mary,217
  , Sarah,156
  , Silas,125
  , William,156
  , Wm.,156
O'NEALE, John B.,216
  , Mary,153
  , Wm.,153
O'NEALL, Ann Jane,167
  , Arthur,167
  , Henry,167
  , Hugh,167 ,176,181
  , John Jr.,217
  , John,137 ,167
  , Mary,167
  , Polly,217
  , Rebecca,217
  , Robert E.,217
  , Sarah,167
  , Thomas,217
  , William,167
O'NEILL, Catherine,032
  , Hannah,366
  , Henry,356 ,358,366
  , Michael,032
  , Nancy,356
OAKMAN, Ann,060
OATES, John,106
OBRYAN, Elizabeth,134
ODAM, Abraham Sr.,061
  , Abraham,061
  , David,061
  , Demsey,061
  , Jacob,061
ODEL, John,138 ,152
ODELL, Barnard,216
  , John,216
  , Margaret,216
  , Mary,216
  , Rignal,216
  , Thomas,216
ODLE, Nancy,204
  , Wm.,204
ODOM, Abraham,061
  , Abram,061
  , Allen M.,061
  , Allen Madison,061
  , Ben,042
  , Benj.,061
  , Benj.Jr.,046 ,067
  , Benjamin Jr.,061
  , Benjamin Sr.,061
  , Benjamin(Maj),061
  , Benjamin,061
  , Daniel D.,062
  , Daniel,038,042,047,061,062,065
  , Darling,061
  , Elizabeth,061
  , Geo.,061
  , George R.,061
  , George Sr.,062
  , George W.,061
  , George,058,061,062,063,071
  , Harriet,065
  , Jane,062
  , John D.,061 ,062
  , John Jr.,128
  , John Sr.,128
  , Julia,061
  , Levica,061
  , Lewis,062
  , Lucy D.,063
  , Lydia,062
  , M.W.,061
  , Mary(Mrs.),062
  , Mary,061 ,062
  , Mich'l,061
  , Michael,062
  , Moses,062
  , Owen,061 ,062
  , Priscilla,062
  , Rebecca,038
  , Rich'd,095
  , Richard,061
  , Sabert,061
  , Sabrad,062
  , Sarah(Mrs.),061
  , Sarah,058,061
  , Seybert,062
  , Whitmill,062
  , William,061 ,062
  , Wyatt,061
ODORN(ADORN), (Mrs),050
OGELVIE, James,102
OGILVIE, Elizabeth Ann,273
  , James,267
  , Priscilla,106
  , Robert,248,273
OGLETREE, Benj.,167
  , Lara-g(Louisa),187
OHANLON, Ann Matilda,253
  , Catherine,253
  , Terrence,253
OLDHAM, Joseph,113
  , Perninah,113
OLIPHANT, David,023
OLIVANT, Jesse,381
OLIVER, Charles,250,308
  , Chas.,266
  , J.A.,274
  , Margaret,282
  , Martha,266 ,308
  , Mary,283
O'BANNON, Harriet C.,060
  , Jennings,060
  , John,062
  , Wm.,138
O'BRIANT, Jesse,087
O'BRIEN, Batt,023
O'DELL, Rachel,228
  , Thos.,228
O'DON, Benjamin,061
O'GILVIE, Elizabeth,250
  , Mary Ann,308
  , Mary,250 ,300
  , Robert,103,250,300,308
O'HANLON, Catherine,260,308
  , Lawrence,260 ,308
  , Margaret,260 ,308,324
  , Matilda,308
  , Samuel H.,260
  , Samuel,308